Edward Feser
Immortal Souls
A Treatise on Human Nature

EDITIONES SCHOLASTICAE

Edward Feser

Immortal Souls

A Treatise on Human Nature

Bibliographic information published by Deutsche Nationalbibliothek
The Deutsche Nationalbibliothek lists this publication in the Deutsche Nationalbibliographie;
detailed bibliographic data is available in the Internet at http://dnb.ddb.de

Our books are distributed worldwide by

EUROSPAN

USA & Canada
Independent Publishers Group IPG
E-mail: orders@ipgbook.com
Tel: +1 800 888 4741
www.ipgbook.com

U.K., Europe, Asia and Africa
Eurospan
Gray's Inn House
127 Clerkenwell Road
London EC1R 5DB
info@eurospan.co.uk

©2024 editiones scholasticae
53819 Neunkirchen-Seelscheid
www.editiones-scholasticae.de

ISBN 978-3-86838-605-9

2024

No part of this book may be reproduced, stored in retrieval systems or transmitted in any form or by any means, electronic, mechanical, photocopying, microfilming, recording or otherwise without written permission from the Publisher, with the exception of any material supplied specifically for the purpose of being entered and executed on a computer system, for exclusive use of the purchaser of the work.

Printed on acid-free paper

Printed in Germany

CONTENTS

Preface	2
Part I: What is Mind?	7
1. The Short Answer	8
2. The Self	17
3. The Intellect	64
4. The Will	111
Part II: What is Body?	171
5. Matter	172
6. Animality	210
Part III: What is a Human Being?	257
7. Against Cartesianism	258
8. Against Materialism	305
9. Neither Computers nor Brains	402
Part IV: What is the Soul?	451
10. Immortality	452
11. The Form of the Body	493
Index	523

Preface

The title of this book is bound to bring to mind two philosophers who are explicitly mentioned only here and there in what follows, but nevertheless loom large in the background throughout. The first is Plato (427-347 B.C.), whose dialogue *Phaedo* is *the* great work on the soul and its immortality in the history of Western philosophy. My longtime readers will not be surprised to find that the names of Aristotle (384-322 B.C.) and Thomas Aquinas (1225-1274 A.D.) appear with greater frequency in the book, and that I favor their position where it differs from Plato's. All the same, though he was mistaken on crucial matters of detail, it was Plato who first got right the *most* important things – that the highest part of human beings is the intellect, that the intellect is incorporeal, that this entails that the soul survives death and is indeed immortal, that it will be rewarded or punished after death, and that all of this can be arrived at by philosophical reasoning independently of any special divine revelation.[1] It would be potentially misleading to describe the book's aim as that of vindicating Plato, but I'll risk doing so anyway (albeit with the qualifications one would expect a Thomist to make).[2] The truth is dearest, but Plato is still dear to me.

The book is also intended to refute the other thinker its title will evoke, namely David Hume (1711-1776). Hume's essay "On the Immortality of the Soul" is perhaps the most eloquent expression in Western thought of the falsehood that belief in life after death can find no rational support short of a special divine revelation (which, of course, he did not think has ever been given us). Hume's *Treatise of*

---

[1] This is not to forget the Pythagorean influences on Plato, but rather to emphasize that it is in Plato that we get the first systematic philosophical articulation and defense of these claims about the soul. For a brief discussion of the Pythagorean background, see David Bostock, *Plato's* Phaedo (Oxford: Clarendon Press, 1986), pp. 11-14.

[2] A "Thomist" being, of course, someone who adheres to Thomism, the system of thought deriving from Thomas Aquinas.

Human Nature, from which I borrow my subtitle, is the most influential source of the errors concerning substance, the self, the intellect, and the will that have led modern man radically to misunderstand his own nature. Clearing away this intellectual rubbish is a prerequisite to establishing that Plato was right and Hume wrong.

As my subtitle indicates, the immortality of the soul is far from the only topic to be treated in the pages that follow. Indeed, immortality is addressed only at the end, in the last two chapters. Even the word "soul" will rarely be used until then. That is deliberate. Nothing I have to say in the first ten chapters strictly requires using the word. Also, "soul" has many connotations, not all of them relevant to the topic of a particular chapter, and some of them unfortunate in any case. Rather than repeatedly and needlessly risking misunderstanding and having to make tiresome qualifications, it seemed better to avoid the word until absolutely necessary. This is not the way discussions of the soul usually proceed. But given the word's ambiguity, my view is that the least potentially confusing approach is first to give as thorough an account of human nature as is possible without using the word, and only then to explain where the notion of the soul fits in.

The book is, then, a general treatment of the metaphysics of human nature. It addresses the main philosophical controversies concerning the self and personal identity, the nature of concepts, the relationship between thought and language, the freedom of the will, embodiment, animal intelligence, perceptual experience, innatism versus empiricism, dualism versus materialism, the philosophical implications of neuroscience and computer science, transhumanism, and so on. To be sure, the book is not exhaustive. Certain matters could have been treated in greater depth. For example, much more could be said about the nature and classification of the sensory powers and the appetites. Certain matters are not treated at all. For example, I say nothing about the distinction between the sexes, which is no small part of human nature. (I will treat that at length in a later book.) I had to draw the line somewhere. But the guiding criterion was to address every topic that needed to be addressed in order to defend the sober Aristotelian-Thomistic middle ground position between Cartesianism on the one hand and materialism on the other.[3] For that reason, the book's length was unavoidable. Because human nature is complex, the ways we can go, and have gone, wrong about it are multifarious. I have tried to refute the errors that are most prevalent today.

The book's eleven chapters are grouped into four parts. Part I addresses the question "What is mind?" Chapter 1 gives a brief overview of what I will argue is the correct answer, which is that a mind is a self or persisting substance having, as its essential attributes, intellect and will. The next three chapters are then devoted to expounding and defending this answer in depth. Chapter 2 defends the reality and irreducibility of the self; chapter 3 explains the nature of the intellect and its irreducibility to any of the powers we share with other animals; and chapter 4 explains the nature of the will and establishes its freedom.

Part II is devoted to the question "What is body?" Chapter 5 explains the nature of the material world in general and shows that the Aristotelian theory of form and matter not only has not been refuted by modern science, but is if anything vindicated by modern science. Chapter 6 addresses the nature of *living* matter, specifically, and in particular discusses what it is to be an animal.

The book defends the traditional Aristotelian view that human beings are by nature *rational animals*, and these first two parts are essentially devoted to explaining what "rationality" and "animality" each amount to. Part III, which is labeled "What is a human being?", refutes the two main modern misconceptions about the relationship between rationality and animality. Chapter 7 is a critique of Cartesian dualism, which radically sunders the human mind from the physical world, making the body something entirely extrinsic and inessential to us. Chapter 8 refutes materialism, establishing that though we are indeed bodily by nature, we are not *entirely* so, and that the intellect in particular is incorporeal or non-physical. Chapter 9 refutes currently popular claims to the effect that neuroscience has vindicated

---

[3] "Cartesianism" is the conception of the mind and its relationship to the body and to the rest of the material world associated with Rene Descartes, the father of modern philosophy.

materialism, and that the mind is a kind of computer program implemented in the hardware of the brain.

The upshot of this part of the book is that a human being is a single psychophysical substance with both corporeal and incorporeal properties and powers. Part IV turns finally to the question "What is the soul?" Chapter 10 argues that, since the intellect is an incorporeal part of a human being, it carries on beyond the death of the body, and that indeed on careful analysis this entails all the main elements of the traditional doctrine of the immortality of the soul. Chapter 11 explains how the position defended in the book relates to the Aristotelian thesis that the soul is the form of the body, and its implications for the origins of the soul and the prospects for its reunion with the body by way of a resurrection of the dead.

Again, many other topics are treated along the way. Many of these are also topics I have addressed in earlier work, such as my book *Philosophy of Mind*, which first appeared almost twenty years ago.[4] They are addressed in greater depth here, and in some cases my views have changed. For example, that earlier book is much too sympathetic to Cartesianism, especially in its treatment of perception. The approach of this book is much more consistently Aristotelian-Thomistic. Having said that, though Aristotle and St. Thomas are by far the greatest influences on my own views, this book is not concerned with exegesis of their work. The claims and arguments I defend in this book are mine, and not always necessarily theirs. If, on some topics, I say something that sounds very much like what they say, that is because I think they were right about it. If, on other topics, I say something that is different from anything they say, or even conflicts with what they say, that is because I think my approach is better. Like other Thomists, I am often accused of following Aquinas too closely, but also of not following him closely enough. In reality, I try only ever to follow an argument wherever it leads.

---

[4] Edward Feser, *Philosophy of Mind: A Beginner's Guide* (Oxford: Oneworld, 2006). This is a slightly revised version of Edward Feser, *Philosophy of Mind: A Short Introduction* (Oxford: Oneworld, 2005).

I also emphasize, again, that this book is concerned only with what *philosophy* can, all by itself, tell us about its subject. It is not about theology, highly relevant though it is to theology. Many are bound to be surprised at just how much can be established by purely philosophical arguments where the existence and nature of the soul are concerned – just as, as I have shown in my book *Five Proofs of the Existence of God*, much can be established by purely philosophical arguments where the existence and nature of God are concerned.[5] *Immortal Souls*, like *Five Proofs*, is intended as a contribution to understanding the *praeambula fidei* or "preambles of faith" – that is to say, the philosophical premises in light of which it can be rationally established that a special divine revelation really has occurred (though exactly how that can be established is a topic for another time).

In this connection I will acknowledge one final lacuna that I think is unavoidable in a philosophical book with the particular purposes this one has, but has been increasingly palpable to me all the same. I refer to the absence of any treatment of the moral and spiritual ramifications of being a creature with an immortal destiny, yet deeply enmeshed in the material world, with the suffering and liability to death that that entails. The years during which I have worked on this book have been especially dark ones, personally as well as for the world in general. Working on the book has played no small part in my own dealing with this darkness, and it is my fervent hope and prayer that my readers will find in it something that is helpful to them.

My usual debts to my beloved wife Rachel and our dear children Benedict, Gemma, Kilian, Helena, John, and Gwendolyn remain, and I thank them for their love and help as I labored over this book. And I'd like to acknowledge a further debt. In the face of the deaths of our father and our sister and the ailments of our mother, my brother Dan Feser has been an exemplar of loyalty and service. I dedicate this book to him, with love and affection.

---

[5] Edward Feser, *Five Proofs of the Existence of God* (San Francisco: Ignatius Press, 2017).

Part I:
What is Mind?

1. The Short Answer

What is the nature of the mind? The question is in one crucial respect different from questions we might ask about the natures of other things, such as stones, trees, or dogs. For in this case, the thing asked about and the thing asking are one and the same. This unique intimacy with its subject matter can hardly fail to facilitate answering the question. Indeed, as Augustine (354-430 A.D.) argued, "the mind knows itself, even when it seeks itself."[6] It can discover something of its own nature merely by reflecting on the fact that it is trying to discover it. What it thereby discovers is that it is a thing that *thinks* and *wills*. For the very attempt to inquire into its own nature involves thinking and willing, and in knowing that it is doing these things, the mind knows that it is a thing *of the kind* that is capable of doing them. If it even tried to doubt this, the exercise in doing so would itself involve thinking and willing.

Augustine puts the point by saying that the mind is a thing that *knows* and *loves*, and that we can be certain of this insofar as it is presupposed even in the act of questioning it. He elaborates as follows:

> For, we are, and we know that we are, and we love to be and to know that we are. And in this trinity of being, knowledge, and love there is not a shadow of illusion to disturb us. For, we do not reach these inner realities with our bodily senses as we do external objects... But, without any illusion of image, fancy, or phantasm, I am certain that I am, that I know that I am, and that I love to be and to know.
>
> In the face of these truths, the quibbles of the skeptics lose their force. If they say; 'What if you are mistaken?' – well, if *I*

---

[6] In Book X, Chapter 10 of *On the Trinity, Books 8-15*, edited by Gareth B. Matthews and translated by Stephen McKenna (Cambridge: Cambridge University Press, 2002), at p. 56.

am mistaken, I am. For, if one does not exist, he can by no means be mistaken. Therefore, I am, if I am mistaken... Nor, as a consequence, am I mistaken in knowing that I know. For, just as I know that I am, I also know that I know. And when I love both to be and to know, then I add to the things I know a third and equally important knowledge, the fact that I love.

Nor am I mistaken that I love, since I am not mistaken concerning the objects of my love. For, even though these objects were false, it would still be true that I loved illusions.[7]

As Augustine points out, if the mind were to doubt its own existence, it would have to exist in order to do the doubting. So, its affirmation of its own existence is not something it can be wrong about. This would remain true even if it turned out that *other* things – such as the physical objects the mind takes itself to see, hear, taste, touch, and smell – were unreal (for example, if the mind were merely dreaming or hallucinating them).

But more relevant to our present purposes is what the mind can know, not about its existence, but about its nature. In reflecting on its knowledge of its own existence, the mind comes to know *that it knows* this. It discovers that it is a *knowing thing*, a thing whose nature makes it capable of knowledge. When it reflects on the further circumstance that it *loves* the fact of its own existence and loves the fact that it has knowledge of its own existence, the mind thereby discovers that it is also a *loving thing*, a thing whose nature makes it capable of love. Even if these objects of its love had been unreal, it would nevertheless be a thing of the sort capable of love, insofar as the love *itself* would still be real even if its objects were not.

In Augustine's view, the mind and its capacities for knowledge and love are therefore parts of a metaphysical package deal, each inseparable from the other. He writes: "But just as there are two things, the mind and its love, when it loves itself, so there are two things, the mind and its knowledge, when it knows itself. Therefore, the mind itself, its love and its knowledge are a kind of trinity."[8] This gives us

---

[7] In Book XI, Chapter 26, of *The City of God*, translated by Gerald G. Walsh, S.J. and Grace Monahan, O.S.U. (Washington, D.C.: Catholic University of America Press, 1952), at pp. 228-29.
[8] *On the Trinity*, Book IX, Chapter 4, at pp. 27-28.

an answer, or at least a partial answer, to our question about the nature of the mind. The mind is a thing of the kind capable of knowing and loving.

While this answer is stated in the third person, it will probably not have escaped the reader's notice that Augustine writes in the *first* person. He talks not only of what his *mind* knows and loves, but of what *he* knows and loves, in a manner that implies that these ways of speaking are interchangeable. Of course, that reflects common usage. As the term is usually understood, your mind isn't merely something you *have*. Your mind just is *you*, or at least it is you considered as a thing that knows, loves, and so forth. You might say, then, that to inquire into the nature of the mind is at the same time to inquire into the nature of the *self*. Thus, to say that the *mind* is a thing of the kind capable of knowing and loving is to say that *you* are a thing of the kind capable of knowing and loving.

Does that entail that there is *nothing more* to your nature than being a thing of the kind that can know and love? Does it entail that having a body is not also part of your nature? No, those conclusions don't follow, and we will see later that they are not true. The point for the moment is just to suggest that whether or not you are *more* than a thing with the capacities to know and to love, you are not *less* than that. The claim is that Augustine's identification of knowing and loving as the characteristic activities of the mind or self gives us at least the rudiments of its nature, the bare minimum a thing must have in order to be a mind or self.

Actually, Augustine's thesis needs a little tidying up. Or at least, even if the terms "knowing" and "loving" are innocent in themselves, today they have connotations which can make his claims about the mind's nature seem narrower than they really are. For one thing, Augustine needn't confine himself to saying that the mind is a thing of the kind capable of *knowledge*. His argument justifies the broader claim that the mind is a thing of the kind capable of *thinking*, whether it has a thought of the sort we would ordinarily count as genuine knowledge, or whether instead it has a thought of the sort we would classify instead as a mere belief. For example, when I falsely believe that I see a tree in the distance, it is still the case that I am *thinking* that there is a tree there, even if I don't in fact *know* that there is.

For another thing, these days the word "love" is commonly taken to connote a kind of emotion, but that is not how ancient writers like Augustine intend it. For these writers, what is essential to loving is to *will* something as good, and the affective state we associate with love can be absent even when we love something in this sense. Consider, for example, the way you might love an enemy. You would not have warm feelings for him; you might even have very negative feelings when you think of him. But if you willed what is good for him (such as his repentance of the evil he has done to you), you could still be said to love him.

It would be less misleading for the modern reader, then, if Augustine's position were formulated instead as the claim that the mind is a thing of the kind capable of *willing*.[9] When you deliberately carry out the exercise of thinking about whether you exist and whether you have knowledge, you are exercising your will. If you resolve to doubt that you have a will, that would itself be a further exercise of the will. Hence the very attempt to doubt that you have a will itself shows that you have one. So, you can conclude that your nature qua mind is to be a thing of the kind capable of willing, as well as of thinking.

I would propose, then, that the lesson we can draw from the considerations raised by Augustine can be formulated by saying that the nature of the mind or the self is to be a thing of the kind capable of thinking and willing. To put it in yet other terms, we can say that it is to be a thing possessing *intellect* and *will*, where the intellect is the capacity to think and the will is (naturally) the capacity for willing.

Readers having some familiarity with the history of philosophy will no doubt have been struck by the similarity of what Augustine says to views famously expressed by René Descartes (1596-1650), commonly regarded as the father of modern philosophy. Descartes' famous Cogito argument (*Cogito, ergo sum*, which is Latin for "I think, therefore I am") was intended to show that one cannot coherently

---

[9] The relationship in Augustine's philosophy between the concept of loving and the concept of willing is more complicated than these remarks let on, but the complications are irrelevant for present purposes. For discussion, see John M. Rist, *Augustine Deformed: Love, Sin, and Freedom in the Western Moral Tradition* (Cambridge: Cambridge University Press, 2014).

doubt one's own existence.[10] He also held that the mind or self is essentially a thing that thinks, and he included willing as a kind of thinking. But it is useful to make Augustine's formulation rather than Descartes' our take-off point, for a couple of reasons. For one thing, doing so helps to underline the point that there is nothing in the thesis that the mind or self is by nature a thing with the capacity to think and will that necessarily entails a commitment to all of Descartes' distinctive views about human nature. For example, it does not entail that one has to agree with Descartes that mind and body are two distinct substances, or that the body is a kind of machine. Augustine would not have accepted either of those claims, and as we will see later, neither of them is true. For another thing, citing Augustine – a thinker who bridged the ancient and medieval worlds – makes it clear that there is nothing distinctively *modern* about that aspect of his conception of the mind or self that he shares with Descartes.[11]

Indeed, there is another thinker from Augustine's era who, I suggest, can also help us to get an initial fix on the nature of the mind or self, namely Boethius (c. 480-524). We owe to him a definition of what it is to be a *person* that was enormously influential in medieval philosophy. A person, says Boethius, is *an individual substance of a rational nature*.[12] Let's break down this definition. In the philosophical sense in which the term is being used here, a *substance* is to be contrasted with its *attributes*.[13] If we take some particular stone as an example, its solidity, color, texture, shape, and weight would be among

---

[10] *Discourse on Method*, Part IV.

[11] It should be added that there is nothing in Augustine's position that would commit us to anything like the use Descartes makes of the Cogito in epistemology or theory of knowledge. That is a good thing, since there is ample reason for anyone sympathetic to the Aristotlelian-Thomistic position I defend in this book to reject Descartes' epistemology. Cf. Reginald Garrigou-Lagrange, "The Thomist Critique of the Cartesian *Cogito*," in *Philosophizing in Faith: Essays on the Beginning and End of Wisdom*, translated by Matthew K. Minerd (Providence: Cluny Media, 2019).

[12] *Liber de Persona et Duabas Naturis*, c. 3.

[13] In traditional Scholastic philosophy it is standard to contrast substances with *accidents*, and in contemporary analytic philosophy it is standard to contrast them with *properties*. But both of those terms have connotations which make them potentially misleading in the present context. So, in order to avoid having to make qualifications and address technical

its attributes, whereas the stone itself is the substance that has those attributes. Attributes exist only *in* a substance rather than in a freestanding way. For example, the color and weight of a stone exist only in the stone and cannot be pulled out and set alongside it, as it were, as separable entities. By contrast, a substance does not exist *in* another thing in the same sense. It is, again, that which bears attributes. It is precisely the sort of entity *in which* things of the kind that cannot exist in a freestanding way must inhere.

What Boethius is saying is that a person is a kind of substance rather than an attribute or collection of attributes. If we think of particular thoughts and acts of will as attributes, then a person is not a collection of such thoughts and acts of will, but rather the substance in which those attributes inhere. Certainly Augustine thinks of a mind or self as a kind of substance.[14] When I first have the thought that I might not exist, and then have the thought that in fact I cannot fail to exist if I am even doubting that I do, Augustine would hold that it is the same one substance that persists from the one thought to the next.

Aristotle distinguished between a *primary substance*, which would be an individual thing, and a *secondary substance*, which would be the species (more specific class) or genus (more general class) into which that thing falls.[15] For example, your pet Collie Fido would be a primary substance, and the species *dog* into which it falls, as well as the genus *Canis* into which that species falls, would be secondary substances.[16] When Boethius says that a person is an *individual* substance, he means that it is a primary substance, a particular thing rather than

---

issues that would be distracting and irrelevant for present purposes, I have opted to use the more anodyne term "attributes." For discussion of the terminological issues and of the substantive metaphysical issues related to them, see Edward Feser, *Scholastic Metaphysics: A Contemporary Introduction* (Heusenstamm: Editiones Scholasticae, 2014), especially pp. 189-93 and 230-35.

[14] For example, he refers to the mind as a "substance" in *On the Trinity*, Book XII, Chapter 1.

[15] *Categories*, Chapter 5.

[16] I am here using the terms *species* and *genus* in their older philosophical senses rather than in the technical senses familiar from modern biology, and for simplicity's sake I am ignoring the subclass into which modern biologists would put dogs, because such details are irrelevant to the specific point I am making at present.

a class of things. (Of course, all individual persons fall under the class *person*, just as all individual dogs fall under the class *dog*. The point is just that *any particular* person, qua *instance* of the class, would be a primary substance or individual.)

What it is to have a *rational nature* is just to be a thing of the kind possessing intellect or the capacity for thought. Now, as medieval thinkers like Thomas Aquinas argued, anything with an intellect must also possess a will. For a substance with an intellect acts by virtue of being inclined toward what its intellect takes to be good, and the will just is (on this analysis) an inclination of that sort. To be a person in the sense that medieval thinkers inherited from Boethius is, then, essentially just to be a mind or self in Augustine's sense.

Combining these ideas, we can say that to *have a mind*, to be *a self*, and to be *a person* are all essentially the same thing, and that what they amount to is being a substance which by nature possesses an intellect and a will. Naturally, this raises many questions, and we will address them in the pages to follow. For the moment let us note what this characterization includes and what it rules out. Non-human animals, plants, and inanimate objects would not count as having minds in this sense, nor as being selves or persons. (That is *not* to say that non-human animals are not sentient or conscious. They are. It is to say only that they lack *intellects* and *wills*, a claim I will defend later on.) Human beings, of course, count as having minds and thus as selves or persons. So too would angels, understood as entirely incorporeal or non-bodily rational substances; intelligent extraterrestrials, if there are any such things; and artificial intelligences or thinking machines, if those are possible. No one denies that extraterrestrial intelligences are at least possible in theory, even if it is controversial whether there really are any. But whether angelic minds or thinking machines really are possible are matters of controversy. We will see later on that in fact angelic minds *are* possible, whereas thinking machines are *not* possible. (I am well aware that that is the reverse of the conventional wisdom these days. The conventional wisdom is wrong.) The point for the moment is that the characterization of mind I have sketched out, though it clearly rules out quite a bit, is still broad enough to include, at least in principle, a fairly wide variety of possible kinds of mind.[17]

It also leaves it open, at least for the moment, whether a purely material substance could have a mind (as materialists hold) and whether any mind, self, or person would instead have to be an entirely immaterial substance (as Descartes' form of dualism holds). We will see that both materialists and Descartes are wrong – that a self or person, something with a mind, could be partly material and partly immaterial, but could never be entirely material.[18] But again, for the moment we do not need to settle those issues.

What we do need to address in this first section of the book are three sets of questions and challenges that arise when considering more closely my proposed characterization of minds, selves, or persons. First, is a mind, self, or person really a substance? Does it really have the kind of *stability or permanence* that is traditionally attributed to substances? Might it not instead be a mere bundle of ever-changing attributes? Indeed, might a persisting self not be a kind of illusion? Second, exactly what is an intellect, and how does it differ from the sentience we share with non-human animals? Might the apparent rationality and meaningfulness of our thoughts not also be a kind of illusion, as eliminative materialists claim? Third, what exactly is the will, and why would something with an intellect have to have a will?

---

[17] There is, of course, an even broader use of the word "mind" on which it covers all sentient creatures, and thus even non-rational animals. But I am using the term in the narrower sense reflected in expressions like: "making up one's mind," "changing one's mind," "losing one's mind," "being of sound mind," "great minds," "a sharp mind," "an enquiring mind," "suspicious minds," "meeting of minds," "open mind," "closed mind," "mind of one's own," "broaden one's mind," "mind-boggling," "of a mind to," "having in mind," "minding one's own business," and so forth. Such expression are only applied to rational creatures and not to non-rational animals, which indicates that there is a more restricted use of the word "mind" that identifies a mind either with a person or a person's intellect.

[18] Here too I follow Augustine rather than Descartes. As Rowan Williams writes, "the mind [or] *mens*, for Augustine, refers to the intelligent and active subject as a whole, *not* 'mind' as opposed to 'body.'" Quoted from his article "Trinitate, De," in Allan D. Fitzgerald, General editor, *Augustine Through the Ages: An Encyclopedia* (Grand Rapids, MI: William B. Eerdmans Publishing Company, 1999), at p. 849.

Thinkers like Aquinas hold that the will's freedom follows from its being a power of a rational substance, but might free will not be an illusion too?

The answer is that none of these things is an illusion. You can know with certainty that you really are a persisting self, and that you possess rationality and free will. Indeed, none of that can coherently be doubted. The next three chapters are devoted to establishing these claims, and thereby expanding upon the short answer to the question "What is mind?" that I have given in this opening chapter.

2. The Self

Its reality and irreducibility

Many debates in the history of philosophy are about whether to accept a *realist*, *reductionist*, or *anti-realist* account of some phenomenon. A realist account of a phenomenon takes it to be real and to have precisely the nature that it appears to have. A reductionist account doesn't quite deny the phenomenon's reality, but holds that its true nature is different from what it seems to be. An anti-realist account takes the phenomenon to be altogether illusory, denying that it corresponds to anything in reality.

For example, consider *thoughts*, such as the thought that the cat is on the mat or the thought that two and two make four. A realist account of thoughts would say that they really do exist, and that they are, as common sense supposes, very different in their nature from anything bodily – from muscular movements, chemical secretions, neural firing patterns, and the like. A reductionist account would not deny that thoughts are real, but would say that common sense is wrong about their nature. For instance, it might hold that, appearances notwithstanding, a thought really is nothing but a firing pattern in the neurons of the brain. An anti-realist account would hold that there really are no such things as thoughts, odd as that may sound. There are *only* the processes occurring in the brain, and what we take to be a thought is merely a kind of misperception of what is really going on there.

Or consider *free will*. A realist account would say that free will is real, and that, as common sense supposes, our having it entails that what we do is up to us and not determined by forces outside our control. A reductionist account would not deny that free will is real, but would hold that its nature is different from what common sense assumes it to be. In particular, it might claim that an action of yours is free as long as you did it because you wanted to do it, even if what you wanted to do was not up to you and was entirely determined by forces outside your control. An anti-realist account, meanwhile, would flatly deny that there is any such thing as free will.

We will have reason to consider the topics of thought and free will in detail in the pages to come, but for the moment I cite them merely as examples meant to illustrate the differences between realist, reductionist, and anti-realist approaches to a phenomenon. I should also note that we could make various further distinctions between approaches (for example, between different specific ways of spelling out a realist or reductionist account of the nature of some phenomenon). But our threefold distinction is sufficient for present purposes.[19]

Now, the *self* is another phenomenon to which these three approaches could be taken. Recall, from the previous chapter, the distinction between *substances* and their *attributes*. Whereas attributes exist only *in* a substance, a substance does not in turn exist *in* anything else in the same sense. For example, the color and weight of a dog don't exist apart from the dog, in a freestanding way, but only *in* the dog. But the dog itself does not exist *in* anything else in the same sense in which its color and weight exist in it. A substance is thus what *stands under* or *grounds* attributes. It can also persist through the gain or loss of an attribute. For example, one and the same dog can at one time be black and at a later time gray, or at one time weigh twenty pounds and at a later time weigh thirty pounds.

A realist view of the self holds that the self really exists, and that it has the nature that common sense takes it to have – the nature of a *substance* that underlies attributes such as *intending to become a comic book artist* or *experiencing pain in one's leg*, and that persists through changes of those attributes. For example, when I was a teenager I intended to become a comic book artist, but a few years later decided to become a philosopher instead. And last night I experienced pain in my leg, but today it is gone. A realist view of the self would say, with common sense, that there really is some *thing* – namely, *me* – that underlies these different thoughts and experiences, and that it

---

[19] For a helpful more detailed account of the varieties of realist, reductionist, and anti-realist approaches that might be taken to various problems in philosophy, see Simon Blackburn, *Spreading the Word: Groundings in the Philosophy of Language* (Oxford: Clarendon Press, 1984), chapter 5.

was the *same* one thing, the same self or person, that had the pain last night but lacks it now, and had the aim of becoming a comic book artist decades ago but decided on a different path (for better or worse) later on.

A reductionist view of the self would agree that the self is real, but would say that common sense is mistaken to think that there is some further entity distinct from the self's thoughts, experiences, etc., which stands under or grounds them. Rather, the self is, on this view, nothing more than the bundle or collection of its attributes. An anti-realist view of the self, meanwhile, would hold that, strictly speaking, there is no such thing. The self, on this view, is an *illusion*, and not something we can identify even with the fleeting bundle of thoughts, experiences, and the like which generate this illusion.

The burden of this chapter is to defend the commonsense supposition that the self is real, and that it is not reducible to a mere bundle of thoughts and experiences (or to anything else for that matter). This will require defending the thesis that the self is a kind of substance. Now, the notion of substance is itself a matter of longstanding philosophical controversy. We will have reason in later chapters to address some of the broader issues that arise in connection with it. But a general treatment of substance is not necessary for present purposes, and is something I have in any event already provided elsewhere.[20] It will suffice for the moment to show that the *self* is a substance, whatever other substances there may or may not be.

The basic argument is straightforward. First, each of us knows with certainty of his own existence simply by way of ordinary self-awareness. Second, reflection on the object of this knowledge makes it evident that it must have the nature of a substance. And third, none of the skeptical attempts to cast doubt on the reliability of self-awareness, nor any reductionist or eliminativist accounts of the self, can be made coherent. Naturally, each of these points needs spelling out.

---

[20] Cf. Edward Feser, *Scholastic Metaphysics: A Contemporary Introduction* (Heusenstamm: Editiones Scholasticae, 2014), chapter 3.

Self-awareness

In an influential account of self-knowledge, Roderick Chisholm links such knowledge to the notion of a proposition that is "self-presenting" and thus "known directly."[21] A proposition is self-presenting to me, and thus directly known by me, when: (a) it is necessarily the case that, if the proposition is true, then I will know that it is true, and (b) it is in fact true. An example would be the proposition that *I seem to see a door*. For it is true at the moment that I seem to see one, and it is necessarily the case that when I seem to see a door, then I *know* that I seem to see one. It would make sense for me to say: "I *seem* to see a door, but in fact I do not *really see* one." (For example, I might say this if I knew that what I was really looking at was a realistic painting of a door.) But it would *not* make sense for me to say: "I *seem* to see a door, but in fact I do not *really seem* to see one." Even if there really is no door there, I can't be wrong when I judge that it at least *seems* to me that there is one, if in fact that is how things seem.

Now, if I know this proposition, argues Chisholm, then I also thereby have knowledge of *myself*. After all, what I know when I know that *I seem to see a door* is an attribute *of me* – namely, my attribute of seeming to see a door. So, if I know that I have this attribute, then I can know that I *exist*. I could hardly have the attribute otherwise. In this way, knowledge of a self-presenting and thus directly known *proposition* affords one knowledge of the *self* which knows it. (We'll consider a possible objection to this in a moment.)

The reader may have noticed that this is similar to the argument from Augustine with which we began the previous chapter. Indeed, I think it is essentially a variation on Augustine's point.[22] Augustine argued that, even when he is mistaken when making some judgment, he must exist in order to be mistaken. Knowledge of the judgment, whether that judgement is mistaken or not, thus suffices to give one knowledge of the self which makes the judgment. Of course, this is also reminiscent of Descartes' *Cogito, ergo sum* ("I think, therefore I am"). What Chisholm is doing is restating the thrust of Augustine's and Descartes' point in a way that makes it explicit that self-

---

[21] Roderick M. Chisholm, *Person and Object* (La Salle, IL: Open Court, 1976), pp. 24-25.
[22] Chisholm quotes Augustine approvingly at p. 33 of *Person and Object*.

knowledge is a byproduct of knowledge of a certain kind of proposition.

However, there is a way of developing this idea which is familiar from the Augustinian and Cartesian traditions and which has evidently influenced Chisholm, but which is not essential to the argument, and which one need not endorse in order to accept it. Augustine holds that, though the mind knows the physical world through sense organs, it knows itself through itself.[23] This might seem to imply that knowledge of the self is direct, and in no way dependent on sensory experience. The Cartesian tradition is associated with the idea of a special faculty of *introspection* or *inner sense*, by which we know the self in a manner that parallels the way perception affords us knowledge of material objects.[24] Chisholm speaks of "direct awareness of the self" or "direct acquaintance" with it.[25]

But one may agree that certain knowledge of the self follows from knowledge of propositions of the kind to which Chisholm appeals, without holding that we are *directly* aware of or acquainted with the self, or that self-awareness involves a special faculty of introspection or inner sense that makes sensory experience unnecessary. An alternative position is that of Thomas Aquinas, who holds that the mind cannot know anything at all, not even itself, without sensory experience. He holds also that when the mind does know itself, this is not a matter of its having direct introspective acquaintance with itself, but rather of knowing its own *acts* and reflecting on their implications. Aquinas writes:

> The first object of its act of understanding... is the nature of a material thing. And therefore that which is first known by the human intellect is an object of this kind, and that which is

---

[23] *On the Trinity*, Book IX, Chapter 3.

[24] Whether Descartes himself actually posited such a faculty is controversial. Cf. Gordon Baker and Katherine J. Morris, *Descartes' Dualism* (London: Routledge, 1996), pp. 18-20 and 39-48.

[25] *Person and Object*, pp. 23-24. The language of "direct acquaintance" is borrowed from Bertrand Russell, in whose epistemology it has a special technical meaning.

known secondarily is the act by which that object is known; and through the act the intellect itself is known.[26]

For example, I look at what is there in front of me and judge that *that is a door*. Then my attention turns from this *object* of my perceptual experience to the perceptual experience *itself*, and I judge that *I seem to see a door*. Finally, reflecting on the fact that this is how things seem to me, I judge that there must therefore be a self or mind *to whom* things seem this way.

Expounding Aquinas's position, Robert Pasnau aptly characterizes this as a process of "cognitive ascent."[27] It is not a matter of perceiving the self by way of a special introspective faculty that is analogous to the visual faculty by which we perceive the door. Rather, "what happens is simply that one thought gives rise to another, in the familiar way we constantly experience."[28] Just as the perceptual experience of the door can trigger the thought that *that door needs to be repainted*, so too it can lead to the thought that *I seem to see a door*, which might in turn lead to the further thought that *there is a self which is having that thought*. Following Aquinas, Pasnau appeals to the analogy of an image in a mirror.[29] When looking at a mirror in which a door is reflected, I may think either "That is a door" or "That is a mirror image of a door," depending on whether my attention is focused on the object being reflected, or on the mirror image itself. But the difference is a difference in what my mind attends to, not a difference in mental faculties being deployed. The same is true, on Aquinas's account, when the mind knows an object outside it, or knows the mental act by which it knows that object, or knows the self which performs that act.

---

[26] *Summa theologiae* I.87.3. Unless otherwise indicated, quotations from the *Summa* are taken from Thomas Aquinas, *Summa Theologica*, in five volumes, translated by the Fathers of the English Dominican Province (New York: Benziger Bros, 1948).

[27] Robert Pasnau, *Thomas Aquinas on Human Nature* (Cambridge: Cambridge University Press, 2002), p. 345.

[28] Ibid.

[29] Cf. Thomas Aquinas, *Quaestiones disputatae de veritate* 2.6.

Because Aquinas's position posits no special introspective faculty, we might, following Therese Scarpelli Cory, speak of it as an account of how "self-awareness" works.[30] She opts for that expression because it has a familiar everyday usage and is not widely associated with a single technical philosophical sense. Now, my aim for the moment is not to argue that the notion of a special introspective faculty is dubious and that Aquinas's alternative account of self-awareness is correct (though that is in fact what I think).[31] The point is merely that arguments of the kind that Augustine and Chisholm give for the certainty of our knowledge of the self do not require positing a special faculty of introspection or inner sense. One could instead adopt Aquinas's account. Hence objections to the notion of a special introspective faculty are not *per se* objections to Augustine's or Chisholm's reasons for claiming that the reality of the self can be known with certainty.

The substantiality of the self

At this point, however, one might raise an objection associated with the 18th-century thinker Georg Christoph Lichtenberg, who directed it against Descartes' Cogito. The most Descartes is entitled to claim, held Lichtenberg, is that *there is thinking going on*, but not that there is an *I* or *self* who is doing the thinking. Similarly, it might be claimed, the most that Augustine or Chisholm is entitled to say with certainty is that *it seems that there is a door*, but not that there is an *I* or *self* to whom it seems this way. Thus, whether we conceive of self-knowledge on the model of introspection or on the model of cognitive ascent, arguments like those of Augustine and Chisholm do not really establish the reality of the self. For its reality simply doesn't follow from the proposition that *it seems that there is a door*, or the proposition that *there is thinking going on*, or any other such proposition.

But Lichtenberg, I would suggest, is on closer inspection not in fact putting forward a clear or even coherent alternative, as can be

---

[30] Therese Scarpelli Cory, *Aquinas on Human Self-Knowledge* (Cambridge: Cambridge University Press, 2014), p. 13.

[31] Cf. Cory's book, and chapter 11 of Pasnau's, for in-depth treatments of Aquinas's position.

seen from some considerations raised by Bernard Williams.[32] Consider the proposition that *it seems that there is a door* and the proposition that *it seems that there is a dog*. Does it follow from these two propositions that *it seems that there is a door and a dog*? No. For the first and second propositions could be true even if the third is not. For example, if I was looking at a door in a room where no dog was present, and you were looking at a dog in the middle of a park where no door was present, the first two propositions would be true, but the third would not.

To explain this lack of entailment, though, I had to make reference to two different *minds* or *selves* – yours and mine – and the different contexts in which they find themselves. And in general, there is no way to make sense of the logical relationships between propositions about how things seem, or about what is being thought, or the like, without making reference to minds or selves *to whom* things seem a certain way, or *who have* the thoughts in question.

Note that it would not help Lichtenberg if we added some further element to each proposition in order to capture the difference in context, but without making reference to minds or selves. For example, suppose we added the word "here" to our three propositions. Would the proposition that *it seems that there is a door here* and the proposition that *it seems that there is a dog here* entail the further proposition that *it seems that there is a door and a dog here*? No, but again, the reason is that the word "here" might in the first proposition indicate the context in which one mind or self finds itself (such as the room with the door in it), and might in the second proposition indicate the different context in which a different mind or self finds itself (such as the park with the dog in it). The reference of the word "here" (which is an example of what philosophers call an *indexical* term) cannot be known until we know which speaker or thinker is using it. Again, reference to minds or selves is essential in order to make sense of the logical relationships in question.

The problem with Lichtenberg's view, however, does not arise merely because of the special natures of minds and their thoughts. It

---

[32] Bernard Williams, *Descartes: The Project of Pure Enquiry* (London: Penguin Books, 1990), pp. 95-101.

runs deeper than that. *Having things seem a certain way* is a kind of *attribute*, as are thoughts in general. They are, in all respects relevant to the present point, metaphysically on a par with non-mental attributes such as *being red, being cold, being round*, and so on. And what all attributes have in common is that they cannot intelligibly be identified or individuated except by reference to a *substance* whose attributes they are. For example, I cannot identify or pick out the particular *whiteness* of the door in front of me without reference to the door whose whiteness it is. And I cannot individuate or distinguish that whiteness from the whiteness of the wall next to the door without reference to the wall in which that separate instance of whiteness inheres. Similarly, we cannot identify or individuate the thought that *it seems that there is a door* without reference to some substance in which that thought, qua attribute, inheres.[33] And to be a substance in which thoughts inhere just is to be a mind or a self. So, if I can know with certainty that *it seems that there is a door*, then I can go on to know with certainty that there is a mind or self to whom it seems that way.

But might there be some alternative way to identify and individuate thoughts, without reference to the self? One proposal is that we can instead identify and individuate a thought by reference to its *causes and effects*.[34] The idea would be that, for example, the thought that *it seems that there is a door* can be picked out and distinguished from other thoughts by reference to the fact that the thought was caused by light from the door striking a certain pair of eyeballs, and that it went on in turn to generate the effect of the writing of the sentence that you are now reading.

But the problem with this might be obvious. For we need to ask: Exactly *whose* eyeballs were struck by the light from the door? And exactly *who* wrote the sentence in question? The answer, of course, is that the eyeballs and act of writing the sentence were *mine*. And I am a self. It is, after all, *substances* that act as causes, and that

---

[33] Cf. E. J. Lowe, *Subjects of Experience* (Cambridge: Cambridge University Press, 1996), p. 25; E. J. Lowe, *More Kinds of Being* (Oxford: Wiley Blackwell, 2009), pp. 134-35; and P. F. Strawson, *Individuals: An Essay in Descriptive Metaphysics* (London: Routledge, 1990), pp. 41ff.

[34] Cf. Christopher Peacocke, *Sense and Content* (Oxford: Clarendon Press, 1983), p. 177.

are affected by other causes. The light from the door affected the organs of a certain substance, namely me; and it was a certain substance, namely me, who wrote the sentence. So, the thought that *it seems that there is a door*, which was generated by the light and produced the writing of the sentence, is an attribute of a substance, namely me. And a substance which has thoughts as attributes just is, again, a mind or self.

The problem, in short, is that in trying to disassociate thoughts from substances, it won't do to appeal instead to causes and effects, because the relevant causes and effects cannot *themselves* be made sense of without reference to precisely the sorts of substances that the view in question is trying to avoid.[35] Of course, those who deny that there is such a substance as the self will disagree, but the problem is that the alternative proposal under consideration fails to provide a non-question-begging reason for the disagreement.

Now, the critic might at this point abandon Lichtenberg's view but still argue that it is possible to avoid the conclusion that the self is a substance. He might concede that there must be a mind or self which has whatever thoughts, experiences, etc. that there may be, but claim that this mind or self is nothing more than a *collection* or *bundle* of the thoughts, experiences, etc. It isn't a substance underlying the collection. This is the "bundle theory" of the self famously associated with David Hume.[36] Whereas Lichtenberg's position suggests an *anti-realist* view of the self, Hume's amounts to a *reductionist* view.

The first thing to say in reply is to reiterate the point that thoughts, experiences, and other mental states are attributes, and attributes cannot be identified or individuated apart from the substance in which they inhere. This objection stands whether we are talking about a particular thought or a collection of thoughts. Nor could Hume solve the problem by identifying and individuating each mental state by reference to the bundle of which it is a part, rather than by reference to a substance in which it inheres. For that would only yield a viciously circular explanation. He would be identifying individual

---

[35] Cf. Lowe, *Subjects of Experience*, pp. 27ff.

[36] *Treatise of Human Nature*, Book I, Part IV, Section VI.

mental states by reference to the bundles of which they are members, and identifying the bundles of which they are members by reference to the individual mental states.

There are yet other problems with identifying and individuating any bundle or collection of mental states (as opposed to an individual mental state). Suppose that there are currently three mental states associated with me: (a) the perceptual experience of seeing a door, (b) the memory of drinking coffee this morning, and (c) the thought that it is almost 2:30 pm. And suppose that there are currently three mental states associated with you: (d) the perceptual experience of seeing a dog, (e) the memory of having pizza for dinner last night, and (f) the thought that you have a flight to catch this evening. On the bundle theory of the self – to oversimplify it a bit in a way that does not affect the present point – I am nothing more than the collection made up of (a), (b), and (c), and you are nothing more than the collection made up of (d), (e), and (f). But exactly what makes it the case that the mental states in question make up just these two discrete bundles? Why isn't (d), say, also part of my bundle rather than yours? Or why don't (c) and (d) make up a third bundle of their own, and thus a distinct self from either you or me, rather being parts of our bundles?

In response, the bundle theorist might point out that from the first-person point of view of my current stream of consciousness, I am aware of seeing a door, of remembering drinking coffee, and of thinking that it is almost 2:30, but am not aware of seeing a dog. That is true, but that does not explain why (d) is not a part of my bundle in a way that will save the bundle theory. For exactly what does this first-person point of view amount to? Is it the point of view of a *substance* which has (a), (b), and (c) as its attributes, but not (d)? The bundle theorist can't say *that*, because his whole point is to avoid having to posit any substance distinct from the collection of mental states. Does this first-person point of view instead reflect some further mental state (g)? In that case, the same problem just arises again: Why is (g) part of my bundle rather than yours, or rather than part of some third bundle?

Hume himself held that we take mental states to be parts of the same one bundle because of relations of *resemblance* and *causation* that hold between them. But this is no help at all. My memory of drinking coffee this morning and your memory of eating pizza last night resemble one another insofar as they are both memories, but they are not parts of the same bundle. Suppose the bundle theorist responds by pointing out that it matters *to whom* two mental states resemble one another. If in fact I had these two mental states – (b) the memory of drinking coffee this morning, and (e) the memory of eating pizza last night – and found that they resembled one another, then I *would* regard them as part of the same bundle. But, as it happens, I don't have both of them. But the problems with such a response should be obvious.

For we need to ask what this self *is* to whom two mental states might resemble one another. If we say that it is a substance, then that will defeat the whole purpose of the bundle theory, which was to avoid having to posit any substance underlying the mental states that make up the bundle. Should we say instead that the self in question is just the bundle itself? Then we will be stuck once again with a viciously circular explanation. We will be purporting to explain why different mental states are part of the same bundle in terms of their resemblance to one another – and then purporting to explain the sense in which two different mental states might resemble one another in terms of their being part of the same bundle.

Suppose the defender of the bundle theory opts instead to posit some further mental state: (h) the experience of finding that (b) and (e) resemble one another. The idea here would be that (b) and (e) will be part of the same bundle if they are associated with the further mental state (h), but not otherwise. But this obviously won't work. For now we need to know how this new mental state (h) does or does not come to be part of the same bundle as (b) and (e). We will have just kicked the problem back a stage, rather than solving it.

Nor does appeal to causal relations between mental states help. For one thing, they have to be causal relations of the right kind. Suppose my memory that I drank coffee this morning leads me to tell you about it, and this in turn triggers in you a memory of having eaten pizza last night. Then there will be a causal relation between (b) and (e), but obviously that would not be enough to make them members of the same bundle. (b) is still my memory and not yours, and (e) is still your memory and not mine. So, suppose we say that two mental states will be part of the same bundle if the specific causal relation that holds between them has to do with their being generated by the same brain, or associated with the same soul. The problem here is that we're now bringing back in the idea of an underlying substance, when the whole point of the bundle theory was to get rid of it. Suppose, then, that we say instead that two mental states will be part of the same bundle if they are causally related to some third mental state. The problem *now* is that we will once again merely have kicked the problem back a stage rather than solved it. For *exactly what* makes their causal relation to this third mental state the right kind – the kind that *will* suffice to make them part of the same bundle (whereas other causal relations do not suffice to do so)?

These problems with Hume's bundle theory of the self reflect problems afflicting reductionist theories of substance in general.[37] There simply is no coherent way to reduce substances to collections of attributes, whether the attributes in question are thoughts, experiences, and the like, or are of some other type. Just as we cannot coherently doubt the reality of the self, neither can we coherently doubt that the self is a substance.

The points made so far establish the incoherence of eliminative and reductionist views of the self considered *synchronically* or at a particular moment of time. Similar points apply to the self considered *diachronically* or over a span of time. Suppose I reason from the premises that *all men are mortal* and that *Socrates is a man* to the conclusion that *Socrates is mortal*. I cannot make sense of this sequence as an *inference* or chain of reasoning without supposing that there is a single self that had all three thoughts, persisting over time from the first through the second and on to the third. Certainly there would be no inference if there were instead three distinct ephemeral selves succeeding one another, any more than there would be if Tom had the thought that *all men are mortal*, Dick had the thought that *Socrates is a man*, and Harry had the thought that *Socrates is mortal*, but none of them had all three thoughts.

---

[37] For more detailed discussion of those problems, see chapter 3 of my *Scholastic Metaphysics*, especially pp. 177-89 and 193-98.

It would be even less plausible to say that an inference had occurred if there were no selves at all, not even of an ephemeral sort, but merely three ownerless thoughts somehow occurring one after another in that sequence. That would be like saying that an inference had occurred if random spills of ink had by chance produced strings of marks that looked vaguely like the sentences "All men are mortal," "Socrates is a man," and "Socrates is mortal" on three adjacent pieces of paper, but with there being no person around to read them much less write them. A sequence of thoughts without a thinker, of the kind posited by Lichtenberg, could never amount to *thinking* in the sense of working through a chain of reasoning – as Lichtenberg himself did in the course of developing his critique of Descartes' Cogito.

Indeed, the problem arises even if we consider just a single thought, let alone a sequence of thoughts. In order even to have the thought that *all men are mortal*, the self needs to persist at least through the short amount of time it takes to think through it.[38] If there is no self that persists through that time, there will be no thought, but at most a sequence of fragments of a thought. And once again, the situation is even more problematic if, following Lichtenberg, we suppose that there are no selves at all, not even a succession of fleeting ones. In the absence of a self, the sequence *all men are mortal* wouldn't constitute a thought any more than a pile of Scrabble letters spilled onto the floor would.

Perhaps, in his defense, Lichtenberg would bite the bullet and suggest that, for all we know, there really *is* nothing that constitutes a thought any more than spilled Scrabble letters do. But this would merely add incoherence to incoherence. To make such a suggestion is *itself* to express a thought and to invite us to agree with it. Or if it isn't, then what exactly would Lichtenberg be doing in saying such a thing? Making noises with no more meaning than a pile of spilled Scrabble letters? If so, then Lichtenberg wouldn't be saying anything *true*, any more than a grunt or a cough is true – in which case, he wouldn't really have offered any defense of his position at all. (We'll have reason later

---

[38] The point is famously developed by Immanuel Kant in the *Critique of Pure Reason*, at B 129-140. Cf. also Geoffrey Madell, *The Identity of the Self* (Edinburgh: Edinburgh University Press, 1981), p. 14; and Stephen E. Braude, *First Person Plural: Multiple Personality and the Philosophy of Mind*, Revised edition (Lanham, MD: Rowman and Littlefield, 1995), pp. 165-69.

on to consider in greater depth the incoherence of denying the reality of thoughts.)

What about a view that doesn't eliminate the persisting self but reduces it to a collection of parts succeeding one another in time? This is the thesis that a person is really nothing but a collection of *person-stages*.[39] There is the stage of me that exists at time t_1, the stage of me that exists at time t_2, the stage of me that exists at time t_3, and so on, and what I am is just the collection of these stages. But this won't work, for the same reason that Hume's "bundle theory" doesn't work. For consider a further sequence of person-stages that might be attributed to *you*, such as the stage of you that exists at time t_4, the stage of you that exists at time t_5, the stage of you that exists at time t_6, and so on. Exactly what is it that makes it the case that all and only stages t_1 through t_3 are stages of me, and all and only stages t_4 through t_6 are stages of you? Why not instead say that t_4 is one of my stages too, or that stages t_3 and t_4 are stages of some third person, or posit any number of other possible combinations?

However we answer such questions (by appealing to causal relations, or whatever), they are going to face exactly the sorts of problems Hume's bundle theory faces. Just as we cannot identify and individuate mental states except by reference to the self whose mental states they are, so too we cannot identify and individuate person-stages except by reference to the person of whom they are stages.[40] Hence the attempt to reduce persons to collections of person-stages, like the attempt to reduce the self to a bundle of mental states, simply gets things the wrong way around.[41]

When considering the self diachronically no less than synchronically, then, there is no way coherently to deny its substantiality

---

[39] On the notion of a "person-stage," see David Lewis, "Survival and Identity," in *Philosophical Papers, Volume I* (Oxford: Oxford University Press, 1983).

[40] Cf. Lowe, *More Kinds of Being*, pp. 137-38.

[41] The view that the self can be reduced to a sequence of person-stages is related to the "four-dimensionalist" view that a physical object can be reduced to a sequence of "temporal parts," and is problematic for similar reasons. For criticism of four-dimensionalism, see pp. 201-8 of *Scholastic Metaphysics*.

and irreducibility. Note that nothing said so far depends on what *kind* of substance the self is. The same points could be made whether we think of the self as essentially bodily, or as essentially incorporeal, or as a mixture of the bodily and the incorporeal. I will return later on to the question of which of these views of the self is correct, but for the moment we can leave it to one side.

Contrary arguments

The case is not complete, however, until we see what is wrong with all the competing views on offer. There have, in the history of philosophy, been three general sorts of challenges to the reality and irreducibility of the self: *metaphysical, phenomenological,* and *scientific.* Let's consider each in turn.

Metaphysical challenges

The most influential metaphysical argument against the substantiality of the self in the history of Western philosophy derives from John Locke (1632-1704). The thrust of the argument is very simple. Locke holds that the same self that at one time is associated with one substance can in principle come to be associated with a different substance. He has in mind scenarios like the one in the movie *Freaky Friday*, wherein a mother and daughter magically exchange bodies. (Locke's own famous example is that of a prince whose consciousness comes to inhabit the body of a lowly cobbler.) Of course, such scenarios are fantasy, but Locke thinks that they are possible at least in theory, and that since a person who first inhabits one body can in such a scenario later come to inhabit another body, it follows that the self cannot be identified with a physical substance. But he holds that a person's consciousness might in principle jump from one *soul* to another no less than from one body to another, so that the self cannot be identified with an *incorporeal* substance either. Therefore, Locke concludes, a person or self cannot be identified with a substance of any kind. Rather, a person is to be identified with that which he imagines jumping from one substance to another – the person's consciousness, the content of which might include memories of having been in one body and awareness of now inhabiting another.[42]

A standard amendment to this account is thought necessary in order to save it from an objection raised by Thomas Reid (1710-1796).[43] Reid asks us to imagine a brave military officer who recalls being flogged as a boy for stealing, and who at an advanced age becomes a general who remembers his exploits as a young officer but has forgotten the boyhood flogging incident. Since the aged general is conscious of having been the young officer, by Locke's criterion he is the same person as the young officer; and since the young officer is conscious of having been the boy, he is the same person as the boy. Now, identity is a transitive relation. That is to say, if A is identical to B and B is identical to C, then A is identical to C. Hence, if the aged general is identical to the young officer and the young officer is identical to the boy, then the aged general is identical to the boy. But since the aged general does not recall having been the boy, it would follow by Locke's criterion that he is *not* the same person as the boy. Hence, Locke's position entails a contradiction.

Commentators on Locke routinely point out that he can get around this problem by simply allowing that the connection of memory between stages of the self need not be direct. He can say that a person A is identical to an earlier person C if *either* A is conscious of having been C, or A is conscious of having been some earlier person B and B was conscious of having been C. With this emendation, the aged general in Reid's example *would* be the same person as the boy by Locke's criterion, and the contradiction disappears.

A far more serious problem, though, is posed by the *circularity objection* commonly attributed to Joseph Butler (1692-1752).[44] Memory can be unreliable. An insane person living in the twenty-first century

---

[42] *An Essay Concerning Human Understanding*, Book II, Chapter 27.

[43] *Essays on the Intellectual Powers of Man*, Essay III, Chapter 6.
[44] *The Analogy of Religion, Natural and Revealed*, Dissertation I, "Of Personal Identity." Though it has been suggested that Butler was not in fact raising the objection commonly attributed to him, but making a more modest point to the effect that we cannot define what personal identity *is* in terms of how we *know* about it. Cf. Harold W. Noonan, *Personal Identity*, Third edition (London: Routledge, 2019), p. 55.

who claims to recall the sting of defeat at Waterloo does not really remember being Napoleon, even if he thinks he does. So, in order for a person A to be identical to an earlier person B, it is not sufficient that A *seems* to remember being B. It has to be the case that A *really does* remember being B. But for A *really* to remember being B presupposes that A and B are in fact identical. Hence, Locke's account is, implicitly, viciously circular. It purports to analyze personal identity in terms of memory, but memory in turn must be analyzed in terms of personal identity.

In an influential analysis, Sydney Shoemaker proposed that Locke's account can be salvaged by appeal to what he calls "quasi-memory."[45] A quasi-memory is a genuine recollection of an experience of some past event or action, but where (to avoid circularity) this does not imply that the person having the quasi-memory is the one who witnessed the event or carried out the action. For instance, if Reid's young officer remembers an experience of being flogged as a boy and there really was such an experience, this could count as a "quasi-memory" even if the officer was not in fact the one who had that boyhood experience. Memories in the ordinary sense are, on this account, treated as a species of quasi-memories. In particular, something will count as a genuine memory in the ordinary sense when it is a quasi-memory *and* the person having the quasi-memory *is* indeed the one who experienced the event or carried out the action.

Now, consider that, in situations where a person falsely seems to remember doing something that he did not in fact do (as in the case of the insane person who thinks he is Napoleon), the pseudo-memory typically has a cause that is very different from the cause of a genuine memory. For example, it might result from a blow to the head, brainwashing, drug abuse, or mental illness. Crucial to genuine memory, then, is the existence of the right sort of causal chain linking one's apparent memory to the event or action that one seems to remember. With these ideas in hand, Shoemaker suggests, we can update Locke's

---

[45] Sydney Shoemaker, "Persons and their Pasts," *American Philosophical Quarterly* 7 (1970): 269-85. Cf. also Derek Parfit, *Reasons and Persons* (Oxford: Clarendon Press, 1984), pp. 219-23.

account by saying that a person A will be identical to some earlier person B if A has a quasi-memory of being B *and* there exists the right kind of causal chain connecting this quasi-memory to B. This, he holds, preserves the spirit of Locke's analysis while avoiding the circularity problem.

Now, one problem with Shoemaker's "quasi-memory" analysis is that it is questionable whether one can coherently be said to have a genuine memory of an experience that was not one's own.[46] But even putting that aside, there is a deeper problem. For what, exactly, will make a causal chain between A and B the "right" kind? It is hard to see how to answer this question in a way that doesn't presuppose a judgment about whether A and B are identical. Shoemaker himself deliberately tailors his account of quasi-memory and its causes so that it will be as close as possible to our ordinary conception of how memory works in cases where A and B are identical. Hence, consider a case where *two* later people seem to remember doing what B did. A famous example is provided by Derek Parfit's "teletransportation" scenario, in which a machine scans a person's body and brain, destroys them, then sends the information to Mars, where a second machine generates an identical copy of the original person.[47] Since the person who steps out of the machine on Mars has the memories of the original, it might seem that by Locke's criterion, he is the same person as the original. But now imagine that the first machine does not destroy the original person's body and brain before sending the information to Mars. Then we'd have *two* people with the memories in question. On our ordinary notion of memory, only one person can remember doing what an earlier person did. Shoemaker thus stipulates that the "right" kind of causal chain will be one that does not involve "branching" of the kind illustrated by Parfit's example. But as Harold Noonan points out, the problem with this procedure is that it gives the lie to

---

[46] For challenges to the coherence of this idea, see Gareth Evans, *The Varieties of Reference* (Oxford: Clarendon Press, 1982), pp. 242-48 and Geoffrey Madell, *The Essence of the Self: In Defense of the Simple View of Personal Identity* (London: Routledge, 2015), pp. 73-76. For defenses of its coherence, see Noonan, *Personal Identity*, chapter 8, and Sven Bernecker, *Memory: A Philosophical Study* (Oxford: Oxford University Press, 2010), pp. 51-61.

[47] Parfit, *Reasons and Persons*, pp. 199-201. Parfit's book appeared after Shoemaker's article, but I use his example because it has become a standard way to illustrate the idea of the "branching" of a stream of consciousness.

the idea that Shoemaker's "quasi-memory" analysis avoids circularity.[48] Shoemaker purports to analyze personal identity in terms of the "right" sort of causal connection, but a causal connection is not allowed to count as the "right" sort if it would entail departing too far from what we would ordinarily count as personal identity.

In response to Noonan, Sven Bernecker suggests that it is because our ordinary understanding of memory and personal identity is more familiar than Shoemaker's "quasi-memory" analysis that the latter seems parasitic on the former. If instead we lived in a world in which "quasi-memories" were common and ordinary memories rare, Shoemaker's analysis would seem natural and our ordinary understanding would seem to be parasitic on *it*.[49] Now, whether "quasi-memory" is a coherent notion in the first place is part of what is at issue. If it isn't, then Bernecker is not in fact describing a genuine possibility. But even apart from that, his reply misses the point. It is comparable to saying that in a world where decorative faux fruit was common and real fruit rare, we would take our conception of the latter to be parasitic on the former. Or it is like saying that in a world where heart disease was so common that healthy hearts were rare, we would take our conception of the latter to be parasitic on the former. In both cases, we probably *wouldn't* make these judgements, but if we did, we would simply be confused, because such judgments would clearly be false. The notion of decorative faux fruit is parasitic on the notion of real fruit, whereas the notion of real fruit is entirely independent of that of decorative faux fruit. We would have the notion of real fruit whether or not we ever started the practice of making decorative faux fruit, but we would never have formed the concept of decorative faux fruit if we hadn't first understood what real fruit is. Similarly, we would have no notion of what heart disease is except by contrast with what we know to be true of healthy hearts, but we would know what a healthy heart is even if there were no such thing as heart disease. There is an *asymmetry* in both cases, and a comparable asymmetry exists between the notion of memory and the notion of "quasi-memory." The latter, if it makes sense at all, cannot be understood except by

---

[48] Noonan, *Personal Identity*, pp. 158-63.

[49] Bernecker, *Memory*, p. 56.

contrast with the former, whereas the former can be understood whether or not we ever conceive of the latter.[50]

But Parfit's "teletransportation" example points to what is in my view the fundamental problem with Locke's account, though not for the reasons usually supposed. Consider a further variation on the scenario. Imagine that after the first machine scans a person's body and brain, destroys them, and sends the information to Mars, the second machine generates *two* identical copies of the original person. Now, since neither copy has the original body, there can be no question of one of them having a more favorable claim to being the same person as the original on that score. By Locke's standard, that doesn't matter anyway. That A is conscious of having been B is sufficient for A to be the same person as B. The trouble is that in this case, *two* later people are conscious of having been the earlier person. Now these two people cannot be identical to each other. After all, if one of them killed the other, it would be absurd to say that the same person would in that case be both dead and alive. But if they are not identical to each other, then neither can either one be identical to the original person. For as noted when discussing Reid, identity is a transitive relation. Hence, if either of the two copies really were identical to the original person, they *would* have been identical to each other.

This "reduplication" objection might seem to be a decisive refutation of Locke's account.[51] But many philosophers have claimed

---

[50] Cf. John McDowell, "Reductionism and the First Person," in Jonathan Dancy, ed., *Reading Parfit* (Oxford: Blackwell, 1997). At pp. 60-1 of *Memory*, Bernecker says in response to McDowell that memory in the ordinary sense is not immune to error, and that in a world where quasi-memory was common and memory in the ordinary sense rare, a person would not habitually conclude, from the fact that he recalls an experience, that he was the one who had the experience. But this is irrelevant to the point at issue. Even in the scenario Bernecker describes, the notion of quasi-memory would still be parasitic on the notion of memory in the ordinary sense, just as, in a world where decorative faux fruit was common and real fruit rare, the notion of decorative faux fruit would still be parasitic on the notion of real fruit.
[51] Bernard Williams presented an influential version of this objection in "Personal Identity and Individuation," *Proceedings of the Aristotelian Society* 57 (1956-7): 229-52. Williams' example didn't involve a teletransportation device, however, but rather a scenario in which two contemporary individuals appear to have equally good claims to being the reincarnation of Guy Fawkes.

that with further tinkering, Locke's alleged insight can still be preserved in the face of this and other problems facing it. Robert Nozick argues that even where two or more later persons have, by Locke's criterion, some claim to being identical to some earlier person, if one of them has at least a somewhat greater degree of continuity with the earlier person than the others do (such as a more complete memory), then this "closest continuer" is the one we should judge identical with the original.[52] Parfit, by contrast, argues that the lesson we should draw from the difficulties facing reductionist theories of the self like Locke's is not that the self is irreducible, but rather that there is no self over and above whatever can be captured in a reductionist analysis.[53] A Lockean, on this view, should simply note that sometimes a single later person A will have quasi-memories of doing what an earlier person B did that are caused in the right kind of way; sometimes several later people might have such quasi-memories, but one will be more closely continuous with B than the others are; and sometimes all of them will be equally continuous. But that is all that can be said. There is no "further fact" of the matter, over and above these various degrees of continuity, about which is identical to the original person. If the self is supposed to be something over above them, then there is no such thing.

Naturally, the various ways of responding to the problems facing analyses like Locke's are controversial. But I submit that the whole debate misses the point, or at least the deepest point. To see what I have in mind, forget about the self for a moment and consider a different example, such as a carrot. Suppose I suggested that the attributes of some particular carrot, such as its orange color, shape, and size, might in theory jump to the substance that had been associated with a different carrot. Suppose I spelled this out by describing carrot A as being of one shade of orange, shape, and size and carrot B has having a slightly lighter shade of orange and slightly larger shape and size, and then proposing that we might find one morning that the attributes that the night before had existed in substance A were now to

---

[52] Robert Nozick, *Philosophical Explanations* (Cambridge, MA: Harvard University Press, 1981), Chapter 1.

[53] Parfit, *Reasons and Persons*, pp. 281-2. Cf. also Derek Parfit, "The Unimportance of Identity," in Raymond Martin and John Barresi, eds., *Personal Identity* (Oxford: Blackwell, 2003).

be found in B, and vice versa. Suppose I then suggested that the carrot *itself* had jumped from A to B, so that what a carrot is is not really a kind of substance after all, but rather a collection of attributes that might be associated with different substances at different times. Suppose someone pointed out in reply that we could imagine *two* carrots, B and C, having the attributes A had the day before, and that this posed a problem for my theory. Suppose I responded by saying that if either B or C was at least slightly more similar to A, then this "closest continuer" of A was the true original carrot. Suppose someone else suggested instead that the real lesson we should draw is that there is no such thing as a carrot over and above whatever degrees of continuity of attributes like color, size, shape, etc. one object has with an earlier one.

This whole discussion would, of course, be silly, but not just because the metaphysics of carrots seems unworthy of such heavy going. The reason it would be silly is that attributes are simply not the sorts of thing that can jump from one substance to another. For example, there is no such thing as the orangeness of a particular carrot jumping to another carrot. To be sure, you could peel off the surface of one carrot and affix it to that of another carrot. But that's not what I'm talking about. That would involve taking a piece of the first carrot and moving it, which can of course happen. And of course, you could alter the shade of the second carrot so that it looks more like the first. But that's not what I'm talking about either. What I'm saying is that the first carrot's orangeness *itself* – not a piece of the carrot but the *orangeness* of the piece – cannot be separated out and moved from one substance to another. That's just not how attributes work. So, whatever we're imagining when we imagine carrot B now looking the way carrot A did, it is not a matter of attributes jumping from one substance to another. It is at most a case of carrot B now having *similar* attributes to those that A had. It is a case of B having somehow been transformed into a *replica* of A, that's all. And the scenario where two carrots, B and C, come to look exactly like A did, reinforces the point. The natural thing to say is that we've now got *two* replicas of A, neither of which (being mere replicas) is actually the same carrot as A. All the chin-pulling about which of them is the "closest continuer" of A, and whether there really is such a thing as a carrot over and above the degrees of continuity, would be for nothing, since it would be based on the erroneous assumption that attributes can jump from one substance to another.

Am I saying that Locke's theory and the entire centuries-long debate it has spawned is based on a similar mistake? Yes, that is exactly what I am saying. Consciousness, memories, personality traits, and the like are attributes. Hence they cannot jump from one substance to another, and the kinds of scenarios Locke and his followers imagine in no way show what they think they do.[54] If someone wakes up in the cobbler's body talking like the prince and seeming to remember what the prince did, then whatever is going on, it is *not* a matter of the prince's consciousness, memories, and personality traits jumping from the prince's body or soul to the cobbler's, because attributes can't do that. It would instead be a matter of the cobbler now somehow having very *similar* memories and personality traits to those of the prince. Similarly, whoever steps out of the machine on Mars in Parfit's teletransportation example, it is not the original person, because memories, being attributes, can't jump from one substance to another. It would merely be a *replica* of the original person, and thus (qua replica) not the original person. The scenario where *two* exactly similar people walk out of the machine on Mars should make that obvious. For clearly *they* are mere replicas, and since they came about in exactly the same way that the single person walking out of the machine does, he is a mere replica too.[55]

The fundamental problem with Locke's position, then, is that it argues for the conclusion that the self is an attribute or collection of attributes, by way of an argument that describes the self doing something (jumping from one substance to another) that an attribute cannot intelligibly be said to do.[56] It also presupposes that we can identify

---

[54] Cf. Chisholm, *Person and Object*, pp. 106-8; and P. M. S. Hacker, *Human Nature: The Categorial Framework* (Oxford: Blackwell, 2007), pp. 297-98 and 301-4.

[55] The point that, in the absence of a persisting substance, even the most similar later person could only ever be a *replica* of an earlier person and never identical to him is emphasized in Antony Flew, *God, Freedom, and Immortality: A Critical Analysis* (Buffalo: Prometheus Books, 1984), pp. 107-8.

[56] For defense of the interpretation of Locke as regarding a person as an attribute or "mode," see E. J. Lowe, *Locke on Human Understanding* (London: Routledge, 1995), pp. 114-15.

and individuate attributes apart from the substance in which they inhere, which, as I have already argued, we cannot coherently do.[57] There are other problems too. For example, if the self is to be analyzed in terms of the continuity of its conscious experiences, what happens to it when a person is entirely unconscious? Barry Dainton proposes dealing with this problem by arguing that the self can be identified with the *capacity* for conscious experience, since a capacity can exist even when it is not exercised.[58] But a capacity too is an attribute, and like other attributes it can neither jump from one substance to another nor be identified and individuated apart from the substance whose capacity it is. The Lockean approach to thinking about the nature of the self simply cannot be extricated from this fundamental and fatal conceptual muddle.

Another famous metaphysical challenge to the reality and irreducibility of the self comes from Buddhism.[59] Whereas the Lockean approach is developed primarily in terms of considerations having to do with the nature of the self specifically, the Buddhist "no-self" doctrine reflects a more general critique of the very notion of substance.[60]

Rightly noting that "modes cannot leap from substance to substance," Robert Pasnau disputes this interpretation of Locke in his *Metaphysical Themes 1274-1671* (Oxford: Clarendon Press, 2011), at p. 718. He suggests that Locke's view is, not that mental attributes that exist in one substance can be transferred to another, but rather that the second substance might have in it a "representation" of a mental attribute that existed in the first (p. 719, note 8). But this interpretation would only reinforce the point that what exists in the second substance is not the original person, but only a *replica* of the original person. For a mental *representation* of a person is not the *person*, any more than a painting or photograph of the person is.

[57] Cf. Lowe, *Locke on Human Understanding*, pp. 116-18.

[58] Barry Dainton, *Self* (London: Penguin Books, 2014), Chapter 5.

[59] Founded by Gautama Buddha (fl. circa 450 B.C.), to whom is attributed the essentials of the Buddhist critique of the self, though later Buddhist thinkers would develop various alternative interpretations of the view.

[60] For some of the relevant classic Buddhist texts, see Sarvepalli Radhakrishnan and Charles A. Moore, eds., *A Sourcebook in Indian Philosophy* (Princeton: Princeton University Press, 1957), pp. 278-89. For useful surveys of the main Buddhist arguments and their metaphysical background, see chapter 12 of John M. Koller, *Oriental Philosophies*, Second edition

Common sense regards tables, chairs, rocks, trees, and other ordinary objects as persisting entities each of which has its own nature or essence sharply demarcating it from other things. Buddhism takes this to be an illusion. In reality, all such entities are entirely reducible to their parts and the causal relations between the parts. For example, what we think of as a tree is really nothing more than a collection of parts causally related in such a way that the resulting composite gives the temporary appearance of corresponding to our concept of a tree. But all that really exists are the parts themselves, and there is in reality nothing corresponding to our concept, or to the purported essence of a tree that that concept captures. The parts that make up the collection are also continually changing, so that the collection corresponding to what we think of as the tree at one moment is not exactly the same as the one that exists at any other moment. Moreover, the character of the composite is ultimately determined by the causal relations its parts bear to everything else that exists, so that a complete description of any one thing would make reference to everything else. Hence there are no essences by which one thing might be neatly distinguished from other things, and no substances that endure over time. This picture of reality is known as the doctrine of "dependent co-origination," since it takes the things that make up the world of everyday experience to be interrelated aspects of one whole rather than the discrete entities they appear to be.[61]

Now, I would argue that Buddhism's general metaphysical picture of the world is false. Substances and essences, I maintain, are real, and most ordinary material objects are not in fact reducible to the sum of their parts. Defending such general metaphysical claims is beyond the scope of a book about human nature, but I have done so at length elsewhere.[62] Fortunately, it will suffice for present purposes to

---

(Englewood Cliffs, NJ: Prentice-Hall, 1985); and chapter 3 of Mark Siderits, *Buddhism as Philosophy: An Introduction* (Indianapolis: Hackett Publishing Company, 2007).

[61] Readers familiar with the early history of Western philosophy will recognize in this a position similar to the dynamic monism of the Pre-Socratic philosopher Heraclitus.

[62] See chapters 3 and 4 of Feser, *Scholastic Metaphysics*.

note the insuperable difficulties facing attempts to apply the general Buddhist metaphysical picture to an analysis of the self.

Buddhism holds that the self too is entirely reducible to its parts, and indeed that strictly speaking it cannot be said to exist at all. For none of the parts count as the self, and there is nothing over and above the parts that could count as the self either. The parts in question are referred to as the "five aggregates," and comprise *bodily processes, sensation, perception, impulses to action,* and *consciousness.* Causal relations between parts in these five classes give rise to the construct we call the "self" in such a way that it seems to have a distinctive essence and to be more than the sum of these parts. But this, it is claimed, is an illusion.

The reader may have noticed that this position is very similar to the ones Locke and Hume would defend more than two millennia after the time of the Buddha. Not only is it open to the same objections that Locke's and Hume's views face, but such objections were raised fifteen centuries ago by critics of Buddhism associated with the *Nyāya* philosophical tradition within Hinduism.[63] For example, the *Nyāya* thinkers note that mental states are attributes, and attributes cannot be identified or individuated except by reference to a substance in which they inhere.[64] They also note that there is no way to identify the relevant causal relations between mental states without reference to a self.[65] For example, suppose I have the thought that the *cat is on the mat* and this triggers in me the desire to utter the sentence "The cat is on the mat." The Buddhist will say that this causal relation between the thought and the desire is what makes them elements of what I take to be the same one self. But suppose my utterance in turn triggers in you the thought that *someone should feed the cat.* Then we have a further mental state that is causally related to the first two. But

---

[63] Cf. *The Nyāya-sūtra: Selections with Early Commentaries,* translated by Matthew Dasti and Stephen Phillips (Indianapolis: Hackett Publishing Company, 2017), chapter 4. Cf. Siderits, *Buddhism as Philosophy,* chapter 5.

[64] Ibid., pp. 79-80.

[65] Cf. Evan Thompson, *Why I Am Not a Buddhist* (New Haven: Yale University Press, 2020), pp. 100-1.

that mental state is *not* part of the same self with which the first two are associated. So, though the Buddhist claims that we can dispense with reference to selves and replace it with reference to causal relations between mental states, in fact we first have to know which mental states are associated with which selves before we can determine which causal relations are relevant. The analysis implicitly presupposes the self and thus hardly eliminates the self.

The Buddhist responds that "mental perception" is what binds the belief that the *cat is on the mat* and the desire to utter the sentence together so that they, but not your belief that *someone should feed the cat*, come to be associated with the same self. But this just raises the same problem over again.[66] For now we need to know what makes this event of "mental perception" part of the same self as the belief that *the cat is on the mat* and the desire to utter the sentence, whereas your belief that *someone should feed the cat* is not part of it. Just as we cannot identify the mental states or relevant causal relations without first knowing which self they belong to, so too we cannot identify the relevant event of "mental perception" without first knowing which self it belongs to. Once again, the analysis presupposes the self and thus cannot be said to eliminate the self.

In order to deal with such problems, the *Pudgalavādin* or "Personalist" school of thought within Buddhism posited the "person" as that which individuates the relevant mental states and causal relations. But the trouble with this approach is that spelling out what it is to be a "person" puts Personalist Buddhism in a dilemma. If a "person" is nothing more than a collection of causally related mental states, then we are back where we started and the Personalist has not added anything to the analysis except some new jargon. But if a "person" is something over and above a collection of causally related mental states, then it appears to be a *self* – in which case, the Personalist will have *abandoned* rather than vindicated the Buddhist no-self doctrine.[67]

---

[66] Ibid., p. 104.

[67] Cf. Koller, *Oriental Philosophies*, pp. 169-70; and Roy W. Perrett, *An Introduction to Indian Philosophy* (Cambridge: Cambridge University Press, 2016), pp. 187-88.

The other points I have already made above in defense of the reality and irreducibility of the self also entail the falsity of the Buddhist analysis. Hence Buddhism does not add anything new to what we have already seen. To be sure, the Buddhist position is older than the views we've considered up to now, and was worked out in detail by thinkers of genius over the course of centuries. For that it deserves our respectful consideration. But that does not entail that Buddhism does not make the same mistakes that Lichtenberg, Locke, Hume, Parfit and company made. It just made them earlier.

Phenomenological challenges

The second of the main challenges to the reality of the self is phenomenological. That is to say, it appeals to what we know from the first-person point of view of conscious experience (as opposed to the third-person point of view of metaphysical inquiry or scientific investigation). It claims that the self is not revealed to us from this first-person point of view, and that we therefore have reason to doubt its reality.

The most famous argument to this effect in the history of Western philosophy comes from Hume. The self, he says, is supposed to be something that underlies the different "perceptions" that we have and that persists through changes from one perception to another. Hence, to be aware of the self from the first-person point of view would entail being aware of something distinct from our perceptions and persisting in this way. Yet the examination of conscious experience reveals no such thing. Hume writes:

> For my part, when I enter most intimately into what I call *myself*, I always stumble on some particular perception or other, of heat or cold, light or shade, love or hatred, pain or pleasure. I never can catch *myself* at any time without a perception, and never can observe any thing but the perception.[68]

Hume suggests that when others carry out this exercise, they will get similar results. For example, when you look within your own mind, you might encounter the thought that *the cat is on the mat*, the experience of seeming to see a door, and so on. But this or that particular

---

[68] *Treatise of Human Nature*, Book I, Part IV, Section VI.

thought, experience, or other mental items is *all* you will encounter, and you will never encounter any *self* in which they inhere.

The first indication that there is something wrong with this argument is that Hume himself reports what is going on by saying things like "*I* always stumble on some particular perception or other." To what does this "I" refer if not the self? It will not do to suggest, as Lichtenberg might, that we can eliminate the first-person reference and instead say something like "Some particular perception is all that is ever observed." For in that case, Hume will be saying something that neither he nor anyone else can support merely from an examination of conscious experience. If an examination of *your* conscious experience fails to turn up anything but particular perceptions, it hardly follows that particular perceptions are all that is *ever observed anywhere*. That would like saying that since I do not ever observe within my own conscious awareness the experience of skydiving, it follows that "The experience of skydiving is never observed." Of course, it *is* in fact observed – by introspective skydivers, even though never by me. Note that the point is not that this by itself shows that there is in fact a self. The point is rather that the force of Hume's argument rests on what he has been able to determine from the first-person evidence. Hence, if he has to reformulate his conclusion in a way that eliminates reference to the first person, he will end up stripping the argument of any force.[69]

There is also the question of what demarcates the perceptions *I* am aware of from the perceptions *you* are aware of if it is not the fact that there are two distinct *selves* who have the respective perceptions. Now, Hume, as we have seen, will say that what demarcates these perceptions is that they are parts of two distinct bundles. This might also seem to legitimate his use of "I" in the passage quoted. It refers to a particular bundle of perceptions, even if not to anything distinct from the bundle in which the perceptions inhere. But this will be an adequate response only if Hume's "bundle theory" of the self is coherent, and as we have seen, it is not.

---

[69] Cf. Chisholm, *Person and Object*, pp. 40-41; and Noonan, *Personal Identity*, pp. 67-68.

The deeper problem with Hume's argument, however, is that it presupposes that the self, if it is real, ought to be knowable to itself in just the way that the other things the self knows are. This is a little like saying that if the eye is real, then it ought to be able to see itself in just the way it sees other things. In fact, of course, while the eye can see other things directly, it can see itself only indirectly, through reflections. What Hume fails to consider is that, like the eye, the self can know itself only indirectly.[70]

Here is how the mistake arises. When you perceive a door, the door is the object of your perception. It is tempting to think that when you are aware of the fact that you are perceiving the door, that is because the perception of the door itself becomes, in turn, the object of something like an *inner* perception or introspective state. "Higher-order" theories of consciousness are based on this supposition, and hold that a mental state like perceiving the door will be unconscious unless it becomes the object of a higher-order mental state.[71] Our knowledge of the internal world of the mind is thereby modeled on our knowledge of the external physical world. With this model in mind, it can seem that the self ought to be directly observable in something like the way the door is, so that when we do *not* in fact observe it, doubts about its reality seem warranted. But in fact this model of self-knowledge is wrong, so that the Humean skepticism about the self that it implies is without foundation.

As philosophers in the phenomenological tradition argue, the self's awareness of itself and its mental states is, in fact, first and foremost "pre-reflective" in nature.[72] Pre-reflective awareness is to be distinguished from reflective awareness on the one hand, and complete unconsciousness on the other. It is clear enough what it is for something to be unconscious. For example, that blood is passing

---

[70] Cf. Plato, *Alcibiades I*, 132d-133c.

[71] Cf. D. M. Armstrong, *A Materialist Theory of the Mind*, Revised edition (London: Routledge, 1993), pp. 92-99; and David M. Rosenthal, "Thinking that One Thinks," in Martin Davies and Glyn W. Humphreys, eds., *Consciousness* (Oxford: Blackwell, 1993).

[72] Cf. Dan Zahavi, *Subjectivity and Selfhood: Investigating the First-Person Perspective* (Cambridge, MA: The MIT Press, 2005).

through your veins and arteries, that food is passing through your intestines, and similar facts are things of which you are usually totally unconscious. Unless something goes wrong, you would normally not be experiencing or thinking about them at all. Reflective awareness, meanwhile, is the sort of thing manifest when you deliberately turn your attention to what you are currently thinking or feeling, when you become self-conscious upon seeing yourself in a mirror or embarrassing yourself, when you rehearse the events of your life to yourself or others, and so on. In such cases, awareness of yourself and your mental states has an *explicit* character.

Pre-reflective awareness, qua awareness, is not unconscious. But neither is it explicit. Suppose that I am driving but have stopped for a red light. Then, while trying to remember what I need to pick up at the supermarket, I notice that the car in front of me has started to move after the light has turned green, and I proceed to drive straight ahead as it turns the corner. A moment later my passenger asks: "What color was that car?" and I pause and say that I think it was silver. In this sequence, a visual experience that had as its object the red light is followed by a visual experience that has a different object, the car. That in turn is followed by a recollection which also has the car as its object. We have a mental state of one type followed by a distinct mental state of the same type followed by a third mental state of a different type, where the object of the third mental state is the same as the object of the second one but different from the object of the first. So, neither any particular mental state, nor any one type of mental state, nor any one object of a mental state persists through the sequence.[73]

Now, let's notice a few things about this example. First, some of what is going on are things I am aware of rather than unconscious of, but not in a reflective way. For example, I was aware of the car in front of me, which is why I could later report on its color. But when I saw it, I was lost in thought trying to remember what I needed to buy,

---

[73] I borrow the basic idea of this sequence (while changing the specific examples) from Dan Zahavi, "The Experiential Self: Objections and Clarifications," in Mark Siderits, Evan Thompson, and Dan Zahavi, eds., *Self, No Self?: Perspectives from Analytical, Phenomenological, and Indian Traditions* (Oxford: Oxford University Press, 2011), pp.57-58.

and thus was not paying much attention to it. Had my passenger asked me the question ten minutes later, I may well have completely forgotten that there was a car, so little did it make an impression on me. In fact, I may remember it later on only precisely because I was asked the question and thereby made to reflect on the experience. But the experience itself was "pre-reflective" rather than reflective, even if it was, again, not unconscious. In fact, this pre-reflective awareness is a precondition of there being anything to reflect *on*. If I had been entirely unconscious of the car, I wouldn't have been aware of it, and thus could hardly reflect later on its color. But had my initial awareness been reflective rather than pre-reflective, I wouldn't have had to think about it for a moment in order to recall the color.

A second thing to note is that despite the fact that no particular mental state, nor any type of mental state, nor any object of a mental state persists through the sequence, they nevertheless are all part of one and the same sequence. What gives the sequence this unity is that each member of it and the sequence as a whole involve the way things are *"for me."* It first seemed *to me* that there was a red light, then it seemed *to me* that the car ahead of me has moved, then it seemed *to me* that the car had been silver, and then as I reflected on its color it seemed *to me* that it was *I* who had seen the red light and then the car. Moreover, the nature of what was experienced, and not merely who was experiencing it, reflect this first-person character. The red light and the car appeared the way one would expect them to appear to someone perceiving them from *my* perspective (from inside the automobile I was driving, given the distance from them that I happened to be at, traveling at the particular speed I was moving at, etc.). The natural way to describe the sequence and each member of it is by reference to the *self* to whom things appear the way they do, and (as we have seen) it is at best extremely difficult to describe them without reference to a self. Here too, though, all of this is typically pre-reflective. I do not explicitly think "It seems to me that there is a red light," then "It seems to me that the car has moved," and so on. I may go on to think such things later on if I reflect on the sequence, but even if I do not, it is still the case that it involved a series of ways that things appeared *for me*.

Writers in the phenomenological tradition emphasize that consciousness is neither something *additional* to pre-reflective awareness nor a matter of taking such awareness as an *object* of thought or perception that would otherwise remain unconscious, as "higher-order" theories of consciousness suppose. Rather, consciousness is *constitutive* of pre-reflective awareness. Nor, they argue, is it merely that the account I have been summarizing *happens* to correspond to the character of the human mind. Rather, our *fundamental* mental states *must* involve pre-reflective awareness. For on the one hand, they cannot be unconscious. If a mental state is unconscious, it is hard to see why it would become conscious simply by virtue of becoming the object of some further mental state that is *itself* unconscious. But on the other hand, if we suppose that our fundamental mental states involve *reflective* awareness, then we will be led into a vicious regress. If a certain mental state is conscious only if it is the object of explicit reflection, then that act of explicit reflection will be conscious only if it is in turn the object of a higher-order act of explicit reflection, which will in turn be conscious only if it is the object of a yet higher-order act, and so on *ad infinitum*.[74]

Now, how does all of this relate to the challenge raised by Hume? In the following way. Hume supposes that in order to be aware of itself, the self would have to become *directly* perceived in an act of *explicit* or *reflective* awareness. But that is not in fact how all awareness works, and indeed it is not how our fundamental mode of awareness works. (Hume, alas, was no better a phenomenologist than he was a metaphysician.) We can be, and usually are, aware of things only implicitly and pre-reflectively, and sometimes (as with the eye which sees itself in a mirror) we can know them only indirectly. In the case of the self, we are initially aware of it pre-reflectively in the manner described by modern phenomenologists. Then we reflect on it by what I referred to earlier as "cognitive ascent" and, while not directly perceiving it, infer that it must not only be real but must have the nature of a substance, for the reasons given above.

Hume, of course, thinks this is all illusory. But the point is that he has given us no good reason to agree with him. His account of what self-awareness would be like is simplistic, and in trying to show

---

[74] Cf. Jean-Paul Sartre, *Being and Nothingness* (New York: Pocket Books, 1966), p. 12.

that we are not aware of the self even *he* cannot entirely avoid reference to it, so tightly is the notion of the self tied to our very conception of awareness. Moreover, Hume's alternative reductionist analysis of the self falls apart upon inspection, as we have seen.

Phenomenological investigation arguably reveals our ordinary notion of the self to be even richer than the points made so far would indicate. Galen Strawson argues that the self is ordinarily experienced or conceptualized as: a *thing*, in some robust sense; *mental* in its nature; *single* or unified both synchronically and diachronically; *distinct* from other things; a *subject of experience*; an *agent*; and having a distinctive character or *personality*.[75] He holds that these aspects of the ordinary phenomenology of the self are so basic that they "are situated below any level of plausible cultural variation."[76] Significantly, he makes these claims despite the fact that he not only does not think that there is anything in objective reality that actually has all of these features, but also denies that he finds all of them in his own introspective awareness of himself. For example, he says that he does not personally have a strong sense of himself as being continuous over long periods of time, even though most other people do.[77] He merely holds that these are in fact aspects of most people's experience of the self, whether or not that experience is delusory.

Naturally, one might dispute Strawson's account of the phenomenological facts. But that even a thinker sympathetic to the reductionist position could concede that that position conflicts with the phenomenology shows that the appeal to introspection simply does not by itself have the force that Hume thinks it does. For one thing, the phenomenology gives much stronger support to the view that the self is real and irreducible than Hume supposes. For another, even if Hume had gotten the phenomenology right, it simply wouldn't follow that the self is not real and irreducible. For two can play at Strawson's game. If Strawson can allow that there *appears* to be a self having all

---

[75] Galen Strawson, "The Self," in Martin and Barresi, *Personal Identity*, at pp. 338-40. Cf. also Strawson's "The Sense of the Self" in his collection *Things That Bother Me: Death, Freedom, the Self, Etc.* (New York: New York Review Books, 2018).

[76] Strawson, "The Self," p. 338.

[77] Strawson, "The Sense of the Self," pp. 34-35.

the aspects he identifies but still argue that the appearance is illusory, then one could also allow, with Hume, that there appears *not* to be a self, and yet still argue that *that* appearance is illusory. At the end of the day, what is decisive is not what the *phenomenology* reveals, but which view has the stronger *metaphysical* considerations in its favor. By that standard, as I have shown, Hume's critic has the better of the argument.

Scientific challenges

It is sometimes claimed that modern science has shown that the irreducibility or even the reality of the self is illusory. Some of these arguments are remarkably shoddy. For example, psychologist Bruce Hood appeals to considerations such as the fact that brain damage can dramatically alter personality, that the neural processes underlying various mental phenomena are distributed throughout the brain rather than centralized in any one part of it, that the brain fills in gaps in the meagre information it receives from the environment when generating conscious awareness of the world and of ourselves, and that the roles we play as men, women, parents, workers, and so on are shaped by our social interactions with others.[78] Such facts, he claims, vindicate the Humean and Buddhist "bundle" theory of the self, and indeed reveal that the self is an "illusion."

But this is a blatant *non sequitur*. The thesis that the self is real and irreducible, you will recall, entails that it is a substance that persists through changes of its attributes and cannot coherently be identified with the collection of attributes themselves. How does the falsity of this claim follow from considerations like those adduced by Hood? Yes, damage to the brain can result in changes in personality, memory, and the like that are so dramatic that the person may even seem unrecognizable. How does it follow that there isn't a single substance in which both the mental attributes that existed before the brain damage, and those that exist after it, inhere? Yes, the neural processes associated with various mental activities are distributed throughout the brain rather than located in one region of it. How does that show that there isn't a single substance to which these various

---

[78] Cf. Bruce Hood, *The Self Illusion: How the Social Brain Creates Identity* (Oxford: Oxford University Press, 2012).

processes themselves, along with the mental states associated with them, can be attributed? Remember that I am not at the moment addressing the question whether the self is an *immaterial* substance, or a material one, or possesses a mixture of material and immaterial attributes. I will return to that later on. The claim is simply that it is a substance of *some* kind, and considerations like those cited by Hood do not show otherwise. (Even Hood, when describing a person's neural processes and mental states, associates them with the same one brain.)

If, in generating conscious experiences of the world around us and of our own minds, the brain fills in gaps in the information supplied by the senses, how does that show that there isn't a persisting substance in which the experiences inhere? If your understanding of what it is to be a man or a woman, a good parent, or a dutiful employee is deeply influenced by the expectations of the fellow members of your society, how does that show that there isn't a single abiding substance to which that understanding can be attributed? Wolves learn how to hunt while still cubs, through play with other cubs. Chimpanzees learn grooming from their mothers. Should we conclude that wolves and chimpanzees are also "illusions"? Again, the conclusion Hood draws doesn't follow from his premises. To identity various internal and external factors that influence how a self comes to conceptualize itself simply does not entail that there is no self, or that the self is nothing but a collection of mental states.

There is also the fact that in spelling out the details of the mechanisms by which the purported illusion of the self is generated, Hood cannot avoid making reference to the very self he says is an illusion. Hood says that it is *your* brain in which can be found the neural activity that generates *your* experiences of the world and *your* sense of self, thereby generating *your* purported "self illusion." So who exactly is Hood talking to, if "you" are only an illusion? How could there fail to be a substance underlying the neural processes and mental states in question, if Hood cannot even identify the latter without making reference to the former? Hood is aware of the problem and responds with hand-waving to the effect that it merely reflects the limits of language.[79] But the problem has nothing to do with the limits of language, any more than the impossibility of round squares has anything to do with the limits of language. Rather, the problem, with the denial of the self as with nonsensical talk about round squares, is conceptual incoherence. For the reasons I've now spelled out at length in this chapter, there is simply no way coherently to articulate the claim that thoughts, experiences, and the like might exist without a substantial self or that the self is nothing but a bundle of such thoughts and experiences.[80]

The weakness of such pop science arguments notwithstanding, it might seem that psychiatry and neuroscience have provided the ingredients for more serious challenges to the reality and substantiality of the self. For example, consider *dissociative identity disorder* (DID) (formerly known as *multiple personality disorder* or MPD). Patients with this disorder appear to shift between several different identities or personalities, each of which has its own distinctive character traits, memories, and the like. Each personality appears to regard the others as distinct persons rather than as roles played by the same one person, and in some cases one personality might have no knowledge of another. Some researchers suggest that different streams of conscious awareness are associated with each personality. All of this might appear to support the Humean claim that the self is really nothing more than an aggregate of mental elements which gives the false appearance of being a single unified substance, where this appearance breaks down in DID cases. Kathleen Wilkes, who is critical of Lockean appeals to bizarre thought experiments, and who judges that less extreme dissociative phenomena like schizophrenia and fugue states do not pose a serious challenge to the reality and unity of the self, nevertheless

---

[79] Ibid., p. ix.

[80] Perhaps scientists like Hood can be forgiven their philosophical howlers on the grounds that they are not philosophers (though in that case one wonders why they see fit to pronounce with such confidence on philosophical matters). Such a howler is less forgivable when committed by a professional philosopher, as it is by Daniel Dennett when he suggests that selves are merely each others' "user-illusions" in chapter 14 of *From Bacteria to Bach and Back: The Evolution of Minds* (New York: W. W. Norton and Company, 2017). For *whom*, exactly, are they "illusions" if all the "users" *themselves* are part of the illusion?

concludes that "the concept 'person' has fractured under the strain" of the evidence concerning dissociative identity disorder.[81]

However, on closer inspection this argument can be seen to have no force. First of all, as even Wilkes acknowledges, the evidence concerning DID can be interpreted in more than one way, and is problematic insofar as at least some of the more exotic DID phenomena can be attributed to role-playing on the part of patients and ideologically-inspired wishful thinking on the part of those treating and studying them.[82] Indeed, some of the more spectacular purported examples of dissociative identity disorder, such as the famous case of "Sybil," have been exposed as fraudulent.[83] Accordingly, whether DID ought still to be included in the American Psychiatric Association's *Diagnostic and Statistical Manual of Mental Disorders* is a matter of longstanding controversy.

But even if we allow that what are characterized as "dissociated identities" or "multiple personalities" are not always the artifacts of a patient's deception or a therapist's prompting but result from a genuine and distinctive disorder of *some* kind, it simply does not follow that there is not a single persisting substance – and indeed, a single *self* – underlying these unusual psychological phenomena. For one thing, none of the phenomena actually entails the existence of distinct streams of consciousness, as opposed to a single stream of consciousness that has become delusional. We are all familiar with the psychological discontinuity and incoherence associated with everyday circumstances like sleep, dreams, drunkenness, senility, and the like. More dramatic disruptions to normal functioning attend disorders like amnesia; schizophrenia, which can involve the experience of hearing thoughts that seem to come from outside oneself; and anosognosia, in which patients seem not to be aware that they are suffering from ailments like blindness or paralysis. In neither these ordinary cases nor the extraordinary ones are we usually tempted to say

---

[81] Kathleen V. Wilkes, *Real People: Personal Identity without Thought Experiments* (Oxford: Clarendon Press, 1988), p. 128.

[82] Ibid., p. 110.

[83] Cf. Debbie Nathan, *Sybil Exposed: The Extraordinary Story Behind the Famous Multiple Personality Case* (New York: Free Press, 2011).

that there is more than one self present. But as Tim Bayne argues, DID phenomena seem to be more extreme instances of the sorts of discontinuity and incoherence associated with these less dramatic sorts of disorder, so that the most natural interpretation of them is that they simply involve a more severe breakdown of continuity and coherence in a single self.[84]

As Bayne suggests, the strange phenomena associated with anosognosia and schizophrenia can be explained in terms of dysfunctions in introspective access to one's conscious states, the mistaking of vivid mental imagery for perception, incapacity for certain kinds of inference, and the like. It is not that there is more than one stream of consciousness, but that the patient is unable to detect or properly interpret everything that is going on in the one stream. Dissociative identity disorder plausibly involves dysfunctions of these sorts together with other factors. For example, there is a more extreme version of the incoherence that results from ordinary self-deception. (Consider the example of a woman who at some level knows that her husband is committing adultery, but will not let herself entertain the thought and instead rehearses to herself other explanations of his suspicious behavior.) There is an exaggerated version of the struggle we often engage in to control our emotions or impulses. (Think of St. Paul's famous characterization of sin as something analogous to an alien force within that leads him to act contrary to the good that he wants to do.[85]) There is a more melodramatic version of the role-playing we engage in when we present ourselves to others in different ways in different contexts, or fantasize about living different sorts of lives. (Think of an actor who can play radically different sorts of character equally convincingly, or even rapidly shift back and forth between different characters as he carries on a dialogue with himself.[86]) Again, one need not hold that DID patients are *knowingly* engaging in deception or make-believe. The confabulation might instead be a consequence of severe dysfunction and delusion. In any event, it would

---

[84] Cf. Tim Bayne, *The Unity of Consciousness* (Oxford: Oxford University Press, 2010), chapter 7.

[85] Romans 7:13-25.

[86] The radio personality Phil Hendrie is famous for being able to do this in an amazingly convincing way.

involve a *single* self mistakenly, if sincerely, believing that it had fragmented into several selves, or even that the several selves had been present all along.

Stephen Braude, who, unlike Bayne, does believe that there are distinct streams of consciousness in cases of dissociative identity disorder, nevertheless rejects the conclusion that there are distinct *selves*, and indeed argues that there must be a single underlying self.[87] He notes, first, that it would be fallacious to infer from the thesis that a person has dissociated into several identities to the conclusion that there must have existed several discrete elements prior to the dissociation of which the person was composed as an aggregate. This is to assume what Braude labels the "principle of compositional reversibility," to which he says there are clear counterexamples.[88] For instance, if you break a table in half with an axe, it doesn't follow that those two halves existed prior to the table and that the table was made by combining them. Rather, the division *creates* parts that didn't previously exist, and something similar can be said to happen with the traumatic events that typically precede dissociative identity disorder. There is also the fact that the character of the identities that result closely reflect the contingent facts about the trauma. For example, sexual abuse might result in the creation of an identity that is either highly prudish or highly sexual, physical abuse might give rise to an identity with a very protective personality, and so on. It is hardly plausible to suppose that identities corresponding to traumatic events in this way just happened to exist already in the person prior to the trauma.

Furthermore, argues Braude, we cannot make sense of the distinct identities that are exhibited in DID cases unless we take them to reside in a single underlying self. For one thing, the multiple personalities tend to share the same language and certain linguistic idiosyncrasies, a common stock of basic abilities (reading, doing arithmetic, understanding social cues, etc.), and certain memories of the pre-dissociated life of the person. This is hard to make sense of unless we suppose that there is a single self which possesses these features, and

---

[87] Braude, *First Person Plural*, chapter 7.

[88] Ibid., chapter 5.

of which the distinct identities are all manifestations.[89] These fundamental features are so tightly integrated into the characters and behaviors of the distinct identities that it is implausible to suppose we could isolate the latter from the former, and treat them as distinct freestanding selves rather than variations on the same one underlying self.[90]

For another thing, the dissociated identities typically arise, again, in response to some kind of trauma. This is hard to make sense of unless we suppose there is a single self which finds itself conflicted and under stress, and generates the identities as a coping mechanism. Such inner psychological conflict could hardly exist if there were two or more irreducible selves present, any more than the existence of two people in the ordinary sense who disagree about something entails inner psychological conflict. The fact that the vast majority of people who go through traumatic events like the ones in question do *not* exhibit DID indicates that DID is simply an extreme means by which a single self might try to cope with a bad situation, where others might opt for other strategies (therapy, fantasy, drugs, or whatever).

We might also note that the distinct identities manifest in DID patients often have access to each other's thoughts (though sometimes they claim not to). It is sometimes suggested that what makes this possible is a kind of *telepathy*, analogous to the ability to know others' thoughts that mind-readers claim to possess.[91] But surely the more obvious and simpler explanation is that the identities are all simply different manifestations of the same one self!

On closer inspection, then, dissociative identity disorder does not cast any serious doubt on the reality and irreducibility of the self.

---

[89] At p. 165 of *The Unity of Consciousness*, Bayne makes the related point that despite the purported existence of multiple personalities competing for control of the body, DID patients typically preserve a high degree of sensorimotor integration.

[90] Cf. Robert Edward Brennan, *Thomistic Psychology* (New York: Macmillan, 1941), pp. 296-99. Brennan distinguishes between a *person*, which is a kind of substance, and a *personality*, which is a collection of attributes. As he suggests, the presence of more than one personality does not entail the presence of more than one person.

[91] Cf. Bayne's discussion in *The Unity of Consciousness*, at p. 168.

But there is another, physiologically grounded sort of dissociation that might seem to do so, namely the strange behavior exhibited by "split-brain" or commissurotomy patients. The procedure in question involves a partial severing of the fibers connecting the two hemispheres of the brain, usually in the corpus callosum. It is sometimes used as a means of alleviating the more severe symptoms of epilepsy. Experiments with these patients have in some cases given rise to behavior indicative of the hemispheres functioning at cross-purposes. For example, a patient's right hand might repeatedly interfere with what his left hand is trying to write, even crossing out and changing it. Or, when a stimulus is hidden from the hemisphere of the brain governing speech, but nevertheless produces an appropriate behavioral reaction (such as laughter) when presented to the other hemisphere, the patient will, when asked, confabulate a sincere but false explanation for this behavior.[92] Such results are sometimes claimed to indicate that what had once been a unified stream of consciousness has divided into two streams, each associated with one hemisphere of the brain. It has even been argued that there are really two persons associated with a human brain even *before* commissurotomy, and that the procedure simply reveals this bifurcation rather than creating it.[93]

Here too, though, closer inspection undermines the more sensational interpretations of the evidence, and certainly gives no grounds for doubting the reality of a single irreducible self. The first thing to note is that commissurotomy patients rarely exhibit odd behavior of the kind in question outside of the highly artificial experimental contexts that researchers have designed in order to elicit it. Typically patients do not like being put in such contexts, and they do not regard themselves as being two persons or otherwise dissociated

---

[92] For detailed discussion of these phenomena and the philosophical issues they raise, see Wilkes, *Real People*, chapter 5; Bayne, *The Unity of Consciousness*, chapter 9; and Michael Lockwood, *Mind, Brain, and the Quantum* (Oxford: Basil Blackwell, 1989), chapter 6.

[93] Cf. Roland Puccetti, "Brain Bisection and Personal Identity," *British Journal for the Philosophy of Science* 24 (1973): 339-55.

in the extreme ways some researchers claim they are.[94] Their everyday behavior is largely normal and would not lead the average observer to judge that there is anything unusual about them.[95]

Commissurotomy patients are also typically already brain-damaged from epilepsy, so that it is not clear that the odd behavior some of them exhibit in experimental circumstances stems from the commissurotomy rather than from the pre-existing brain damage.[96] The two hemispheres of their brains are also never literally entirely split off from one another. For one thing, sometimes the corpus callosum is not entirely cut. But even when it is, there remain many other connections between the two hemispheres at other places in the brain. Moreover, there is nothing necessarily special about the fact that two brain states or processes exist in different hemispheres in the brain. Neural states and processes in different parts of the *same* hemisphere can be more remotely connected to one another than neural states and processes in different hemispheres sometimes are.[97] Hence it is somewhat arbitrary to posit exactly two streams of consciousness, each associated with one of the two hemispheres of the brain – as opposed, say, to many streams of consciousness associated with the many different sub-hemispheric areas of the brain. But if we are not going to attribute different streams of consciousness to different parts of the same hemisphere, why attribute different streams to the different hemispheres?

Even Wilkes, despite being overly impressed by the evidence from dissociative identity disorder, urges a more cautious interpretation of "split-brain" behavior. As she points out, there are many phenomena of both an everyday and an abnormal sort that involve a greater degree of dissociation than commissurotomy patients usually exhibit, but where we would not be tempted to posit more than one

---

[94] Cf. Bayne, *The Unity of Consciousness*, p. 196.

[95] Ibid., pp. 199f.

[96] Wilkes, *Real People*, p. 140.

[97] Cf. Lockwood, *Mind, Brain, and the Quantum*, p. 81.

person.[98] For example, there is the fact that it often takes a person time fully to realize or admit to himself the reality of some unpleasant circumstance, so that he may act in a manner inconsistent with what at some level he knows to be true. There is the fact of divided attention, wherein a person can carry out two very different complex tasks at the same time (such as negotiating traffic while carrying on a philosophical conversation). There is the phenomenon of "being of two minds" about some matter. There is weakness of will, wherein we do things that in some sense we do not want to do. There is outright self-deception, wherein one gets himself to believe something that at some level he knows to be false. Among abnormal cases, there is the amnesia associated with fugue states and the odd behavior that can be elicited via hypnosis. Now, in all of these normal and abnormal cases, we have a person who acts in a unified way overall, and simply exhibits a certain degree of dissociation under special circumstances. We don't treat any of it as evidence of more than one self, but rather interpret it as the multitasking of, or confusion within, a single self. There is no reason not to interpret the behavior of "split-brain" patients and simply an extension of the same sort of thing. We don't have more than one self in these cases. We simply have behavior on the part of a single self, the oddity of which is perfectly understandable given that the self in question is, after all, brain-damaged. The oddity of the behavior no more gives us reason to deny a single self then does the oddity of the gait of someone whose legs are damaged, or the oddity of the speech of someone whose teeth, jaw, or facial muscles have been damaged.

Then there is the fact that the two hemispheres of the brain, just as any other two parts of the brain, are built to *complement* one another's functioning. They are not built to operate independently, but rather work as a unit.[99] Moreover, the rest of the human body is simply not constructed in a way that would make it suited to be operated by two minds, but also functions as a unit.[100] All things considered, then, attributing two selves (as opposed to a single confused self)

---

[98] Wilkes, *Real People*, pp. 145-52.
[99] Ibid., pp. 151-52.

[100] Ibid., p. 166.

even to a commissurotomy patient (let alone to the pre-commissurotomy person) is by no means the natural interpretation of the behavioral and physiological evidence, but on the contrary is a highly unnatural interpretation.

Finally, as Braude points out, even if we were to go along with the suggestion that two selves come to exist post-commissurotomy, it simply wouldn't follow that there was not a single unified self pre-commissurotomy, or that the single self that then existed has now divided into two. We could say instead that the previous self simply went out of existence after the commissurotomy and was replaced by two new selves, in a manner comparable to cell division or the slicing of a flatworm into two new worms.[101] The point isn't that this is plausibly what actually happens in commissurotomy (I don't think it is), but rather to reinforce the lesson that there is nothing in the scientific evidence *itself* that forces on us an interpretation contrary to the reality and irreducibility of the self. There are alternative ways to interpret it, and given that, as we have seen, there is independent reason to affirm the reality and irreducibility of the self, we ought to opt for one of those alternatives.

Reductionists and eliminativists might insist that the most I have shown is that we have to *think* about the self as if it were real and irreducible, but not that there actually *is* such a self. Contemporary naturalist philosophers commonly assume that if a metaphysical claim is not grounded in natural science, then the only thing left for it to be is a deliverance of "conceptual analysis." But such analysis, claims the philosophical naturalist, can only ever tell us about how we *conceptualize* reality, and not how reality is in itself.

The fundamental problem with this objection is that it is simply false to suppose that metaphysical reasoning cannot be a third source of knowledge distinct from either natural science or conceptual analysis. This is a large issue that I cannot settle in a book that is about human nature, specifically, but I have addressed it at length

---

[101] Braude, *First Person Plural*, p. 138.

elsewhere.[102] In any event, it will suffice for present purposes to make a narrower point.[103] It is not enough for the reductionist or eliminativist merely to *assert* that there may be no irreducible self despite our having to think as if there is. In order for us to take this assertion seriously, we need some coherent account of *what it would be* for there to exist no irreducible self even though we have to think as if there is. But the arguments I have given in this chapter claim precisely to show that we *cannot* give a coherent account of such a scenario. Hence, to respond to these arguments by suggesting that reductionism or eliminativism might still be true, even if we cannot see how, merely begs the question.

So much, then, for challenges to the reality and irreducibility of the self. Let us turn now to challenges to the reality of the self's thoughts and free choices.

---

[102] Cf. Feser, *Scholastic Metaphysics*, chapter 0, and *Aristotle's Revenge: The Metaphysical Foundations of Physical and Biological Science* (Neunkirchen-Seelscheid: Editiones Scholasticae, 2019), pp. 139-51.

[103] I borrow it from Howard Robinson, *From the Knowledge Argument to Mental Substance* (Cambridge: Cambridge University Press, 2016), pp. 242-43.

3. The Intellect

Intellect versus sentience

The intellect is that power by which we are able to entertain *concepts*, to affirm the truth or falsity of *propositions*, and to assess the cogency of *arguments*. For example, we can entertain the concept of *being a man*; we can affirm the truth of the proposition that *all men are mortal*; and we can determine that from the propositions that *all men are mortal* and that *Socrates is a man*, the conclusion that *Socrates is mortal* logically follows. Traditionally, the act of entertaining a concept is known as *simple apprehension*; the act of affirming or denying the truth of a proposition is known as *judgment*; and the act of inferring a proposition from other propositions is known as *reasoning*. Simple apprehension, judgment, and reasoning are the intellect's basic operations.[104] Being *rational* or capable of *thought* is essentially a matter of having the capacity for these operations of the intellect.

To be sure, things are more complicated than this summary indicates. In Aristotelian-Thomistic philosophy, a distinction is drawn between *active intellect*, which is the power by which we first form a concept, and *passive intellect*, which stores concepts once they are formed. In addition to judgment, contemporary philosophers of mind typically distinguish a variety of further *propositional attitudes*, so called because they involve a thinker's taking a certain attitude toward a proposition. For example, you might *believe* that the cat is on the mat, *desire* that the cat is on the mat, *fear* that the cat is on the mat, and so on. These would be different possible attitudes one could take toward the same proposition. Or you might believe that the *cat is on the mat*, believe that *the dog is on the log*, believe that *all men are mortal*,

---

[104] Cf. Thomas Aquinas, *Summa Theologiae* I.85.5.

and so on. These would be different propositions toward which one might take the same attitude. In contemporary philosophy of mind, the capacity for thought is usually analyzed primarily in terms of this notion of the propositional attitudes.[105]

We will return to such details later on, but for the moment we can focus on the capacity to grasp concepts, propositions, and arguments as what is fundamental to having an intellect or being a rational or thinking being. Now, of these three, concepts are the most basic. For a proposition involves combining concepts. For instance, in order to formulate the proposition that *all men are mortal*, we need first to have the concept of *being a man* and the concept of *being mortal*. Arguments, in turn, are built up out of propositions, such as the propositions that *all men are mortal*, that *Socrates is a man*, and that *Socrates is mortal*. In order to understand the intellect, then, the first thing we need to understand is what a concept is.

The easiest way to begin is to contrast what the intellect does when entertaining concepts with what the mere *sentience* that we share with other animals makes possible. So, a brief account of sentience is in order. A further distinction traditionally drawn in Aristotelian-Thomistic philosophy is that between the *external senses* and the *internal senses*, both of which are typically possessed by sentient organisms. The external senses are the familiar ones: sight, hearing, taste, smell, and touch. Each of them is associated with its own characteristic range of sensations. For example, sight might yield a sensation of a rectangular red expanse; hearing might yield a sensation of a loud bang; taste, a sensation of bitterness; smell, a sensation of a sweet

---

[105] Cf. Tim Crane, *The Mechanical Mind: A Philosophical Introduction to Minds, Machines and Mental Representation*, Third edition (London: Routledge, 2016), pp. 17-19. As Crane points out, though, not *all* thoughts are propositional attitudes, since they don't all take *propositions* as their objects. For example, I might desire a cup of coffee just as I might desire that the cat is on the mat. But whereas the object of the latter desire is a proposition, the object of the former is a thing (the cup of coffee) and not a proposition. Yet it would still be a *thought* of the kind of which rational beings alone are capable, insofar as the coffee is *conceptualized* as such. (Of course, a dog, cat, or other non-rational creature might desire something too, but not in the same sense that we do, insofar as such animals would *not* conceptualize the objects of their desires. More on this topic presently.)

fragrance; touch, of warmth.[106] Obviously, this is very elementary. Much more could be said about the external senses at the neurological, psychological, and philosophical levels of description, and we will have more to say later on. But this will suffice for present purposes.

The internal senses are the *synthetic sense*, *instinct*, the *imagination*, and *sensory memory*. Some of the jargon may be unfamiliar, but the capacities it refers to are not. The synthetic sense is what unifies the deliverances of the five external senses into a coherent conscious experience. For example, when sight yields a sensation of an elongated yellowish expanse, touch a sensation of a smooth and solid surface, taste a sensation of sweetness, and so on, the synthetic sense combines these in a way that gives rise to the conscious awareness of a banana. It presents the diverse qualities revealed by sight, touch, taste, etc. not as a mere aggregate, but rather as aspects of one and the same object.[107]

Instinct is also known as the "estimative power," though while that expression might be at least a little more informative, it is less familiar. Instinct in the sense I am talking about is the capacity of an organism to apprehend something sensed as either beneficial or harmful, and to be inclined, accordingly, either to pursue it or to avoid it. For instance, once you have a sensory experience of a banana, you might "estimate" it to be desirable and therefore be at least somewhat inclined to get hold of it so as to eat it either at that moment or later on (though, of course, competing inclinations might override that one, or you might happen to be someone who doesn't like bananas). By contrast, sensory experience of a snake might lead you to estimate or

---

[106] The distinction between external and internal senses is a loose one insofar as touch can yield information not only about objects external to us, but also about internal states of the body. But this looseness does not affect the points being made in this section.

[107] The more traditional name for the synthetic sense is the "common sense." But because this expression has come to have a very different meaning in modern English, it is potentially misleading, and some Aristotelian-Thomistic philosophers accordingly prefer to use a different label. I borrow the phrase "synthetic sense" from Thomas Verner Moore, *Cognitive Psychology* (New York: J. B. Lippincott Company, 1939), pp. 237-44. Other alternatives sometimes used are "unifying sense" (cf. George P. Klubertanz, *The Philosophy of Human Nature* (New York: Appleton-Century-Crofts, Inc., 1953), pp. 124-28) and "central sense" (cf. Celestine Bittle, *The Whole Man: Psychology* (Milwaukee: The Bruce Publishing Company, 1945), chapter VII).

apprehend it as dangerous, and therefore to be at least somewhat inclined to flee from it (though of course, that inclination too may be overridden by a competing one).

The imagination, in the sense we are concerned with, is the capacity to form images (also traditionally known as "phantasms"), understood as copies of what we experience in sensation. For example, we can not only have a visual sensation of an elongated yellow expanse, but, after it is no longer present, can also bring to mind a mental image of what that yellow expanse looked like. We can not only have a tactile experience of a smooth and solid surface, but can also later bring to mind what that surface felt like. We can not only taste sweetness, but can call to mind what tasting sweetness is like even when we are not currently eating anything sweet. We can not only have a sensory experience of a banana, but can form a mental image of a banana. And so on. As these examples indicate, there is mental imagery associated with all five external senses and with the synthetic sense. We can also form images of things we have never had sensory experience of, by combining aspects of things we have experienced. For example, we can combine the image of a banana with the image of redness, and thereby imagine what a red banana would look like.

Sensory memory retains what is known via instinct or the estimative power, just as imagination retains what is sensed. In this way, sensory memory goes beyond imagination. For example, merely to imagine a yellow banana is not necessarily to remember it. (Suppose I had only ever seen green bananas and yellow things of other kinds, and form the mental image of a yellow banana by combining images of these other things.) In sensory memory, the triggering of such an image will be causally linked to the past event of actually having experienced a yellow banana, and will be associated with an inclination toward bananas that have not been experienced (say, an inclination to seek out other bananas in the future given that the one experienced before tasted good).

Much more could be said about these "internal senses" as well, but here too what has been said will suffice for present purposes. In any event, it is not terribly controversial that sentient organisms possess *something* like the capacities just described, even if contemporary philosophers and scientists would not use the jargon that Aristotelian-Thomistic philosophers traditionally do, nor carve the conceptual territory up in precisely the same way.

The point is that organisms without concepts, and thus without intellects, can and do possess the external and internal senses. For instance, a dog can see a triangle, but it does not conceptualize it as *a closed plane figure with three straight sides*. A dog can see, hear, smell, touch, and (if it is an angry mood!) taste a human being, but it does not conceptualize a human being as *a rational animal*.[108] For that reason, it does not entertain propositions about triangles or human beings, much less reason from one proposition to other propositions. But a dog *can* do things like instinctively estimate the piece of food a particular human being is holding out to it as desirable, and thus be inclined to approach it. It *can* have images of sights, odors, tastes and the like that it has experienced in the past triggered in its consciousness. It *can* by virtue of such experience come to associate a certain human being with food, and thereby be moved in future to seek that human being out.

Of course, human beings possess these external and internal senses too, but on top of that, we *do* conceptualize the deliverances of these senses. We can see a particular triangle and can form mental images of that triangle and of other possible particular triangles. But in addition, we can grasp the *concept* of a triangle as *a closed plane figure with three straight sides*, and are enabled thereby to entertain propositions about triangles and to engage in geometrical reasoning that reveals to us further things about their nature. We can see, hear, and touch a particular human being, and can form mental images of other actual and possible human beings. But in addition, we can grasp the *concept* of a human being as *a rational animal,* and are enabled thereby to entertain propositions and to reason about human beings. And so on.

---

[108] For the moment I use the traditional Aristotelian definition of what a human being is merely as an example. I will defend it later on. But for present purposes, nothing rides on whether this particular definition is correct.

Against imagism

But might our ability to entertain concepts not be merely an extension of what other sentient organisms are capable of, differing from it in degree rather than kind? That is the implication of a view known as "imagism," which holds that concepts are just mental images. It is commonly associated with the early modern empiricist tradition.[109] To see why imagism cannot be true illuminates the nature of concepts and of how the intellect differs from mere sentience.

To be sure, one does not need to be an empiricist or a philosopher of any other school of thought in order to suppose that a concept is a kind of mental image. The average person may think that to have the concept of a triangle, for example, is to have a picture of a triangle before the mind's eye. Certainly it is true that when we think about triangles, we tend to form such imagery, and that when we think about trees, dogs, or whatever, we tend to form images of those things. All the same, the concept is not and cannot be the same thing as any image, for several reasons.[110]

Consider first that concepts are *universal*. For example, the concept of a triangle as *a closed plane figure with three straight sides* applies to all triangles, whether right, acute, or obtuse, whether isosceles, scalene, or equilateral, whether drawn in ink, pencil, or chalk,

---

[109] That Berkeley and Hume were imagists is generally acknowledged. See Berkeley's *A Treatise Concerning the Principles of Human Knowledge*, Part I, Paragraph 33; and Hume's *A Treatise of Human Nature*, Book I, Part I, Sections I and VII. There is greater controversy over how to interpret Locke's views. For the evidence that he too was an imagist, see Michael Ayers, *Locke: Epistemology and Ontology* (London: Routledge, 1991), Volume I, Chapter 5. For an opposing view, see David Soles, "Is Locke an Imagist?" *The Locke Newsletter* 30 (1999): 17-66. For a survey of the views of all three of these major empiricists, see Michael Tye, *The Imagery Debate* (Cambridge, MA: The MIT Press, 1991), pp. 5-11. For a more recent defense of imagism, see Bertrand Russell, *The Analysis of Mind* (New York: Macmillan, 1921), Lecture XI.

[110] Points like the ones that follow are commonly made in works of Aristotelian-Thomistic philosophy. See, for example, George Hayward Joyce, *Principles of Logic*, Third edition (London: Longmans, Green, and Co., 1949), pp. 15-17; P. Coffey, *The Science of Logic*, Volume I (London: Longmans, Green, and Co., 1918), pp. 2-5; Michael Maher, *Psychology: Empirical and Rational*, Ninth edition (London: Longmans, Green, and Co., 1933), pp. 235-38; Celestine N. Bittle, *The Science of Correct Thinking: Logic*, Revised edition (Milwaukee: Bruce Publishing Company, 1951), pp. 24-28; and Raymond J. McCall, *Basic Logic*, Second edition (New York: Barnes and Noble, 1967), pp. 3-6.

whether black, red, or green in color, and so on. The concept *abstracts from* these varying features that particular triangles might possess and captures only what is common to every member of the class. But no mental image of a triangle can be similarly abstract and universal. Any image will be, say, of a green equilateral triangle, or a red right triangle, or what have you. It will always be an image of some particular triangle, having concrete features that not all triangles have in common. Hence the concept cannot be identified with any image.

The point is even more obvious when we consider more abstract concepts – that is to say, concepts applying to even wider varieties of thing. For example, the concept of *being a living thing* applies to bacteria and algae, dandelions and oak trees, snails and spiders, mice and lions, frogs and sharks, starfish and Tyrannosaurus Rex, human beings and (if there are any) extraterrestrials. But there is no image one can form that comes remotely close to resembling all of these things. For any mental picture of a living thing will have too many concrete features unique to living things of the kind pictured, and will be missing features possessed by living things of other kinds.[111]

A second difference between concepts and mental images is that many concepts have a *clarity and distinctness* that no image can possess. Consider, for example, the mental pictures you might form of a crowd of five hundred people, a crowd of seven hundred and fifty people, and a crowd of one thousand and twenty-four people. The images are all bound to be roughly the same. But the *concept* of a crowd of five hundred is clearly and distinctly different from the *concept* of a crowd of seven hundred and fifty, which is clearly and distinctly different from the *concept* of a crowd of one thousand and twenty-four. Or consider an example famously used by Descartes to make the same point.[112] A chiliagon is a geometrical figure with one thousand sides, and a myriagon is a geometrical figure with ten thousand sides. A mental picture you might form of one of these will look more or less

---

[111] The point applies not only to highly abstract concepts, though, but even to concepts of individual things. For example, no *mental image* you might form of some particular person can capture all the ways that he might appear or act that your *concept* of that person captures. Cf. Jerry A. Fodor and Zenon W. Pylyshyn, *Minds without Meanings: An Essay on the Content of Concepts* (Cambridge, MA: The MIT Press, 2015), pp. 24-25.

[112] Rene Descartes, *Meditations on First Philosophy*, Meditation Six.

the same as the image you form of the other, and they will resemble too any mental image you might form of a one thousand and twenty-four sided figure, or indeed of a circle. There is no clear and distinct difference between any of these images. But there *is* a clear and distinct difference between the *concept* of a chiliagon, the *concept* of a myriagon, the *concept* of one thousand and twenty-four sided figure, and the *concept* of a circle.

So far we have been considering examples of things of which we can form at least some image, however limited its applicability to all the members of a class. But a third problem with imagism is that there are some things of which we have concepts, but of which we can form no image at all. Consider, for example, the notion of a geometrical point, which has a location in space but no length, width, or depth. When we try to form an image of a point, we are bound to picture a dot, like the period at the end of this sentence. But that is not, strictly speaking, a point, since it has length and width and a point does not. Or consider the geometrical notion of a line, which has length but no width or depth. This too cannot strictly be imagined, for when we try we always end up picturing something with length and some minimal width.

Consider also abstractions like the concept of *law*. Law is not a physical object you can see or otherwise perceive, and thus it is not something of which you could form an image. Of course, you might picture in your mind a courtroom, jurors, and someone in a judge's robe. But that is merely to imagine things that are contingently associated with law, not law *itself*. Law might exist even if these things did not. Or you might call before your mind the *word* "law," either its appearance as written or the sound you hear when it is spoken. But that too is not the same thing as law itself. Law existed in ancient China and ancient Rome, but the English word "law" did not. Even more abstract is a concept like the *validity* of an argument. You can easily grasp the validity of an argument like: *All men are mortal, and Socrates is a man; therefore, Socrates is mortal.* The conclusion plainly follows of necessity from the premises. But you cannot *imagine* validity in the sense of forming a mental picture of it. Validity is simply not the sort of feature that has a certain shape or color, sound or taste, texture or smell.

Concepts, then, simply cannot be identified with mental images of any kind. Nor, for similar reasons, can the propositions or complete thoughts that we build out of concepts be identified with images or sets of images. Take, for example, a thought the content of which is the proposition that *snow is white*. You might at first suppose that to have that thought is nothing more than to call before your mind the sentence "Snow is white." But on further reflection that clearly cannot be correct. Someone who speaks German but no English can nevertheless entertain exactly the same proposition and in that sense have exactly the same thought. He would express that proposition in a sentence like "Schnee ist Weiss," but the proposition *itself*, and its constituent concepts, are the same as those you express in English.[113]

It might seem that propositions could nevertheless be identified with images of things other than words and sentences. Take a thought the content of which is the proposition that *the cat is on the mat*. Might that not be identified with a mental picture of a cat sitting on a mat? But on closer consideration, this clearly won't work either.[114] Mental images, like all pictorial representations, are inevitably ambiguous or indeterminate in their content. For example, suppose what you picture mentally is a gray cat sitting on a brown mat. Exactly which proposition is supposed to be identified with this mental picture? Is it the proposition that *the cat is on the mat*? Or the proposition that *an animal is on the mat*? Or the proposition that *a gray cat is on a mat*? Or the proposition that *a cat is on a brown mat*? Or the proposition that *Tabby is on the mat* (assuming that that is the cat's name)? Or one of any number of other propositions that might be taken to describe the state of affairs pictured? There is nothing in *the image itself* that can tell you. An image is always at best ambiguous between alternative possible propositional contents. But a thought

---

[113] Gottlob Frege famously argues for this distinction between propositions on the one hand and mental images on the other in his classic essay "The Thought: A Logical Inquiry," *Mind* 65 (1956): 289-311.

[114] For recent surveys of points of the kind made in this and the next few paragraphs, see Crane, *The Mechanical Mind*, pp. 10-14, and Jesse J. Prinz, *Furnishing the Mind: Concepts and Their Perceptual Basis* (Cambridge, MA: The MIT Press, 2002), pp. 28-32.

can be *unambiguous* in its propositional content – in which case a thought cannot be identified with any pictorial mental image.[115]

Then there are propositions the content of which is not even prima facie plausibly captured by any pictorial image. For example, consider propositions about a particular point in time, such as the proposition that *it will rain at noon*. You might call to mind a mental picture of rain falling during the daytime. But what in the image could capture the idea that it is raining at *noon*, exactly, as opposed to 11 am or 1 pm? What about cases where it is raining at noon, but there is no sunlight at all (for example, because the rain is occurring during the winter months in Alaska)? You might suppose that you could capture the time by adding to the mental picture an image of a clock that reads "12 pm." But what is there in this new image that can determine that it corresponds to the (future tense) proposition that *it will rain at noon*, as opposed to the (present tense) proposition that *it is raining at noon* or the (past tense) proposition that *it rained at noon* – or indeed, as opposed to the proposition that *it is raining at 11 am and there is a broken clock nearby that reads "12 am"*? How would we represent a situation where it is raining at noon and there is no clock present?

Consider also *negations*, which are propositions about what is *not* the case. For example, how could the proposition that *it will not rain at noon* correspond to a mental picture? By imagining, say, an ordinary contemporary street scene from which rain is absent? But why would that correspond to the proposition that *it will not rain at noon* as opposed, say, to the proposition that *there are no extraterrestrials in the city*, or the proposition that *there are no dinosaurs in the city*, or to any other of a countless number of propositions about what is not true of an ordinary street scene?

Or consider the difference between *conditionals* (which are if-then propositions), *conjunctions* (which are both-and propositions), and *disjunctions* (which are either-or propositions). How would the proposition that *if it is raining, then there will be bad traffic* be conveyed in a mental picture? By imagining a scene in which it is raining next

---

[115] Cf. Ludwig Wittgenstein, *Philosophical Investigations* (New York: Macmillan, 1953), p. 54; and Jerry A. Fodor, *The Language of Thought* (Cambridge, MA: Harvard University Press, 1975), pp. 179-81.

to a scene in which there is bad traffic? But why would this correspond to the proposition that *if it is raining, then there will be bad traffic*, rather than the proposition that *it is raining and there is bad traffic*, or the proposition that *either it will rain or there will be bad traffic*? Here too, nothing in the mental images themselves can determine which of several alternative propositional contents is the one being conveyed.

Now, some philosophers have denied that mental images are best thought of on the model of pictures. Against this "pictorialist" conception of imagery, they have proposed the "descriptionalist" thesis that a mental image is best thought of on the model of a linguistic description of what is represented by the image.[116] Would imagism be more plausible given this alternative account of the nature of imagery? It would not be. For what exactly does a linguistic description of the sort in question amount to? If it amounts to a mental image of a spoken or written sentence, then the account will have exactly the same problems we've already considered. On the other hand, if we think of the linguistic description on the model of a proposition that might be expressed by a sentence, then we are no longer really talking about a theory that reduces thoughts to mental images, but rather one that goes in the opposite direction – that is to say, one that assimilates mental images to thoughts. Perhaps we even have a theory that implicitly denies that there are mental images, and instead posits *only* thoughts.[117] Whatever one thinks of such a view, it hardly amounts to a defense of imagism.

It is important to emphasize that none of these critical remarks about imagism are meant to deny the familiar fact that when we entertain concepts and propositions, we do tend to call appropriate images to mind. For example, when you have the thought that *the cat is on the mat*, you may well "hear" in your mind the sentence "The cat is on the mat," or you may visualize a cat on a mat. When you entertain the concept of *being a triangle*, you may well form a mental picture

---

[116] For overviews of the debate between these accounts, see Ned Block, ed., *Imagery* (Cambridge, MA: The MIT Press, 1981), and Tye, *The Imagery Debate*.

[117] Daniel Dennett characterizes the debate between pictorialism and descriptionalism as a debate over whether mental images are real, though Ned Block thinks this is a misleading way of conceiving of the dispute. See their respective essays in Block, ed., *Imagery*.

of a triangle. And so on. Indeed, we will see later on that such imagery is a necessary precondition of the normal functioning of the human intellect. The point, though, is that forming images is nevertheless *distinct from* entertaining concepts and propositions, even if it is associated with it. It is at most a *necessary* condition for thinking, and cannot be a *sufficient* condition.[118]

It is no less important to emphasize that the rejection of imagism by no means entails a commitment to the doctrine of *innate ideas*, which holds that at least some concepts are built into the human mind before anything enters into it via the senses. To be sure, in early modern rationalism, this doctrine came to be associated with the rejection of imagism. The assumption was that if concepts are not images, then they cannot have gotten into the mind via the sensory experiences of which images are faint copies. Meanwhile, the early modern empiricists, who rejected innate ideas and held that there can be no concepts in the mind without antecedent sensory experiences, concluded that concepts must be nothing more than images or copies of such experiences. The assumption was that one had to take either the rationalist option of rejecting imagism and adopting innate ideas, or the empiricist option of rejecting innate ideas and embracing imagism.

But this is a false choice. A third option would be the Aristotelian-Thomistic position that predated the modern rationalist/empiricist dichotomy. It holds that there can be no concepts in the mind without antecedent sensory experience and the imagery to which it gives rise, but also that the intellect can by abstraction draw concepts *out of* images, where the abstracted concepts are distinct from any image. Hence it rejects both innate ideas and imagism, both rationalism and empiricism in its modern, post-Lockean form.[119] Contemporary

---

[118] E. J. Lowe vigorously defends what he characterizes as the "neo-Lockean" thesis that mental imagery is the "medium" in which thinking must take place if it is to have the conscious character we experience it as having. See Lowe's *Locke on Human Understanding* (London: Routledge, 1995), pp. 165-70, and also his *Subjects of Experience* (Cambridge: Cambridge University Press, 1996), chapter 6. But Lowe makes it clear that he does not intend thereby to defend the sort of imagism I have been criticizing in this section.

[119] I add the qualifier "in its modern, post-Lockean form" because Aristotle and Aquinas are themselves sometimes classified as empiricists of a sort, on the ground that they reject the rationalist doctrine of innate ideas. This is fair enough, but it cannot be emphasized too

neo-empiricist philosophers like Jesse Prinz, who agree that imagism is false, nevertheless argue that some modified form of post-Lockean empiricism must be correct, on the grounds that rationalist accounts of concepts face serious philosophical and empirical difficulties.[120] What they fail to see is that the Aristotelian-Thomistic position provides another alternative. Indeed, Aristotelian-Thomistic philosophers would argue that the insuperable problems facing both imagism and innate ideas imply that there *must* be such an alternative.[121]

We will have reason to return to these issues presently and in later chapters. Again, the point to emphasize for the moment is simply that rejecting imagism does not entail denying that sensation and imagination play crucial roles in the operation of the human intellect.

What are concepts?

To reject imagism is to say something about what concepts are *not*. Can we say more about what they *are*? We can, and we can start by noting what contemporary neo-empiricists and neo-rationalists alike agree on concerning their nature.[122]

First of all, a concept is a *mental representation* of the most fundamental sort. Take the concept of *being a triangle*. It represents triangles, just as the *word* "triangle" does. In the case of both the word and the concept, we therefore have what contemporary philosophers call *intentionality*. This is a technical term which must not be confused

---

strongly that their rejection of imagism is no less important than their rejection of innate ideas. From the Aristotelian-Thomistic point of view, both rationalism *and* empiricism in its modern form get the nature of the human intellect seriously wrong.

[120] Prinz, *Furnishing the Mind*, chapter 5.

[121] For a useful treatment of the differences between the Aristotelian and modern empiricist positions, see Alexander Greenberg, "Concept Empiricisms, Ancient and Modern," in Christina Thomsen Thörnqvist and Juhana Toivanen, eds., *The Aristotelian Tradition: Cognition and Conceptualization* (forthcoming).

[122] For a survey of this common ground written from a neo-empiricist point of view, see chapter 1 of Prinz, *Furnishing the Mind*. For a survey written from a neo-rationalist point of view, see chapter 2 of Jerry A. Fodor, *Concepts: Where Cognitive Science Went Wrong* (Oxford: Clarendon Press, 1998).

with what we have in mind when, in everyday contexts, we use words like "intentional" or "intentionally." In particular, it has nothing to do with acting on purpose. Rather, for something to have intentionality in the technical philosophical sense is for it to *aim at*, be *directed toward*, or be *about* something (typically, though not always, something distinct from itself). For example, the word "triangle" *aims at*, is *directed toward*, or *about* geometrical figures of a certain kind, and the word "cat" *aims at*, is *directed toward*, or *about* animals of a certain kind. By contrast, the nonsensical sequence of letters "shmat" is not aimed at, directed toward, or about anything. As these examples indicate, it is the possession of intentionality that makes words *meaningful*, whereas it is the lack of intentionality that makes a sequence of letters like "shmat" *meaningless*.

Now, though words like "triangle" and "cat" possess intentionality, they do not have it in a built-in or inherent way, but only as a matter of convention. Considered just by itself, the sequence of letters "cat" has no more inherent meaning than the sequence "shmat" has. Had the history of the English language gone differently, we might have used "shmat" to refer to animals of the feline type and "cat" as an example of a meaningless string of letters. Mental representations like concepts are unlike linguistic representations in this respect. Unlike the word "triangle," the concept of *being a triangle* does have its intentionality in an inherent or built-in way. To aim at, be directed toward, or be about triangles is simply part of *what it is to be* the concept of *being a triangle*. There is just no such thing as a concept of *being a triangle* that doesn't have such intentionality. To borrow John Searle's way of putting the distinction, whereas linguistic representations like words have only "derived intentionality," mental representations like concepts have "intrinsic intentionality."[123]

Keep in mind that the concept of *being a triangle* is *not* to be identified with any mental *image*, including a mental image of the way

---

[123] John R. Searle, *The Rediscovery of the Mind* (Cambridge, MA: The MIT Press, 1992), pp. 78-82. Searle also identified a third category, which he calls "as-if intentionality." This is the sort of thing we attribute to something that does not genuinely have even derivative intentionality let alone intrinsic intentionality, but which in some contexts it is useful to describe *as if* it did. For example, when we say that the thermostat thinks it is too hot in the room, we describe it *as if* it had a thought with a certain conceptual content, even though it does not in fact have any thoughts or concepts at all.

the English word "triangle" looks when written or the way it sounds when spoken. So, when I say that the concept of *being a triangle* has intrinsic intentionality rather than merely derived intentionality, I am *not* saying that the image you form when you see the word "triangle" in your mind's eye, or the sound you bring to mind when you think about someone uttering it, has intrinsic intentionality. The intentionality of such mental imagery is as derived as that of a written or spoken word. Again, someone who speaks a language other than English and has never seen or heard that particular English word can nevertheless have the *concept of being a triangle*. He would call to mind different images than an English speaker would when contemplating triangles, but the concept would be identical to the one that an English speaker possesses. (If you're trying to *visualize* concepts and finding it difficult, then you need to stop trying. A concept is not the sort of that *can* be visualized. If you are visualizing something, then what you've got is an *image* – and again, *concepts are not images*.)

It is important to emphasize that to characterize a concept as a "mental representation" does not commit one to everything that has been associated with that phrase in the history of philosophy. In particular, it does not commit one to the view that concepts or any other mental representations are themselves the primary objects of our thoughts. When you think about triangles, it is indeed *triangles* that you are thinking about, rather than the concept of *being a triangle*. The concept is (usually) not itself the object of your thought, but rather that *by which* you grasp the object of your thought (just as eyeglasses are usually not themselves the object you are looking at, but rather that *by which* you perceive the object you are looking at). To characterize concepts as mental representations entails only that they are that by which the intellect represents things. It does not entail the rightly maligned early modern rationalist and empiricist model of the mind as directly aware only of its own ideas as they flit across the stage of an inner theatre.[124]

---

[124] For a useful treatment of the differences between the Aristotelian-Thomistic approach to concepts and much else that has gone under the "mental representation" label in the history of philosophy, see John O'Callaghan, *Thomist Realism and the Linguistic Turn* (Notre Dame, IN: University of Notre Dame Press, 2003).

A second area of common ground between different theories of concepts is that concepts are that by which we *categorize* or *classify* things. Triangles are set apart from squares insofar as the former fall under the concept of *being a triangle* and the latter do not; cats differ from dogs insofar as they fall under the concept of *being a cat* and dogs don't; and so on. (The class of things that fall under a concept is referred to by philosophers as the *extension* of the concept.) As with intentionality, this is an *inherent* feature of concepts. If something is the concept of *being a cat*, then it simply could not be the case that cats did not fall under it, or that non-cats (dogs, say) did. (That is not to say that there couldn't, as a matter of contingent fact, be a situation where nothing fell under the concept. For example, if cats went extinct, then the extension of the concept of *being a cat* would be empty. The point is rather that even in that case, there could still *in principle* be something that fell under it, and if something did so, it would have to be a cat.)

Note that I am not here addressing the question of *how we know* whether something falls under a certain concept. Nor am I addressing the question of whether all, or even any, of the classes represented by our concepts are objectively real or merely constructs of the mind. Those are very important questions, but they are beside the present point, which is simply that to be a concept is to be the sort of thing under which a class of things falls (*however* we know that something falls under it, and *whether or not* the class in question is something we invent rather than discover).

A third widely acknowledged feature of concepts is what philosophers refer to as their *compositionality*. They can be combined into more complex concepts and, as noted already, into propositions.[125] For instance, the concept of *being a triangle* and the concept of *being equilateral* can be combined to yield the concept of *being an equilateral triangle*. The concept of *being a man* and the concept of *being mortal* can (together with what is called the universal quantifier) be combined to form the proposition that *all men are mortal*. (In fact, appeal to the role

---

[125] Some contemporary writers essentially define concepts as the constituents of propositions. Cf. Christopher Peacocke, *A Study of Concepts* (Cambridge, MA: The MIT Press, 1992), p. 2; and Georges Rey, "Concepts," in Samuel Guttenplan, ed., *A Companion to the Philosophy of Mind* (Oxford: Blackwell, 1994), at p. 185.

they play in propositions is another way in which contemporary philosophers often explain what it is to be a concept. A concept can be thought of as a constituent of a proposition, in something like the way a brick can be understood as a constituent of a wall.)

As Jerry Fodor and Zenon Pylyshyn have emphasized, the compositionality of concepts accounts for two important features of thought, namely its *productivity* and *systematicity*.[126] Thought is productive or fertile in the sense that, out of a finite number of primitive concepts and rules of combination, we can construct an infinite number of compound concepts and propositions. To consider some trivial examples, we can combine concepts in such a way as to yield the proposition that *there are two cats on the mat*, or the proposition that *there are three cats on the mat*, or the proposition that *there are four cats on the mat*, and so on *ad infinitum*. Using connectives like "and" and "or," we can construct compound propositions out of elementary ones. For example, from the proposition that *the cat is on the mat* and the proposition that *the dog is on the log*, we can form the compound proposition that *the cat is on the mat and the dog is on the log*. We could add another "and" and another proposition to yield the more complex proposition that *the cat is on the mat and the dog is on the log and the mouse is in the house*. And so on *ad infinitum*. Thought is systematic in the sense that the capacity to entertain one proposition typically goes hand in hand with the capacity to entertain others. For instance, I can entertain the proposition that *the dog is on the log*, but also the proposition that *the log is on the dog*. I simply put the same concepts together using the same rules of combination, but in a way that yields a different compound.

A fourth attribute of concepts widely acknowledged by theorists of different stripes is their *public* character. One and the same concept can be entertained by different people, and by the same person at different times. For example, when you entertain the concept of *being a triangle* and I entertain the concept of *being a triangle*, it is

---

[126] Cf. Jerry A. Fodor and Zenon W. Pylyshyn, "Connectionism and Cognitive Architecture," in Alvin I. Goldman, ed., *Readings in Philosophy and Cognitive Science* (Cambridge, MA: The MIT Press, 1993).

one and the same concept that we are entertaining. By the same token, when each of us entertains the proposition *that triangles have three sides*, it is one and the same proposition we are entertaining. It is not that you are entertaining your own private concept or proposition and I am entertaining mine. If concepts were private, we could not so much as communicate with one another. We not only could not agree with one another, we could not disagree either. Unless you and I had the same thing in mind when we entertained the concept of *being a triangle*, we could neither agree that *all triangles have three sides* nor disagree about whether *Feser overuses the triangle example*.

Now, it might seem that people often do *not* have the same concepts, given the very different beliefs and levels of knowledge they have about things. For example, a chemist has a much richer understanding of what it is to be water than a layman does, and libertarians and socialists have very different ideas about what justice requires. Can we really say, then, that the chemist and the layman have one and the same concept of *water*, or that libertarians and socialists have one and the same concept of *justice?* Yes, we can. Philosophers sometimes draw a distinction between *concepts* and *conceptions*.[127] A libertarian and a socialist might agree that a just society is one in which each person has what he is entitled to. But whereas the libertarian might say that people are entitled only to what they work for or are freely given, the socialist might say that they are entitled to an equal share of society's wealth. We might in that case say that they have the same *concept* of justice, but different *conceptions* of what justice requires. A layman and a chemist might agree that water is a clear, tasteless, odorless substance that is liquid at room temperature, freezes when very cold, is the stuff found in lakes and rivers, and so on. But whereas that is more or less all that the layman has to say about the nature of water, the chemist will be able to go on to explain that water is a composition of hydrogen and oxygen, to say exactly how it will behave under various conditions and why, and so forth. We might say that the layman and the chemist have the same *concept* of water, but the chemist has a much more detailed *conception* of what water is. There are different

---

[127] For an influential application of this distinction in the context of political philosophy, see John Rawls, *A Theory of Justice* (Cambridge, MA: Belknap Press, 1971), pp. 5-6. For an influential application in the context of philosophy of mind, see Georges Rey, "Concepts and Conceptions," *Cognition* 19 (1985): 297-303.

ways in which this distinction between concepts and conceptions might be spelled out, but for present purposes it will suffice simply to note that the differences in the beliefs and levels of knowledge people have about a class of things do not by themselves entail that they are operating with different concepts.[128]

So much for what the different sides in the debate over concepts tend to agree about. Let us turn now to an issue they do *not* agree about. Apart from the question of whether any concepts are innate, the main point of contention between contemporary neo-rationalists and neo-empiricists is whether concepts are mental representations of a kind distinct from the representations associated with the different sensory modalities. The neo-rationalist view is that they *are* of a distinct kind – that concepts are "amodal" representations, representations in a "central code" unique to thought and distinct from the diverse ways information is coded in the different sensory modalities. The neo-empiricist view is that there are no such amodal representations, so that a concept is a representation in a modally-specific code. Hence, for the neo-rationalist, the concept of *being a cat* is a mental representation that is amodal in the sense of being distinct from any visual, auditory, tactile, gustatory, or olfactory perceptual representation of a cat. But for the neo-empiricist, the concept of *being a cat* is not amodal, but is instead encoded in one or more perceptual representations – for example, in a visual representation of how a cat looks or an auditory representation of the sound it makes.[129]

To be sure, and as noted already, neo-empiricists agree that concepts cannot be identified with mental images. Hence they do not regard the perceptual representations that encode concepts as representations of an imagistic kind, specifically. They would characterize the relevant representations in some alternative way. For example, a visual perceptual representation of a cat might be identified with a

---

[128] For a discussion of different ways of spelling out the distinction, see Elisabetta Lalumera, "On the Explanatory Value of the Concept-Conception Distinction," *Rivista Italiana di Filosofia Del Linguaggio* 8 (2013): 73-81.

[129] Cf. Prinz, *Furnishing the Mind*, chapter 5, and Jesse J. Prinz, "The Return of Concept Empiricism," in Henri Cohen and Claire Lefebvre, eds., *Handbook of Categorization in Cognitive Science* (Amsterdam: Elsevier Academic Press, 2005).

neural mechanism in the visual processing center of the brain that is causally related in the right sort of way to some cat in the external environment. An auditory perceptual representation of the cat would be identified with a mechanism in the auditory center of the brain that has the right sort of causal relation to the cat. And so forth. Distinct perceptual representations of various cats can then get linked together and stored in what Prinz calls a "long-term memory network" in the brain.[130] Activity in this network might in turn later generate a new perceptual representation that functions as a "simulation" of the sort of representation that might be triggered in the presence of a cat.[131] Insofar as this simulation can serve as a proxy for the long-term memory network causally correlated with cats, Prinz labels it a "proxytype."[132] The concept of *being a cat* can, on his version of neo-empiricism, be identified with such a proxytype. But the same simulation might serve as a different proxytype, and thus a different concept, depending on which long-term memory network triggers it. For example, a simulation of a visual perceptual representation of a cat that is generated by the long-term memory network causally correlated with cats in general will count as the concept of *being a cat*. But the same simulation would, if generated instead by the long-term memory network causally correlated with *Persian* cats, specifically, count as the concept of *being a Persian cat*.

This account of concepts is less crude than the imagism of early modern empiricism, but it is nevertheless in the same spirit. Like imagism, neo-empiricism essentially reduces the intellect to the activity of what the Aristotelian-Thomistic tradition calls the "internal senses." It can capture at best the capacities of the most sophisticated sentient but non-rational forms of life, but not what is distinctive about concepts and the cognitive activities that concepts make possible, such as the entertaining of propositions and reasoning

---

[130] Prinz, *Furnishing the Mind*, p. 144.

[131] Ibid., p. 150.

[132] Ibid., chapter 6.

through arguments. In fact, despite its eschewal of imagism, neo-empiricism is open to objections that are analogous to those that it acknowledges are fatal to imagism.

Consider first the question of what gives a proxytype the specific conceptual content it is supposed to have – for example, what makes it the concept of *being a cat*, as opposed to the concept of *being a Persian cat*. Prinz's answer, again, is that it has to do with which "long-term memory network" in the brain causes it. But this is no answer at all. For one thing, a proxytype will be causally related to all sorts of *other* mechanisms in the brain as well. So why is it the long-term memory network that determines the content of the proxytype, rather than one of these other mechanisms? For another thing, even if we concede that it is the proxytype's causal relation to the long-term memory network that is relevant, this just kicks the problem back a stage. For what, exactly, gives a particular long-term memory network the precise content that *it* has? Suppose such a memory network is causally linked with cats. It will also be causally linked with all sorts of other things. For example, it will be causally linked with the ancestors of cats, with the light and sound waves that mediate our perceptual awareness of cats, and so on. So what makes it a memory network related to *cats*, as opposed to a memory network related to *ancestors of cats*, or one related to *light and sound waves*?[133]

The problem, then, is that proxytypes and the sets of causal relations they enter into are, considered by themselves, systematically ambiguous or indeterminate in their content. There is nothing in them that can suffice to determine that they represent *being a cat*, say, as opposed to *being a Persian cat*. But concepts can have an umambiguous or determinate content. Hence concepts cannot be identified with proxytypes. Now, the problem of the ambiguity or indetermi-

---

[133] Cf. pp. 294-95 of Dan Ryder's contribution to Jonathan M Weinberg, Daniel Yarlett, Michael Ramscar, Dan Ryder, and Jesse J. Prinz, "Making Sense of Empiricism?" *Metascience* 12 (2003): 279-303, a symposium on Prinz's book *Furnishing the Mind*. The problem Ryder raises for neo-empiricism is an instance of a more general problem of indeterminacy of content that faces all causal theories of intentionality, as we will see in a later chapter.

nacy of the content of imagism was among the problems facing imagism. Hence neo-empiricism is in this respect no improvement over imagism after all.

Like imagism, neo-empiricism also has difficulty accounting for concepts that are highly abstract – in particular, those that are so abstract that they do not plausibly correlate with any perceptual representation any more than they correlate with any image. Earlier we considered examples like the concept of *law*, the concept of the *validity* of an argument, the notions of the *negation* and *disjunction* of propositions, and so on. None of these corresponds to a concrete physical object that might be seen, heard, tasted, touched, or smelled, and thus there can be no perceptual representations of them even of the kind the neo-empiricist speaks of, any more than there can be images of them. Prinz suggests that the neo-empiricist could appeal instead to perceptual representations of *words*, such as written and spoken instances of the English words "law," "validity," and so forth.[134] But this is as hopeless a strategy as identifying concepts with images of such words. For the meanings of these words are entirely conventional. "Law," for example, has the meaning it does only because it is conventionally used to express the *concept* of law. Hence we already have to have some grasp of that concept independently of and prior to the introduction of the word. There is also the problem, noted earlier, that those who don't speak English and have never encountered the *word* "law" can nevertheless have the very same *concept* of law that English speakers have.

Then there is the problem that neo-empiricism cannot account for the way concepts enter into propositions and arguments. Consider the following inference:

All tigers are cats.

Tony is a tiger.

Therefore, Tony is a cat.

---

[134] Cf. the discussion of this problem in the last section of Prinz, "The Return of Concept Empiricism."

This inference is clearly valid. Now, its validity presupposes that each of the terms expresses the same concept from step to step. Otherwise we would have a fallacy of equivocation. For example, if "cat" conveyed the concept of *being a cat* in the first premise, but the concept of *being a Persian cat* in the conclusion, then the conclusion would not follow. According to Prinz's theory of proxytypes, though, the same simulation of a perceptual representation can count as a different concept depending on which long-term memory network triggers it. For example, if causally linked to one such network, it will count as the concept of *being a cat*, and if causally linked to another, it will count as the concept of *being a Persian cat*. So what would guarantee that the same proxytype, and thus the same concept, is being deployed in both the first premise and the conclusion of the inference above, thereby preserving validity?

Prinz's answer would be that the relevant perceptual representations associated with the first premise and with the conclusion of the inference are triggered by the same long-term memory network. But now we have a problem. For causal relations of the kind in question are *contingent*. They could have been other than they are. But logical relations between concepts are *necessary*. If *all tigers are cats* and *Tony is a tiger*, then it *cannot possibly* fail to be the case that *Tony is a cat*. Proxytypes simply don't bear the sorts of relations to one another that concepts bear to one another, and thus the latter cannot be identified with the former. The most the neo-empiricist can identify are contingent causal relations which we might for some purposes treat *as if* they had the logical form a valid inference has. But what we need for an account of concepts is something that *does in fact* have that form.[135]

---

[135] This sort of objection is developed at pp. 284-85 of Weinberg's contribution to Weinberg, et al., "Making Sense of Empiricism?" and in Edouard Machery, "Neo-Empiricism and the Structure of Thoughts," in Paco Calvo and John Symons, eds., *The Architecture of Cognition: Rethinking Fodor and Pylyshyn's Systematicity Challenge* (Cambridge, MA: The MIT Press, 2014). Weinberg and Machery take the problem to be an instance of a more general point about the systematicity of thought made in Fodor and Pylyshyn, "Connectionism and Cognitive Architecture."

Nor does the empirical evidence neo-empiricists appeal to in defense of their position show what they think it does. Studies indicate that when asked to carry out conceptual tasks (such as listing a thing's features), subjects will form simulations of perceptual representations of the things the concepts are concepts of.[136] But the most this shows is that the entertaining of concepts is *associated with* simulations of perceptual representations. It does not show that the entertaining of concepts is *reducible to* simulations of perceptual representations, any more than the fact that we tend to form mental images when we entertain concepts shows that concepts are reducible to mental images. With simulations of perceptual representations as with images, even if they were *necessary* for the entertaining of concepts, it would not follow that they were *sufficient*.

There is also empirical evidence that at least some cognitive tasks are *not* tied to simulations of perceptual representations. For example, there seems to be no difference in the performance of subjects asked to estimate how many members there are in a set, whether the set involves visible objects or sounds. Nor is there difference in performance when they are asked to add their estimations of the number of things in two sets of objects known via the same sensory modality, or to add their estimations of the numbers of things in two sets known via different modalities. Hence such cognitive tasks do not seem tied to any particular sensory modality, but rather to involve some amodal form of representation.[137]

In short, the empirical arguments for neo-empiricism are weak at best and non sequiturs at worst, and the conceptual problems with it are as grave as those facing imagism.[138] To that extent, in the

---

[136] Cf. Laurence W. Barsalou, Karen Olseth Solomon, and Ling-Ling Wu, "Perceptual Simulation in Conceptual Tasks," in Masako K. Hiraga, Chris Sinha, and Sherman Wilcox, eds., *Cultural, Psychological and Typological Issues in Cognitive Linguistics* (Amsterdam: John Benjamins, 1999).

[137] Cf. Edouard Machery, "The amodal brain and the offloading hypothesis," *Psychonomic Bulletin and Review* 23 (2016): 1090-1095.

[138] Yet another contemporary proposal is the "mental map" theory according to which a collection of states in the brain can stand in an isomorphic relation to a collection of things in the world in a manner analogous to how the elements of the map of a country correspond to its cities, roads, etc. Cf. David Braddon-Mitchell and Frank Jackson, *Philosophy of*

debate between contemporary neo-empiricists and neo-rationalists, the latter have the better of the argument. Neo-rationalists are correct to regard concepts as mental representations of an amodal kind, in the sense of being different from perceptual representations of any sort (whether images, proxytypes, or whatever). Now, one way in which the notion of an amodal mental representation might be developed is in terms a distinction drawn by the Thomist philosopher John Poinsot, also known as John of St. Thomas (1589-1644). Poinsot distinguished between *instrumental signs* and *formal signs*.[139] Both sorts, being signs, *signify* or represent things. Accordingly, they have what I referred to earlier as intentionality. Now, an instrumental sign is a sign that is also something *other* than a sign. For example, a written or spoken instance of the word "cat" is a sign or representation of cats. But it is also something else, such as a set of ink splotches or sound waves. That is why its intentionality is of what Searle calls the "derived" kind. A formal sign, by contrast, is a sign that is *nothing but* a sign. Its entire nature is to represent or be about something, and there is nothing to it over and above its doing so. Its intentionality is therefore of what Searle calls the "intrinsic" kind. Its specific intentional content or meaning is built into it precisely insofar as it exhausts what it is. Now, concepts (and also the complete thoughts we entertain, which are built up out of concepts) are in Poinsot's view signs of this type, formal rather than instrumental signs. There is nothing more to them than their representational content, which makes them not only unlike words in a language like English, but also unlike images and

---

Mind and Cognition, Second edition (Oxford: Blackwell, 2007), pp. 177-84. The process of thought is, on this view, analogous to what happens when a cartographer updates a map or combines maps. But this theory is no more plausible than the ones we've already rejected. For one thing, purported maps in the brain, no less than maps of the ordinary kind, are bound to be as inherently ambiguous or indeterminate in content as mental images and proxytypes are. For another, as José Luis Bermúdez objects, maps don't have the specific kind of structure that propositions have, and the logical transition from one proposition to another is not like the updating of a map. Cf. Bermúdez, *Thinking without Words* (Oxford: Oxford University Press, 2003), pp. 160-62.

[139] For a useful brief overview, see Francis H. Parker and Henry B. Veatch, *Logic as a Human Instrument* (New York: Harper and Brothers, 1959), pp. 13-23. Parker and Veatch propose "material signs" as a better label for what Poinsot calls "instrumental signs," but I prefer Poinsot's original terminology.

proxytypes, which have some nature over and above their representational content (such as resemblance in the case of images, and causal relations in the case of proxytypes).

Thinking of concepts as formal signs gives us a way to see what is wrong with an objection raised by Prinz, who suggests that the view that concepts are amodal representations faces the same problems that its empiricist rivals do.[140] If something could be a mental image of a cat or a simulation of a perceptual representation of a cat, and yet nevertheless fail to represent cats in general (as the concept of *being a cat* does), then why couldn't an amodal mental representation fail to do so too? But the problem with this objection is that it implicitly assumes that amodal mental representations too would be *instrumental* signs, signs that have some nature over and above their representational content – so that, like images and proxytypes, they might in principle exist even if they did not have the representational content they do. But that is precisely what Poinsot's proposal denies. What sets concepts qua formal signs apart from words, mental images, proxytypes, etc. is that there is no gap between their nature as signs and their representational content, precisely because, again, there is nothing more to their nature than their representational content. They are, to borrow an apt phrase from P. M. S. Hacker, "all message and no medium."[141]

The key argument for the existence of formal signs is that without them there could not be any signs at all. Instrumental signs, such as words in a natural language like English, derive their intentionality from other signs, as when a new word is defined in terms of existing words. Some of these other signs too might be instrumental, as when the existing words in question are defined in terms of yet other existing words. But not *all* of the signs from which these instru-

---

[140] Prinz, "The Return of Concept Empiricism."

[141] P. M. S. Hacker, *The Intellectual Powers: A Study of Human Nature* (Oxford: Wiley Blackwell, 2013), p. 390. Hacker himself applies the phrase to thoughts rather than to concepts. He also holds that, precisely because they have no medium, they are not representations or signs (which, he claims, of their nature require a medium). But it seems to me that Hacker is confusing what happens to be true of representations or signs of the ordinary sort with what must be true of all representations or signs as such.

mental signs derive their meaning can be instrumental, on pain of vicious infinite regress or circularity. There must be signs which simply have their intentional content in an intrinsic or built-in way, or there would be nothing that signs with merely derived intentionality could derive it *from*. But to be a sign with such intrinsic intentionality is to be something whose entire nature just is its intentional content, something which does not have some distinct nature to which intentional content must be added. It is to be a *formal* sign. Now, concepts are precisely the sources of the derived intentional content possessed by merely instrumental signs like words in a natural language. They are what in fact do the job that only formal signs can do. Hence concepts are formal signs.[142]

Now, the contemporary neo-rationalist thesis that concepts are amodal mental representations is also often associated with a linguistic conception of these representations. The idea is that the right way to model concepts and propositions is on *words* and *sentences*, as in Fodor's influential "Language of Thought Hypothesis."[143] Does our discussion so far commit us to this? Certainly concepts are like words in that they represent without bearing any sort of physical resemblance to what is represented, and insofar as they exhibit a kind of semantic compositionality which, as Fodor has rightly emphasized, makes possible a productivity and systematicity in the case of thought that parallels the productivity and systematicity of natural languages. Because concepts and propositions are in such respects analogous to linguistic phenomena, language provides at least a useful heuristic model for thought.

However, this by no means entails a commitment to everything associated with the notion of a Language of Thought or to other themes of contemporary neo-rationalism.[144] It does not entail supposing that any concepts are innate. Nor does it entail agreement with

---

[142] Cf. Parker and Veatch, *Logic as a Human Instrument*, pp. 19-20.

[143] Cf. Fodor's *The Language of Thought*, and also *LOT 2: The Language of Thought Revisited* (Oxford: Clarendon Press, 2008).

[144] It is also worth noting that there are some clear differences between thoughts on the one hand and sentences on the other. For example, one can interpret and misinterpret a sentence but one cannot interpret or misinterpret one's own thoughts; and there can be a gap between what one *says* when using a sentence and what one means, but there can be

Fodor's physicalist supposition that mental representations are material symbols encoded in the brain. For that reason, it does not entail supposing that thinking is to be identified with the processing of symbols according to the rules of a computer program. In fact, all of these suppositions are false, as I will argue later. But it suffices for present purposes simply to note that what has been said so far leaves such questions open.[145]

Thought and language

This naturally leads us to the question of the relationship between the intellect and language. Is the possession of language a necessary condition for having the capacities to grasp concepts, entertain propositions, and reason from one proposition to another? Might the possession of these intellectual capacities even be entirely reducible to the possession of a capacity for linguistic behavior?

The latter proposal is famously associated with *behaviorism*. It is widely understood to be a further variation on the modern empiricist project of giving a reductionist account of the intellect. Instead of identifying the possession of concepts and thoughts with the having of mental images or simulations of perceptual representations, the behaviorist essentially identifies them with the capacity for certain kinds of linguistic utterance and other forms of behavior. For example, to have the concept of *being a cat* or the thought that *the cat is on the mat* would, on the behaviorist analysis, amount to the disposition to sort cats from dogs and other animals, to utter or assent to the sentence "The cat is on the mat" under certain circumstances, and so forth. Behaviorism is widely rejected today, but it is useful for the sake of completeness at least briefly to summarize the main problems with it. B. F. Skinner's book *Verbal Behavior* is perhaps the best-known at-

---

no such gap between what one *thinks* and what one means. Cf. Hacker, *The Intellectual Powers*, p. 390.

[145] For a helpful discussion of the ways in which the Thomistic account of thought (which I am defending in this book) is similar to and different from medieval and contemporary theories of mental language, see Joshua P. Hochschild, "Mental Language in Aquinas?", in Gyula Klima, ed., *Intentionality, Cognition, and Mental Representation in Medieval Philosophy* (New York: Fordham University Press, 2015).

tempt to provide a behaviorist account of thought and language, precisely because it was the target of a famously devastating critique by linguist Noam Chomsky.[146] The objections raised by Chomsky and his followers against Skinner are applicable to behaviorism in general.

Perhaps the most fundamental problem with behaviorism is that it has proved impossible to replace attributions of thoughts and other mental states with nothing more than descriptions of behavior and dispositions for behavior. Consider, for example, the suggestion that to believe that *the cat is on the mat* is to have a disposition to utter or assent to the sentence "The cat is on the mat." A person will have such a disposition only under certain conditions, such as his having a *desire* to utter or assent to the sentence (which he might not have if, say, he wants to hide the presence of the cat from someone). So, analyzing one propositional attitude (the belief that the cat is on the mat) in terms of a behavioral disposition leads us to posit a further propositional attitude (the desire to utter or assent to a certain sentence). For the behaviorist reduction to be carried out completely will thus require an analysis of that further propositional attitude in terms of a behavioral disposition. But it turns out that such further attempted reductions only ever seem to raise the same problem over again. The behaviorist reduces a given propositional attitude to the having of a disposition for a certain kind of behavior, where the having of that disposition cannot be made sense without reference to a further propositional attitude, which the behaviorist attempts to reduce to a further disposition, which *itself* cannot be made sense of without reference to a propositional attitude, and so on *ad infinitum*.

As Chomsky pointed out, the problem afflicts even the application of the behaviorist's own fundamental theoretical notions. Skinner and other behaviorist psychologists hoped to explain the acquisition of language in terms of the *responses* of the language user to *stimuli*, and in particular in terms of those responses that are *reinforced* by

---

[146] Cf. B. F. Skinner, *Verbal Behavior* (New York: Appleton-Century-Crofts, 1957), and Noam Chomsky, "A Review of B. F. Skinner's *Verbal Behavior*," in Ned Block, ed., *Readings in the Philosophy of Psychology, Volume I* (Cambridge, MA: Harvard University Press, 1980). For a useful survey of the behaviorist analysis and the Chomskian critique, see chapter 4 of Georges Rey, *Contemporary Philosophy of Mind* (Oxford: Blackwell, 1997). For a popular account of language influenced by Chomsky's ideas, see Steven Pinker, *The Language Instinct* (New York: HarperPerennial, 1995).

rewards and punishments. The idea was to model even the most sophisticated linguistic behavior on the same basic mechanism by which behaviorists attempted to mold the behavior of rats and pigeons in the laboratory. A rat might be trained to press a certain bar (a response) in reaction to hearing a bell (a stimulus) by way of rewarding such behavior with a food pellet (a reinforcement). Once such conditioning is in place, further behavioral dispositions can be established by way of "response chaining," in which a stimulus associated with a certain reward itself comes to reinforce a further response. For example, because of its association with the food pellet, the rat's hearing of the bell might come to reinforce some further response like doing a dance upon seeing a light.[147] Mastery of language can, on the behaviorist analysis, be explained in terms of the operation of similar mechanisms.

But what counts as a *stimulus* or a *response* in the case of distinctively human behavior? To borrow an example from Chomsky, suppose someone makes a remark in the presence of a painting.[148] What exactly is the stimulus? We have no way of saying without first knowing the content of the remark. If the person says "It clashes with the wallpaper," we might identify the stimulus as the color of the painting; if he says "It's tilted," we might identify the stimulus with the frame; if he says "It's beautiful," "Hideous," or "I thought you liked abstract work," we might identify yet some other feature as the stimulus (though *which*, exactly, is not so clear). But this means that we can't characterize the stimulus in a way that is independent of the *response* of the person. Moreover, the characterization will presuppose facts about the *mental states* of the person – about how the painting looks to the person, what features he is concentrating his attention on, and so forth. This is even more obvious when the stimulus is claimed to be some complex phenomenon remote from the person whose utterance is the response, as when (to borrow another example

---

[147] Cf. Rey, *Contemporary Philosophy of Mind*, p. 98.

[148] Chomsky, "A Review of B. F. Skinner's *Verbal Behavior*," p. 52.

from Chomsky) a confusing international situation triggers the comment "This is war."[149]

What counts as the verbal *response* is no easier to determine in a way that is independent of the mental states of the speaker. Suppose someone utters "The cat is on the mat" in the presence of a cat. Why is *that* to be regarded as the response to the stimulus, as opposed to just the words "on the," or as opposed to some longer string of sounds made in the course of uttering the sentence (a cough, followed by a stammered "Um, the cat is on the mat," followed by a grunt)? It is hard to see how to answer that question without making reference to the content of the speaker's *thought* that the cat is on the mat, the *convention* we have of using words like those that make up "The cat is on the mat" to convey meaning (whereas there are no such conventions in the case of coughs and grunts), and so on.

Then there is the fact that even the behaviorist tends to understand what counts as a reinforcement of a piece of behavior in terms of how we perceive and conceptualize things. Chomsky notes, for example, that Skinner characterizes what will reinforce a response in an artist or writer in terms of what the artist or writer *hopes for* or *imagines* happening in the future.[150] Again, the behaviorist's own basic conceptual tools for re-describing human beings in a way that makes no reference to what is going on in their minds (notions like *stimulus*, *response*, and *reinforcement*) end up *presupposing* facts about what is going on in their minds.

There are other serious problems. For example, we exhibit many responses that are entirely novel and thus have never been reinforced in the past. For example, someone who has never been mugged or otherwise in physical danger before will turn his wallet

---

[149] Ibid., p. 53. That behaviorists, when characterizing stimuli, tend to do so in terms of how things appear to the human mind (which they are supposed to be analyzing away) is a point emphasized in F. A. Hayek, *The Counter-Revolution of Science* (Indianapolis: LibertyPress, 1979), chapter 5.

[150] Ibid., p. 56.

over to a mugger if refusing to do so might cost him his life.[151] It is easy to understand this if we think of the victim as playing out the scenario in his mind, but not if, like the behaviorist, we confine our explanation to appeals to stimulus and response patterns that have been set up in the past.

Then there are the details of distinctively linguistic behavior. Even response chaining cannot account for how we are able to put together *sentences*, as opposed to mere strings of related words (such as "up, down" or "north, south, east, west").[152] Neither can it account for our mastery of the difference between disjunctives and conditionals. For instance, consider the two sentences "Either the cat is on the mat, or the dog is on the log" and "If the cat is on the mat, then the dog is on the log." Building up a verbal response word-by-word via stimulus-response conditioning will not guarantee that a sentence that begins with "either" will continue with "or" as opposed to "then" after the word "mat" is reached, because the mechanism will be sensitive only to that immediately preceding word, and not to what was emitted by the speaker several words previously.[153] Especially influential is the "poverty of the stimulus" objection to behaviorist accounts of language, which notes that children are able to produce an indefinite number of grammatical sentences with a very high degree of accuracy (notwithstanding the occasional cute mistakes they are prone to make) on the basis of a relatively small number of examples provided by adults, some of which are themselves grammatically deficient.[154]

Reducing thought to language, then, is out of the question. We cannot make sense of linguistic behavior unless we take the intellect to be something real and distinct from that behavior even if its

---

[151] Cf. Daniel C. Dennett, "Skinner Skinned," in *Brainstorms* (Cambridge, MA: The MIT Press, 1981), at p. 67.

[152] Rey, *Contemporary Philosophy of Mind*, p. 110.

[153] Ibid., p. 110 and Pinker, *The Language Instinct*, pp. 94-95.

[154] Cf. Rey, *Contemporary Philosophy of Mind*, pp. 116-121 for discussion of this problem and related problems for behaviorism. Note that these facts about linguistic capacity parallel the productivity and systematicity of thought referred to earlier.

thoughts are expressed through it. Might we posit an even more radical separation of thought and language? Is thought not only distinct from language, but something that might exist entirely in the absence of language?

Some arguments for this conclusion are certainly weak. For example, it sometimes pointed out that human infants and adults with certain cognitive impairments lack the ability to use language but nevertheless appear to possess some concepts.[155] The trouble with this argument is that human beings in their mature and healthy state *do* have the ability to use language, and even immature or impaired human beings are surrounded by fellow human beings who do in fact use it. So, for all the argument shows, infants and the impaired adults in question would *not* possess concepts if this larger linguistic context were not present.

What about non-human animals which lack language altogether but nevertheless appear able to recognize and sort things? Doesn't the presence of this ability show that they possess concepts? No, because such recognitional abilities are neither sufficient nor even necessary for the possession of concepts.[156] To grasp a concept, it is not enough to be able to put things into different groups (even a coin sorting machine can do that). One must have a grasp of the logical connections between concepts, as evinced in the capacity to make correct inferences, and that is typically manifested linguistically. (Whether any non-human animals possess language is a question I'll address in a later chapter.) One can also possess a concept without knowing how to recognize or sort things that fall under it. To borrow some examples from Hacker, one can have the concept of *being old* without knowing how to identify pre-Cambrian rocks, and one can have the concept of *being fake* without knowing how to identity a fake painting.[157]

---

[155] Prinz, *Furnishing the Mind*, p. 18.

[156] Hacker, *The Intellectual Powers*, p. 129.

[157] Ibid.

As followers of Ludwig Wittgenstein (1889-1951) emphasize, beings with the capacity for language are our *paradigms* for beings who possess the capacity to think (in the sense of grasping concepts, being able to entertain propositions, and being able to reason logically from one proposition to another).[158] It is precisely in the ability to use a word or phrase correctly that we typically manifest our possession of a concept, and certain intellectual activities (keeping records, codifying laws, sophisticated mathematics, etc.) would not be possible without written language.

A powerful defense of the view that the cognitive abilities most distinctive of human beings cannot exist in animals without language has been developed by José Luis Bermúdez – powerful, and also ironic insofar as Bermúdez defends this conclusion in the context of a larger argument for attributing thoughts of other kinds to animals that lack language.[159] Consider first what Bermúdez characterizes as *second-order* cognition, or thinking about thought processes themselves, as we do when we recognize a defect in some plan or argument, try to come up with ways to remedy it, reflect on the logical connections between steps in an argument we find compelling, and so forth. Here the objects of our thoughts are not things outside the mind, but, again, thoughts themselves, and so in order to reflect on them we need some way to represent them to ourselves. Now, unconscious mental representations, like those posited in Fodor's Language of Thought hypothesis, cannot be the form this representation takes, precisely *because* they are unconscious and the second-order cognitive processes in question are conscious. Mental images cannot do the job either, since images do not have inferential relationships to one another the

---

[158] Some thinkers inspired by Wittgenstein's views on the relationship between thought and language are also influenced by the Aristotelian tradition that informs my own position in this book. Cf. e.g. Hacker, *The Intellectual Powers*, pp. 101-6 and 384-85, and David Braine, *The Human Person: Animal and Spirit* (Notre Dame, IN: University of Notre Dame Press, 1992), pp. 351-67.

[159] Bermúdez, *Thinking without Words*, chapters 8 and 9.

way propositions do.¹⁶⁰ The only sorts of representations that seem suited to represent thoughts and their inferential relations are *linguistic* representations. Language is, after all, compositional, productive, and systematic in a way that, as we noted earlier, thought is. Words combine into sentences and sentences into arguments in a manner that parallels the way in which concepts combine into propositions and propositions into chains of inference. This gives to language a fitness for representing thought that other media of representation lack. We are able to engage in second-order cognition precisely insofar as we can linguistically represent thoughts and their logical relationships.

As Bermúdez argues, what is true of second-order cognition is true also of other distinctively human cognitive activities. For example, we are capable of *higher-order desire*, or the desire to have or to be free of certain desires.¹⁶¹ This requires us to be able to represent to ourselves what having a certain desire involves and what its logical implications are for circumstances we have not experienced. We are capable of attributing beliefs, desires, and other propositional attitudes to other people (or as the jargon would have it, we possess a "theory of mind"). That requires entertaining propositions we may neither regard as true ourselves nor want to be true, but which we think others have the attitudes of belief or desire towards. We are able to entertain *compound propositions* of the kind discussed earlier, such as conjunctions, disjunctions, and conditionals. That too requires us to be able to entertain propositions in the abstract, and consider how their truth or falsity determines the truth or falsity of the more complex propositions they make up. We are able to consider the *modal* status of a proposition (that is to say, whether it is true or false of necessity or merely possibly), and we can grasp *tense* (that is to say, whether a proposition *is* true, *was* true, or *will be* true). This also requires us to grasp the proposition in the abstract and determine whether or not to attach a certain modal status or tense to it. All of

---

¹⁶⁰ Neither, in Bermúdez's view, can "mental maps" of the kind proposed by Braddon-Mitchell and Jackson do the job, because the way a map gets modified is simply not like the logical transition from one proposition to another in a chain of inference.
¹⁶¹ Cf. Harry Frankfurt, "Freedom of the Will and the Concept of a Person," *Philosophical Review* 68 (1971): 5-20.

these cognitive abilities require us to be able to represent to ourselves not particular things in the world (as we do in perception and imagination), but thoughts or propositions *about* things. Again, sentences provide a vehicle for doing so that no other medium of representation can.

Now, Bermúdez does not deny that animals without language are in some sense capable of having beliefs and of changing them in the light of the evidence. He gives the example of a rat which comes to realize that a food reward will appear whether or not it presses a lever, and adjusts its future behavior accordingly. But he characterizes such belief modification as "direct" rather than "reflective."[162] It such a case, a perceptual encounter with the world produces an immediate alteration in how the world is represented. It does not involve the entertaining of propositions and considering their logical or evidential relations to one another. Non-linguistic animals obviously can also have desires, but only what Bermúdez calls "goal-desires" rather than "situation-desires."[163] The object of the former sort of desire is some *thing* in the world (such as water, or prey), whereas the object of the latter sort of desire is that some proposition be true or situation obtain (for example, that it be true that one always has enough to eat and drink). Non-linguistic animals can also possess a rudimentary sort of "theory of mind." Take the distinction between "simple seeing" and "epistemic seeing."[164] Characterizing the former entails identifying some object or situation that the perceiver is aware of, as when we say that the dog sees the food in front of it or sees that there is a man in the vicinity. But to characterize the former requires goes beyond this and attributing *propositional content* to the state of the perceiver that the perceiver might go on to relate to other propositions. For example, we might say of a human being not only that he sees that a man is present but that he thereby grasps perceptually the truth of the proposition *that a man is present* and can therefore go on to infer that, since all men are mortal, a mortal thing is present. Non-linguistic animals are capable of simple seeing and of being aware that other

---

[162] Bermúdez, *Thinking without Words*, p. 169.

[163] Ibid., p. 173.

[164] Ibid., p. 174.

animals are engaged in simple seeing. An ape might not only see a banana but see that another ape sees the banana. But that is not the same thing as epistemic seeing or the attribution to other animals of epistemic seeing. Epistemic seeing and the attribution to others of epistemic seeing, like reflective belief modification and situation-desires, requires taking thoughts or propositions themselves as the object of one's thoughts, and that requires linguistic representation.

As Bermúdez notes, we can also distinguish between believing a general proposition, and having a disposition to form a certain kind of belief about particular things of a general type.[165] An example of the former would be believing that *all tigers are dangerous*. An example of the latter would be having a disposition, when in the presence of tigers, to form the belief that *this thing is dangerous*. To be capable of the latter does not entail being capable of the former. While non-linguistic animals are capable of something analogous to the latter, they are, argues Bermúdez, not capable of the former. The reason is that grasping a universal generalization requires representing a proposition in thought and breaking it down into its components, as when in modern formal logic we analyze the proposition that all tigers are dangerous as having the structure: *For any x, if x is a tiger then x is dangerous*. Again, to do this sort of thing requires representing the proposition in a sentence, and thus linguistically.

Much more could be said, but the key point to emphasize is that words like "thought," "belief," and the like are not univocal, so that we need to disambiguate when addressing the question whether thinking requires language. If by "thinking" we mean the capacity for what Bermúdez calls direct belief modification, goal-desires, simple seeing, dispositions to form beliefs about things of a general type, and so forth, then non-linguistic animals are capable of thinking. But all of this falls within the range of capacities made possible by what Aristotelians traditionally call the "internal senses." It doesn't follow that non-linguistic animals are capable of what Bermúdez calls second-order cognition, higher-order desires, the attribution to others of propositional attitudes, reflective belief modification, a grasp of compound, modal, tensed, and general propositions, situation-desires and epistemic seeing, and so forth. These capacities are characteristic of

---

[165] Ibid., p. 183.

human beings as animals with distinctively intellectual rather than merely sentient powers. If *that* is the sort of thing we mean by "thinking," then there is good reason to conclude that non-linguistic animals are not capable of thinking.

The word "language" is also not univocal and must be disambiguated before we can fruitfully address the question whether non-linguistic animals can think. Karl Popper drew a distinction between four main functions of language.[166] The first is the *expressive* function, which involves the outward expression of an inner state. Here language operates in a way comparable to the sound an engine makes when it is revved up, or an animal's cry when in pain. The second is the *signaling* function, which adds to the expressive function the generation of a reaction in others. Popper compares it to the danger signals an animal might send out in order to alert other animals, and to the way a traffic light signals the possible presence of cars even when there are none about. The third is the *descriptive* function, which involves the expression of a proposition, something that can be either true or false. The paradigm here would be the utterance of a declarative sentence, such as "Roses are red," "Two and two make four," or "There is a predator in the area." Notice that the latter example differs from an animal's cry of warning in having a conceptual structure. A bird's squawk might cause another bird to feel fear and take flight. What it does not do is convey an abstract concept like eagle, predator, or danger, and thus it does not convey the sort of propositional content that presupposes such concepts. The fourth is the *argumentative* function, which involves the expression of an inference from one or more propositions to another in a manner than can be said to be either valid or invalid, as when we reason from the premises that *all men are mortal* and *Socrates is a man* to the conclusion that *Socrates is mortal*.

While the most primitive of animals may be incapable of behavior that performs even the first two of these functions, there are also obviously animals that can perform them, and in that sense they

---

[166] Cf. Karl Popper and John C. Eccles, *The Self and Its Brain* (London: Routledge, 1990), pp. 57-59, and Karl R. Popper, *Knowledge and the Body-Mind Problem* (London: Routledge, 1994), pp. 81-92. Popper borrows the distinction between the first three of these four functions from the psychologist Karl Bühler.

can be said to have language. But to be capable of performing the expressive and signaling functions of language does not entail being capable of the descriptive and argumentative functions. *Those* functions require linguistic representations that mirror what we have called the compositionality, productivity, and systematicity of thought, such as the words by which we express concepts and the sentences by which we express propositions. Whether animals lacking *that particular sort of language*, can be said to think *in the sense of entertaining concepts, propositions, and logical inferences* is the most interesting and important way of interpreting the question of whether non-linguistic animals can think. As we have seen, there is good reason to conclude that, when the question is interpreted that way, the answer must be in the negative.[167] (Note that the question whether any non-human animals possess language of that sort, and thus can think in that sense, is a *separate* question. Again, I will address that issue in a later chapter.)

These results are perfectly compatible with the irreducibility of thought to linguistic behavior. Certainly nothing in the critique of behaviorism summarized above entails that the capacity for concepts, thought, and reasoning could exist in the absence of language. I have noted already that even though concepts and propositions cannot be *reduced* to mental imagery, it could still be true that human beings require imagery as an aid to entertaining concepts and propositions. Similarly, even though thought cannot be *reduced* to the capacity for language, it could still be true that the capacity for language is a precondition for human thought.

On the other hand, as I will argue in later chapters, it is certainly possible for there to be intellects (albeit ones very different in their operation from our own) entirely divorced from matter, and thus without language of the kind with which we are familiar (embodied in spoken utterances and written marks, and thus presupposing bodily organs and material media). For the moment we can simply note that we needn't settle this particular issue for the purposes of this chapter, which requires showing only that the intellect is not reducible to the

---

[167] Similarly, when arguing for a difference in kind rather than degree between human beings and other animals, Mortimer Adler is careful to assert that "at this moment, there are no scientific data infirmative of the proposition that only man has a *propositional* language" (emphasis added). Cf. Mortimer J. Adler, *The Difference of Man and the Difference It Makes* (New York: Holt, Rinehart, and Winston, 1967), p. 113.

capacity for language any more than it is reducible to the capacity for mental imagery or the simulation of perceptual representations.

Eliminativism

Much more radical than the view that concepts, thoughts, etc. can be reduced to mental imagery, perceptual representations, or linguistic behavior is the thesis that there simply are no such things – that we should not bother trying to reduce them to something else, but rather ought partially or entirely to *eliminate* such notions from our account of human nature.

The standard argument for this sort of view appeals to the premise that one or more of the notions in question cannot plausibly be accommodated by science – say, by neuroscience,[168] or by the best computational models of the mind developed by cognitive scientists,[169] or by experimental psychology.[170] The idea is that if concepts, propositional attitudes, intentionality, or some other aspect of the mind are not to be found in what Wilfrid Sellars famously called the "scientific image of man,"[171] then they must not really be there in man himself.

This kind of argument rests on a number of assumptions. First of all, it presupposes, at least implicitly, that science commits us to a "mechanistic" conception of the natural world which attributes to matter only those properties susceptible of mathematical description (size, spatial location, velocity, etc.), and which takes the world to be devoid of what Aristotelians call final causality or teleology (i.e. directedness toward an end). Second, it presupposes scientism, accord-

---

[168] Cf. Paul M. Churchland, "Eliminative Materialism and the Propositional Attitudes," in *A Neurocomputational Perspective* (Cambridge, MA: The MIT Press, 1989).

[169] Cf. Stephen P. Stich, *From Folk Psychology to Cognitive Science: The Case against Belief* (Cambridge, MA: The MIT Press, 1983).

[170] Cf. Edouard Machery, *Doing without Concepts* (Oxford: Oxford University Press, 2009).

[171] Wilfrid Sellars, "Philosophy and the Scientific Image of Man," in *Science, Perception, and Reality* (Atascadero, CA: Ridgeview Publishing Company, 1991).

ing to which we should not regard as real anything but what is captured in the picture of the world provided by science, interpreted in broadly mechanistic terms. Third, it assumes that one or more of the key mental notions we have been discussing (concepts, the propositional attitudes, intentionality, etc.) cannot be fitted into this scientific picture of the world (again, interpreted mechanistically).

This last assumption is controversial even among those committed to the first two assumptions. Many contemporary materialist philosophers hold that the mind *can* be explained in terms compatible with a mechanistic conception of nature. However, as I will argue in later chapters, they are wrong, and the eliminativist's third assumption is correct. If you exclude teleology or directedness to an end from your picture of nature, there is no way you are going to fit notions such as intentionality (the directedness of thought toward an object) into it.

But the specific purposes of the present chapter don't presuppose this rejection of materialism, and in any event, the third assumption will support eliminativism only given the first two assumptions. Those assumptions, however, are essentially simply taken for granted by eliminativists rather than argued for rigorously. Moreover, the assumptions are false. The mechanistic conception of nature has *not* been proved true by science, and there *is* more to the world than can be captured by science interpreted in mechanistic terms. Hence, even if concepts, propositional attitudes, intentionality, etc. cannot be explain in terms of mechanistic science, that gives no support at all to eliminativism.

Naturally, to defend these claims requires a treatment of deep issues in metaphysics and the philosophy of science that cannot be addressed thoroughly in a book on human nature, specifically. But I have defended these claims in depth elsewhere,[172] and we will have reason to address some of the relevant issues in later chapters. For the purposes of the present chapter, it will suffice to note some more

---

[172] Cf. Edward Feser, *Scholastic Metaphysics: A Contemporary Introduction* (Heusenstamm: Editiones Scholasticae, 2014) and, especially, my *Aristotle's Revenge: The Metaphysical Foundations of Physical and Biological Science* (Neunkirchen: Editiones Scholasticae, 2019).

specific problems with eliminativist arguments – and to show that eliminativism simply cannot, in any event, be true.

To begin with a less radical form of eliminativism, consider Edouard Machery's view that psychology ought to abandon the notion of a *concept*.[173] This suggestion is not quite as extreme as it might seem. Machery notes that psychologists have developed several theories of what a concept is. Some take a concept to be a *prototype*, in the sense of a representation of a set of properties that a standard example of a member of some class will tend to have. Some take a concept to be an *exemplar*, in the sense of a representation of some remembered instance of a category. Some take a concept to be a *theory*, in the sense of a body of knowledge about members of a class. These different approaches each have their strengths, and Machery allows that there really are prototypes, exemplars, and theories. But he suggests that psychological research does not give us reason to think that there really is some *one* kind of thing, concepts, of which the prototype view, the exemplar view, and the theory view are all alternative accounts. Rather, psychology should just affirm that there are prototypes, exemplars, and theories, and leave it at that, giving up the assumption that the notion of a *concept* is needed to tie these three kinds of thing together.

Machery's argument simply takes it for granted that what matters is what contemporary psychologists happen to need or find useful when developing their theories. But this assumption is problematic even apart from the usual general difficulties with scientism. As Machery himself emphasizes, contemporary psychologists and philosophers are often talking past one another when discussing concepts. The former are typically not even addressing the issues that concern the latter (where the sorts of issues that concern philosophers are the ones we've been addressing in this chapter). Why, then, conclude from the state of play in psychology that the notion of a concept should be dispensed with? Why not conclude instead that psychologists ought to address the issues that philosophers are concerned about, in which case they may find that the notion of a concept is indispensable? Or why not conclude that psychology and philosophy

---

[173] Cf. Machery, *Doing without Concepts*, especially chapter 8.

are complementary approaches to the subject, so that even if the former does not need the notion of a concept, the notion is still indispensable when dealing with the issues addressed by the latter?

Nor is it plausible in the first place that psychology really can do without the notion of a concept. As Georges Rey points out, it seems impossible even to characterize the variety of phenomena that psychology must account for without deploying the notion.[174] Rey observes:

> On the face of it, concepts are the stuff of which psychological claims and explanations are made. Generalizations and explanations of, e.g., cognitive development, fallacies in reasoning, vision and language understanding (to take some of the more successful areas of recent psychology) – all these *presuppose* concepts as shared constituents of the propositional attitudes the explanations concern. It's not clear how even to *describe* the phenomenon of the Müller-Lyer illusion unless we can presume that people share a concept of *longer than*, or the gambler's fallacy, without them sharing [the concept of] *more likely*. Concepts seem to be natural kinds at least to the extent that they are the kinds of entity over which psychology generalizes.

Moreover, people's prototypes, exemplars, and theories differ, yet they are still able to engage in fruitful debate with one another. That implies that there are *concepts* over and above these that they share and that provide a common reference point for agreement and disagreement. Indeed, Machery and his critics themselves could hardly disagree if there were not some shared conceptual content by reference to which they could understand what their dispute is about in the first place. In these ways, looking to psychology for grounds to deny the reality of concepts seems inevitably self-defeating.

The self-defeating nature of eliminativism is even more obvious, indeed notorious, when its more extreme versions are considered. These would be views which claim that there are no such things

---

[174] Cf. Rey's July 2009 review of Machery's *Doing without Concepts* in *Notre Dame Philosophical Reviews*, online at: https://ndpr.nd.edu/reviews/doing-without-concepts/ Accessed June 15, 2021.

as beliefs, desires, or other propositional attitudes, and in general nothing that possesses the intentionality or representational content definitive of concepts and thoughts – where this view is, again, put forward on the grounds that propositional attitudes and intentionality cannot be reduced to properties of the kind recognized by neuroscience or other natural sciences.

That there is something fishy about this line of reasoning should be obvious from the fact that it is never pushed through consistently. As Stephen Stich (himself a former eliminativist) and Stephen Laurence emphasize, there are all sorts of notions for which we have no good reductionist analysis (they give examples like *couch, car, war, famine, ownership, mating,* and *death*) but which few would propose we eliminate from our picture of reality.[175] But the fact is that we simply *could not possibly* coherently eliminate from that picture everything which cannot be given a reductionist analysis. In particular, the very attempt to eliminate intentionality and related notions will always implicitly *presuppose* them.

The simplistic or "pop" way of making this point is to say that eliminativists claim to believe that there are no beliefs, which is a performative self-contradiction. As eliminativists rightly point out, by itself this is not a very impressive objection, because the eliminativist can always avoid using locutions like "I believe that..." and make his point in other terms instead. However, the real question is whether the eliminativist can spell out his position in a way that *entirely* avoids terms that explicitly or implicitly presuppose intentionality. That *cannot* be done. Even if you get rid of intentionality in one area it will, like the proverbial whack-a-mole, always rear its head somewhere else.[176]

---

[175] Stephen P. Stich and Stephen Laurence, "Intentionality and Naturalism," in Stephen P. Stich, *Deconstructing the Mind* (Oxford: Oxford University Press, 1996), p. 176.

[176] Cf. Lynne Rudder Baker, *Saving Belief: A Critique of Physicalism* (Princeton, NJ: Princeton University Press, 1987), chapter 7; Paul A. Boghossian, "The Status of Content," *Philosophical Review* 99 (1990): 157-84; Paul A. Boghossian, "The Status of Content Revisited," *Pacific Philosophical Quarterly* 71 (1991): 264-78; Edward Feser, *The Last Superstition: A Refutation of the New Atheism* (South Bend, IN: St. Augustine's Press, 2008), pp. 229-37; William Hasker, *The Emergent Self* (Ithaca: Cornell University Press, 1999), chapter 1; Angus Menuge, *Agents Un-*

Hence, consider the eliminativist's central claims – that intentionality is *illusory*, that descriptions of human beings as possessing intentionality are *false*, that it is a *mistake* to try to reduce rather than eliminate it, etc. All of these notions are as suffused with intentionality as any the eliminativist wants to overthrow. They presuppose the *meaning* of a thought or of a statement that has failed to *represent* things accurately, or a *purpose* that one has failed to achieve or that one should not have been *aiming* to achieve in the first place. Yet we are told by the eliminativist that there are no purposes, meanings, representations, aims, etc. of any sort whatsoever. So, how can there be illusions, falsehoods, and mistakes?

For that matter, how can there be *truth* or *correctness*, including the truth and correctness the eliminativist would ascribe to science? For these concepts too presuppose the meaning of a thought or statement that has represented things accurately, or the realization of a purpose. Thus, "Water is composed of hydrogen and oxygen" is true, while "Water is composed of silicon" is false, and the reason has to do with the meanings we associate with these sentences. Had the sentences in question had different meanings, the truth values would not necessarily have been the same. By contrast, "Trghfhhe bgghajdfsa adsa" is neither true nor false, because it has no meaning at all. Yet if eliminativism is right, "Water is composed of hydrogen and oxygen" is as devoid of meaning as "Trghfhhe bgghajdfsa adsa" is – in which case it is also as devoid of a truth value as the latter is. Moreover, if eliminativism is right, every statement in the writings of elminativists themselves, and every statement in every book of science, is as devoid of meaning as "Trghfhhe bgghajdfsa adsa" is, and thus just as devoid of any truth value. But then, in what sense do either science or eliminative materialist philosophy give us the *truth* about things?

Logic is also suffused with intentionality, insofar as inferences *aim* at truth and insofar as the logical relationships between statements presuppose that they have certain specific *meanings*. "Socrates is mortal" follows from "All men are mortal" and "Socrates is a man"

---

der Fire (Lanham: Rowman and Littlefield, 2004), chapter 2; and Victor Reppert, "Eliminative Materialism, Cognitive Suicide, and Begging the Question," *Metaphilosophy* 23 (1992): 378-92.

only because of the meanings we associate with these sets of symbols. If we associated different meanings with them, the one would *not* necessarily follow from the others. If each was as meaningless as "Trghfhhe bgghajdfsa adsa" is, then there would be no logical relationships between them at all – no such thing as the one set of symbols being *entailed* by, or *rationally justified* by the others. But again, if eliminativism is right, then every sentence, including every sentence in every work of eliminativist philosophy and every sentence in every book of science, is as meaningless as "Trghfhhe bgghajdfsa adsa" is. In that case there are no logical relations between any of the sentences in any of these writings, and thus no valid arguments (or indeed any arguments at all) to be found in them. So in what sense do either science or the assertions made by eliminativist philosophers constitute *rational defenses* of the claims they put forward?

Notions like "theory," "evidence," "observation," and the like are as suffused with intentionality as the notions of truth and logic are. Hence if there is no such thing as intentionality, then there is also no such thing as a scientific theory, as evidence for a scientific theory, as an observation which might confirm or disconfirm a theory, etc. Eliminativism makes of *all* statements and *all* arguments – scientific statements and arguments no less than metaphysical ones, and indeed every assertion of or argument for eliminativism itself – a meaningless string of ink marks or noises, no more true *or* false, rational *or* irrational than "Trghfhhe bgghajdfsa adsa" is. As M.R. Bennett and P.M.S. Hacker put it, the eliminativist "saws off the branch on which he is seated," undermining the very possibility of science in the name of science.[177]

The eliminativist owes us an explanation, then, of how he can so much as *state* his position in a coherent way in the absence of all these notions his position requires him to jettison. The stock eliminativist move at this point is to claim that future neuroscience will provide new categories to replace these old ones, at which point the view can be stated in a more consistent way. But that is like someone asserting that 2 + 2 = 23 and then, when asked what exactly this claim

---

[177] M. R. Bennett and P.M.S. Hacker, *Philosophical Foundations of Neuroscience* (Oxford: Blackwell, 2003), p. 377.

can mean given what it is to add, what it is for numbers to be equal, etc., responding that he can't really say but that future mathematicians will come up with a way of making sense of it. Until we have such an explanation, we don't even know so much as *what the claim is* that we are being asked to consider, much less whether it is correct. The same can be said for eliminativism. Until we are given a coherent way of *formulating* the thesis, we don't really have anything that *amounts to* a thesis, much less one we have reason to take seriously.

Hilary Putnam reports that the eliminativist Paul Churchland once acknowledged in conversation that he needs a "successor concept" to the notion of truth, and that he doesn't know what it will be.[178] This is doubly problematic. For one thing, if an eliminativist like Churchland is admitting both that he cannot claim that eliminativism is *true* (since a consistent eliminativist has to regard the notion of truth as illusory as that of intentionality) and that he has nothing to put in place of truth, then it is not clear exactly what he is trying to say about eliminativism or to convince *us* to say about it. (It cannot be "Eliminativism is true," but at best something like "Eliminativism is _____ ," with no explanation of how to fill in the blank. Until we have such an explanation, what is it that are we supposed to do with this utterance?) For another thing, the notion of a *concept* is as suffused with intentionality as the notions of truth, meaning, etc. are. So, if Churchland is consistent, he cannot say that he needs a "successor concept" for the notion of truth, but rather a "successor _____ ," where we now have a second blank to fill in with a term that does not entail the existence of intentionality, and where we are once again at a loss as to what that term might be.

The upshot of our discussion in this chapter, then, is that the intellect, like the self whose intellect it is, is real and irreducible. Whether it is material or immaterial in nature is a question to which we will return. But if it should turn out that no materialist account of our intellectual powers can succeed, it will follow that the problem is in that case with materialism and not with the commonsense supposition that we really do have concepts, thoughts, and rationality.

---

[178] Hilary Putnam, *Representation and Reality* (Cambridge, MA: The MIT Press, 1988), p. 60.

4. The Will

What is the will?

As we saw in chapter 1, according to Boethius's classic definition, a person is *an individual substance of a rational nature*. The subsequent two chapters defended the commonsense view that we are indeed persons in this sense. I argued in chapter 2 that it cannot coherently be denied that the self is a substance that persists over time. I argued in chapter 3 that it cannot coherently be denied that this substance has the rational or intellectual powers of grasping concepts, putting them together into propositions, and reasoning logically from one proposition to another. I also claimed in chapter 1 that free will is no less real and irreducible than the self and the intellect. I defend that claim in this chapter. But before we can understand why and in what sense the will is *free*, we need first to understand what the will *is*.

The short answer is that the will is the power or capacity of a rational substance to pursue what the intellect judges to be good. (Not necessarily *morally* good, but at least good in the broad sense of being suitable or desirable in some way.) It is also traditionally known as the "rational appetite." It is an *appetite* insofar as it involves an inclination or tendency toward some object or end. It is a *rational* appetite insofar as the object is pursued as something conceptualized in a certain way, and thus as something about which we might reason and come to know true propositions. This distinguishes the will from the appetites that non-human animals possess, which involve inclinations toward *non*-conceptualized objects of sensory perception; and from the sorts of inclinations or tendencies that a plant or an inanimate substance might exhibit, which are not even conscious, let alone conceptualized. A dog can see water and desire what it sees, but it cannot desire it *as water*, because it does not have the concept of water or any other concept. A tree can be inclined to sink its roots in the direction of the water below ground, but it cannot see or otherwise perceive the water or consciously desire it, much less conceptualize it. Water itself has an inclination or tendency to move toward the lowest point it can reach, but when it does so it is not exercising some organic capacity (as a tree is when it sinks roots into the ground), much less perceiving, desiring, or conceptualizing anything. A human being, by contrast, can not only perceive and desire water, but can know *that it is water*, and desire it precisely *as* something conceptualized in that specific way. To be able to do that sort of thing is just what it is to have a will. This is, in any event, the account of the will famously associated with Aquinas, and the aim of this chapter is to establish the reality and freedom of the will in this sense of "will."[179]

Again, that is the short answer to the question about what the will is. A longer answer will have to address various further questions raised by the short answer, such as: What is a substance? What is a power? What is it for a power to be inclined or tend toward some object or end? Now, these are issues of general metaphysical import, a thorough treatment of which is beyond the scope of a book devoted to human nature, specifically. But for present purposes, a brief overview will suffice (and in any event, I have provided a more thorough treatment of these topics elsewhere).[180]

In fact we have already discussed the notion of a substance in chapter 2, but let's say a little more. One way to understand what a substance is is to contrast it with what it is not. A substance is not an *attribute*, nor an *aggregate*, nor an *artifact*. For example, redness is an attribute rather than a substance, insofar as it exists only *in* other things – in an apple, say, or in a Stop sign – whereas a substance does

---

[179] Cf. Thomas Aquinas, *Summa Theologiae* I.19.1 and *Summa Contra Gentiles* IV.19. For detailed discussion of Aquinas's account of the will and related matters, see Steven J. Jensen, *The Human Person: A Beginner's Thomistic Psychology* (Washington, D.C.: Catholic University of America Press, 2018), chapters 12-14; Robert Pasnau, *Thomas Aquinas on Human Nature* (Cambridge: Cambridge University Press, 2002), chapters 7 and 8; and Eleonore Stump, *Aquinas* (London: Routledge, 2003), chapters 9 and 13.

[180] Cf. Edward Feser, *Scholastic Metaphysics: A Contemporary Introduction* (Heusenstamm: Editiones Scholasticae, 2014).

not exist *in* another thing in the same sense. It has a kind of *independence* that an attribute lacks. A pile of stones is an aggregate rather than a substance, insofar as it is really nothing over and above the sum of the stones that make it up, each of which would be exactly as it is whether or not it was part of the pile. A substance has a kind of *unity* that an aggregate lacks, insofar as it is more than the sum of its parts, each of which is what it is only relative to the whole substance of which it is a part. A watch is an artifact rather than a substance, insofar as its characteristic end or purpose of telling time is observer-relative, something imposed on it from outside by the designers and users of the watch. A true substance is directed toward the ends that are characteristic of it in an *intrinsic* way, of its very nature rather than merely by virtue of the purposes of some artificer.

The technical Aristotelian-Thomistic way of capturing the difference between a true physical substance and a mere aggregate or an artifact is to say that a physical substance has qua substance a *substantial form,* whereas an aggregate or an artifact has qua aggregate or artifact a merely *accidental form.* But let's pause to say something about the notion of *form* in general before explaining the distinction between substantial and accidental form in particular. The form of a thing is, to a first approximation, its essence or nature, as contrasted with the matter that takes on that form, essence, or nature. For example, there is the form of being a sphere, which is distinct from the different kinds of matter (plastic, rubber, stone, wood, etc.) that might take on that form. In Aristotelian-Thomistic philosophy, to identity the form and matter of a thing is to identify two of its *four causes,* namely its *formal cause* and its *material cause.* The remaining two are its *efficient cause,* which is whatever brought it into existence, and its *final cause,* which is the end or set of ends toward which it tends. In the case of a ball, for example, we might say that its formal cause is its spherical shape, its material cause is the rubber it is made out of, its efficient cause is the manufacturing process in some factory that brought it about, and its final cause is to roll down incline surfaces, bounce when hitting a solid object, and so on.

Now, a substantial form is a form that makes something a substance of a certain kind (such as a stone or a dog), and thereby gives it its fundamental character. An accidental form (such as the shape of some stone or the color of a certain dog) is a secondary feature that merely modifies a substance that would still be a substance of the same kind even without the feature. A mark of a thing's having a substantial form (and thus of its being a true substance rather than a mere modification of a substance) is the presence in it of irreducible properties and causal powers. Any example is bound to be controversial, but suppose for the sake of argument that water is a true substance, and thus has qua water a substantial rather than merely accidental form. The idea would be that the properties and causal powers of water (being liquid at room temperature, acting as a solvent, and so on) are irreducible to the properties and causal powers of hydrogen, oxygen, or any mere aggregate of hydrogen and oxygen. By contrast, the properties and causal powers of a random pile of ice cubes made out of frozen water are reducible to the aggregate of the properties and powers of the cubes that make up the pile, and the properties and causal powers of an igloo constructed out of blocks of ice are reducible to the aggregate of the properties and powers of the blocks. Hence to be an aggregate like a pile of ice cubes or an artifact like an igloo is to have a merely accidental rather than substantial form. As these examples indicate, things with merely accidental forms presuppose the existence of things having substantial forms. You can't have random piles of ice cubes and igloos unless you first have frozen water. Hence substances are metaphysically more fundamental than aggregates and artifacts.

I've brought up powers again, so let's turn to those. A power is a capacity to act or operate in a certain way, such as acting on another thing so as to bring about a change in it. For example, frozen water or ice has the power to cool down the surrounding air. Now, a power is a kind of attribute, and like other attributes it exists only *in* a substance rather than in a freestanding way. The power to cool down the surrounding air is a power *of* the ice. Strictly speaking, it is not the *power to cool* that cools down the air; it is the *ice* that cools down the air, by virtue of having the power to do so.

The French playwright Molière (1622-73) famously mocked this sort of talk as tautological or uninformative, but it is not. Consider his example of opium, to which we can attribute a dormitive power, or power to cause sleep. To attribute such a power to opium is not a tautology, as it would be a tautology to say that opium causes sleep because it causes sleep. When we attribute such a power to opium, we are saying that there is something *about the opium itself* that produces sleep, that it is not something merely in the circumstances under which it is ingested that does so (even if the circumstances play some role). We are also saying that it is not merely something in a particular sample of opium that causes sleep, but something in opium as such that does so. Of course, this is not the most informative claim in the world. We would also like to know *exactly what* it is about opium that gives it this effect, and a chemist might tell us that. But the claim really does give us at least some information about opium.

Now, as I have indicated, the powers of a physical substance are grounded in its substantial form, and different kinds of substance will have different powers, as water and opium obviously do. Powers themselves differ insofar as they *aim at* or are *directed toward* different outcomes, as being cooled and being made to sleep are different outcomes. It is through its powers that a substance manifests its final causality, also known as its teleology (as we saw in chapter 3). Indeed, a causal power is a kind of link or middle man between a substance's substantial form and its teleology. As Aquinas says, "some inclination follows every form,"[181] and "every agent acts for an end."[182] That is to say, an agent (a substance considered as an efficient cause) will, by virtue of its distinctive substantial form, be inclined toward, and act to bring about, some particular kind of end or set of ends. But a substance's substantial form aims it toward those ends *through* its causal powers, as it were.

Early modern philosophers eschewed the notions of formal and final causality, and, especially after David Hume, they tended to throw out the notion of causal powers as well. For post-Humean philosophy of causation, causes and effects are conceived of as inherently "loose and separate" in the sense that, in principle, any effect or none might follow upon any cause. This is precisely what we should expect if no cause has a substantial form or teleology by virtue of which it

---

[181] *Summa theologiae* I.80.1.

[182] *Summa theologiae* I-II.9.1.

naturally aims at the production of some particular effect or range of effects. Hence, if a certain kind of effect B does *in fact* happen always to follow from a certain cause A, that must, for the post-Humean philosopher, be attributed to some "law of nature" *extrinsic* to A and B, rather than to some power intrinsic to A. It is something *outside of* A (the law in question) rather than something *internal to* it (a causal power) that accounts for what it does. This conceptual shift could hardly fail to have repercussions for the modern understanding of how the will is related to the agent whose will it is and to the actions that follow upon its operation (an understanding very different from that of Aquinas).

Before we get to that, one last general point must be made about causal powers, which is that whether and how they operate depends crucially on circumstances. We must distinguish between a power and its manifestation on any particular occasion. A sample of opium has the power to cause sleep even if it is never ingested and thus never in fact causes sleep. Even if it is ingested, it may not cause sleep if this outcome is blocked by some other causal factor – say, by your having taken a handful of amphetamines before taking the opium. The manifestation of a causal power may depend on its operating in tandem with other causal powers, and also on the absence of the operation of yet other powers.

As contemporary theorists of causal powers often point out, such facts have dramatic implications for our understanding of laws of nature. It is often assumed that laws of nature are fundamental to physical reality, and that at least the paradigmatic examples of laws of nature operate in a strict or exceptionless way. But in fact, physical phenomena will exhibit the regularities described by a law of nature only *given* that certain causal powers are acting in tandem or failing to do so, and in some cases this condition never actually holds. For example, Newton's first law tells us that an object in motion, if it is not acted upon, has a tendency to remain in motion forever. But objects never actually do remain in motion forever, because all of them always are in fact acted upon by other objects. Hence the regularity described by the law never really holds. As this indicates, causal powers are actually more fundamental to physical reality than laws of nature are. A law is really just a description of how things will go *if* substances manifest their causal powers in such-and-such a way. As philosopher of science Nancy Cartwright famously put it, the laws of physics "lie."[183] They do not describe physical reality as it really is, but only some idealization of physical reality.[184]

As we will see, this has implications for the traditional debate over determinism and free will. Determinism holds that what happens in the physical world at any given moment is necessitated by what was happening at earlier moments. This presupposes a picture of the world on which the laws of nature are metaphysically fundamental, and causal processes are secondary, operating in a way that conforms strictly to the laws. But for the Aristotelian-Thomistic picture of the world that I am describing, this has things backwards. It is substances and their powers that are fundamental, and laws are secondary, describing the patterns that will result *if* certain combinations of powers manifest or fail to manifest. Hence determinism simply gets nature fundamentally wrong. Note that it is not only human beings that it gets wrong, but also non-human animals, plants, and inanimate phenomena. Since much of the modern debate about free will presupposes this deterministic picture of nature, that debate simply gets off on the wrong foot.[185]

We'll come back to that. For the moment, note that while the behavior of non-human animals is not deterministic, neither is it random or arbitrary. It is perfectly intelligible given their causal powers together with the powers of the things they interact with. Yet non-human animals do not have wills, much less free will. So, being non-determined but also non-random is not sufficient for having a will, free or otherwise. What more is needed? Aquinas's answer is that the

---

[183] Nancy Cartwright, *How the Laws of Physics Lie* (Oxford: Clarendon Press, 1983).

[184] For defense of this view of laws of nature and discussion of the relevant contemporary literature, see Feser, *Scholastic Metaphysics*, pp. 63-72 and Edward Feser, *Aristotle's Revenge: The Metaphysical Foundations of Physical and Biological Science* (Neunkirchen-Seelscheid: Editiones Scholasticae, 2019), pp. 177-90.

[185] Cf. Rani Lill Anjum and Stephen Mumford, *What Tends to Be: The Philosophy of Dispositional Modality* (Abingdon: Routledge, 2018), chapter 10; and Steven Horst, *Laws, Mind, and Free Will* (Cambridge, MA: The MIT Press, 2011).

will is a power of the kind of thing whose activity arises from *within* it in a certain way – specifically, by way of having *knowledge* of the kind of which a rational substance alone is capable.[186] To act voluntarily is to *know what you are doing* in the way that human beings do.

But it will be useful, before we say more about what this involves, to say something about intermediate cases – intermediate, that is to say, between inanimate things like opium and water on the one hand and human beings on the other. A living thing is distinguished from non-living things in being self-perfecting.[187] That is to say, in addition to having powers by which it affects other things, it also has powers to complete and maintain itself, as a plant does when it grows and takes in water and nutrients. In this thin sense, any living thing, including even a plant, can be said to be a kind of self-mover, and thus to act by virtue of something within it. (The technical way of putting this is that it exhibits *immanent* causality as well as *transeunt* causality.) Still, a plant, like water or opium, does not know what it is doing, and thus cannot be said to act voluntarily or from will.

Now, though the behavior of non-human animals is not quite voluntary either, animals are closer than plants are to possessing the crucial characteristic that makes for will, in a way that is instructive. Suppose I yank a plant from the ground, or tie one of its branches back so that the leaves are kept permanently in the shade. Of course, no one would regard these movements of the plant as voluntary. The plant's natural tendencies would be to sink its roots *into* the ground, and to grow toward the light. Being contrary to its natural tendencies, the movements I've caused in it are violent, and violent movements are *ipso facto* involuntary. But even when the plant does do what is natural to it, we wouldn't say that it acts voluntarily. It sinks its roots into the ground and grows toward the light, but again, we would say that even then it *doesn't know* what it is doing. That is why we wouldn't blame a plant for failing to sink its roots into the ground or grow toward the light. We would judge such a failure to be the result of the

---

[186] *Summa theologiae* I-II.6.1-2.

[187] For a more detailed exposition and defense of the account of what it is to be a living thing that I will summarize here, see pp. 375-83 of Feser, *Aristotle's Revenge*. We will also return to this topic in chapter 6.

plant's being afflicted by some sort of damage or disease, rather than anything analogous to choice. We wouldn't say that the plant should know better, because it doesn't know anything at all, and you have to know something before you can be held responsible.

Again, for Aquinas, voluntary behavior is behavior that arises from *within* the agent in a certain specific way. The plant's roots being yanked from the ground is a movement that does not arise from within the plant in any sense, since, in my example, I am the one who makes them move that way. The plant's roots sinking into the ground is a movement that does arise from within the plant in a sense, since it results from the plant's natural self-perfective powers qua plant. However, though the power and inclination are in the plant, the *end toward which* the power is inclined is in no sense present within the plant, nor even represented within it. An end's being represented within an agent in some way is, Aquinas holds, a necessary condition for the agent's behavior arising from within it in the relevant sense.

Now, in a non-human animal, the ends toward which its powers are inclined *are* represented within it. For an animal can *perceive* a thing toward which it is naturally inclined, such as the food it eats. Even before it actually eats it, the food is in the animal *qua perceived*. Of course, an animal can *mis*perceive things, as when a greyhound in a race chases a fake rabbit. But that reinforces the point that it is something in a sense internal to the animal, namely the end *as perceived* (or misperceived), that moves it to act. A plant, by contrast, doesn't even rise to the level of misperception, let alone perception.

So, unlike a plant, an animal has a *kind* of knowledge of the end it is pursuing. However, we still wouldn't say that an animal *knows what it is doing*, and thus wouldn't hold it morally responsible for what it does, any more than we would hold a plant morally responsible. For while the animal knows *the end* that it pursues, it doesn't *know that* it knows it. It doesn't know the end *as* an end, for it does not have the concept of an end, nor indeed any concepts at all. Hence it also lacks the concept of being a *means* to an end, and thus doesn't *know* that its action is a means to the end it pursues, much less that other means might be possible. This lack of concepts entails a certain inflexibility in the animal's behavior. Like a plant, an animal cannot do otherwise than whatever it in fact does. If the animal is hungry and there are no countervailing circumstances present (such as a predator's being in the vicinity of the food, and frightening the animal away), the animal's perception of the food will result in it trying to eat it. Because of this lack of concepts and consequent inflexibility in behavior, Aquinas says that a non-human animal acts voluntarily only in an imperfect sense.

Now, a rational substance is a substance with an intellect, and to have an intellect is precisely to have the capacity to conceptualize what one knows. A human being qua rational animal not only knows the food that he tries to eat, but knows it *as* food of a certain kind (an apple, say) and *as* something that would be good for him to eat given his need for nutrition. He also knows that biting into it straightaway would be one possible means of eating it, and that this has certain advantages and disadvantages compared to other means such as baking it into a pie, turning it into applesauce, or squeezing the juice out of it and drinking it. What all of this makes possible, as Aquinas emphasizes, is *deliberation*. Since a rational being possess universal concepts, he can identify particular ends and means as instances of general kinds.[188] He can make *comparisons* between these different possible ends and different possible means to the ends.[189] He can arrive at judgments about which ends and means are best, and also make judgments *about those judgments themselves*.[190] Hence, when he decides to eat the apple, he *knows what he is doing* in a way that opium, or a plant, or a non-human animal does not know what it is doing.

We have, then, a hierarchy of degrees to which the source of a thing's behavior is to be found within it. Inanimate things like frozen water and opium have causal powers which are directed toward certain ends (for example, cooling down the surrounding air and causing sleep, respectively), but these ends are entirely external to the inanimate things themselves. Merely vegetative forms of life have powers directed toward ends internal to them (such as growth), but without any sort of knowledge of these ends. Given their inherent directedness toward an end, the powers of these animate and inanimate

---

[188] *Summa Theologiae* I.59.3.

[189] *Summa Theologiae* I.83.1.

[190] *De Veritate* 24.1.

non-sentient substances can be thought of as *appetites* of a sort, but as merely *natural appetites* (to use the Aristotelian-Thomistic jargon) insofar as they reflect a thing's natural tendencies rather than any sort of knowledge. Since a non-human animal perceptually represents the ends toward which it is directed, it does have a kind of knowledge (albeit an imperfect kind). Its powers are classified as *sensory appetites*. Human beings as rational animals have a more perfect knowledge of the ends toward which they are directed, insofar as they can conceptualize them, make judgments about them, and draw inferences about them. They know these ends *as* ends, deliberate about whether they are worthy of pursuit and about the best means to pursue them, and decide how to act on the basis of this deliberation. The activity of rational beings thus arises from within them in the most perfect possible way. They possess a kind of causal power which we can classify as *rational appetite*.

To have a will is, for Aquinas, precisely to have rational appetite, to have in the most perfect way possible the source of one's activity within one. To be a rational substance entails having a will, because every kind of substance has its own distinctive causal powers, and a will just is the kind of appetite or power characteristic of a rational substance. Because rational substances have, in this way, the source of their activity within them, they possess a kind of *self-determination* that nothing else has.[191] What we rational substances do is *up to us*, whereas what non-rational things do is not up to them. This is, as we will see, crucial to understanding the nature of the will's freedom.

The thesis that the will is to be understood as a power of a rational substance is by no means merely some idiosyncratic or arbitrary claim of Aquinas's. It is implicit in the very concept of choice and in the phenomenology of our experience of choosing. As John Searle notes, we cannot make sense of choice except as the activity of an irreducible self with reason and agency that persists over time.[192]

---

[191] For a detailed analysis, see Thomas Pink, *Self-Determination: The Ethics of Action, Volume I* (Oxford: Oxford University Press, 2016).

[192] John R. Searle, *Rationality in Action* (Cambridge, MA: The MIT Press, 2001), chapter 3; and John R. Searle, *Freedom and Neurobiology* (New York: Columbia University Press, 2007), pp. 32-33 and 53-55.

For choice is the outcome of deliberation, which is a rational process extended over time, and it presupposes a continuing subject who persists from the beginning of that process through to the end of it. Choice is also *active*, a *bringing of something about* rather than passively experiencing it as occurring. The subject of this activity cannot be merely a *bundle* of events or properties of the kind posited by Hume, because there must be something that ties together the various cognitive acts that enter into the deliberative process, and makes of them a single chain of reasoning that results in choice. Of course, the skeptic might insist that all of this is illusory. But the point for the moment is that the notion of will is necessarily tied to the notions of a persisting self with rationality, so that we cannot coherently affirm the reality of the will without affirming the reality of a rational self. I have, in any event, already argued in chapters 2 and 3 for the reality of such a persisting self and for its rationality. We will return presently to the question of why we should affirm that it does indeed possess will.[193]

Aquinas holds that the intellect is prior to the will, a thesis sometimes called *intellectualism* (where *voluntarism* is the rival view that the will is prior to the intellect). What has been said should make it clear what this means and why he holds it. For the will is a power of a substance, and a power is ontologically less fundamental than the substance of which it is a power. And the *kind* of substance of which it is a power is a rational or intellectual substance. Hence, the will is posterior to the intellect in just the way that the power to cause sleep is posterior to opium, or the power to sink roots into the ground is posterior to a plant. To say that the will is prior to the intellect would be like saying that a plant's power to sink roots is prior to its vegetative nature. It would get things the wrong way around, putting the volitional cart before the intellective horse. Moreover, a thing cannot be willed unless it is known, and it is the intellect that knows. An appetite is an appetite for some object, and if the object is not known intellectually, then the appetite would be a natural appetite or a sensory appetite rather than a rational appetite, and thus would not be a will. By contrast, if, *per impossibile*, an intellectual substance lacked a

---

[193] By arguing that choice is the activity of a substance or irreducible self, I am committed to what is in contemporary philosophy often called an *agent-causal* account of the will rather than an *event-causal* account. More on this issue below.

will and therefore were not inclined toward or away from what it knows, it would still *know* what it knows.

To be sure, there is a *sense* in which the will can move the intellect, as even Aquinas allows. But when properly understood, this does not in any way conflict with what has been said so far. For the will cannot move the intellect, any more than it can do anything else, unless the intellect first judges such movement to be good and worthy of pursuit. For example, suppose we say that the will moves the intellect to contemplate some topic. That is precisely because the intellect judges such contemplation to be worth pursuing, and the will simply follows its lead. When we speak of the will doing this or that, it is easy to fall into the trap of thinking of the will as if it had a mind of its own, which somehow competes with the intellect. In fact the only mind the will has is the intellect itself. When the will moves the intellect, it is really the *intellect* moving the intellect by means of the will. Or, better still, it is the rational substance moving itself, by means of the same power by which it moves other things, namely the will. To think that the will somehow moves the intellect on its own is like thinking that, when I pull a rug out from under myself and fall down, it is the rug that has knocked me down. In fact I knocked myself down by means of pulling the rug, and in the same way, I move my intellect myself when I will either to contemplate or not contemplate some topic.

Here we must avoid a fallacy of hypostasization, of thinking of the will as if it were a substance in its own right as opposed to being a power of a substance. To speak of the will doing this or that is like speaking of the power of opium causing sleep. Properly understood, it is really just a shorthand for speaking of what a substance is doing. It is the opium that causes sleep by virtue of its dormitive power, and it is a rational substance as a whole to which the will's activity is properly attributed. It is not really my will that does anything. *I* do things, by virtue of having a will. Reductionist theories of the self can facilitate the fallacious tendency to hypostasize the will. If we think of the person, not as a unity but rather as an aggregate of parts, then the intellect, the will, our various bodily parts, and the other aspects of human nature come to seem like quasi-substances in their own right, interacting like billiard balls knocking into one another. We end up with a model of action on which the intellect directing the will to pick up an apple is conceptualized on analogy with the cue ball knocking the eight ball into a third billiard ball. One then can start wondering whether it might not really be the eight ball that is knocking into the cue ball, and be led thereby into voluntarism. But this model is a travesty. Strictly speaking, there is just one agent here, the human being himself, who picks up the apple by virtue of knowing it and willing to acquire what it knows.

We must also avoid confusing the will with the emotions that are often associated with its exercise.[194] When you will to take a bite of an apple, this may be associated with a strong desire for the apple, and when you will to run away from a snake, this may be associated with fear. But the act of will is distinct from the desire and the fear. The will is related to the intellect in a way that is analogous to the relationship between emotions and the sensations and mental imagery that can trigger them. The sight of a snake can generate fear, and forming a mental image of an apple can generate desire. In the same way, when the intellect conceptualizes something as an apple or a snake, the will might be drawn toward it in the first case or repelled by it in the second. But just as it would be a mistake to identify the concept of an apple or a snake with the mental images associated with these things, so too would it be a mistake to identify the will with the desire or the fear. Desire and fear, like sensation and imagination, can exist in creatures without intellects. Will cannot.

Volitions and teleology

I have been elaborating upon what it means to hold, as Aquinas does, that the will is the rational appetite, the power or capacity of a rational substance to pursue what the intellect judges to be good. But is will, in this sense, real? I have already argued, in chapter 2, that we are indeed persisting substances, and, in chapter 3, that we do indeed have intellect or rationality.[195] Does that not suffice to establish the

---

[194] Cf. Jensen, *The Human Person*, pp. 67-69 and 224-27.
[195] So as to give the lay of the conceptual land, I have spoken of material causes as well as formal, efficient, and final causes. But I have not yet addressed the question whether we really are material substances, or immaterial substances, or substances with both material and immaterial attributes. Just as I did not need to settle that question in order to establish the reality of the self and of the intellect, I do not need to settle it in order to establish

reality of the will too, given that it is essentially just what a rational substance exercises when it acts? For example, isn't it obvious that you have just now *willed* either to read on or to put this book down?

Some philosophers think not. What I have been saying implies that the will is a capacity over and above our capacities to *believe* something, to *desire* that it be the case, or to take any of the other propositional attitudes referred to in chapter 3. I have also said that the will has a teleological character, that its objects serve as the final causes of the actions that result from willing. An exercise of the power of will – an *act of willing* something – is commonly referred to in the philosophical literature as a *volition*. Some philosophers deny that there are any such things as volitions, and hold that action can be entirely explained instead in terms of propositional attitudes like belief and desire. Some philosophers also deny that action is inherently teleological, and hold that it can instead be analyzed entirely in terms of efficient causation (unsurprisingly given that, as I noted above, modern philosophy has tended to eschew the notion of teleology or final cause). In order to see that the will as I have characterized it is real, then, we need to see why these philosophers are mistaken.

One objection raised against the notion of a volition is that in order for a volition to be the cause of some piece of behavior, it would have to be something we could characterize independently of that behavior, since causes and their effects are, in general, distinct things. For example, heat from the sun might cause a certain ice cube to melt, but we can describe the sun completely independently of its relation to this particular effect. Now, in the case of volitions, it seems we *cannot* characterize them apart from the behavior of which they are said to be the causes. For example, I cannot describe the specific volition that is my *willing* to raise my arm without making reference to my behavior of raising it. Thus, the objection holds, there is a tight conceptual connection between volitions and the behaviors they purportedly cause of a kind that does not hold in the case of things genuinely related as cause and effect.[196]

---

the reality and freedom of the will. But I will address it in later chapters, and in this chapter I will have reason to say something about how the will relates to our material attributes *if* we have such attributes.

[196] Cf. A. I. Melden, *Free Action* (London: Routledge and Kegan Paul, 1961), chapter 5.

The trouble with this objection is that while we can concede that a cause and its effect must be distinct entities, it doesn't follow that we must in every case be able to characterize the former independently of the latter. For while this is possible in some cases (as in the example of the sun and the melting of the ice cube), there may be special features of other cases that make it impossible. In the case of volitions, they have (as beliefs and desires do) a kind of *intentionality* or directedness toward an object, and specifying a particular volition's intentional content is, naturally, going to part of how we identify it. Thus do we characterize the volition we have taken as our example as *willing to raise my arm*, specifically. But it doesn't follow that the volition is not a distinct entity from the behavior of raising my arm (just as a belief or desire is a distinct entity from what it represents). I might, after all, will to raise my arm without my arm actually being raised, if damage to the relevant nerves prevents this (just as I might believe that it is raining or desire that there be rain even if it is not in fact raining). In that case, the volition is clearly a distinct entity from the behavior toward which it points, and which in the normal case it causes.[197]

An especially influential set of objections to the notion of a volition was raised by Gilbert Ryle (1900-1976).[198] He notes that volitions are said to explain what makes a piece of behavior voluntary. For example, if my arm goes up as a result of a muscular spasm, we would say that such a motion was involuntary. But when I deliberately raise my arm, the claim is that this counts as a voluntary action because it was caused by a volition. Now, Ryle raises a dilemma for this account. Are volitions *themselves* voluntary? Either way we answer, the notion of a volition seems problematic. For if we say that they are *not* voluntary, then how can they explain what makes a piece of behavior voluntary? (After all, the neural processes that cause a muscular spasm are not voluntary, and they hardly make the spasm itself voluntary.) But if we say that volitions *are* voluntary, then it seems we are faced with a vicious regress. For if what makes a piece of behavior voluntary is that it was caused by a volition, wouldn't it follow that what makes that volition itself voluntary is a further volition?

---

[197] Cf. E. J. Lowe, *Locke on Human Understanding* (London: Routledge, 1995), pp. 124-26.

[198] Gilbert Ryle, *The Concept of Mind* (New York: Barnes and Noble, 1949), pp. 62-69.

Wouldn't that further volition itself be made voluntary by yet another volition, and so on ad infinitum?

But the dilemma is bogus, for in fact there is no problem for the notion of a volition either way we answer. For suppose we do say that volitions are themselves voluntary. It doesn't follow that they are, or need to be, voluntary *in the same sense* in which the behavior they explain is voluntary. We can say that the sidewalk is wet, and that water is wet, but they are obviously not wet in the same way. The sidewalk is wet because it is covered with water, but water is wet, not because it is covered with water, but rather because it is that by virtue of which other things are wet. Similarly, both the raising of my arm and my act of willing to raise my arm can be said to be voluntary, but in different senses. The raising of my arm is voluntary because it was caused by the volition or act of will, and the volition is voluntary because it is that in virtue of which the behavior it causes is voluntary.[199]

Suppose instead that we say that a volition is *not* itself voluntary. It doesn't follow that it would not be capable of explaining how the behavior it causes is voluntary. That would follow if the sense in which a volition is involuntary is the same as the sense in which a muscle spasm or a reflex is involuntary, but volitions are not involuntary in that sense. Volitions do, after all, have features that spasms and reflexes don't have, such as being conceptually related to the cognitive processes that give rise to them, and this gives volitions and the behavior they cause a rationality that spasms and reflexes lack.[200] It is precisely this rationality that accounts for the difference between voluntary action and mere spasms and reflexes. Even if volitions are not themselves voluntary, they can still intelligibly be said to be *that by virtue of which* behavior is voluntary, and thereby play an explanatory role. By way of analogy, consider that the moon is illuminated, and that because it is it can illuminate other things, such as a tree you see outside your window when the moon is full. On a moonless night, let us imagine, the tree is not illuminated. Now, the sun is not illuminated

---

[199] Cf. Hugh McCann, "Volition and Basic Action," *Philosophical Review* 83 (1974): 451-73.

[200] Cf. Lowe, *Locke on Human Understanding*, p. 127. See also E. J. Lowe, *Subjects of Experience* (Cambridge: Cambridge University Press, 1996), pp. 153-54.

either. But obviously, the sense in which the sun is unilluminated is not the same as the sense in which the tree is unilluminated on a moonless night, and neither is the sun unilluminated in a sense that would prevent it from illuminating other things. Rather, the sun is *that by which* things like the moon are illuminated. It is not less than illuminated, but rather more than being merely illuminated. Volitions are like that. If they are not themselves voluntary, that is not because they are less than voluntary, but rather because they are more than merely voluntary, being that by virtue of which other things count as voluntary.

Ryle also objects that the notion of a volition is the product of philosophical theorizing rather than something derived from experience. The average person is familiar with thoughts, feelings of boredom, headaches, and the like, but not volitions. But as E. J. Lowe points out, we are in fact sometimes aware of volitions, especially when they are inefficacious (as when injury prevents us from doing what we will to do).[201] Moreover, the reason we are usually not aware of them is not because they are rare, but precisely because they are so common. As Lowe says, they are like one's nose, which is rarely noticed in one's field of vision precisely because it is always there.[202]

Ryle claims that it is often difficult to say exactly how many volitions are involved in a particular case, such as when reciting a poem backwards. One problem with this objection, as Lowe notes, is that it would prove too much. It is no less difficult to say how many *utterances* are involved in reciting a poem backwards, but Ryle and other critics of the notion of volition wouldn't deny that utterances are real.[203] Another problem noted by Lowe is that Ryle's question is not as unanswerable as he supposes. How many volitions are involved in a case like the one he mentions may be clearer once we further spec-

---

[201] Lowe, *Subjects of Experience*, pp. 154-55.

[202] Lowe, *Locke on Human Understanding*, pp. 127-28.

[203] Lowe, *Subjects of Experience*, pp. 155-56. Cf. Lawrence H. Davis, *Theory of Action* (Englewood Cliffs, NJ: Prentice-Hall, 1979), p. 23.

ify the circumstances. Reciting the poem backwards would presumably involve fewer volitions for someone well-rehearsed than it would for someone who is attempting this for the first time, and who may thus have to stop several times to try to remember the next line, and then will to continue the recitation.

Critics of the notion of volition allege, in any event, that it is simply not needed in order to account for action. It is often claimed, for example, that we can explain an action instead in terms of what the agent *believes* together with some "pro-attitude" he takes, such us *desiring* or *wishing*. Hence, we can explain why Bob went to the liquor store by noting that he desired some gin, believed that he could get it there, and that this conjunction of belief and desire caused him to act.[204] But the trouble with such an account, as Lowe observes, is that belief and desire are not by themselves sufficient to generate action.[205] Obviously, I can believe that gin is available at the liquor store without that prompting me to go there. But even if I desire some gin, that won't necessarily generate the action either. I may, after all, judge that the desire would be a bad one to indulge (if, say, I am trying to overcome a drinking habit). Nor would it help to appeal to a mental event like forming the *intention* to go to the liquor store, since, like a desire, an intention need not result in action either immediately or at all. (Even if I sincerely intend to go to the liquor store, I may do so only long after forming the intention, or may forget about it and not do it at all.) What we need to posit is something with an inherent tendency *immediately* to generate action (which desires and intentions lack) and that is precisely what a volition or act of will is.[206] This is not to deny that beliefs, desires, and intentions play a role in generating volitions, which then go on to trigger behavior. But we shouldn't conclude from this that the volition is somehow unnecessary, and that belief, desire, and intention can trigger behavior without this middle

---

[204] For an influential defense of such an analysis of action, see Donald Davidson, "Actions, Reasons, and Causes," in his *Essays on Actions and Events* (Oxford: Clarendon Press, 1980).

[205] Lowe, *Locke on Human Understanding*, pp. 137-39 and *Subjects of Experience*, pp. 157-61.

[206] Of course, that is not to say that a volition actually will always result in action, for it might be frustrated (e.g. by neurological damage). The point is that a volition will immediately result in action *unless* frustrated, whereas a desire or intention might not immediately result in action even when not frustrated.

man. As Lowe notes, this would be like saying that since a spark might cause an explosion which in turn causes a building to collapse, we might as well suppose that a spark could directly cause the collapse without the middle step of the explosion.[207]

As Searle notes, in rational action there is always a "gap" between the having of a certain belief and desire on the one hand, and the carrying out of the action on the other.[208] I may desire some gin and believe that I can get it at the liquor store, but the action of going to the liquor store will count as rational precisely only if the having of that desire and belief does *not* causally necessitate it – that is to say, only if I might nevertheless refrain from the action despite having that desire and belief. For if the mere having of the desire and belief does suffice to guarantee that I will carry out the action, then we would have a case in which I am acting out of addiction, obsession, or the like, and thus in a paradigmatically irrational way. Of course, sometimes we do act in such ways. But not in the normal case. As Searle concludes, the thesis that actions are caused by beliefs and "pro-attitudes" alone is true not of actions in general and certainly not of rational actions, but only of irrational and non-rational actions.

The thesis that action is not irreducibly teleological is also commonly spelled out in terms of the idea that behavior can be explained in terms of beliefs and "pro-attitudes." For example, that Bob went to the liquor store can, on this view, be explained in terms of his

---

[207] One could acknowledge that the will is real and argue that it is nevertheless *reducible* to some other mental phenomenon, such as desire. This is essentially the view defended in Harry G. Frankfurt's influential essay "Freedom of the Will and the Concept of a Person," in Gary Watson, ed., *Free Will* (Oxford: Oxford University Press, 1982). Frankfurt identifies willing with having a second-order desire, viz. a desire that one have a certain desire. But there are serious problems with this view even apart from the points made already about the need for the notion of volition over and above that of desire. (Cf. Pink, *Self-Determination*, p. 143.) For one thing, there are many cases where a person can be said to will something even though there is no second-order desire present. For another, it is not clear that Frankfurt can avoid a vicious regress, in which a second-order desire counts as volitional only if it is the object of a yet higher-order desire, and so on *ad infinitum*. In short, there are either too few desires or too many to make Frankfurt's account work.

[208] Searle, *Rationality in Action*, pp. 12-17 and chapter 3; and Searle, *Freedom and Neurobiology*, pp. 50-58.

desire for gin and his belief that gin is available at the liquor store acting in tandem as *efficient causes* of his behavior.[209] No reference to *final cause* is needed. Even if Lowe's point is conceded that reference need also be made to a volition or act of will that comes between the belief and desire on the one hand and the behavior on the other, the opponent of teleology might insist on interpreting this volition as simply one further *efficient* cause in the chain.

But there is a well-known problem with this sort of analysis, having to do with cases involving "deviant causal chains." To take a different example, consider an explanation like: *Bob knocked over the glass of water for the purpose of distracting Fred.* The phrase "for the purpose of" is teleological. But the opponent of teleology would suggest that the explanation can be reformulated as: *Bob had the intention of distracting Fred and this caused him to knock over the glass of water,* where this new description eliminates the teleological element. Bob's intention is characterized as the *efficient* cause of his action, and this, it might seem, suffices to explain his behavior. But on closer inspection, we can see that this reformulation won't work. For consider the case where Bob's intention to knock over the glass makes him so nervous that his hand shakes uncontrollably, and knocks over the glass before he otherwise would have.[210] Then it is certainly true that *Bob had the intention of distracting Fred and this caused him to knock over the glass of water,* but it is *not* true that *Bob knocked over the glass of water for the purpose of distracting Fred.* For in this case, Bob knocked over the glass not *for the purpose of* distracting Fred (even though he did want to do that at some point), but rather because he lost control of his hand. So, the two descriptions are not equivalent after all. That is to say, there is content to the statement that *Bob knocked over the glass of water for the purpose of distracting Fred* that is not captured in the reformulation *Bob had the intention of distracting Fred and this caused him to knock over*

---

[209] Again, Davidson's "Actions, Reasons, and Causes" is the *locus classicus* for this view.

[210] The example is from Alfred R. Mele, *Springs of Action: Understanding Intentional Behavior* (Oxford: Oxford University Press, 1992), p. 182.

the glass of water. The teleological language captures a crucial aspect of the situation that is not conveyed in the reformulation.[211]

To try to salvage the reformulation, one might add to it the idea that the intention in question causes the resulting action only via bodily motions that the agent has *guidance* of or *control* over, rather than by involuntary shaking and the like.[212] But the trouble with this is that "guidance" and "control" are *themselves* teleological notions – for guidance or control is always guidance or control *towards* an end or goal – so that the revised analysis will not truly have eliminated teleology at all.[213]

Alternatively, Alfred Mele suggests that the reformulation might stipulate that the intention is the *direct* cause of the behavior, whereas in the case in which Bob nervously knocks over the water prematurely, the intention causes the behavior only indirectly.[214] Now, even in the case where nervousness plays no role, there is presumably neural activity that comes between the intention and the behavior. So why wouldn't that make the intention only an indirect cause even in that case? Mele's response is to *include* all of that neural activity as part of the behavioral effect that the intention directly causes. But now another problem for the reformulation arises. For if, in this case, the neural activity that generates the knocking over of the glass is to be included in the behavioral effect that the intention directly produces, why couldn't Bob's nervousness in the other case also be included as part of the behavioral effect that the intention directly produces? And if it is, then Mele's appeal to what the intention *directly* causes will fail to salvage the reformulation. Bob's intention will be the direct cause of the effect in *both* cases, so that directness

---

[211] Cf. Scott R. Sehon, *Teleological Realism: Mind, Agency, and Explanation* (Cambridge, MA: The MIT Press, 2005), pp. 91-93.; and Scott Sehon, *Free Will and Action Explanation: A Non-Causal, Compatibilist Account* (Oxford: Oxford University Press, 2016), pp. 90-93.

[212] Cf. Mele, *Springs of Action*, pp. 202-203.

[213] Sehon, *Teleological Realism*, pp. 96 and 99.

[214] Mele, *Springs of Action*, p. 202.

will not suffice to explain what makes the purposive behavior different from the case where Bob is nervous.[215]

Another option might be simply to stipulate, in the reformulation, that nervousness played no role. In other words, we can reformulate the statement that *Bob knocked over the glass of water for the purpose of distracting Fred* by saying instead that *Bob had the intention of distracting Fred and this caused him to knock over the glass of water (but without nervousness playing a causal role)*. But it turns out that even this won't work. For there are cases of purposive action in which nervousness *does* play a role. For instance, consider a weightlifter who is able to lift an extremely heavy barbell only because his intention to do so is associated with nervous excitement that provides an extra burst of energy.[216] Since that is possible, it is not correct to say that purposive action is distinguished by the absence of nervousness, in which case reference to such an absence cannot salvage the reformulation.

G. F. Schueler notes another problem facing the thesis that any action can be explained in non-teleological terms by citing the belief and desire that served as efficient causes of the action.[217] The problem is that identifying the desire in question will itself inevitably bring back in an implicit appeal to teleology. Suppose I donate to a charity, you ask me why I did so, and I respond: "Because it's a worthy cause." You, as an observer of my action, might reasonably attribute to me the desire to support the cause and explain my action by reference to this desire. But from my first-person point of view, I may, nevertheless, not conceptualize my reason for acting in terms of such a desire. That is to say, when I consider whether I should make the donation, what occurs to me would in normal cases be a judgment like the judgement *that this is a worthy cause*, rather than the judgment *that donating to it will satisfy a desire I have*. The fact that I have such a desire, even when it is obvious that I do, would normally not enter into my

---

[215] Sehon, *Teleological Realism*, pp. 95-96.

[216] Ibid., p. 98. Cf. Sehon, *Free Will and Action Explanation*, p. 101. Sehon borrows the example from George M. Wilson, *The Intentionality of Human Action* (Palo Alto: Stanford University Press, 1989), p. 252.

[217] G. F. Schueler, *Reasons and Purposes: Human Rationality and the Teleological Explanation of Action* (Oxford: Clarendon Press, 2003), pp. 56-68.

deliberative process. What enters into the process are questions like "Is this a worthy cause?" rather than questions like "What sorts of desires do I have?"[218]

Moreover, the third-person description of me as having such a desire is parasitic on the first-person conceptualization of my action. There are, after all, several possible desires you could attribute to me in order to explain my action. For example, you could attribute my action to *the desire to be seen by others as generous,* or even (though this would be strange!) *the desire to get rid of some excess cash.* The reason you in fact attribute to me instead the desire to support the cause is that I have told you that the reason I made the donation is that the cause is worthy. In other words, it is *that I have the end or goal of supporting the cause* that justifies the attribution to me of a desire to support it. But that is a teleological description of my action. Hence the attribution of the desire *presupposes,* at least implicitly, such a teleological description. It hardly makes sense, then, to suggest that an explanation of my actions in terms of my beliefs and desires, considered just as efficient causes, can entirely replace a teleological description of my action. For such a description is implicit in the very attribution to me of a desire.

The lesson of all this is, again, that there is an aspect to volitional behavior that cannot be captured in a description that makes reference only to efficient causality. As Scott Sehon observes after surveying the relevant contemporary philosophical literature:

> The [efficient] causal theory of action is still the dominant theory... But despite the hegemonic status of the causal theory, the problem of deviant causal chains has yet to be successfully addressed, and, thus, the alleged elimination of teleology has not been carried through. Moreover, it appears that there is a steady pattern in the failed attempts, consistent

---

[218] As Thomas Pink writes: "The idea of motivation – of being moved by something to act as one does... includes the idea of being moved, not by an attitude, but by the object of an attitude – by the desirability of an outcome, as well as by a desire for that outcome" (*Self-Determination,* p. 219). In the case at hand, what motivates me is *the promotion of a worthy cause,* which is the *object* toward which my action aims. The motivation is not, primarily or perhaps even at all, the aim of fulfilling the *desire* I have to promote the worthy cause.

with what we would expect if there is an irreducibly teleological element to human agency.[219]

But might not the critic of teleology at this point simply dig in his heels and argue that if we can't give a reductionist account of the teleology of human action, we should just dismiss it as an illusion? No, because this eliminativist move is no more coherent than is the eliminativist approach to concepts criticized in the previous chapter. Even to propose doing this is itself to posit an end or goal – the goal of solving the problem teleology poses for the reductionist – and thus to manifest teleology in the very act of denying it! As Sehon says of eliminativists who suggest that they are speaking of teleology only for the sake of formulating a *reductio ad absurdum* against it: "When we argue by reductio, we assume the truth of something *in order to* show that it leads to a contradiction and thus must be false after all. That is, to argue by reductio is to do something for a purpose."[220] Similarly, if the eliminativist says that he uses teleological language to describe his proposal only *for the sake of argument*, or only *for the sake of communicating his position*, he is manifesting teleology in the very act of denying that it is real. As Alfred North Whitehead (1861-1947) once observed, those who are "animated by the purpose of proving that they are purposeless constitute an interesting subject for study."[221]

---

[219] Sehon, *Free Will and Action Explanation*, pp. 107-8.

[220] Sehon, *Teleological Realism*, p. 230.

[221] Alfred North Whitehead, *The Function of Reason* (Princeton, NJ: Princeton University Press, 1929), p. 16.

What is freedom?

On analysis, then, we simply cannot make coherent sense of the suggestions that there are no volitions or that action involves only efficient causality rather than teleology. Hence we must conclude that the will is real and that it really is directed towards the ends grasped by the intellect, as toward a final cause. Let's turn now to the question of whether the will is free. Here too I need to begin by defining my terms, and once again the conception I will be defending is Aquinas's. Modern discussions of free will often identify two conditions, one or both of which are taken to be necessary and sufficient for an agent's acting freely: first, that the agent is the source of his own actions (sometimes called the "principle of ultimate authorship"[222]); and second, that the agent could have acted otherwise than he does (often called the "principle of alternate possibilities"[223]). Aquinas too characterizes free choice in terms of these conditions.[224] But he doesn't regard them as equally fundamental. As I have said, for Aquinas, to

---

[222] Cf. Anjum and Mumford, *What Tends to Be*, p. 162. Philosophers writing on this topic use a variety of phrases to describe what Anjum and Mumford call "ultimate authorship." Richard Taylor says that I am free if "it is up to me" what I do (*Metaphysics*, Second edition (Englewood Cliffs, NJ: Prentice-Hall, 1974), p. 44). Similarly, Pink speaks of freedom as entailing "control or up-to-usness" (*Self-Determination*, p. 30). Tobias Hoffman and Peter Furlong talk of "perfect sourcehood" ("Free Choice," in M. V. Dougherty, eds., *Aquinas's Disputed Questions on Evil: A Critical Guide* (Cambridge: Cambridge University Press, 2016), p. 58). Robert Kane speaks of "ultimate responsibility" (at pp. 13-16 of "Libertarianism," in John Martin Fischer, Robert Kane, Derk Pereboom, and Manuel Vargas, *Four Views on Free Will* (Oxford: Blackwell, 2007)). Michael McKenna and Derk Pereboom suggest that for persons to have free will is for them "to exercise the strongest sense of control over their actions necessary for moral responsibility" (*Free Will: A Contemporary Introduction* (London: Routledge, 2016), p. 6). The reference to moral responsibility may seem to add a further condition beyond what is identified by the other authors quoted, but McKenna and Pereboom go on to make clear that they intend their characterization of free will to apply also to actions that do not have moral significance. Their point is merely to emphasize the *strength* of the "control" over action entailed by free will, viz. that it is strong enough that one could be held morally responsible. What all these accounts have in common is the idea that free will entails a maximum degree of control over what one does.

[223] Harry Frankfurt, "Alternate Possibilities and Moral Responsibility," *Journal of Philosophy* 66 (1969): 829-39. Frankfurt himself is famously critical of the principle, but his terminology has become standard.

[224] Cf. Hoffmann and Furlong, "Free Choice," pp. 57-60.

have a will is to be the source of one's own activity in the fullest possible way, which entails acting from intellectual knowledge (as opposed to acting from natural appetite or from sensory knowledge). And that is also, in his view, what it is to have freedom of choice. The ability to do otherwise is a byproduct of this.[225]

We'll come back to that, but let's begin by noting that though I have been speaking both of free will and of free action, the former is the more fundamental notion and the latter is not meant to be understood independently of it. For there is a *sense* in which one might be said to act freely and yet not have free will, and a sense in which one might be unable to act freely and still have free will.[226] For example, a dog that slips the leash and runs off can be said to act freely insofar as it is doing what it wants to do, but since it lacks an intellect, it is not acting from free will. A human being might be bound and thus prevented from acting freely, but his will would nevertheless remain free insofar as he can still *will* to perform the acts he is prevented from carrying out. When I speak of "free action," I mean, specifically, action that flows from free will, and thus action of which a rational substance is the ultimate author.

Note also that freedom as I understand it does not entail the will's utter indifference to the ends toward which it might aim. Like every other substance, a rational substance is of its nature directed toward some end. Aquinas would say that that end is its happiness, which is the realization of what is good for it. Some might dispute this, but for present purposes we needn't settle the question of what, specifically, is our natural end. We need note only that in the case of a rational substance, an end toward which it is directed can be known intellectually, and that the will or rational appetite *just is* that power by virtue of which such a substance can aim at an end qua grasped by the intellect.[227] A will that was not of its nature directed toward what

---

[225] Robert Kane is another influential defender of free will who takes ultimate authorship to be more fundamental to free will than the ability to do otherwise. Cf. Kane, "Libertarianism," p. 14.

[226] Cf. Frankfurt, "Freedom of the Will and the Concept of a Person," p. 90.

[227] We can, of course, also aim at ends that are not grasped by the intellect. For example, any human being aims at the end of circulating blood through his body, just by virtue of

the intellect takes to be good would be like an acorn that was not of its nature directed toward becoming an oak. The latter just wouldn't really be an acorn, and the former just wouldn't really be a will.[228]

We have here a kind of necessity that Aquinas calls *natural necessity*, since it has to do with what a thing *cannot not* do given its nature or essence.[229] This contrasts with what he calls the *necessity of coercion*, which has to do with a thing's being forced to do what is contrary to its natural tendencies, as when I imagined tying a plant's branches back so that its leaves were kept in the shade. Obviously, necessity of coercion is incompatible with freedom of choice, since it would involve forcing a rational substance to do something contrary to what its intellect takes to be good, and thus contrary to what it wills. But *natural* necessity is not contrary to freedom of choice. On the contrary, just as you might say that a plant is more free if I do not tie its branches back – that is to say, if I let it do what it "wants" to do, what it cannot help aiming to do given the kind of thing it is – so too a will is more free if it is not prevented from doing what *it* cannot help doing given the kind of thing it is, namely pursuing what the intellect takes to be good. A tree that did not aim at getting its branches toward the sun would not be a freer tree, but just a defective tree. And a will that did not aim at the good would not be a freer will, but just a defective will.

Now, Aquinas distinguishes a third kind of necessity, which, perhaps somewhat confusingly, he calls *necessity of the end*. The reference here is not to our ultimate natural end, which, as I have said, Aquinas takes to be happiness, understood as the realization of what is *in fact* good for a rational substance. The reference is rather to what

---

having a heart and blood vessels, and does so even if he is completely unaware of the existence of this circulatory system. It is precisely because we can aim at such ends without the intellect being cognizant of them that their pursuit is not subject to the will.

[228] For further discussion and defense of the thesis that the will always aims at what the intellect takes to be good, see Edward Feser, "Being, the Good, and the Guise of the Good," in Daniel D. Novotny and Lukas Novak, eds., *Neo-Aristotelian Perspectives in Metaphysics* (London: Routledge, 2014).

[229] *Summa theologiae* I.82.1-2.

is *perceived* to be good, or to the *means* by which the good might be attained. Now, the intellect can be mistaken about what is in fact good, and it might note that several different means to attaining what it takes to be good are possible. In that sense, it is not necessitated toward the ends it pursues. Necessity of the end in the present sense would exist if the intellect had such a penetrating grasp of what is in fact good that it could not *not* perceive it to be good, or if there were no possible means of attaining the good other than the one the intellect takes to be a means. In this sort of situation, the will cannot will otherwise. Importantly, for Aquinas, this kind of necessity, like natural necessity, is not contrary to the will's nature and not contrary to freedom.

This is why I say that, for Aquinas, ability to do otherwise is a *byproduct* of acting from intellectual knowledge, and thus of freedom. But it is not itself the essence of freedom. The essence of freedom is acting from intellectual knowledge, and in cases where we *are* capable of misperceiving what is in fact good, or of entertaining alternative means of achieving the good, this yields alternative possible courses of action. The deep underlying reason for this is that knowing things intellectually entails bringing them under concepts, and there are different ways that the same things can be conceptualized. As Elizabeth Anscombe notes in a slightly different context, "a man may know that he is doing a thing under one description, and not under another,"[230] and there are typically alternative possible descriptions under which we might know a thing or an action. John Haldane writes:

> [T]o think of an item is always to think of it via some conception... For any naturally individuated object or property there are indefinitely many non-equivalent ways of thinking about it. That is to say, the structure of the conceptual order, which is expressed in judgements and actions, is richer and more abstract than that of the natural order.[231]

---

[230] G. E. M. Anscombe, *Intention*, Second edition (Cambridge, MA: Harvard University Press, 2000), p. 11.

[231] J. J. C. Smart and J. J. Haldane, *Atheism and Theism*, Second edition (Oxford: Blackwell, 2003), p. 107.

To borrow an example from Haldane, every triangle is necessarily a trilateral and vice versa. Hence, triangles and trilaterals are not different objects. Nevertheless, the *concept* of *being a triangle* is distinct from the *concept* of *being a trilateral*. Thus, one might think about a given object in terms of one of these concepts and yet not think about it in terms of the other. To borrow a famous set of phrases from Wilfrid Sellars (1912-1989), the intellect always brings things into "the logical space of reasons," of which the conceptual order is a part, and that space is wider than the "space of causes" into which our behavior and the objects we interact with also fall.[232] The same one natural order of causally related physical objects can be carved up conceptually by the intellect in innumerably different possible ways.

This reflects what contemporary philosophers call the thesis of the *indeterminacy of meaning*, which generalizes what we saw in chapter 3 about the impossibility of reducing concepts to either mental images or patterns of behavior. As we there noted, there are always alternative possible ascriptions of conceptual content to any mental imagery or behavioral pattern. Conceptual content *outstrips* anything that could be captured in a description of mental images or behavior. But it turns out that it also outstrips any description we could give, however thorough, of a thinker's mental imagery and behavior *together with* the details of his neurophysiology and of the larger physical world with which the thinker causally interacts. No matter what this collection of facts turns out to contain, there are always alternative possible ways the thinker might conceptualize the world, consistent with this set of facts. The collection of physical facts is therefore *indeterminate* between different possible ascriptions of concepts, beliefs, etc. to a thinker – that is to say, it is not by itself sufficient to determine what a thinker is thinking. (We will have reason in a later chapter to revisit this thesis of the indeterminacy of meaning, and to

---

[232] Wilfrid Sellars, "Empiricism and the Philosophy of Mind," in Herbert Feigl and Michel Scriven, eds., *Minnesota Studies in the Philosophy of Science, Volume I* (Minneapolis: University of Minnesota Press, 1956). As John McDowell, writing under Sellars' influence, puts it in *Mind and World* (Cambridge, MA: Harvard University Press, 1994), "the space of reasons is the realm of freedom" (p. 5).

see why philosophers of very different basic metaphysical commitments, materialist no less than dualist, have affirmed it.[233])

Now, since the intellect can in principle conceptualize or describe the same one thing in different ways and thus, depending on the conceptualization or description, judge the very same thing either as a good end (or means), or judge instead that some other end (or means) is better, it follows that the agent could in principle *either will or not will* the same end (or means). Thus he has the ability to do otherwise, just as a consequence of having an intellect. Non-human animals and inanimate things lack this ability to do otherwise precisely because they do not bring things under concepts, and therefore don't have alternative *ways* of conceptualizing things and the flexibility of action that that entails.

This gives us a way to understand the role of circumstances in choice and action.[234] Recall that I said that whether and how the causal powers of a substance will manifest depends crucially on context, and in particular on which of the causal powers of *other* things are either manifesting or not manifesting. This, you might also recall, is why I said that it is a mistake to think of laws of nature as the fundamental level of physical reality. Laws of nature are instead a description of the way things will go *if* there obtains a (typically idealized) situation in which substances and their powers are operating in tandem in a certain specific way. Hence determinism, which presupposes that laws of nature are fundamental and that they describe the way things always actually go, gets nature wrong. However, this does not entail that there is no necessitation in nature. On the contrary, though the

---

[233] It is important to note that the term "indeterminacy" in this context does not have the same meaning as the term "indeterminism" does in the context of the traditional debate over free will and determinism. The debate between determinism and indeterminism has to do with whether the totality of physical facts at any given time *causally necessitates* what will occur at later times. But the indeterminacy of meaning has to do instead with whether a complete description of the facts about a thinker's mental imagery, behavior, neurophysiology, and causal relations to the larger physical world by itself *logically entails* one ascription of conceptual content to his thoughts to the exclusion of another possible ascription. To be sure, I am suggesting that the latter issue is *relevant to* the debate over determinism and free will, but it is nevertheless a different issue.

[234] Cf. *Summa theologiae* I-II.7.1-4.

idealized situation described by a law may not in fact obtain, *if* it obtains, *then* things really will go the way the law says they will. That is why it is possible to discover at least idealized laws of nature.

But though this is true of the order of inanimate things, and of plants and non-human animals, it is not true of human beings. For the context in which our causal powers operate does not include *merely* the other substances, together with their powers, with which we may interact. It also includes the way we actually *conceptualize* all of this other context, and, again, there are typically alternative possible ways in which we might conceptualize it. Whatever particular conceptualization we adopt is part of what governs how we act, but because there is nothing in the intellect as such that entails that one conceptualization rather than another will prevail, there is nothing that necessitates a particular outcome, the way that a certain outcome *will* be necessitated when non-human physical substances and their powers interact in just the right way.

This is the reason for what Donald Davidson (1917-2003) famously called the "anomalism of the mental" – the fact that there are no strict laws correlating mental and physical phenomena, the way there are strict laws of physics and chemistry.[235] That the conceptual order outstrips the physical order rules out there being such laws. Now, one might argue, on the basis of this anomalism, that our intellectual capacities are immaterial. Indeed, I will argue for that conclusion in a later chapter. But Davidson himself did not draw that conclusion, and we need not insist upon it for present purposes. We need not appeal to mind-body dualism in order to defend free will, any more than we needed to do so in order to defend the reality and irreducibility of the self or the reality and irreducibility of the intellect. What has been said so far commits us only to rejecting a *reductionist* brand of materialism, even if we were to grant for the sake of argument that the mind might in some way be material. One alternative to materialist reductionism would be an account that relates mind to body in terms of the Aristotelian four-causal explanatory framework described earlier. For example, consider the action of my typing up this chapter. That my intellect *conceptualizes* what I am doing *as* an act

---

[235] Cf. Donald Davidson, "Mental Events," in *Essays on Actions and Events*.

of typing (as opposed, say, to the typing being an involuntary spasm) is the *formal* cause of the action; the end or goal of typing up the chapter, toward which my will is directed, is the *final* cause; and the relevant bodily processes are the *material* and *efficient* causes. I am a single substance of which these four irreducibly different factors are aspects.[236]

That is the case, anyway, if indeed I am a substance with bodily properties. But as I have said before, for the purposes of the first four chapters of this book, we can bracket off the question of whether the substance that I am is wholly material, wholly immaterial, or some compound of the material and immaterial. This is a question that naturally arises when we consider the relationship of the intellect and will to human physiology, and it is one I will address in later chapters. But it can largely be put to one side when considering the nature of free will *per se*. On the Thomistic conception that I am defending, the will is free insofar as it is oriented toward an end that the intellect conceptualizes as worth pursuing (which entails that volition arises from within the agent in the fullest possible way, as the "principle of ultimate authorship" requires); and there are typically alternative ways the intellect might conceptualize an end (which entails that the agent could have willed otherwise, as the "principle of alternate possibilities" requires). This is so whether the actions that result take the form of bodily movements (as when I type up this chapter) or exercises in thought (as when I lie back in bed and think through what I want to write before getting up to do it). How this relates to physiological processes is of secondary importance (albeit I will have reason to say a little more about that presently, and will say a lot more about it later in the book). The will could be free in the sense described whether we go on to spell out its relation to human physiology in a Cartesian manner, a materialist manner, or the Aristotelian hylemorphist manner I favor.

Some contemporary philosophers have suggested that the key to understanding the nature of free will is the insight that action must

---

[236] Cf. *Summa Theologiae* I-II.17.4; and John Haldane, "A Return to Form in the Philosophy of Mind," in David S. Oderberg, ed., *Form and Matter: Themes in Contemporary Metaphysics* (Oxford: Blackwell, 1999).

be analyzed in teleological terms, and not merely in terms of efficient causality.[237] Since I have emphasized the irreducibly teleological character of action, I would agree with this as far as it goes. However, it is crucial to emphasize that teleology *as such* is merely a necessary condition for freedom, not a sufficient condition. As I have suggested, non-human animals, and even plants and inanimate things, can be said to be directed towards ends or goals, but they do not have wills, let alone free will. What makes the will free is that it is directed, specifically, toward an end *as conceptualized by the intellect*.[238]

Now, given the way I have characterized the nature of free will, its reality follows straightaway from what I have argued for so far. In particular, I have argued that we are substances of the kind that have intellects; that the actions of these substances are (at least in some cases) directed toward what the intellect judges to be worth pursuing (which satisfies the "principle of ultimate authorship");[239] and that there are typically alternative ways in which the intellect could conceptualize the ends it considers and, consequently, alternative ends the will might pursue (which satisfies the "principle of alternate possibilities"). Since that is just what it is to have free will, it follows that we have free will.

But more can be said. Aquinas offers an argument for the reality of freedom.[240] It begins like this: "Man has free choice. Otherwise, deliberations, exhortations, precepts, prohibitions, rewards, and

---

[237] Cf. Sehon, *Free Will and Action Explanation*, especially Part II; and Stewart Goetz, *Freedom, Teleology, and Evil* (London: Continuum, 2008). That action cannot be understood except in teleological terms is also implicit in Jean-Paul Sartre's analysis of freedom in *Being and Nothingness* (New York: Pocket Books, 1966), Part Four, Chapter 1.

[238] I don't mean to imply that the contemporary writers cited would disagree with this, and they do characterize the ends that move the will precisely as *reasons* (Goetz) or as *rationalizable* (Sehon), which implies that those ends are conceptualized. Still, they tend to emphasize teleology as the key to the analysis, and my point is that it is not teleology as such that is crucial, but rather the specific *kind* of teleology of which rational agents alone are capable.

[239] I say "at least in some cases" because, again, if we are indeed material or partially material substances, then we also carry out activities of which the intellect is typically unaware, such as the circulation of the blood.
[240] For discussion of the argument, see H. D. Gardeil, *Introduction to the Philosophy of St. Thomas Aquinas, Volume III: Psychology* (St. Louis: B. Herder, 1956), pp. 211-16. Gardeil treats

punishments would make no sense."²⁴¹ Now, you might think that what he is doing here is really just giving an argument for why it would be horrible if free choice were an illusion, insofar as the basic presupposition of morality and related practices would in that case be undermined. And you may go on to point out that this doesn't really show that free choice is *real*, but merely gives a motivation for *wanting* it to be real.

But I don't think that that is Aquinas's argument at all. I would suggest that what he is saying is that it is simply a datum that our practices of deliberating, exhorting, and so forth do in fact make sense. If anyone claims to doubt this, we can point out that such doubt is, on analysis, incoherent – that one has actually to engage in deliberation and the like precisely in the act of trying to justify one's denial of it. Now, if this datum makes sense only on the assumption that we have free choice, then, Aquinas concludes, we must have free choice.²⁴² Aquinas elaborates as follows:

> Now a man acts by judgment, since through his cognitive power he judges that something should be pursued or avoided. But the reason why he acts by *free* judgment and is able to go in alternative ways is that in the case of a particular action this judgment arises from a comparison made by reason and not from natural instinct. For with respect to contingent matters, reason has an openness with respect to opposites, as is clear from dialectical syllogisms and rhetorical persuasions. But particular actions are contingent matters, and so with respect to them the judgment of reason is related to

---

the passage from Aquinas that I will be quoting as if it contained two or even three arguments, of which the first lines from the passage constitute the first argument. But it seems to me that that is a mistake, and that the rest of the passage is simply elaborating on the one argument summarized in the first lines.

²⁴¹ *Summa theologiae* I.83.1, quoted from the translation by Alfred J. Freddoso, available online at: https://www3.nd.edu/~afreddos/summa-translation/TOC.htm

²⁴² An argument to the effect that there is an inconsistency in denying free will while engaging in the practice of deliberating is also developed by Peter van Inwagen in *An Essay on Free Will* (Oxford: Clarendon Press, 1983), at pp. 153-61.

different alternatives and is not determined to just one. Accordingly, by the very fact that he is rational, man must have free choice.[243]

Aquinas's reference to reason's "openness with respect to opposites" and to its being "related to different alternatives and... not determined to just one" is, I suggest, essentially an appeal to the way that the conceptual order outstrips the order of things conceptualized. And it is this outstripping that entails the possibility of willing otherwise. Because the intellect is not necessitated to conceptualizing things one way rather than another, the will is not necessitated to being moved to one end rather than another. But neither is choice random or arbitrary. For choice is always *for a reason*, even if the reason is not necessitated. And to act for a reason is precisely not to act randomly or arbitrarily.[244]

Searle presents an argument which is similar to Aquinas's, and which elaborates on the idea that engaging in rational deliberation while denying the freedom of the will is ultimately incoherent.[245] He notes, first, that even when we have reasons for action that we take to be decisive, we cannot help but judge that it is up to us whether or not to go ahead and act on those reasons, and that the reasons by themselves don't suffice to generate action.[246] We experience action as a matter of our *making things happen*, rather than of our merely observing that they happen. We experience a reason for action as something which we ourselves have to *make* effective, rather than being effective on its own. And we experience actions that simply occur *automatically* as a consequence of our having a reason for doing them (such as acting from a *compulsion* to seek a certain end) precisely as *outside* our control. Here Searle is describing what, as we noted earlier, he calls the "gap" between having a belief and desire on the one hand,

---

[243] *Summa theologiae* I.83.1, Freddoso translation.

[244] Cf. Goetz, *Freedom, Teleology, and Evil*, pp. 19-20.

[245] Searle, *Rationality in Action*, pp. 13-14 and 70-73; and Searle, *Freedom and Neurobiology*, pp. 43 and 77.

[246] Searle, *Rationality in Action*, pp. 62-67.

and actually deciding and acting on the other, that exists whenever we take ourselves to act freely.

Now, Searle argues that even if I judge that these features of the phenomenology of choosing are illusory, I nevertheless cannot possibly act except in a way that presupposes that they are *not* illusory.[247] For example, I cannot "sit back" and passively wait for my actions to happen rather than actively trying to make them happen. For one thing, even when, after "sitting back" in this way, some action finally does occur, it will be experienced precisely as *something I myself did* rather than something I merely observed occurring. For another thing, even deciding to carry out this policy of "sitting back" and waiting for action to occur is *itself* experienced as an active choice on my part. We cannot avoid having to choose, and we cannot experience the choices we make except as *up to us*, and thus free.

Searle himself stops short of claiming that this argument establishes the reality of free will, but in my estimation he is wrong to do so. His view seems to be that, even if I cannot coherently deliberate and choose while at the same time taking myself to lack free will, it might for all that still be that this is just a matter of finding it psychologically irresistible to believe in something that is not in fact real. But it is no good merely to *say* that it might be unreal. The skeptic needs to provide for us a coherent scenario on which freedom is unreal even though we seem to experience it. And I submit that there is no such scenario. Searle says that, though at the *psychological* level there is nothing that necessitates what I will choose, it may at least in principle be the case that there is something at the *neural* level that does so, of which I am unaware.[248] But this cannot be right, and we have already seen the reason why. It has to do with the "anomalism of the mental," the fact that there is nothing at the physical level of description that necessitates any particular description at the mental level (where, you will recall, this will be the case *even if materialism is true*). Hence, no matter what is going on at the neural level, it will not suffice to determine my choice. The anomalism of the mental entails that the

---

[247] Ibid., pp. 70-73.

[248] Ibid., pp. 73-74.

"gap" described by Searle is *metaphysical* in nature rather than merely epistemic – that it is a gap in reality itself rather than in our knowledge of reality. (And again, this is so even if materialism is true.) So, it's not just that we cannot help but *believe* that free will is real. It's that *there is no coherent scenario* in which free will merely seems to be real but is not.

I have said that acting from intellectual knowledge is the essence of the will's freedom, and that the ability to do otherwise is a byproduct of this, rather than being itself the essence of freedom. I have also qualified the claim that there are alternative ways in which the intellect might conceptualize things by saying that this is *typically* the case. That leaves it open that there might be cases where the intellect is *unable* to conceive of something other than as a good to be pursued, or where it might know there to be only one possible means to attaining some good. In such cases, I have said, the will is subject to what Aquinas calls *necessity of the end*. Even in these cases, since the end the will is fixed on is an end grasped by the intellect, the agent is the source of his own activity in the fullest possible way. The agent thus remains free, on the Thomistic conception of freedom that I have been advocating.[249]

Does this entail that the ability to do otherwise drops out as irrelevant to free will? By no means. For we have to consider *how* an agent comes to be unable to conceive of some end except as good, and thus unable to will otherwise. Suppose someone could, initially, will either to perform some action or not to perform it, but through habitually choosing not to perform it molds his character in such a way that he eventually becomes unable to will it. Robert Kane describes the actions that result from such choices as "self-forming actions."[250] And as he notes, it is natural to characterize the actions that flow from our having a certain kind of moral character as done "of our own free will," even if we could not have done otherwise. For it is precisely

---

[249] Cf. Stump, *Aquinas*, pp. 297-300. On Stump's reading of Aquinas, the principle of alternate possibilities is not a necessary condition for free will and the principle of ultimate authorship suffices. But for the reasons I will give presently, I think this needs qualification.

[250] Cf. Kane, "Libertarianism," pp. 13-16.

because of earlier actions where we *could* have done otherwise that we have come to have such a character. This does not entail that we could at some point in the past have willed otherwise in absolutely *every* respect. As I noted earlier, for Aquinas, the will is as a matter of natural necessity oriented toward what the intellect (correctly or incorrectly) *takes to be* good. But to the extent that exactly *what* the intellect takes to be good can vary, so too can what the will chooses vary.

Readers familiar with the modern philosophical debate over free will might wonder whether Aquinas's position amounts to a *compatibilist* theory of freedom.[251] I would answer that it most certainly does not. For one thing, compatibilism holds that freedom is consistent with determinism, and as we have seen, from a Thomistic point of view, determinism is a wrongheaded conception of the natural world. So, reconciling freedom with determinism is simply not the sort of project that a thinker like Aquinas has in view. For another thing, precisely because of its determinism, compatibilism makes something outside the agent – namely the laws of nature together with the state of the universe prior to the agent's existence – the source of his activity. That conflicts with what I have said is Aquinas's account of the essence of free choice. Again, for Aquinas, the *agent himself*, and not the laws of nature or the state of the physical universe prior to the moment of choice, is the ultimate author of his actions.[252]

Is Aquinas's view of free choice what philosophers call a "libertarian" view, then?[253] As Eleonore Stump notes, this depends on how one understands libertarianism.[254] If libertarian free will is taken to entail the ability to do otherwise *without qualification*, then Aquinas's

---

[251] Anthony Kenny suggests that it does, in his book *Aquinas on Mind* (London: Routledge, 1993), at p. 77. So too does Pasnau, at p. 221 of *Thomas Aquinas on Human Nature*.

[252] Cf. Stump, *Aquinas*, p. 286.

[253] "Libertarianism" in the context of the debate over free will is the view that the will is free in the sense that no matter what has happened in the past or what is true of the agent at the moment of choice, he could always have chosen other than the way he does in fact choose. This should not be confused with "libertarianism" in the sense in which the term is used in political contexts, which is a different view addressing different issues.

[254] Ibid., pp. 300-2 and 304-6.

account is not libertarian. But Stump seems to think that a view according to which it is sufficient for freedom that an action originate in the intellect and will of the agent could reasonably be construed as a version of libertarianism. And on this construal, Aquinas's account would be libertarian. Specifically, it seems closest to what is in contemporary philosophy called an "agent-causal" libertarian position.[255] Perhaps the issue is, at the end of the day, semantic. But I would point out that participants on all sides of the contemporary debate about free will, compatibilism, and libertarianism usually make philosophical assumptions that Aquinas and other Thomistic philosophers would reject. Hence it is not easy to situate Aquinas's position within that debate, and trying to do so can threaten to obscure his position as much as it might illuminate it. In any event, the conception of free will that I have been defending in this chapter is Aquinas's conception, specifically. Whether or not it corresponds to free will as others conceive of it is, for my purposes, neither here nor there.

Arguments against free will

Let us turn now to arguments purporting to show that free will is an illusion. As Mark Balaguer notes, there have historically been three main arguments of this sort, which he labels *the classical argument, the random-or-predetermined argument,* and *the scientific argument.*[256] Let's

---

[255] Cf. Stefaan E. Cuypers, "Thomistic Agent-Causalism," in John Haldane, ed., *Mind, Metaphysics, and Value in the Thomistic and Analytical Traditions* (Notre Dame, IN: University of Notre Dame Press, 2002). Influential defenses of agent-causal libertarianism include Roderick M. Chisholm, "Human Freedom and the Self," in Watson, ed., *Free Will*; Roderick M. Chisholm, *Person and Object* (LaSalle, IL: Open Court, 1976), chapter II; Taylor, *Metaphysics*, chapter 5; Timothy O'Connor, *Persons and Causes* (Oxford: Oxford University Press, 2000); and Randolph Clarke, *Libertarian Accounts of Free Will* (Oxford: Oxford University Press, 2003). Naturally, in characterizing Aquinas's position as "agent-causal," I don't mean to imply that there are no important differences between it and modern agent-causal views. As Cuypers notes, whereas modern agent-causal libertarians emphasize the efficient causality of agents, there is in Aquinas an emphasis on teleology or final causality. Pink (at pp. 259-64 of *Self-Determination*) rejects agent-causalism for missing the essentially goal-directed nature of free action, but it seems to me that what he is objecting to is not a feature of agent-causalism as such.

[256] Mark Balaguer, *Free Will* (Cambridge, MA: The MIT Press, 2014), chapter 2.

consider each of them in turn. We'll then consider some further, less well-known but nevertheless important arguments against free will.

The classical argument

The classical argument is the traditional argument from determinism. Determinism holds that the state of the physical universe at any particular moment, together with the laws of nature, necessitate what occurs at any later moment. The claim of the classical argument against free will is that given this determinist thesis, our choices and actions cannot be free. One influential response to this argument is the compatibilist position that properly understood, free will is compatible with determinism. Another is to appeal to the Cartesian dualist conception of the mind as an immaterial substance, and argue that free will is secured by virtue of this immaterial substance's causal interference with the material world. But as I have indicated, I do not accept compatibilism, and I do not think that an appeal to dualism is necessary in order to uphold the reality of free will.[257]

The first thing to say in response to the classical argument is that it rests on a false premise. In particular, and as I have already suggested, determinism is simply mistaken about the nature of material substances and their causal relationships. As causal powers theorists Rani Lill Anjum and Stephen Mumford argue:

> Causes genuinely produce their effects. But this does not require that they necessitate them. Causing an effect is not the same as guaranteeing it. Causal dispositionalism offers an alternative account of causal production... Causes tend or dispose toward their effects with varying degrees of strength in different cases. They often succeed in producing these effects but, even when they do so, they did not through any necessitation.[258]

---

[257] To be sure, I do think that the intellect and will are immaterial, and I will argue for that claim in a later chapter. I also think that their immateriality is, at the end of the day, crucial to understanding why the will is free. But one could in principle accept the defense of free will that I am setting out in this chapter without agreeing with me about any of that.

[258] Anjum and Mumford, *What Tends to Be*, p. 166.

When physical substances get into relatively stable relationships so that their causal powers operate in tandem, the result is what Nancy Cartwright calls a "nomological machine," a system whose behavior approximates the description given by a law of nature.[259] An example would be the solar system, whose constituents are related to one another in such a way that their causal powers, operating together, give rise to a pattern of behavior that approximates Kepler's laws of planetary motion. On this account, laws of nature are not fundamental features of the natural world, and the world does not behave in the rigidly deterministic way the laws describe. Rather, a law of nature is an idealized description of how a system of physical objects will behave *if* the causal powers of those objects are activated in tandem.

This account has many able advocates in contemporary philosophy, and is motivated independently of the debate over free will. Naturally, it requires a detailed exposition and defense. Given the treatment of issues in general metaphysics and philosophy of science that that would require, this is beyond the scope of a book on human nature, though I have provided such exposition and defense elsewhere.[260] The point to emphasize for present purposes is that determinism can hardly be taken for granted. It too requires defense, and in fact (I and other contemporary causal powers theorists maintain) is mistaken in its account of the natural world and its causal properties. Hence, insofar as the classical argument against free will takes determinism for granted, it begs the question at best and rests on a false premise at worst.

Nor, even apart from these issues in philosophy of science, can determinism claim to have modern science on its side. As Balaguer points out, a major problem with the classical argument against free will is that while it seemed to have scientific support in the heyday of

---

[259] Nancy Cartwright, *The Dappled World: A Study of the Boundaries of Science* (Cambridge: Cambridge University Press, 1999), chapter 3.

[260] Again, see my *Scholastic Metaphysics*, pp. 63-72 and *Aristotle's Revenge*, pp. 177-90 for further exposition and defense as well as an overview of the relevant contemporary literature.

153

Newtonian physics, it no longer does so after the rise of quantum mechanics.[261] For quantum physics contains laws that are *probabilistic* rather than deterministic. To be sure, some would speculate that there might be deeper laws that have not yet been discovered but which would be consistent with determinism. But the point is that science itself does not currently support such a speculation.

Others would propose that even if determinism does not hold at the quantum level, at the macroscopic level of the brain, quantum effects cancel out and the physical world operates more or less as determinism describes it.[262] One problem with this reply is that it too is open to challenge. Some have argued that there are physical mechanisms by which quantum effects can be amplified sufficiently to make a difference at the macroscopic level of the brain.[263] But a deeper problem is that the concession that at least the quantum level is probabilistic rather than deterministic effectively undermines the classical argument against free will. For the appeal is now no longer to the thesis of universal determinism, but rather to the purported features of some specific part of the natural world. That makes it a different argument from the classical argument against free will – specifically, a version of the scientific argument, which we'll consider below.

If the classical argument gets matter wrong, it also presupposes a mistaken conception of the mind's relationship to it. Given the "anomalism of the mental" referred to earlier, the totality of physical facts at a given time would not determine the *mental* facts at any later time *even if* they determined the physical facts at every later time. Hence they would not determine what we think and will at any later time. Davidson thus took his thesis of the anomalism of the mental to secure free will.[264] As I have noted, Davidson did not take this

---

[261] Balaguer, *Free Will*, pp. 18-19.

[262] Cf. Ted Honderich, *How Free Are You? The Determinism Problem* (Oxford: Oxford University Press, 1993), pp. 65-66.

[263] Cf. Robert Kane, *The Significance of Free Will* (Oxford: Oxford University Press, 1996), pp. 128-30; and Robert C. Bishop, "Chaos, Indeterminism, and Free Will," in Robert Kane, ed., *The Oxford Handbook of Free Will* (Oxford: Oxford University Press, 2002).

[264] Davidson, "Mental Events," pp. 207 and 225.

anomalism to entail metaphysical dualism. For Davidson, the physical and the mental comprise two irreducibly different *modes of description* of human beings and their behavior, but they do not correspond to two irreducibly different *realities*. Rather, they are different ways of describing the same one reality, which Davidson took to be physical. His view is thus known as "anomalous monism." It is a kind of "monism" insofar as it posits a single, physical reality to which both physical and mental predicates can be ascribed. It is "anomalous" insofar as it denies that there can be any laws of nature by which the totality of physical facts would entail the mental facts.

Some readers are bound to wonder whether such a position can work. It might seem that either anomalous monism makes of mental descriptions mere ways of talking that capture nothing in objective reality or, if they do capture something real, that the view entails a kind of dualism in disguise. I sympathize with this suspicion, and will argue in a later chapter that the considerations that motivate Davidson's anomalism do in fact entail the immateriality of the intellect and will. But as is evident from the fact that Davidson and his followers would not agree, this claim requires further argumentation. Commitment to the anomalism of the mental does not *by itself* entail dualism, but does support free will. Hence to appeal to it in rebutting the classical argument does not require insisting that the mind is immaterial.

The random-or-predetermined argument

The second of the main arguments against free will purports to show that we don't have free will even if determinism is false. It takes the form of a dilemma. Either determinism is true, or it is not true. If it is true, then our choices are predetermined by forces outside our control, and free will is an illusion. But if determinism is not true, then our choices are uncaused. In that case, they amount to random occurrences, and a random occurrence cannot amount to a free choice. Hence, even if determinism is false, free will is an illusion.[265]

---

[265] As Balaguer points out at pp. 25-28 of *Free Will*, a more precise version of the argument would acknowledge that there is a third option, on which our choices are neither caused deterministically nor entirely random, but instead caused in a *probabilistic* way. The argu-

As Anjum and Mumford point out, one problem with this sort of argument is that it rests on a false dilemma.²⁶⁶ It assumes that if an effect is not causally predetermined, then it must be random. But as we have seen, there is an alternative way to understand causality, according to which causes *tend* or *dispose* toward their effects. Because they tend toward their effects, the effects are not random. It isn't the case that just any old effect could have followed. But because causes *merely* tend or dispose rather than necessitate, effects are not predetermined either.

Another problem is that the argument presupposes that the intelligibility of a choice is to be found only in identifying its *efficient* cause. Hence, in the scenario where a choice is not determined by some antecedent efficient cause, the argument claims that the choice must be random. But as I emphasized earlier, there is in human action an irreducible element of *final* causality or teleology, and this is crucial to its intelligibility. If an action is not predetermined but is nevertheless done for the sake of some particular end, then it is hardly random. That the agent decided to carry out the action with that end in view makes the action intelligible. Again, on the Thomistic account of free will that I am defending, freedom is a matter of our choices resulting from our *rational deliberation about ends and means*. And it makes no sense to regard as "random" a choice that reflects such deliberation.

Balaguer makes the additional point that as long as *I* made the choice I did, the fact that nothing outside me caused me to make it is hardly inconsistent with free will; on the contrary, that is precisely what it is to *have* free will. Hence the random-or-predetermined argument's interpretation of the "random" side of the purported dilemma that it poses is just confused. Properly understood, the scenario in which our choices are not determined by forces outside us is not inconsistent with free will but rather *just is* our having free will.²⁶⁷

---

ment would then assert that a choice with a probabilistic cause is one that is in part predetermined and in part random, so that the scenario is just a combination of the first two and no more consistent with free will than they are.

²⁶⁶ Anjum and Mumford, *What Tends to Be*, pp. 161-62.

²⁶⁷ Balaguer, *Free Will*, pp. 80-86.

I think this is correct as far as it goes, insofar as it reflects the point that having free will is fundamentally about being the *ultimate author* of one's actions. But it is important to emphasize that *what it means* to be the ultimate author of one's actions is for those actions to flow from one's rational deliberation about ends and means. This is crucial to understanding why an agent's not being caused to choose as he does by anything outside him does not entail that the choice is arbitrary or unintelligible, as the accusation of randomness implies.

For the same reason, it is also crucial that Anjum and Mumford's point be supplemented with an emphasis on the fact that it is, specifically, rational deliberation that tends or disposes us toward the choices we make. It is this consideration, and not tending or disposing as such, that makes freedom possible, since inanimate objects and non-human living things also have tendencies or dispositions but lack free will. To be sure, Anjum and Mumford recognize that mere tending or dispositionality is not sufficient for free will, and that reference to deliberation and the normative considerations it takes account of is also essential.[268] However, I would add that the teleological element that I have emphasized is no less essential. I have allowed that there is something at least approximating causal necessitation in the case of non-rational substances, when the conditions are right for the triggering of their causal powers in tandem. But there is not even an approximation of such necessitation in the case of human beings. If we are thinking of rational deliberation entirely as a matter of the efficient causation of our actions, this might seem to entail a residue of randomness or unintelligibility. This disappears when we keep in mind that action is ultimately to be understood in terms of *final* causes.

The scientific argument

Of the three most influential arguments against free will, it is the scientific argument that has in the contemporary debate gotten the most

---

[268] Anjum and Mumford, *What Tends to Be*, pp. 166-71.

attention from the general public. Recent years have seen the popularization of the claim that neuroscience and psychology, in particular, have shown free will to be an illusion.[269]

The first thing to note in response to such claims is that determinism turns out to be as much of a red herring in this context as it did in the case of the classical argument. Recall that, in response to the point that quantum mechanics has undermined the scientific case for determinism, it is often suggested that quantum effects cancel out at the macroscopic level, so that the brain might more or less operate in a deterministic way even if determinism does not hold at the quantum level. As Balaguer points out, the problem with this suggestion is that modern neuroscience, like quantum mechanics, is at least in part probabilistic rather than deterministic.[270] In particular, both a neuron's release of a neurotransmitter and the neurotransmitter's triggering of a neural firing operate in a probabilistic rather than deterministic way.

Indeed, even to speak of probabilities here is potentially misleading if it is taken to imply that neural causes always make their effects *highly* probable. A historically influential conception of scientific explanation known as the "covering-law model" claims that the way science explains a phenomenon is to show that it is entailed by, or at least made probable by, a description of the conditions holding antecedent to the phenomenon together with some law of nature. But as philosopher of neuroscience Carl Craver notes, this model simply does not fit the way explanations in neuroscience actually work.[271] Rather, such explanations typically involve identifying the underlying mechanisms by which some higher-level phenomenon is brought about, where the phenomenon often not only does not follow with necessity from the operation of the mechanism, but (given all the factors that

---

[269] For example, in books like Michael Gazzaniga's *Who's In Charge? Free Will and the Science of the Brain* (New York: HarperCollins, 2011) and Sam Harris's *Free Will* (New York: Free Press, 2012).

[270] Balaguer, *Free Will*, pp. 94-96.

[271] Carl F. Craver, *Explaining the Brain: Mechanisms and the Mosaic Unity of Neuroscience* (Oxford: Clarendon Press, 2007), pp. 7-8, 39-40, and 66-69.

need to be in place together with possible interfering circumstances) may even occur with well under fifty percent probability.

Hence contemporary neuroscience gives no more support to the deterministic premise of the classical argument than contemporary physics does. If opponents of free will are going to find support in neuroscience, they have to look elsewhere. However, some of them claim to find it in the work of neuroscientist Benjamin Libet (1916-2007).[272] In Libet's famous experiments, subjects were asked to flex a wrist whenever they felt like doing so, and then to report on when they had become consciously aware of the urge to flex it. Their brains were wired so that the activity in the motor cortex responsible for causing their wrists to flex could be detected. While an average of 200 milliseconds passed between the conscious sense of willing and the flexing of the wrist, the activity in the motor cortex would begin an average of over 500 milliseconds before the flexing. Hence the conscious urge to flex, it is suggested, seems not to be the *cause* of the neural activity which initiates the flexing, but rather to *follow* that neural activity.

Now, Libet himself qualified his conclusions, allowing that though we don't *initiate* movements in the way we think we do, we can at least either *inhibit* or *accede to* them once initiated. But according to philosopher Alex Rosenberg, the work done by Libet and others "shows conclusively that the conscious decisions to do things never cause the actions we introspectively think they do" and "defenders of free will have been twisting themselves into knots" trying to show otherwise.[273] Similarly, biologist Jerry Coyne assures us that:

> "Decisions" made like that aren't conscious ones. And if our choices are unconscious, with some determined well before

---

[272] Cf. Benjamin Libet, *Mind Time: The Temporal Factor in Consciousness* (Cambridge, MA: Harvard University Press, 2004), chapter 4.

[273] Alex Rosenberg, *The Atheist's Guide to Reality* (New York: W.W. Norton and Co., 2011), p. 152.

the moment we think we've made them, then we don't have free will in any meaningful sense.[274]

However, as several critics have pointed out, this line of argument commits a number of fallacies.[275] The first problem is that Libet didn't show that the kind of neural activity he measured is *invariably* followed by flexing. Given his experimental setup, only cases where the activity was actually followed by flexing were detected. He didn't check for cases where the neural activity occurred but was not followed by flexing. So, we have no evidence that that kind of neural activity is *sufficient* for the flexing. For all Libet showed, it may be that the neural activity in question leads to flexing (or doesn't) depending on whether it is conjoined with a conscious free choice to flex.[276]

A second problem is that the sorts of actions Libet studied are highly idiosyncratic. The experimental setup required subjects to wait passively until they were struck by an urge to flex. But many of our actions don't work like that, especially those we attribute to free choice. Instead, they involve active deliberation, the weighing of considerations for and against different possible courses of action. It's hardly surprising that conscious deliberation has little influence on what we do in an experimental situation in which deliberation has been explicitly excluded. And it's a fallacy of hasty generalization to extend conclusions derived from these artificial situations to all human action, including cases which *do* involve active deliberation.[277]

Third, even if the neural activity Libet identified had invariably been followed by a flexing of the wrist, that still wouldn't show

---

[274] Jerry A. Coyne, "Why You Don't Really Have Free Will," *USA Today* (January 1, 2012).

[275] Cf. M.R. Bennett and P.M S. Hacker, *Philosophical Foundations of Neuroscience* (Oxford: Blackwell, 2003), pp. 228-31; Raymond Tallis, *Aping Mankind: Neuromania, Darwinitis, and the Misrepresentation of Humanity* (Durham: Acumen, 2011), pp. 54-56 and 247-50; Alfred R. Mele, *Free: Why Science Hasn't Disproved Free Will* (Oxford: Oxford University Press, 2014), chapter 2; Balaguer, *Free Will*, pp. 97-101; and Christian List, *Why Free Will is Real* (Cambridge, MA: Harvard University Press, 2019), pp. 141-47.

[276] Mele, *Free*, pp. 12-13.

[277] Ibid., pp. 13-16.

that the flexing wasn't a product of free choice. For why should we assume that a choice is not free if it registers in consciousness a few hundred milliseconds after it is made?[278] Think of making a cup of coffee. You don't explicitly think: "I will now proceed to move my hand toward the kettle; now I will pick it up; now I will pour hot water through the coffee grounds; now I will put the kettle down; now I will pick up a spoon." You simply do it. You may, after the fact, bring to consciousness the various steps you just carried out; or you may not. We take the action to be free either way. After all, you are not having a muscle spasm, or sleepwalking, or hypnotized, or under duress, or in any other way in circumstances of the sort we would normally regard as incompatible with acting of your own free will. The notion that a free action essentially involves a series of fully conscious episodes of willing, each followed by a discrete bodily movement, is a straw man.[279]

It is also simply wrongheaded to think of voluntary actions as prompted by feelings and urges. (Recall the point made earlier that a volition should not be confused with the feelings or emotions associated with it.) As M. R. Bennett and P. M. S. Hacker point out, feeling an urge to sneeze does not make a sneeze voluntary.[280] Since Libet is willing to allow that we might at least inhibit actions initiated by unconscious neural processes, even if we don't initiate them ourselves, Bennett and Hacker observe that:

> Strikingly, Libet's theory would in effect assimilate all human voluntary action to the status of inhibited sneezes or sneezes which one did not choose to inhibit. For, in his view, all human movements are initiated by the brain before any aware-

---

[278] Ibid., pp. 16-17.

[279] Cf. McKenna and Pereboom, *Free Will*, p. 269.

[280] Bennett and Hacker, *Philosophical Foundations of Neuroscience*, p. 229.

ness of a desire to move, and all that is left for voluntary control is the inhibiting or permitting of the movement that is already under way.[281]

As Bennett and Hacker go on to emphasize, being moved by an urge – such as an urge to sneeze, or to vomit, or to cough – is in fact the *opposite* of a voluntary action. Once again, Libet's model of voluntary action is simply a straw man, so that his experiments have dubious relevance to the question of free will.

A fourth problem is that Libet and those who draw sensationalistic conclusions from his work fail to consider alternative interpretations of the neural activity in question. Perhaps it correlates, not with the *intention* to flex, but rather with *preparing* to flex without necessarily intending to do so, or with *imagining* or *thinking about* flexing. Or perhaps it correlates with a *general intention* to flex as opposed to a *proximal intention* to do so.[282] Think again of the coffee example. Suppose when you got up in the morning, you decided you wanted to make some coffee. You could be said to have formed a general intention to do so. But suppose also that you don't actually make it until several minutes later, after using the bathroom, getting dressed, and going to the porch to get the newspaper. Only then did you decide it was time to go to the kitchen and actually make the coffee. At that point you formed a proximal intention to make the coffee. Similarly, the participants in Libet's experiments could be said to form both a general intention that they will flex their wrists once they have a certain feeling, and then a proximal intention once the feeling actually arises. Nothing in Libet's experiment tells us that the neural activity he cites correlates with the one kind of intention rather than the other, even if we were to concede (as we should not) that there is any reason to correlate it with an intention in the first place.

As Raymond Tallis points out, the nature of the intentions involved even in this simple action of flexing the wrist is actually more

---

[281] Ibid., p. 230.

[282] Mele, *Free*, pp. 20-23.

complex than this last point indicates.²⁸³ There is a sense in which the intention to perform the action could be said to have been formed many minutes before the subject flexed his wrist, when he had the experimental setup explained to him; or hours before, when he left the house to come take part in the experiment; or even days or weeks before, when he first agreed to participate. A long and complex series of psychological and physiological events played a role in what happened when the wrist was actually flexed. So why fixate on one particular bit of neural activity taken in isolation as *the* cause of the action? After all, neural activity and bodily movements do not *by themselves* entail action, free or otherwise. The spasmodic twitch of a muscle involves both neural activity and bodily movement, but it is not an action.

So, the precise significance that a bit of neural activity or a bodily movement has for a given action cannot be read off from the physiological facts alone. It is only within the larger psychological context that we can make sense of it. For it is only *the person as a whole*, and not some sub-personal part of him such as an isolated bit of neural activity, who can properly be said to intend and to act. And so it is only the person as a whole, and not the neural activity, who can be said to be the cause of his actions. In pretending otherwise, Libet and those who appeal to his research in order to cast doubt on free will are simply presupposing a reductionist account of human nature – an account which defenders of free will would reject. Hence they cannot claim that Libet's research supports reductionism and undermines free will without begging the question.²⁸⁴

---

²⁸³ Tallis, *Aping Mankind*, pp. 248-50.
²⁸⁴ As List observes (*Why Free Will is Real*, pp. 4-7), a question-begging reductionism is common in arguments that appeal to science in order to cast doubt on free will. The skeptic notes that free will is not to be found at some lower-level description of human beings (e.g. at the level of fundamental particles, or at the neural level) and concludes that it must not exist. But part of the free will defender's point is that that is the wrong place to look, and that it is at the higher-level description of persons as a whole that free will is to be found. The fallacy is the same as the one which, as we saw in chapter 3, is committed by eliminative materialists who deny the reality of intentionality on the grounds that it cannot be found at the neural level of description.

Another influential argument against free will appeals to the work of neuroscientist J. D. Haynes and his colleagues, but it essentially commits the same fallacies as Libet's argument.[285] To be sure, on the surface, Haynes's results seem more impressive than Libet's. Subjects in the Haynes study were asked to decide whether to press one of two buttons while their brain activity was measured using fMRI. It was found that activity in two brain regions predicted which button would be pressed up to ten seconds before the conscious decision was reported. The problem for free will seems obvious: If a person's choice can be predicted from brain activity ten seconds before the choice is made, how can the choice be free?

But there is much less to this argument than meets the eye. For one thing, the accuracy of the predictions in question is in fact only about 60 percent (where 50 percent would be pure chance). That is consistent with an interpretation of the relevant brain activity as corresponding, not to an unconscious decision to press a certain button, but rather to a mere unconscious bias or inclination toward pressing it, an inclination the subjects can and often do go on to resist.[286] Indeed, there is independent evidence that the brain regions in question are associated, not with willing, but with *planning*.[287] If the subjects in question are merely planning to press a certain button up to ten seconds before they do, it is hardly surprising if they often then go on to press it – but also, around forty percent of the time, change their minds. Certainly there is nothing in that that is incompatible with free will.

As with Libet's argument, the argument from Haynes's study simply makes tendentious philosophical assumptions about how to interpret the brain activity in question. And as with Libet's experimental setup, the action studied by Haynes is highly idiosyncratic. It involved choosing one action rather than another for no particular reason. Again, the actions we typically regard as free are not like that,

---

[285] Cf. Balaguer, *Free Will*, pp. 101-17; and Mele, *Free*, chapter 3.

[286] Mele, *Free*, pp. 28-30.

[287] Balaguer, *Free Will*, p. 104.

but instead involve conscious deliberation. Hence it would be a fallacy to generalize from cases like the ones studied by Haynes to *all* action.

Other influential scientific arguments against free will appeal to psychological research that shows that unconscious factors, social pressure, and the like can influence the choices we make. But these arguments are even feebler than the ones considered so far.[288] For example, consider psychologist Stanley Milgram's famous obedience experiments, in which participants were instructed to administer what they falsely supposed were genuine electric shocks to people who gave incorrect answers to questions put to them. Many participants reluctantly obeyed these commands even when they seemed to be causing severe pain. Some have argued that such data casts doubt on the reality of free will. But as Mele says, "it's [hard] to see exactly what the argument is supposed to be."[289] Is the claim that Milgram's experimental setup made it *inevitable* that participants would obey? That can't be it, because not every participant obeyed the commands. Is the idea merely that situations exist in which people find it difficult to disobey authority figures? If so, what defender of free will ever denied that?

Social psychologist Daniel Wegner studied unusual cases in which subjects perform actions they are not conscious of.[290] He suggests that these cases show that free will is an illusion. But here too the argument is a *non sequitur*. That *some* of our behavior is not caused by conscious choices simply does not entail that *none* of our behavior is ever caused by such choices.[291] And it is especially fallacious to draw such a sweeping conclusion from idiosyncratic examples. Moreover, social scientific research on what are called "implementation intentions" shows that of two groups assigned to do a certain task, the one instructed consciously to decide how to carry it out is more likely actually to do it than the group that is not so instructed. This indicates

---

[288] Cf. Balaguer, *Free Will*, pp. 90-93; and Mele, *Free*, chapters 4 and 5.

[289] Mele, *Free*, pp. 71-72.

[290] Daniel M. Wegner, *The Illusion of Conscious Will* (Cambridge, MA: The MIT Press, 2002).

[291] Mele, *Free*, pp. 50-51.

that conscious intentions do in fact influence what we do.²⁹² Of course, that is in any case just common sense. But the point is that, even if we are looking at the issue simply from the perspective of social psychology, the evidence does not point in the direction of Wegner's extreme conclusion.

Other arguments

Let's turn, finally, to some arguments that are less well-known to the general public, but which have gotten attention in academic philosophy. I have suggested that the Thomistic conception of free will that I have been defending is similar to what in contemporary philosophy is called "agent-causal libertarianism." Against this view, Derk Pereboom has raised what has come to be known as "the luck objection."²⁹³ The state of the physical universe at any particular time together with the laws of nature, whether conceived of in deterministic or probabilistic terms, would lead us to expect agents to behave in the future in certain specific ways. Meanwhile, agent-causal libertarianism claims that the behavior of these agents is the result of their free choices, where these choices have no causal antecedents external to the agent. Together these claims seem to imply that the behavior that results from these choices happens to correspond to what we would expect it to be from the laws of nature. But this entails "wild coincidences," according to Pereboom, and "the proposal that agent-caused free choices do not diverge from what the statistical laws predict for the physical components of our actions would be so sharply opposed to what we would expect as to make it incredible."²⁹⁴ Now, Pereboom acknowledges that agent-causal libertarians could deny the assumption that free choices will in fact generally correspond to what the

---

²⁹² Ibid., pp. 45-49.

²⁹³ Pereboom, "Hard Incompatibilism," in Fischer, Kane, Pereboom, and Vargas, *Four Views on Free Will*, at pp. 110-14; and McKenna and Pereboom, *Free Will*, pp. 271-72.

²⁹⁴ McKenna and Pereboom, *Free Will*, p. 271.

laws of nature would lead us to expect.[295] And in my opinion, we should indeed deny it. But the trouble with this move, says Pereboom, is that "we have no evidence" that there really are any actions that diverge from what the laws of nature would lead us to expect.[296]

The problem with Pereboom's claim that "we have no evidence" of this is not that it is false, but that it is true only in a trivial and uninteresting sense. For in fact the laws of nature as science knows them today give us no evidence *one way or the other* for *any* claim about how, specifically, any of us will act. Pereboom makes it sound as if we actually know of physical laws that entail or make probable what we will do at any given point in the future, and as if the question is what the agent-causal libertarian can say in the face of these laws. But of course, we know of no such laws. Reductionists *assume* that such laws must exist, but the assumption is based on a general metaphysical theory, not on any actual scientific findings. Hence the "evidence" no more favors Pereboom's position than it undermines the agent-causal position. Talk of the "evidence" is thus a red herring. The dispute between Pereboom and the agent-causal libertarian is not going to be settled by existing empirical evidence, but by philosophical argumentation.

Now, I would say that what a sound philosophical analysis of the situation really shows is the following. Laws of nature are not fundamental to physical reality. Rather, the natural world is, at the fundamental level, made up of substances of various kinds with their distinctive causal powers. When certain kinds of substance get into proximity to one another in a stable way, the result is what Cartwright calls a "nomological machine," whose behavior approximates laws of nature. That is true, anyway, of relatively simple collections of substances, such as a solar system. With much more complex systems, there are no known laws, though in some cases that might change with further scientific investigation. But with human beings, not only are there no known laws, there can be no laws. The reason is that human beings are *rational* beings, and the "anomalism of the mental" makes

---

[295] Ibid., and Pereboom, "Hard Incompatibilism," p. 113. Pereboom notes that this is the position taken by Chisholm in "Human Freedom and the Self."
[296] Pereboom, "Hard Incompatibilism," p. 113.

it impossible in principle to subsume rational deliberation and its outcomes under laws of nature. Hence human beings and collections of human beings can never be "nomological machines," so that there cannot be laws of psychology the way there are laws of planetary motion, laws of chemistry, and the like.

If this is correct, then there can be no question of agent-causal libertarianism predicting that human actions will be contrary to what the laws of nature would lead us to expect them to be, because there not only *are* no laws of the relevant sort, but *never could be* such laws in the first place. Pereboom may disagree with this analysis, but the point is that his objection merely *assumes* it is wrong, and does nothing to *show* that it is. Hence he simply begs the question.

Galen Strawson has developed a variation on the random-or-predetermined argument, holding that free will is impossible whether or not determinism is true.[297] In particular, he argues that the kind of self-determination that is essential to free will is in principle impossible. For what such self-determination requires is not just that the agent choose to act the way he does for certain reasons, but also that he is responsible for having those reasons in the first place. That requires him to have *chosen* those reasons, and in order for him rationally to have done so, there must be yet *further* reasons in light of which the reasons were chosen. But those reasons too will have to have been chosen, in light of yet further reasons, and so on *ad infinitum*. So, self-determination requires the making of an infinite series of choices, which is impossible. Hence the free will that depends on self-determination is also impossible.

But the defender of free will need not accept Strawson's assumption that freedom requires that the agent has chosen the reasons for which he acts.[298] Certainly the defender of Aquinas's conception of free will need not accept it. As I have said, on Aquinas's conception, freedom of the will is consistent with the *natural necessity* by which the will is directed toward what the intellect takes to be good. We don't *decide* that the will will be directed toward what the intellect takes to

---

[297] Galen Strawson, *Freedom and Belief*, Revised edition (Oxford: Oxford University Press, 2010), chapter 2.
[298] Cf. Goetz, *Freedom, Teleology, and Evil*, p. 27; and McKenna and Pereboom, *Free Will*, p. 152.

be good; it just *is* so directed, of its very nature. Free will as Aquinas understands it is also consistent with *necessity of the end*, which obtains when the intellect cannot fail to conceive of some end as good or where there is only one possible means by which the end it takes to be good can be realized. In such cases, the agent cannot choose reasons other than those that are present to the intellect. There may also be cases where the agent simply judges some end to be worth pursuing for its own sake, rather than for the sake of anything else, even if some other judgement was possible. For example, you might on some occasion find it worthwhile for its own sake to tap your fingers on a certain glass.[299] Now, whether it is the will's general directedness toward what the intellect perceives to be good, or the intellect's inability to conceive of some specific end except as good or of some means as an avoidable way of achieving a good, or the intellect's simply finding some good as worth doing for its own sake, we have in each case reasons for action that are simply given, as it were, rather than chosen. The agent is nevertheless free. For one thing, the reasons, even if they are in one of these ways just given, are *the agent's* reasons, so that he is still the source of any action that they give rise to (as the "principle of ultimate authorship" requires). For another thing, it is still up to the agent *whether or not* to act on those reasons (as the "principle of alternate possibilities" requires).

Now, this implies (to borrow some terminology from Stefaan Cuypers) a distinction between the *object* of the will and the *exertion* of the will.[300] When I say that some reasons are simply given rather than chosen, I am saying that the *object toward which* the will is directed can simply be given rather than chosen, consistent with the will's freedom. There is a termination to any regress of final causes for the sake of which the will acts. I may pursue one end for the sake of another, and that for the sake of yet another, but at some point I simply have certain ends which are not chosen but in some sense are just given. Hence the regress posited by Strawson is not after all infinite, but this is consistent with the self-determination required for free will, both

---

[299] I borrow both the point and the example that illustrates it from Pink, *Self-Determination*, pp. 231-32.

[300] Cuypers, "Thomistic Agent-Causalism," p. 101.

because the reasons in question are still my reasons and because it is up to me whether I act on them.

But it might now seem that *another* vicious regress looms. For what about the *exertion* of the will? What makes it the case that I do in fact act or refrain from acting on the reasons in question? Doesn't a choice to act require a cause, and if the act is to be a free and thus self-determined one, doesn't that entail that the cause must be some further choice on my part? If that is the case, doesn't that further choice itself require yet another choice as a cause, and so on *ad infinitum*? The answer is that this does not follow. Just as the will's ultimate ends in the order of final causes are simply given rather than pursued for the sake of yet further ends, so too its ultimate acts in the order of efficient causes can bring about effects (such as bodily movements) without themselves being caused. The will is in this sense an uncaused cause or unmoved mover.[301]

This does *not* entail that its operation is random, either in the sense of being an exception to the principle of causality or in the sense of being unintelligible or devoid of explanation. It is not an exception to the principle of causality, because events require causes insofar as they contain some passive potentiality that requires actualization. For example, a statue requires a cause because the material out of which it is made initially only potentially has the shape of the statue. Something has to actualize that potential in order for the statue to exist. The exertion of the will, by contrast, is entirely *active* rather than passive. It is a *bringing about* that is not *itself* brought about by anything else. Yet it is not unintelligible or devoid of explanation, because it is done *for a reason* – in particular, for the sake of the end grasped by the intellect – and something done for a reason is the opposite of unintelligible. Hence the defender of agent-causal free will

---

[301] Ibid., pp. 95-97. As Cuypers goes on to note, this is consistent with holding that the will is *ultimately* moved by God, just as, for the Thomist, *everything* other than God ultimately exists and acts at any moment only insofar as God conserves it in being and concurs with its causal activity. If we accept this theological picture (as I happen to), the will would count as an unmoved mover only in a relative sense, with God alone being an unmoved mover in an absolute sense. But important though it is, this issue can be bracketed off for present purposes, and the argument of this chapter does not rest on any theological premises. In my view, how divine causality relates to the will is in any event more a question about the nature of divine causality than it is a question about the nature of the will.

is not stuck with the dilemma of having to posit either "an infinite regress or a nonrational flip-flop."[302]

This completes the *long* answer to the question "What is mind?", the short answer to which I gave in chapter 1. That short answer, you will recall, is that to have a mind is to be a self or a person, and that this entails being a substance which by nature possesses an intellect and a will. We have, over the course of the subsequent chapters, now seen in much greater detail what this means, and why it cannot coherently be denied that we have minds in this sense. We turn now to consider the nature of the body.

---

[302] I borrow the phrase from the discussion of Strawson in Clarke, *Libertarian Accounts of Free Will*, p. 170.

Part II:
What is Body?

5. Matter

What is matter?

Having now examined the nature of mind in some detail, we turn to the body and the mind's relationship to it. Our ultimate aim is to answer questions like: Are mental states and processes reducible to brain activity? Is the body essential to the self or merely a kind of vehicle in which it moves about? Do we survive the deaths of our bodies? But we cannot effectively address such questions without first understanding what the body is. That, in turn, requires an account of material things in general, since whatever else the body is, it is a material thing. So, in this chapter, we consider the nature of matter.

Of course, nothing could be more familiar than material objects – tables and chairs, rocks and trees, dogs and cats and human bodies themselves. But what exactly *is* matter? The history of philosophy and science shows surprisingly little consensus on how to answer that question. As Stephen Toulmin notes in the article on "Matter" in *The Encyclopedia of Philosophy*, "it is highly doubtful whether one can isolate a single concept of matter shared by, say, Anaximander and Aquinas, Democritus and Descartes, Epicurus and Einstein."[303]

Here I will discuss what I take to be the three historically most influential and well-developed general approaches to the nature of matter. The first is the *hylemorphism* originally articulated by Aristotle in response to the views of his predecessors from Thales to Plato, and later refined by Thomas Aquinas and other Scholastic thinkers. I have had reason to say something about this account in earlier chapters, but now we need to examine it in greater depth. The second approach is the *mechanical philosophy* that the founders of early modern philosophy and science put in place of hylemorphism (though its roots lay

---

[303] Stephen E. Toulmin, "Matter," in Paul Edwards, ed., *The Encyclopedia of Philosophy*, Volume 5 (New York: Macmillan and Free Press, 1967), p. 213.

in ancient Greek atomism, which was among the views Aristotle rejected). The third is the account of matter offered by contemporary physics, and in particular by quantum mechanics. I will not only defend hylemorphism, but will argue that its rival the mechanical philosophy is plagued by insuperable problems, and that what modern physics tells us about matter is not only compatible with hylemorphism but if anything vindicates it.[304]

Needless to say, this is a large issue, a full treatment of which requires discussion of a variety of issues in metaphysics and philosophy of science (not to mention physics and chemistry) that go well beyond what can be addressed in a book about human nature. It will suffice for present purposes to set out the main lines of argument, and in any event I have provided a fuller discussion elsewhere.[305]

Hylemorphism

Actuality and potentiality

Hylemorphism occupies the middle ground between two extremes that had developed in Pre-Socratic philosophy, the *dynamic monism* of Heraclitus and the *static monism* of Parmenides and Zeno. Heraclitus denied the permanence and unity of everyday objects. To illustrate,

---

[304] When I say that these have historically been the three most influential and well-developed views, I primarily have in mind the history of Western philosophy and science. The topic has, of course, also been addressed in non-Western philosophy. But the main views developed in the non-Western traditions seem to parallel the views taken in the West. For example, something like hylemorphism has been defended in the history of Chinese philosophy, and atomism has been influential in the history of Indian philosophy. On the former, see James Dominic Rooney, *Material Objects in Confucian and Aristotelian Metaphysics: The Inevitability of Hylomorphism* (London: Bloomsbury Academic, 2022). On the latter, see Sahotra Sarkar, "Aggregates versus Wholes: An Unresolved Debate between the Nyāya-Vaiśeṣika and Buddhist Schools in Ancient Indian Atomism," in Ugo Zilioli, ed., *Atomism in Philosophy: A History from Antiquity to the Present* (London: Bloomsbury Academic, 2021).

[305] Cf. Edward Feser, *Scholastic Metaphysics: A Contemporary Introduction* (Heusenstamm: Editiones Scholasticae, 2014), chapter 3; and *Aristotle's Revenge: The Metaphysical Foundations of Physical and Biological Science* (Neunkirchen-Seelscheid: Editiones Scholasticae, 2019), chapters 1 and 5.

I'll borrow an example from physicist Richard Feynman, who gives the following lucid description of the evaporation of a glass of water:

> Above the surface we find... *water vapor*, which is always found above liquid water... In addition we find some other molecules – here two oxygen atoms stuck together by themselves, forming an *oxygen molecule*, there two nitrogen atoms also stuck together to make a nitrogen molecule. Air consists almost entirely of nitrogen, oxygen, some water vapor, and lesser amounts of carbon dioxide, argon, and other things. So above the water surface is the air, a gas, containing some water vapor. Now... [t]he molecules in the water are always jiggling around. From time to time, one on the surface happens to be hit a little harder than usual, and gets knocked away... Thus, molecule by molecule, the water disappears – it evaporates. But if we *close* the vessel above, after a while we shall find a large number of molecules of water amongst the air molecules. From time to time, one of these vapor molecules comes flying down to the water and gets stuck again. So we see that what looks like a dead, uninteresting thing – a glass of water with a cover, that has been sitting there for perhaps twenty years – really contains a dynamic and interesting phenomenon which is going on all the time. To our eyes, our crude eyes, nothing is changing, but if we could see it a billion times magnified, we would see that from its own point of view it is always changing: molecules are leaving the surface, molecules are coming back...
>
> Not only does the water go into the air, but also, from time to time, one of the oxygen or nitrogen molecules will come in and "get lost" in the mass of water molecules, and work its way into the water. Thus the air dissolves in the water; oxygen and nitrogen molecules will work their way into the water and the water will contain air.[306]

Now, though the terms of this description are modern, I think Heraclitus would interpret it as a fine illustration of his basic claims. Common sense would regard the water in the glass as a single unified

---

[306] Richard P. Feynman, *Six Easy Pieces* (New York: Basic Books, 2011), pp. 11-13.

substance that persists over time and can be sharply distinguished from what surrounds it. But in fact, Heraclitus would say, it is an aggregate of constantly changing parts that persists no longer than any particular configuration of the parts does, and the boundaries of which blur into those of its surroundings. Indeed, for Heraclitus the only genuinely abiding substance is the world as a whole, of which the ordinary objects of our experience are merely the ever-shifting appearances. To be sure, I am not saying that Feynman's description actually vindicates dynamic monism (and that was certainly not what Feynman himself was trying to do). In fact the scientific evidence can be given alternative philosophical interpretations, as we'll see.

In any event, if such empirical considerations might at least seem to offer support to Heraclitus, Parmenides and Zeno notoriously appeal instead to abstract rational arguments in support of their contention that it is change and multiplicity, rather than permanence and unity, which are illusory. Take Parmenides first. He argued that for change to occur would require *non-being* to give rise to *being*. For example, when the water in the glass cools, the coolness has to go from non-being to being. But for being to arise from non-being is for something to come from nothing, and from nothing comes nothing. Therefore, Parmenides concludes, change is impossible. But so too is multiplicity. For two or more things to be distinct objects, there would have to be something that sets them apart, and in Parmenides' view this would be the empty space between them. Now, empty space, he claims, would be the absence of anything, or non-being. But precisely because it is the absence of anything, non-being does not exist. And in that case, empty space does not exist, so that there is nothing that can set apart purportedly different things. So, there really are no different things, but just one thing: being, undifferentiated and unchanging.

Zeno famously defends Parmenides' teaching with a set of ingenious paradoxes, of which we'll consider two. In the *dichotomy* paradox, Zeno asks us to consider a runner trying to get from point A to point B. Common sense supposes that nothing could be easier, but Zeno holds that on analysis, the journey can be seen to be impossible. For in order to get from A to B, the runner first has to get from A to the midpoint between A and B. But to get to the midpoint, he first has to get to the quarter-point, and to get to that he first has to get to the eighth-point, and so on ad infinitum. So he can never reach B, and indeed cannot even get his foot off of point A, since even to move an inch would require traversing an infinite series of ever smaller distances. This sort of paradox shows, in Zeno's view, that motion is an illusion.

Zeno's *paradox of parts* begins with the thesis that if there really were multiple objects in the world, then either they would have size or they would have no size. If they have no size, then nothing has any size, because combining any number of things with no size can only ever yield something with no size. Hence everything would be the same size, namely no size at all. But that is absurd. But supposing that there are multiple things that do have size also leads to absurdity. For if they have size, then they are divisible into parts of smaller size, and those of yet smaller parts, and so on ad infinitum. But then they each have an infinite number of parts, and since a thing is bigger the more parts that are added to it, it would follow that they are of infinite size. Hence everything would be of the same size, namely of infinite size. But this too is absurd. So, either way, the assumption that there are multiple objects leads to absurdity and must be rejected.

Now, Aristotle's hylemorphism is grounded in a crucial distinction he develops when explaining where dynamic monism and static monism go wrong. Their mistake is failing to note the difference between *actuality* and *potentiality*. Consider an ice cube. In describing it we might note that it is solid, transparent, a cubic inch in size, cold to the touch, sitting motionless on the table, and so on. Those are the different ways it *actually* is. But that would not be a full description, which would require noting also the ways it *potentially* could be. For example, potentially it is liquid (if you melt it), potentially it is flying through the air (if you throw it), potentially it is smaller (if you break a piece off of it), and so on. A potentiality is not an actuality, but it is not nothing either. It is really there in the ice cube even if not actualized. For example, if you keep the ice cube in a freezer for ten years and it never in fact melts, it still has the *potential* to melt in a way that it does not have the potential to turn into gasoline, or to grow legs, or to solve equations.

Aristotle would say that while Parmenides is correct to hold that being cannot arise from non-being, his error is to suppose that that is what change would involve. What change really involves is one kind of being or reality coming from another kind – *being-in-actuality* arising from *being-in-potentiality*. Or to speak a little more plainly, change involves the actualization of a potential. It is also wrong for Parmenides to characterize the space between objects as nothingness or non-being, because it has potentialities and potentialities are not nothing. Once we identify potentiality as a kind of reality distinct from actuality, Parmenides' arguments against change and multiplicity collapse.

Zeno makes a similar error, in Aristotle's view. While it is true that there is an infinite number of ever smaller distances between points A and B, these smaller distances are there only potentially rather than actually. Hence there is not an actual infinite number of distances for a runner to traverse, and the dichotomy paradox falls apart. Similarly, the infinite number of parts in an object are there only potentially until we do something to divide it. Until we divide it, there is in actuality just the one object. Hence the paradoxical consequences of an object having an actually infinite number of parts are blocked.

The error of Parmenides and Zeno is essentially to collapse all reality into actuality, ignoring potentiality. Now, Heraclitus makes the opposite error, of collapsing all reality into potentiality and denying actuality. For he holds that there is only endless becoming, change that is not change *to* anything, that never congeals into anything determinate. In effect, he posits a world of potentialities which only ever give way to other potentialities, without any of them being actualized. But this cannot be. For potentialities, though distinct from actualities, are grounded in actualities. For example, it is because the ice actually has the unique chemical structure it does that it has the potentiality to melt when the temperature rises above 32 degrees Fahrenheit. If it had some other structure, it would have a different melting point.

Form and matter

We'll come back to some of these issues, but for the moment let's see at last how all of this gives rise to hylemorphism. As Scholastic followers of Aristotle like Thomas Aquinas point out, the distinction between actuality and potentiality is completely general, applying to all possible kinds of substance. For example, suppose there are angelic intellects, which would be minds that exist apart from matter. They would go from potentiality to actuality when created by God. But the notions of potentiality and actuality apply in a special way to physical things, the objects of perceptual experience. Unlike angelic intellects, physical objects are susceptible of both generation and corruption and occupy specific locations in space and time. What makes this possible is that they are composites of potentiality and actuality of special kinds, namely *matter* and *form* (where the Greek words for matter and form – *hyle* and *morphe* – give us the word "hylemorphism," sometimes spelled "hylomorphism").[307]

In change, there is, again, both a potential that is to be actualized and the actualization of that potential. Consider the ink in a dry-erase marker. While still in the pen it is actually liquid. But it has the potential to dry into a triangular shape on the surface of a marker board. When you use the pen to draw a triangle on the board, that potential is actualized. Having dried into that shape, the ink has yet other potentials, such as the potential to be removed from the board by an eraser and in the process to take on the form of dust particles. When you erase the triangle and the dried particles of ink fall from the board and/or get stuck in the eraser, those potentials are actualized.

Now, what we have in this scenario is, first of all, a determinable substratum that underlies the potentialities in question – namely, the ink. We also have a series of determining patterns that that substratum takes on as the various potentials are actualized – patterns like *being liquid*, *being dry*, *being triangular*, and *being particle-like*.

---

[307] The Neo-Confucian philosopher Zhu Xi (1130-1200) drew a parallel distinction between *li*, the pattern or structure that gives a thing its nature, and *qi*, the material substrate in which *li* inheres. For defense of the view that Zhu Xi's position amounts to a variety of hylemorphism, see Rooney, *Material Objects in Confucian and Aristotelian Metaphysics*, chapter 4.

The determinable substratum of potentiality is what in hylemorphism is meant by the term "matter," and a determining pattern that exists once the potential is actualized is what is meant by a "form." Matter is, essentially, that which needs actualizing in change; form is, essentially, that which results from the actualization. Note that *any* determining, actualizing pattern counts as a "form" in this sense. A form is not merely the shape of a thing, nor is it necessarily a spatial configuration of parts (though shape and spatial configuration are kinds of forms). *Being blue, being hot, being soft*, etc. are also forms in the relevant sense.

Change is not the only phenomenon that points to the distinction between matter and form. Note that a form or pattern like *triangularity* is universal rather than particular. It is the same pattern that one finds in green triangles and red ones, triangles drawn in ink and those drawn in pencil, triangles used as dinner bells and those used on a billiards table, and so forth. Triangularity is also perfect or exact rather than approximate. For example, being triangular in the strict sense involves having sides that are straight rather than wavy. Now, the triangle you draw on the marker board has straight sides, but only imperfectly or approximately. It is also a particular instance of triangularity rather than triangularity as such. Hence there must not only be something by virtue of which the thing you've drawn is triangular, but also something by virtue of which it is triangular in precisely the imperfect way that it is. There must also be something by virtue of which triangularity exists in *this particular* point in time and space.

Now if being triangular is a way of being *actual*, being triangular only in an imperfect way is a way of being *potential*. For insofar as the triangle's sides are only imperfectly straight, the ink in which you have drawn it has, you might say, only partially actualized the potential for triangularity. And insofar as the triangle has been drawn in some particular time and place, the potential in question is a potential at *that* time and place, rather than at another, that has been actualized. Now that by virtue of which what you have drawn is actually triangular to the extent that it is, is its *form*; while that by virtue of which it is limited, or remains merely potential, in the extent to which it is triangular is its *matter*.

Insofar as form accounts for whatever permanence, unity, and actuality there is in the natural world, it represents, as it were, the Parmenidean side of things. The triangle drawn on the marker board persists to the extent that it retains its triangular form, is identical to other triangles insofar as it is an instance of the same form they instantiate, and is perfect or complete in its actuality to the degree that it approximates that form. Insofar as matter accounts for the changeability, diversity, and potentiality that exists in the natural world, it represents the Heraclitean side of things. The triangle drawn on the board is impermanent insofar as its matter can lose its triangular form, is distinct from other things having the same form insofar as it is one parcel of matter among others which instantiate it, and is imperfect or potential to the extent that it *merely* approximates the form.

Matter is passive and indeterminate, form active and determining. The same bit of matter can take on different forms, and the same form can be received in different bits of matter. Hence matter and form are as distinct as potentiality and actuality. Still, just as potentiality is grounded in actuality, so too does matter always have *some* form or other. If the ink in our example is not in a liquid form, it is in a dry, triangular form, and if not that then in the form of particles. And if the particles are broken down further so that the ink is in no sense still present, then the form of the chemical constituents of the ink would remain. If matter lacked *all* form it would be nothing but the pure potentiality for receiving form; and if it were *purely* potential, there would be no actuality to ground it and it would not exist at all.

Now, several further distinctions are needed in order to flesh out the hylemorphic analysis of what it is to be a physical substance. First, there is the general distinction between any substance and its attributes. Consider a solid, gray, round, smooth stone of the sort you might pluck from a river bed. The solidity, grayness, roundness, and smoothness are *attributes* of the stone, and the stone itself is the *substance* which bears these attributes. The attributes exist *in* the stone whereas the stone does not exist *in* any other thing in the same sense. Substances, in general, just are the sorts of things which exist in themselves rather than inhering in anything else, and which are the subjects of the attributes which do of their nature inhere in something else. This is true of physical or corporeal substances like stones, and it is true of incorporeal substances too if there are any such things.

Physical substances are, again, composed of form and matter, but here two further distinctions must be made. If we abstract from our notion of matter *all* form, leaving nothing but what I have called the pure potentiality to receive form, we arrive at the idea of *prime matter*. (More on this in a moment.) Matter already having some form or other – that is to say, matter which is actually a stone, or wood, or water, or what have you, and is not merely potentially any of these things – is *secondary matter*. There is a corresponding distinction between kinds of form. A form which makes of what would otherwise be utterly indeterminate prime matter some determinate concrete thing of a certain kind is a *substantial form*. A form which merely modifies some secondary matter – and in particular, which modifies matter which already has a substantial form – is an *accidental form*. Stated more precisely, the basic claim of hylemorphism is that a physical substance is a composite of *prime matter* and *substantial form*.

The distinction between substantial form and accidental form is illuminated by comparison with the different but related Aristotelian distinction between *nature* and *art* – that is to say, between natural objects on the one hand, and everyday artifacts on the other. Hence, consider a *liana vine* – the kind of vine Tarzan likes to swing on – as an example of a natural object. A *hammock* that Tarzan might construct from living liana vines is a kind of artifact, and not a natural object. The parts of the liana vine have an inherent tendency to function together to allow the vine to exhibit the growth patterns it does, to take in water and nutrients, and so forth. By contrast, the parts of the hammock – the liana vines themselves – have no inherent tendency to function together as a hammock. Rather, they must be arranged by Tarzan to do so, and left to their own devices – that is to say, without pruning, occasional rearrangement, and the like – they will tend to grow the way they otherwise would have had Tarzan not interfered with them, including ways that will impede their performance as a hammock. Their natural tendency is to be liana-like and not hammock-like; the hammock-like function they perform after Tarzan ties them together is extrinsic or imposed from outside, while the liana-like functions are intrinsic to them.

Now the difference between that which has such an intrinsic principle of operation and that which does not is essentially the difference between something having a substantial form and something having a merely accidental form. Being a liana vine involves having a substantial form, while being a hammock of the sort we're discussing involves instead the imposition of an accidental form on components each of which already has a substantial form, namely the substantial form of a liana vine. A liana vine is, accordingly, a true *substance*, as Aristotelian hylemorphism understands substance. A hammock is not a true substance, precisely because it does not qua hammock have a substantial form – an *intrinsic* principle by which it operates as it characteristically does – but only an accidental form. In general, true substances are typically natural objects, whereas artifacts are typically not true substances. A dog, a tree, and water would be true substances, because each has a substantial form or intrinsic principle by which it behaves in the characteristic ways it does. A watch, a bed, or a computer would not be true substances, because each behaves in the characteristic ways it does only insofar as certain accidental forms have been imposed on them from outside. The true substances in these cases would be the raw materials (metal, wood, glass, etc.) out of which these artifacts are made.

It is important to emphasize, however, that the correlation between what occurs "in the wild" and what has a substantial form, and the correlation between what is man-made and has only an accidental form, are only rough correlations. For there are objects that occur in nature and apart from any human intervention and yet have only accidental forms rather than substantial forms, such as piles of stones that gradually form at the bottom of a hill and beaver dams. And there are man-made objects that have substantial forms rather than accidental forms, such as water synthesized in a lab and breeds of dog. Of course, no one would be tempted in the first place to think of these as "artifacts" in the same sense in which watches and computers are artifacts. But even objects that are "artificial" in the sense that they not only never occur "in the wild" but require significant scientific knowledge and technological expertise to produce can count as having substantial forms rather than accidental forms. Styrofoam would be one possible example.[308]

The basic idea is that it seems to be essential to a thing's having a substantial form that it has properties and causal powers that are irreducible to those of its parts.[309] Hence water has properties and causal powers that hydrogen and oxygen do not have, whereas the properties and causal powers of, say, an axe seem to amount to nothing over and above the sum of the properties and powers of the axe's wood and metal parts.[310] When water is synthesized out of hydrogen and oxygen, what happens is that the prime matter underlying the hydrogen and oxygen loses the substantial forms of hydrogen and oxygen and takes on a new substantial form, namely that of water. By contrast, when an axe is made out of wood and metal, the matter underlying the wood and the matter underlying the metal do not lose their substantial forms. Rather, while maintaining their substantial forms, they take on a new accidental form, that of being an axe. The making of Styrofoam seems to be more like the synthesis of water out of hydrogen and oxygen than it is like the making of an axe. Styrofoam has properties and powers which are irreducible to those of the materials out of which it is made, which indicates the presence of a substantial form and thus a true substance.

There is a further complication to the story. Among the attributes of a thing, we need to distinguish those that are *proper* to it from those which are not. It is the former alone which are labeled "properties" in Aristotelian-Thomistic philosophy, with the others referred to as "contingent" attributes.[311] (This contrasts with the very loose way the term "property" is used in contemporary analytic philosophy, to refer to more or less any feature we might predicate of a thing.) The properties or proper attributes of a substance are those which "flow" or follow from its having the substantial form it does.

---

[308] Cf. Eleonore Stump, *Aquinas* (London: Routledge, 2003), p. 44.

[309] Cf. Eleonore Stump, "Substance and Artifact in Aquinas's Metaphysics," in Thomas M. Crisp, Matthew Davidson, and David Vanderlaan, eds., *Knowledge and Reality: Essays in Honor of Alvin Plantinga* (Dordrecht: Springer).

[310] Stump, *Aquinas*, p. 44.
[311] Cf. Feser, *Scholastic Metaphysics*, pp. 230-35.

Being four-legged, for example, flows or follows from having the substantial form of a dog. It is a natural concomitant of "dogness" as such, whereas being white (say) is not, but is merely a contingent attribute of any particular dog. Now this "flow" can, as it were, be blocked. For instance, a particular dog might, as a result of injury or genetic defect, be missing a leg. But it wouldn't follow from its missing that leg that being four-legged is not after all a true property of dogs, nor would it follow that this particular creature was not really a dog after all. Rather, it would be a *damaged or defective instance* of a dog. When determining the characteristic properties and causal powers of some kind of thing, then, we need to consider the *paradigm* case, what that kind of thing is like when it is in its mature and normal state.

So, a thing counts as a true substance when it has a substantial form rather than a merely accidental form, and the mark of its having the former is that in its mature and normal state, it exhibits certain properties and causal powers that are irreducible to those of its parts. Aquinas's interpretation of hylemorphism insists on the doctrine of the *unicity* of substantial form, according to which a substance has only a single substantial form.[312] Suppose A is a substance, and has B and C as parts. Since A is a substance, it has a substantial form. Do B and C have further substantial forms of their own? If they did, then they too would be substances. In that case, though, A's form would relate to B and C as an accidental form relates to secondary matter. But then A wouldn't really have a substantial form after all, and thus not really be a substance. So, if A really is a substance, then its parts B and C must not themselves have substantial forms or amount to true substances in their own right. There is only the single substantial form, the form of A, which informs the prime matter of A. Another way to look at it is that if B and C had substantial forms, then they would be what actualizes the prime matter so that it constitutes a substance (or two substances in this case, namely B and C). In that case, the prime matter wouldn't *potentially* be a substance, but would already *actually* be a substance. That is to say, it would be secondary matter. But then there would be nothing left for the substantial form of A to do qua actualizer of prime matter. It would serve merely to

---

[312] Cf. John Goyette, "St. Thomas on the Unity of Substantial Form," *Nova et Vetera* 7 (2009): 781-90.

modify an already existing substance and thus amount to an accidental form rather than substantial form. So, again, a substance *A* can really only have one substantial form.

To see the implications of this, consider once again our example of water, which has hydrogen and oxygen as its parts. Suppose for the sake of argument that water is a true substance rather than an aggregate, and thus has a substantial form. Since a substance can have only a single substantial form, it follows that the hydrogen and oxygen in water don't have substantial forms. That entails in turn that hydrogen and oxygen don't exist in water as substances. Now, this may seem odd, since hydrogen considered *by itself* and oxygen considered *by itself* each do seem to be substances. They have their own characteristic irreducible properties and causal powers, after all. But the lesson we should draw from these considerations, according to the doctrine of the unicity of substantial form, is that hydrogen and oxygen do not exist *actually* in water, but only *virtually*. Notice that the claim is *not* that they don't exist in water *at all*. It is rather that they don't exist in water *in the way* that they exist when they exist on their own. The situation is comparable to the Aristotelian account of what is really going on in Zeno's paradox of parts scenario, in which the parts are present – they are not nothing or non-being – but only potentially rather than actually.

This too may sound odd, but it should sound less so upon reflection. Consider that if hydrogen and oxygen were actually present in the water, then they should possess their characteristic properties and powers.[313] That means that we should be able to burn the hydrogen, and to boil the oxygen at -183°C. But we cannot do either. Hence the substantial forms of hydrogen and oxygen cannot be present, in which case the *substances* hydrogen and oxygen cannot be present. Furthermore, if hydrogen and oxygen were actually present, then for something to be water would be for it to have a merely accidental form, and properties and causal powers reducible to those of hydrogen and oxygen. But that is also not the case, since water has powers and properties that a mere aggregate of hydrogen and oxygen does not. Hydrogen and oxygen are present in water, then, in the sense

---

[313] Cf. David S. Oderberg, *Real Essentialism* (London: Routledge, 2007), p. 75.

that water has the *potentiality* to have hydrogen and oxygen drawn out of it – by electrolysis, say.

As I've indicated, two of the motivations for hylemorphism have to do with its application to the critique of static monism's denial of multiplicity and of change. These lines of argument for hylemorphism are sometimes labeled the *argument from limitation* and the *argument from change*.[314] The basic idea of the first line of argument is, again, that a form is *of itself* universal, so that we need a principle to explain how it gets tied down, as it were, to a particular thing, time, and place. For example, *roundness* can be instantiated in multiple objects and at different times and spatial locations, and the geometrical truths pertaining to it remain true whether or not any particular round thing or group of round things comes into existence or remains in existence. *Roundness* is thus not *as such* limited, so that something needs to be added to it if we do in fact find it limited in some way. Matter – the matter of this individual bowling ball, of that individual wheel, and so forth – is what does this job. For example, it is the matter of some individual wheel that accounts for the fact that roundness is instantiated in some particular automobile, in a way it is not instantiated in (say) the tree next to the automobile or the road under it. Matter also accounts for limitation in another respect. The *roundness* of a circle as defined in geometry is perfect or exact, yet any particular triangle drawn on a chalkboard, in a book, or what have you, is always at least to some extent imperfect. Matter accounts for this kind of limitation too insofar as, qua the potentiality to receive form, it is never fixed or locked on to any one particular form, but always ready to take on another.

For the moment, however, it is the argument from change about which more must be said. On an Aristotelian analysis, a real change involves the gain or loss of some attribute, but also the persistence of that which gains or loses the attribute. For example, when a banana goes from being green to being yellow, the greenness is lost and the yellowness is gained, but the banana itself persists. If there

---

[314] Henry J. Koren, *An Introduction to the Philosophy of Nature* (Pittsburgh: Duquesne University Press, 1962), chapter 2. Cf. Margaret Scharle, "A Synchronic Justification for Aristotle's Commitment to Prime Matter," *Phronesis* 54 (2009): 326-45, whose distinction between "synchronic" and "diachronic" arguments for prime matter roughly corresponds to the distinction between the argument from limitation and the argument from change.

were no such persistence, we would not have a *change* to the banana, but rather the annihilation of a green banana and the creation of a new, yellow one in its place.

Matter, for hylemorphism, essentially *just is* that which not only limits form to a particular thing, time, and place, but also that which persists when an attribute is gained or lost. It is absolutely crucial to understand that the characteristics of matter identified so far – its correspondence to potentiality (as contrasted with form's correspondence to actuality), its status as the principle of the limitation of form, and its status as the principle of persistence through change – are *definitive* of matter as hylemorphism understands it. That is to say, the hylemorphist is using the term "matter" in a *technical sense*. He is *not* saying that matter *as it has independently come to be understood in modern physics and chemistry* is what turns out to be the stuff that plays the roles of persisting through change, limiting form, and corresponding to potentiality. He is, so far, not saying anything about matter in the modern sense at all. Rather he is *defining* "matter" as *that which plays these roles*. (Nor is this some eccentric usage; in fact it is an *older* usage than that familiar from modern physics and chemistry.) Of course, how "matter" in this sense relates to "matter" in the modern sense is a good question, and it is one I'll address presently. The point for the moment is simply to forestall irrelevant objections and misunderstandings.

Now, one sort of change that takes place is change *to* a persisting substance. The subject of this sort of change is secondary matter, matter already having a substantial form. For the Aristotelian, we can identify three kinds of change falling into this class. There is, first of all, *qualitative* change, as when the banana in our example changes color, from green to yellow. Second, there is *quantitative* change, as when the banana, having begun to rot, shrinks in size. Third, there is *local motion* or change with respect to location or place, as when the banana flies through the air when you toss it toward the waste basket.

Another, more radical kind of change is change *of* a substance, *substantial* change. It is change that involves, not a substance gaining or losing some attribute while still persisting, but rather a substance going out of existence and being replaced by a new one. This is what happens when the banana is eaten, digested, and incorporated into the flesh of the animal that ate it, or when it is burned and reduced to ash. Because change requires some underlying persisting subject that does not change, there must be such a subject in the case of substantial change no less than in the case of the other kinds. But because it is the substance itself that goes out of existence in this case, it is a substantial form that is lost, not a merely accidental form. Hence it is not any kind of secondary matter that is the subject of this sort of change, but rather prime matter.[315]

Now, since prime matter is that which underlies the loss of one substantial form and the gain of another, it does not of itself have a substantial form and is therefore is not any kind of substance. Nor, since the having of accidental forms and attributes in general presupposes being a substance, does it possess any attributes or accidental forms. It is not *actually* any *thing* at all. But that does not entail that it is nothing, for remember that between actuality and nothingness or non-being, there is potentiality, which is a kind of being. *That* is what prime matter is – the pure potentiality to receive form.

Because potentiality cannot exist without actuality, prime matter does not exist without actuality. That is to say, it does not exist on its own, but only together with some substantial form or another. All matter as it exists in reality, outside the mind, is secondary matter. But that does not entail either that prime matter is not real or that it is not really distinct from the substantial forms with which it is conjoined. Being *trilateral* (having three straight sides) is a different geometrical feature from being *triangular* (having three angles) even though a closed plane figure cannot have the one without having the other. We can distinguish them in thought and what we thereby distinguish are features that are different in reality, even if outside the mind the one cannot be separated from the other. Similarly, prime matter and substantial form differ in reality even if they cannot be separated in reality, but only in thought.[316]

---

[315] Oderberg, *Real Essentialism*, pp. 71-76.

[316] For more on the idea of a real distinction in Aristotelian-Thomistic philosophy, see Feser, *Scholastic Metaphysics*, pp. 72-79.

Without prime matter, there could be no substantial change, because there would be no subject of change that persists through the change. There would rather be the complete annihilation of one substance and the creation of another utterly novel substance in its place. That the world does not work like that is evident from the continuity that substantial change no less than the other sorts of change exhibits. For example, wood that is burned reliably turns to ash, not to water or cheese or rose petals. Why would this be the case if there were absolutely *nothing* that carries over from the wood to the ash, but rather the complete disappearance of the first and the appearance out of nothing of the second? Why wouldn't just any old thing appear in place of the wood?

The mechanical philosophy

This brings us to the "mechanical philosophy," which is a generic label for a set of views about the nature of matter that began to supplant hylemorphism in the thinking of philosophers and scientists in the 17th century.[317] The paradigmatic version is *atomism*, first developed by ancient Greek philosophers like Democritus and revived by early moderns like Pierre Gassendi and Thomas Hobbes. Atomism holds that all observable physical objects can be broken down into unobservable particles which cannot in principle be broken down further (the idea of such an indivisible particle being the original meaning of the word "atom," which has in modern science come to have a different sense). Differences between observable objects are just differences in the configurations of the atoms, and all changes to an object and changes of one object into another can be accounted for in terms of changes in the configurations of atoms as they move through space. Being indivisible, the atoms are the unchanging substrate of all change.

---

[317] For a brief overview of the transition from the hylemorphic conception of matter to the mechanical conception in its various forms, see Patrick Suppes, "Aristotle's Concept of Matter and its Relation to Modern Concepts of Matter," *Synthese* 28 (1974): 27-50. For a book-length treatment of the variety of positions taken in the early modern period, see Thomas Holden, *The Architecture of Matter: Galileo to Kant* (Oxford: Clarendon Press, 2004). I survey the main themes and arguments of the mechanical philosophy at greater length than I can here in *Aristotle's Revenge*, at pp. 42-64.

Now, other versions of the mechanical philosophy have different conceptions of the particles. Descartes thought that no particle could be indivisible in principle, so that there is no bottom level of particles. The corpuscularianism of Robert Boyle and John Locke agrees that all particles are divisible in principle, but nevertheless posits a bottom level of particles that happen to be undivided in fact. The force-shell atom theory of Roger Boscovich takes the particles to be unextended and thus indivisible points projecting shells of force. And there are yet other differences between these variations, such as their divergent accounts of the nature of space. What they have in common is the idea that all observable objects are really just aggregates of particles whose properties and powers can be reduced to the sum of those of the particles, in something like the way that a machine is an aggregate of parts whose properties and powers can be reduced to the sum of the properties and powers of the parts.[318] (That is the reason for the "mechanical philosophy" label.)

In other words, the view essentially treats ordinary natural objects as having what hylemorphism would call accidental forms rather than substantial forms. It also treats all the parts out of which they are composed, including the ultimate parts, as actual rather than merely potential. Once again to refer to our water example, the mechanical philosophy would say that oxygen and hydrogen are actually rather than merely virtually in water, and that its ultimate constituents are actual particles of some sort, rather than the pure potentiality of prime matter. All of this distinguishes it not only from hylemorphism, but also from Heraclitus's dynamic monism (since it takes the ultimate particles to be discrete and unchanging unities) and from the static monism of Parmenides and Zeno (since it affirms that the particles are distinct and move through space). It would take Feynman's description of evaporation, which I quoted earlier, to be a

---

[318] Paul Humphreys proposes "generative atomism" as a generic label for views of this sort, whether they conceive of the fundamental entities to which everything else can be reduced as atoms in the original, Greek atomist sense or instead in some other way. See Humphreys' *Emergence: A Philosophical Account* (Oxford: Oxford University Press, 2016), pp. 11-18. Colin McGinn proposes the label "combinatorial atomism with lawlike mappings" (or CALM). See McGinn's *Problems in Philosophy: The Limits of Inquiry* (Oxford: Blackwell, 1993), pp. 18-20.

paradigmatic illustration and indeed vindication of the mechanical philosophy's mode of explanation.

A related component of the mechanical philosophy is its "mathematization" of nature. Galileo attributed to matter only *quantitative* properties such as size, shape, position in space, and movement through space. Irreducibly *qualitative* features such as color, sound, heat, and cold he took to exist only in the mind's representation of matter rather than in matter itself. The book of nature, Galileo famously said, "is written in the language of mathematics, and its characters are triangles, circles, and other geometric figures without which it is humanly impossible to understand a single word of it."[319] Similarly, Descartes held that "extension in length, breadth and depth constitutes the nature of corporeal substance" whereas "weight, colour, and all other such qualities that are perceived by the senses... can be removed from it, while the matter itself remains intact" so that "its nature does not depend on any of these qualities."[320] All the matter that exists in the universe has this same basic nature of extension, and "any variation in matter or diversity in its many forms depends on motion" in the sense of *"the action by which a body travels from one place to another."*[321] As one historian writes, of the centrality of this view to the mechanical world picture:

> In the second half of the [seventeenth] century the distinction between the primary, geometrico-mechanical qualities, which were considered to be really inherent in a physical body as such, and the secondary qualities, which were mere names for the perceptive sensations and the feelings of pleasure and pain experienced in consequence of, or in connexion

---

[319] *The Assayer*, excerpted in *Discoveries and Opinions of Galileo*, translated by Stillman Drake (New York: Random House, 1957), p. 238.

[320] *Principles of Philosophy*, in *The Philosophical Writings of Descartes*, Volume I, translated by John Cottingham, Robert Stoothoff, and Dugald Murdoch (Cambridge: Cambridge University Press, 1985), at pp. 210 and 224.

[321] Ibid., pp. 232-33.

with, physical processes in the external world, was universally accepted, and in fact considered to be almost self-evident.[322]

Indeed, "the total rejection of all non-geometrico-mechanical qualities... is the essence of mechanistic natural philosophy."[323]

To attribute to matter only properties of a geometrical or more broadly mathematical character affords it a crisp determinacy it cannot have if it is a principle of mere potentiality rather than actuality, and makes it possible for material objects to be governed by exact laws of the kind enshrined in equations.[324] It also allows for a precise and elegant way of conceiving of how simpler bits of matter combine to form more complex objects, and of how changes in the material world occur. It can all be described in terms of the spatial relationships between particles, their movement from one position in space to another, adding or subtracting particles to or from existing configurations of particles, and so on.[325] To be sure, contemporary physics has moved beyond the relatively simple model of matter and local motion that this suggests. Space is no longer conceived of in Euclidean terms. Particles are not modeled on little billiard balls or the like. But what has survived is the idea that nature can be captured in a mathematical description, and that what cannot be so captured is to be interpreted as merely the way conscious experience presents matter to us rather than the way matter really is in itself.

---

[322] E. J. Dijksterhuis, *The Mechanization of the World Picture* (Oxford: Oxford University Press, 1961), p. 431.

[323] Ibid., p. 432.

[324] Cf. Roberto Torretti, *The Philosophy of Physics* (Cambridge: Cambridge University Press, 1999), pp. 13-14.

[325] Though mechanistic reductionism facilitates a mathematized conception of nature no less than a mathematized conception of nature facilitates mechanistic reductionism. As Humphreys writes: "Generative atomism is a formidable position, the enormous advantages of which are most directly evident in its ability to represent systems and their states by formal, extensional, mathematical techniques – something that is made possible by a parallel between the generative aspects of the systems and the generative aspects of the representations we use" (*Emergence*, p. 13).

A further crucial element of the mechanical philosophy is its expulsion of teleology from the material world. I have noted, in this chapter and the previous one, that hylemorphism attributes to an object having a substantial form an *inherent* tendency toward a certain end or range of ends, whereas an object having an accidental form thereby has a purely *extrinsic* or externally imposed tendency toward whatever ends it aims at. Again, a liana vine has built-in tendencies to grow toward the forest canopy and take in water through its roots, but no built-in tendency to function as a hammock. On the mechanical conception of nature, however, there is in material things no built-in teleology of *any* kind. Just as the mechanical philosophy effectively makes the forms of ordinary objects accidental rather than substantial, so too does it effectively attribute to them at most extrinsic rather than intrinsic teleology.

To be sure, the mechanical philosophy's banishment of teleological notions from the study of nature was not, at first, thoroughgoing.[326] On the one hand, Bacon and Descartes thought final causes useless for purposes of physics, while Spinoza denied their reality altogether. But on the other hand, William Harvey thought them essential to understanding the circulatory system, and Boyle held that the study of nature revealed God's purposes. Still, the tendency was, increasingly, to regard a natural object's directedness toward an end as something *externally* imposed rather than (as Aristotelian hylemorphism would have it) as intrinsic to natural objects as such. Moreover, as scientific explanations ceased to make any reference to God, so too did reference even to externally imposed teleology disappear. As philosopher of science David Hull summarizes what eventually became the standard view, "explanations were designated as mechanistic to indicate that they included no reference to final causes," and in this sense "all present-day scientific explanations are mechanistic."[327]

---

[326] For discussion of the persistence of teleological analysis at the beginning of the history of modern science, see Steven Shapin, *The Scientific Revolution*, Second edition (Chicago: University of Chicago Press, 2018), pp. 155-61; and Jeffrey K. McDonough, "Not Dead Yet: Teleology and the 'Scientific Revolution,'" in Jeffrey K. McDonough, ed., *Teleology: A History* (Oxford: Oxford University Press, 2020).

[327] David L. Hull, "Mechanistic explanation," in Robert Audi, general editor, *The Cambridge Dictionary of Philosophy* (Cambridge: Cambridge University Press, 1995), p. 476.

The average educated person may suppose that the mechanical philosophy has been confirmed by modern science. Nothing could be further from the truth. In fact the mechanical philosophy's conception of matter faces a number of grave problems. Again, I have addressed these issues at length elsewhere, but here I will summarize the most important lines of criticism. The first is what we might call the *reductionism problem*. Because the mechanical philosophy treats ordinary physical objects as having accidental rather than substantial forms, it entails that dogs, trees, stones, and the like are not really substances. The true substances are the fundamental particles, and to be a dog, a tree, or a stone is just for these particles to take on a certain kind of accidental form. A dog, a tree, or a stone is entirely reducible to the sum of the particles of which it is made.

The problem is that it turns out to be extremely difficult at best – and indeed, probably most philosophers and scientists today would acknowledge, impossible in principle – entirely to describe a dog (for example) in terms of nothing more than the particles that make it up and their properties and powers. Dogs and the like simply have properties and causal powers that are irreducible to the sum of those of their parts.[328] Now, many contemporary philosophers who acknowledge this opt for non-reductionist but also non-hylemorphist positions such as "non-reductive physicalism."[329] But the trouble with such views is that on analysis they turn out to be ambiguous between hylemorphism and reductionism.[330] As I have said, the irreducibility of a thing's properties and causal powers to those of its parts is for hylemorphism a mark of the presence of a substantial form rather than a merely accidental form. The non-reductive physicalist doesn't want to go so far as to revive the notion of substantial form, and wants to treat the parts of a substance as actually rather than virtually in the substance. But this, the hylemorphist argues, implicitly entails reductionism after all. For either it directly treats an object as having only

---

[328] Cf. Feser, *Scholastic Metaphysics*, pp. 177-84; Oderberg, *Real Essentialism*, pp. 65-76.

[329] The Nyāya-Vaiśesika tradition in Indian philosophy, though atomist, took something like this position in opposition to the more thoroughgoing reductionism of some strains of Buddhist philosophy. Cf. Sarkar, "Aggregates versus Wholes."

[330] Cf. Feser, *Scholastic Metaphysics*, pp. 184-89.

an accidental form and thus as not a true substance, or it indirectly does so by virtue of denying the unicity of substantial form.

A second and related problem for the mechanical philosophy is what we might call the *identification problem*. If we say that a dog or a stone is really just a collection of particles, we have to ask exactly *which* collection of particles that is. For example, does the collection of particles that make up a stone include those that are floating in the air two inches out from the surface of the stone? Does it include only those particles that exist half an inch or deeper below the surface of the stone? Presumably the answer in each case is No. But then it seems that we can identify the relevant particles only by reference to the stone of which they are parts. We can't pick out the relevant particles except by reference to the stone as a whole, whereas the whole point of the mechanical philosophy was to show how that there is nothing more to the whole than the particles.[331] In this way too, it turns out to be extremely difficult or impossible to reduce physical objects to collections of particles.

A third problem is that from the point of view of hylemorphism, the atomist doesn't really get rid of substantial form and prime matter at all, but simply relocates them. Call this the *relocation problem*. Suppose that to be a dog, a tree, or a stone really is to have a merely accidental form, and that the only true substances are the fundamental particles. We would still have to regard *them* as composites of substantial form and prime matter, for the reasons given in the arguments from limitation and from change. For one thing, like any other form, the form of being a particle is universal, and so there must be something that ties that form down to some individual thing time, and place – to *this* particular particle at this particular time and place, that particular particle at that time and place, and so on. That is the job matter does, and since the particles in question are fundamental rather than composites of some more fundamental substances, it is only prime matter than can do the job rather than any kind of

---

[331] Cf. Crawford L. Elder, *Real Natures and Familiar Objects* (Cambridge, MA: The MIT Press, 2004), pp. 50-58; and Elder, *Familiar Objects and their Shadows* (Cambridge: Cambridge University Press, 2011), pp. 118-24.

secondary matter. And only this prime matter together with the substantial form of a particle would give us an actual substance.

For another thing, as long as it is even in *principle* possible for a fundamental particle to come into existence or go out of existence, there will have to be something that underlies this substantial change, which brings us back to prime matter and substantial form. Of course, the ancient atomists held that the fundamental particles could be neither generated nor corrupted. But merely to assert this does not make it so, and it is hard to see how there could be such particles. Any particle is going to be limited in various ways – to being of this particular size and shape, at this particular location at any moment, and so on. But what is limited in such ways is a mixture of actuality and potentiality rather than pure actuality. It is actually of *this* shape and merely potentially of some other shape, actually at this location and only potentially at that one, and so on.

Now, only what is pure actuality – something which has no potentials that need to be or indeed could be actualized, but which is, as it were, always already actual – could exist in a necessary way. (The idea of pure actuality is in fact the philosophical core of the Aristotelian-Thomistic conception of God.) Anything less that that could exist only in a contingent way. But then the fundamental particles would have to be contingent rather than necessary, and thus the sorts of thing which could in principle either exist or not exist. This capacity either to exist or fail to exist must have an underlying basis, which brings us back to the conclusion that the particle is composed of prime matter and substantial form.

A fourth problem is posed by the mechanical philosophy's commitment to the thesis that all the parts of an object exist in it actually rather than virtually. For the parts in question are material parts that are extended in space, and anything extended is in principle capable of being divided into smaller extended parts. Now, if extended parts are divisible into smaller extended parts *ad infinitum*, and if all the extended parts are *actually* rather than merely virtually in physical objects, then it follows that every such object has an infinite number of parts. In that case, the paradoxes identified by Zeno will follow – every physical object would be infinitely large and they would all be the same size. Call this *Zeno's problem*.

It is sometimes claimed that the problem here is illusory, on the grounds that infinite divisibility is merely an artifact of geometrical models and does not apply to concrete physical reality. But as philosopher Thomas Holden points out, this response misses the point.[332] The paradoxes arise not from the geometry alone, but from the geometry combined with the premise that the parts of an object are all actual rather than potential. That is why Aristotle can accept that a physical object is infinitely divisible without falling into Zeno's paradoxes. He doesn't deny the mathematics, but rather simply rejects the assumption that the parts of an object are in it actually rather than potentially. And the mechanical philosophy opens itself back up to the paradoxes precisely by taking on board that assumption. Moreover, as Holden judges, its doing so "was rooted more in unreflective prejudice than well-grounded argument" and the tendency of contemporary philosophers to make the same assumption "perhaps... is itself simply a prejudice inherited from our early modern forebears."[333]

A fifth objection to the mechanical philosophy might be called the *abstraction problem*. As I've said, the mechanical philosophy characterizes the material world in terms of its abstract mathematical structure. But a description of its abstract mathematical structure can no more tell us everything about concrete material reality than the geometry of triangles can tell us everything about pyramids, dinner bells, and billiard ball racks. Like a blueprint, it isolates certain features while leaving out others. The absence of substantial forms, teleology, and the like from its *representation* of nature thus no more

---

[332] Holden, *The Architecture of Matter*, pp. 2-3 and 19-21. Holden's book contains a very useful extended discussion of the paradoxes that arise when the geometrical conception of matter is combined with the thesis that the parts of an object are in it actually rather than potentially. While the basic idea goes back to Zeno, Holden shows how the early modern critics of hylemorphism grappled with the problem too, and that the controversy has not been resolved by their present-day successors so much as forgotten by them.

[333] Ibid., p. 278. To be sure, Holden himself does not judge the controversy to have been settled in favor of hylemorphism either. The point is that it has not, contrary to what contemporary philosophers tend to assume, been settled against it.

shows that those features are absent from nature *itself* than the absence of people, furniture, pets, and the like from the blueprint of some house shows that those things are absent from the house itself.[334]

Then there is the *teleology problem*, which is that it is not in fact possible entirely to eliminate final causes even from a complete account of the phenomena described by physics (let alone those described by biology or psychology). What I have in mind is not the well-known controversy about whether the "principle of least action" is teleological, though that is not without interest.[335] The point has to do instead with the thesis that *every agent acts for an end* (known in Aristotelian-Thomistic philosophy as the "principle of finality"), which was briefly discussed in the previous chapter. Physics describes entities (such as particles of various kinds) each of which has distinctive causal powers.[336] But we cannot make sense of some thing A's having a power to produce an effect of some type E unless we think of A as being *directed toward* or *aiming at* E. Otherwise it is unintelligible how A in fact reliably produces E as its effect, rather than some alternative effect F or G or no effect at all. Nor is this merely a line of argument defended by Aristotelian-Thomistic philosophers. Similar lines of argument have been rediscovered by cotemporary philosophers having no Aristotelian-Thomistic ax to grind.[337] Naturally, like the

---

[334] That the mathematical description of the material world afforded by modern physics is highly abstract and therefore necessarily incomplete is by no means a point made by Aristotelian-Thomistic philosophers alone, but was emphasized by early twentieth-century philosophers like Bertrand Russell and scientists like Arthur Eddington, and has been given renewed attention by several contemporary philosophers and scientists. I say much more about this issue and the literature surrounding it in *Aristotle's Revenge*, especially at pp. 158-94 of chapter 3 and in several sections of chapters 4 and 5.

[335] Cf. McDonough, "Not Dead Yet: Teleology and the 'Scientific Revolution,'" pp. 169-76; and A. d'Abro, *The Rise of the New Physics*, Volume I (New York: Dover Publications, 1951), pp. 265-66.

[336] Bertrand Russell at one point in his career argued that modern physics had banished the notion of causation from the scientific picture of the world, though he later changed his mind. Some philosophers have tried to revive his earlier position. See *Aristotle's Revenge*, pp. 124-32 for discussion and criticism of such arguments.

[337] Influential examples include George Molnar, *Powers: A Study in Metaphysics* (Oxford: Oxford University Press, 2003), chapter 3, and U. T. Place, "Dispositions as Intentional States,"

other lines of argument I've been summarizing, this one too calls for more detailed development and defense, but I've provided that elsewhere.[338]

Quantum mechanics

Let us turn to quantum mechanics, because that, I want to argue, poses a further problem for the mechanical philosophy and indeed vindicates hylemorphism. To see how, recall first that hylemorphism takes prime matter on its own to be wholly indeterminate. By itself it is not an actual particular physical thing of any kind, but rather the pure potentiality to be a particular physical thing of some kind. If we think of matter on the analogy of the position of a needle on a dial and the values on the dial as representing the various specific kinds of material thing that might exist, prime matter is like a needle that is flitting wildly all across the face of the dial. It has no intrinsic tendency to stop at any particular value, though potentially it could be made to stop at any of them. Substantial form is what actualizes that potential and makes of otherwise indeterminate prime matter a substance of some determinate kind – a molecule, a rock, a tree, a dog, or what have you.

Now, if prime matter is like the needle flitting wildly across a dial's face, then for hylemorphism a fundamental particle, considered in isolation and apart from any substance it might partially constitute, is like a needle which has narrowed its flitting somewhat to a certain range of possible values. For example, fermions do not have the indeterminacy of prime matter, for they are matter of a certain *kind*, with properties and causal powers distinctive of that kind. However, they do maintain a very high degree of indeterminacy insofar as there is an extremely wide variety of more complex kinds of matter that they

---

in D. M. Armstrong, C. B. Martin, and U.T. Place, *Dispositions: A Debate*, ed. Tim Crane (London: Routledge, 1996). For discussion of the relationship of this recent work to the Aristotelian-Thomistic approach to the subject, see David S. Oderberg, "Finality Revived: Powers and Intentionality," *Synthese* 194 (2017): 2387-2425.

[338] See *Scholastic Metaphysics*, pp. 88-105. A related but distinct consideration is that notions like "computation" and "information," to which physicists sometimes appeal when describing natural processes, are also irreducibly teleological. Cf. pp. 366-74 of *Aristotle's Revenge* and Edward Feser, "From Aristotle to John Searle and Back Again: Formal Causes, Teleology, and Computation in Nature," *Nova et Vetera* 14 (2016): 459-94.

might constitute.[339] They do not flit back and forth past *every* possible value on the dial, but they do still flit past most of them. A fermion qua fermion can be a constituent of water, a stone, a dog, or what have you. Water and stone, by contrast, are like a needle that has settled down to flitting only across a very narrow range of possible values. Water may take a liquid, solid, or gaseous state; stone may be arranged in a pile or used to construct a wall. Compared to a fundamental particle, though, there is relatively little transformation they can undergo consistent with remaining what they are (viz. water or stone). Whereas prime matter is the pure potentiality to be any material thing, fermions have a somewhat narrower range of potentiality, and water a much narrower range.

Now, hylemorphism's treatment of the lower-level material constituents of a thing as a kind of *potentiality* requiring actualization by higher-level features is one of its essential differences with the mechanical philosophy, which treats all the material constituents of a thing as equally actual all the way down. And here quantum mechanics is clearly closer to hylemorphism than to the mechanical philosophy. Indeed, the neo-Aristotelian character of quantum mechanics was recognized by Werner Heisenberg. Echoing the hylemorphic account of the relationship between prime matter and fundamental particles, Heisenberg writes:

> All the elementary particles are made of the same substance, which we may call energy or universal matter; they are just different forms in which matter can appear.
>
> If we compare this situation with the Aristotelian concepts of matter and form, we can say that the matter of Aristotle, which is mere "potentia," should be compared to our concept

---

[339] As Joseph Bobik notes in *Aquinas on Matter and Form and the Elements* (Notre Dame, IN: University of Notre Dame Press, 1998), "many of the particles of today's physics are almost property-less" and thus "as close to prime matter as one can get" without actually getting there (pp. 284-85).

of energy, which gets into "actuality" by means of the form, when the elementary particle is created.[340]

Regarding the "statistical expectations" quantum theory associates with the behavior of an atom, Heisenberg says:

> One might perhaps call it an objective tendency or possibility, a "potentia" in the sense of Aristotelian philosophy. In fact, I believe that the language actually used by physicists when they speak about atomic events produces in their minds similar notions as the concept "potentia." So the physicists have gradually become accustomed to considering the electronic orbits, etc., not as reality but rather as a kind of "potentia."[341]

And again:

> The probability wave of Bohr, Kramers, Slater... was a quantitative version of the old concept of "potentia" in Aristotelian philosophy. It introduced something standing in the middle between the idea of an event and the actual event, a strange kind of physical reality just in the middle between possibility and reality.[342]

To be sure, Heisenberg's way of expressing the point needs tidying up. For one thing, he appears in these passages to *contrast* "potentia" with "reality." But as I have said, for the Aristotelian, potentiality is itself a kind of reality, albeit distinct from the reality that is actuality. Indeed, Heisenberg himself clearly agrees that "potentia" have a kind of reality, for elsewhere he notes that they "are completely objective, [and] do not depend on any observer."[343] Heisenberg's identification of "mere 'potentia'" or pure potentiality with energy also may need qualification. As Stanley Grove has pointed out,

---

[340] Werner Heisenberg, *Physics and Philosophy* (New York: HarperCollins, 2007), p. 134.

[341] Ibid., pp. 154-5.

[342] Ibid., p. 15.

[343] Ibid., p. 27.

energy is *quantifiable*, whereas prime matter, being wholly indeterminate, is not – in which case, energy would be a kind of secondary matter that is "at least one structural level above that of prime matter."[344] On the other hand, David Oderberg suggests that it is arguably not energy *as such* that is quantifiable, but only energy *qua* measured as a constituent of objects, processes, systems, etc.[345] If we think of energy as having "no determinate form in itself," then in Oderberg's view one *might* be able to argue that it is identical to prime matter.[346] Indeed, it shares other characteristics with prime matter, such as being conserved through changes and not existing in concrete objects apart from form (though Oderberg judges the arguments for identifying prime matter with energy to be less than conclusive even if strong).[347]

Robert Koons identifies several further respects in which quantum mechanics might be said to support an Aristotelian conception of matter (yielding a synthesis Koons labels "quantum hylomorphism").[348] First of all, the Copenhagen interpretation treats microphysical phenomena, and in particular the position and momentum of a particle, as merely potential apart from interaction with macro-level systems (such as observers who measure the micro-level phenomena). Hence, like hylemorphism, the Copenhagen interpretation implies that the microphysical level is not metaphysically more fundamental than macro-level objects, nor sufficient by itself to

---

[344] Stanley F. Grove, *Quantum Theory and Aquinas's Doctrine on Matter*, Ph. D. dissertation, Catholic University of America, 2008, pp. 282-83.

[345] David S. Oderberg, "Is Prime Matter Energy?" *Australasian Journal of Philosophy* (2022).

[346] Oderberg, *Real Essentialism*, p. 76.

[347] See Oderberg, "Is Prime Matter Energy?" for a detailed analysis of the arguments for and against the identification.

[348] Robert C. Koons, "Hylomorphic Escalation: An Aristotelian Interpretation of Quantum Thermodynamics and Chemistry," *American Catholic Philosophical Quarterly* 92 (2018):159-78; and "Knowing Nature: Aristotle, God, and the Quantum," in Andrew B. Torrance and Thomas H. McCall, eds., *Knowing Creation: Perspectives from Theology, Philosophy, and Science, Volume 1* (Grand Rapids: Zondervan, 2018).

ground all facts about the macro-level. Rather, the micro- and macro-levels are mutually interdependent, just as the Aristotelian claims.

Second, there is the holism implied by quantum entanglement phenomena. The properties of a system of entangled particles are irreducible to the properties of the particles considered individually or their spatial relations and relative velocity. The whole is more than the sum of its parts, as it is on the hylemorphic account of physical substances. Third, quantum statistics treats elementary particles of the same kind as indiscernible and essentially *fused* within a larger system, thereby losing their individuality and "merging into a kind of quantum goo or gunk."[349] As philosopher of physics Dean Rickles puts it, in quantum mechanics, such particles "are really excitations of one and the same basic underlying field" and best thought of "as 'dollars in a checking account' rather than 'coins in a piggy bank': they can be *aggregated* but not counted and distinguished."[350] This echoes the Aristotelian position that parts exist in a substance virtually or potentially rather than actually.

Grove proposes that the wave-particle duality famous from quantum interference phenomena reflects precisely the greater indeterminacy that matter exhibits the closer it is to the level of prime matter.[351] A photon can readily flit back and forth between wave-like and particle-like manifestations in a way that a cow cannot readily flit back and forth between cow-like and hamburger-like manifestations, because particles, being closer to prime matter, are (to use my analogy from earlier) like the needle on a dial flitting across a wide range of possible values. By contrast, a cow is far from the level of prime matter insofar as there are several intermediate levels of kinds of physical substance between it and prime matter (e.g. purely vegetative substances, middle-sized inorganic substances, particles of greater or lesser complexity). A cow is like a needle that flits only across a very

---

[349] Koons, "Hylomorphic Escalation," p. 163.

[350] Dean Rickles, *The Philosophy of Physics* (Cambridge: Polity Press, 2016), pp. 161-3.

[351] Grove, *Quantum Theory*, pp. 252-59.

narrow range of possible values on the dial. As Grove notes, the probabilistic nature of quantum events also reflects proximity to the level of prime matter.[352] Again, the closer a substance is to the level of prime matter, the greater its indeterminacy (its tendency to flit across the dial, as it were), and thus the greater its unpredictability.

Grove also points out that the abrupt or discontinuous changes described by quantum physics (such as an atom gaining an electron, or an electron being boosted to a higher energy level within an atom) are reminiscent of hylemorphic substantial change, which is also abrupt or discontinuous.[353] The gain or loss of a substantial form is all or nothing, unlike the gain or loss of an accidental form, which can be continuous. Now, the mechanical philosophy, as I have indicated, essentially reduces changes that the Aristotelian regards as substantial to accidental changes, and thus interprets what the Aristotelian would take to be discontinuous transitions as in fact continuous ones. Insofar as quantum physics affirms abrupt or discontinuous transitions, it confirms an Aristotelian rather than mechanical philosophy understanding of matter, at least in a very general way.

Heisenberg's famous uncertainty principle is also, in Grove's view, something that should not be surprising on a hylemorphic conception of matter.[354] A particle's momentum implies a potentiality toward a range of possible positions, and its position implies a potentiality toward a range of possible momenta. But since momentum and position yield only potentialities rather than actualities, we should expect that knowledge of the one will yield less than certainty vis-à-vis the other.

Summing up the implications of the results of contemporary physics for the dispute between the mechanical philosophy and Aristotle, philosopher of science Patrick Suppes wrote:

---

[352] Ibid., pp. 263-66.

[353] Ibid., pp. 259-63.

[354] Ibid., pp. 266-72.

The empirical evidence from macroscopic bodies and also from high energy particles is that the forms of matter continually change. There is no reason to think that there is a spatial buildup of electrons, for example, from some more elementary objects. The collisions of electrons and other particles to produce new particles as observed, for example, in cloud-chamber and other experiments is simply good Aristotelian evidence of the change of form of matter. The cloud-chamber data especially support Aristotle's definition of matter. As we observe change there must be a substratum underlying that which is changing. What is the substratum underlying the conversion of particles into other particles, or the conversion of particles into energy? The answer seems to me clear. We can adopt an Aristotelian theory of matter as pure potentiality. The search for elementary particles that are simple and homogeneous and that are the building blocks in some spatial sense of the remaining elements of the universe is a mistake.[355]

N. R. Hanson, another prominent twentieth-century philosopher of science, suggested that the surprising properties quantum theory attributes to particles entail a "dematerialization of matter."[356] But that is because he, like other contemporary philosophers and scientists, is operating with the conception of matter inherited from the mechanical philosophy, which removed from matter the potentiality that Aristotle took to be its very nature. By putting potentiality back into matter, quantum physics, from an Aristotelian point of view, is in fact *re*materializing rather than *de*materializing it.

Corporeality

The mathematization of matter, as I have said, is one of the hallmarks of the mechanical philosophy. Descartes famously took this in the direction of a *geometrization* of matter, specifically. Matter, he held, is

---

[355] Suppes, "Aristotle's Concept of Matter and Its Relation to Modern Concepts of Matter," pp. 46-47.

[356] N. R. Hanson, "The Dematerialization of Matter," in Ernan McMullin, ed., *The Concept of Matter* (Notre Dame, IN: University of Notre Dame Press, 1963).

nothing more than *extension*, viz. the property by which something is located in space, has one or more dimensions, and possesses adjacent parts. Now, what has been said already shows that this cannot be *all* there is to matter. Matter, as I have argued, cannot properly be understood except in terms of *potentiality*, along with the *ends* or *final causes* toward which potentialities are directed. These features cannot be captured in a purely geometrical description of matter. Furthermore, a purely geometrical description by itself captures only abstract patterns, and there must be in matter some additional, concrete reality in which the abstract patterns are instantiated.

There are additional reasons why extension cannot be all there is to matter.[357] A material object can change its geometrical characteristics (as when a plant or animal increases or decreases in size), and yet remain numerically the same object. Hence there must be more to it than these characteristics. Material objects can share the same nature despite differing in their geometrical features, as when two dogs differ in size despite both being dogs. There must then be more to being a material object of a certain kind (such as a dog) than merely having geometrical features.

All the same, though material substances are *more than* mere extension, they are not *less than* that. Descartes was wrong to suppose that extension exhausts the nature of matter, but he was correct in thinking that all material substances are extended.[358] More precisely, while extension is not the essence of matter, it is what Aristotelian-Thomistic philosophers call a *proper accident* or *property* of matter. A proper accident or property is a characteristic that naturally flows or follows from a thing's essence. For example, the capacity to use language is not our essence as rational animals, but it does flow or follow

---

[357] Cf. Henry J. Koren, *An Introduction to the Philosophy of Nature* (Pittsburgh, PA: Duquesne University Press, 1962), pp. 80-81.

[358] Ibid., pp. 85-86. Cf. James A. McWilliams, *Cosmology*, Second revised edition ((New York: Macmillan, 1950), chapter IX; Vincent Edward Smith, *Philosophical Physics* (New York: Harper and Brothers, 1950), chapter 12; and P. Henry van Laer, *Philosophico-Scientific Problems* (Pittsburgh, PA: Duquesne University Press, 1953), pp. 23-26.

from that essence.³⁵⁹ Similarly, while extension is not the essence of matter, it does flow or follow from its essence.³⁶⁰ Indeed, extension is what Aristotelian-Thomistic philosophers traditionally regard as the "first" or most fundamental of matter's properties.³⁶¹

Here is one way to see why.³⁶² In the case of observable physical objects, we know precisely *from* observation that they are extended, and any extended object is divisible in principle into smaller parts. Now, if these smaller parts were non-extended or dimensionless, they could never add up to something extended.³⁶³ Hence the parts have to be extended as well (and even if *per impossibile* they were dimensionless points, they would still have other features characteristic of extension, such as being located in space and adjacent to one another). In this way, extension is characteristic of material things "all the way down," as it were, not just of the material things that we can observe. (To be sure, *prime* matter is not extended, but that is because, *qua* pure *potentiality* to take on substantial form, it is not itself an actual, concrete material *thing* in the first place. Rather it is, together with substantial form, one of the two main *constituents* of any actual, concrete material thing.)

Moreover, the other features of matter presuppose extension. For example, a material thing can have color only insofar as it has a colored *surface*, and any surface is extended. A material thing is said

---

³⁵⁹ Here I am using "property" in the technical Aristotelian-Thomistic sense, which differs from the sense in which other philosophers use the term. Cf. *Scholastic Metaphysics*, pp. 191-92 and 230-35.

³⁶⁰ One Aristotelian-Thomistic philosopher argues that, strictly speaking, it is "not actual extension, but the aptitude for it" that is a proper accident of matter (McWilliams, *Cosmology*, p. 91), where an immaterial substance would lack even the aptitude. For present purposes we can put this qualification to one side.

³⁶¹ A common formulation is that "quantity is the first accident" of material things, but I have avoided it so as to avoid confusion. "Quantity" is in this context being used as a synonym for extension, but not all readers will understand it that way, and the technical Scholastic tern "accident" is even more likely to be misunderstood.

³⁶² Cf. Smith, *Philosophical Physics*, pp. 412-34.

³⁶³ Cf. Feser, *Aristotle's Revenge*, pp. 204-8.

to be impenetrable only insofar as it occupies some extended area which cannot at the same time be occupied by another material thing. And so on. Now, observable objects and their parts are our paradigms for what counts as "material." Hence, given that any observable object must be extended (and wouldn't be observable otherwise) and any concrete part of a material object must also be extended, we have our conclusion that matter in general is extended.[364]

The discussion of this chapter yields the following general characterization of material substance (also called "physical substance" or "corporeal substance"). Any material substance is a composite of substantial form and prime matter. A mark of its having a substantial form (and thus being a true *substance*, as opposed to an aggregate or artifact) is the possession of properties and causal powers which are irreducible to the sum of the properties and powers of its parts. Any such substance will, whatever other properties it has, have the property of extension. It will also have distinctive teleological properties insofar as its causal powers will aim or direct it toward the bringing about of certain distinctive effects, given the appropriate triggering circumstances. A material substance of a certain kind is *generated*, or comes into being, when prime matter takes on the substantial form definitive of that kind (where the resulting object's having the properties and powers distinctive of that kind is an indicator that this has occurred). A material substance of a certain kind is *corrupted*, or goes out of existence, when prime matter loses the substantial form definitive of that kind (as is evidenced by the disappearance of the powers and properties distinctive of that kind).

Accordingly, an *incorporeal* or *immaterial* substance would be a substance that lacked any material substrate and any extension. Whether there are substances of this kind, and what they would be like, are questions to which we will return in later chapters. But for

---

[364] Quantity is also, on the traditional Thomistic view, essential to understanding how matter individuates different members of the same species. (Cf. Feser, *Scholastic Metaphysics*, pp. 198-201.) We'll have reason to return to this point in a later chapter.

the moment, having now given an account of what corporeal substance in general is like, we need to consider the nature of *living* corporeal substances in particular.

6. Animality

What is a living thing?

Human beings, the Aristotelian-Thomistic tradition argues (and I am going to argue) are by nature *rational animals*. Naturally, properly to understand what this entails, we need to understand what it is to be rational and what it is to be an animal. I addressed the first of these attributes in chapters 1 through 4. Here I address the second. Now, an animal is a kind of material substance, and I explained in chapter 5 what that involves. More specifically, an animal is a kind of *living* material substance. So, let us begin our consideration of animality with a discussion of what it is for a thing to be alive.

A living thing, according to the traditional Aristotelian view, is a self-moving thing. But given the ambiguity of the term "moving," what this amounts to is better expressed by the Scholastic language of *immanent causation*.[365] A causal process is immanent when it originates within the agent and terminates within it in a way that tends toward the agent's own self-perfection or completion. This is to be contrasted with *transeunt* (or *transient*) *causation*, which terminates outside the

---

[365] Useful expositions of the Aristotelian-Thomistic understanding of the nature of living things can be found in George P. Klubertanz, *The Philosophy of Human Nature* (New York: Appleton-Century-Crofts, Inc., 1953), pp. 47-50; chapter 1 of Henry J. Koren, *An Introduction to the Philosophy of Animate Nature* (St. Louis: B. Herder, 1955); chapter 2 of H. D. Gardeil, *Introduction to the Philosophy of St. Thomas Aquinas, Volume III: Psychology* (St. Louis: B. Herder, 1956); and J. F. Donceel, *Philosophical Psychology*, Second edition (New York: Sheed and Ward, 1961), pp. 26-28. For recent defense, see David S. Oderberg's *Real Essentialism* (London: Routledge, 2007), pp. 177-83, and "Synthetic Life and the Bruteness of Immanent Causation," in Edward Feser, ed., *Aristotle on Method and Metaphysics* (Basingstoke: Palgrave Macmillan, 2013). For a historical study of how the Aristotelian conception of living things had developed in the era just before early modern philosophers began to move away from it, see Dennis Des Chene, *Life's Form: Late Aristotelian Conceptions of the Soul* (Ithaca: Cornell University Press, 2000).

agent. A snake's digestion of the mouse it has eaten would be an example of an immanent causal process. Digestion begins when the meal is eaten and ends when its nutrients have all been absorbed into the bloodstream, and the result of the process is that the animal is enabled to survive, grow, and reproduce. A boulder's rolling down a hill during an earthquake and bumping into another boulder, which in turn bumps into a third, would be an example of a transeunt causal process. The source of the boulders' motion is entirely outside them, and does not terminate in anything like completion or self-perfection in any of them.

Living things no less than non-living things exhibit transeunt causation. Like a boulder, an animal might roll down a hill and bump into another animal. An immanent causal process might also have transeunt effects as a byproduct, such as the waste that an animal defecates after digesting a meal, which might contribute to polluting a nearby body of water. But living things are living because they alone exhibit immanent *as well as* transeunt causation. It is in this sense that they are self-movers. They move or change themselves in the sense that they carry out activities that contribute to their own completion or perfection.

As the talk of completion and self-perfection indicates, immanent causation is *teleological*. Digestion results in the nourishment of *the snake*, not of the mouse and not of some hybrid of snake and mouse.[366] Indeed, the mouse has altogether disappeared by the end of the process, whereas the snake continues. Hence the process *points* or *aims toward* the realization of the ends of the snake, specifically. Now, it might seem that non-living things exhibit a similar kind of teleology. For example, we say that a coffee machine can turn itself on in the morning, that a computer can run a self-diagnostic routine, and so on. But these are examples of artifacts, which (as I explained in the previous chapter) have merely accidental forms and derivative teleology. Living things, by contrast, are true substances, with substantial forms and intrinsic teleology. The parts of a coffee machine or computer have no *built in* tendency to pursue the ends distinctive of those kinds of devices. They have to be made to do so by human designers.

---

[366] Cf. Robert Pasnau and Christopher Shields, *The Philosophy of Aquinas* (Boulder, CO: Westview Press, 2004), p. 34.

A snake *does* have a built in tendency to pursue ends such as digestion. Machines seem life-like only if we ignore this crucial distinction between substantial and accidental form.

It is important to add at once, however, that it is not intrinsic teleology *per se* that is definitive of immanent causation or of life. Recall that, for the Aristotelian, there is teleology wherever there is even the simplest inorganic causal regularity. The sulfur in the head of a match *aims* or *points toward* the outcome of generating flame and heat; the brittleness of a glass *aims* or *points toward* a manifestation such as shattering; and so forth. These are examples of transeunt causation despite their teleological character, because they do not involve anything like the *perfection* or *completion* of an agent in the way that digestion involves the perfection or completion of the snake. It is directedness toward that particular *sort* of end – again, the perfection or completion of the causal agent itself – that is definitive of immanent causation and thus definitive of life.

These examples of inorganic teleology also show that it is not a good objection to the Aristotelian account of life to allege that, precisely *because* that account is teleological, it does not sit well with modern physics' non-teleological conception of nature. For one thing, as I emphasized in the previous chapter, the absence of some feature from physics' *representation* of nature simply does not entail that that feature is absent from nature *itself*. That physics eschews teleological explanation merely reflects its mathematically oriented methodology, and by itself has no metaphysical implications. For another thing (and as I also noted in the previous chapter), there are powerful arguments for attributing teleological features to nature in general and not just to living things, arguments which I have defended elsewhere.[367] Of course, the critic of Aristotelianism will reject these arguments, but the point is that it is no good to reject the Aristotelian account of life *merely* on the grounds that it is teleological, since the Aristotelian has independent arguments which purport to show that we need to affirm teleology anyway, whatever we say about the nature of life.

---

[367] Edward Feser, *Scholastic Metaphysics: A Contemporary Introduction* (Heusenstamm: Editiones Scholasticae, 2014), pp. 88-105.

Another possible objection would be that we don't need the Aristotelian account of life, because there are better alternatives available. Mark Bedau suggests that there are four main accounts of the nature of life in play in contemporary biology and philosophy.[368] The first is the view that to be alive is to have a metabolism. The second holds that life is to be defined in terms of a longer list of characteristics, which may include metabolism but must refer to other characteristics as well – for example, reproduction, purposeful behavior, the possession of parts with functions, and/or capacity for evolution. The third holds that there is no one characteristic or set of characteristics that all and only living things have in common, but at best a "family resemblance" between living things. On this view, any living thing will have *some* of the characteristics found on lists like the ones adherents of the second view would draw up, but there won't be a common core that every single living thing possesses. The fourth view, which is the one Bedau favors, holds that life is to be defined in terms of "supple adaptation" to changes in the environment, of the kind seen in evolution.

One problem with appealing to such accounts in criticizing the Aristotelian view is that these alternatives are all themselves problematic. As Bedau notes, one problem with accounts like the second and third is that they raise the question *why* the characteristics they cite tend to be clustered together in living things. Whatever the answer to that question is would seem to be a more plausible candidate for revealing the nature of life than the cluster of characteristics themselves is. A problem with the appeal to metabolism, Bedau notes, is that there are, arguably, metabolizing entities that are not living, such as a candle flame. One problem with the "supple adaptation" appealed to by Bedau is that it seems to apply not only to living things, but also to cultures and economic markets, which adapt to their environments but would not ordinarily be regarded as alive. Bedau seems willing to bite the bullet and regard these things as alive, but as Mar-

---

[368] Mark A. Bedau, "The Nature of Life," in Margaret A. Boden, ed., *The Philosophy of Artificial Life* (Oxford: Oxford University Press, 1996).

garet Boden points out, even if we were to go along with this implausible proposal, there are other problems.[369] First, Bedau's account implies that it is *populations* of organisms that are alive in the most fundamental sense – since they are what adapt in the relevant respect – with individual organisms alive only in a secondary sense. But this gets things the wrong way around. Second, his account would seem to imply, implausibly, that a population that ceased evolving would no longer count as living. Third, and equally implausibly, it seems to imply that an organism or population that arose in a way other than evolution (such as direct creation by God) would not count as living.[370]

But as David Oderberg points out, another and deeper problem with these accounts of the nature of life is that on analysis they tend to *presuppose* rather than replace immanent causation.[371] For example, metabolism "is probably the paradigmatic example of immanence: the organism takes in matter/energy, uses it for its sustenance, growth, and development, and expels what is noxious or surplus."[372] Moreover, understanding metabolism in terms of immanent causation explains why fire doesn't count as metabolizing and thus is not alive. For unlike agents engaged in immanent causation, fire is not a *substance*, but merely a modification of a substance or substances. Meanwhile, the "supple adaptation" to its environment of a population of organisms presupposes various kinds of activity in the individual organisms that make up the population, and this activity will involve immanent causation (metabolism, growth, etc.). A characteristic like reproduction also involves immanent causation insofar as it is an active process internal to the organism that is an ordinary function of mature or perfected members of its kind. This differentiates it from processes that might superficially appear similar to reproduction – such as the splitting of a rock, which is something that *happens to* the rock rather than an activity it carries out, which occurs due to causes

---

[369] See Boden's "Introduction" to *The Philosophy of Artificial Life*, pp. 23-24.
[370] Cf. John Dupré, *The Metaphysics of Biology* (Cambridge: Cambridge University Press, 2021), p. 61.

[371] Oderberg, "Synthetic Life and the Bruteness of Immanent Causation," pp. 214-16.

[372] Ibid., p. 214.

entirely *external* to it, and which *damages* or *diminishes* rather than perfects or completes the rock.[373]

The point is best understood by recalling the Aristotelian distinction (introduced in the previous chapter) between the *essence* of a thing and the *properties* or *proper accidents* that flow or follow from that essence. To take a stock example, the essence of a human being is to be a rational animal (if, for the sake of argument, the reader will go along with the traditional Aristotelian definition) and the capacity for humor is a property that flows from this essence. The capacity for humor is not itself part of the essence, but is rather a byproduct of it, a consequence of rationality. The manifestation of a property can be blocked, which is why some people can appear virtually humorless.

Now, the trouble with the alternative accounts of the nature of life under consideration is that they all focus on what are really at best *properties* of life rather than the *essence* of life.[374] By contrast, the Aristotelian account of life in terms of immanent causation captures precisely the essence of which the other characteristics are properties. This is, the Aristotelian proposes, the right way to understand Bedau's insight that to define the essence of life in terms of either a necessary and sufficient cluster of characteristics or a looser "family resemblance" cluster only raises the problem of explaining why the characteristics in question tend to be found together in living things. The Aristotelian answer is that the items on the right list of characteristics (whatever that turns out to be) are not parts of the essence of life but rather properties that flow from the essence, which is immanent causation. And it is because the manifestation of a property can be frustrated that some items on these proposed lists don't always appear in every single organism, even if they appear in most of them. For example, the reason some individual organisms and species of organism do not reproduce is not because reproduction is not a true property of living things, but rather because in some living things the

---

[373] Oderberg, *Real Essentialism*, pp. 179-80.

[374] Ibid., pp. 177-78.

manifestation of this property has been blocked (e.g. by chromosomal abnormalities).[375]

What should we say of borderline cases, such as viruses? Oderberg argues, quite plausibly, that viruses lack immanent causal activity and thus are not truly alive.[376] They do not take in or process nutrients, as truly metabolizing entities do; they do not grow; and even their capacity to replicate is arguably not true reproduction, insofar as it does not involve an active internal process:

> Virus replication, to [speak] metaphorically, is more like a genetic version of photocopying than genuine biological reproduction. The paper does not put itself into the copier – outside forces do that. And it is not the paper that expends energy in being copied – it is the copier that expends the energy.[377]

But whether viruses are alive is, of course, a matter of controversy. Whatever the right answer, the Aristotelian does not claim that the matter can be settled from the armchair. What he does claim is that the *way* empirical considerations can settle the matter is by telling us whether or not viruses exhibit immanent causation.

Are living substances as the Aristotelian conceives of them *reducible* to non-living ones? The answer, naturally, hinges on whether immanent causation is reducible to transeunt causation. The answer to *that* question is that it is not reducible.[378] The first problem for the reductionist here is an "apples and oranges" problem. Immanent and transeunt causation are simply different in kind, and not merely in degree. The difference between causal activity that perfects the agent and causal activity that does not is like the difference between a circle and a polygon. You can add as many sides to a polygon as you like,

---

[375] Ibid., pp. 178-79.

[376] Ibid., pp. 191-92.

[377] Ibid., p. 284, note 20.
[378] Cf. Koren, *Introduction to the Philosophy of Animate Nature*, pp. 18-19; Oderberg, *Real Essentialism*, pp. 193-200; and Oderberg, "Synthetic Life and the Bruteness of Immanent Causation," pp. 216-23.

and you will never get a circle. Of course, you might get something that *looks like* a circle to sense organs that are incapable of making sufficiently fine discriminations, but that is not the same as getting an actual circle. Similarly, you can add to a transeunt causal process all the further transeunt causal processes you like, but you will never get immanent causation out of it. The most you will get is something that might *look like* immanent causation, just as a polygon with sufficiently many sides might look like a circle. That is precisely what we have in the case of computers, robots, and other complex machines that might appear superficially to be alive. As I have already said, in fact these are not truly alive, because they are artifacts with mere accidental forms rather than genuine substances with substantial forms, and a living thing is a kind of substance. Naturally, the critic of Aristotelianism would reject the distinction between substantial and accidental forms, but *merely* to reject it as a way of rebutting the argument I'm developing here would be to beg the question.

A further consideration is that, as I emphasized in the previous chapter, any attempted reductionist account of an entity is going to fail whenever it has properties and causal powers that are unanalyzable in terms of the sum of the properties and causal powers of its parts. But we clearly do have that in the case of living things. For example, the self-perfecting or self-completing nature of an immanent activity like a snake's digestion of a mouse cannot be captured except by reference to the snake considered as a whole. It is true that the parts of the snake – eyes, skin, and so on – are also thereby nourished, but since these parts themselves exist only for the sake of the whole, that they are nourished is not the primary end of the immanent activity, but a secondary end, subordinate to the end of nourishing the snake.

To forestall some irrelevant objections, note that nothing that has been said has anything at all to do with vitalism or any other commitment to some non-physical principle. On the contrary, for the Aristotelian, most kinds of living things – plants and non-human animals, for example – are entirely physical or corporeal. To say that living things are irreducible is not to hold that they are non-physical, but entails merely that there are irreducibly different kinds of physical things. If someone points out to you that circles are irreducible to polygons, it would be quite ridiculous to accuse him of holding that circles must possess some mysterious non-physical principle that makes them different from polygons, or that circles are not geometrical figures the way polygons are. It is equally silly to accuse someone who argues that living things are irreducible to non-living things of being committed thereby to the existence of *élan vital* or otherwise denying that they are entirely physical.

Note also that the irreducibility of immanent causation to transeunt causation has nothing at all to do with complexity. An extremely simple thing will exhibit immanent causation and therefore life as long as its activity is self-perfective. A thing will fail to be alive as long as it exhibits only transeunt causation, no matter how many and how complex are the chains of transeunt causation to be found within it. The difference between a circle and a polygon has nothing to do with the former having greater complexity; indeed, there is an obvious sense in which it is simpler. Similarly, the difference between immanent and transeunt causation, and thus between living and non-living things, has nothing essentially to do with complexity.

For that reason, nothing in what has been said hinges on what one thinks of "design arguments" for God's existence of the kind associated with William Paley and contemporary "Intelligent Design" theorists. If someone pointed out to you that circles differ in kind from polygons, it would be absurd to accuse him of insinuating thereby that circles must have been specially created by a divine designer. It is similarly absurd to accuse someone who regards immanent causation as irreducible to transeunt causation as insinuating thereby that living things are too complex to have arisen except by intelligent design. Whether circles are a kind of polygon, and where circles come from, are entirely separate questions. Whether immanent causation is reducible to transeunt causation, and where entities exhibiting immanent causation come from, are also entirely separate questions.[379]

Now, a critic might give up reductionism without embracing the Aristotelian position. He might opt instead for eliminativism.

---

[379] For further discussion of the important differences between "Intelligent Design" theory and the Aristotelian-Thomistic position I am defending here, see Edward Feser, *Aristotle's Revenge: The Metaphysical Foundations of Physical and Biological Science* (Neunkirchen-Seelscheid: Editiones Scholasticae, 2019), pp. 432-42.

That is to say, he might concede both that immanent causation is definitive of life and that immanent causation is irreducible to transeunt causation, but then deny that there really is any such thing as immanent causation. He will thereby be committed to denying that there is any such thing as *life*, but he may be willing to bite that bullet. He may say that, *strictly* speaking, there really are no living things, but only things that *seem* to be alive.[380] This would be analogous to admitting that circles are irreducible to polygons but at the same time insisting that only polygons actually exist and that what we think are circles are really all just polygons that have so many sides that they seem to be circles.

But this cannot be right. Note first of all that the consistent eliminativist will have to deny that *he is himself* alive. More to the point, he will have to deny that he himself really carries out any immanent causal activity. But that is manifestly false, for thinking – including thinking about the nature of life, eliminativism, and so on – is itself an immanent causal activity. Gathering evidence, reasoning through the steps of an argument, and so forth all have as their end the perfection of the thinker as a rational creature. The thinker goes from ignorance to knowledge, is thereby perfected qua thinker, and this outcome remains the same whether or not it goes on to have any transeunt causal byproducts, such as the relating of his knowledge to other people. Thus, the eliminativist has to carry out immanent causal activity in the very act of denying that there is such a thing as immanent causal activity. His position is simply incoherent. To get around

---

[380] Cf. Ferris Jabr, "Why Nothing is Truly Alive," *The New York Times* (March 12, 2014). Descartes's conception of material things (including animals and human bodies) as pure extension entails an eliminativist position, certainly given the Aristotelian understanding of the nature of life. As Dennis Des Chene writes in *Spirits and Clocks: Machine and Organism in Descartes* (Ithaca: Cornell University Press, 2001): "In Cartesianism there are two separate domains, joined only by way of the union of the human soul and its body. In neither do you find living things in the Aristotelian sense. The body-machine does not live, since it has no powers, but only passive qualities derived from the modes of extension; nor does the soul, since it has no part in nutrition, growth, or generation" (p. 3). To be sure, that last remark isn't quite right. The human soul as Descartes conceives of it, even given that it is a *res cogitans* or thinking substance divorced from any corporeal features, would still count as living from an Aristotelian point of view. For it still thinks, and thinking is an immanent or self-perfective activity. All the same, as Des Chene goes on to write, for Descartes "the living world, *humans aside*, has no property, and includes no entity, that would distinguish it from the nonliving" (pp. 3-4, emphasis added).

this problem, the eliminativist might of course decide to deny the existence of himself or of his thoughts just as he denies the existence of life, but I already argued in earlier chapters that these positions are incoherent too.

Notice that I am *not* giving a simplistic argument to the effect the eliminativist breathes, moves his arms and legs, and does other things that common sense regards as the hallmarks of living things. Obviously the eliminativist would respond that he regards these activities as differing only in degree and not in kind from the activities that machines and other non-living things carry out, so that this commonsense retort begs the question. I am appealing, not to untutored common sense, but rather to the notion of immanent causation; and I am saying that, whatever one wants to say about breathing, moving one's limbs, and the like, *thinking* is an activity that cannot coherently be analyzed in terms of transeunt causation alone. So, there is no way to be a *consistent, across-the-board* eliminativist. The would-be eliminativist will have to admit that he and other rational creatures are alive, at least qua thinking substances (where the relation of our bodily attributes to thought is another question, to be addressed in later chapters).

Even given that the organic cannot be either eliminated altogether from our picture of the natural world or reduced to the inorganic, reductionists and eliminativists might still try to press one further line of argument. They might hold that the living things most familiar to us – the flowers and trees, birds and fish, dogs and cats of everyday experience – are still reducible to some primitive level of organic phenomena even if the latter cannot be either reduced or eliminated themselves. To be sure, as John Dupré notes, "in recent years, philosophers of biology have tended strongly towards the rejection of reductionism."[381] However, there has also been a renewed interest among philosophers of biology in the idea that biological explanation is a matter of identifying the "mechanisms" by which organisms carry

---

[381] Dupré, *The Metaphysics of Biology*, p. 4.

out their activities.³⁸² A mechanism in the sense in question is a structure which fulfills a certain function by virtue of the operation of component parts which are organized in a certain way. Now, it is important to note that this basic idea does not by itself entail a conception of living things of the kind associated with the "mechanical philosophy" criticized in the previous chapter. Aristotelian-Thomistic philosophers do not for a moment deny that there are biological "mechanisms" in the sense in question. What they find objectionable in the mechanical philosophy is rather its rejection of substantial forms and intrinsic teleology. Nevertheless, the reductionist philosopher of biology Alex Rosenberg suggests that the renewed emphasis on the search for mechanisms in contemporary philosophy "is very close to reductionism, perhaps even being an old wine in a newer bottle."³⁸³ He thinks that, by analyzing organisms into mechanisms and those mechanisms into yet more basic mechanisms, it is possible to reduce all biological phenomena to the kinds and causal powers described at the level of molecular biology.³⁸⁴

Rosenberg acknowledges, though, that the identification of mechanisms can vindicate reductionism only if it can avoid positing "downward causation."³⁸⁵ More precisely, it will have to explain higher-level features of organisms in terms of lower-level mecha-

---

[382] For surveys of the recent literature, see section 4 of Alex Rosenberg, *Reduction and Mechanism* (Cambridge: Cambridge University Press, 2020), and Daniel D. De Haan, "Hylomorphism and the New Mechanist Philosophy in Biology, Neuroscience, and Psychology," in William M. R. Simpson, Robert C. Koons, and Nicholas J. Teh, eds., *Neo-Aristotelian Perspectives on Contemporary Science* (London: Routledge, 2018). Carl Craver, whose work we had reason briefly to consider in chapter 4, is one prominent proponent of this new "mechanism."

[383] Rosenberg, *Reduction and Mechanism*, p. 57.

[384] Cf. Alex Rosenberg, *Darwinian Reductionism, Or, How to Stop Worrying and Love Molecular Biology* (Chicago: University of Chicago Press, 2006). Indeed, Rosenberg is an even more radical reductionist, who holds that the biological can indeed be reduced to the kinds described by physics. But the point for present purposes is that a less extreme reductionist could disagree with him about that and still hold that higher-level biological phenomena can be reduced to lower-level biological phenomena.

[385] Rosenberg, *Reduction and Mechanism*, pp. 60-61.

nisms, without also having in any way to explain lower-level mechanisms in terms of higher-level features. As Dupré notes, however, the identification of biological mechanisms does *not* in fact satisfy this reductionist demand.[386] Consider, for example, the explanation of an organism's ability to move itself around. It will, of course, make reference to mechanisms such as those comprising muscles, bones, motor neurons, and the like. But we cannot understand the natures of these organs except by reference to the whole organism of which they are parts, and indeed the organs cannot function or even survive apart from their integration into the larger organism.

Dupré also notes additional problems facing a reductionist reading of the biologist's search for mechanisms, and in particular facing the idea that an organism can be reduced to the sum of the functional parts that compose it just as a machine (such as an apple peeler, to borrow Dupré's example) can be reduced to the sum of the functional parts that compose *it*.[387] For one thing, a machine and its parts can sit inactive indefinitely without losing its basic character, as does an apple peeler that lays in a drawer unused. By contrast, an organ (such as the heart) in the normal case persists only insofar as it is continuously functioning as part of the larger organism. For another thing, organisms always operate not only by virtue of what is going on at the level of the mechanisms that compose them, but also by virtue of interactions with the surrounding environment, such as the taking in of food and oxygen. "Reductionism," says Dupré, "can only apply fully to closed systems, but there are no closed systems, at least in biology."[388] At the same time, the *stability* of a machine's operation depends on outside forces (such as a person's skillful use of the apple peeler) whereas an organism's stability derives from within, as with the "regeneration and self-repair of parts."[389]

---

[386] Dupré, *The Metaphysics of Biology*, pp. 10-11.

[387] Ibid., pp. 11-13.

[388] Ibid., p. 11.

[389] Ibid., p. 68.

Now, from an Aristotelian-Thomistic point of view, these distinctive features of organisms identified by Dupré reflect the fact that they have substantial forms by virtue of which they exhibit immanent causation. That is to say, the mechanisms identified by biologists are parts *of a substance* existing and operating *for the sake of the perfecting of* that substance. Dupré, though opposed to reductionism, nevertheless resists such a conclusion. He holds that an organism is a kind of "process" rather than a substance. In defense of this claim, he develops the following points.[390] First, a substance, he says, is supposed to persist through time by virtue of the persistence of certain essential properties. But there are, he claims, no such persisting properties, and an organism persists instead by virtue of "causal links between [its] temporal stages."[391] Second, the default condition of a substance, he says, is stasis, whereas organisms, like processes, involve constant change. Third, a substance is supposed to have a kind of independent existence, but organisms are highly dependent on their environments. Fourth, a substance has definite boundaries, but there are cases in the biological realm (for example, symbiosis in lichens) where the boundaries of an organism are not clear.

To see what is wrong with these arguments, recall first what was said in chapter 2 about attempts to analyze a person as an aggregate of person-stages related by cause and effect. The problem, we saw, is that there is no way to identify and individuate person-stages or the relevant causal relations between them except by reference to the person as a whole. But exactly the same problem afflicts Dupré's attempt to analyze an organism as a "process" consisting of temporal stages related by cause and effect. There is no way to identify and individuate these temporal stages or the relevant causal relations except by reference to the organism as a whole. We can no more coherently deny that an organism is a substance than we can deny that the self is a substance.

---

[390] Ibid., p. 47.

[391] Ibid. Cf. also p. 45.

Each of Dupré's other points is either a *non sequitur* or rests on a false supposition about the nature of substance, at least as Aristotelian-Thomistic philosophers understand substance. Recall the distinction between a thing's essence or nature and the properties or proper accidents that flow from that essence. For example, having four legs is a property of dogs insofar as any dog in a fully mature and undamaged condition will have four legs. But it is nevertheless possible for a particular dog to lack four legs insofar as it is not fully mature or has in some way been damaged. It is a mistake, then, to think that the persistence of a substance entails its actually manifesting its properties at every moment. An organism's substantial form, understood as its essence or nature considered concretely rather than in the abstract, is a not a cluster of properties but rather that which grounds the organism's properties.

Furthermore, no Aristotelian-Thomistic philosopher would agree with Dupré's claim that stasis is the default condition of all substances as such. To be sure, if "stasis" is interpreted broadly enough to include the bare persistence of a substance over time, then the Aristotelian-Thomistic philosopher would agree that stasis will be a feature of any material substance to *that* extent. But it doesn't follow that the default condition of substances is stasis in *every* respect. In particular, no Aristotelian-Thomistic philosopher would deny that an organic material substance is constantly changing insofar as it is (in the case of an animal, say) continuously taking in oxygen, shedding cells and growing new ones, and so on. On the contrary, it is of the very nature of such a substance continually to change in such respects even as it endures through those changes (and thus remains unchanged in *that* respect).

Similarly, the Aristotelian-Thomistic philosopher does not claim in the first place that every substance must be independent in *every* respect. To be sure, it will not be dependent *in the manner* in which, say, an attribute is dependent on the substance in which it inheres, or in the manner in which an accidental form depends on there being a substantial form already informing the substance that the accidental form modifies. But that doesn't mean that a substance will not be dependent in other respects (such as the respects in which an organism might depend on its environment for food, oxygen, mating opportunities, or what have you).

As to the boundaries of organisms, while there are indeed cases where they seem difficult to determine (as with lichens) there are also cases where they do not (as with dogs, cats, and the like). The question of whether to assimilate the former cases to the latter or the latter to the former is not one that can be settled by empirical biological considerations alone, but requires bringing to bear independently motivated philosophical assumptions.[392] But in that case, Dupré cannot, without begging the question, appeal to the difficult cases as if by themselves they settled the matter in favor of his position. As we have seen, the Aristotelian has independently motivated arguments for the hylemorphic account of substance, and in light of that account the most natural way of understanding organisms is as substances rather than processes. What to say about problematic examples would require case-by-case analysis. But given hylemorphism, the Aristotelian has grounds for the general conclusion that where boundaries are unclear, we are either not really dealing with a true organism at all, or are dealing with an organism that has definite boundaries but simply lack sufficient knowledge of where those boundaries are.[393]

Contemporary philosophy of biology's new interest in mechanisms, which Rosenberg wrongly characterizes as the heir of reductionism and Dupré rightly takes to provide no support for reductionism, in fact if anything positively vindicates Aristotelian hylemorphism. As Daniel De Haan argues, some of the key themes of this movement (which he calls the "New Mechanist Philosophy" or NMP), despite the label, actually recapitulate some of the main themes

---

[392] Cf. David S. Oderberg, "The Great Unifier: Form and the Unity of the Organism," in Simpson, Koons, and Teh, eds., *Neo-Aristotelian Perspectives on Contemporary Science*, p. 215.

[393] Where we are not dealing with a true organism, the Aristotelian holds that we are dealing instead with either a *part* of an organism or a *collective* of organisms. For analysis of various problem cases from an Aristotelian-Thomistic point of view, see Oderberg's "The Great Unifier," and also his article "Siphonophores: A Metaphysical Case Study," in Anne Sophie Meincke and John Dupré, eds., *Biological Identity: Perspectives from Metaphysics and the Philosophy of Biology* (London: Routledge, 2021).

of hylemorphism.[394] I noted in chapter 4 that, for the Aristotelian, it is the causal powers of substances, rather than laws of nature, that are fundamental to physical reality. NMP too takes genuine explanation to involve identifying a thing's causal powers rather than the laws that govern it. I also noted there that for the Aristotelian, determinism is a mistaken way of understanding causation in general (let alone human action). Some NMP writers too take the causal powers of the mechanisms they identify to operate in a stochastic rather than deterministic manner.

NMP writers typically do not see the search for the underlying mechanisms of the phenomena they seek to explain as an attempt to *reduce* the phenomena to these mechanisms. They don't regard the entities identified at lower levels of description as more real than those identified at higher levels, and the former are seen as *constituting* the latter in a way that is reminiscent of the hylemorphist's notion of the material cause of a substance. NMP typically does not regard wholes as aggregates, but regards them as more than merely the sum of their parts. It takes the *organization* of the parts to be an ontologically basic fact about the whole, in a way that parallels the hylemorphist's conception of form's relation to matter. Some NMP writers take a teleological conception of mechanisms to be at least pragmatically invaluable, and others are even willing to consider a realist account of teleology.

This is not to say that NMP writers have endorsed or would endorse every aspect of Aristotelian hylemorphism or that everything they say is compatible with it. The point is just that it tells in favor of hylemorphism that contemporary philosophers with no Aristotelian axe to grind have independently rediscovered some of its central themes and judged them essential to a proper understanding of living things.

---

[394] De Haan, "Hylomorphism and the New Mechanist Philosophy in Biology, Neuroscience, and Psychology."

Sentient versus vegetative life

A living thing, I have argued, is a substance characterized by immanent causation or self-perfecting activity. Traditionally, Aristotelian philosophers have taken the most fundamental kinds of living thing to be substances of the *vegetative* sort, in the technical Aristotelian sense of that term. That is to say, they are substances that metabolize, or take in nutrients and eliminate wastes so as to sustain themselves; that grow in the sense of increasing in size from within rather than merely by accretion; and that reproduce in the sense of generating new, distinct individuals of the same kind as themselves. For example, a tree does these things, and insofar as its carrying out of these operations is irreducible to the aggregate of the activities of its parts, it counts as a true substance. Any living substance that carries out some variation of these activities, but nothing further that differs in kind from them, is a purely vegetative substance. (Of course, things other than plants carry out such activities, such as fungi. But again, "vegetative" is being used here in a technical sense, and does not correspond in meaning to terms like "vegetable" or "plant" in the familiar senses of those terms.)

The traditional Aristotelian position is that an *animal* or *sensory* substance is a further kind of living substance, irreducible to the vegetative kind. Animals or sensory substances possess the basic vegetative capacities but, in addition, three irreducibly different capacities of their own. The first and most fundamental is *sentience*, which is the capacity for conscious awareness of stimuli. The second is *appetite*, which is the capacity either to seek or to avoid the stimuli one is aware of. The third is *locomotion*, which is the capacity to move oneself either toward or away from the object of appetite. Obviously, these three form a kind of package. The final cause of locomotion is to allow the organism to react to sensed stimuli, with appetite being the bridge between locomotion and sentience.

The empirical evidence bears this out insofar as these three capacities all tend to be found together in organisms that have any one of them.[395] But as Aristotelian philosophers argue, the connection

---

[395] There can be significant variation in the underlying physiology. The sensory receptors may not always be as complex as the eyes, ears, and other sensory organs possessed by

is metaphysically stronger than a mere empirical correlation.³⁹⁶ Locomotion would be positively harmful in organisms that lacked sentience, since they would move about without being able to know whether what they are moving themselves toward was beneficial or dangerous. Appetite would result in nothing but frustration in a creature that lacked locomotion. Sentience would be pointless, at least with respect to stimuli that it was beneficial for the organism either to acquire or to avoid, in the absence of locomotion – though perhaps one might argue that there could, at least in theory, be creatures that were sentient but existed in a world of stimuli that could neither benefit nor harm them and which they merely contemplated.³⁹⁷

In chapter 3, I discussed how, where sentience is concerned, the Aristotelian would draw further distinctions between the *external senses* (which are the familiar five senses of sight, hearing, taste, smell, and touch) and the *internal senses* (which are the *synthetic sense, instinct, the imagination,* and *sensory memory*). I explained in that chapter what each of these involves. Where appetites are concerned, Aristotelians distinguish between *concupiscible appetite* and *irascible appetite*.³⁹⁸ Concupiscible appetite is a matter of being drawn toward something

---

paradigmatically sentient organisms. The connecting link between sensory input and behavioral output may not always be a nervous system. Where there are nervous systems, we can, as Peter Godfrey-Smith points out, distinguish between those that are of a "sensory-motor" nature and those of an "action-shaping" nature. (See his *Other Minds: The Octopus, the Sea, and the Deep Origins of Consciousness* (New York: Farrar, Straus, and Giroux, 2016), pp. 22-27.) Both involve receptivity to the external environment, but in the former this role is primary whereas in the latter the main function is coordination of an organism's internal activities. But whatever the details, in a sentient organism "one part of it must be *receptive*, able to see or smell or hear, and another part must be *active*, able to make something useful happen. The organism must also establish a connection of some sort, an arc, between these two parts" (p. 16).

[396] Cf. Klubertanz, *The Philosophy of Human Nature*, p. 58; Koren, *An Introduction to the Philosophy of Animate Nature*, p. 139; and Oderberg, *Real Essentialism*, pp. 185-86.

[397] Cf. Galen Strawson, *Mental Reality* (Cambridge, MA: The MIT Press, 1994), chapter 9.

[398] Cf. Klubertanz, *The Philosophy of Human Nature*, chapters IX and XI; Robert Edward Brennan, *Thomistic Psychology* (New York: Macmillan, 1941), chapter 6; Steven J. Jensen, *The Human Person: A Beginner's Thomistic Psychology* (Washington, D.C.: The Catholic University of America Press, 2018), chapter 5.

straightforwardly pleasant or repelled by something straightforwardly unpleasant. Examples would be the desire to eat or copulate and disgust at the sight of a dead body or feces. Irascible appetite is a matter of being drawn toward something pleasant but difficult to attain, or repelled by something unpleasant but difficult to avoid. These are in play when, for example, an animal in a hot desert hopefully searches for water that is nowhere in sight or angrily lashes out at a predator that cannot be avoided. Needless to say, what today are usually called "emotions" fall under the categories of concupiscible and irascible appetites.

Some animals exercise the full range of powers I have been describing – the external senses, the internal senses (the synthetic sense, instinct, imagination, and sensory memory), concupiscible and irascible appetites of various kinds, and locomotion. Some animals exhibit only some of these. But fundamental to all of them is the basic capacity for conscious awareness of stimuli. Now, is this really irreducible to anything of which merely vegetative forms of life are capable?[399] It might seem that it is *not* irreducible insofar as plants grow toward the light and sink roots in the direction of water, a Venus fly trap will react to the presence of an insect and the *Mimosa pudica* will respond to touch, and so forth. Isn't this evidence that something like sentience exists in plants?

---

[399] Before addressing this question, it is worthwhile noting that even those who are more sympathetic to reductionism than I am can acknowledge that the traditional Aristotelian distinction between vegetative, sensory, and rational forms of life is heuristically useful and marks fundamental transitions in nature. The scientists Simona Ginsburg and Eva Jablonka do in *The Evolution of the Sensitive Soul: Learning and the Origins of Consciousness* (Cambridge, MA: The MIT Press, 2019). They argue (at pp. 35-40) that a similar distinction is drawn by Daniel C. Dennett in his *Darwin's Dangerous Idea: Evolution and the Meanings of Life* (New York: Simon and Schuster, 1995), at pp. 373-80. Dennett distinguishes between what he calls *Darwinian creatures*, which possess only rudimentary organic properties; *Skinnerian creatures*, which can respond behaviorally to their immediate environments; *Popperian creatures*, which can represent and respond to environments other than those immediately present; and *Gregorian creatures*, which make use of culturally embodied information. Ginsburg and Jablonka propose that Darwinian creatures correspond to the Aristotelian category of purely vegetative forms of life. Skinnerian and Popperian creatures, they suggest, correspond to the category of sensory forms of life – Skinnerian creatures to those possessing mere sensation, Popperian creatures to those which add imagination to the repertoire. Finally, Gregorian creatures correspond to the Aristotelian category of rational animals.

No, it is not. The Aristotelian does not deny that merely vegetative forms of life can in certain ways be sensitive to external stimuli. The claim is rather that they lack *conscious awareness* of these stimuli – that, as contemporary philosophers of mind would put it, they lack *qualia* (where examples of qualia would be *the way thirst feels* and *what it is like to see blue*). And sensitivity to external stimuli of the kind plants exhibit doesn't entail the presence of qualia. For example, that the roots of a plant grow in the direction of water doesn't entail that it feels thirst, and that the Venus fly trap reacts to the presence of an insect doesn't entail that it feels hunger – any more than a smoke alarm experiences the smell of smoke, or the motion detector in an outdoor security lamp has a visual experience of someone crossing in front of it.

Moreover, plants lack crucial features that lead us to attribute conscious awareness to animals.[400] In animals there are specialized sense organs associated with their various forms of awareness – eyes with visual awareness, ears with hearing, and so on. Plants lack such organs. Furthermore, sensation in animals is associated with a variability of response that is not present in plants. Unless it is in some way damaged, a plant will simply grow toward the light or sink its roots downward in response to the relevant stimuli. A properly functioning animal, by contrast, may respond in a number of ways to stimuli presented to it. For example, it might immediately leap toward the prey it sees, or sneak up toward it slowly, or refrain from acting at all if it sees another, stronger predator in the vicinity or some barrier it is afraid to cross. A conscious experience functions as a kind of *intermediary* between external stimuli and different possible behavioral responses, an intermediary that makes this variability of response possible. That plants lack such variability is thus a reason to think they lack anything like such intermediary conscious experiences. Furthermore, as Oderberg notes, a sentient plant could not move itself *as a*

---

[400] Koren, *An Introduction to the Philosophy of Animate Nature*, pp. 72-73; and Michael Tye, "Qualia," *Stanford Encyclopedia of Philosophy* (2017), at: https://plato.stanford.edu/entries/qualia/ [last accessed 15.9.2018]

whole either toward or away from anything it sensed in its environment that was either beneficial or dangerous.[401] As noted already, in the absence of such locomotion, sentience would be pointless or even harmful. Hence the movements of which plants are capable are best thought of as merely mechanical rather than on the model of animal locomotion.

Contemporary philosophers are likely to judge the notorious intractability of the "qualia problem" (also known as the "hard problem of consciousness") to be the chief consideration in favor of the irreducibility of sentience. A battery of influential arguments set out the problem from a variety of angles. The "zombie argument" holds that it is possible in principle for there to be a world physically identical to ours down to the last particle, such that the creatures who occupy it are physiologically and behaviorally indistinguishable from those in the actual world. The difference is that none of these creatures is conscious, and in particular none has any qualia whatsoever. Hence the facts about qualia in our world must be further facts, over and above the physical facts.[402] The "knowledge argument" asks us to imagine a woman who has for her entire life been held in a black and white room, never experiencing color. We are also asked to imagine that she has nevertheless been able, through textbooks and the like, to learn everything there is to know about the physical facts associated with color vision – facts about the physics of light, the surface reflectance properties of objects, the way the brain processes information received through the retina, and so on. Suppose she eventually leaves the room, sees a red object, and thereby learns for the first time what it is like to see red. Since she already knew all the physical facts, facts about the red qualia she has now been made aware of must be further facts over and above the physical facts.[403] Thomas Nagel

---

[401] Oderberg, *Real Essentialism*, pp. 186-88.

[402] Cf. David J. Chalmers, *The Conscious Mind* (Oxford: Oxford University Press, 1996), chapter 4.

[403] Cf. Frank Jackson's articles "Epiphenomenal Qualia" and "What Mary Didn't Know," in Peter Ludlow, Yujin Nagasawa, and Daniel Stoljar, eds., *There's Something About Mary: Essays on Phenomenal Consciousness and Frank Jackson's Knowledge Argument* (Cambridge, MA: The MIT Press, 2004).

argues that no amount of scientific knowledge could reveal to us *what it is like* to have the experiences characteristic of a species whose sensory apparatus is very different from ours, such as bats. Hence facts about conscious experience are of a very different nature from facts of the kind to which the methods of physics, biology, physiology, etc. give us access.[404] And there are yet other arguments that develop the theme that facts about conscious experience, and in particular facts about the qualia distinctive of conscious experience, are irreducible to physical facts.[405]

Is any of these arguments sound? Naturally, that depends in part on exactly what they are taken to be arguments *for*. If nothing else, they are intended to establish the thesis that conscious experience cannot be reduced to any property of the kind recognized by current physics, chemistry, neuroscience, or the like. My own view is that, so understood, the arguments are successful, though of course they are highly controversial. But a major reason why they are controversial is that they are also often claimed to establish the dualist thesis that conscious experience is something *non-physical* or *incorporeal*. That does not follow from the first thesis (as some proponents of the arguments, such as Nagel, recognize), and it is not true. The correct judgment, I would argue, is that the conscious awareness characteristic of animal life is irreducible to the properties possessed either by inorganic substances or purely vegetative living substances, but that it is nevertheless an entirely physical or corporeal phenomenon.

To understand how both of these things can be true, it must be kept in mind that the conception of matter that contemporary philosophers tend to take for granted is one they have inherited from Galileo, Descartes, and the other early modern proponents of the mechanical philosophy. Recall from chapter 5 that one of the key components of this view is the idea that matter is devoid of color, sound,

---

[404] Thomas Nagel, "What Is It Like to Be a Bat?" in *Mortal Questions* (Cambridge: Cambridge University Press, 1979).

[405] I survey the main arguments and counterarguments in chapters 4 and 5 of *Philosophy of Mind* (Oxford: Oneworld Publications, 2006). An especially detailed and helpful analysis of the contemporary literature and main lines of argument can be found in Joseph Levine, *Purple Haze: The Puzzle of Consciousness* (Oxford: Oxford University Press, 2001).

odor, taste, heat, cold, etc. as common sense understands them. These are "secondary qualities," and there is, according to the mechanical philosophy, nothing in matter itself that resembles our experiences of them. If, for example, we follow modern physics in defining an object's color in terms of the electromagnetic radiation that is either reflected or absorbed by its surface, then we can say that material things have color. But if by the "color" of an object we mean what common sense means – namely, *the way a color looks* to the average observer – then, so it is claimed, there is nothing corresponding to that in material things themselves. Colors as common sense understands them exist only in the mind of the observer, as the qualia of his conscious awareness of physical objects rather than as qualities of the objects themselves. There is really nothing and nowhere else for them to be if they are not taken to be features of mind-independent physical reality. As Tim Crane writes:

> For contemporary thinkers, to deny that [qualia] are properties of physical objects leaves them with no alternative to thinking that [qualia] are properties of experience... It turns out, then, that when one is aware of a red thing in experience, one is also aware – in some sense – of a feature of one's experience.[406]

Now, if qualia are not features of physical objects, then it follows that they are not features of the *brain* or the body more generally, since these are physical objects. But they are features of the *mind*, and in particular of its conscious experiences. It follows, then, that the mind, or at least conscious experiences, are not physical. Thus does the mechanical philosophy's account of matter yield a kind of dualism. Indeed, some early modern philosophers explicitly argued for dualism

---

[406] Tim Crane, "The Origins of Qualia," in Tim Crane and Sarah Patterson, eds., *History of the Mind-Body Problem* (London: Routledge, 2000), p. 188. Crane's account of the origins of the notion of qualia emphasizes its roots in the sense-datum tradition in twentieth-century epistemology. But that tradition was in turn rooted in assumptions inherited from early modern thinkers like Descartes, Locke, et al., whose conception of the mind's epistemological and metaphysical relationship to the material world was deeply informed by their commitment to the mechanical philosophy.

on the basis of the mechanical philosophy.[407] Nagel is one contemporary critic of materialism who has noted that it is precisely the conception of matter that we have inherited from the early moderns, and to which materialists are themselves committed, that underwrites the conclusion that qualia cannot be physical. On a superficial reading of Nagel, it might seem that his point is merely that the conscious experiences of bats, specifically, are alien and that current neuroscience does not help us to understand them. But Nagel is in fact making a point about conscious experience *in general*, and about *any* scientific knowledge that confines itself to facts of the kind compatible with a mechanistic account of nature. As he emphasizes, modern science operates with a conception of the "physical" that strips away from it anything that reflects the point of view of the conscious observer. It is this conception that, by definition as it were, makes the conscious observer himself impossible to fit into the physical world.

I would submit that the zombie argument, the knowledge argument, and other contemporary expressions of the "qualia problem" are best interpreted as different ways of expressing this insight that conscious experience cannot be reduced to any property or collection of properties of the physical kind, *if* we understand "physical" the way that most philosophers and scientists have at least implicitly understood it since the mechanical conception of nature came to be taken for granted. But it does not follow that conscious experience cannot be physical in some *other* sense of "physical." Here too Nagel is, among contemporary exponents of the qualia problem, especially insightful. He does not present his argument as a demonstration that consciousness is not physical, full stop, but rather as showing that it is not clear what it could mean to call it "physical" *given* the way modern science and philosophy tend to conceive of consciousness and of the physical.

Noting that it is the early moderns' desiccated conception of matter that excludes conscious awareness from it, some contemporary philosophers have proposed reintroducing consciousness into

---

[407] Ralph Cudworth (1618-1688) was one early modern thinker who developed such an argument, as noted by Michael Ayers in *Locke, Volume II: Ontology* (London: Routledge, 1991), pp. 171-72. Another was Nicolas Malebranche (1638-1715), whose version is discussed in Tad M. Schmaltz, *Malebranche's Theory of the Soul* (Oxford: Oxford University Press, 1996), pp. 136-39.

the material world in a wholesale way, arguing that *all* matter, inorganic and vegetative no less than animal, is conscious. This view is known as *panpsychism*, an influential recent proponent of which is Philip Goff.[408] Goff begins with considerations about the nature of modern physics of the kind that I set out in chapter 5. In particular, he notes that the reason features like color, odor, sound, heat, cold, etc. as common sense understands them are absent from physics' picture of the natural world is that Galileo and his successors, for methodological purposes, decided to focus only on those features of reality susceptible of a mathematical description.[409] Following Bertrand Russell and Arthur Eddington, Goff also emphasizes that physics therefore reveals to us only the abstract mathematical structure of the material world, but not the intrinsic nature of the entities that bear this structure.[410] Other sciences, such as chemistry and neuroscience, also fail to reveal the intrinsic nature of material things. The reason is that they merely describe causal relations between the entities they are concerned with, where these entities are themselves constituted by lower-level entities, and ultimately by the lowest-level entities described by particle physics. And again, physics itself gives us only abstract mathematical structure. Hence from the top of nature down to the bottom, structure is really all that even science as a whole, at the end of the day, reveals to us. It does not tell us about the intrinsic nature of the entities that make up the structure.

So far so good. But now Goff borrows a further idea from Eddington and Russell, who held that introspection of one's own conscious experiences does reveal the intrinsic nature of at least one physical object, namely the brain.[411] That is to say, when you look within and encounter qualia – the way red looks, the way heat feels,

---

[408] See Philip Goff, *Galileo's Error: Foundations for a New Science of Consciousness* (New York: Vintage Books, 2019), and his more academic presentation of his views in *Consciousness and Fundamental Reality* (Oxford: Oxford University Press, 2017). Cf. Chalmers, *The Conscious Mind*, pp. 293-301, and Galen Strawson, "Realistic Monism: Why Physicalism Entails Panpsychism," in *Real Materialism and Other Essays* (Oxford: Clarendon Press, 2008).

[409] Goff, *Galileo's Error*, chapter 1, and *Consciousness and Fundamental Reality*, pp. 11-14.

[410] Goff, *Galileo's Error*, pp. 122-28, and *Consciousness and Fundamental Reality*, pp. 135-37.

[411] Goff, *Galileo's Error*, pp. 130-31.

the way a musical note sounds, and so on – what you are directly aware of are the entities that "flesh out" the abstract causal structure of the brain that is revealed by science. Now, if qualia are the intrinsic properties of at least this one physical object, and we know nothing from physics about the intrinsic properties of any other part of physical reality, then, Goff proposes, we can speculate that qualia are also the intrinsic properties of all other physical reality.[412] Physics leaves a "huge hole" in our picture of nature that we can "plug" with qualia.[413] But since qualia are the defining features of conscious experience, it follows that conscious experience exists throughout the material world. To be sure, Goff is keen to emphasize that the conscious awareness associated with, say, an electron is bound to be radically unlike, and more primitive than, ours. He also notes that a panpsychist need not attribute conscious awareness to all everyday physical objects (such as a pair of socks) but only to the more elementary bits of matter of which they are composed. Still, he is attributing something like sentience to physical reality well beyond the animal realm, indeed well beyond the realm of living things.

But this line of argument is fallacious, and the bizarre solution panpsychism proposes to the problem of how to fit consciousness into the natural world is completely unnecessary. For one thing, it is hard to imagine a more stark example of the fallacy of hasty generalization than Goff's inference from what (he claims) *brains* are like to a conclusion about what *matter in general* is like. Suppose we allow for the sake of argument that introspection of qualia involves direct awareness of the intrinsic properties of the matter that makes up brains. Brains are an extremely small part of the matter that makes up even just the Earth, let alone the rest of the universe (from which, as far as we know, they are entirely absent). They are also the most complex things in the universe. Why suppose that *all* matter, and especially the most elementary matter, is plausibly modeled on them? Surely the prima facie far more plausible bet would be that most matter is radically *unlike* brains.

---

[412] Goff, *Consciousness and Fundamental Reality*, pp. 169-71.

[413] Goff, *Galileo's Error*, p. 132.

A second problem is that Goff's argument takes for granted that what contemporary philosophers call "qualia" really are features *of conscious experience* rather than of the external objects that conscious experience is experience *of*. And that assumption is open to challenge. As Crane writes:

> It is not at all obvious that when we learn what it is like to taste retsina, we are learning about a property of an experience. Isn't it slightly more obvious, at least at first sight, that we are learning something about retsina: viz.,what *it* tastes like, or what it is like to taste it? [414]

The point is not that what seems obvious to common sense must be correct, but rather that it shouldn't simply be taken for granted that contemporary philosophers' habit of talking about the way retsina tastes, the way red looks, the way heat feels, etc. as if these were features *of the mind* (and thus as if they were "qualia") – as opposed to features *of mind-independent reality* – reflects an accurate carving up of the conceptual territory.[415] Goff himself emphasizes that Galileo's treatment of these qualities as mind-dependent was motivated by his project of developing a purely mathematical conception of nature; that this was a philosophical thesis rather than one that has been established by science; and that it created the very problem of consciousness that Goff thinks panpsychism solves. Why not solve it instead by simply not following Galileo in making the conceptual move that created the problem? Goff says that "Galileo took the sensory qualities out of the physical world" and that panpsychism is "a way of

---

[414] Crane, "The Origins of Qualia," p. 186.

[415] A third option would be to hold that there are properties of the relevant kind to be found both in the mind and in mind-independent reality. Consider what happens when you look at a red apple. Some writers propose labeling properties like the redness we attribute to the apple "phenomenal" properties, and properties like the redness we attribute to your experience of the apple "qualitative" properties. Cf. Austen Clark, *A Theory of Sentience* (Oxford: Oxford University Press, 2000), pp. 1-4, and Galen Strawson, "Red and 'Red'" in *Real Materialism and Other Essays*. As Clark warns, however, some philosophers use these expressions in different, or even opposite, senses.

putting them back."[416] Why not instead merely refrain from taking them out in the first place?

Or, if we're going to speak of putting them back after Galileo took them out, why not put them back *in the specific places he took them from*? Why instead put them into every *other* bit of matter, including unobservable particles, when that is not where they came from? For example, Galileo (and the mechanical philosophy more generally) hold that the redness you see when you look at an apple is not in the apple itself, but only in your mind. Goff tells us that, in order to solve the problem this sort of view raises, we should say that the redness you see is in your *brain*, and that something analogous to it is in *electrons and other particles*. Why not just say instead that it really is *in the apple* after all, and leave it at that? Goff's "solution" is analogous to trying to rectify the injustice caused by a theft by giving the stolen money back to everyone *except* the person it was taken from!

It might be replied that to reject Galileo's move in this way would conflict with the findings of modern physics. But as Goff himself says, the move is at bottom *philosophical* rather than scientific in nature. To be sure, scientific considerations (about the physics of light, the neuroscience of vision, etc.) are relevant. But they do not by themselves establish the correctness of the mechanical philosophy's distinction between primary and secondary qualities, because the scientific evidence is susceptible of different philosophical interpretations. Nor could Goff object that reversion to something like the conception of color, sound, etc. that prevailed before the rise of the mechanical philosophy would be too radical a departure from philosophical orthodoxy. For he acknowledges that *panpsychism* represents a radical departure from it, and argues that such a departure is necessary in order to solve the problem posed by Galileo's conceptual revolution.

Moreover, some mainstream contemporary philosophers would, for reasons independent of debates about either panpsychism or Aristotelianism, defend the "naïve realist" view about qualities that

---

[416] Goff, *Galileo's Error*, p. 138.

was overthrown by Galileo and the mechanical philosophy.[417] To be sure, this is a large issue, an adequate treatment of which is beyond the scope of a book about human nature. But I have defended this naïve realist position elsewhere.[418] Suffice it for present purposes to note that Goff not only reasons fallaciously *to* the conclusion that conscious experience pervades inorganic reality, but reasons *from* assumptions about the nature of color, sound, heat, cold, etc. that his own critique of the mechanical philosophy should have led him to question.

A further problem is that the suggestion that there is something analogous to consciousness in fundamental physical particles and other inorganic entities is simply prima facie implausible, and not just because it sounds bizarre. As I argued above, sensation is closely tied to appetite and locomotion, so that the absence of the latter from plants tells strongly in favor of the absence of sensation from them as well. What is true of plants is *a fortiori* true of electrons and other particles too, to which it is even more implausible to attribute appetite or locomotion. There are simply no good empirical grounds for attributing anything like sentience to the inorganic realm, any more that there are for attributing it to plants.

The attribution also turns out to be completely pointless, given other things Goff says. Consider that the panpsychist's attribution to basic physical particles of something analogous to consciousness is alleged to make it more intelligible how the *brain* could be conscious. For if matter is already conscious "all the way down," as it were, then there should be no surprise that the complex organ that is the brain is conscious too. We need simply to work out how the more elementary forms of consciousness that exist at lower levels of physical reality add up to the more sophisticated form with which we are

---

[417] Cf. Hilary Putnam, *The Threefold Cord: Mind, Body, and World* (New York: Columbia University Press, 1999), and Keith Allen, *A Naïve Realist Theory of Colour* (Oxford: Oxford University Press, 2016). Barry Stroud, in *The Quest for Reality: Subjectivism and the Metaphysics of Color* (Oxford: Oxford University Press, 2000), develops a powerful critique of the mechanical philosophy's thesis that color does not exist in the material world in the way common sense supposes it to, though he stops short of claiming positively to demonstrate that that the commonsense or naïve realist view about color is correct.

[418] *Aristotle's Revenge*, pp. 340-51.

familiar from our own everyday experience. This is known as the "combination problem," and while Goff thinks there are promising approaches to solving it, he acknowledges that panpsychists have not yet done so.[419]

You might suppose, then, that Goff is committed to a kind of reductionism according to which higher-level features of the natural world are intelligible only if reducible to lower-level features, where Goff differs from materialist reductionists only in positing the existence of consciousness at lower levels as well as at higher levels. But in fact, Goff explicitly rejects this reductionist assumption, citing in support the work of contemporary critics of reductionism like Nancy Cartwright (which we had reason to consider in chapter 4).[420] Goff allows that physical objects can have properties that are irreducible to the sum of the properties of their parts. But then, what is the point of positing consciousness at the level of basic particles as part of an explanation of how animals and human beings are conscious? Why not instead merely take the consciousness that exists at the level of an organism as a whole to be one of those properties irreducible to those of its parts? That is exactly what the traditional Aristotelian position does.

Goff says that there must be something that fleshes out the abstract structure described by physics, and alleges that "there doesn't seem to be a candidate for being the intrinsic nature of matter other than consciousness."[421] But in fact there is no great mystery here in need of some exotic solution. We need only to see what is in front of our nose, which, as Orwell famously said, requires a constant struggle. The concrete reality that fleshes out the abstract structure described by physics is nothing other than *the world of ordinary objects revealed to us in everyday experience*. Physics is an abstraction *from that*, just as the representation of a person's face in a pen and ink sketch is an abstraction from all the rich concrete detail to be found in the actual, flesh-and-blood face. No one thinks that the existence of pen and

---

[419] Goff, *Galileo's Error*, pp. 144-48.

[420] Ibid., pp. 161-69.

[421] Ibid., p. 133.

ink drawings raises some deep metaphysical puzzle about what fleshes out the two-dimensional black-and-white representation, and neither is there any deep metaphysical mystery about what fleshes out the abstract structure described by physics. The bizarre panpsychist solution is no more called for in the latter case than in the former. Does that mean there is nothing more to be said about the intrinsic nature of matter beyond what common sense would say about it? Not at all, and we have seen in the previous chapter what more there is to be said about it. The Aristotelian hylemorphist account of material substances as compounds of substantial form and prime matter, possessing efficient causal powers and directed toward characteristic ends, etc. gives us a rich account of matter's intrinsic nature.

There are, then, good grounds for taking sentience or conscious awareness to be an irreducible property of animals, but also (contra Goff) for denying that it exists in anything other than animals. Note, though, that I am here using "animals" in its traditional Aristotelian sense, which is broader than the sense in which "*Animalia*" is used in modern biology. Consider that bacteria, for example, would in modern systems of biological classification constitute their own kingdom distinct from *Animalia*. However, they clearly exhibit primitive forms of sensing and locomotion, as well as the flexibility of response to their environment characteristic of appetite.[422] Hence in the older, Aristotelian sense of the term, they count as animals.[423] That is by no means to deny that there are important differences between bacteria and *Animalia* in the modern sense of the term, nor to reject the classifications made by modern biologists. Despite the overlap in terminology, the older Aristotelian distinction between vegetative and animal forms of life is intended to track a different sort of divide in the biological realm than the ones that modern biologists are interested in.

---

[422] Cf. Godfrey-Smith, *Other Minds*, pp. 15-20.

[423] Cf. Oderberg, *Real Essentialism*, p. 190.

To be sure, exactly how this Aristotelian metaphysical distinction relates to modern scientific systems of biological classification is an important question. But it is irrelevant for present purposes.[424]

As I have emphasized, antireductionist arguments give no reason to conclude that sentience entails any *non-physical* or *incorporeal* properties (as opposed to irreducible but still corporeal properties). There are also positive grounds for judging sentience to be physical or corporeal. Consider what neuroscience reveals about the mechanisms by which sensations are generated.[425] With taste, for example, the process beings when, say, a piece of food excites the sweet, sour, salty, and bitter receptors on the tongue. The activation level in some of these four sets of receptors will be high and in the others low, and precisely how high or low it will be in any of the four will depend on exactly what kind of food it is (an apple, a piece of steak, or whatever). Suppose there are ten levels of activation in each of the four sets of receptors. One sort of taste might be associated with an activation level of 8 in the sweet receptors, 5 in the sour receptors, and 2 in both the salty and bitter receptors. Another sort of taste will be associated with a different combination of values in each of the four receptors. All of the different possible combinations of values will comprise what we might call a "taste space," within which all the taste sensations possible for organisms with tongues like ours can be located. Something similar can be said of color sensations. There are three sorts of receptors in the retina, each sensitive to a distinct wavelength of light. The activation levels in the neurons downstream from these three sets of receptors vary depending on the object seen, and the possible combinations of activation levels correspond to the different possible colors that might be seen, each locatable in the "color space" they comprise. A similar story can be told about the other senses and sensory qualities.

---

[424] For detailed treatment of this issue, see Oderberg, *Real Essentialism*, pp. 183-93 and chapter 9.

[425] Cf. Paul M. Churchland, *The Engine of Reason, the Seat of the Soul: A Philosophical Journey into the Brain* (Cambridge, MA: The MIT Press, 1995), chapter 2.

Sensation also presents the world as a domain of corporeal objects of which the perceiver is a part. Consider, for example, the aspect of perception known as *constancy*.[426] An object will *look* larger or smaller as we move toward or away from it, but we nevertheless treat it as being of the same one size throughout. Similarly, even though two objects of the same color often *look* different when in different light, we can nevertheless judge the two to be of the same color and interact with them accordingly. Variations in appearance notwithstanding, sizes and colors are *perceived as* stable features of an external, physical reality rather than as fleeting modifications of the perceiver's own subjective consciousness. As Mohan Matthen writes:

> Animals can perform these feats of discrimination too. Suppose for instance that you are able to train a bird or a fish to seek food on yellow-coloured discs. They will not be deterred by lighting conditions different from those that you used during the training: they will recognize yellow even in shadow, in reddish or bluish illumination, discs even at oblique angles, and from far away. Regardless of environmental variations that affect the signal that is received by their eyes, they will forage on yellow discs and ignore other stimuli.[427]

Bodily behavior itself determines how things will be perceived. To take an especially dramatic example, blind people fitted with cameras that transform visual images into a set of vibrations or electrical stimulations felt on their skin will come to experience these *as objects located in space* rather than as mere touches on the skin.[428] Or to be more precise, they will do so *when* they are able to control the positon and angle of the camera in a way that influences what is presented to it. The sensory systems of fish and earthworms, which will cancel the effects on their senses of their own actions so as to distinguish them from stimulation arising from external objects, illustrate how the bodily behavior of non-human animals too influences how they perceive

---

[426] Godfrey-Smith, *Other Minds*, pp. 83-84, and Mohan Matthen, *Seeing, Doing, and Knowing: A Philosophical Theory of Sense Perception* (Oxford: Clarendon Press, 2005), pp. 4-5.
[427] Matthen, *Seeing, Doing, and Knowing*, p. 4.

[428] Godfrey-Smith, *Other Minds*, p. 80.

the world.[429] All of this dovetails with the Aristotelian thesis that sensation is inherently tied to locomotion, which is obviously a corporeal power. And it illustrates how sense perception presents its objects as what psychologist James J. Gibson calls "affordances" for bodily action on the part of the perceiver qua *embodied entity* alongside other bodies or physical objects.[430]

It is thus unsurprising that, as Nagel's critics have noted, scientific investigation can in fact tell us a great deal about the experiences of bats and other animals.[431] Our knowledge of the retinal receptors of different kinds of animals allows us to infer whether and how they perceive colors. Given what we know about the physics of light and the focusing role that the lens plays in the eye, we can determine exactly how vision allows for perception of the spatial position of a light source, whereas auditory perception allows for no similarly precise identification of the source of a sound. The physics of sound gives us reason to judge that the mustached bat probably cannot perceive objects farther than about three feet away, that the depth of its auditory field likely gets smaller the closer it gets to its prey while the information about the prey available to it gets more detailed, and that objects moving away from it will suddenly disappear from the perceptual field rather than fade out. And so on.

None of this implies that a description of the conscious experiences of animals is *reducible* to a description couched in the language of physics, physiology, neuroscience, ethology, and the like. Again, I don't think that is possible any more than the dualist does. What it does show, however, is how close and fine-grained is the connection between the nature of conscious experience and the specifics of the relevant physical facts, just as we'd expect if consciousness is physical

---

[429] Ibid., p. 83.

[430] James J. Gibson, *The Ecological Approach to Visual Perception* (Boston: Houghton Mifflin, 1979).

[431] Cf. Kathleen Akins, "What Is It Like to Be Boring and Myopic?" in Bo Dahlbom, ed., *Dennett and His Critics* (Oxford: Blackwell, 1993); and Clark, *A Theory of Sentience*, pp. 122-29.

or corporeal (even if, to repeat, it is not reducible to *lower-level* physical facts).

I will have more to say in the next chapter about the corporeal nature of sentience. In the chapter after that, we will see that there are compelling reasons for concluding that the *intellect* is *non*-physical or *incorporeal*. But these reasons have to do with characteristics of the intellect that it does not share with sentience. Hence while human or rational animals are partly incorporeal, non-human animals are entirely corporeal.

Animal intelligence?

This naturally brings us to the question of whether any non-human animals are intelligent. Certainly some of them are, in a *loose* sense of "intelligent." For some of them solve problems, produce crude tools, and so forth. But as I noted in chapter 3, non-human animals no less than human ones can be said to possess not only the familiar external senses of seeing, hearing, tasting, touching, and smelling, but also the *internal* senses – the *synthetic sense*, *instinct* or the estimative power, the *imagination*, and *sensory memory*. Many of the clever things that non-human animals can do can be attributed to the operation of the internal senses, and thus give no evidence of intelligence in the strict sense that entails the possession of *intellect*. To have an intellect, you will recall, entails the ability to grasp *concepts*, to put them together into *propositions*, and to *reason logically* from one proposition to another.

I also argued in chapter 3 that for an animal to be intelligent in this strict sense requires *language*. But here too, you will recall, there is a crucial ambiguity. We noted Karl Popper's distinction between the *expressive*, *signaling*, *descriptive*, and *argumentative* functions of language. Some non-human animals are clearly capable of the first two of these functions. But it is only a capacity for the descriptive and argumentative functions that marks an animal as intelligent in the sense of having an intellect. So, the question of whether any non-human animals are intelligent in the strict sense ultimately boils down to the question of whether any of them exhibits linguistic behavior that is plausibly interpreted as conveying abstract concepts, propositions, and logical inferences.

The answer is that none of them does. The best known and most promising examples are apes to whom researchers have tried to teach American Sign Language (ASL) or some other system of linguistic symbols. But as Noam Chomsky observes, there are five crucial differences between human language and what such apes are capable of.[432] Two of them are biological. In human beings, Chomsky observes, language is associated with specific language centers in the brain that have no apparent parallel in apes. He also says that language developed in human beings long after their evolutionary separation from other primates.

But the remaining considerations are the more philosophically fundamental ones. In human beings, Chomsky points out, language is used in a way that is largely independent of immediate stimuli, the satisfaction of needs, or instrumental purposes. That is to say, we talk about things that are distant in time and space, and typically do so without intending that our utterances will get us some reward (e.g. food). Our use is also governed by rules determining the structure of utterances, in a recursive way that allows for a potentially infinite number of sentences. The alleged cases of language use by apes exhibits none of these key features. Furthermore, human children come to learn language by mere exposure to it, without the need for explicit training. Apes, by contrast, can be made to do things that look vaguely like simple human language use only after considerable training by human beings. To think this reflects a genuine capacity for language that lay dormant until human researchers came along to coax actual performance out of them is, Chomsky says, like supposing that there might be a species of birds who have the capacity to fly but won't exercise it until people teach them how to use it.

Careful examination of well-known cases of apes who have purportedly mastered language (such as Washoe, Nim Chimpsky, and Kanzi) reinforces this skepticism.[433] Wishful thinking, dubious inferences, problematic methodology, and conceptual imprecision are rife

---

[432] Noam Chomsky, *Rules and Representations* (New York: Columbia University Press, 1980), pp. 239-40. Chomsky develops the comparison at greater length in "Human Language and Other Semiotic Systems," in Thomas A. Sebeok and Jean Umiker-Sebeok, eds., *Speaking of Apes: A Critical Anthology of Two-Way Communication with Man* (New York: Plenum Press, 1980).
[433] Cf. Joel Wallman, *Aping Language* (Cambridge, MA: Cambridge University Press, 1992).

in the work of researchers who claim to have taught ASL or some other linguistic system to apes. In some cases, researchers have counted as examples of language use natural gestures that already existed before the training began.[434] Steven Pinker observes that:

> To arrive at their vocabulary counts in the hundreds, the investigators would also "translate" the chimps' pointing as a sign for *you*, their hugging as a sign for *hug*, their picking, tickling, and kissing as signs for *pick, tickle*, and *kiss*. Often the same movement would be credited to the chimps as different "words," depending on what the observers thought the appropriate word would be in the context. In the experiments in which the chimps interacted with a computer console, the key that the chimp had to press to initialize the computer was translated as the word *please*.[435]

Researchers have also been found to have been inadvertently prompting the signs that an ape would then go on to produce.[436] Failure correctly to produce actual ASL signs has sometimes been claimed to result merely from lack of sufficient dexterity rather than a lack of understanding of the signs.[437] In one study, cases where researchers disagreed about whether an ape's performance counted as an error, or about precisely what error was committed, were left out of the record of the ape's error rate.[438] There is no solid evidence in the apes' behavior of "displaced reference," or reference to things distant in space or time.[439] Nor, where a word for something close at hand is used, is there a distinction drawn between that thing and things associated

---

[434] Ibid., pp. 53-54.

[435] Steven Pinker, *The Language Instinct* (New York: HarperCollins, 1994), p. 338.

[436] Herbert S. Terrace, *Why Chimpanzees Can't Learn Language and Only Humans Can* (New York: Columbia University Press, 2019), pp. ix, 21, and 41-48.

[437] Wallman, *Aping Language*, p. 62.

[438] Ibid., p. 63.

[439] Ibid., pp. 65 and 69-70.

with it (e.g. between an apple, the knife used to cut it, and the location where it is kept).[440] Nor is there behavior clearly exhibiting anything more than mere conditioning to carry out an action so as to secure some reward (as opposed to genuine understanding of a name), or simple associations of the kind a dog exhibits when it carries its leash over to its owner so as to go out for a walk.[441] Nor is there any serious evidence that apes follow grammatical rules when emitting sequences of symbols (as opposed, say, to rote repetition of paired terms).[442]

Hardly less significant than the failure of apes to duplicate even the most rudimentary human linguistic competence are all the many glaring differences between human language of a slightly more sophisticated kind and the symbolic systems researchers have attempted to teach apes, even on a generous interpretation of those attempts. As Chomsky writes:

> As far as has been reported, they are strictly finite systems in principle (apart, perhaps, from trivial devices such as conjoining), with no significant notion of phrase and no recursive rules of embedding or structure-dependent operations... Similarly, elements basic to the semantics of human language, such as modality and propositional attitude, description and presupposition, aspect and anaphora and quantification, and so on, seem to be entirely lacking...
>
> [S]uch elementary and primitive uses of language as telling a story, requesting information merely to enhance understanding, expressing an opinion or a wish (as distinct from an instrumental request), monologue, casual conversation, and so

---

[440] Cf. Noam Chomsky, *What Kind of Creatures Are We?* (New York: Columbia University Press, 2016), pp. 42-43; Robert C. Berwick and Noam Chomsky, *Why Only Us: Language and Evolution* (Cambridge, MA: The MIT Press, 2016), pp. 145-46; and Pinker, *The Language Instinct*, p. 340.

[441] Wallman, *Aping Language*, pp. 64-76.

[442] Ibid., chapter 6. Cf. Berwick and Chomsky, *Why Only Us*, pp. 146-48; and Pinker, *The Language Instinct*, p. 339.

on, all typical of very young children, seem utterly unrelated to the functions of the ape systems.[443]

Nor do apes emit the alleged linguistic behavior they exhibit in a spontaneous way, as opposed to under prompting.[444] Nor do they take turns in conversation, but sign simultaneously with their partner and in a manner that is not clearly visible to him.[445] Nor, once they gain whatever facility with words human trainers are able to impart to them, do they pass it on to other chimpanzees.[446] Nor, unlike human beings, are they able to introduce new words by use of existing words.[447]

Arguments for linguistic competence in apes seem to get off the ground only because such obvious differences are ignored, while relatively trivial analogies between human and ape performance are overemphasized. As Chomsky says, appealing to such analogies to justify applying the "language" label to what apes and human beings have in common is like supposing that there is an interesting notion of "flight" on which "humans can 'fly' about 30 feet, chickens about 300 feet, Canada geese far more."[448] In reality, of course, "the study of broad jumping probably has little to offer concerning the flight of birds, or conversely."[449] Neither do the vague similarities between human and ape performance provide any interesting evidence that apes possess language of the kind that evinces intellect.

It is also fallacious to suggest, as is often done, that there is a close similarity between the best ape linguistic performance and the

---

[443] Chomsky, "Human Language and Other Semiotic Systems," pp. 435-36.

[444] Pinker, The Language Instinct, p. 340.

[445] Ibid.

[446] Mortimer J. Adler, Intellect: Mind Over Matter (New York: Collier Books, 1990), p. 32.

[447] Ibid., p. 33.

[448] Chomsky, "Human Language and Other Semiotic Systems," p. 430.

[449] Ibid., p. 440.

worst human performance, such as that exhibited by mentally impaired human beings or very small children. As Chomsky says, to think this shows that such apes are exhibiting the early stages of genuine linguistic development is like supposing that a human child flapping his arms "is exhibiting 'incipient flight motions.'"[450] From an Aristotelian point of view, what matters to determining what capacities an organism of a certain kind possesses is what it does naturally when in its mature and healthy state. Human beings in their mature and healthy state naturally manifest a capacity for language. Apes in their mature and healthy state do not. That supports the judgment that even a small child or mentally impaired human being has a capacity for language – even if one that has not yet been developed, and perhaps never will be – whereas an ape coached by human beings to clever mimicry does not have such a capacity.

Chomsky's critique focuses on the absence of grammar from apes' purported linguistic performance. But as psychologist Herbert Terrace argues, a more fundamental problem is that apes do not even truly learn individual words, let alone the ability to combine them in a rule-governed way.[451] The reason, he maintains, is that they lack two factors crucial to the way human children learn language: the *intersubjectivity* and *joint attention* characteristic of early bonding between mothers and their infants.[452] Intersubjectivity has to do with the capacity to share psychological states (such as emotions), and develops by way of an infant's imitation of his mother's facial expressions. A baby smiling in response to seeing his mother's smile would be an example. Joint attention builds on intersubjectivity, and has to do with the capacity of mother and infant together to perceive some external object. An example would be a baby pointing at some object, and the laughter that she and the baby share confirming that they both see

---

[450] Ibid., p. 437.

[451] Terrace, *Why Chimpanzees Can't Learn Language and Only Humans Can*.

[452] Ibid., pp. 25-28 and chapter 4.

it.⁴⁵³ This understanding of what is going on in each other's minds is necessary for mother and child to come to *refer* to the same objects, and reference is essential to coming to learn words. Terrace judges that, lacking intersubjectivity and joint attention, apes also lack reference. This is why they never exhibit what he calls the "declarative" use of language that is characteristic of humans – talking about something simply for its own sake, as opposed to the "imperative" practice of emitting noises so as to secure something one wants, such as food.⁴⁵⁴ (To use Popper's language, apes are capable of only the *expressive* and *signaling* functions of language, not the *descriptive* function, let alone the *argumentative* one.)

But are non-human animals truly devoid of mental states like the ones in question? Might there not be behavioral criteria apart from language that would justify the attribution of such states to them? For instance, couldn't it be said that a dog comes running because it *believes* that you have put food in its bowl, or that when it brings over its leash it *wants* to go for a walk and *understands* that you will see that that is what it wants? Examples like this might seem to justify attributing *propositional attitudes* to non-human animals after all.⁴⁵⁵

But appearances here are deceptive. To begin to see the problem, note that, as is acknowledged by at least one defender of this view, if a non-human animal possesses a belief or propositional attitude of some other kind, we should be able to identify its *content*, and this is by no means an easy task.⁴⁵⁶ Suppose a dog runs after a cat who

---

⁴⁵³ As Terrace points out (pp. 125-30), *joint attention* is to be distinguished from *gaze following*, which non-human animals do possess. Gaze following is a matter of an animal seeing what another animal sees, perhaps as a result of seeing that the other animal sees it. But it lacks the quality of *sharing* the experience that is distinctive of joint attention.

⁴⁵⁴ Ibid., p. 129.

⁴⁵⁵ For an overview of recent debate on this issue, see chapter 4 of George Graham, *Philosophy of Mind: An Introduction*, Second edition (Oxford: Blackwell, 1998); and the readings in Part 7 of Brie Gertler and Lawrence Shapiro, eds., *Arguing About the Mind* (London: Routledge, 2007).

⁴⁵⁶ Graham, *Philosophy of Mind*, pp. 76-80.

appears to have scampered up a tree, and starts to bark as it looks up. Should we say that the dog believes that a *cat* has run up the tree? That it believes that *a small furry animal* has run up the tree? That it believes that *its enemy* has run up the tree? Should we say that it believes that it has run up *a tree*, or that it has run up *an elongated beige object with lots of green stuff at the top*? Exactly which *concepts* should we attribute to the dog?

It is simply not plausible to attribute *any* of these concepts to it. Possessing a concept entails the ability logically to relate it to other concepts. If, for example, you know that John is a bachelor, then you know, among other things, that John does not have a wife, and that he is a man. To possess the concept bachelor entails such knowledge, and thus entails having further concepts like the concept *having a wife* and the concept *man*. It also involves being able to draw inferences such as that *if John gets married, he will no longer be a bachelor*. Now, there is no reason to think that a dog is capable of relating concepts like *cat, tree, small furry animal*, etc. to other concepts in ways like these. Hence there is no reason to attribute such concepts to a dog – and in that case, no reason to attribute a belief to it.

What would give evidence of such mastery of concepts is language, and there is hardly any better reason to think that dogs possess language than there is to think that apes possess it. Indeed, as I argued in chapter 3, possession of language is a necessary condition for having concepts. Hence, if a non-human animal lacks language, it is not just that we lack any reason to think it possesses concepts and beliefs. We have positive reason to judge that it does not possess concepts or beliefs.

Roger Fellows has developed an argument to this effect, modifying a line of argument first presented by Donald Davidson.[457] Consider first that, in order to have a belief, one must have concepts. But

---

[457] Roger Fellows, "Animal Belief," *Philosophy* 75 (2000): 587-98. The relevant articles by Davidson are "Thought and Talk" and "Radical Interpretation," in Donald Davidson, *Inquiries into Truth and Interpretation* (Oxford: Clarendon Press, 1984), and "Rational Animals," in Davidson's *Subjective, Intersubjective, Objective* (Oxford: Clarendon Press, 2001). Fellows's argument is Davidsonian, but not exactly Davidson's, since he modifies what he takes to be incomplete or erroneous aspects of Davidson's position.

in order to have a concept, one must be able to entertain *counterfactuals* – that is to say, one has to be able to know what *would* be the case *if* certain conditions were to obtain. For example, in order to have the concept of *cat*, one must know that if something is a cat, then it will be alive, it will have whiskers, and so on. Now, to entertain counterfactuals requires grasping the difference between truth and falsity (since, for example, to know counterfactuals like the ones in question requires understanding that it is false to classify something as a cat if it is not a living thing). But to grasp the difference between truth and falsity entails having the concept of *belief*, since truth and falsity have to do with whether a belief accurately represents reality or not. Hence, the capacity to have beliefs ultimately presupposes having the *concept* of belief.

That's one premise in Fellows's main argument. Another premise is that to have the concept of belief requires being a language user. Again, to have the concept of belief goes hand in hand with grasping the difference between truth and falsity. But to grasp that difference entails the ability to hold before the mind the content of the "that" clause in a statement of the form *X believes that p*. Take, for example, the statement that *John believes that the cat is on the mat*. In order to understand the difference between this belief's being true and its being false, one must be able to hold before one's mind the notion *that the cat is on the mat* and compare it to reality in order to determine whether or not it accurately represents it. But the only way to hold that before the mind is *linguistically*, for example, by entertaining a sentence like the English sentence "The cat is on the mat." Thus, again, Fellows concludes that to grasp the concept of belief entails being a language user.

We have, then, the premises of Fellows's main argument, to the effect that *the capacity to have beliefs presupposes having the concept of belief* and that *having the concept of belief requires being a language user*. From these two premises, it follows that if something is not a language user, then it cannot have beliefs. Hence, since non-human animals are not language users, they cannot have beliefs. Again, this dovetails what we saw in chapter 3 about the close connection between the possession of concepts and the capacity for language.

Empirical considerations lend further support to this philosophical line of argument. Biologist Daniel Povinelli argues that the evidence reveals apes to be incapable of grasping what is unobservable.[458] For example, the way chimpanzees come to learn that there is no point in signaling to a fellow chimpanzee who is blindfolded indicates that they are responding merely to outward physical features rather than entertaining the idea that others have or lack the *experience* of seeing. They seem to lack anything like a notion of causal *power*, as opposed to the mere observed conjunction of a cause with its effect. Even after attempts to teach them numerical notions, they appear incapable of genuine counting (as opposed to merely noting that one collection is larger or smaller than another), or of grasping numbers as entities in their own right. The empirical evidence also undermines the sensationalistic claims often made about the alleged intelligence and linguistic capacity of other animals, such as dolphins.[459] Such results are consistent with the Aristotelian thesis that while some non-human animals possess imagery, sensory memory, and instinct, they lack true *concepts*, which, unlike the former powers, outstrip anything that is observable.

The reader might still find it plausible that there is *something* to the idea that animals have beliefs – for instance, that the dog in my example possesses at least something *like* a belief that the cat is in the tree. But as Fellows points out, it is perfectly possible to acknowledge the validity of this intuition while denying that dogs have beliefs in the sense in which we have them:

> The denial of animal belief does not entail the truth of behaviorism... There is no difficulty with the idea that the brains of non-linguistic animal kinds contain (non-semantic) infor-

---

[458] Daniel Povinelli, "Behind the Ape's Appearance: Escaping Anthropocentrism in the Study of Other Minds," in Gertler and Shapiro, eds., *Arguing about the Mind*. Cf. Raymond Tallis, *Aping Mankind: Neuromania, Darwinitis, and the Misrepresentation of Humanity* (Durham: Acumen, 2011), pp. 157-61.

[459] Cf. Justin Gregg, *Are Dolphins Really Smart? The Mammal Behind the Myth* (Oxford: Oxford University Press, 2013).

mation-bearing states, which function in ways which are analogous, within a restricted domain, to the ways in which beliefs function in the human community.[460]

Again, such animals possess mental imagery, instinct or "estimative power," and sensory memory. This gives their behavior a flexibility and sophistication that goes well beyond that of creatures capable only of responding to immediate stimuli. Because imagery can resemble more than merely the particular sensed object that initially generated it, some non-human animals can even respond to classes of objects rather than merely to individuals, despite lacking mental representations with the strict universality of concepts. For these reasons, there is in such animals something *analogous* to what we call beliefs, desires, etc. in us. But it is only wishful thinking or conceptual imprecision to suppose that what they are doing is the same or continuous with what we do. It is comparable to supposing that adding sides to a polygon can yield a circle. In fact this can in principle only ever yield an approximation to a circle, and what non-human animals do at most only ever approximates what beings with intellects can do. As Fellows notes, when we go beyond the claim of a mere analogy, and attribute to non-human animals beliefs with conceptual content (as we do when we say, for example, that a dog believes that its master is present) we are merely *projecting* the way *we* conceptually carve up the world onto the animal, which does not itself conceptualize anything at all.[461] Certainly we are going beyond the evidence, which can be entirely explained by reference to sub-intellectual powers like the ones traditionally attributed by Aristotelians to non-human animals.[462]

Let's summarize the results of this chapter. A living thing is a substance characterized by immanent or self-perfective activity, and an animal is a corporeal living thing characterized by sentience. Sentience is entirely corporeal, but it is nevertheless irreducible to the properties and powers possessed by inorganic substances or by merely

---

[460] Fellows, "Animal Belief," p. 589.

[461] Ibid., p. 594.

[462] Cf. James M. Stedman, Matthew Kostelecky, Thomas L. Spalding, and Christina L. Gagné, "Animal Cognition: An Aristotelian-Thomistic Perspective," *The Journal of Mind and Behavior* 38 (2017): 193-214.

vegetative forms of life. Hence animals alone are sentient. But no non-human animals rise above mere sentience, and in particular, none of them possesses an intellect.

Having now set out in detail the natures of both *rationality* and *animality*, we are ready to consider their relationship in human beings. The next two chapters aim to refute two common errors: the *Cartesian* error, which entirely separates our rationality from our animality; and the *materialist* error, which entirely assimilates our rationality to our animality. For the Cartesian, a human being is a composite of two substances, one corporeal and one incorporeal; for the materialist, a human being is a single entirely corporeal substance. The truth, as I will argue, is that a human being is a single substance with both corporeal and incorporeal properties and powers. We are neither angels nor apes, but something in between.

Part III:

What is a Human Being?

7. Against Cartesianism

The Cartesian prison

We have now examined in some detail what it is to have a mind and what it is to have a body. And we have made our analysis more precise by speaking, more specifically, of *rationality* and *animality* and what each entails. Now, what is the relationship between them in human beings? According to a view historically associated with Plato and Descartes, it is our rationality alone that is essential to us, with animality, and indeed corporeality, being no more truly a part of a person than his clothing is. A human being, on this view, is an *incorporeal* or immaterial substance, with which the body is only contingently associated. This view is commonly known as *substance dualism*.

It is only fair to note that there are nuances in the views of Plato and Descartes, and important differences between their accounts, which are often ignored in discussions of their views about human nature.[463] But our interest here is not in Plato or Descartes exegesis. It is in a certain conception of human nature that, in modern philosophy, evolved out of their dualism, and out of Descartes' version in particular. Because of Descartes' special influence on this conception, I will follow standard practice by referring to it as *Cartesianism*, bracketing off questions about how closely its details correspond to the views of Descartes himself.

There are three key elements of the Cartesian conception of human nature, the first of which I have already mentioned. The self,

---

[463] For a detailed treatment of Plato's position, see Lloyd P. Gerson, *Knowing Persons: A Study in Plato* (Oxford: Oxford University Press, 2003). For discussion of the nuances in Descartes' position, see Gordon Baker and Katherine J. Morris, *Descartes' Dualism* (London: Routledge, 1996) and Marleen Rozemond, *Descartes's Dualism* (Cambridge, MA: Harvard University Press, 1998).

for Cartesianism, is a wholly incorporeal substance. Arms and legs, eyes and ears, the digestive and nervous systems, and animal organs and functions in general are as entirely extrinsic to it as tables, chairs, rocks, and trees. Like the latter, the human body is regarded as part of the "external world," viz. the realm of material objects distinct from the immaterial *res cogitans* or "thinking substance" that is the human mind. (That external world, including the human body, is in turn conceived of by the Cartesian along the lines of the mechanical world picture I criticized in the preceding two chapters.)

This first element of Cartesianism is metaphysical. The second is epistemological. It is the thesis that the foundation of the self's knowledge of anything, including the external world, is to be found in *innate ideas*. Following the Aristotelian-Thomistic tradition, I argued in chapter 3 that concepts differ in kind and not merely in degree from mental imagery, so that the intellect differs in kind and not degree from sentience. Early modern rationalist thinkers like Descartes agree with this judgment, but draw the conclusion that concepts, or at least the most basic of our concepts, must in no way derive from the senses or imagination, and instead are *built into* the mind. For this reason, these concepts, and certain propositions built out of them, are and indeed must be knowable independently of the senses might tell us. In this way, knowledge of the self and its ideas is prior to knowledge of anything else.

The third element is simultaneously metaphysical and epistemological, and concerns the notion that what the self is directly aware of are only ever *representations* of things rather than things themselves. The epistemological aspect of this idea is known as *indirect realism* or *representative realism*, because it doesn't deny that there really is a world independent of our representations of it. It is, in that respect, realist. What it claims is rather that we know that mind-independent reality only *indirectly, by way of* the representations that external objects cause in our minds. But the causal relation between these objects and our representations of them is taken to be contingent insofar as the representations would have exactly the same character whether or not they had been caused by those objects, and indeed whether or not there were any external world at all. It would, on this view, still seem to me that I am sitting here typing these words even if the computer in front of me, my body, and indeed the entire material world were entirely illusory. There is in this way a "self-containedness" to mental representations, and this amounts to a metaphysical or ontological thesis additional to the epistemological one.[464] For it is a claim about the *nature* of these representations, albeit one that underlies the epistemological claim that we cannot directly know the world beyond them.

The first of these three theses is, again, known as *substance dualism*, and the other two are often referred to as *innatism* and *representationalism*, respectively. They might seem to be independent claims insofar as one could, in principle, accept one without committing oneself to either of the others. But there is at the very least a natural affinity between them that makes it unsurprising that they came together to define the broadly Cartesian conception of human nature. We can see how in light of the Scholastic philosophical principle *agere sequitur esse*, or "action follows being."[465] What this means is that what a thing *does* reflects what it *is*, so that we can infer something about the activities of a thing from what we know about its nature, and vice versa. If the self is a wholly incorporeal thinking substance, complete just as it is whether or not any body is associated with it, then it is hard to see how its capacity for knowledge could depend on a body's sense organs. Innatism thus seems to follow from substance dualism. Since such a substance and its activities would be complete whether or not any body or material world in general existed or not, the "self-containedness" of thought posited by representationalism seems to follow as well.

Because much depends on how the details of each of these three views is worked out, I stop short of claiming that there is a strict entailment from substance dualism to the other two theses. Moreover, each of them has at least a grain of truth. I will argue in the next

---

[464] Cf. Gregory McCulloch, *The Mind and Its World* (London: Routledge, 1995), pp. 11-17. Cf. John McDowell, "Singular Thought and the Extent of Inner Space," in Philip Pettit and John McDowell, eds., *Subject, Thought, and Context* (Oxford: Clarendon Press, 1986), especially the discussion at pp. 145-55.

[465] For exposition and defense of this principle, see Edward Feser, *Five Proofs of the Existence of God* (San Francisco: Ignatius Press, 2017), pp. 174-76.

chapter that a human being's intellectual powers are indeed incorporeal, even if this does not entail that he is a wholly incorporeal substance. I will also argue that we have an innate *capacity* for forming concepts, even if concepts themselves are not innate. And there is a sense in which we perceive the world outside us *by way of* mental representations, even if mental representations are not themselves the direct *objects* of perception. But the Cartesian takes the incorporeality of the human *intellect* to entail the incorporeality of the human *person* as a whole, and this distortion of human nature naturally suggests the other two distortions as well.

The upshot of these distortions is a radical alienation of the self from the body and from the material world more generally. In Plato's *Phaedo*, this alienation is conveyed in the image of the body as the soul's prison. In the centuries since Descartes wrote, his conception of the mind has seemed to his critics to make of *it* a kind of prison. If the self is entirely whole regardless of the existence of the body and the material world more generally, if it need not rely on information from them in order to know anything, and if its own ideas are all it can directly know in the first place, how can it be certain that there really *is* anything distinct from it? Notoriously, the Cartesian ego seems trapped within itself. And as John McDowell has emphasized, the problem is not just that the Cartesian picture appears to make the external world *unknowable*, but that it seems to make it *unthinkable*. It's not merely that we're locked in a Cartesian theater, having direct access only to mental representations of the external world, and cannot be certain that there really is anything outside the theater, anything which corresponds to the representations. It's also that the Cartesian picture threatens to make it unintelligible how our experiences could count as true *representations* in the first place – how they could have the *intentionality* they do, how they could so much as *stand for* or be *about* external objects (whether or not those objects exist).

The problem derives from the *contingency* of the connection between mind and world posited by the Cartesian picture. Here's an analogy (mine, not McDowell's). Words like "dog" and "cat" have no inherent or necessary connection to dogs and cats. They are, of themselves, just meaningless strings of shapes or noises (depending on whether they are written or spoken). The connection of these symbols to the dogs and cats they represent is a matter of convention. Now, the convention gets set up because our thoughts about dogs and cats *do* have some kind of necessary connection to the things they are about, and the linguistic symbols inherit this connection by standing in for the thoughts – or so it seems. But on the Cartesian model of the mind, mental states too have only a contingent connection to external reality. For, again, the model holds that the mental realm could be exactly as it is even if there were no external world corresponding to it. So, how do mental states have, in that case, any more power to represent external reality than meaningless strings of shapes or sounds do? How can they have what philosophers call any "intentional content" at all? McDowell concludes that "it [is] quite unclear that the fully Cartesian picture is entitled to characterize its inner facts in content-involving terms – in terms of its seeming to one that things are thus and so – at all," so that the mental realm it posits is "blank or blind" rather than having any genuine intentionality or aboutness.[466] If the Cartesian conception were correct, our own experience would have the character of what William James called, in another context, "one great blooming, buzzing confusion."[467] It would not even *seem to be* an experience of a world of tables, chairs, dogs, cats, trees, clouds, and people.

Properly to understand human cognition, however, is to see that the connection between the mind and the material world is *not* contingent. Rather, human intellection and perception are *essentially embodied*. As we will see in a later chapter, this does not rule out the possibility of abnormal circumstances in which the intellect exists and operates apart from the body. The point is that such circumstances would be *abnormal*. The norm even for human intellection, and certainly for perception, is for the mind to operate only in tandem with – indeed, one might say, only utterly *immersed* in – the corporeal realm.

---

[466] McDowell, "Singular Thought and the Extent of Inner Space," p. 152.

[467] William James, *The Principles of Psychology, Volume One* (New York: Dover Publications, 1950), p. 488.

Being in the world

We can begin with the most obvious ways in which the mind seems dependent on the body, which are commonly emphasized by materialists.[468] We know from everyday experience that drugs and alcohol, lack of sleep, aging, and damage to the brain all have dramatic effects on mental functioning, including the most abstract of rational thought processes. We know that the mental capacities we share with other animals, such as perception, are in them entirely dependent on bodily organs to which our own organs are similar in all relevant respects. We know from neuroscience that there are correlations between specific mental capacities (for visual experience, language use, etc.) and specific areas of the brain. The substance dualist will insist that all of this reflects nothing more than the brain's role as *mediator* between the immaterial *res cogitans* and the rest of the body. But the dependence of the mind on the brain is much stronger than one would expect if the brain were merely a mediator. Descartes holds that the mind is a complete substance in its own right, the very essence of which is to think, and that the body is a distinct substance wholly devoid of thought. If that were true, one would suppose that no matter how grave the damage to the body and brain, at least the most abstract of intellectual processes would be completely unaffected, even if they would no longer be able to guide bodily behavior. But that is not in fact what we find.

Frederick Olafson notes several other ways, obvious upon reflection, in which a person's relationship to his body has an intimacy that his relationship to other physical objects lacks.[469] With a tool or other piece of equipment, you can lay it down and take it up again at will, but you cannot do that with your body. You cannot view your body from outside, the way you can view other physical things, but

---

[468] See e.g. Paul M. Churchland, *Matter and Consciousness*, Revised edition (Cambridge, MA: The MIT Press, 1988), pp. 18-21. Some writers who are critical of materialist reductionism nevertheless also emphasize these manifest ways in which mind depends on body. See e.g. Raymond Tallis, *I Am: A Philosophical Inquiry into First-Person Being* (Edinburgh: Edinburgh University Press, 2004), chapter 6.

[469] Frederick A. Olafson, *What Is a Human Being? A Heideggerian View* (Cambridge: Cambridge University Press, 1995), chapter 6.

only from within, by way of inhabiting it. But neither, for the most part, do you know what is going on with it by way of viewing it even from within. Rather you simply know it without need of observation, just by virtue of its being *your* body. You don't *come across* or *encounter* your body. Rather, it is itself *that by which* you come across or encounter things. In the ordinary case, there is nothing you need to do in order to move your body, as when you walk or pick something up. Your deliberately moving your arm, for example, just *is* an action, rather than some *effect* of an action. (Contrast your movement of a stick or a chair, which *is* an effect of your action.) Similarly, when you spontaneously laugh or cry at something, these are not further effects in your body of some prior effect on you (as if your body were some external object that would not exhibit this behavior unless you made it do so). Rather, they themselves just are part of the effect on you. Such aspects of everyday experience of the body are just what one would expect if the body just is the person or part of the person, but not what one would expect if, as the Cartesian claims, a person and his body are utterly distinct substances.

There are, however, also subtler but no less philosophically significant ways in which human intellection and perception are essentially embodied. They were explored in depth by twentieth-century philosophers like Ludwig Wittgenstein, Martin Heidegger, Gilbert Ryle, Maurice Merleau-Ponty, and Michael Polanyi.[470] Needless to say, these are thinkers of diverse and sometimes conflicting commitments. As that fact indicates, one need not endorse everything said by any of them in order to see the force of the lines of thought they have in common. The recurring theme most relevant to our purposes is that of *tacit knowledge*. The idea is that the explicit content of all our cognitive states presupposes a body of *in*explicit knowledge, where this knowledge is fundamentally a matter of *knowing how* to interact with

---

[470] Cf. Ludwig Wittgenstein, *Philosophical Investigations*, Third edition (New York: Macmillan, 1968); Ludwig Wittgenstein, *On Certainty* (New York: Harper and Row, 1972); Martin Heidegger, *Being and Time*, translated by John Macquarrie and Edward Robinson (New York: Harper and Row, 1962); Gilbert Ryle, "Knowing How and Knowing That," *Proceedings of the Aristotelian Society* 46 (1945-46): 1-16; Gilbert Ryle, *The Concept of Mind* (New York: Barnes and Noble, 1949); Maurice Merleau-Ponty, *Phenomenology of Perception*, translated by Donald A. Landes (London: Routledge, 2012); Michael Polanyi, *Personal Knowledge* (Chicago: University of Chicago Press, 1962); and Michael Polanyi, *The Tacit Dimension* (Garden City, NY: Doubleday, 1966).

the world, rather than a matter of *knowing that* such-and-such propositions are true. It is knowledge essentially embedded in *bodily capacities*.

This conception of human knowledge contrasts with what I have called Cartesianism's "representationalist" conception.[471] Now, representationalism was fundamental to the epistemological side of the early modern intellectual revolution, of which the mechanical world picture was the metaphysical side. Like the mechanical philosophy, it became common ground between modern views otherwise at odds – empiricist and rationalist, materialist and dualist alike. Hubert Dreyfus and Charles Taylor have developed a penetrating analysis of this generic representationalism, and identify four key components.[472] First, the representationalist holds that our knowledge of objective reality is *mediated* by knowledge of representations of some sort – whether ideas in a Cartesian *res cogitans*, or patterns encoded in neural structures, or the formal symbols of a computer program, or whatever. Second, the content of these representations is taken to be clearly and explicitly defined rather than tacit. Third, it is held that the justification of all knowledge claims can never get beyond or below these explicitly formulated representations – especially the subset of foundational or "given" representations, if there is one (though on some versions of representationalism, there is not).

The fourth component of representationalism is what Dreyfus and Taylor call the "dualist sorting" of reality into the representations themselves on the one hand and the physical world they represent on the other, where the latter is conceived of in terms of the mechanical world picture. Descartes put this dualism forward as an ontological

---

[471] Again, the point is not to deny the existence of mental representations themselves, as should be obvious from what was said in chapter 3, but only to reject a Cartesian conception of them. Some writers put such emphasis on cognition's embodied nature that they deny that mental representations need play any role at all in understanding human cognition. (See e.g. Anthony Chemero, *Radical Embodied Cognitive Science* (Cambridge, MA: The MIT Press, 2009.) But this eliminativist conclusion doesn't follow from the considerations to be adduced below, and in any event the arguments marshalled in chapter 3 show it to be false.

[472] Hubert Dreyfus and Charles Taylor, *Retrieving Realism* (Cambridge, MA: Harvard University Press, 2015), pp. 10-12.

thesis, carving the world into the material and the immaterial, *res extensa* and *res cogitans*. Materialists reject this aspect of the Cartesian picture, holding that the representations ought to be identified instead with some subset of the denizens of the material world (such as brain processes), construed mechanistically. As we've seen in earlier chapters, since this mechanistic picture characterizes matter as devoid of teleology and secondary qualities, this leaves the materialist with the problem of explaining *how* the intentionality and qualia that characterize these representations could be properties of matter so defined. In these ways, as Dreyfus and Taylor note, representationalism generated the modern "mind-body problem."

Though representationalism is an epistemological thesis, it has, as I noted above, a metaphysical aspect as well. Materialists suppose the representations in question to be mere bits of matter alongside all the others, construed mechanistically. By contrast, the Cartesian takes the representations to be essentially disembodied, since he supposes that their conceptual and perceptual content would be entirely transparent to the mind even in the absence of a material world. For critics of representationalism like Wittgenstein, Heidegger, and the others named above, neither of these suppositions is correct, so that neither the materialist nor the Cartesian account of human nature can be correct either. These thinkers argue (contra the Cartesian) that there is content to human cognition and perception that is not transparent to the mind, but rather necessarily exists below the level of consciousness and in an essentially embodied form. But the way it exists there entails (contra the materialist) that the body cannot be understood mechanistically, as a clockwork-like aggregate of insentient and meaningless parts. What these thinkers are engaged in is, in effect, a rediscovery of the Aristotelian conception of human nature, even if they do not always think of themselves as doing this and even if some of them would resist this characterization.[473]

---

[473] Neglect of the Aristotelian tradition sometimes leads such thinkers into non sequiturs. For example, John Haugeland takes the considerations revealing the embodied nature of cognition to show that there are no clear boundaries between mind, body, and world, so that they are best thought of as a single system. (Cf. "Mind Embodied and Embedded," in Haugeland's *Having Thought: Essays in the Metaphysics of Mind* (Cambridge, MA: Harvard University Press, 1998).) Among his reasons for this judgment is the observation that things in the world, no less than representations in the mind, are "meaningful" and part of a "web

Embodied intellection

The considerations indicating the embodied nature of intellectual activity and those indicating the embodied nature of perception are related but distinct. Let us begin with intellectual activity, which, as noted in chapter 3, involves three main capacities: first, the capacity to form abstract concepts; second, the capacity to combine concepts into a complete thought or proposition; and third, the capacity to reason from one proposition to another in accordance with canons of logical inference. Critics of representationalism like those mentioned above sometimes present their objections in the form of *regress arguments*.[474] These arguments come in different versions, which emphasize different intellectual capacities among the three I just identified.

Consider first the regress entailed by the grasp of a concept, and John Searle's way of spelling it out.[475] In order for you to grasp any one concept, you need to grasp others. For example, to understand the concept of a *bachelor*, you need to understand the concept of a *man* and the concept of *being unmarried*; and understanding these further concepts requires grasping yet other concepts in turn. *Applying* a concept also presupposes background knowledge. To borrow an example from Searle, in order to have the intention of running for President of the United States, you have to know that in order to become the President one has to win an election, that to win one needs to run a successful campaign, and so forth. Our understanding and

---

of significance," even if they aren't themselves representations. But the Aristotelian would say that this is a mark of their exhibiting *teleology or final causality*, not evidence that the mind is somehow "embedded" in the external world, whatever exactly that would mean. Though intending to escape the Cartesian tradition, Haugeland inadvertently presupposes the Cartesian-cum-mechanistic anti-teleological assumption that "directedness" or "aboutness" only exists in the mind. Hence when he notes the presence of directedness or aboutness in the physical world, he wrongly concludes that the *mind* must therefore in some way extend into the physical world.

[474] For a useful overview, see Neil Gascoigne and Tim Thornton, *Tacit Knowledge* (Durham: Acumen, 2013).

[475] Cf. John R. Searle, *Intentionality: An Essay in the Philosophy of Mind* (Cambridge: Cambridge University Press, 1983), chapter 5; and John R. Searle, *The Rediscovery of the Mind* (Cambridge, MA: The MIT Press, 1992), chapter 8.

application of concepts thus takes place within what Searle calls a *Network* of beliefs, intentions, etc.

Now, when applying a concept, we obviously don't bring to consciousness all the other concepts and beliefs that it presupposes. When you have the conscious thought "Fred is a bachelor," you don't necessarily at the same time consciously think "That Fred is a bachelor entails that Fred is a man," etc. That is one sense in which the explicit content of our thoughts presupposes something inexplicit. But there is a deeper sense in which it does so. To borrow another example from Searle, suppose you go into a restaurant and say "Bring me a steak with fried potatoes." Even if both you and the waiter do bring to consciousness the concept of *steak*, the concept of *bringing something*, etc. and consciously relate these concepts to the further concepts in terms of which they are to be defined, the precise way to *apply* all of this explicit knowledge is still as yet undetermined. For there is nothing in the Network of concepts and beliefs that go into defining what it is to be steak, etc. that by itself determines that when the waiter brings you the steak, it will be on a plate rather than encased in concrete, that he will place it on the table rather than shoving it into your pocket, and so on. Of course, in ordinary circumstances we would never for a moment expect these bizarre things to happen. The point, though, is that the supposition that they won't happen is one which is usually not *explicit* or conscious. We simply take it for granted that the steak will be on a plate, will be placed on the table, and so forth.

Naturally, we could make these assumptions explicit if we wanted to. You could consciously think "When the waiter brings me the steak, it will be on a plate and he will place it on the table." The waiter could consciously think "When I take the steak to the customer, I will not shove it into his pocket and it will not be encased in concrete." But as Searle points out, even if this happens, there will always be yet *further* assumptions that are not conscious or explicit. Precisely because there will be, the regress through the Network is not infinite. It ends with a set of capacities, dispositions, and ways of acting which Searle calls the *Background* against which the Network operates. The Background involves our behaving *as if* we were explicitly and consciously affirming propositions, when in fact we are not doing so. The waiter does not consciously entertain the thought that he needs to put the steak on the table and not in your pocket. He is simply unconsciously *disposed to act* in that particular way rather than some other way. You do not consciously entertain the proposition that the waiter will put the steak on the table rather than try to put it into your pocket. You are simply *disposed to act* in a way that presupposes this. For example, when you see him coming, you clear the area of the table directly in front of you, and you do not pull your pocket open. Insofar as the Background involves the exercise of capacities, the manifestation of dispositions, and the like, rather than the conscious entertaining of propositions, its operation is a matter of our *knowing how* to act rather than *knowing that* such-and-such propositions are true.

Searle draws a further distinction, between the "local Background" and the "deep Background." The local Background has to do with those unconscious capacities, dispositions, and ways of acting which are culturally and historically contingent, and thus which at least in principle can change from time to time and place to place. The custom of placing a customer's steak on the table rather than in his pocket and not encasing it in concrete first would be an example. There could be cases (even if very odd ones) where these particular Background dispositions change. For example, imagine that someone opens a theme restaurant devoted to performance art or pranks, where customers are told that they should expect the unexpected.

The deep Background, by contrast, involves capacities, dispositions, and ways of acting that are hardwired into us. For example, they might reflect our specific biological constitution. Even if cultural and historical circumstances change, we are not going to form a Background disposition to fly by flapping our arms, because the physical and biological facts simply do not allow for that. Or the deep Background dispositions might go even deeper than that, as those which presuppose realism about the material world outside our minds do. Even a reader of Descartes' *Meditations* who starts to wonder whether tables, chairs, rocks, trees, and even his own body are hallucinations will unthinkingly exercise capacities that presuppose that they are real. For example, he might put the book down momentarily and rub his chin pensively. He might walk over to the refrigerator to grab a beer to drink before he reads any further. If his roommate throws a baseball at him while he is reading, he will duck. And so forth. The deep Background dispositions that presuppose that his chin, the floor under his feet, the refrigerator, the beer, the baseball, etc. are all real run far deeper than any doubts about them he might entertain in his philosophical moments.

Now, these Background capacities, dispositions, and ways of acting, and especially the deep Background ones, are essentially *bodily* capacities, dispositions, and ways of acting. For they involve ways of speaking, gesturing, walking, picking things up, eating, etc. all of which involve use of the body and its organs. In this way our grasp of abstract concepts presupposes embodiment.

A second sort of regress argument involves our assent to propositions and our deployment of canons of logical inference. Suppose I explicitly assent to the proposition that *Socrates is mortal* upon considering the proposition that *all men are mortal* and the proposition that *Socrates is a man*. I have reasoned through what logicians call an AAA-1 form categorical syllogism, but it may be that I am unaware of having done so. After all, most people would draw that conclusion from those premises even if they had never taken a logic class and know nothing about the standard classification of forms of reasoning. When they entertain the propositions that *all men are mortal* and that *Socrates is a man*, it just strikes them as obvious that Socrates must therefore be mortal. Their explicit knowledge that *Socrates is mortal* rests on inexplicit or tacit knowledge of the validity of reasoning of the AAA-1 type.

Now, a person could, of course, become self-conscious about what sort of reasoning he is deploying in cases like these, as logic students do. The fact that he is conscious of it may even play a role in his justification for believing the conclusion. Whereas the untutored reasoner might say "Socrates is mortal, *because* all men are mortal and Socrates is a man," the logic student might say "Socrates is mortal, *because* all men are mortal and Socrates is a man, *and* an AAA-1 form syllogism is always valid." But even if this knowledge becomes explicit, there will always be yet further knowledge that is not explicit. As Ryle points out, a very slow student may explicitly know that *Socrates is a man*, that *all men are mortal*, and that *AAA-1 form syllogisms are valid*, and still not put all this knowledge together in the right way. It might somehow just not "click" for him that *Socrates is mortal*. What this student lacks is the inexplicit knowledge that the normal student has. Suppose we try to solve the problem by making this knowledge explicit and teaching it to the slow student that way. We might formulate it as the proposition that *if AAA-1 form syllogisms are valid and all men are mortal and Socrates is a man, then Socrates is mortal*, and then add this new explicit proposition to the already explicit set of propositions that *AAA-1 form syllogisms are valid, all men are mortal*, and *Socrates is a man*. But even if the student now sees that this new proposition is true, if he is very, *very* slow he may *still* not see that the conclusion that *Socrates is mortal* follows. And so on for any further proposition we make explicit and add to the mix.[476]

So, adding further explicit propositions will not solve the problem, and it is not what solves the problem in the case of the normal student. If it were, then since there is always yet another further explicit proposition we could add, what the normal student would be doing is explicitly grasping an infinite series of explicitly formulated propositions, all at once, when he judges that *Socrates is mortal*. Obviously, that is not what is going on. What is going on, Ryle argues, is that the normal student's explicit *knowledge that* the propositions in question are true and the inference rule valid leads the student to draw the right conclusion only because he also possesses practical *knowledge how* to apply that theoretical knowledge. This *knowing how* cannot be a matter of grasping explicit propositions, on pain of infinite regress, but rather involves (as it does for Searle) the having of certain capacities, dispositions, and the like.

For Ryle, what is true of logical reasoning is true of all intelligent behavior – playing chess, driving a car, operating machinery, or whatever. It cannot *merely* involve knowledge of explicitly formulated propositions, such as propositions stating rules for action. For one thing, there is always a gap between knowing the rule and actually applying it. For another, a rule can always be applied either intelligently or unintelligently, and intelligent application cannot be a matter merely of applying yet further rules, on pain of the same sort of infinite regress just mentioned. All intelligent behavior thus ultimately rests instead on *knowing how* – again, on dispositions and the like. Since playing chess, driving a car, and for that matter carrying

---

[476] Cf. Lewis Carroll, "What the Tortoise Said to Achilles," *Mind* 4 (1895): 278-280.

out a conversation with someone about whether Socrates is mortal are all *bodily* activities, the dispositions in question are *bodily dispositions*.[477]

Now, Searle's analysis is in part inspired by Wittgenstein's philosophical anthropology, to which Ryle's position also bears a family resemblance. Other thinkers arguing for the essentially embodied nature of human intellectual activity have been primarily inspired instead by phenomenology.[478] In both cases the considerations marshaled are of a philosophical rather than scientific character. However, similar conclusions have been arrived at by writers motivated precisely by findings in empirical science. Andy Clark has usefully summarized some of the key points.[479]

For example, consider the *action loop* phenomena studied by psychologists, in which bodily action plays a crucial role in the solving of a cognitive task. Clark gives the example of trying to figure out where a certain piece fits in a jigsaw puzzle. The way we typically do this is not merely by intellectually representing the shape of the piece and the shapes of the spaces into which it might fit and then deducing which of the latter is the correct place to put it, though of course we do this to some extent. Rather, we also *physically manipulate* the piece by rotating it and trying actually to fit it into a certain space, adjusting our intellectual representations accordingly if we cannot. Our thought processes not only guide our bodily behavior but are influenced in turn *by* that behavior.

Then there is what Clark calls the phenomenon of "*soft assembly.*" A "hard-assembled" system is one whose behavior is determined in a top-down way by a centralized body of information and cognitive

---

[477] Jason Stanley and Timothy Williamson criticize Ryle's argument in "Knowing How," *Journal of Philosophy* 98 (2001): 411-444. But their objections rest on a number of misunderstandings, as I show in *Aristotle's Revenge: The Metaphysical Foundations of Physical and Biological Science* (Neunkirchen-Seelscheid: Editiones Scholasticae, 2019), at pp. 102-5.

[478] See e.g. Hubert L. Dreyfus, *What Computers Still Can't Do: A Critique of Artificial Reason* (Cambridge, MA: The MIT Press, 1992).

[479] Andy Clark, *Being There: Putting Brain, Body, and World Together Again* (Cambridge, MA: The MIT Press, 1997), chapters 1 and 2.

"blueprint" for action, and is thus ill-equipped to deal with circumstances that are not included in the body of information or covered by the blueprint. A "soft-assembled" system, by contrast, is more decentralized, sensitive to information coming in from the periphery of the system and thus more flexible in its responses and adaptable to unforeseen circumstances. Scientific study of human behavior shows that it is largely soft-assembled. For example, the specific way we walk across a certain surface is not determined entirely by centralized neural processes or conscious thought, but is highly sensitive to such localized factors as leg mass, muscle strength, the kind of shoes one is wearing, the presence or absence of blisters, the specific physical characteristics of the surface, and so on. All of these factors "partner" together to generate a particular gait, with the centralized neural and cognitive processes adjusting themselves to the deliverances of the body.

In these ways, *bodily factors* provide a kind of "scaffolding" for cognition, and as Clark emphasizes, material phenomena outside the body provide further *"external* scaffolding." For example, books, notes, pictures, or even just the having of certain specific physical objects around us all function as aids to memory. The presence or absence of physical objects of certain kinds also provides a context that both facilitates and delimits the actions we might perform and thus the practical reasoning we might engage in. To cite an example from Clark, the presence in a kitchen of certain specific spices, oils, eating utensils, etc. determines the range of the sorts of cooking options one will entertain and the decisions one will make about what specifically to cook.

Of course, much of this is just common sense, but it is common sense confirmed by psychological and neuroscientific study of human action, and also by research in robotics, insofar as application of principles like action loops, soft assembly, and external scaffolding often turn out to provide the most efficient solutions to the problem of getting a machine to simulate human behavior.

Embodied perception

Let's turn now to the ways in which perceptual experience too is essentially embodied. I briefly addressed this topic in chapter 6, but much more can be said. Once again, Clark provides a useful summary of some of the relevant considerations from contemporary psychology and neuroscience. There is, for example, the phenomenon of *niche-dependent sensing*, by which a creature's sense organs are adapted to detecting a specific range of environmental features. For instance, a tick is sensitive to the butyric acid on the skin of mammals, the olfactory detection of which will cause it to drop from a tree onto a passing mammal. Contact with the skin then initiates in the tick heat-detecting behavior, and the actual detection of heat will in turn initiate burrowing into the skin. Within the larger physical world, there is only a specific subset of phenomena that constitute the tick's *"effective environment,"* with the rest of the world being largely invisible to it. Now, like other creatures, human beings too have sense organs that are keyed to certain features of the world and not others, and which determine for them their own unique effective environment.

Another example involves what researchers call *animate vision*, or visual sensing of a sort which crucially involves bodily engagement with the world. Saccades are quick movements of the eyes back and forth between fixation points, and they play a key role in visual perception. In viewing a particular scene, frequent saccades allow us, in the view of some researchers, to avoid having to construct an enduring and detailed neural model of the immediate environment. Instead we simply access the needed information by returning to the environment repeatedly during the course of the visual experience, letting the things in the environment code for themselves, as it were. In this way it is the things themselves, rather than our internal representations of them, that we deal with in perception.[480]

Then there is the fact that we typically do not take gaps in sensory information to correspond to gaps in the thing sensed. Clark gives the example of grasping a bottle without looking at it, in which

---

[480] In *Seeing, Doing, and Knowing: A Philosophical Theory of Sense Perception* (Oxford: Clarendon Press, 2005), Mohan Matthen notes that the neuroscientific and psychological evidence indicates that there are distinct neural pathways in the brain associated with "descriptive vision" and "motion-guiding vision" (pp. 293-300). These operate in tandem, but the latter pathway allows us to respond behaviorally to visual information without that information registering in consciousness, the way that information processed by the former does. In this way, vision has a component that is inherently geared toward bodily interaction with the world as well as a component geared more toward the descriptive function emphasized by representationalism.

the absence of information about the areas of the bottle's surface between one's fingers is not interpreted as indicating that there are holes in those areas. What such examples show, some researchers suggest, is that sensation is not the mere passive intake of information, but rather an active bodily engagement with the world. The sense organs are essentially used as *tools* for exploring objects which are experienced as independent of us, and as extended beyond what we immediately perceive of them. As psychologist James Gibson famously argued, things in our environment are perceived as "affordances" for action.[481] We feel a bottle as something that affords us the possibility of picking it up and drinking from it, we see a doorknob as something which affords us the possibility of turning it and leaving the room, and so forth. In short, we perceive things precisely *as accessible to the body*.

This scientific work recapitulates and reinforces lines of argument developed along phenomenological lines by philosophers like Heidegger, Merleau-Ponty, and Polanyi. Dreyfus summarizes three respects in which, according to this tradition, perception presupposes our being embodied subjects within a larger world of physical objects.[482] First, there is the figure-ground phenomenon, in which the thing perceived is always perceived *as* distinct from some surrounding context. Dreyfus gives the example of the Rubin's vase image familiar from Gestalt psychology, which can be seen either as a white vase against a black background or as two black faces in profile against a white background. What is taken to be the background constitutes what Edmund Husserl called the "outer horizon" of the thing perceived, by contrast with the "inner horizon" or those aspects of the thing which are not perceived but are nevertheless presupposed in

---

[481] James J. Gibson, *The Ecological Approach to Visual Perception* (Boston: Houghton Mifflin, 1979). That's not to endorse everything Gibson said in connection with this notion. Cf. Chemero's *Radical Embodied Cognitive Science* for discussion of the philosophical issues that arise in interpreting Gibson's work (though Chemero takes Gibsonian considerations in an eliminativist direction that, as I have said, I reject).

[482] Dreyfus, *What Computers Still Can't Do*, chapter 7.

our perception of the thing.[483] To borrow another example from Dreyfus, when we perceive a house we perceive it *as* something having a back and an inside rather than taking the front of the house as a mere façade, even though the front is all we directly see. Now, all of this presupposes embodiment insofar as what we take to be a thing's inner and outer horizons depends on how we regard our bodies to be situated with respect to the things perceived, and how we take those things qua physical objects to be situated with respect to one another. I take what I see to be the front of a house rather than a mere façade because I see what I see *from this angle*, and I note that it is next to *this other house*, behind *this driveway*, and so forth. Perception involves a particular perspective on the rest of the physical world, taken by one thing among others situated within that world.

Second, perception involves *anticipation* of a larger whole, of which what is immediately sensed is only a part. A musical note is perceived *as* a part of a piece of music, a nose or eye *as* a part of the face, and so forth. Furthermore, as Heidegger famously emphasized, we perceive things fundamentally in terms of their "readiness-to-hand," i.e. the way they might be deployed by us as "equipment" by which we might realize our ends. Now, at least much of the anticipation such perception involves is of a bodily nature. It is primarily in the act of *grasping* and *using* a hammer, in *feeling* in one's hand its weight and solidity, that we anticipate what might be done with it. It is primarily in *feeling in one's body* the rhythm of a piece of music that we anticipate the beats and notes that will follow, and in *moving our fingers* across a piece of silk that we anticipate that the rest of the fabric will have a similarly smooth texture.

Third, this anticipation is transferable across the body, from one sensory modality or organ of action to another. What is first learned through touch comes to be knowable also by sight; what is seen or touched thereby becomes graspable and otherwise subject to possible manipulation; what is heard coming toward us can thereby be avoided or approached via bodily movement; and so on.

---

[483] Edmund Husserl, *Ideas: General Introduction to Pure Phenomenology* (New York: Routledge, 2002), Part III.

Now, it might seem that such phenomenological descriptions of perceptual experience in terms of embodied subjects acting within a world of other physical objects could be replaced by descriptions couched either in the entirely "first-personal" and "subjective" terms of a sense datum language (as a Cartesian might propose), or in the entirely "third-personal" and "objective" terms of the theoretical entities postulated by physical science (as a materialist might propose). But such a replacement could never be carried out consistently, because the re-descriptions in question are parasitic on the phenomenological description.

For example, suppose I am looking at a tomato that I am holding in my hand, and that I try to describe the experience in terms of sense data such as *a roundish red patch in the center of my field of vision*, etc. It is only because I *first* have the experience of what I take to be a tomato situated in such-and-such a way relative to other external physical objects, and to me as an embodied subject, that I can go on to identify the sense data in question in just the way I do. For example, I have to say such things as that the redness of the patch is specifically of the sort that is typically seen on a tomato-like surface; that the red patch is surrounded by other color patches of a shape and texture that are typical of what one would normally take to be part of a hand; that all these patches have the appearance that a tomato and hand would have if looked at from above; and so forth. The sense datum description involves *abstracting* certain features *from* the commonsense phenomenological description of ordinary physical objects, and then treating these abstracted features as if *they*, rather than the physical objects, were what one is really perceiving. But the commonsense phenomenological description always remains lurking in the background, as that by reference to which we identify the sense data we are supposedly replacing it with.[484]

Something similar is true of any attempt to replace the phenomenological description in terms of a description couched instead in the language of scientific theory. Hence, suppose I try to replace

---

[484] Cf. Dreyfus and Taylor, *Retrieving Realism*, p. 53; Wilfried Sellars, "Empiricism and the Philosophy of Mind," in H. Feigl and M. Scriven, eds., *Minnesota Studies in the Philosophy of Science*, Volume I (Minneapolis, MN: University of Minnesota Press, 1956), p. 274; and P. F. Strawson, "Perception and its Objects," in G. F. Macdonald, ed., *Perception and Identity: Essays Presented to A.J. Ayer with His Replies* (Ithaca: Cornell University Press, 1979), pp. 43-44.

any reference to tomatoes, hands, etc. with references to collections of particles organized in such-and-such ways. There is no way to identify exactly *which* collections of particles I have in mind in any particular case except by reference to the ordinary objects they are supposed to be replacing. I have to refer to particles arranged specifically in a *tomato-like way*, or to particles which to a normal observer would be *perceived as a tomato*, etc., and to the relations that collections of particles so described have to further collections of particles organized in an *eye-like way*, a *hand-like way*, etc. Once again, the attempted re-description is parasitic on the commonsense phenomenological description.[485]

But even if such purported alternative descriptions are parasitic on the commonsense phenomenological description, might the latter not still be false? Might the external physical world and indeed one's own body not be illusory? Yet this familiar skeptical proposal presupposes what Dreyfus and Taylor characterize as the first, "mediational" assumption of representationalism. It supposes that we can abstract human cognitive and perceptual activity out of its bodily context and then intelligibly reify it as a set of "representations" which may or may not match up with a physical reality external to them. And that is precisely what the arguments we have been considering deny. These arguments maintain that the very idea that human cognitive processes and perceptual experiences might have just the content they do, yet without there actually being a physical world in which we are embedded as embodied subjects, is *itself* an illusion. The skeptic presupposes the possibility of a gap between the thinking and perceiving subject on the one hand and the corporeal world on the other that is not in fact intelligible.

So, the "mediational" assumption on which the skeptical objection rests simply begs the question. Worse, insofar as it is put forward in the name of science (or, more precisely, in the name of the mechanical world picture wrongly taken to have been established by

---

[485] Polanyi, *The Tacit Dimension*, pp. 20-21; Crawford L. Elder, *Real Natures and Familiar Objects* (Cambridge, MA: The MIT Press, 2004), pp. 50-58; and Crawford L. Elder, *Familiar Objects and their Shadows* (Cambridge: Cambridge University Press, 2011), pp. 118-24.

science), the "mediational" conception of perceptual experience leads to incoherence, in a way suggested by Frederick Olafson.[486] (The remarks to follow are inspired by Olafson, anyway, though I will not be stating things exactly the way he does.) Science crucially depends upon observation. But what exactly is presented to us or given in observation? The commonsense view – traditionally known as "direct realism" or "naïve realism," and called by Olafson the "natural attitude" – takes ordinary physical objects themselves to be what we are directly aware of. The "mediational" component of representationalism rejects this assumption, and traditionally held that sense data or the like are in fact what are presented or given to us in perception, with the physical world known at best only *indirectly, through* our direct knowledge of sense data.

Now, contemporary philosophers have largely abandoned the sense datum theory, in part because the very notion of a sense datum faces problems like those summarized above. What is purportedly "given" to us on a sense datum account turns out to be no less "theory-laden," and thus subject to challenge, than commonsense or naïve realism is according to the "mediational" picture. Furthermore, if the sense datum theory is interpreted in Cartesian dualist terms, then we have to add the interaction problem to the list of difficulties. But if sense data are not what is presented or given to us in perception, what is? A naturalist might propose substituting some materialistically respectable representations in place of the notion of a sense datum – neural processes, computational symbols, or what have you. But these can hardly be taken to be *given* or *presented* to us in perception, since most people have no idea what is going on in their brains, and have no idea what a computational symbol is. It takes a lot of sophisticated theorizing to come to the conclusion that what one is "really" aware of when introspecting one's conscious experiences are brain states of a certain type, or computational symbols. To postulate neural or computational representations is therefore to open up a further gap between appearance and reality, in addition to the initial gap opened up by the original sense datum theory. Just as the original theory posits inner representations through which we get at the external world, we

---

[486] Frederick A. Olafson, *Naturalism and the Human Condition: Against Scientism* (London: Routledge, 2001), chapter 3.

would now have to posit second-order inner representations through which we get at the (neural or computational) representations.

This puts the "mediational" picture in a dilemma. What motivated the picture in the first place was the idea that everyday perceptual judgments are so riddled with challengeable assumptions (the assumption that one is not dreaming, that secondary qualities correspond to real features of physical objects, etc.) that we cannot take physical objects to be what are presented to us in perception, but must replace them with sense data. But sense data themselves, and alternatives such as neural or computational representations, turn out to be no less theory-laden and thus no less subject to challenge. Hence if the theory-ladenness of ordinary perceptual judgments is taken to undermine the commonsense view that physical objects are presented to us in perception, then the theory-ladenness of judgments framed instead in terms of sense data or neural or computational representations should lead us to conclude that *they* are not what is given to us in perception either.

This generates a regress in which what is given or presented to us in perception keeps getting pushed back. There are two ways the "mediational" picture can deal with this regress, but both are fatal to it. On the one hand, one could break the regress by simply postulating that there is a stage that terminates it, despite involving judgments that are theory-laden and challengeable. One could say, for example, that sense data really are what is given to us or presented in perception, even though sense datum judgments are theory-laden and open to challenge. The problem with this move, however, is that it makes the abandonment of direct realism entirely pointless and unjustified. If theory-ladenness and the possibility of error do not suffice to show that sense data are not given or presented to us in perception, then how could they suffice to show that *ordinary physical objects* are not what is given or presented to us in perception? If we are going to end up admitting at the end of the day that there is after all some level at which things are just given in perception despite the possibility of error, we might as well take those things to be what common sense has always taken them to be – tables, chairs, rocks, trees, etc. – rather than philosophically problematic and unmotivated theoretical entities like sense data, neural or computational representations, or what have you. This way of dealing with the regress simply undermines the whole point of the "mediational" picture.

The second, alternative way of dealing with the regress would be to deny that we ever get to *anything* that is given or presented to us in perception. There is just the regress of representations themselves, which either proceeds to infinity or loops back around in a circle, and we cannot get beyond it. But if that is the case and nothing is really given or presented to us in perceptual experience, then perception loses all contact with external reality and cannot serve as an evidential basis for science.

This *epistemological* dilemma for representationalism parallels a *metaphysical* dilemma that afflicts naturalist versions of the mechanical world picture – unsurprisingly, given that representationalism and mechanism have, as noted earlier, gone hand in hand in modern philosophy. As noted in earlier chapters, the mechanical philosophy banishes from the material world any features that are irreducibly qualitative and cannot be accommodated to a purely quantitative or "mathematicized" conception of nature. Hence color, sound, heat, cold, etc. as common sense understands them are taken to exist only as the qualia of conscious experience rather than as features of physical objects themselves, and "directedness" toward an object is taken to exist only as the intentionality of thought rather than as the teleology or final causality of physical processes.

Now, this seems straightaway to entail Cartesian dualism, since if irreducibly qualitative features and "directedness" do not exist in matter but do exist in the mind, then that implies that the mind must not be material. But the naturalist, of course, wants to resist this conclusion. This leaves him with two options. On the one hand, he could expand his notion of what counts as "natural" so as to include irreducibly qualitative features and "directedness." This is essentially the option taken by contemporary non-reductive naturalists and by property dualists and panpsychists who regard themselves as naturalists. The trouble with this position, though, is that it makes the original move in the direction of mechanism pointless. If you are going to have to put irreducibly qualitative features and "directedness" back into the natural world at the end of the day, why take them out in the first place? What, in that case, would justify resisting the commonsense and Aristotelian claim that they have *always* been there?

The other option would be simply to deny that irreducibly qualitative features and "directedness" really exist at all, even in the mind. This is the option taken by eliminativists who deny the existence of qualia and intentionality. But this is to deny the existence of perceptual experience and intellectual activity themselves, and thus to undermine the evidential basis of the science in the name of which eliminativists take this extreme position – thereby "immolating themselves on the altar of their theory," as Olafson puts it.[487]

As Erwin Schrödinger said of the extrusion of the sensory qualities from the modern scientific picture of the natural world:

> We are thus facing the following strange situation. While all building stones for the [modern scientific] world-picture are furnished by the senses qua organs of the mind, while the world picture itself is and remains for everyone a construct of his mind and apart from it has no demonstrable existence, the mind itself remains a stranger in this picture, it has no place in it, it can nowhere be found in it.[488]

Thomas Nagel makes essentially the same point when he notes that modern science works with a conception of the physical world that excludes from it anything that reflects the first-person point of view of the conscious observer, so that that point of view cannot *itself* be fitted within, or explained in terms of, the physical.[489] Though we arrive at what Wilfrid Sellars called the "scientific image" (the world as described in terms of the concepts of physical science) only from *within* the "manifest image" (the world as it appears to us in ordinary

---

[487] Ibid., p. 51.

[488] Erwin Schrödinger, "On the Peculiarity of the Scientific World-View," in *What is Life? and Other Scientific Essays* (New York: Doubleday, 1956), p. 216.

[489] Thomas Nagel, "What Is It Like to Be a Bat?" in *Mortal Questions* (Cambridge: Cambridge University Press, 1979).

perceptual experience), the manifest image cannot in turn be reconstructed from the scientific image.[490] Accordingly, the scientific image *cannot account for its own existence* and thus cannot possibly give us an exhaustive description of reality.[491]

Now, it is sometimes claimed that it is not merely philosophical theory, but the findings of neuroscience too, that establish that in perception, the mind presents us with what is largely an illusion rather than the external world as it really is. Alva Noë notes that there are two main lines of argument offered in support of this thesis.[492] First, it is argued that the brain puts together a representation of the world that, in its detail, goes well beyond what could be gleaned from the data that actually makes it to the sensory organs. For example, since we have two eyes, the brain receives information about two retinal images. Moreover, these images are inverted. Yet what we see is only a single world, and we see it upright rather than upside-down. So, the brain must be altering the input it gets from the senses in order to generate the representation of the world we actually experience. Furthermore, the retinal images are unstable given the eyes' constant movements, the resolving power of the eye is limited insofar as there are fewer rods and cones at the periphery of the eye, each eye has a blind spot where there are no photoreceptors, it takes time for light to reach the eye, and so forth. Yet the world as we experience it seems stable, continuous, rich in detail, and immediately present. So, the brain must be filling in the gaps in the information it receives from the senses so as to create the representation that we experience.

Second, there are the phenomena of "change blindness" and "inattentional blindness," in which subjects fail to notice even dramatic things sometimes happening around them. For example, in one

---

[490] Wilfrid Sellars, "Philosophy and the Scientific Image of Man," in *Science, Perception and Reality* (London: Routledge and Kegan Paul, 1963).

[491] Olafson, *Naturalism and the Human Condition*, pp. 20-21.

[492] Alva Noë, *Action in Perception* (Cambridge, MA: The MIT Press, 2004), chapter 2; and Alva Noë, *Out Of Our Heads: Why You Are Not Your Brain, and Other Lessons from the Biology of Consciousness* (New York: Hill and Wang, 2009), chapter 6.

experiment, a person who is asked by a stranger for directions is temporarily distracted, and doesn't realize that the stranger he finishes the conversation with is not the same person as the one who initially asked for the directions. Again, the lesson some take from such examples is that the brain constructs a perceptual representation of the world that does not correspond to reality.

As Noë notes, there are in fact two kinds of skeptical conclusion that have been drawn from such considerations. The traditional skeptical lesson is the one already indicated, to the effect that the brain puts together a detailed perceptual representation of the external world that doesn't correspond to reality. But a different skeptical lesson more recently drawn by some writers is that it only *seems* to us like the brain has constructed a detailed perceptual representation, when in fact it has not.[493] On this view, we not only get the external world wrong, we get the internal world of experience itself wrong too.

But as Noë argues, both of these conclusions are mistaken, and certainly don't follow from the neuroscientific evidence. In fact, for all the neuroscientific evidence shows, we don't construct an internal representation of the world, and we don't seem to do so either. That is just bad phenomenology. Rather, what we *seem* to encounter in experience is precisely the *external world itself*, not some representation of it. The external world seems to us to be *directly accessible*, rather than hidden beyond some perceptual representation. What we take to be detailed is, not our perceptual representation of the world, but, again, the world itself. When we fill in the gaps in our experience of the world, we do so precisely by adverting to further experience *of the world itself*, rather than fleshing out some internal representation. We do so by virtue of *actively engaging* in the world rather than being passive spectators of an internal representation. To the extent that experience seems to us to be rich and orderly, that is simply because *the world itself* is presented to us in experience as rich and orderly. And the best explanation of why all of this seems to be the case is that it really is the case.

---

[493] Cf. Daniel C. Dennett, *Consciousness Explained* (Boston: Little, Brown, 1992); and S. J. Blackmore, G. Brelstaff, K. Nelson, and T. Troscianko, "Is the Richness of Our Visual World an Illusion? Transsaccadic Memory for Complex Scenes," *Perception* 24 (1995): 1075-81.

Again, nothing in the neuroscientific evidence itself shows otherwise. It seems to show otherwise only if we *read into it* a representationalist account of knowledge. But then it is this representationalist philosophical assumption, and not the scientific evidence itself, that is doing the work. Moreover, casting doubt on the reliability of introspection and on our knowledge of the external world has, once again, the paradoxical consequence of undermining the neuroscientific evidence that was claimed to justify these skeptical conclusions. For we need to have knowledge of the external world in order to study the brain, and we need to be able to rely on introspection in order to correlate physiological processes with perceptual states.

The way to avoid such paradoxes is to abandon the anti-Aristotelian representationalist and mechanistic assumptions that inevitably lead to them. Contra representationalism, we need to acknowledge that it is physical objects themselves that are presented or given to us in perception. Contra mechanism, we need to put the first-person point of view of the conscious subject back into the body.

Social animality

Our immersion in the corporeal world goes deeper still. It is not merely that human beings, considered individually, are essentially embodied subjects. It is also that they depend for the exercise of their cognitive capacities on interaction with *other* embodied subjects. Everyday human life requires the mastery and deployment of a preexisting body of social knowledge, and this includes not only book learning but also tacit knowledge embodied in ways of perceiving and acting, which becomes part of the individual's "local Background" (once again to deploy Searle's expression). Neither the book learning nor the tacit embodied knowledge is spun out of whole cloth by the individual, but rather is acquired from other human beings – parents, siblings, teachers, and society at large.

Obviously, it is largely by way of *language* that this existing body of knowledge is transmitted to the individual. Now, language is an essentially social phenomenon, and presupposes an objective world which different language users together occupy. In an influential analysis, Donald Davidson speaks of a "triangulation" between the language user, other language users, and objects in their common environment.[494] For one speaker to interpret another's utterances requires, in the most fundamental case, noting what is going on in that common environment and attributing to the other speaker thoughts that would, given what is going on, be the sort that would naturally be expressed by way of such utterances. To take a trivial example, if someone says "That must be John" in a context in which there has just been a knock on the door, we would naturally interpret his utterance as an expression of the thought that John is the one who knocked on the door. Knowledge even of the meaning of one's *own* utterances is similarly grounded, insofar as one takes oneself to be expressing the sorts of thoughts people would normally express by way of the words one is using, given the way those words are typically used in one's linguistic community. In this way, the very practice of using language presupposes that one is a thinking subject in a world of commonly accessible objects that is also occupied by other thinking subjects.

Moreover, it presupposes that together we mostly *get things right* when thinking and speaking about that world. Of course, people disagree about many things, and often get things wrong even when they agree. But Davidson's point is that these errors and disagreements make sense only against a background of a much larger body of shared truths. The basic idea is that in order to interpret your utterances as *language*, I have to regard them as the expression of beliefs and other propositional attitudes, and in order to identify which beliefs those are, I have to be able to relate them to things in our common environment. To use W. V. Quine's famous example, in order for a field linguist to interpret a native speaker's utterance of "Gavagai" as meaning "Lo, a rabbit," he has to be able to attribute to the speaker the belief that a rabbit is present, and relate that belief to the rabbit that actually *is* present to the both of them as they try to communicate.[495]

But that entails, Davidson argues, that we cannot so much as communicate with others unless we regard most of what they believe

---

[494] Cf. Donald Davidson, "Rational Animals," in his anthology *Subjective, Intersubjective, Objective* (Oxford: Clarendon Press, 2001).
[495] W. V. Quine, *Word and Object* (Cambridge, MA: The MIT Press, 1960).

as true.[496] If I were to regard your body of beliefs as *fundamentally* out of sync with the objective world we both share – if I thought that what was going on in your thoughts had little connection at all to the world of tables, chairs, rocks, trees, and other people that we both occupy – then I could have nothing to ground any attribution to you of any specific beliefs or other propositional attitudes, and thus no basis for attributing any particular content to your utterances. I would have to regard them as gibberish. Again, we can and do of course regard *some* of what other people say and think as mistaken, especially where the utterances and beliefs concern matters remote from directly observable reality. But this disagreement makes sense only against a background of agreement on more basic matters. I can judge that you are *mistaken* when saying "That guy across the street is John" only because I also judge that you *correctly* perceive that there is a street in front of us and a man standing across it, and have simply misperceived exactly who that man is. If I did not think that you were getting things right at least about the street and the presence of a person across it, I could not attribute to you the belief that John is the person across the street and then go on to judge your belief to be false.

Here too, what goes for my understanding of what other people say goes also for what I say. I could not understand *my own* utterances as language unless I took myself to be largely correct about the mind-independent world those utterances are about. In this way, the Cartesian notion of the mind's "self-containedness" turns out on closer inspection to be incoherent. For again, it supposes that the content of my thoughts could be exactly as it is even if those thoughts were all mistaken, indeed even if there were no mind-independent world at all. But Davidson's argument entails that consistently to follow out such a scenario would render me unable to take my thoughts to have any content at all, even a mistaken content. Obviously, though, they *do* have content, otherwise I could not even entertain the Cartesian doubt about whether the world really is the way my experience presents it to me.

---

[496] Donald Davidson, "A Coherence Theory of Truth and Knowledge," in Ernest Lepore, ed., *Truth and Interpretation: Perspectives on the Philosophy of Donald Davidson* (Oxford: Basil Blackwell, 1986).

Wittgenstein famously developed a similar line of argument in his critique of the notion of a logically private language.[497] By a "logically private language," I don't mean one that merely *happens* to be understood by only a single person, like the words a child might make up for fun without explaining their meaning to anyone else. No one denies that that is possible. Rather, a logically private language is one that *cannot even in principle* be understood by anyone else. The reason this is relevant to our discussion, and the reason Wittgenstein was interested in it, is that the Cartesian conception of the mind seems to entail that a logically private language *is* possible. For, again, it holds that the content of our thoughts and experiences could be exactly as they are whether or not any other people, and any external world at all, existed. And it holds that the material world, including human bodies and behavior, could be exactly as they are even if there were no genuine thoughts or experiences associated with them (this being the "zombie" scenario discussed in the previous chapter). The divide between mind and world is so complete on this picture that it is possible, at least in principle, that there might be no one else who truly does or could understand what I do when I use language, in which case my language is logically private. But if, as Wittgenstein holds, the notion of a logically private language is incoherent, then the "self-containedness" that the Cartesian picture attributes to the mind is also incoherent.

Exactly how to interpret Wittgenstein's argument is notoriously controversial, and I have no intention of resolving or even addressing that controversy here.[498] Suffice it for present purposes to make the following points. As Wittgenstein emphasizes, it is crucial to linguistic competence that a speaker be able to tell the difference between *getting things right* and merely *seeming* to get them right. In linguistic usage of the familiar kind, the public domain of other lan-

---

[497] Wittgenstein, *Philosophical Investigations*, §§243-315.

[498] For a brief overview of the main issues that arise in interpreting the argument, see chapter III of Malcolm Budd, *Wittgenstein's Philosophy of Psychology* (London: Routledge, 1989). For a detailed treatment, see chapters I-III of P. M. S. Hacker, *Wittgenstein: Meaning and Mind, Part I: Essays* (Oxford: Blackwell, 1990).

guage users and their shared physical world is what makes this possible. We can check utterances against a common environment and common criteria of usage and thereby make sense of them. But in the Cartesian scenario, there is no common environment and no common criteria, but just the way things seem to me – which would, again, be exactly the same whether or not the way they seem is the way they really are. The external physical world cannot provide such a common reference point, because none of us has direct access to it, but knows only our own private subjective representation of it. The internal mental world cannot provide such a common reference point either, because each of us has access only to his own thoughts and experiences, and cannot directly know whether there really *are* any thoughts and experiences associated with anyone else, let alone what their content might be.

Hence, in a logically private language, the very distinction between *actually* correct usage and only *apparently* correct usage dissolves. But in that case there can be no such thing as correct usage, and thus no such thing as meaningful language at all. It might seem that one could solve the problem by establishing rules for correct usage for oneself in the privacy of one's own consciousness, and then determining that future uses are correct by consulting one's memory. But this is an illusion. Suppose, for example, that one introduced some term S into one's private language by saying inwardly "By S I will mean *this*," while focusing one's attention on a certain sensation. Exactly what does S refer to? That *particular* sensation? Sensations *like* it? Like it in what respect, exactly? (Like it in being a *sensation*? In being a sensation of a *certain sensory modality*? Like it in intensity? In duration?) Perhaps the answer will be that it just seemed that one meant to understand S this way rather than that way – and that it now seems to memory that that is what one seemed to mean at the time. But once again we are stuck with the way things *seem*, and no way to check that against the way they really *are*. As Wittgenstein says, appealing to memory in order to confirm the correctness of usage in a logically private language is like supposing that one can verify the truth of what today's newspaper says by buying a second copy and noting that it says the same thing.[499]

---

[499] Wittgenstein, *Philosophical Investigations*, §265.

The illusion that a logically private language is possible is sustained by our practice of using our familiar everyday terms for sensations and the like to try to describe the scenario. We say, for example, that it seems perfectly possible that I could have words in such a language for pain, for red or green color sensations, that I could focus my attention on a sensation and thereby attach a word to it, and so on. But "pain," "red," "green," "sensation," etc. are, of course, words borrowed from ordinary language, and their meanings are all established by reference to public objects and criteria for usage – red and green physical objects, the behavior people exhibit when they are in pain or having other sensations, and so on. Hence when we seem to be intelligibly describing a scenario in which someone is using a logically private language, the meaning of the terms we use is parasitic on the public criteria by which these familiar terms are understood.[500]

A thorough treatment of arguments like Davidson's and Wittgenstein's would require a detour into issues in the philosophy of language that are beyond the scope of a general book on human nature. But we can address what is perhaps the main objection to such arguments, which is that they fall short of establishing the falsity of the Cartesian picture. What they show at most, it is claimed, is that we have to think and speak *as if* there really is a world external to the mind to which its thoughts and experiences correspond, but not that there really is one.[501] But this objection misses the point. It presupposes that we can make sense of a scenario on which the mind represents the world in just the way it does, yet where the world is not at all like that or even fails to exist. And the whole point of the argument

---

[500] Wittgenstein is sometimes accused of behaviorism, according to which there is nothing more to pain and other sensations than certain patterns of behavior or dispositions to behavior. But there is nothing in the points I have been making that entails that, and in fact behaviorism presupposes precisely the denuded, mechanical conception of behavior that Wittgenstein and other opponents of the Cartesian picture reject.

[501] Cf. Barry Stroud, *The Quest for Reality: Subjectivism and the Metaphysics of Color* (Oxford: Oxford University Press, 2000), pp. 192-93. Stroud develops a Davidson-style argument in defense of the commonsense view that colors really exist in the world outside the mind, but he judges that the argument shows only that we have to think about color *as if* this were true, and fails to demonstrate that it really is true. For further discussion of Stroud's argument and naïve realism about color in general, see Feser, *Aristotle's Revenge*, pp. 340-51.

is that we *cannot* really make sense of such a scenario. Hence the objection begs the question.

Turning to the phantasms

In chapter 3, I noted that the dispute between early modern empiricists and rationalists over innate ideas was closely connected to their respective positions on *imagism*, the thesis that concepts are to be identified with mental images (or "phantasms," to use the Scholastic term). The empiricists held that no concepts are innate and all must derive from experience, and concluded from this that imagism must be true. The rationalists held that imagism is false, and concluded from this that at least some concepts must be innate or built into the mind rather than deriving from experience. The empiricists completely assimilated concepts to mental imagery, and the rationalists completely divorced concepts from mental imagery. I also noted that this is a false choice. A third alternative is the Aristotelian-Thomistic view that imagism is false, but that, nevertheless, no concepts are innate and all must in some way be derived from experience. As the medieval Scholastic slogan put it, *nihil est in intellectu quod non prius fuerit in sensu* ("nothing is in the intellect which was not first in the senses"). Moreover, even after the intellect first derives its concepts from the senses, it must normally "turn to the phantasms" or imagery when entertaining them later on.[502]

Hence, to agree with the Cartesian's rejection of imagism does not entail accepting his innatism, and it is now time to see why the latter is in any case false. But first it is important to say a little more about the Aristotelian-Thomistic position that the early modern rationalists and empiricists rejected, so as to be clear about exactly what the dispute is about.[503] For the Aristotelian-Thomistic tradition, the

---

[502] Thomas Aquinas, *Summa Theologiae* I.84.7, in *Summa Theologica*, translated by the Fathers of the English Dominican Province (New York: Benziger Bros, 1948). Cf. *Summa Theologiae* I.85.1.

[503] For a useful exposition of the Aristotelian-Thomistic position, see Robert Edward Brennan, *Thomistic Psychology* (New York: Macmillan, 1941), chapter 7. For discussion of the relationship between early modern rationalist and empiricist views and their Aristotelian-Thomistic predecessor, see Robert Merrihew Adams, "Where Do Our Ideas Come From? – Descartes vs. Locke," in Stephen P. Stich, ed., *Innate Ideas* (Berkeley and Los Angeles: University of California Press, 1975).

human intellect starts out devoid of concepts. Cognition begins when physical objects stimulate the sense organs, which in turn leads the "synthetic sense" (briefly discussed in chapter 3) to unify the various deliverances of these external senses into a single coherent conscious experience. For example, vision might register a yellowish elongated expanse, touch a smooth and solid surface, taste a sensation of sweetness, etc. and the synthetic sense combines these into conscious awareness of a banana. The imagination then goes on to generate an image or phantasm of the banana, which represents its sensory qualities to the mind but in a way that abstracts them from the specific time and place that any actual particular banana would have to occupy.

It is here that the intellect enters the picture. In particular, what I briefly referred to in chapter 3 as the *active intellect* abstracts out from the phantasm a representation of the banana that goes beyond what the senses or the imagination can detect. Suppose, for example (and to borrow from *The Merriam-Webster Dictionary*), that the content of this representation is: *an elongated, usually tapering, tropical fruit with soft pulpy flesh, enclosed in a soft usually yellow rind*. This applies not only to all the actual bananas that you have seen and imagined, but to all the existing bananas that you have not seen or imagined, to all the bananas that have existed in the past, all those that will exist in the future, and all those that never have and never will exist but which would have existed had things gone differently. The representation counts as a true *concept*, with all the properties of concepts noted in chapter 3, and it enables you to entertain propositions about bananas that go well beyond anything that you have experienced or could experience, and to draw inferences from those propositions. It does so by capturing (albeit imperfectly) the *form* or *essence* that makes a banana a thing of the kind that it is. But whereas, in this or that particular banana, this form or essence is embedded in a certain bit of matter confined to a certain time and place, the form is abstracted out of those individualizing conditions and considered instead as a universal, multiply realizable pattern. Once these forms are abstracted out and concepts formed, they enter into *passive intellect*, the storehouse of concepts generated by active intellect.[504]

Just as the eye is always ready to see, but cannot do so unless light hits it, so too is the active intellect always ready to abstract forms out from images or phantasms so as to form a concept, but cannot do so unless an image is actually present. It is like a magnet which, however powerful, cannot draw metal to it unless there is some metal in the vicinity. Imagery, in turn, requires prior sensation. Hence there can be noting in the intellect without prior sensation. Furthermore, even after the concepts are formed, they are normally entertained together with some image or phantasm. For example, even when you are considering the most abstract scientific or metaphysical truths pertaining to bananas, you typically at the same time *imagine* bananas. And even if you don't, you will at the very least form a visual or auditory image of a *word* like "banana." In this way too, the intellect, though differing in kind and not merely in degree from the imagination, in its ordinary operations works in conjunction with imagination. But imagination, like sensation, is for the Aristotelian-Thomistic tradition a corporeal faculty. In this way too, then, that tradition takes even the most abstract cognition to be embodied.

Obviously, this account raises various questions, and some of them will be addressed presently. The main question being addressed here, however, is, specifically, whether any concepts are *innate* in a sense in which the Aristotelian-Thomistic tradition denies that they are. The view that some concepts are innate is, as I have said, sometimes called "innatism," and in contemporary philosophy it also goes by the label "nativism" (since it takes at least some concepts to be "native" to the mind rather than acquired). It should be obvious that any interesting form of innatism or nativism must say more than merely that we have certain innate or built-in *powers* or *capacities*. As we have seen in earlier chapters, Aristotelian-Thomistic philosophers themselves attribute all sorts of inherent powers or capacities to natural

---

[504] Active intellect and passive intellect are also sometimes referred to in the literature as "agent intellect" and "possible intellect," respectively. But it seems to be that talk of active and passive intellect is likely to be at least somewhat less opaque and misleading to most modern readers.

substances, as do many philosophers of other schools of thought. Indeed, the active and passive intellects themselves are powers or capacities of a sort, as are sensation and imagination. Innatism makes a stronger claim. It holds that, in some way, at least some concepts are *already* present in the intellect *prior to* any exercises of our powers of sensation and imagination. That does not mean that an innatist must hold that we actually consciously entertain a concept before having experiences of things of the sort the concept represents, and innatists typically would not hold that. But for a theorist who takes a certain concept to be innate, experience does not *generate* the concept, but rather merely triggers our awareness of what was already there in the intellect before the triggering. For example, if such a theorist took the concept of *being a banana* to be innate, the claim would be that this concept was present in the intellect even before we ever experienced any bananas, and that such experience merely called it forth from the mind. Experience is in this way like taking water from a well in which it was already waiting to be drawn out, rather than filling a well that was previously empty.

It is only fair to acknowledge that innatists typically have reasons for taking this view beyond just their rejection of imagism.[505] In the contemporary debate, one such reason stems from "poverty of the stimulus" considerations like those which, as we saw in chapter 3, Noam Chomsky famously raises against behaviorism. Chomsky argues that the linguistic capacity even of children extends far beyond what one would expect it to be given the relatively meager evidence concerning usage to which experience has exposed them. It is simply not plausible, in his view, that their understanding of grammar could result from generalizations from observed instances. As he puts it, their linguistic output vastly outstrips the experiential input.[506] This leads him to posit an innate universal grammar. Now, a grammar consists

---

[505] One traditional argument suggests that innateness best explains the *universality* of certain concepts. But the standard response is that the concepts in question are universal, not because they are innate rather than derived from experience, but rather because certain features are universal to experience itself. Hence experience universally gives rise to concepts representing those features.

[506] Noam Chomsky, "Recent Contributions to the Theory of Innate Ideas," in Stich, ed., *Innate Ideas*. Cf. also Stich's discussion of Chomsky in his introduction to the volume.

of rules and definitions. These are propositional in form, and propositions have concepts as constituents. Hence Chomsky's argument might seem to provide grounds for concluding that at least some concepts are innate. A similar argument is advanced by psychologists who propose that certain *theories* about how the natural world works are innate. They note, for example, that even infants appear to know that objects move separately from one another, that they maintain their size and shape, that they typically act on one another only on contact, and so on. Since, it is claimed, infants have not had sufficient experience to support such generalizations, this knowledge must be built in to the mind.[507]

Several things can be said in response to such arguments, but the first thing to note is that they are, even prima facie, less threatening to the Aristotelian-Thomistic position than they are to the modern versions of empiricism at which they are usually directed. For example, Chomsky's argument is certainly a powerful objection to behaviorism, which sought to account for linguistic competence in terms of stimulus-response conditioning. As Chomsky rightly insists, there must be more going on in between sensory input and behavioral output than the behaviorist is willing to acknowledge. But for the Aristotelian-Thomistic position, what is going on has nothing to do with innate ideas, but rather with the generation of phantasms by the imagination, the abstracting out of forms by the active intellect, and the storage of the resulting concepts in passive intellect. "Poverty of the stimulus" considerations may tell *against* behaviorism and other heirs of early modern empiricism, but it does not follow that they tell *in favor* of innatism as opposed to the Aristotelian-Thomistic position.

Jesse Prinz identifies a second problem with arguments like the ones in question. Perceptual representations, he points out, are merely "receptive," whereas concepts are, by contrast, "spontaneous" or "under the endogenous control of the organism."[508] For example, a perceptual experience of a banana is something that *happens* to you,

---

[507] For a useful overview of the linguistic and psychological literature on arguments like those summarized in this paragraph, see Jesse J. Prinz, *Furnishing the Mind: Concepts and Their Perceptual Basis* (Cambridge, MA: The MIT Press, 2002), pp. 198-228.
[508] Ibid., p. 197.

but the concept of a banana is something you can actively bring to mind, can combine with other concepts so as to entertain a proposition, and so on. Now, the purportedly innate concepts posited by the linguistic and psychological theories just described are not under the endogenous control of the infants and children to whom they are attributed.[509] Infants do not actively bring to mind and engage in abstract reasoning about the concepts of *maintaining size and shape, acting by way of contact*, and the like. Young children with merely rudimentary linguistic competence do not actively bring to mind and reason about grammatical concepts. But if infants and children lack this important capacity characteristic of the having of concepts, that is evidence against the claim that they have them. It indicates that, even if there are innate representations and capacities of some sort, they are *sub*-conceptual in nature. They may even be representations and capacities that *facilitate* the acquisition of concepts like the ones posited, but the concepts themselves would not be innate.

The most influential defender of innatism or nativism in contemporary philosophy is Jerry Fodor.[510] Fodor observes that when we learn a new complex concept, we are able to do so because we already know the simpler concepts of which it is composed. For example, I can learn the concept BACHELOR by combining the concepts UNMARRIED and MAN if I already have those. (I'll follow the convention observed by Fodor and other contemporary writers on this topic of signifying concepts by putting them in capital letters.) But then, he argues, there must be some primitive concepts that are innate, otherwise I could not learn new ones in this way. Fodor emphasizes that this does not entail that experience is irrelevant to one's ability to deploy such concepts. But its role is to trigger what is already there in the mind, rather than to introduce it into the mind. Triggering is a "brute-causal" process which, unlike the introduction of new concepts by way of existing

---

[509] Ibid., pp. 200 and 214.

[510] Jerry A. Fodor, *The Language of Thought* (Cambridge, MA: Harvard University Press, 1975), chapter 2; and "The Present Status of the Innateness Controversy," in Jerry A. Fodor, *Representations: Philosophical Essays on the Foundations of Cognitive Science* (Cambridge, MA: The MIT Press, 1981).

ones, does not involve adverting to the logical relations the new concept bears to existing ones.[511]

As it happens, though, Fodor later moved away from innatism, and a problem with his account to which he became sensitive is that it raises the question of *why*, exactly, a concept will be triggered by precisely a thing of the kind it represents. To borrow his example, why is the concept DOORKNOB triggered by *doorknobs*, specifically, rather than by some other kind of thing?[512] If the triggering of innate concepts is merely a "brute-causal" process, it is hard to see why this should be so. For example, it is hard to see why it couldn't have turned out instead that the concept DOORKNOB was, just as a brute causal fact, triggered by dogs or donuts. This has come to be known as "the doorknob/DOORKNOB problem," and Fodor's solution is to propose that there is in the first place *nothing more to being* a doorknob than being the kind of thing that triggers the concept DOORKNOB. Hence there is no mystery about why doorknobs trigger DOORKNOB. Since to do that sort of thing is *just what it is to be* a doorknob, the connection between doorknobs and DOORKNOB is *necessary* rather than contingent, and thus we are not dealing with a connection that could have been otherwise and thus calls for explanation.

One implication of this is that it makes *being a doorknob* a *mind-dependent* property rather than an objective one. To be a doorknob, on Fodor's account, is nothing more than to be the sort of thing that *strikes us as being* a doorknob. But Fodor also now concludes that what needs to be innate in order for his causal account of concepts to succeed is not the *concept* DOORKNOB, but merely a *mechanism* for generating the concept.[513] And as we've noted already, someone who rejects innate *ideas* could nevertheless accept that there are innate features of a sub-conceptual sort, and a causal mechanism like the kind Fodor

---

[511] Fodor, "The Present Status of the Innateness Controversy," p. 280.

[512] Jerry A. Fodor, *Concepts: Where Cognitive Science Went Wrong* (Oxford: Clarendon Press, 1998), p. 132. As Prinz notes (*Furnishing the Mind*, p. 232), this isn't an ideal example, since DOORKNOB is plausibly a complex concept rather than a primitive one.

[513] Fodor, *Concepts*, pp. 142-43.

posits would be exactly that. Indeed, such a mechanism is precisely what the Aristotelian-Thomistic position posits, even if its details are different from those of Fodor's account. Active intellect is an innate power to generate concepts, but it is not *itself* a concept.

Now, doorknobs are human artifacts, so that treating DOORKNOB as the concept of something mind-dependent is not entirely implausible. But what about natural kind concepts like WATER, which represents something that exists objectively, apart from human minds? Though water itself is not mind-dependent, the concept WATER is initially triggered in us by surface properties of water that tend in a law-like way to trigger it, given the way our minds happen to operate.[514] In that respect it's like DOORKNOB, and Fodor's account of its acquisition requires only an innate mechanism, rather than that the concept itself be innate. With scientific investigation, Fodor notes, our concept WATER comes to represent the *essence* that underlies the surface properties that initially triggered the concept.[515] And that essence captures something entirely mind-independent. However, this does not involve acquiring a new concept, but rather a new way of applying the existing concept, WATER. Hence our coming to learn the essence of water, like our initial acquisition of the concept WATER, does not involve innate ideas.[516]

Naturally, the Aristotelian-Thomistic philosopher is bound to regard this retreat from innatism by its foremost contemporary defender as at least a partial vindication. But even more can be said. As Prinz notes, a difficulty facing Fodor's revised position is that it cannot account for our possession of concepts that apply to *atypical* instances as well as typical ones.[517] Consider that a very unusual looking doorknob might fail to trigger the concept DOORKNOB. Hence, Fodor has to hold that *being a doorknob* "is that property that we form concepts

---

[514] Ibid., pp. 154-59. Here I follow M. J. Cain's reading of Fodor in *Fodor: Language, Mind and Philosophy* (Cambridge: Polity, 2002), pp. 75-76.

[515] Fodor, *Concepts*, pp. 159-61.

[516] Cf. Cain, *Fodor*, pp. 76-77.

[517] Prinz, *Furnishing the Mind*, p. 233.

of after experiencing *typical instances*."⁵¹⁸ Now, the concept applies to atypical instances too, of course, and once we have it we can go on to judge that what initially seemed not to be a doorknob really is one after all. But how can this be? If a concept is a concept of just whatever it is that triggers it, then why is the resulting concept in this case DOORKNOB (which applies to both typical and atypical cases), rather than the concept TYPICAL DOORKNOB (which, naturally, applies only to the typical ones)?⁵¹⁹

Prinz rightly concludes that the concept that experience triggers must capture a *common essence* that both the typical and atypical cases share, so that the intellect can go on to apply it to the atypical cases after acquiring it from the typical ones. Fodor's position cannot account for this. Now, Prinz himself tries to spell out what such a concept would be like in the neo-empiricist terms that I have already criticized in chapter 3. But the basic idea that experience generates a concept capturing a common essence is one the Aristotelian-Thomistic position heartily agrees with. Again, what this involves, the view says, is active intellect's abstracting out from what is perceived its form or essence, and considering it in isolation from the individualizing conditions in which it is embedded in this or that particular spatiotemporal object. On this picture, *the very same* form or essence that makes, for example, a particular banana a thing of the kind it is, with the very same nature that other members of that kind possess, comes to exist in the intellect, but as a concept rather than as that which informs the banana's matter. A concept *just is* a form abstracted from matter and entertained by an intellect. In this way, the intellect's understanding

---

⁵¹⁸ Ibid.

⁵¹⁹ In fact, this is but an instance of a more general problem of indeterminacy for Fodor's account. Doorknobs are a kind of door hardware (alongside hinges, etc.) and door hardware in turn is a subclass of hardware in general. So why does a doorknob trigger the concept DOORKNOB, as opposed to the concept DOOR HARDWARE or the concept HARDWARE? Cf. Fiona Cowie, *What's Within? Nativism Reconsidered* (Oxford: Oxford University Press, 1999), pp. 114-16.

of a thing involves a "formal identity" between it and the thing known, without material identity.[520]

Naturally, all of this raises various questions.[521] Some might wonder, for example, whether this account is vulnerable to an influential objection raised by Peter Geach.[522] It is often said that to abstract a concept from individual instances is to attend to certain of their features while ignoring others (for example, by focusing attention on what is common to various bananas while ignoring the fact that this one is green and that one yellow, this one eight inches long and that one shorter, and so forth). The problem with this, though, is that to attend only to those features contained in a concept is itself an exercise of one's grasp of that concept. Hence abstraction presupposes concepts and therefore cannot account for them. As John Haldane points out in response, however, we need to distinguish abstraction's presupposing a concept *logically* from its presupposing it *temporally*.[523] To understand the distinction, consider Haldane's example of riding a bike. Actually riding a bike *logically* presupposes having the ability to ride it. All the same, it is only when one first actually rides one that one acquires, in the very doing of this, the ability to ride it. The ability is not present earlier in time than the first exercise of it. Hence actually riding a bike does not *temporally* presuppose the ability. But in the same way, though selectively attending to certain features of a banana may logically presuppose having the concept of a banana, it does not follow that it temporally presuppose it. The acquisition and first exercise of the concept can instead be simultaneous, just as the acquisition and first exercise of the ability to ride a bike are. And the Aristotelian-Thomistic account, as Haldane and I understand it, is

---

[520] Cf. John Haldane, "Mind-World Identity Theory and the Anti-Realist Challenge," in John Haldane and Crispin Wright, eds., *Reality, Representation, and Projection* (Oxford: Oxford University Press, 1993).

[521] I have more to say about the subject in "Truth as a Transcendental," in Joshua P. Hochschild, Turner C. Nevitt, Adam Wood, and Gábor Borbély, eds., *Metaphysics Through Semantics: The Philosophical Recovery of the Medieval Mind: Essays in Honor of Gyula Klima* (Dordrecht: Springer, 2023).

[522] Peter Geach, *Mental Acts* (London: Routledge and Kegan Paul, 1971), pp. 18ff.

[523] John Haldane, "Chesterton's Philosophy of Education," in *Faithful Reason: Essays Catholic and Philosophical* (London: Routledge, 2004), at pp. 192-93.

committed only to the claim that concepts are not in the intellect *temporally* prior to abstraction.

The point for the moment, though, is not to present a general exposition and defense of Aristotelian-Thomistic epistemology, but rather to emphasize that any non-innatist must take experience to generate a concept capturing a common essence, and that the Aristotelian-Thomistic position proposes that what this involves is a transfer of a form or essence *from* the thing in which it is instantiated *to* the intellect. Operating in the background here is hylemorphism, as well as the Scholastic principle that whatever is in an effect must in some way have preexisted in its total cause (sometimes called the "principle of proportionate causality").[524] Now, early modern empiricists and rationalists alike rejected the picture of causality and of nature in general that this account of concept acquisition presupposes, replacing it with the mechanical world picture discussed in previous chapters. But as Robert Adams has observed, this did not involve the replacement of the Aristotelian-Thomistic account of how experience causes concepts with some *alternative* account.[525] Rather, the moderns gave *no account at all* of how this happens. The early modern empiricists simply assert that it does somehow happen, whereas the rationalists denied that it did and opted instead for innatism.[526] The result was that both views made it utterly mysterious how the mind gets in any sort of cognitive contact with the external world. Say what one will about the Aristotelian-Thomistic account, its notion of a "formal identity" between the intellect and the object it knows prevents the mind-world gap that has plagued modern philosophy from opening up in the first place.

In fact, things are even worse for the modern empiricist than this lets on. Recall that the mechanical world picture holds that there

---

[524] For exposition and defense of this principle, see Edward Feser, *Scholastic Metaphysics: A Contemporary Introduction* (Heusenstamm: Editiones Scholasticae, 2014), pp. 154-59.

[525] Adams, "Where Do Our Ideas Come From? – Descartes vs. Locke," p. 83.

[526] For discussion of how the early modern rationalists' general conception of how nature operates led them to conclude that concepts could not arise via experience and must be innate, see Cowie, *What's Within? Nativism Reconsidered*, chapter 3.

is nothing in the external world that resembles our experiences of colors, sounds, heat, cold, and other secondary qualities. Recall also that it rejects the Aristotelian four-causal framework for understanding the relations between natural phenomena, and instead thinks of causation in terms of the motions and interactions of particles, as described by physics' mathematical models. As Colin McGinn has noted, these aspects of the mechanical world picture positively point *toward* innatism rather than away from it.[527] For if there is nothing in the external world resembling our ideas of secondary qualities, those ideas can hardly come from outside the mind. Indeed, when we add Berkeley's famous point that our ideas of primary qualities cannot be separated from our ideas of secondary qualities, it follows that the former too cannot come from outside the mind. For example, we cannot make sense of a color like red except as occupying some extended area with a certain shape, so that if our idea of the former is innate so too must be our idea of the latter. Meanwhile, the majority of our concepts bear no resemblance at all to what an empiricist committed to the mechanical world picture must regard as their proximate causes. For example, an abstract geometrical concept like *circularity* or *triangularity* hardly resembles any of the motions of particles or electrochemical activity in the brain that such an empiricist regards as its trigger. This is precisely why early modern rationalists like Descartes judged that the mechanical conception of nature pointed to innatism rather than empiricism.

Nor can a non-Aristotelian contemporary critic of innatism reasonably level against Aristotelianism the accusation that its appeal to capacities like active and passive intellect saddles us with "dormitive power" pseudo-explanations. For these critics of innatism too often find that they need to posit similar capacities. For example, Fiona Cowie allows that, in order to account for how we acquire some concept F, we may have to posit "unlearned recognitional capacities" such that "one can be born (hence not have to learn how to be) a detector of Fs by having an F-sensitive cognitive reflex."[528] "One's brain and

---

[527] Colin McGinn, *Inborn Knowledge: The Mystery Within* (Cambridge, MA: The MIT Press, 2015), pp. 22-28.

[528] Cowie, *What's Within? Nativism Reconsidered*, p. 135.

perceptual apparatus can simply be structured such that they react reliably and characteristically to that property," she says, so that "one can be an F-detector simply in virtue of how one is built."[529] It's hard to see how positing a "recognitional capacity," "cognitive reflex," or "F-detector" is any less suspect than the notion of active intellect. Of course, the latter is tied up with the Aristotelian hylemorphist conception of nature, which most modern philosophers reject. But the point is that the Aristotelian's positing of *capacities* or *powers* cannot reasonably be dismissed as pseudo-explanatory by those who find that they too have to posit capacities and powers. There are, in any case, independent reasons to accept hylemorphism, as I have shown in earlier chapters. Hence the Aristotelian-Thomistic account of concept acquisition is still on the table as a non-innatist alternative to modern empiricism, over which, as we have seen, it has definite advantages.

That innatism is, in any event, false, is evidenced by one final consideration, alluded to at the beginning of this section. Even after concepts are acquired, we must, as Aquinas puts it, "turn to the phantasms" whenever we entertain them. Everyday experience attests to this.[530] We find that, even when entertaining the most abstract concepts and propositions, we must bring imagery before the mind, even if only a visual or auditory image of the words expressing the concept or proposition. For example, though the proposition *that snow is white* is not identical with either the English sentence "Snow is white" or any parallel sentence in another language, such as the German "Schnee ist weiss," we nevertheless cannot entertain this proposition without bringing some sentence or other to mind. When we think through a problem, we also tend to form sequences of mental images. E. J. Lowe offers the example of giving someone directions, where we typically call to mind images of each step along the journey as we verbally relate them to the other person.[531] Resort to imagery is typical even with more abstruse exercises in intellection. As Lowe observes:

---

[529] Ibid., p. 133.

[530] Cf. Brennan, *Thomistic Psychology*, p. 193.

[531] E. J. Lowe, *Locke on Human Understanding* (London: Routledge,1995), p. 167.

> We should never underestimate the importance of imaginative models and metaphors in our understanding of even the most abstract and sophisticated subjects. Consider, for instance, the heuristic value of graphs and diagrams in mathematics and logic, and the historical role of visual and even physical models in the development of scientific theories of atomic and molecular structure.[532]

We also find that confusion in the order of our sensory experiences, as in dreams and hallucinations, goes hand in hand with confused intellection. Though the intellect is distinct from both sensation and imagination, its operation does not float free of them.

Now, if recourse to imagery is unavoidable even after we already have concepts, then *a fortiori* it can hardly be less necessary when we first acquire them. That does not entail the early modern empiricist thesis that concepts just *are* images – a thesis which, as we saw in chapter 3, is false. It does sit poorly with the innatist claim that concepts somehow exist in the intellect prior to the formation of imagery, but sits well with the Aristotelian-Thomistic thesis that concepts are abstracted from imagery. That thesis retains its power as the middle ground position that remains when the alternative rationalist and early modern empiricist extremes have been rejected.

The case I have been spelling out in this chapter for the immersion of human cognition in the material world supports the conclusion that we are, contra Cartesianism, corporeal substances. But it does not entail the materialist claim that we are *wholly* corporeal substances. And that claim is false, as we will see in the next chapter.

---

[532] E. J. Lowe, *Subjects of Experience* (Cambridge: Cambridge University Press, 1996), p. 170.

8. Against Materialism

The immateriality of the intellect

We saw in chapter 3 that our intellectual powers cannot be reduced to those characteristic of sentience (such as perception and imagination), which we share with other animals. We saw in chapter 6 that there is no good reason to attribute these irreducible intellectual powers to any non-human animals. Thus, human beings differ in kind and not merely in degree from the other animals. Now, it is possible to exaggerate this difference, as Platonists and Cartesians do. They effectively reduce us human beings to our intellects, and deny any corporeal properties to the purely intellectual substances they claim we are. In effect, they characterize human beings as if they were angels (where an angel just is a purely intellectual and incorporeal substance). We saw in chapter 7 that this is a mistake, and that the corporeal properties characteristic of animals in general are among the properties of human beings.

But it is also possible to exaggerate the corporeality of human nature, and that is the mistake that materialists make. To be sure, the irreducibility of the intellect does not by itself suffice to show that it is incorporeal. After all, we saw in chapter 5 that ordinary physical substances are not reducible to their microstructural parts, and in chapter 6 that living substances are not reducible to inorganic ones. All the same, water and stone, trees and grass, dogs and cats are all entirely corporeal. But the intellect has properties that make it irreducible in a much stronger sense than these other things are – properties that no purely corporeal thing can possibly have.

The upshot is that a human being is a substance with both corporeal *and* incorporeal properties. If we are not quite angels, neither are we mere clever apes. There is in us a dash of both, so that we straddle the divide between the material and immaterial realms.

There are several powerful arguments for the immateriality of the intellect, and their basic thrust is as old as Plato and Aristotle. But modern readers, unfamiliar as they typically are with the broader metaphysical and epistemological assumptions that inform the presentation of ancient and medieval arguments for the intellect's immateriality, often badly misunderstand those arguments. So, I will begin with arguments couched in terms more familiar from contemporary academic philosophy. Later in the chapter I'll turn to considerations of the kind emphasized by Aristotle and Aquinas, and show how they can be understood in light of these more familiar ideas and arguments.

The indeterminacy of the physical

The first argument is one that derives from the late James Ross, and that I have defended and developed myself in earlier publications.[533] Given Ross's formulation and the themes from twentieth-century analytic philosophy that informed it, we might label it the argument from "the indeterminacy of the physical." But it is crucial to understand that "indeterminacy" in this context has nothing at all to do with the debate over causal determinism (which I addressed in chapter 4). It concerns instead the notion of indeterminacy with respect to *semantic and conceptual content*. Something has *determinate* semantic or conceptual content when it has an *exact* or *unambiguous* meaning, when there is what contemporary philosophers sometimes call a "fact

---

[533] See James Ross, "Immaterial Aspects of Thought," *Journal of Philosophy* 89 (1992): 136-50; and James Ross, *Thought and World: The Hidden Necessities* (Notre Dame, IN: University of Notre Dame Press, 2008), chapter 6. My most detailed previous development and defense of Ross's argument can be found in Edward Feser, "Kripke, Ross, and the Immaterial Aspects of Thought," *American Catholic Philosophical Quarterly* 87 (2013): 1-32. This essay was reprinted in Edward Feser, *Neo-Scholastic Essays* (South Bend, IN: St. Augustine's Press, 2015). The argument has also recently been expounded and defended in Adam Wood, *Thomas Aquinas on the Immateriality of the Intellect* (Washington, D.C.: Catholic University of America Press, 2020), at pp. 239-54; and in Antonio Ramos-Diaz, "Logical and Mathematical Powers," in William M. R. Simpson, Robert C. Koons, and James Orr, eds., *Neo-Aristotelian Metaphysics and the Theology of Nature* (London: Routledge, 2022). In chapter 3 of *The Last Word* (Oxford: Oxford University Press, 1997), Thomas Nagel develops a criticism of naturalistic accounts of thought that is in some respects similar to Ross's argument.

of the matter" about what it means. To borrow a famous example from W. V. Quine, suppose a linguist is attempting to translate the utterance "gavagai," spoken by a member of some heretofore unknown tribe in the presence of a rabbit.[534] Suppose that in light of the evidence provided by the speaker's behavior, what is going on around him, and so on, the linguist is able to determine with certainty that what the native speaker was saying is "Lo, a rabbit!" and that no other translation was possible even in principle. We could say in that case that there is a fact of the matter about what the speaker meant – that the utterance had an utterly unambiguous, exact, or determinate meaning, and that the thought the utterance expressed had a similarly unambiguous, exact, or determinate conceptual content.

Ross's argument

Now, arguments famously developed within contemporary analytic philosophy, and especially arguments deriving from Quine and from Saul Kripke, demonstrate that no purely material entity, system, or process possibly *could* have an unambiguous, exact, or determine semantic or conceptual content in this sense. There is no fact of the matter to be determined *from the physical facts alone* about what a speaker means by his utterances or what thoughts are being expressed by these utterances. This is the thesis of the indeterminacy of the physical that Ross grounds his argument on.

The other key component of Ross's argument is the thesis that our thoughts at least sometimes *do* have a determinate, exact or unambiguous content. For the purposes of the argument, Ross focuses on *formal* thinking of the kind familiar from mathematics and formal logic. Examples would be adding, squaring a number, and applying the inference rule *modus ponens*. When we engage in such arithmetical or logical reasoning, there is indeed a fact of the matter about what we are doing, about the conceptual content of our thoughts. For example, such a thought process can be determinately or unambiguously an instance of *adding* (rather than subtracting, multiplying, or whatever) or an instance of applying *modus ponens* (rather than *modus tollens*, a fallacious affirming of the consequent, or whatever).

---

[534] Willard van Orman Quine, *Word and Object* (Cambridge, MA: The MIT Press, 1960), p. 51f.

This much puts us in a position to state Ross's basic argument, which is very simple and can be put in the form of the following syllogism:

1. Formal thought processes can have an exact or unambiguous conceptual content.

2. Nothing material can have an exact or unambiguous conceptual content.

3. So, formal thought processes are not material.

The syllogism is valid. If we accept the premises, we must accept the conclusion. The bulk of Ross's discussion is devoted to defending the premises. With regard to the first premise, it is important to note that Ross takes intellectual activity of *all* kinds to have an exact and unambiguous conceptual content, not merely thinking of the logical and mathematical kind.[535] But determinacy of content is most obvious in the case of logical and mathematical examples, which is why the argument focuses on them.

Let's begin with the second premise, and with a very elementary and intuitive example, to set the stage for the more technical and abstract sorts of examples to which Ross appeals. Consider a simple pictorial representation, such as a drawing of a triangle: ∆ What is the content of this representation? Does it represent *triangularity* in the abstract? Or only *black* triangles, specifically? Or maybe only *black isosceles* triangles, specifically? Does it represent something else instead, such as a pyramid, or a dunce cap, or a slice of pizza? There is nothing in the physical properties of the representation that can tell us. Studying the size of the image, the thickness of its lines, the chemistry of the ink in which it is drawn, or the like, will not provide an answer to the question, for whatever the list of the image's physical properties turns out to contain, they will all be compatible with various alternative possible attributions of conceptual content to the picture.

---

[535] Ross, "Immaterial Aspects of Thought," pp. 149-50 and *Thought and World*, p. 123.

Notice that the situation does not change even if we add something to the picture, such as the word "triangle" written under the image. For one thing, that that particular sequence of shapes or sounds counts as a word in the first place, let alone a word with the specific meaning the word "triangle" has, has nothing to do with its physical properties. It is entirely a matter of convention. For another thing, even given the customary meaning of the word, there are still alternative possible interpretations of the revised image with the word written under it. For example, it could represent triangles themselves, or it could represent instead the *English word* "triangle," or it could even represent the obscure 1970s Japanese pop band Triangle. Again, nothing in the physical properties of the word and image can suffice to tell us precisely what conceptual content they convey. This will be true no matter what further details we add to the image. There will always be alternative possible interpretations. The physical properties of any material representation are *indeterminate* or *ambiguous* with respect to its content. Whatever conceptual content it turns out to have will have to be determined by something *outside* these properties.

The reader may have noticed that the point is reminiscent of what was said in chapter 3 about the irreducibility of concepts to sensations and mental images. Indeed, I concede to the materialist that sensations and mental images are physical (albeit my conception of the physical is not quite the same as the materialist's, as I explained in chapter 5). The claim to be established presently is that concepts and other intellectual phenomena are irreducible even to physical properties beyond those possessed by sensations and mental images, indeed to any set of physical properties whatsoever.

Now, Ross deployed an example borrowed from the contemporary philosopher Saul Kripke to drive the point home.[536] Suppose you had never computed any numbers as large as 57, but are asked to compute "68 + 57." You answer "125," confident not only that this is

---

[536] Saul Kripke, *Wittgenstein on Rules and Private Language* (Cambridge, MA; Harvard University Press, 1982), pp. 7-9. Some important questions about how to interpret Kripke and Ross's use of Kripke are raised in Peter Dillard, "Two Unsuccessful Arguments for Immaterialism," *American Catholic Philosophical Quarterly* 85 (2011): 269-86. I put them to one side here because they are tangential to the concerns of this chapter, but I do address them in "Kripke, Ross, and the Immaterial Aspects of Thought."

the arithmetically correct answer, but also that it accords with the way you have always used the word "plus," namely to denote the addition function, which, when applied to the numbers 68 and 57, yields 125. But now, Kripke says, imagine that a bizarre skeptic asks you how you can be sure that this is really what you meant by the word "plus" in the past, and therefore how you can be sure that "125" really is the right answer. Perhaps, our skeptic suggests, what you really meant in the past by "plus" and the symbol "+" was not addition, but rather what Kripke calls the "quus" function, which can be defined as follows:

$$x \text{ quus } y = x + y, \text{ if } x, y < 57;$$
$$= 5 \text{ otherwise.}$$

In that case, what you would always have been carrying out was really "quaddition" rather than addition, since quadding and adding numbers will always yield the same result when the numbers are smaller than 57. That would entail that now that you are computing "68 + 57," the correct answer would be "5" rather than "125"; and perhaps, the skeptic proposes, you think otherwise because you are now misinterpreting all your previous usages of "plus" and "+." This all seems absurd, of course, but how can you know the skeptic is wrong?

Kripke has his own uses for this example, but what Ross emphasizes is that nothing in the facts about your behavior, your neurophysiology, or any other physical aspect of human nature can determine that what you were really doing was addition rather than quaddition. For example, it is no use appealing to the fact that what you always have *said* in the past is "Two plus two equals four" rather than "Two quus two equals four," because what is at issue is what you *meant* by "plus." The skeptic will say that it may be that every time you said "plus," what you really meant was the quaddition function. Nor will it help even to call to mind memories of your having had visual or auditory mental images of the sentence "Two plus two equals four" rather than the sentence "Two quus two equals four," because what is in question is the *meaning* you attached to those sounds and shapes.

Even if you were to insist that, whatever you meant in the past, what you *now* mean by "plus" is addition rather than quaddition, the skeptic will still ask how you know *that*, and Ross and Kripke would point out that to answer the question it will not suffice to point out that you *here and now* utter sentences like "Two plus two equals four" rather than "Two quus two equals four," or that you *here and now* bring mental images of the first sentence to mind rather than the second, because the question is what meaning you attach *here and now* to those sounds and shapes. Nor will it help to appeal to what is going on in your nervous system, because in order to know that such-and-such neural activity is associated with addition rather than quaddition, we first have to know that you really *are*, at any particular moment, carrying out addition rather than quaddition, so that we can establish a correlation between addition and the neural activity in question. In other words, any neurophysiological criterion we could appeal to would have to *presuppose* that we already know that you are adding rather than quadding, and thus couldn't by itself *establish* that you are.

Notice that it is completely irrelevant that most of us have in fact computed numbers larger than 57, because for any person, there is always *some* number, even if a very large one, higher than which he has never computed, and Kripke's imagined skeptic can always run his argument using that number instead of 57. Notice also that there is nothing special about the word "plus." An example parallel to Kripke's could be constructed for *any* term, so that the lesson Ross draws is that there is nothing in the material facts about human nature than can suffice to determine the meaning or conceptual content of any sentence or of any other material representation. Again, the physical properties of any material representation are by themselves ambiguous with respect to their conceptual content.

Quine used the example of his cited earlier to establish a similar conclusion. Again, imagine a linguist attempting to translate a native's utterance of "gavagai" in the presence of a rabbit. He could take the correct translation to be "Lo, a rabbit!," and might construct a manual of translation of the native's entire language that is consistent with this translation. But in principle he might replace "rabbit" with a more exotic option like "undetached rabbit part" or "temporal stage of a rabbit," and construct alternate manuals of translation each consistent with one of these possible translations.[537] Quine argues that there is nothing in the native's linguistic behavior and environment that can by itself determine which of these three alternative

---

[537] Quine, *Word and Object*, p. 51f.

translation schemes is correct. But there is, in Quine's view, no evidence to go on other than such behavioral evidence. Hence, he concluded, there is no fact of the matter about which translation is correct, and the meaning of the utterance is indeterminate. The example is unusual, but the point applies equally well to the translation of anyone's speech. Indeed, as John Searle has noted, given Quine's behaviorist assumptions, there is no difference in principle between Quine's example and the first-person case in which one considers what one means by one's *own* words.[538] There will be alternative interpretations of one's own use of "rabbit" that are all equally compatible with one's behavioral dispositions. And in that case there will be, given Quine's behaviorist assumptions, no fact of the matter about what one means.

Now as Kripke points out, a non-behaviorist could take this to be merely a *reductio ad absurdum* of Quine's behaviorist approach to language (as, indeed, Searle does).[539] But the upshot of Kripke's own example is that even an appeal to introspection of one's sensations and mental images (which a behaviorist would eschew) won't solve the problem raised by Quine.[540] For example, suppose that one calls to mind a mental image of a rabbit or of the word "rabbit" whenever one uses that word. There is nothing in the content of such images that by itself will determine that what one *means* really is "rabbit" as opposed to "undetached rabbit part" or "temporal stage of a rabbit."

To reinforce the point that no physical properties of *any* kind can determine meaning, Ross, again following Kripke, notes that there are no physical features of an adding machine, calculator, or computer that can determine whether it is carrying out addition or quaddition, no matter how far we extend its outputs.[541] As Kripke emphasized,

---

[538] John R. Searle, "Indeterminacy, Empiricism, and the First Person," in *Consciousness and Language* (Cambridge: Cambridge University Press, 2002). Cf. W. V. Quine, *Ontological Relativity and Other Essays* (New York: Columbia University Press, 1969), pp. 47-48.

[539] Kripke, *Wittgenstein on Rules and Private Language*, p. 57.
[540] Ibid., pp. 14-15 and 55-57.
[541] Ross, "Immaterial Aspects of Thought," 141-44; Kripke, *Wittgenstein on Rules and Private Language*, 32-37. Cf. Jeff Buechner, "Not Even Computing Machines Can Follow Rules: Kripke's Critique of Functionalism," in Alan Berger, ed., *Saul Kripke* (Cambridge: Cambridge University Press, 2011).

appealing to the intentions of the programmer will not solve the problem, because that just raises the question of whether the programmer really had addition or quaddition in mind, as in the original paradox. But Kripke makes a deeper point. No matter what the past behavior of a machine has been, we can always suppose that its *next* output – "5," say, when calculating numbers larger than any it has calculated before – might show that it is carrying out something like quaddition rather than addition. Now it might be said in response that if this happens, that would just show that the machine was *malfunctioning* rather than performing quaddition. But Kripke points out that whether some output counts as a malfunction depends on what program the machine is running, and whether the machine is running the program for addition rather than quaddition is precisely what is in question. We might find out by asking the programmer, but there is nothing in *the physical properties of the machine itself* that can tell us.

Let's turn now to Ross's defense of the first premise of his basic argument, viz. the claim that formal thought processes can have an exact or unambiguous conceptual content. Adding, squaring a number, inferring via *modus ponens*, and the like are some of the examples of formal thinking Ross appeals to. Anyone who agrees that material processes are indeterminate in the way Kripke's and Quine's arguments imply but who wants to avoid the conclusion that thought is immaterial will have to deny that any of our thoughts is ever determinate in its content; and philosophers like Bernard Williams and Daniel Dennett essentially do deny this.[542] But then they will also have to deny that our thoughts are ever really determinately of any of the forms just cited. They will have to maintain that we only ever *approximate* adding, squaring, inferring via *modus ponens*, etc. "Now that," Ross says, "is expensive. In fact, the cost of saying we only simulate the pure functions is astronomical."[543] In particular, Ross identifies

---

[542] See Bernard Williams, *Descartes: The Project of Pure Inquiry* (London: Penguin Books, 1978), p. 300, and Daniel C. Dennett, "Evolution, Error, and Intentionality," in Dennett's *The Intentional Stance* (Cambridge, MA: The MIT Press, 1989). Cf. Dennett's *Darwin's Dangerous Idea* (New York: Simon and Schuster, 1995), chapter 14. In addition to Quine, Dennett identifies Paul and Patricia Churchland, Donald Davidson, John Haugeland, Ruth Millikan, Richard Rorty, Wilfrid Sellars, and Robert Stalnaker as philosophers who essentially take the same position.
[543] Ross, "Immaterial Aspects of Thought," 145-6.

four problems with the suggestion that we only ever approximate adding, squaring, *modus ponens*, etc. (Some of these are only hinted at, but what I will have to say in developing them is, I think, faithful to Ross's intentions.)

First, it is, from a phenomenological point of view, bizarre to suppose that there is no fact of the matter about whether any of us is, for example, really adding right now. Compute ten plus ten in your mind. Is it remotely plausible to say that there is no objective right answer to the question whether you were just now carrying out addition rather than quaddition? Suppose we were to allow for the sake of argument that that is possible at least in principle. Why should we have *more* confidence in the theory that leads us to such a bizarre result than we have in the phenomenological evidence that we really are adding? Moreover, if the phenomenology could be wrong about something like this, how can we be confident that it is right about anything else? For example, if we are getting it wrong when making judgements about the conceptual content of our very thoughts, how do we know we aren't also getting it wrong when making judgments about the conceptual content of our perceptual experiences? And in that case, what happens to the observational and experimental evidence upon which physical science rests? For example, if a scientist takes himself to be having a perceptual experience of seeing that the needle on a dial is pointing to a certain number, how could he be sure that he isn't really having an experience of some very different sort?

Second, it isn't just common sense that the critic's view conflicts with. The claim that we never really add, apply *modus ponens*, etc. is hard to square with the existence of the vast body of knowledge that comprises the disciplines of mathematics and logic. Nor is it just that mathematics and logic constitute genuine bodies of knowledge in their own right; they are also presupposed by the natural sciences. Now, it is in the name of natural science that philosophers like Quine and Dennett draw the extreme conclusions about the indeterminacy of meaning that they do. But if natural science presupposes mathematics and logic and mathematics and logic presuppose that we do indeed have determinate thought processes, it is hard to see how they can consistently draw this conclusion.

A third and related problem is that if we never really apply *modus ponens* or any other valid argument form, but at best only approximate them, then *none of our arguments is ever really valid.* That includes the arguments of those, like Quine and Dennett, who say that none of our thoughts is really determinate in conceptual content. Hence the view is self-defeating. Even if it were true, we could never be rationally justified in believing that it is true, because we couldn't be rationally justified in believing *anything.*

Fourth, the claim that we never really add, square a number, or apply *modus ponens* or the like is self-defeating in an even more direct and fatal way. For coherently to deny that we ever really do these things presupposes that we have a grasp of what it would be to do them. And that means having thoughts with conceptual content as determinate or unambiguous as those the skeptic says we do not have. In particular, to deny that we ever really add requires that we unambiguously grasp *what it is* to add and then go on to deny that we really ever do it; to deny that we ever really apply *modus ponens* requires that we unambiguously grasp what it is to reason via *modus ponens* and then go on to deny that we ever really do that; and so forth. Yet the whole point of denying that we ever really add, apply *modus ponens*, etc. was to avoid having to admit that we at least sometimes have thought processes with an unambiguous or determinate conceptual content. So, to deny that we have them presupposes that we have them. It simply cannot coherently be done.

And so we have Ross's argument. Again, premise 1 tells us that formal thought processes can have an exact or unambiguous conceptual content – as is evidenced by the fact that, as we have just seen, even the act of denying that they have such a content commits us implicitly to affirming that they do have it. Premise 2 tells us that nothing material can have an exact or unambiguous conceptual content – as even materialists like Quine and Dennett acknowledge, on the basis of arguments like Quine's and Kripke's. From these premises we get our conclusion, namely that formal thought processes are not material.

Objections and replies

In order better to understand Ross's argument, it will be useful to consider some objections that have been leveled against it, and how Ross would or could respond to them. Robert Pasnau has raised an objection to one of Aquinas's arguments for the immateriality of the intellect which might seem applicable to Ross's argument as well.[544] Aquinas argued that the intellect "is not a thing composed of matter and form, because the species of things are received in it in an absolutely immaterial way, as is shown by the fact that the intellect knows universals, which are considered in abstraction from matter and from material conditions."[545] Pasnau claims that this argument commits what he calls the "content fallacy," which involves "conflating two kinds of facts: facts about the content of our thoughts, and facts about what shape or form our thoughts take in our mind."[546] A crude example of such a conflation would be reasoning from *Bob is thinking about a red sports car* to the conclusion that *Bob's thought is red*. In the passage at hand, Pasnau says, Aquinas's "conclusion pertains to intellect's intrinsic qualities: [such as] being immaterial," and this is "inferred from intellect's intentional qualities: being 'concerned with universals.'"[547] In other words, Aquinas (so Pasnau seems to be claiming) is fallaciously inferring from the premise that *the intellect grasps universals, which are immaterial* to the conclusion that *the intellect is immaterial*. Now Ross might seem to be committing a similar fallacy. In particular, it might seem that he is reasoning from the premise that *formal thought processes are about determinate functions like adding, modus ponens, etc., which are immaterial* to the conclusion that *formal thought processes are immaterial*.

---

[544] Robert Pasnau, "Aquinas and the Content Fallacy," *The Modern Schoolman* LXXV (1998): 293-314. Cf. Pasnau, *Thomas Aquinas on Human Nature* (Cambridge: Cambridge University Press, 2002), pp. 315-16. To be sure, Pasnau himself does not raise this objection against Ross. Indeed, a passing reference to Ross's argument in *Thomas Aquinas on Human Nature* is positive, if noncommittal (p. 411). But when I have defended Ross's argument in earlier work, some readers have suggested that Pasnau's objection applies to it.
[545] *Quaestiones disputatae de anima* XIV, as translated by John Patrick Rowan in *The Soul: A Translation of St. Thomas Aquinas's* De Anima (St. Louis: B. Herder, 1949), at p. 182.

[546] Pasnau, "Aquinas and the Content Fallacy," p. 293.

[547] Ibid., p. 304.

But Ross is committing no such fallacy, and neither is Aquinas for that matter. Certainly there is a more charitable way to read them. I would suggest that they are both reasoning in something like the following way:

The objects of thought have property X, which entails that they are immaterial.

But thought itself also has property X.

So, thought must also be immaterial.

And this argument form is valid. For Aquinas, the X in question *universality*, and for Ross the X is *having determinate conceptual content*. Aquinas can be read as saying that, just as the universal *circle* applies to every circle without exception, so too do the *thoughts* we have about circles (when doing geometry, say) apply to every circle without exception; and just as the former could not do so if it were material, neither could the latter. Ross can be read as saying that, just as the abstract form of inference *modus ponens* as studied in logic has a determinate content, so too do we have thoughts that have a determinate content; and just as the former could not be determinate if it were material, neither could the latter.

Brian Leftow cites Ross's argument explicitly in the course of discussing Aquinas, and tentatively suggests a possible difficulty.[548] Quinean considerations of the sort raised by Ross do indeed imply, Leftow allows, that the content of our thoughts cannot be determined by physical processes in the brain. But a materialist who endorses what is called an "externalist" theory of conceptual content could accept this, consistent with maintaining his materialism: "Information not present in the brain could be present in a physical sum, the brain plus its physical environment."[549] One problem with this objection is that it fails to see that Quine himself has already addressed it insofar

---

[548] Brian Leftow, "Soul, Mind, and Brain," in Robert C. Koons and George Bealer, eds., *The Waning of Materialism* (Oxford: Oxford University Press, 2010).

[549] Ibid., p. 410.

as he notes that a native's utterance of "gavagai" is indeterminate between alternative translations *even given* the facts about his environment that the field linguist has to go on.

But a response to Leftow closer to Ross's own manner of arguing is suggested by Kripke's point about adding machines. For any such machine, we can always ask whether a given output is a malfunction. Perhaps what we take to be an output consistent with the machine's adding is really a malfunction in a machine that is "quadding" instead. Nothing in the physical aspects of the machine itself can tell us, and this will be true no matter how large or complex the machine is. But then, if we think of an individual's brain and the various parts of his environment as related like the parts of the machine, then even if that environment includes the entire physical universe, there will be nothing in the collection of these physical facts taken by itself to tell us whether the individual's next utterance really is an expression of addition rather a malfunction in a system that is really carrying out quaddition.[550]

Peter Dillard, borrowing an example from computer science, says that there is a determinate or unambiguous difference between an and-gate, an or-gate, and other logic gates, and holds that this falsifies Ross's claim that physical phenomena are inherently indeterminate in content.[551] But this overlooks Kripke's point that whether a machine has certain computational properties – in this case, whether a given electrical circuit really instantiates an and-gate or is instead malfunctioning – is not something that can be read off from the physical properties of the circuit itself, but depends on the intentions of the designer.

---

[550] To be sure, as a hylemorphist, I do not regard either the brain or a human being of which the brain is an organ as in every relevant respect comparable to a computer, since the latter is an artifact whose parts do not have the kind of organic relationship to one another that the parts of a living thing do. But I am not here comparing the brain or a human being to a computer, but rather the brain or human being *together with the various aspects of its physical environment* to a computer. And those aspects of the environment are not related to an individual human being or his brain in the organic way that the parts of a living thing are related to one another.

[551] Dillard, "Two Unsuccessful Arguments for Immaterialism," pp. 274-5.

Dillard also suggests that the upshot of Kripke's example is merely epistemological rather than metaphysical – that his argument shows at most only that the claim that someone is thinking in accordance with a certain function (such as addition) is underdetermined by the physical evidence, and not that the physical facts are themselves indeterminate.[552] But as both Kripke and Ross emphasize, the implications of the quus example are indeed metaphysical rather than merely epistemological.[553] As Kripke puts it, "not even what an omniscient God would know... could establish whether I meant plus or quus,"[554] because for the reasons given above, everything about my past behavior, sensations, mental imagery and the like is compatible (not just compatible *as far as we know*, but compatible *full stop*) with my meaning either plus or quus. Nor does Dillard say anything to show otherwise.

A further objection raised by Dillard begins by noting that Ross is committed to the Aristotelian view that causal powers are aimed or directed toward the generation of their characteristic effects (a view I defended in earlier chapters). Dillard holds that this thesis is inconsistent with Ross's claim that physical processes are inherently indeterminate. Consider, for example, the tendency of the sulfur in the head of a match to produce flame and heat, specifically, when struck (rather than frost and cold or some other effect). Isn't this an instance of a determinate physical phenomenon?[555] But the problem with this objection is one that Dillard himself inadvertently hints at when he alludes to the distinction between natural powers and rational powers.[556] Consider a dog and a human being who are both looking at the same food. Each is in a perceptual state that is "directed at" the food. But there is a *conceptual* element to the human being's perceptual experience of the food that isn't present in the case of the dog.

---

[552] Ibid., p. 273.
[553] Kripke, *Wittgenstein on Rules and Private Language*, 21 and 39; Ross, *Thought and World*, pp. 119-20. In fairness to Dillard, it should be noted that he makes no reference to Ross's *Thought and World* and relies entirely on Ross's earlier discussion in "Immaterial Aspects of Thought."

[554] Kripke, *Wittgenstein on Rules and Private Language*, p. 21.
[555] Dillard, "Two Unsuccessful Arguments for Immaterialism," p. 275.
[556] Dillard, "Two Unsuccessful Arguments for Immaterialism," p. 275, n. 17.

The dog's causal powers, however complex relative to those of non-sentient material substances, are nevertheless sub-rational.

To borrow an example from Hilary Putnam, suppose it is suggested that a certain neural "data structure" evolved in dogs to facilitate their getting meat, and that this justifies us in attributing to them what Putnam calls a "proto-concept" of meat.[557] As Putnam points out, the dog will be satisfied and nourished whether it is given fresh meat, canned meat, or some textured vegetable protein that looks, smells, and tastes exactly like meat. For that reason, there is no fact of the matter about whether its putative "proto-concept" represents any one of these in particular, and thus no sense to be made of the question of whether the dog has a true belief about what it is eating when it eats the vegetable protein rather than meat. "Evolution didn't 'design' dogs' ideas to be true or false, it designed them to be successful or unsuccessful."[558] But in that case the suggestion that the dog really *has* a "proto-concept" of meat in the first place is groundless:

> [T]he whole idea that a unique correspondence between the data structure and meat is involved in this bit of natural selection is an illusion, an artifact of the way we described the situation. We could just as well have said that the data structure was selected for because its action normally signals the presence of something which has a certain smell and taste and appearance and is edible.[559]

In short, there is nothing in the situation described that entails that anything in the dog's brain corresponds to *meat* specifically, and thus there is nothing in the situation that entails that the dog has a *concept* (or "proto-concept") of meat. The point is completely general, applying to *any* concept. What a dog's neural wiring and corresponding perceptual experiences facilitate is survival, not truth or falsity. Hence we are not going to read off true or false beliefs from a dog's neural-

---

[557] Hilary Putnam, *Renewing Philosophy* (Cambridge, MA: Harvard University Press, 1992, pp. 27-33.
[558] Ibid., p. 31.

[559] Ibid.

cum-perceptual states, and neither will we read off from them the *concepts* that true or false beliefs presuppose. It follows that, contra Dillard, the existence in purely material substances of causal powers which are directed toward certain outcomes does not suffice for the kind of determinacy characteristic of concepts.[560]

Now, the solution to his "quus" paradox that Kripke himself took the most seriously is the one he (controversially) attributes to Wittgenstein, a so-called "skeptical solution." The skeptical solution concedes that there is no fact of the matter about what we mean by "plus," and thus no way to give *truth-conditions* for the claim that by "plus" one means addition. It is then suggested that we can nevertheless give *assertibility-conditions* for this claim, and that these conditions are to be found in what a linguistic community actually agrees upon. That you mean addition rather than quaddition by "plus" is just a matter of your using "plus" in a way that the linguistic community counts as addition.[561] Dillard suggests that Ross's argument might be resisted simply by denying his first premise – that formal thinking has a determinate content – and embracing instead Kripke's skeptical solution, or the related Quinean view that to count a speaker's usage of "plus" as addition is just to note that his usage does not elicit "bizarreness reactions" in his fellow language users.[562]

But as we have already seen, Ross argues that it is simply self-defeating to deny that our formal thought processes are determinate. Dillard offers no response to this other than the insinuation that by biting the bullet, the Kripkean or Quinean can stalemate Ross. Yet the views are *not* thereby left at a stalemate, for that would require that each view is at least internally consistent and thus as coherent as its rival, and neither Kripke's skeptical solution nor Quine's position *is* coherent. For one thing, and as Searle has emphasized, both Kripke and Quine have implicitly to presuppose precisely what they deny.

---

[560] That directedness does not entail determinacy should be obvious enough from the existence of vague and ambiguous expressions. Such expressions "point" to a certain possible range of meanings – a large range in the case of vague expressions, a smaller one in the case of ambiguous ones – but not determinately to any particular meaning within the range.

[561] Kripke, *Wittgenstein on Rules and Private Language*, chapter 3.

[562] Dillard, "Two Unsuccessful Arguments for Immaterialism," pp. 277-8.

Even to get his "gavagai" scenario off the ground, Quine has to presuppose that we can understand the difference between meaning *rabbit* by "rabbit" and meaning *undetached rabbit part* by "rabbit," at least in our own case.[563] Something similar could be said about the difference between adding and quadding in Kripke's example. Indeed, Kripke himself insists that "the sceptical problem indicates no vagueness in the *concept* of addition... or in the word 'plus', *granting* its usual meaning" and that, again, granting this meaning, "the word 'plus' denotes a function whose determination is *completely* precise."[564] (This is obviously related to Ross's point that we have to have a determinate grasp of what addition, *modus ponens*, etc. are even to deny that we have such a grasp.) And as Searle points out, Kripke's skeptical solution presupposes that I can know what I mean by "agreement" with the community (though given the skeptical paradox, *how* do I know that by "agreement" I really do mean *agreement* rather than *quagreement*?)[565]

For another thing, as Ross points out, to deny that our thoughts are ever determinate is to deny that we ever really reason validly. Now, both Kripke and Quine are eminent logicians, and paradigmatic analytic philosophers who would not be caught dead putting forward a bold philosophical thesis without claiming to be able to give a solid argument for it. And yet their position entails that there are no solid arguments for any philosophical position, including their own. How can it seriously be maintained that such a position stalemates Ross's? As Thomas Nagel has argued, what Kripke's argument really amounts to is a *reductio ad absurdum* of the reductionist assumption that meaning must somehow be explicable in terms of something

---

[563] Searle, "Indeterminacy, Empiricism, and the First Person," p. 234.

[564] Kripke, *Wittgenstein on Rules and Private Language*, p. 82.

[565] John R. Searle, "Skepticism About Rules and Intentionality," in Searle's *Consciousness and Language* (Cambridge, MA: Cambridge University Press, 2002), p. 260. Thomas Nagel makes a similar point about "fact," "word," "mean," and other terms needed even to state the skeptical paradox and its solution. See *The Last Word* (Oxford: Oxford University Press, 1997), p. 44.

else – behavior, physiology, mental imagery, dispositions, or what have you.[566]

Now, Kripke has a response to the suggestion that meaning something by a word is *sui generis* and not to be assimilated to sensations, dispositions, or the like, and it is a response Dillard seems to think effectively rebuts Ross's argument:

> Such a move may in a sense be irrefutable... But it seems desperate: it leaves the nature of this postulated primitive state – the primitive state of 'meaning addition by "plus"' – completely mysterious... Such a state would have to be a finite object, contained in our finite minds... Can we conceive of a finite state which *could* not be interpreted in a quus-like way? How could that be?[567]

Commenting on Kripke's objection, G. W. Fitch characterizes the suggestion that meaning is *sui generis* as an appeal to a "brute fact."[568] Arif Ahmed suggests that Kripke's objections to explaining meaning by reference to sensations or mental images would apply to any appeal to a *sui generis* mental state as well.[569]

But all of this simply begs the question against the view that meaning is *sui generis*. Fitch's and Ahmed's claims presuppose that the *sui generis* state in question is one that could at least in principle come apart from meaning addition. They presuppose that there are two things in question here – the mental state itself and a certain conceptual content, where it is a "brute fact" that the two are conjoined in a particular case, and where we can imagine a case where the state exists with some different content instead. But that is precisely what the *sui generis* view denies. It holds that we should *not* think of meaning

---

[566] Nagel, *The Last Word*, pp. 41-7.

[567] Kripke, *Wittgenstein on Rules and Private Language*, pp. 51-2. Cf. Dillard, "Two Unsuccessful Arguments for Immaterialism," p. 276, n. 20 and p. 279.

[568] G. W. Fitch, *Saul Kripke* (Montreal and Kingston: McGill-Queen's University Press, 2004), p. 153.

[569] Arif Ahmed, *Saul Kripke* (London: Continuum, 2007), p. 122.

something by a word as an otherwise content-free mental state which has somehow been fitted with a detachable content. Similarly, when Kripke alleges that the view is "mysterious," he seems to assume that a *non*-mysterious view would be one that reduces meaning to something else – again, to behavior, sensations, dispositions, or what have you. And that too is just what the view of meaning as *sui generis* denies. Kripke and his commentators Fitch and Ahmed really offer no *argument* against the *sui generis* view. They merely express an undefended prejudice in favor of a reductionist approach, and pretend that it constitutes an objection.

It is, in any event, quite rich for someone who says that our thoughts never have any determinate content – and therefore implies that we never really add, square a number, reason in accordance with *modus ponens*, etc. but only seem to – to accuse the other side of mystery-mongering! The retort open to Ross is obvious: We *know* that there must be such a thing as a *sui generis* state of meaning addition by "plus" (or of meaning something else by another word), because arguments like Kripke's show that denying that there is reduces to absurdity. Even if we are left with a sense of mystery about the nature of meaning, mystery is different from, and far better than, the self-defeating incoherence that Ross's critic is forced into.

That there is nothing arbitrary or ad hoc about the *sui generis* response to arguments like Kripke's and Quine's is evidenced by the fact that Scholastic philosophers took something like that view, on independent grounds, long before the arguments in question came on the scene. As we saw in chapter 3, John of St. Thomas distinguished between *instrumental* signs and *formal* signs.[570] As Francis Parker and Henry Veatch explain, an instrumental sign is "double-natured"; that is to say, it "is a sign and also something else, namely, an entity in its own right."[571] The smoke that we take to be a sign of fire, the red and white striped pole that functions as a sign of a barber shop, and writ-

---

[570] Francis H. Parker and Henry B. Veatch, *Logic as a Human Instrument* (New York: Harper and Brothers, 1959), pp. 16-22.

[571] Ibid., pp. 16-17.

ten and spoken words are all material signs in that they can be characterized entirely apart from their status as signs – in terms of their chemical composition, say, or texture, or shape. Formal signs, by contrast,

> do not have traits which must be known before their significance is known. They are not *means* – things which *have* meaning. They are themselves meanings; they are signs and nothing but signs... [They] have no nature other than their signifying nature. [572]

Examples would be concepts and propositions. Neither a concept nor a proposition has any nature other than being about whatever it is about. It makes sense to suppose that a material sign might not have been about anything. But it makes no sense to suppose that a concept or proposition might not have been about anything. These are signs that are *nothing but* signs.

Notice that this a perfectly natural distinction to draw, and one which has been drawn for centuries, just given what we know pretheoretically about the difference between words, material symbols, and the like on the one hand and concepts and propositions on the other. There is also, if there were really any doubt about whether there are any formal signs, a fairly intuitive argument for their existence, one suggested by Parker and Veatch.[573] Precisely because material signs and their conceptual content are separable, we cannot read off the content from the nature they have apart from their status as signs, and have to determine their meaning by reference to other signs (as we do when we check a dictionary to see how one word is defined by reference to other words). But if every sign were a material sign, we would be led into a vicious regress. Hence there must be signs which *just are* their meanings, and which therefore need not be known by reference to other signs and can serve as the terminus of explanation of those signs which do need to be explained by reference to others.

---

[572] Ibid., p. 18.

[573] Ibid., pp. 19-20. What follows is my paraphrase of their argument.

Now, this notion of a formal sign corresponds more or less exactly to what Kripke calls a *sui generis* conception of meaning, a conception in which there is simply no gap between a sign and its conceptual content of the sort Kripke's skeptic needs in order to get his skepticism off the ground. Whatever one thinks of the notion, it is motivated independently of the desire ("desperate" or otherwise) to find a response to arguments like Kripke's. And its very existence obviously bolsters Ross's case. Not only can he argue that the *sui generis* conception of meaning is unavoidable if we want to avoid the self-defeating incoherence of Ross's critic; he can argue that there is in the notion of formal signs a preexisting, independently motivated account of meaning that corresponds to the *sui generis* conception, already waiting there "on the shelf" as it were rather than being concocted ad hoc. We had good reason to accept it even apart from the arguments of Quine, Kripke, and Co. Their arguments show it to be not merely worthy of consideration, but unavoidable on pain of incoherence.

Dillard raises yet another objection, to the effect that Ross's position opens up "an apparently unbridgeable gulf between thought and behavior."[574] And materialists will insist that the view that thought is immaterial does not sit well with what we know from modern neuroscience. In response it must, first of all, be emphaized that the Aristotelian position Ross represents (and that I am defending in this book) does not deny that, in the normal case, material processes are *necessary* for thought. Rather, it denies that they are *sufficient* for it.

To see how a human thought has, in the normal case, material aspects as well as the immaterial aspects we have been considering so far, consider the analogy of *sentences*. The English sentence "Snow is white" conveys the same proposition whatever material form it takes, whether spoken, written, or typed into a word processor. The spoken, written, or typed German sentence "Schnee ist weiss" also conveys the very same proposition, and that proposition could be conveyed too not only in some other natural language but in even more exotic ways – through Esperanto, say, or encoded in some computer language. So, the propositional content of a sentence cannot be reduced to any of

---

[574] Dillard, "Two Unsuccessful Arguments for Immaterialism," p. 279.

its material or linguistic properties. All the same, we typically convey and entertain a proposition via the *medium* of a sentence. As Frege put it: "The thought, in itself immaterial, clothes itself in the material garment of a sentence and thereby becomes comprehensible to us. We say a sentence expresses a thought."[575] We do not "see" propositions "naked," as it were; they rarely if ever leave the house except in sentential garb. Thus, while what we grasp when we grasp the proposition that snow is white is not *identical* with the English sentence "Snow is white," what we grasp is nevertheless grasped *through* that English sentence (or through the German sentence "Schnee ist weiss" or a sentence of some other language).

Now when the sentence is spoken, written, or typed, the material medium will be compression waves in the air, ink marks, pixels, or the like. When it is entertained mentally, the medium will be a phantasm or mental image (whether visual or auditory), and the Aristotelian regards that as something material. The conveying or entertaining of concepts without putting them together into complete thoughts will not involve the use of sentences but it will still involve the use of either individual words, or pictures, symbols, or the like, whether written, spoken, drawn, or imagined. In this way our intellectual activity, though it cannot in principle be entirely material, is nevertheless always conducted through material media. As Aquinas writes:

> Although the intellect abstracts from the phantasms, it does not understand actually without turning to the phantasms.[576]

> [I]t is clear that for the intellect to understand actually, not only when it acquires fresh knowledge, but also when it applies knowledge already acquired, there is need for the act of the imagination and of the other powers. For when the act of the imagination is hindered by a lesion of the corporeal organ, for instance in a case of frenzy; or when the act of the memory is hindered, as in the case of lethargy, we see that a man is

---

[575] Frege, "The Thought: A Logical Inquiry," 292.

[576] *Summa theologiae* I.85.5, as translated by by the Fathers of the English Dominican Province in St. Thomas Aquinas, *Summa Theologica* (Notre Dame, IN: Christian Classics, 1981).

> hindered from actually understanding things of which he had a previous knowledge.[577]
>
> [I]n the present state of life whatever we understand, we know by comparison to natural sensible things. Consequently it is not possible for our intellect to form a perfect judgment, while the senses are suspended, through which sensible things are known to us.[578]

That Aquinas is right about this is something I argued for in the previous chapter.

From an Aristotelian-Thomistic point of view, then, it is hardly surprising that modern neuroscience has uncovered intimate correlations between neural activity and mental activity, or that damage to the brain can severely impair thought – any more than it is surprising that if we physically damage a sentence, its ability to convey its propositional content is diminished or destroyed despite that content's being irreducible to the sentence's physical properties. For the Aristotelian or Thomist to acknowledge that there is a physiological component to thought is not to make a desperate concession to modern scientific advances. On the contrary, it is merely to reaffirm something that Aristotle and Aquinas themselves already recognized.

It must also be kept in mind that for the Aristotelian-Thomistic tradition, human beings and their operations are, like other natural substances and processes, to be analyzed in terms of formal, material, efficient and final causes, which together form an irreducible unity. In the case of a thought (such as the thought *that snow is white*) the neural processes associated with the relevant phantasms might be regarded as the material cause of a single event of which the intellective activity is the formal cause. To be sure, the analysis of human thought and action in terms of the Aristotelian four-causal explanatory framework is a more complicated business than that suggests. But it is only if that framework is rejected that to acknowledge that there are immaterial aspects of thought can seem to open up what

---

[577] *Summa theologiae* I.84.7.

[578] *Summa theologiae* I.84.8.

Dillard calls "an apparently unbridgeable gulf between thought and behavior." And to reject it without argument would simply be to beg the question against the Aristotelian-Thomistic view.

Having said all that, an implicit neuroscientific refutation of Ross's argument might nevertheless seem to be suggested by the subtitle of Paul Churchland's book *Plato's Camera: How the Physical Brain Captures a Landscape of Abstract Universals*.[579] Can it be that neuroscience has after all finally shown that something with the determinacy and strict universality of a concept could be embodied in "muscle-manipulating *trajectories* of... collective neuronal activities" and the like?[580]

No, it cannot be, and Churchland does not actually try to show otherwise. Rather, what he does is to change the subject. He tells us that, contrary to what philosophers have supposed historically, the "fundamental unit of cognition" is not the judgment, with its susceptibility of truth or falsity and its logical relationships to other judgments, but rather "the *activation pattern* across a proprietary *population* of neurons."[581] Nor does "theoretical understanding" consist primarily in the grasp of sentences or propositions, but rather in "an *unfolding sequence of activation-vectors*" within the brain.[582] Nor does knowledge fundamentally involve justified true belief. Rather, a "conceptual framework" turns out to be "a hierarchically structured, high-dimensional activation space," and a "perceptual representation" turns out to be "a 10^6-element neuronal activation vector."[583] And Churchland tells us that while such neurological "representational vehicles... can have, or lack, sundry representational virtues," they "are

---

[579] Paul M. Churchland, *Plato's Camera: How the Physical Brain Captures a Landscape of Abstract Universals* (Cambridge, MA: The MIT Press, 2012).

[580] Ibid., p. 3.

[581] Ibid., p. 4.

[582] Ibid., pp. 22-23.

[583] Ibid., p. 32.

not the sorts of things to which the notion of Tarskian truth even applies."[584]

Now, little or nothing in the way of argument is actually given by Churchland for any of these claims. A general materialism is simply taken for granted, and it is insinuated that since processes of the sort Churchland describes are the ones neuroscientists are discovering within the brain, they must be what cognition essentially consists in. To his credit, Churchland sees that the properties in terms of which thought is typically characterized – propositional content, truth and falsity, logical interrelationships, and so forth – simply cannot intelligibly be ascribed to the brute physiological processes he is interested in. But in that case, what reason can there be to characterize such processes as embodying "cognition," "understanding," "knowledge," or the having of a "conceptual framework" in the first place? When stripped of propositional content, truth or falsity, logical connections, and the like, how does a pattern of neural activity constitute a "cognition" any more than the flexing of a tendon or the secretion of bile constitutes a cognition? In fact Churchland is simply equivocating, using terms like "cognition," "concept," etc. in a novel way, as *stand-ins* for physiological descriptions. He is in no way *explaining* cognition in terms of physiology. He is instead simply *ignoring* (or even *eliminating*) cognition altogether and talking about physiology instead, using the vocabulary of cognition but in a way that is mostly contrary to its usual sense.

I say "mostly" rather than "entirely" contrary because it is crucial to Churchland's account that he retains the notion of "representation" in something like its traditional sense. Now, he does nothing to *justify* his use of the notion of representation; again, why a neural process counts as a "representation" any more than the flexing of a tendon or the secretion of bile counts as a representation is something Churchland does not tell us. (Indeed, he is critical of existing materialist attempts to explain representation in terms of the causal relations between neural processes and properties of the external world, in part for indeterminacy reasons of the sort canvassed

---

[584] Ibid.

above.⁵⁸⁵) Churchland simply *assumes* that the neural processes he describes constitute representations of a sort, and goes from there. In particular, he supposes that the brain embodies something like a "map" of the external world.

Now, with this an Aristotelian writer like Ross can readily agree, at least for the sake of argument. But the map-like representations Churchland postulates do not amount to *concepts* of the sort Ross and other Aristotelian writers are concerned with. They are instead better identified with *phantasms*, which such writers have always acknowledged to be physiological. And they are no less indeterminate and less than universal than phantasms as traditionally conceived of are. Churchland makes heavy use of the analogy of a road map, and of the notion that the "homomorphism" between such a map and the streets and highways it represents is a model for the homomorphism between the "maps" embodied in the brain and features of the external world. But of course, a road map is as indeterminate as any of the other material symbols and images we have considered. For instance, there is nothing in the material properties of the lines on a map that of themselves determine that an inch represents a mile (say) rather than ten miles; and a legend placed on the side of the map to explain this will itself be comprised of material symbols that are *themselves* indeterminate in their meaning.

Churchland gives us no reason to think that any "map" encoded in the brain will be any less indeterminate. And thus his position is no challenge at all to Ross's argument. To be sure, it is only fair to acknowledge that arguments like Churchland's may indeed help to elucidate the *material* aspects of thought, the role that phantasms and physiology play in cognition. But that there are also, and more importantly, *immaterial* aspects of thought is a thesis that no neuroscientific discovery has refuted or could refute.

In response to my defense of Ross, Dillard has in follow-up work presented three lines of criticism.⁵⁸⁶ The first raises once again

---

⁵⁸⁵ Ibid., pp. 97-98.

⁵⁸⁶ Peter Dillard, "Ross Revisited: Reply to Feser," *American Catholic Philosophical Quarterly* 88 (2014): 139-47.

the charge that Ross is entitled to only an epistemological conclusion, not a metaphysical one. In particular, according to Dillard, the most Ross can say is that you cannot *know from* the physical facts what you or anyone else means. But it doesn't follow that the physical facts don't suffice to make it the case that our thoughts and utterances *actually have* some determinate conceptual content. For all Ross has shown, maybe our thoughts *are* purely physical but nevertheless do have some determinate meaning, even if we can't know what that meaning is. Hence (Dillard concludes) Ross hasn't really established that formal thinking is not physical.

Dillard defends this claim by appealing to what he takes to be a parallel example. Consider the mitosis that a cell undergoes, and an imaginary Kripke-style parallel process which Dillard labels "schmitosis." Schmitosis is just like mitosis, except that:

> "[S]chmitosis"... yields nuclei containing an exact copy of the parental nucleus's chromosomes for the first 10^n cell divisions but an entirely different set of chromosomes for any cell divisions > 10^n. No matter how many mitotic divisions the cells undergo, their behavior will also conform to an incompatible, non-mitotic process.[587]

What we've got here, Dillard suggests, is a scenario in which it is indeterminate from the lower-level physical facts whether a cell is undergoing mitosis or schmitosis. But it doesn't follow that there is no objective fact of the matter about whether a cell is really undergoing mitosis, and it doesn't follow that, if there is a fact of the matter, something *non*-physical is happening here. What we should say instead, in Dillard's view, is that mitosis is *irreducible* to the lower-level physical facts, but is still itself physical.

Now, so far I am happy to agree with what Dillard says, at least for the sake of argument. Indeed, though he doesn't put it this way, he is essentially making a very Aristotelian claim. For it is part of the Aristotelian theory of substantial form that a true substance has properties and causal powers that are irreducible to those of its parts. And

---

[587] Ibid., p. 140.

that has nothing essentially to do with immateriality. The causal powers and properties of a dog or a tree are irreducible to those of their parts, but a dog and a tree are still purely material substances. The causal powers and properties of water are irreducible to those of a mere aggregate of distinct parcels of hydrogen and oxygen, but water is still a purely material substance. And so forth.

So, if so far Dillard has made a point that an Aristotelian like Ross or me would agree with, how is it supposed to pose a problem for Ross's argument? The answer is that the irreducibility of mitosis to lower-level physical facts has, Dillard evidently thinks, only *epistemological* rather than metaphysical significance. And this in his view supports the judgment that the indeterminacy of meaning too has only epistemological significance. Just as mitosis is a purely material process even if irreducible to lower-level physical facts, so too might formal thinking be purely material even if its content is indeterminate from the physical facts.

But Dillard is making two mistakes here. The first is in supposing, without argument, that irreducibility has only epistemological significance. He seems to think that if a higher-level feature is physical despite being irreducible to lower-level physical features, then the gap between the levels cannot in any way be metaphysical and thus must be epistemological. But the Aristotelian hylemorphist denies that. There are, on the Aristotelian view, metaphysical gaps *within* the material world itself and not just between the material and the immaterial. For example, there are the traditional Aristotelian distinctions between the inorganic and the organic and between merely vegetative and animal forms of life. So, unless he provides some argument for the supposition he is making, Dillard is here begging the question against the Aristotelian.

More importantly, the issue doesn't really have anything to do with irreducibility per se in the first place. Dillard is essentially conflating questions about indeterminacy and questions about irreducibility, and thereby misunderstanding Ross's argument. Ross isn't arguing that thought is *irreducible* and therefore immaterial. Again, as an Aristotelian he would not make such an inference. Rather, he is arguing that thought has *a determinate conceptual content* and is therefore immaterial. So, the mitosis/schmitosis example is simply not relevantly parallel to Ross's examples, because there is no conceptual content involved in mitosis.

Dillard's second objection questions Ross's claim that it is incoherent to deny that our thoughts ever have any determinate conceptual content. Here Dillard makes two main points. First, he notes that a Quinean naturalist would express the claims to which he is committed in terms of a formal language, and in summarizing how this would go Dillard speaks of what he calls the "L-sentences" of such a language. Dillard then says:

> Whether an L-sentence is logically valid or whether an L-sentence is a logical consequence of other L-sentences has nothing to do with whether there are determinate facts about human thinking, any more than whether ferns in the Smoky Mountains are undergoing photosynthesis has anything to do with determinate facts about Tasmanian devils.[588]

Now, Dillard's point here, if I understand him correctly, is that whether an argument in such a formal language is valid or not is just an objective fact that has nothing to do with what anyone thinks about it. Hence the determinacy or indeterminacy of human thought is irrelevant.

But if this is what Dillard is saying, then he is missing Ross's point. The question isn't whether there might still, as a matter of objective fact, be logical connections between propositions even if human thought was material (if we understand these objective facts in Platonic terms, say). The question is whether *human thought could ever get in contact* with these facts. And what Quinean and Kripkean indeterminacy arguments entail, Ross argues, is that human thought could not do so *if* it were material. For while there might still in that case be a fact of the matter about whether *modus ponens* is objectively a valid form of inference, there would be *no* fact of the matter about *whether anyone's thoughts actually conform* to modus ponens or to some other, invalid inference form instead. And *that's* the sort of result that generates the incoherence Ross is talking about.

---

[588] Ibid., p. 144.

Dillard's second move here is to appeal to the "skeptical solutions" that naturalist philosophers have proposed in order to deal with indeterminacy puzzles like Kripke's and Quine's. He puts particular emphasis on the Quinean idea that we can take others to mean the same thing we do when our utterances don't produce in them "bizarreness reactions" like blank stares, eye-rolling, puzzled looks, etc. Writes Dillard:

> The austere naturalist grants that we can be said to assert, mean, and understand things in the minimal sense that our utterances and inscriptions which either contain the relevant expressions or are made in response to others' utterances and inscriptions containing them do not provoke bizarreness reactions.[589]

As far as I can tell, what Dillard is saying here is that as long as your utterances don't produce such "bizarreness reactions" in others, then, the materialist can argue, you can be said to be adding, applying *modus ponens*, etc., and the indeterminacy problem is thereby solved. Hence the incoherence problem won't arise.

But there are several problems with this proposal. First, we need to distinguish (a) the thesis that there is no objective fact of the matter about what anyone means, from (b) attempts to deal with the practical problems this thesis generates by way of appealing to the absence of "bizarreness reactions" or the like. Now, what Dillard seems to be saying is that a materialist could hold that as long as we have (b), then we needn't worry about the practical problems posed by (a). But this completely misses Ross's point. Ross is not saying that (a) *could* in principle be true but that it would pose intractable practical problems for the materialist – in which case the materialist's appeal to (b) would be to the point. Rather, Ross is saying that (a) is incoherent and *cannot* in principle be true, so that we never even get to the stage of having to deal with indeterminacy problems by appealing to bizarreness reactions, etc. (Of course, Ross allows that there would be no fact of the matter about what anyone means *if human thought were material*. But he does *not* grant that there might in principle be no fact of the matter

---

[589] Ibid.

about what anyone means *full stop*. He thinks there *is and must be* a fact of the matter, which is why human thought has to be *im*material.)

Another problem is that the very idea that the absence of "bizarreness reactions" suffices to solve the indeterminacy problem is simply a non-starter, for several reasons. For one thing, the absence of bizarreness reactions in others is neither necessary nor sufficient for one's reasoning to count as conforming to a valid logical form. As all logic teachers know, if you present an argument like the following to beginning students:

> Either 2 + 2 = 5 or the sky is blue.
>
> It is not true that 2 + 2 = 5.
>
> Therefore, the sky is blue.

that will certainly produce "bizarreness reactions" in them. They will think it a very odd way to speak, and they may even go so far as to say that it is not a logical way to speak. But of course, in fact it is a perfectly valid and even sound argument of the logical form *disjunctive syllogism*. Arguments that are not sound but still valid also provoke bizarreness reactions in people. If you say:

> If the sky is green, then water is flammable.
>
> The sky is green.
>
> Therefore, water is flammable.

you will once again provoke bizarreness reactions in beginning students, and it takes a little effort to explain why, for all its obvious faults, this is at least a valid argument in the sense in which the word "valid" is used in logic.

You can also say and do things that do not produce bizarreness reactions in others, yet do not amount to logical reasoning. For example, if you give an argument like the following:

> If it is raining, then the streets are wet.

The streets are wet.

Therefore, it is raining.

many will nod approvingly and think it in no way bizarre. But in fact it is an argument of the invalid form *affirming the consequent*. And it would remain invalid even if you somehow got all logicians to start agreeing with it. Furthermore, we say and do all sorts of other things that do not produce bizarreness reactions in others – walking, yawning, saying "Have a nice day," etc. – but which do not amount to valid forms of reasoning, precisely because they don't involve *reasoning* of any sort at all.

Then there is the fact that what the Quinean calls "bizarreness reactions" *are themselves just as indeterminate in their significance as any utterance is*. For example, it is no good to say: "The looks people give me when I say that two and two make four don't seem to express puzzlement; therefore I must be adding and not quadding." For just as the Kripkean skeptic can always ask: "But what do you or anyone else *really mean* when you use words like 'plus,' 'add,' etc.?" so too can he ask: "But what do you or anyone else *really mean* when you smile, nod, stare blankly, grimace, etc.?" The Quinean appeal to "bizarreness reactions" doesn't solve the indeterminacy problem at all, but merely pushes it back a further stage.

Dillard's third objection is that if thought processes are immaterial, but all we ever observe of other people are their bodies and behavior, then we could never know the meaning of anyone else's thoughts. "Ross's immaterialism appears to open up an unbridgeable gulf between thinking and behavior," says Dillard.[590] But there are several problems with this objection. First, what Dillard is raising here is just a variation on the traditional "problem of other minds." And it is difficult to see why Dillard thinks this is a special problem for *Ross*. It can be and often is presented as a problem *whatever* one's view about the metaphysics of mind, whether dualist or materialist. For on either view there is arguably at least an epistemological gap between bodily and physiological facts on the one hand and facts about the mind on the other.

---

[590] Ibid., p. 145.

This would be especially true of the non-reductive form of naturalism that Dillard pits against Ross. As we saw above, in his first objection against Ross, Dillard suggests that the meaning of our thoughts might still be physical even if it could not be inferred from physical facts about behavior, brain activity, etc. He claimed, contra Ross, that this has only epistemological rather than metaphysical significance. But in that case *Dillard himself* is affirming an epistemological gap between thinking and behavior that poses just the sort of problem he thinks Ross's position lands Ross in. So, again, there is nothing about Ross's position that raises the problem of other minds in a unique way.

Second, it would be rather absurd for a materialist who accepts Quinean or Kripkean indeterminacy results to raise this sort of objection against Ross. Ross could respond: "At least given my view there *is* a fact of the matter about what a person means, even if one could not know what that meaning is except in one's own case. But if materialism were true, we couldn't say even that much. There would be *no fact of the matter at all*, not just a fact of the matter that we couldn't know about."

Dillard also suggests that Ross's position no less than anyone else's is vulnerable to Kripke's imagined skeptic. He says that the "*sui generis* acts of thinking" entailed by Ross's argument would be problematic as purported anchors of meaning even in the first-person case, in just the way Kripke's argument says that sensations and behavior are problematic even in the first-person case. To be sure, Dillard seems to allow that Ross's "*sui generis* acts of thinking" *would* suffice to determine the content of the thoughts I am having *here and now*. But he thinks they would not suffice to tell me what the true content of my past thoughts was. He writes:

> But since my earlier behavior associated with the "+" sign does not determine whether I was actually adding as opposed to quadding or even thinking of nothing at all, I also have no idea whether yesterday I was adding, quadding, or thinking of nothing at all.[591]

---

[591] Ibid., p. 146.

But there are two problems with Dillard's argument here. First, it is not at all clear *why* he thinks that Ross's "*sui generis* acts of thinking" would suffice to determine meaning in the first-person case here and now, but nevertheless would *not* suffice to determine what I meant in the past. For, contrary to what Dillard says in the sentence just quoted, I don't have *merely* my memory of past behavior to go on. I also have my memory of these past *sui generis* acts. And if present *sui generis* acts suffice to determine the content of what I am thinking now, why don't past *sui generis* acts suffice to determine the content of what I was thinking then? (True, in theory I could be forgetting what past *sui generis* acts of thought I actually engaged in. But that's a *different* problem, merely a special case of the more general question of how I can know memory is reliable. It has nothing to do with Ross's account, specifically.)

The second problem with Dillard's objection is that (depending on how one reads him) he may be overlooking the crucial difference between sensations, behavior, etc. on the one hand and Ross's "*sui generis* acts of thinking" on the other. As we saw above, with sensations, behavior, etc., there is a gap in principle between the sensation or behavior itself on the one hand, and whatever conceptual content it is associated with on the other. But with the *sui generis* acts of thinking (or "formal signs," as John of St. Thomas characterizes them), there is no such gap. The thought *just is* its content. Now it is the gap that exists in the former case that is essential to the sorts of problems Kripke raises. But since the gap doesn't exist in the case of *sui generis* thoughts, the problems in question don't apply to them.

The failure of naturalistic theories of content

It might be supposed that determinate or unambiguous conceptual content can be secured by causal relations of the kind posited by contemporary naturalistic theories of content.[592] Nothing could be further from the truth. In fact, such theories notoriously face indeterminacy problems precisely like those emphasized by Ross. Indeed, defenders of such theories are themselves well aware of the difficulty, and while they have developed various purported solutions, there is no consensus on any of them – unsurprisingly, since, I would argue, no solution is possible.

The most straightforward sort of naturalistic theory of content is a causal theory, the basic idea of which is that *B will represent A when B is caused by A*. For example, suppose we identified thoughts with brain states of a certain kind, and that in a particular case some such state was triggered by the presence of a cat on a mat. Then, the story goes, that thought will have the content that *the cat is on the mat*. But it is widely acknowledged that to leave it at that would be woefully inadequate. Jerry Fodor calls such an unadorned account the "Crude Causal Theory," and there are several immediate problems with it.[593] For example, suppose Grandma owns a cat and has the thought that *the cat is on the mat* whenever she thinks she sees the cat sitting on the mat. But suppose also that she has bad eyesight, and that unbeknownst to her, the cat is only on the mat half the times she thinks it is. The other times it is really the neighborhood dog, who has wandered in through the cat door, that is sitting on the mat. If the Crude Causal Theory were correct, the content of Grandma's thought should be the disjunctive proposition that *either the cat is on the mat or the dog is on the mat*, since both the cat and the dog cause the thought with the same regularity. But in fact she only ever has the thought that *the cat is on the mat*, and never thinks about the dog at all. How can a causal theory account for this? This is known as the "disjunction problem." Or suppose that Grandma has never had a cat and that there are no cats in her neighborhood, but that she still thinks that *the cat is on the mat* whenever the neighborhood dog wanders in, again because of her

---

[592] Adam Wood briefly considers this possible reply to Ross at pp. 252-53 of *Thomas Aquinas on the Immateriality of the Human Intellect*, and rejects it for reasons like those I will spell out here.
[593] Jerry A. Fodor, *Psychosemantics: The Problem of Meaning in the Philosophy of Mind* (Cambridge, MA: The MIT Press, 1987), p. 99.

poor eyesight. This example too conflicts with the Crude Causal Theory, which falsely implies that she must be thinking about the dog, since it is only ever the dog that is causing her thought. This is the "misrepresentation problem."

These problems reflect different ways the factors in terms of which the Crude Causal Theory hopes to explain the content of our thoughts are *indeterminate* in a way the thoughts themselves are not. Grandma's thought is specifically about *the cat being on the mat*, and there is nothing in the causal facts appealed to that can explain why her thought has *exactly that content* and no other. The work of contemporary naturalistic theorists of content is devoted to identifying additional physical factors that might remove the indeterminacy.[594]

It is worthwhile surveying some of this work, both so as to give the naturalist a fair shake and also to illustrate how deep and intractable are the indeterminacy problems facing such theories. There is, for example, Fred Dretske's approach to solving the misrepresentation problem.[595] He begins by introducing the notion of a "natural sign," which is a more or less reliable indicator of the presence of a thing insofar as it is typically caused by that thing in a law-like way. Hence, expanding metal is a natural sign of a rise in temperature; a northerly-flowing river is a natural sign of a downward gradient in that direction; spots on the face are a natural sign of measles; and so forth. Natural signs can be said to have a kind of "natural meaning," which Dretske abbreviates as meaning$_n$: spots on the face mean$_n$ that measles are present, expanding metal means$_n$ that the temperature is rising, etc. Dretske takes the notion of meaning$_n$ to be a plausible starting point for a naturalistic account of content, but it can, as he acknowledges, hardly be the whole story insofar as it does not suffice to account for misrepresentation. For a natural sign cannot *misrepresent* anything, precisely because it represents whatever causes it. To

---

[594] For an introduction to the contemporary debate, see Tim Crane, *The Mechanical Mind: A Philosophical Introduction to Minds, Machines, and Mental Representation*, Second edition (London: Routledge, 2003), chapter 5; and Edward Feser, *Philosophy of Mind* (Oxford: Oneworld, 2006), chapter 7.

[595] Fred Dretske, "Misrepresentation," in Radu J. Bogdan, ed., *Belief: Form, Content and Function* (Oxford: Clarendon Press, 1986). See also Fred Dretske, *Explaining Behavior: Reasons in a World of Causes* (Cambridge, MA: The MIT Press, 1988), chapter 3.

use Dretske's example, when the doorbell malfunctions, what its ringing means$_n$ is not that the doorbell button has been pushed (since it hasn't been), but rather that there is electrical current flowing in the doorbell circuit. Of course, *we* might interpret the ringing as meaning that the button has been pushed and thus (under the circumstances) take it to count as a misrepresentation, but in that case the "meaning" in question derives from us, and in particular from the purposes to which we put doorbells, and is not there naturally in the material processes themselves.

A theory that appealed only to meaning$_n$ would therefore be no advance on the Crude Causal Theory. What the naturalist needs to add, Dretske says, is the notion of "functional meaning" or meaning$_f$. As indicated, we ordinarily count even the malfunctioning doorbell's ringing as meaning that the button has been pushed because it is the *function* of the doorbell to tell us when someone is pushing it. In this case the function derives, again, from us, but Dretske suggests that there are also natural functions that might provide a naturalistic ground for meaning$_f$ and, in turn, for the possibility of misrepresentation. Such functions most plausibly derive from *biological need*. Dretske gives the example of marine bacteria possessing a sensory mechanism called magnetotaxis, by which they are able to propel themselves along the earth's magnetic field. For example, such bacteria living in the northern hemisphere are able to propel themselves toward magnetic north. Now, the function of this mechanism may be to allow the bacteria, who thrive only in oxygen-free environments, to avoid oxygen-rich surface water. We might say, then, that the meaning$_f$ of such a sensory state in one of these bacteria is that *oxygen-free water is present in this direction*. And this is what the state will mean$_f$ even in the case where no such water is present, because (say) we have placed a bar magnet near the bacterium and thereby disoriented it. Hence, it might seem that we have a naturalistic conception of meaning which can account for misrepresentation.

Yet as Dretske himself acknowledges, this will not quite do. One problem is that it is not obvious how it accounts for meaning where biological need is not in question, though Dretske thinks the account might be extended in a way that does account for such cases. But what he allows is a more serious problem is an indeterminacy that remains in factors like those considered so far. *If* we say that the function of the bacterium's sensory states is to indicate where oxygen-free environments are, then it seems we have an account of misrepresentation of the sort the naturalist is seeking. But why describe the function of the sensory states this way? Why not say instead that their function is to indicate the direction of geomagnetic north, or even just to indicate the direction of magnetic north? But if we take the last of these options, then the bacterium's sensory state does *not* misrepresent the environment when we place the bar magnet near it. For it really does detect (the bar's) magnetic north in that case.

That what the bacterium ultimately *needs* is oxygen-free water rather than to propel itself to magnetic north *per se* does not help to eliminate the indeterminacy. To borrow another example of Dretske's, if what I need is vitamin C, it doesn't follow that any state of my perceptual-cognitive apparatus has to mean$_f$ or represent something as containing vitamin C; representing it as a lemon or orange will suffice, since being a lemon or orange is correlated with having vitamin C.

Thus, to find a naturalistic ground for the possibility of misrepresentation, some further element needs to be added to the story. Dretske proposes that this further element has to do with an organism's having (unlike the bacterium, which is sensitive only to magnetic north as an indicator of oxygen-free environments) more than one way to detect the presence of some thing that it needs either to seek or to avoid. So, suppose a creature needs to avoid a certain kind of tree that is poisonous to it, and that it can identify the tree either by its leaf pattern or by the texture of its bark. When it has either an internal sensory state I_1 which means$_n$ that the leaf pattern is present, or an internal state I_2 which means$_n$ that the bark is present, the creature will go into a further state R that leads it to run away. Now R itself in this case does *not* mean$_n$ either that the leaf pattern is present or that the bark is present, because there is no regular correlation between either one of those, specifically, and R; either one could cause R. But R *does* mean$_n$ that the tree is present, because whether it is via the leaf pattern or via the bark that the tree causes R, it will reliably cause R. And since it is its need to avoid the tree that causes the creature to go into state R, what R *functionally* means, means$_f$, is specifically that a tree of the sort in question is present, rather than that the leaf pattern is present or that the bark is present. The indeterminacy that characterized the bacteria example has been eliminated. Moroever, R will have this meaning$_f$ even if we present the creature with a fake tree with the same leaf pattern or the same bark texture. Hence we will have, in that circumstance, a case of misrepresentation – and one that, it might seem, can be accounted for in naturalistic terms.

However, Dretske acknowledges that even this supplemented account is not free of difficulty. For even if R does not mean$_n$ that *the leaf pattern is present*, specifically, or mean$_n$ that *the bark is present*, specifically, why could we not say that R has a disjunctive meaning$_n$ – that R means$_n$ that *either the leaf pattern is present or the bark is present*? But if we say that, then indeterminacy enters the picture yet again: R could mean$_f$ (that is to say, *functionally* mean) either that *a tree of such-and-such a kind is present* or it could mean$_f$ that *either the leaf pattern or the bark is present*, and there will be, in this case as in the bacteria case, no non-arbitrary way to favor one over the other as the "true" function or meaning$_f$ of R. And if we say that the latter, disjunctive meaning$_f$ is the true one, then once again we do not really have a case of misrepresentation at all: When we present the creature with a fake tree, since at least the leaf pattern or bark texture *will* in that case be present, the creature's sensory state represents things accurately. Misrepresentation has, therefore, still not been explained naturalistically.

Dretske further acknowledges that this indeterminacy problem will reappear for any even more complex system as long as we can identify for it some corresponding more complex disjunctive property the detection of which might be characterized as its function. His response to the problem is to propose one final wrinkle to the theory. Suppose now that we have a creature capable, through conditioning, of continually adding to the number of properties of the tree to which it is sensitive. Hence, while at one point it is sensitive only to the leaf pattern and to the texture of the bark, it might come later to be able to detect also the tree's visible root structure, still later its average size, and so forth. If, as in our previous example, we think of the meaning$_n$ of R in this case as some disjunctive property, then since the disjunctive property in question will change as the creature adds to the properties to which it is sensitive, the meaning$_n$ of R will also change over time. And that would entail that, if we thought of the function of R as the detection of this disjunctive property, then that function, and thus the meaning$_f$ of R, would also change over time.

Nonetheless, R will still be a reliable indicator of the *tree* over time, and thus mean$_n$ that *a tree of such-and-such a sort is present* over time. Hence, if we are to regard R as having some stable meaning$_f$ or *functional* meaning over time, Dretske says, the only such meaning available for it to have – since the disjunctive property is *not* stable over time – is that *a tree of such-and-such a sort is present*. And since it will have that meaning$_f$ even when triggered by something other than the tree (e.g. a fake tree having the same leaf pattern, or whatever), we have at last a naturalistic basis for explaining misrepresentation.

But not so fast. For there are several problems with Dretske's final revision too. For one thing, if it really shows anything at all, the most it shows is that *if* R has some meaning$_f$ that is stable over time, *then* that meaning$_f$ must have to do with the detection of the tree. But why not say instead that R has *no* stable meaning$_f$ over time? What is there *in the physical facts* that determines that R means$_f$, stably, that *a tree of such-and-such a sort is present*, as opposed to having an ever-changing series of disjunctive meanings$_f$? Dretske offers no answer. But if what R really has is nothing more than an ever-changing series of disjunctive meanings$_f$, then at any particular moment of time, R will *not* be misrepresenting that which triggers it. Even Dretske's final account is really no less subject to indeterminacy problems than are the accounts he acknowledges to be inadequate.

For another thing, it is not clear how the sorts of examples Dretske develops are relevant in the first place to explaining the determinacy of conceptual content. Recall that Dretske claims that what he calls "natural signs" have at least a kind of "natural meaning," even if not the kind of meaning that might explain misrepresentation. But why should we accept even that modest claim? What licenses a description of expanding metal (say) as a "sign" of a rise in temperature, or as "meaning" that the temperature is rising? True, when we observe the expansion, we can (given our background knowledge) infer that the temperature is rising. But how does that show that the expanding metal has, by itself and apart from our knowledge of it and its properties, a semantic property like "meaning"? Did it have "meaning," or count as a "sign," before any human beings were around? "Meaning" to whom, in that case? A "sign" to whom? In fact there would be no "meaning" or "sign" literally present at all until intelligent creatures like us come along and, discovering that a rise in temperature causes metal to expand, come to *take* expanded metal to "mean" or be a "sign" of a rise in temperature.

Yet even if we were to concede this point to Dretske, it still would not do the work he needs it to do. For even the biological examples to which he appeals (let alone the inorganic ones) could plausibly account only for the content of the sub-rational perceptual states of non-human animals. It would not suffice to explain the distinctively *conceptual* content of human intellects, let alone *determinate* or unambiguous conceptual content.

For philosophers like Ruth Millikan, David Papineau and Karen Neander, the key to solving the misrepresentation problem lies in an *etiological* analysis of the notion of function.[596] Take a trait like the heart. It both pumps blood and makes a thumping sound, but biologists would say that only the former is its function. What justifies this judgement? According to the etiological analysis of biological function, the answer is that it is because the heart pumps blood, rather than because it makes a thumping sound, that it was favored by natural selection. Now, whether such an etiological analysis of the notion of function is correct is itself a matter of controversy. I think it is not correct, but let's suppose for the sake of argument that it is.[597] The way it is claimed to solve the misrepresentation problem is as follows. Suppose once again that we identify the thought that *the cat is on the mat* with a brain state of a certain kind. Suppose also that brain states

---

[596] Ruth Garrett Millikan, *Language, Thought, and Other Biological Categories* (Cambridge, MA: The MIT Press, 1984); Ruth Garrett Millikan, "Biosemantics," in *White Queen Psychology and Other Essays for Alice* (Cambridge, MA: The MIT Press, 1993); David Papineau, *Philosophical Naturalism* (Oxford: Blackwell, 1993), chapter 3; Karen Neander, *A Mark of the Mental: In Defense of Informational Teleosemantics* (Cambridge, MA: The MIT Press, 2017).

[597] I discuss the literature on and problems with such analyses in Edward Feser, *Aristotle's Revenge: The Metaphysical Foundations of Physical and Biological Science* (Neunkirchen: Editiones Scholasticae, 2019), at pp. 387-91.

of that kind were favored by natural selection precisely because they enabled our ancestors to identify cats. Then we can say that their function is to indicate the presence of cats, and take this function to determine their *content*. Now, an organ retains its biological function even if it is used for some other purpose. For example, if a cannibal used someone's heart for a meal, it would still be the case that its biological function is to pump blood, rather than to serve as a meal. By the same token, the brain state's function of indicating cats – and thus, according to the theory under consideration, its having a *content* that represents cats – remains the same even if in some cases the brain state is triggered by something other that a cat, such as the neighborhood dog. Thus, it is proposed, the etiological notion of function allows for a naturalistic account of misrepresentation.

A number of objections have been raised against this "biosemantic" account of content (as Millikan characterizes it). For example, if having a biological function gives brain states like the kind in question conceptual content, why does it not also give hearts, lungs, kidneys and the like conceptual content, given that they too have functions?[598] But the problem that is most relevant to our present concerns is that this account too faces the indeterminacy problem. To borrow an example from Fodor, consider the neural mechanism in frogs that causes them to snap their tongues out when a fly goes by. Given the biosemantic theory, it might seem that the function of this mechanism is to catch flies, specifically, and thus that we should also take it to *represent* flies, specifically. But as Fodor suggests, nothing in the biological facts strictly requires this way of conceptualizing the mechanism. We could equally well say that the function of the mechanism is to catch *little ambient black things*, and thus that *little ambient black things* is what it represents.[599] It is true that it is only because the little ambient black things that frogs snap at happen to be flies that natural selection favored its snapping at them. But the point is that there is no need for the frog to conceptualize them *as flies* in order for natural selection to favor this (or indeed to conceptualize them in any

---

[598] Jerry A. Fodor, *A Theory of Content and Other Essays* (Cambridge, MA: The MIT Press, 1990), p. 66.

[599] Ibid., pp. 71-73.

way at all). Etiology is thus insufficient to establish a determinate content.

Defenders of this approach have developed various replies to Fodor, but, tellingly, they concede the crucial point at issue. Biting the bullet, Daniel Dennett agrees that function analyzed in terms of natural selection cannot secure determinate content, but proposes that what we should conclude from this is that our thoughts do not *have* determinate conceptual content.[600] But I have already explained earlier why this position is incoherent. Neander thinks there are ways to qualify the appeal to etiology so as to eliminate indeterminacy, but in a way she acknowledges would account at most for the *perceptual* content we share with other animals, not the *conceptual* content that is distinctive of the human intellect.[601] Similarly, Millikan acknowledges several respects in which the representational states she thinks an etiological account explains differ from distinctively human cognition.[602] She notes, for example, that unlike the non-human animals which provide illustrations of her "biosemantic" approach, human beings can store representations for future use, put them together into propositions, and draw inferences from them. Needless to say, these are precisely features of the kind that are characteristic of concepts.

This is precisely what we should expect given the point made by Putnam cited earlier, to the effect that what natural selection favors is *survival value* rather than truth or falsity, so that the conceptual content presupposed by truth and falsity is not something that we can read off from the causal factors involved in natural selection. Hence there is nothing in those factors that can tell us that what a frog represents are *flies* or *little ambient black things*, or (to return to Putnam's own example) that what a dog represents is *meat* rather than *textured vegetable protein*. After all, gazelles' legs were favored by natural selection because they allowed gazelles to run fast and thereby to escape predators. But no one suggests that this shows that a gazelle's leg has

---

[600] Dennett, "Evolution, Error, and Intentionality."

[601] Neander, *A Mark of the Mental*, pp. 149 and 237.

[602] Millikan, "Biosemantics," pp. 97-101.

the concept of running fast, or the thought that *now would be a good time to run*. As Putnam writes:

> Isn't it with dogs as with gazelles? Dogs which tended to eat meat rather than vegetables when both were available produced more offspring (gazelles which ran faster than lions escaped the lions and were thus able to produce more offspring). Just as we aren't tempted to say that gazelles have a proto-concept of running fast, so dogs don't have a proto-concept of meat... The "reference" we get out of this bit of hypothetical natural selection will be just the reference we put in our choice of a description. Evolution won't give you more intentionality than you pack into it.[603]

In other words, in order to make the evolution of certain neural structures relevant to the explanation of conceptual content, the etiological account has to *presuppose* that such neural structures possess conceptual content in the first place in a way that the gazelle's leg structure (say) does not. It fallaciously reads such content *into* the physical facts, rather than (as it purports to be doing) deriving it *from* those facts.

Fodor's own preferred approach to solving the indeterminacy problem is to appeal to the idea of "asymmetric dependence."[604] Suppose that Grandma has long owned a cat, but that it is only in recent months that the neighborhood dog has started occasionally to wander into her house. Suppose that the dog's presence comes to trigger in Grandma a brain state of the relevant kind only because of the longstanding causal relationship that already existed between the cat's presence and brain states of that kind. There is in this case an asymmetry between the two causal relationships, insofar as the relationship between the dog and such brain states depends on the preexisting relationship between the cat and such brain states, whereas the latter causal relationship in no way depends on the former. Fodor suggests that what determines content in such a case is a causal relationship of the latter kind. That is to say, *B* will represent *A* if *B* is caused

---

[603] Putnam, *Renewing Philosophy*, pp. 32-33.

[604] Fodor, *Psychosemantics*, chapter 4, and *A Theory of Content*, chapter 4.

by *A* and this causal relationship is not asymmetrically dependent on some other causal relationship (as the relationship involving the dog is dependent on that involving the cat). And that is why Grandma's thought has the content that *the cat is on the mat*, rather than having the disjunctive proposition as its content.

Here too, however, there are several problems.[605] Suppose that whenever Grandma sees a cat, a certain characteristic pattern of stimulation occurs in her retinas, which in turn goes on to trigger the brain state in question. Why, in that case, does the brain state represent *cats*, as opposed to representing *retinal stimulation patterns of that particular kind*? Consider also that cats have many properties, not all of which are captured in my conceptualization of them but any of which could be said to be causally related to the brain state in question. So why does that brain state represent what causes it as *cats*, specifically – as opposed, say to *furry things*, or *mammals*, or any of a number of other ways of conceptualizing them? Or suppose that though the causal link between dogs and the brain state is asymmetrically dependent on the causal link between cats and the brain state, the latter brain state is in turn asymmetrically dependent on a causal link between mammals and the brain state.[606] Why should we take the brain state in that case to represent cats rather than mammals? Once again, the causal factors to which the naturalist appeals, however characterized, do not suffice to determine that a brain state has *this* content rather than *that*.

But such counterexamples are symptoms of a deeper problem identified in a line of criticism developed by Putnam and, earlier, by

---

[605] For useful discussion of which, see M. J. Cain, *Fodor: Language, Mind and Philosophy* (Cambridge: Polity, 2002), pp. 134-47.
[606] I borrow the point from Lynne Rudder Baker, "Has Content Been Naturalized?" in Barry Loewer and Georges Rey, *Meaning in Mind: Fodor and His Critics* (Oxford: Blackwell, 1991), p. 29.

Karl Popper.⁶⁰⁷ Popper's example involves an *utterance* that is triggered by the presence of a cat, but the point applies no less to a brain state that is so triggered. He states his basic argument as follows:

> Consider a machine which, every time it sees a ginger cat, says 'Mike'. It represents, we may be tempted to say, a *causal model* of naming, or of the name-relation...
>
> We admit that the machine may be described as realizing what we may loosely call a 'causal chain' of events joining Mike (the cat) with 'Mike' (its name). But there are reasons why we cannot accept this causal chain as a representation or realization of the relation between a thing and its name.
>
> It is naive to look at this chain of events as beginning with the appearance of Mike and ending with the enunciation 'Mike'.
>
> It 'begins' (if at all) with a state of the machine prior to the appearance of Mike, a state in which the machine is, as it were, ready to respond to the appearance of Mike. It 'ends' (if at all) not with the enunciation of a word, since there is a state following this... It is our *interpretation* which makes Mike and 'Mike' the extremes (or terms) of the causal chain, and not the 'objective' physical situation. (Moreover, we might consider *the whole process of reaction* as name, or only the last letters of 'Mike', say, 'Ike'.) Thus, although those who know or understand the name-relation may choose to interpret a causal chain as a model of it, it is clear that the name-relation is not a causal relation, and cannot be realized by any causal model.⁶⁰⁸

As I understand Popper, what he is saying here is this. In order to explain conceptual content in causal terms, we would need to

---

⁶⁰⁷ I discuss Popper's version at greater length in "Hayek, Popper, and the Causal Theory of the Mind," in Leslie Marsh, ed., *Hayek in Mind: Hayek's Philosophical Psychology*, a special issue of *Advances in Austrian Economics*, Vol. 15 (2011). The article is reprinted in Feser, *Neo-Scholastic Essays*.
⁶⁰⁸ Karl R. Popper, "Language and the Body-Mind Problem," in *Conjectures and Refutations. The Growth of Scientific Knowledge* (New York: Harper and Row, 1968), pp. 297-98. I have removed Popper's paragraph numbers.

be able to identify some specific, determinate cause *A* as "the beginning" of the relevant causal chain and thus as that which is being represented, and some specific, determinate effect *B* as "the end" of the causal chain and thus as that which does the representing. For a causal theory says that some effect *B* will represent whatever *A* causes it in just the right way (where what counts as "the right way" is to be spelled out in terms of details like those the naturalistic theories of content we've been examining would add to the Crude Causal Theory).

Now, objectively, as it is in itself and apart from human interests, the world contains an enormously complex network of causal chains. In the example at hand, there are the states and processes of the machine prior to the cat's appearance, the motion of the cat as it enters the room, the journey of the light from the cat's body to the electric eye affixed to the machine, the electrical current's passage from the eye to the machine's innards, the machine's emitting of the sound "Mike," the cat's perking up its ears on hearing this sound and perhaps fleeing the room as a consequence, and so forth. There are also all the events that occurred prior and subsequent to these ones, and the events occurring simultaneously which have some influence on them – the traveling of the electrical current from the wall socket to the machine it is powering, a mouse scurrying along the floor which the cat is hoping to catch, and so on and on. But what is it that makes any of this count as a "beginning" or an "end" of a causal chain? In particular, what is it that makes the *cat*, specifically – rather than the cat's surface or its motion, or the mouse, or the light traveling from the cat, or the electrical current, or one of a million other things – "the beginning" of some chain? And what is it that makes the sound *"Mike,"* specifically – rather than the electrical current passing through the machine, or the sound "Ike" (i.e. the last part of the sound "Mike"), or the perking up of the cat's ears, or one of a million other things – "the end" of some chain?

The answer, Popper argues, is that there is nothing in the objective physical facts *themselves* that determines which if any of these things is the "beginning" or "end" of a causal chain. Objectively there is just the complex network of causes extended forward and backward in time indefinitely. Rather, it is because *the causal theorist* has, for the purposes of spelling out his theory, an interest in the cat and in the name "Mike" – an interest which he does not have in cat surfaces, or electrical current, or the mouse – that *he* picks out the cat and the utterance of the name as especially significant, and labels the former "the beginning" of a causal chain and the latter "the end." But that means that the identification of the relevant causal chain *presupposes* the conceptual content in terms of which the causal theorist characterizes the situation. And in that case he cannot intelligibly appeal to such causal chains in order to *explain* this conceptual content. The point applies *mutatis mutandis* when we replace the machine's utterance of "Mike" with some brain state that the causal theorist would identify a thought about the cat with.

Putnam developed a similar line of argument.[609] Criticizing Fodor's causal account of content, Putnam notes that in everyday claims about causation, we typically distinguish between "contributory causes" or "background conditions," on the one hand, and "*the* cause" of an event on the other. For example, if we say that a stuck valve caused a certain pressure cooker to explode, we are treating the stuck valve differently than the way we treat (say) the lack of holes in the vessel of the pressure cooker, even though the latter also played a role in the explosion. The lack of holes we treat as a contributory cause or background condition; the stuck valve we treat as "*the* cause," as being of special significance. Putnam observes:

> Yet, in the physics of the explosion, the role played by the stuck valve is exactly the same as the role of [the lack of holes]: the absence of either would have permitted the steam to escape, bringing down the pressure and averting the explosion.[610]

---

[609] Putnam, *Renewing Philosophy*, especially chapter 3. Cf. Hilary Putnam, *The Many Faces of Realism* (La Salle, IL: Open Court, 1987), pp. 37-39; Hilary Putnam, "Is the Causal Structure of the Physical Itself Something Physical?" in *Realism with a Human Face* (Cambridge, MA: Harvard University Press, 1990); and Hilary Putnam, "Aristotle after Wittgenstein," in *Words and Life* (Cambridge, MA: Harvard University Press, 1994). Ideas similar to Putnam's are developed in Josep E. Corbí and Josep L. Prades, *Minds, Causes and Mechanisms: A Case Against Physicalism* (Oxford: Blackwell, 2000).

[610] Putnam, *The Many Faces of Realism*, pp. 37-38.

> For in fundamental physics, at least, one usually ignores the distinction between contributory causes and "the cause", and tries to provide a formalism which shows how all of the factors interact to produce the final result.[611]

Though it has no unique significance to the physics of the situation, we treat the stuck valve as special, Putnam says, because of our interests. We take it that

> the valve 'should have' let the steam escape – that is its 'function', what it was designed to do. On the other hand, the surface element [present where a hole might otherwise have been] was not doing anything 'wrong' in preventing the steam from escaping; containing the steam is the 'function' of the surface of which [this element] is a part. So when we ask 'Why did the explosion take place?', knowing what we know and having the interests we do have, our 'explanation space' consists of the alternatives:
>
> (1) Explosion taking place
>
> (2) Everything functioning as it should
>
> What we want to know, in other words, is why 1 is what happened *as opposed to* 2. We are simply not interested in why 1 is what happened *as opposed to* such alternatives as:
>
> (3) The surface element ... is missing, and no explosion takes place.[612]

Insofar as the distinction between "*the* cause" and contributing or background conditions is in this way "interest-relative" and "context-sensitive," it *presupposes* our conceptualizing the situation in a certain way. For "to be interested in something, in this sense, you have to be able to think about it – you have to be able to refer to it, in

---

[611] Putnam, *Renewing Philosophy*, p. 50.

[612] Putnam, *The Many Faces of Realism*, p. 38.

thought or in language."⁶¹³ Now the aim of a naturalistic theory like Fodor's is to *explain* conceptual content in purely physical terms, and in particular in terms that make no reference to notions other than those recognized by physical science. Yet given their actual examples, such theories in fact help themselves to a "notion of things 'causing' other things [which] is not a notion... simply handed to us by physics" – namely, a notion that presupposes the interest-relative distinction between "*the* cause" and contributing or background conditions.⁶¹⁴ That is to say, these theories make reference to ordinary objects – cats, the valves on pressure cookers, and the like – in a way that gives them a causal significance they do not have in the sorts of explanations physical science offers. Nor can these theories avoid doing this, given that their aim is precisely to explain how we can represent such everyday objects in thought and language. But in doing it they are subtly *presupposing* the existence of conceptual content – the very phenomenon they are supposed to be explaining.

Now, the conception of the physical world implicit in naturalistic theories of content is what I have referred to in earlier chapters as a *mechanistic* conception, one that denies the reality of Aristotelian formal and final causes. Putnam holds that the specific causal notions naturalistic theories require are simply not available to them, given this conception. As Putnam puts it, "nature, or 'physical reality' in the post-Newtonian understanding of the physical, has no semantic preferences."⁶¹⁵ There is nothing in the physical facts so conceived that can determine why any particular causal chain "can be singled out as 'the' relation between signs and their referents."⁶¹⁶ What is required for such a chain, Putnam says, is an "intrinsic distinction" between the cause of an event and mere background conditions, but this "has much

---

[613] Putnam, *Renewing Philosophy*, p. 50.

[614] Ibid.

[615] Putnam, "Is the Causal Structure of the Physical Itself Something Physical?,", p. 83.

[616] Ibid., p. 89.

more to do with medieval (and Aristotelian) notions of 'efficient causation' than with post-Newtonian ones."[617] In particular, it presupposes an "Aristotelian conception of form" – of a "self-identifying structure" which objectively demarcates an object from others in a way objects are not demarcated in the mechanical world picture.[618] It is this form or structure which, on the Aristotelian account of concept-formation, is abstracted by the intellect from an object consequent upon perceptual contact with it. To identify what naturalistic theories need in order to solve the indeterminacy problem thus provides, in Putnam's view, "grist for the mill of a possible latter-day Aristotelian metaphysics. The natural Aristotelian response to the difficulties just canvassed is to say, 'I told you so. You cannot do without the notion of *form*.'"[619] But were such theories to take this notion on board, they would cease being naturalistic. Certainly they would cease to be materialist, since to abstract a form upon concept-formation is precisely to *dematerialize* it.

To be sure, Putnam himself rejects both naturalistic theories and neo-Aristotelianism alike, though not, in the latter case, for good reasons. But I will say more later on about the nature and defensibility of the neo-Aristotelian account. The point for the moment is just to emphasize the intractability of the indeterminacy problem facing naturalism, and that the only way to solve it is effectively to endorse precisely the positon I am arguing for in this chapter.

The nature of thought

I have addressed the issue of the indeterminacy of the physical in considerable detail, both because it has received an enormous amount of attention in contemporary analytic philosophy and because it affords a powerful argument for the intellect's immateriality. But it is by no means the only such argument. While the determinate character of conceptual content is one aspect of thought that makes it impossible

---

[617] Putnam, *The Many Faces of Realism*, p. 26.

[618] Putnam, "Aristotle after Wittgenstein," pp. 68-69. Cf. the comparison of causal theories of reference to the notion of "substantial form" in Hilary Putnam, *Reason Truth, and History* (Cambridge: Cambridge University Press, 1981), p. 47.

[619] Putnam, "Aristotle after Wittgenstein," p. 69.

to assimilate to a materialist account of human nature, there are others that are more neglected in contemporary philosophy.

The storage problem

There is, for example, what David Oderberg has called the "storage problem" facing materialism.[620] The problem concerns what Oderberg describes as an "ontological mismatch" between concepts on the one hand, and any place in the brain at which the materialist might claim to locate concepts on the other. There just is no intelligible way in which the brain could be said to store concepts. In particular, Oderberg identifies five features of concepts that fundamentally differentiate them from anything in the brain (or anywhere else in the physical world, for that matter). Concepts are *abstract, unextended,* and *universal,* whereas material things are concrete, extended, and particular. Some concepts are *simple,* but any remotely credible candidate material loci for them are composite. And the intellect can grasp a potential *infinity* of concepts, while no potentially infinite powers can be attributed to a material object like the brain. Let's elaborate on each of these points in turn.[621]

---

[620] David S. Oderberg, "Concepts, Dualism, and the Human Intellect," in A. Antonietti, A. Corradini, and E. J. Lowe, eds., *Psycho-Physical Dualism Today* (Lanham, MD: Rowman and Littlefied, 2008). See also David S. Oderberg, "Hylemorphic Dualism," in E. F. Paul, F. D. Miller, and J. Paul, eds., *Personal Identity* (Cambridge: Cambridge University Press, 2005) and David S. Oderberg, *Real Essentialism* (London: Routledge, 2007), pp. 250-55.

[621] Antonio Ramos Diaz, "How Not to Argue against Materialism: On Oderberg's Storage Problem Argument," *American Catholic Philosophical Quarterly* 90 (2016): 455-76, wrongly alleges that Oderberg's argument does not sit well with a Thomistic conception of the intellect, for reasons we will consider presently. But though Oderberg's neat and helpful way of tying the differences between concepts and candidate material loci together under the "storage problem" label is, as far as I know, original with him, it is important to emphasize that the basic line of argument is not some idiosyncratic invention of his own but is longstanding in the Thomistic tradition. For example, the argument from the potential infinity of concepts that can be grasped by the intellect is presented by Aquinas in *Summa Contra Gentiles*, Book II, Chapter 49. A version of the argument from the universality of concepts versus the particular nature of material loci is presented by Aquinas in *Summa Theologiae*, Part I, Question 75, Article 5. Another version of that argument is presented in Mortimer J. Adler, *Intellect: Mind Over Matter* (New York: Macmillan, 1990), chapter 4. Yet other versions of that argument, as well as the argument from the simplicity of concepts versus the composite nature of material loci, are given in Celestine N. Bittle, *The Whole Man: Psychology* (Milwaukee: Bruce Publishing Company, 1945), at pp. 505-7 and 512-13, and in Michael Maher, *Psychology: Empirical and Rational*, Ninth edition (London: Longmans, Green, and Co., 1933), at pp. 466-69 and 470-72. The argument from the abstract nature of

We saw in chapter 5 that extension, though it does not exhaust the nature of matter (as Descartes held) is nevertheless a property of all matter. That is to say, material things are locatable in space and typically occupy some region of space, and as a consequence typically exhibit features like length, width, and depth.[622] This in turn makes them concrete and particular. Consider, for example, a triangle drawn in black ink on a marker board in some classroom. It occupies a region of space distinct from the regions occupied by other material things, including other triangles. Hence it is one particular triangle alongside the others, and alongside particular things of other kinds.

Contrast this with the concept *triangularity*. It is universal rather than particular insofar as it cannot be identified with any individual triangle or collection of triangles, capturing as it does the nature or essence (viz. being a closed plane figure with three straight sides) which all triangles have in common. It is abstract in the sense that the intellect forms the concept by *abstracting* triangularity from particular individual triangles and considering it in isolation from them. (Nor is what it thereby considers merely some exotic further individual triangle existing in the mind, for in that case the intellect would just be aware of some further particular thing rather than what all the particulars have in common.) For that reason it is also abstract in the sense that it does not have a spatial location in the way that

---

concepts versus the concrete nature of bodily states is presented in Cardinal Mercier et al., *A Manual of Modern Scholastic Philosophy*, Volume I, Third English edition (St. Louis: B. Herder Book Company, 1932), at pp. 296-97. Arguments from the universality, abstractness, infinity, and simplicity of concepts are developed in James E. Royce, *Man and His Nature* (New York: McGraw-Hill, 1961), at pp. 91-97 and 312-13.

[622] I say "typically" in case someone wants to object that quantum phenomena can lack a determinate location in space. This does not affect the present argument, for several reasons. First, to lack a determinate location in space (being not determinately *here* rather than *there*) is not the same as being non-spatial or outside of space altogether (the way that, say, Platonic Forms are said to be outside of space altogether). Quantum phenomena are not non-spatial in the latter sense, which makes them locatable in space in the sense that is relevant to the present argument. Second, as I argued in chapter 5, the quantum phenomena in question involve *potentialities* in matter whereas what is relevant for present purposes is what is true of matter as *actualized* (for example, matter having a substantial form of the kind that actualizes its potential to constitute a human brain). Third, and relatedly, the candidate purported material loci for concepts would exist only in material things of the kind associated with intellectual activity, specifically (such as human brains), and not at the quantum level underlying all material things.

particular individual triangles do. You can locate *this particular* individual triangle here and *that particular* individual triangle over there (which is what makes them concrete), but you cannot locate *triangularity* in the abstract here, there, or anywhere else in space. And neither can you locate the *concept* triangularity at any particular location in space. For that reason it is not an extended thing, whereas the things that occupy space are extended.

It might be thought that this begs the question against the materialist, who would hold that the concept can be located in, say, some particular area of the brain. Now of course, there is no *obvious* way that this is so. Locating the concept *triangularity* in the brain is not like locating the hippocampus or amygdala in the brain. But might it nevertheless be located there in some more subtle way? Reflection shows that it cannot be. Suppose it turned out that whenever we entertain the concept, neural firings in the brain trace out some triangular pattern (across the surface of the brain, for example). To be sure, materialists would not claim that this is what actually happens or even that it is remotely plausible, but it would arguably be the best case scenario for materialism. Yet even such a pattern could not be identified with the concept *triangularity*, because it would be just one particular individual triangle among others, rather than something that captures what is common to all triangles. Should we think instead of the concept existing in the brain as something like the *word* "triangle," perhaps encoded neurally in something analogous to the way the word might be encoded in an electrical pattern in a computer? But that cannot be right either, because the connection between triangles and the English word "triangle" is entirely conventional. Indeed, we give the word "triangle" meaning precisely by using it to express the concept *triangularity*, in which case it must be *distinct from* that concept. Might we instead identify the concept not with a word in English or in any other of the familiar natural languages, but rather in a "Language of Thought" encoded as some neural structure within the brain? But then we would need to explain how such a structure comes to have the content *triangularity*, specifically, rather than some other content or no content at all. And we saw in the previous section that no materialist account of content can succeed.

So, the claim that concepts are universal, abstract, and unextended remains standing, as does the claim that material things are by contrast particular, concrete, and extended. Hence concepts cannot be identified with anything material. Hence they are not *in* the brain in the way that neural structures, blood vessels, etc. are in the brain. There is, however, clearly a sense in which they *are* in the intellect. When we note, for example, that you possess the concept *triangularity* and a three-year-old child does not, we naturally judge that the concept is in your mind but not in the child's mind. To be sure, given what I've been saying, the sense in which concepts can be said to be *in* the intellect cannot be the same as the sense in which a material part is in the brain (i.e. by virtue of having spatial location). But they are in the intellect in a sense that is *analogous* to the sense in which something can be said to be in the brain. Compare the way that physicists talk about the curvature of space. Obviously, space cannot be curved in the way that, say, a basketball has a curved shape. For the curvature of the basketball is a property of the surface of a physical object, whereas space is not itself a physical object but rather that in which physical objects are located. But there is something about space that is *analogous* to the curvature of a surface, and so too can there be something about the location of concepts in the intellect that is analogous to the location of physical parts in the brain.

Naturally, we might raise questions about precisely what *is* the nature of the intellect and of the locatability of concepts within it, given its differences from the brain. But as Oderberg emphasizes, we do not need to be able to answer those questions in order to draw the conclusion that they are indeed different – that the intellect is simply not the same thing as the brain or any part of the brain, and that its activities are not identifiable with any sort of brain activity (even if its activities are causally related to brain activity in a way we will address later on).

Now, Antonio Ramos Diaz has objected that this line of argument is not compatible with a Thomistic conception of the intellect (the conception to which Oderberg is committed, and which I am defending in this book).[623] For though Thomists take the intellect to be

---

[623] Diaz, "How Not to Argue against Materialism."

immaterial, they also take it to be a concrete, particular thing. Yet Oderberg's argument, claims Diaz, holds that concepts cannot be located in any concrete, particular thing (which is why it goes on to conclude that they cannot be located in the brain, specifically). But as Oderberg explains in a reply to Diaz, it is not particularity and concreteness *as such* that are at issue, but rather particularity and concreteness of the kind exhibited by *material* things specifically.[624] Material things are particular in the sense that they *instantiate* universals, whereas a concept, by contrast, does not instantiate a universal. For example, the black triangle drawn on the marker board in some classroom is one particular instantiation of triangularity alongside others, but your concept *triangularity* is not such an instantiation. Rather, it involves considering triangularity *apart from* all instantiations. Concepts are abstract in the sense that they capture universal natures considered as *abstracted from* particular instantiations, and in the sense that they do not have a spatial location, as concrete material things do. But that does not prevent the intellect from being concrete in the sense that it is not itself a universal nature abstracted from particulars (whatever that would mean), while *not* being concrete in the sense of being locatable in space.

Let's turn now to the sense in which concepts can be simple in a way that material things are not. Some concepts are analyzable into simpler concepts. For example, the concept of *being a bachelor* is analyzable into the concepts of *being a man* and *being unmarried*. At some point we reach concepts that are simple in the sense of not being analyzable into further concepts. With some concepts it will be controversial whether they are truly simple in this sense, but suppose for the sake of argument that concepts like *being*, *unity*, and *identity* are simple. Then, if such concepts were located in the brain, there would have to be some simple material loci corresponding to them. However, as Oderberg argues, there are no such loci, for material things are all divisible into parts and thus not simple.

As Oderberg notes, it will not do to suggest that there might be fundamental material parts that are unextended and thus indivisible, because unextended parts could never add up to an extended

---

[624] David S. Oderberg, "The Storage Problem Revisited: A Reply to Diaz," *American Catholic Philosophical Quarterly* 92 (2018): 97-105.

thing (and thus to a material thing). Nor will it do to suggest that there are fundamental material parts that are extended yet indivisible, even if we granted the dubious assumption that an extended thing could be indivisible. For if such parts were extended, they would themselves still have at least *geometrical* parts or distinct sub-regions (even if these could not be divided from one another) and thus would not be simple in the relevant sense. Again, there just are no simple material loci for simple concepts to correspond to.

We had reason in chapter 4 to cite John Haldane's observation that "for any naturally individuated object or property there are indefinitely many non-equivalent ways of thinking about it... [so that] the structure of the conceptual order, which is expressed in judgements... is richer and more abstract than that of the natural order."[625] For example, every triangle is necessarily a trilateral and vice versa. Hence, triangles and trilaterals are not different objects. Nevertheless, the *concept* of *being a triangle* is distinct from the *concept* of *being a trilateral*. But what is true of this particular object is true of all concrete entities in the physical world. There are more concepts that might be formed of these entities than there are entities. Now, if the number of concepts outstrips the number of concrete entities there are in the natural world, then it obviously outstrips the number of concrete entities there are in the *brain*. This brings us to the last of the ontological mismatches between the intellect and the brain identified by Oderberg, which is that the number of neural phenomena is finite, whereas the number of concepts we might form is not just larger but *infinite*.[626]

That the intellect can grasp a potential infinity of concepts is obvious just from the fact that the series of numbers is infinite, and there is no number in the series of which we are incapable in principle

---

[625] J. J. C. Smart and J. J. Haldane, *Atheism and Theism*, Second edition (Oxford: Blackwell, 2003), p. 107.

[626] Joshua Rasmussen's "counting argument" against physicalism is similar to the point Oderberg makes here. See Joshua Rasmussen, "Against Nonreductive Physicalism," in Jonathan J. Loose, Angus J. L. Menuge, and J. P. Moreland, eds., *The Blackwell Companion to Substance Dualism* (Oxford: Wiley Blackwell, 2018); and Joshua Rasmussen, *Who Are You, Really? A Philosopher's Inquiry into the Nature and Origins of Persons* (Downers Grove, IL: InterVarsity Press, 2023), pp. 60-73.

of forming a concept. Of course, it is true that no one *actually* has entertained or could entertain the concept of each and every number in this infinite series. But the fact that, for each one of them, we have the *potential* to form a concept of it is enough to make the point. For no material thing, including the brain, could even potentially entertain them. Though enormously complex, the brain is nevertheless finite in its size, powers, etc. As Oderberg notes, it is hardly plausible to suppose that the more complex a concept is, the smaller is the region of the brain in which it is to be located. But if we make the more plausible assumption that the more complex a concept, the larger is the region of the brain in which it is to be located, then the materialist faces the problem that the finite size of the brain would then entail a limit in principle to how many concepts can be stored in it. But there is no limit in principle to how complex are the concepts the intellect might come to entertain.[627]

Again, Oderberg emphasizes, rightly, that we do not need to be able to give much in the way of a positive characterization of the intellect in order to establish its immateriality. Still, we can understand something about its nature by recalling once again John of St. Thomas's notion of a *formal sign*, a sign that is nothing but a sign (in contrast to an *instrumental sign*, which is a sign that is also something else). We saw in chapter 3 why concepts are best understood as formal signs, whether or not we go on to regard them as immaterial; and we saw earlier in this chapter how appeal to the notion of a formal sign shows why a certain sort of objection to Ross's argument for the intellect's immateriality fails. But the notion also clarifies how concepts can have the features Oderberg focuses on whereas material loci in the brain cannot. A material representation (such as a written or spoken word, a pictorial image, or the like) is an instrumental sign insofar as it is a representation *and also* something else – an ink splotch, a light pattern on a screen, compression waves in the air, or a physical entity of some other kind. As such, it is, like any other physical entity, a particular rather than a universal, a concrete thing occupying space, extended through space, and composite rather than simple. A concept

---

[627] As Oderberg notes, this is consistent with recognizing that there are *extrinsic* limits to what concepts a human intellect might entertain, given its dependence on the sensory information it happens to have access to. What matters is that the intellect is free of the *intrinsic* limits that characterize the brain.

(such as the concept *triangularity*) is a formal sign insofar as it is a representation that is *not* also something else, a representation that is *nothing but* a representation. As such, it lacks any further features that would prevent it from being universal, abstract, unextended, and simple.

The notion of a formal sign also helps us to see what is wrong with a further objection that might be leveled against the "storage problem" argument. Earlier in this chapter I briefly addressed Pasnau's "content fallacy" objection, considered as a potential criticism of Ross. It might be thought that Oderberg commits the fallacy. Consider the concept *triangularity*. It represents not merely this or that particular triangle, but rather the nature or essence they have in common. But though the *content* of the concept is in this way universal, the critic may object that it would be fallacious to conclude from this that the concept *itself* is universal. And if it is not, then the ontological mismatch Oderberg claims to detect is illusory, and concepts might be locatable in material loci after all.

But as John Haldane has noted when defending Aquinas's version of the argument from the universality of thought, this sort of objection assumes that where concepts are concerned, there is a distinction to be drawn between the concept qua *vehicle* of content and the concept's content *itself*, yet this assumption can be challenged.[628] And the notion of a formal sign is precisely the notion of a representation in which the distinction between vehicle and content, which exists in instrumental signs, collapses. Again, a formal sign is a sign that is nothing but a sign. It makes no sense to think of it as a vehicle from which its content might be detached, for it just *is* its content. If concepts are formal signs, then, there can be no question of committing any "content fallacy" with respect to them. If the content is universal, the concept itself is universal, just as Oderberg holds, because there is nothing more to the concept than its content.

---

[628] John Haldane, "The Metaphysics of Intellect(ion)," *Proceedings of the American Catholic Philosophical Association* 80 (2006): 39-55, at p. 53.

The space of reasons versus the space of causes

There is yet more work to be done by the notion of a formal sign, as is made evident by a line of argument developed by Laurence BonJour.[629] He begins with the following observation:

> [A] certain general view of the nature of thought... is regarded by many not only as correct, but in fact as virtually the only conceivable account: the view that thought is essentially a symbolic or linguistic process that employs a representational system at least strongly analogous to a natural language...
>
> [A]ccording to the symbolic view of thought, what happens when I think about redness and greenness is only that either the English *words* 'red' and 'green' or close analogues of these words in a "language of thought" occur in my mind or brain.[630]

Now, this needs qualification. As we saw in chapter 3, there are philosophers who hold that concepts are better understood as images, or proxytypes, or mental maps, rather than on a linguistic model. But we also saw there that there are insuperable difficulties with such views and that something *like* the "Language of Thought" model is hard to avoid, certainly if one is a realist (as opposed to an eliminativist) about the propositional attitudes and is committed to the project of "naturalizing" thought. And naturalizing it will also require identifying the symbols posited by this model with neural states or some other material substrate.

But as BonJour argues, this model simply does not and cannot capture the nature of thought. In particular, it cannot make sense of how our thoughts have the specific content they do or how that content is accessible to us. The problems are related. Suppose we say that to have the thought that *the cat is on the mat* is to have the sentence "The cat is on the mat" (or some corresponding sentence in the Language of Thought or "Mentalese," as it is often labeled in the literature) encoded in the brain. How does that string of material symbols

---

[629] Laurence BonJour, *In Defense of Pure Reason* (Cambridge: Cambridge University Press, 1998), pp. 162-86.

[630] Ibid., p. 162.

come to have *that particular* content, specifically, rather than some other? And how do we come to have access to that content, as you do when you are *aware that* you are thinking that the cat is on the mat? As we've seen, a causal theory like Fodor's would say that it is the causal relations the Mentalese sentence bears to objects in the world outside the brain that determines the content, and other theories would trace the causal relations back to the time our ancestors' brains were molded by natural selection. We've already considered some of the grave problems facing such theories, but BonJour calls attention to another one. What I have direct access to on the model in question is the Mentalese symbols themselves, rather than to their distal causes. If I know anything about those distal causes, it is precisely because I have Mentalese symbols that represent them, my knowledge of the causes being mediated only through those symbols. So it would put the cart before the horse to suppose that I know the causes first and then, on that basis, come to know the content of the symbols. But it cannot be that I know the content of the symbols by reference to yet other Mentalese symbols, because that would just raise the question of how I know the content of *those* symbols. We would be led into a vicious infinite regress.

BonJour notes that one possible reply would be to deny that we really do have access to the contents of our thoughts, on the basis of arguments for *externalist* theories of content. There is, for example, Putnam's influential "Twin Earth" thought experiment, in which we are asked to imagine a world exactly like ours except that the stuff there referred to as "water" is not composed of H_2O molecules but rather of XYZ molecules.[631] Now, suppose you have no knowledge of the chemical composition of what you call "water" and that your twin on Twin Earth has no knowledge of the chemical composition of what he calls "water." Hence what you are aware of introspectively when you think about what you call "water" is identical to what your twin is aware of when he thinks about what he calls "water" – thoughts to the effect that "water" is the stuff that fills lakes and rivers, that it quenches thirst, and so on. All the same, what you *mean* when you use the word "water" (namely H_2O) is different from what your twin means by it (namely XYZ). Since you are both unaware of this, the

---

[631] Hilary Putnam, "The Meaning of 'Meaning,'" in *Mind, Language, and Reality: Philosophical Papers, Volume 2* (Cambridge: Cambridge University Press, 1975).

meaning of your thoughts is, the argument claims, not in fact accessible to you. There's a lot that has been and could be said about this, but as BonJour points out, what matters for present purposes is that the claim that we flatly don't have access to the content of the thoughts we express when using "water" simply doesn't follow. The most that follows (if anything) is that we don't have access to *part* of the content of our thoughts, not that we have access to *none* of the content. (To use the standard jargon, we have access to the "narrow content" that is known to introspection, even if not to the "wide content" that is determined by causal relations to the broader environment.) Indeed, it is hard to make sense of the thought experiment at all, and in particular of the assumption that you and your twin are otherwise identical, unless we suppose that you have access to at least part of the content. But if we have access even to part of the content of our thoughts, the problem BonJour identifies has not been solved.

Another possible response, notes BonJour, would be to appeal to what is called "conceptual role semantics."[632] On this view, the content of a symbol of Mentalese is determined by its inferential relations to other symbols. For example, the content of the sentence "All men are mortal" is determined by the fact that it entails the sentence "All men are subject to death"; the fact that, together with the sentence "Socrates is a man," it entails the further sentence "Socrates is mortal"; and so on. Now, the theory cannot leave it at that if it is to vindicate naturalism, because a sentence can bear inferential relations to other sentences in the first place only if it already *has* semantic content; meaningless sounds or marks on paper don't bear inferential relations of any kind. So, the theory has to appeal to something outside the network of inferential relations in order to explain how the system of symbols as a whole counts as embodying any inferential relations at all. The standard approach is to claim that there are *causal* relations between the symbols of Mentalese that parallel, and account for, the inferential relations between them. The idea would be that there are, for example, causal relations between instances of the Mentalese equivalents for "All men are mortal," "Socrates is a man," and "Socrates is mortal" that account for the inferential relations between them.

---

[632] Cf. Ned Block, "Advertisement for a Semantics for Psychology," in Stephen P. Stich and Ted A. Warfield, *Mental Representation: A Reader* (Oxford: Blackwell, 1994).

But as BonJour argues, this approach too is utterly hopeless as a solution to the problems he raises. For one thing, conceptual role semantics has problems even apart from the question of its relevance to the problem BonJour is concerned with. For example, if the content of a sentence of Mentalese is determined by its inferential relations to other symbols, and we consider that no two human beings have exactly the same set of beliefs (and thus do not, on the Language of Thought analysis, assent to exactly the same sentences of Mentalese) it would follow that the inferential relations one person's Mentalese sentences bear to one another is never exactly the same as those another person's Mentalese sentences bear to one another. It would follow that no two persons attribute exactly the same content to their thoughts. But how, then, is it ever possible for them to communicate? How could they so much as agree or disagree about whether (say) the cat is on the mat, if they do not in the first place attach the same meaning to the sentence "The cat is on the mat"?

But there are other problems more directly relevant to the subject at hand. Conceptual role theories presuppose that there is an isomorphism between the system of logical relations between propositions, on the one hand, and the system of causal relations between sentences of Mentalese, on the other. For example, consider the logical relations between the proposition that *all men are mortal*, the proposition that *Socrates is a man*, and the proposition that *Socrates is mortal*. The theory requires that these relations map onto some unique set of causal relations between Mentalese symbols encoded in the brain (such as the Mentalese equivalents of the English sentences "All men are mortal," "Socrates is a man," and "Socrates is mortal").

Yet there is no such mapping. Obviously, there is no necessary connection between the propositions that *all men are mortal*, that *Socrates is a man*, and that *Socrates is mortal* on the one hand, and any instances of the English sentences "All men are mortal," "Socrates is a man," and "Socrates is mortal" on the other. There is, for example, nothing in the shapes of the letters or in the chemistry of the ink marks or the physics of the compression waves in which those sentences are embodied that gives the sentences the specific meanings they have. Their meaning is entirely a matter of arbitrary convention, and very different propositions (or no propositions at all) could have been associated with those shapes, ink marks, and compression waves instead. But neither is there any necessary connection between those propositions and the material symbols encoded in the brain posited by the Language of Thought hypothesis. The intrinsic physical properties of brain states no more entail any unique propositional content than the chemistry of ink marks or the physics of compression waves do. That is precisely why Fodor has to develop a causal theory to account for how such brain states acquire the content the Language of Thought hypothesis attributes to them.

But as we have seen, no such theory can solve the indeterminacy problem. And the entire system of symbols in the brain posited by the Language of Thought hypothesis is no less indeterminate in its conceptual content than an individual symbol is. Hence there is nothing in the causal relations between the Mentalese sentences corresponding to "All men are mortal," "Socrates is a man," and "Socrates is mortal" that can determine that they correlate with the logical relations between the propositions that *all men are mortal*, that *Socrates is a man*, and that *Socrates is mortal*, specifically, as opposed to correlating with logical relations between some very different set of propositions, or no propositions at all. Moreover, as BonJour points out, even if such a unique mapping could somehow be established, that would not suffice to show that thoughts *just are* sentences in Mentalese, as opposed to being *correlated with* sentences in Mentalese.

But there is yet another problem. The number of inferential relations any one thought has to all the others is vast, and the vast majority of them are not accessible to consciousness all at once. If the content of any thought is determined by these relations, then, that content would not be accessible to consciousness either. You would not be able to know the content of any of your thoughts. Nor could anyone coherently propose simply accepting this skeptical conclusion, rather than regarding it as a *reductio ad absurdum* of the premises that lead to it. For to draw the conclusion that *I do not know the content of any of my thoughts*, I would have to be able to know the content of *that* thought, the thought in which I draw the conclusion.

As BonJour points out, if the Language of Thought theorist attempts to solve this problem by appealing to some further symbol in the brain, access to which somehow gives us knowledge of all the inferential relations determining the content of some particular thought, that will just raise the same problem again. For now we need to know how we are able to access the content of *that* symbol. Yet if the Language of Thought theorist appeals instead to some factor other than a symbol encoded in the brain, he will in effect be giving up his theory. For in that case, why is it not that additional factor, rather than symbols in the brain, that is the key to understanding the nature of thought?

The gap identified by BonJour between causal relations on the one hand and logical relations on the other is also emphasized by what is sometimes called the "argument from reason" against naturalism.[633] The argument has been developed in different ways by different writers, but I would propose that the basic idea can be summarized as follows. Naturalism must take thinking to consist of nothing more than the transition from one material symbol to another in accordance with causal laws (whether the details are spelled out along the lines of Fodor's Language of Thought hypothesis or in some other way). Now, the explanation of how this works cannot make reference to the meaning or conceptual content associated with such symbols, but only to physical properties of the symbols of the kind identified by physics, chemistry, neuroscience and the like. For the whole point of a naturalistic theory is to *explain* features like conceptual content in such terms, and such a theory could not do that if it *presupposed* meaning or conceptual content.

But these physical properties and the causal relations they entail will remain the same whatever meaning or conceptual content is associated with them. To see this, consider the parallel example of a calculator. Punching the symbols "1," "+," "1," and "=" into it will generate the further symbol "2" whether we associate the usual arithmet-

---

[633] Cf. William Hasker, *The Emergent Self* (Ithaca: Cornell University Press, 1999), pp. 64-75, and Victor Reppert, "The Argument from Reason," in William Lane Craig and J. P. Moreland, eds., *The Blackwell Companion to Natural Theology* (Oxford: Wiley-Blackwell, 2009). Versions of the argument can be found in C. S. Lewis, *Miracles* (New York: Macmillan, 1978); Karl Popper, *Objective Knowledge*, Revised edition (Oxford: Clarendon Press, 1979), chapter 6; and Alvin Plantinga, *Warrant and Proper Function* (Oxford: Oxford University Press, 1993), chapter 12.

ical meanings with these symbols or instead assign to them some eccentric meanings, because the electronic properties of the calculator alone are what determine what symbols get displayed. Similarly, neurally encoded symbols of Mentalese paralleling the English sentences "All men are mortal" and "Socrates is a man" would still generate a symbol paralleling the sentence "Socrates is mortal" whether we associate the usual meanings with them or instead assign to them some eccentric meanings, because the neurophysiological properties of the symbols alone are what determine which further symbols get generated.

However, a symbol could serve as a *rational justification* of another symbol *only* by virtue of the meaning or conceptual content associated with the symbols. After all, it is only because we associate the symbols "1," "+," "1," "=," and "2" with the usual meanings that "1 + 1 = 2" expresses an arithmetical truth. Similarly, it is only if Mentalese symbols paralleling "All men are mortal," "Socrates is a man," and "Socrates is mortal" have the usual meanings that the first two will *logically entail*, and thus rationally justify, the third. If instead the first two symbols conveyed the propositions that *it is raining in Cleveland* and that *the movie was boring*, respectively, while the third symbol conveyed the proposition that *robots will take over the world*, the latter would hardly follow logically from the former.

In that case, though, a naturalistic theory of thought cannot account for how any of our thought processes is ever rational. For such a theory entails that our thoughts would generate each other in just the way they do whether or not these transitions corresponded to any valid inference patterns. It would be no good to appeal to the fact that our inferences *seem* valid, because they might seem that way even if they were not (just as an insane person's illogical inferences seem perfectly reasonable to him). Causal relationships of the kind a naturalistic theory posits in order to account for our thought processes could at most explain why, as a matter of *psychological* fact, we *consider* an inference to be reasonable. But they cannot underwrite the supposition that, as a matter of *logical* fact, it really *is* reasonable.

Nor is the problem merely that we could not *know* whether our thought processes are really rational. The point is not merely *ep-*

istemic, but *ontological*. It is that our thought processes would not actually *be* rational. They would on the best case scenario only *parallel* genuinely rational thought processes. We would be like a machine that, just as a matter of sheer accident, happened to produce the symbol "4" when the symbols "2," "+," "2," and "=" were punched into it. This would not really be adding, but just something that looked like adding, and if naturalism were true, then the most we would ever be capable of is something that looked like logical inference but wasn't genuine logical inference. Actual logical relationships between propositions would drop out of the story as irrelevant to what happens, leaving only brute causal relations between symbols.

If the facts recognized by the naturalist were all the facts there are, then, we would never actually make any logical inferences at all. Our apparent inferences would be illusory. But that would include the apparent inferences the naturalist himself makes in defense of his position. Naturalistic accounts of thought are, accordingly, self-defeating. Nor will it do for the naturalist to suggest that we might bite the bullet and give up on the idea of rational inference. For to do even that much you have to first grasp what truly rational inference would involve and go on to judge, on the basis of naturalism and its implications, that we don't have any reason to judge that we ever really do that – which would itself be an exercise in doing it. The whole position simply collapses into incoherence, in a way that is similar to the way that (as we saw above and in chapter 3) it is incoherent to suppose that our thoughts never really have any determinate conceptual content.

This is an example of what is sometimes called a *retorsion* argument, the aim of which is to refute a view by showing that it entails a performative self-contradiction. It is sometimes suggested that such an argument amounts to a *tu quoque* fallacy of rejecting a claim merely because the person making it behaves in a hypocritical manner (in this case, rejecting naturalism on the basis of the naturalist's hypocritically engaging in logical inference despite holding, or at least having a view that implies, that such a thing is impossible). Another criticism claims that retorsion arguments can show at most that we have to *think* about things a certain way (in this case, that we have to think of ourselves as engaging in logical inference), but not that they really *are* that way. But such objections misunderstand the nature of retorsion arguments, which are simply a species of *reductio ad absurdum* arguments, the probative force of which is generally acknowledged. The point is not that the naturalist's position is hypocritical or that we have to think of ourselves as if we engaged in logical inference. The point is that naturalism entails the proposition that *logical inference is impossible*, whereas the fact that there are people who defend naturalism entails the proposition that *logical inference actually does occur*, and both those propositions cannot be true. Hence the very act of defending naturalism refutes it.[634]

The lesson of both BonJour's argument and the argument from reason is (again to apply a distinction from Wilfrid Sellars that I cited in chapter 4) that the "logical space of reasons" is wider than the physical "space of causes."[635] The former cannot be mapped onto the latter and thus cannot be reduced to or entirely explained in terms of it. BonJour notes that the problem for naturalism derives from the supposition that thought is "composed entirely of elements whose content is imposed upon them from the outside in some relational way," such as the symbols of Fodor's Language of Thought or physical representations of some other kind.[636] For once that is assumed, we are stuck with the problems of explaining how these elements get their conceptual content and how we can have access to that content, problems which, we've seen, are insuperable. We have to acknowledge instead that "at least some of the elements of thought must be *intrinsically* meaningful or contentful, must have the particular content that they do simply by virtue of their intrinsic, non-relational character."[637] In other words, we need to acknowledge that thought is composed of *formal* rather than instrumental signs – signs

---

[634] I defend retorsion arguments at greater length in *Aristotle's Revenge*, at pp. 80-84.

[635] Wilfrid Sellars, "Empiricism and the Philosophy of Mind," in Herbert Feigl and Michel Scriven, eds., *Minnesota Studies in the Philosophy of Science, Volume I* (Minneapolis: University of Minnesota Press, 1956).

[636] BonJour, *In Defense of Pure Reason*, p. 180.

[637] Ibid.

that are nothing but signs, that have no nature other than their content, so that there can be no question of the signs being present but with some different content or no content at all. And if to have these signs in the intellect just is to have their *content* in the intellect, there is no longer any mystery about how the intellect gets access to that content.[638]

The simplicity of the self

I have in previous chapters argued for the reality and irreducibility of the self or person as an intellectual substance. I have in this chapter argued that its intellectual powers are immaterial. Recall that to have an intellect is to have the capacities to grasp concepts, to entertain propositions, and to reason from one proposition to another in accordance with canons of logical inference. The storage problem argument and the argument from the indeterminacy of the physical show that concepts are immaterial. These arguments also show that entertaining propositions is an immaterial activity. For if concepts cannot be stored in the brain, then the propositions of which concepts are constituents can hardly be stored there either. And Ross's argument entails that no set of physical facts could suffice to determine that I am, for example, entertaining the proposition that *one plus one equals two* as opposed to the proposition that *one quus one equals two*. Ross's argument from the indeterminacy of the physical, the argument from reason, and BonJour's argument entail that reasoning from one proposition to another cannot be a material process. So, all three of the characteristic powers or capacities of the intellect have been shown to be immaterial.

Now, from this it follows that the substance whose powers they are is immaterial, at least given the Scholastic principle *agere sequitur esse* or "action follows being." That is to say, what a thing *does* reflects what it *is*, so that if a substance carries out an immaterial activity, it must itself be an immaterial substance. Note that this does not entail that it is *wholly* immaterial, and I argued in the previous chapter that human persons are not wholly immaterial. But they are immaterial in part.

---

[638] Ibid, p. 167.

I will develop and defend these points in a later chapter. For the moment I want to argue that the immateriality of the self can be established in a more direct manner, by way of appeal to the *simplicity* of the self. What it means to be simple in the sense operative here is to be non-composite or not made up of parts. The basic idea is that the self is simple or non-composite, but nothing material can be simple or non-composite. From that it follows that the self is not a material thing.

Before spelling the argument out in greater detail, though, I need immediately to qualify the claim that the self is simple. Simplicity in the sense in question comes in degrees. I do not claim that the self is simple or non-composite in an absolute sense (the way God is said to be simple in classical theism). For example, given what I have said in earlier chapters, I obviously do not deny that there are distinct powers within the self. The claim is rather that the self is simple in certain specific ways in which material things are not simple. Furthermore, I am also not claiming that the self is, without qualification, simple even in this narrow sense. Rather, the claim is that the self considered *qua intellect* is simple in a way no material thing can be. I have, after all, said that the human person is in part bodily, and the body is composed of parts. But bodily parts are themselves composed of parts. For example, the brain is composed of neurons or nerve cells, the heart is composed of cardiomyocyte cells, and both kinds of cells are composed of parts of their own. Hence the self qua *blood-circulating* thing is not simple or non-composite. But the intellect, unlike the brain or the heart or any other bodily organ, is not composed of parts. Hence the self qua *thinking* thing *is* simple or non-composite.

To be precise, the intellect lacks what Scholastic writers call *quantitative* parts and *constitutive* parts.[639] Quantitative parts are parts of an extended kind, such as the smaller bits of matter a bone or muscle can be broken down into, and the yet smaller bits those parts can in turn be broken down into. Constitutive parts would those of which,

---

[639] Cf. Bittle *The Whole Man*, pp. 510-14; Maher, *Psychology*, pp. 466-69; Mercier et al., *A Manual of Modern Scholastic Philosophy*, pp. 299-300; and Royce, *Man and His Nature*, pp. 312-23. Quantitative parts are sometimes also called "integrant" parts or "spatial" parts, and constitutive parts are also called "essential" parts.

according to Aristotelian-Thomistic metaphysics, all physical things are essentially composed, namely form and matter. My claim that the intellect is simple or non-composite is thus to be understood as the claim that it is neither extended nor composed of form and matter. Since being extended and being composed of form and matter are, as I argued in chapter 5, essential to physical things, it follows that the intellect is not a physical thing.

A key traditional argument for this claim appeals to the *unity of consciousness*.[640] The basic idea is that the self's knowledge both of other things and of itself would not be possible if it were composed of parts.[641] Now, in recent literature on the argument, the emphasis has

---

[640] Versions of this argument were defended in ancient philosophy by Plotinus, in *Enneads* IV, 7, 1-3; in medieval philosophy by Avicenna in the *Kitab al-Najat* and by Aquinas in the *Commentary on Aristotle's De Anima*, III, 3; in early modern philosophy by Leibniz in the *Monadology*, section 17; in the nineteenth century by Hermann Lotze, in *Metaphysic*, Book III, Chapter 1; and by twentieth-century Thomists like Bittle, Maher, Mercier, and Royce, cited in the previous note. In recent philosophy, it has been defended in Hasker, *The Emergent Self*, pp. 122-46; John Haldane, "(I Am) Thinking," *Ratio* 16 (2003): 124-39; David Barnett, "You are Simple," in Robert C. Koons and George Bealer, eds., *The Waning of Materialism* (Oxford: Oxford University Press, 2010); and J. P. Moreland, "Substance Dualism and the Unity of Consciousness," in Loose, Menuge, and Moreland, eds., *The Blackwell Companion to Substance Dualism*. Though his general epistemological views prevent him from taking the argument to succeed as a demonstration, Kant's treatment of it in the Second Paralogism in the *Critique of Pure Reason* (A 352) is not entirely unsympathetic. For discussion of Kant's complicated relationship to the argument, see Karl Ameriks, *Kant's Theory of Mind: An Analysis of the Paralogisms of Pure Reason*, New edition (Oxford: Clarendon Press, 2000), chapter II. For a collection of essays on the history of the argument, see Thomas M. Lennon and Robert J. Stainton, eds., *The Achilles of Rationalist Psychology* (Springer, 2008).

[641] Several kinds of unity are discussed in the literature on the unity of consciousness, and it is important to distinguish between them. (Cf. Moreland, "Substance Dualism and the Unity of Consciousness," and Tim Bayne and David J. Chalmers, "What is the Unity of Consciousness?" in Axel Cleeremans, ed., *The Unity of Consciousness* (Oxford: Oxford University Press, 2003.) For example, there is *objectual phenomenal unity*, which is illustrated by the way you might perceive the color and shape of a ball as features of one and the same object, the ball. The difficulty of explaining this kind of unity is known in neuroscience as "the binding problem." There is also *subject phenomenal unity*, which has to do with the way different mental states or different aspects of the same mental state are all attributable to one and the same subject. It is the second sort of unity that I am addressing here. As Moreland notes, however (p. 203), subject phenomenal unity accounts for objectual phenomenal unity insofar as the reason why perception of the color of the ball and perception of the shape of the ball are united into a single perceptual experience of the ball is that there is a single unified subject whose perceptual experience it is.

tended to be on the unity of perceptual experience, specifically. And where the perceptual experience of a *rational* animal is in view, I would agree that this unity implies simplicity. But I do not hold that the perceptual consciousness of *non*-human animals has the kind of unity that would entail simplicity, and thus it is in my view a mistake for recent defenders of the argument to focus as they have on perceptual consciousness. What is crucial is the unity of mental acts of a distinctively *intellectual* kind, such as the entertaining of a proposition or the distinctively *conceptualized* sort of perceptual experience of which rational animals alone are capable. The way earlier writers in the tradition formulated the argument often reflected this.

Naturally, one reason for the emphasis on intellectual rather than perceptual acts is that simplicity entails immateriality, and I have argued in the previous chapter for the corporeality of perception. But there are also independent grounds for thinking that it is intellection rather than perception that is key to seeing why the self has a kind of unity that entails immateriality. Jerry Fodor famously argued that perception is *modular*, whereas cognition of the kind we characterize as thinking is not.[642] A module in Fodor's sense is a special-purpose psychological faculty, sensitive only to information about a certain narrow domain and processing that information in a way that is "encapsulated" from information that exists elsewhere in the mind. For example, consider visual perception, which is sensitive to light but not to the information that hearing and touch allow us to detect. Think also of the way that a visual perceptual illusion will persist even after you come to know that it is an illusion. For instance, in the Mueller-Lyer illusion, two lines of the same length appear to be of different lengths, and they retain this appearance even after the perceiver learns that the lengths are in fact the same. In this way the visual perceptual module is encapsulated from the information that exists elsewhere in the mind about the true length of the lines. Modules have various further properties, such as being driven by input (such as that provided by sense organs), largely confined to bottom-

---

[642] Jerry A. Fodor, *The Modularity of Mind* (Cambridge, MA: The MIT Press, 1983). Cf. the essays in Part II of Fodor's *A Theory of Content*. The relevance of Fodor's arguments to the argument from the unity of consciousness is noted by Lennon and Stainton in their introduction to *The Achilles of Rationalist Psychology*, at p. 7.

up information flow (as perception provides information for more abstract thought processes), and relatively superficial in what they reveal about their domains. They also tend to be associated with specific, localized neuroanatomical mechanisms. The higher cognitive processes we call "thinking," Fodor points out, are very different.[643] They take in and integrate information from across domains, are not limited to either bottom-up or top-down information flow, yield a deeper grasp of their objects, and are not so closely associated with specific neuroanatomical mechanisms. For these reasons, he notes, higher cognitive processes are not susceptible of analysis in terms of the kinds of computational models and localized neural mechanisms that have shed light on perception.[644]

The relevance of all this to the issue at hand is that it provides independent grounds for judging that it is *intellectual* rather than perceptual acts that most clearly unify information in a way that makes them difficult to locate in some particular material structure or collection of structures, such as in the brain (even if, to be sure, Fodor himself did not draw an anti-materialist conclusion from this).

As I have said, the basic idea of the argument from the unity of consciousness is that the self's knowledge both of other things and of itself would not be possible if it were composite. To see why, let's start with its knowledge of other things, such as the proposition that *the cat is on the mat*. When you entertain this proposition, what you entertain is a single unified thought. But this would not be possible if you qua thinking thing were composed of parts. For suppose you were made up of two parts A and B. Suppose further that A is entertaining the concept of *the cat* and B is entertaining the concept of *being on the mat*. This would no more amount to *you* entertaining the thought that *the cat is on the mat* than two people standing next to each other, one of them entertaining the concept of *the cat* and the other entertaining the concept of *being on the mat*, would amount to a single person entertaining the proposition that *the cat is on the mat*. Suppose instead

---

[643] Fodor, *Modularity of Mind*, pp. 101-19.

[644] Specifically, he thinks this is true of non-demonstrative inference. Whether computational models shed light on demonstrative inferences (like those characteristic of mathematics) is an issue to be addressed in the next chapter.

that each part, A and B, was entertaining the entire proposition that *the cat is on the mat*. That too would no more amount to *you* entertaining the proposition than two people standing next to each other, each of them entertaining the proposition that *the cat is on the mat*, would amount to a single person entertaining the proposition.

Could it somehow be only A and B together which entertain the complete thought that *the cat is on the mat*? But what exactly does this suggestion amount to? What do A and B each contribute to the entertaining of the thought? If each contributes a part of the thought (with A entertaining the concept of *the cat* and B entertaining the concept of *being on the mat*), then we are back to the first scenario. If instead A and B each entertains the complete thought, then we are back to the second scenario. So the suggestion that A and B together somehow entertain the complete thought doesn't really amount to a third possibility. Nor, as William Hasker points out, will it help to posit a neural "scanning mechanism" of some kind that collects and integrates the information from A and B, since this will simply raise the same problem again at a higher level.[645] For how does the information encoded in the parts of the scanning mechanism get unified? Hence there is simply no sense to be made of a composite thing entertaining a proposition.

Nor, for similar reasons, could the self qua thinking thing know *itself* if it were composite. Suppose your intellect were composed of parts A and B. It can't be that self-awareness involves A being aware of A and B being aware of B, any more than two people standing next to each other, each aware of himself, amounts to one person being aware of himself. Nor can it involve A being aware of B and B being aware of A, any more than two people standing in front of each other, each aware of the other, amounts to one person being aware of himself. Suppose instead that A is aware of both A and B and B is aware of both A and B. This would not amount to *one* self being aware of itself any more than two people standing next to each other, each being aware of himself and of the other person, amounts to one person being aware of himself. Nor will it help to suggest that A and B together know A and B, for this will reduce to the other scenarios, just as the

---

[645] Hasker, *The Emergent Self*, pp. 128-9.

analogous proposal in the case of the self's knowledge of the proposition that *the cat is on the mat* collapsed into the other scenarios. There is simply no sense to be made of the intellect's being aware of itself except in terms of a single non-composite whole knowing that same one non-composite whole.

As David Barnett has noted, it will not do to propose that the *number* of parts, the *causal* or *structural relations* between them, or their *natures* could somehow account for the unity of a self composed of them.[646] Again, two people standing next to each other, one of them entertaining the concept of *the cat* and the other entertaining the concept of *being on the mat*, do not amount to a single intellect entertaining the proposition that *the cat is on the mat*. And adding a third, fourth, or any number of other persons would not give rise to such an intellect. Suppose that such persons exhibited causal and structural relations to one another that paralleled the relations holding between the brain states that mediate between sensory inputs and behavioral outputs. For example, suppose that when light from a cat on a mat triggered the sensory receptors in a certain robot, this alerted the persons to send signals to one another in a way that parallels neural processing of visual information, and these signals in turn were fed back to the robot in such a way that they caused it to utter the sentence "The cat is on the mat." Though this would suffice to *simulate* behavior like that of a single intellect which had the thought that *the cat is on the mat*, it wouldn't suffice actually to *give rise to* such an intellect, any more than the two people standing next to each other in our original example would. Nor, again, would the natures of the parts make any difference. If even the two people standing next to each other in our example, each explicitly entertaining the relevant concepts, would not amount to a single intellect having the thought that *the cat is on the mat*, how would parts of some other nature (such as neurons or some other *sub*-personal entities) amount to such an intellect? As Barnett points out, it is the fact that the parts would be *multiple* (a pair, or

---

[646] Barnett, "You are Simple."

three, or whatever), and not the natures of the parts, that poses the problem of how a unified whole could arise out of them.⁶⁴⁷

Naturally, a critic might respond to the argument from the unity of consciousness by suggesting that there is in fact no such thing as a unified self, so that whether materialism can explain its unity is moot. But I have already established the reality, irreducibility and unity of the self in chapter 2, so such a response will not do. However, the materialist might raise other objections. For example, commenting on the versions of the unity of consciousness argument put forward by Leibniz and discussed by Kant, Margaret Wilson suggests that

---

⁶⁴⁷ Andrew Bailey responds to Barnett in "You Needn't be Simple," *Philosophical Papers* 43 (2014): 145-60, proposing some theses in mereology (the theory of parts and wholes) that he claims block the inference to simplicity. Why can't two persons (what Bailey calls a "person-pair") make up a single unified intellect? Perhaps, Bailey suggests, because it is impossible for an entity such as a person-pair to exist. For if it is impossible for it even to exist, then, naturally, it would be impossible for it to do anything else, such as amount to a single unified consciousness. But in that case we would have an alternative explanation of why it would not amount to such a consciousness, one that did not require us to affirm the simplicity of conscious subjects.

In a separate line of argument, Bailey asks us to consider a certain human being sitting in a chair (which he calls Org, for "organism"), and the collection that consists of all the parts of that human being except his left pinky (which he calls Org-minus). It is plausible that while Org is conscious, Org-minus is not a separate conscious entity and indeed that it is impossible for it to be one. But then, just as Org cannot have such a part that is conscious, perhaps any single unified consciousness cannot have parts that are conscious (such as parts like the members of a person-pair). In that case, we would again have an alternative explanation of why a person-pair would not amount to a single unified consciousness, one that does not require affirming simplicity (since Org does have parts).

One problem with this curious response is that, as Bailey concedes, it is "far from obvious" that it *is* in fact impossible for "person-pairs" to exist (p. 151). (Certainly they *seem* to exist wherever there are two people.) The thesis seems to have no motivation other than finding a way to block the inference to simplicity. Similarly, it is far from obvious that the case of Org and Org-minus is an interesting and helpful analogue to the case of two people standing next to each other, since Org-minus is a dubious entity at best. It is hard to see why the defender of the argument from the unity of consciousness should be impressed by objections that make crucial use of such eccentric and artificial examples.

But even apart from their eccentricity and artificiality, it is hard to see the point of the mereological rigmarole. There being two oranges next to each other doesn't amount to there being a single orange. There being two geometrical points in proximity to one another doesn't amount to there being a single geometrical point. And there being two persons next to each other doesn't amount to there being a single person. These are straightforward logical facts, and Bailey's examples shed no more light on (and cast no more doubt on) the unity and simplicity of the self than they shed (or cast doubt) on the unity of an orange or the simplicity of a geometrical point.

they beg the question.[648] For in order to reason confidently from the nature of the self to the falsity of materialism, we'd first have to have sufficient knowledge the nature of the self. But knowing whether materialism is true is part of what would be required in order have such knowledge. Hence the argument must *presuppose* the falsity of materialism in order to argue for its falsity.

To see what is wrong with this objection, consider first that it would prove too much. In particular, if it was effective against anti-materialist arguments like the one in question, it would be no less effective against materialist arguments. The critic of materialism could say that all such arguments beg the question, because in order to argue confidently from premises about the nature of the mind to a conclusion that the mind is material, you'd first have to have sufficient knowledge of the nature of the mind, and that knowing whether the mind is material is part of what such knowledge would entail. Indeed, arguments for all sorts of conclusions would be undermined. Any time someone argued that things of type X are identical with (or not identical with) with things of type Y, or that they can be explained (or cannot be explained) by reference to things of type Y, the critic could respond that we'd need sufficient knowledge of the natures of X and/or Y in order to get such an argument off the ground – and that that would include knowledge of whether the claim in question is in fact true, so that such arguments beg the question.

In fact, the argument from the unity of consciousness does not beg the question and in particular does not presuppose the falsity of materialism. It does not and need not begin with any claim about the nature of the self other than that it exhibits unity of the kind in question. If a detective knows that Smith was not in Los Angeles on January 1, he can conclude that Smith could not have committed a certain crime that occurred in Los Angeles on that date, and he can do so even if he initially knows little if anything else about Smith. Similarly, we can reason from the unity of consciousness to the conclusion that the self cannot be material even if we initially know little or anything else

---

[648] Margaret Dauler Wilson, "Leibniz and Materialism," in *Ideas and Mechanism: Essays on Early Modern Philosophy* (Princeton, NJ: Princeton University Press, 1999), at pp. 400-1.

about the self. In any event, Wilson's objection does not show otherwise.[649]

In a Kantian vein, one might object that the argument shows at most only that we have to *think* of the self as simple, not that it really *is* simple.[650] Now, if this objection presupposes Kant's general epistemology, it will beg the question, since no one convinced by arguments like those I've been defending in this book is likely to agree with that epistemology. Yet if it is meant instead as a freestanding objection, independent of a more general Kantian framework, then like Wilson's objection it will prove too much. For one might as well suppose that any argument for any conclusion (including the conclusion that materialism is true), no matter how powerful, can be rebutted simply by suggesting that it shows only that we have to *think* of the conclusion as true, not that it actually *is* true. Obviously it would be silly to suppose that this is a serious response to arguments in general. But, unless backed by some tendentious epistemology like Kant's, it is no less silly a response to the argument from the unity of consciousness.

Yet another objection would be to suggest that there may be some unknown metaphysical relation between parts such that a unified self could emerge from them.[651] But by itself this is mere handwaving. The argument from the unity of consciousness purports to show that a unified self *could not* emerge from parts of the kind in question. In order to rebut the argument, one has to show that this conclusion does not in fact follow, or that a premise of the argument is false. It is no good merely to propose that some unknown relation might allow for emergence when the argument implies that there could be no such relation. And once again we have an objection that would prove too much. If the objection were any good, then *any* reductionist claim, no matter how far-fetched and open to obvious objections, could be defended merely by suggesting that there may be

---

[649] In fairness to Wilson, she presents the objection as one that Leibniz's version of the argument from the unity of consciousness is subject to given the epistemological assumptions Leibniz makes when criticizing other arguments for immaterialism. But if one does not share the epistemological assumptions in question (as I do not) then the objection fails.

[650] Cf. Ameriks, *Kant's Theory of Mind*, pp. 55-56.
[651] Ibid., pp. 58-59.

some unknown relation that solves the problems facing it. For example, despite the well-known and apparently insuperable objections to phenomenalism's attempt to reduce physical objects to collections of sense data, or behaviorism's attempt to reduce mental states to patterns of behavior, one could propose that there might be some as-yet unknown relation between sense data and physical objects or behavior and mental states by which the reductionist analyses could be made plausible. But no one would regard this as a serious defense of phenomenalism or behaviorism. Neither, then, should anyone regard the proposal under consideration as a serious objection to the argument from the unity of consciousness.

It might be claimed that findings in modern neuroscience point the way to a materialist explanation of the unity of consciousness. The relevant literature has been surveyed by Christopher Viger, Robyn Bluhm, and Sharday Mosurinjohn.[652] As they note, there are two main approaches to neuroscientific accounts of how information gets unified. The first is structural, positing hierarchies of neurons that trace up to some single unifying structure or cell. The second is operational, holding that it is the simultaneity of activity in certain key cells that accounts for unity. A problem with the first approach is that in order to capture all the information that is to be unified, a structure at the top of the hierarchy would have to exhibit greater neural complexity, not less. A problem with the second approach is that there is always some simultaneous neural activity in the brain anyway, so that there must be more than that to the unification of information.

That these neuroscientific accounts would face such problems is entirely predictable, since they are really just variations on the problems which the argument from the unity of consciousness has traditionally claimed must plague any materialist theory. Any such theory is going to have to associate different bits of information with different material parts, but be unable to account for how these parts get unified into the whole we know in consciousness, any more than

---

[652] Christopher Viger, Robyn Bluhm, and Sharday Mosurinjohn, "The Binding Problem: Achilles in the 21st Century," in Lennon and Stainton, eds., *The Achilles of Rationalist Psychology*.

ideas in the minds of two or more people standing next to each other amount to a single intellect's having a unified thought. Viger, Bluhm, and Mosurinjohn propose that the solution is to hold that the information in diverse neural locations is bound by virtue of being *represented as* bound. In support, they cite Dennett's view that the self is not a "Cartesian theater" but a "center of narrative gravity," a useful fiction constructed by the brain out of the "multiple drafts" of the story it tells itself about the goings on within the body and its relations to its environment.[653] But the obvious problem (apart from the fact that the self is not a fiction, as we saw in chapter 2) is that this just pushes the problem back a stage. For how does the information scattered across the brain get unified into a single coherent representation? How does the information spread across multiple drafts get unified into a single self-description (fictional or otherwise)? The proposal no more explains the unity of consciousness in materialist terms than writing a second IOU to back up a first IOU pays a debt.

So, we cannot avoid the conclusion that the self qua intellect is simple or non-composite in the sense of not being made up of extended parts or of form and matter. But physical things, as we saw in chapter 5, are essentially extended and composed of form and matter. Hence it follows that the self qua intellect is not a physical thing. Now, Tim Bayne objects that this conclusion does not follow, even if one grants the premises.[654] It would follow only if the materialist identified the mind with a physical *substance* like the brain. But while identity theorists would make such an identification, other materialists would not. In particular, functionalists would say that we should not reify the mind, holding instead that "minds are not substances, but are *systems* that *emerge* from the appropriate functioning of an organism (or a part thereof)."[655] To be sure, Bayne concedes that the emergence might not result from a mere aggregation of parts, and that "it

---

[653] Cf. Daniel C. Dennett, *Consciousness Explained* (Boston: Little, Brown and Company, 1991), especially chapter 13.

[654] Tim Bayne, "Problems with Unity of Consciousness Arguments for Substance Dualism," in Loose, Menuge, and Moreland, eds., *The Blackwell Companion to Substance Dualism*, at p. 211.

[655] Ibid. Emphasis added.

could turn out that the fundamental unit of consciousness is the entire conscious stream" considered as a whole.[656] He also concedes that the relevant facts about what he calls "the appropriate functioning of an organism" do not strictly *logically entail* the facts about consciousness and its unity.[657]

The trouble is that these concessions give the game away. For what is at issue is precisely *how* the diverse components of a system, whatever the functional relations they bear to one another, could generate the essentially unified whole that is conscious awareness. Bayne gives no answer to this question, but simply proposes that, in some as yet unknown way, unified minds "emerge from" certain organic systems. Yet as J. P. Moreland writes, "punting to emergence is simply to slap a label on the problem" rather than to solve it.[658] It is just a variation on what I characterized a moment ago as the hand-waving move that simply ignores rather than addresses the problem and would prove too much if accepted.

Bayne also claims that, whatever problems the unity of consciousness poses for materialism, it poses no less serious problems for those who take the mind to be immaterial.[659] For the materialist's appeal to "the operations of a complex system" affords at least the *beginnings* of an explanation of consciousness, whereas insisting on the simplicity of the intellect deprives the critic of materialism of these explanatory resources.[660] One problem with this objection is that it presupposes a conception of explanation that begs the question against the argument from the unity of consciousness, and certainly against the larger philosophical traditions in which it arose. For philosophers of a Neoplatonic, Aristotelian, or Scholastic orientation, the deepest

---

[656] Ibid., p. 217.

[657] Ibid., p. 214, where Bayne distances himself from behaviorism and analytical functionalism, which do posit such an entailment (quite implausibly, as is widely acknowledged).

[658] Moreland, "Substance Dualism and the Unity of Consciousness," p. 188.

[659] Bayne, "Problems with Unity of Consciousness Arguments for Substance Dualism," p. 223.

[660] Ibid.

explanations always involve appeal to what is metaphysically *simpler* (again, in the sense of being non-composite) rather than to what is more complex.

To be sure, this raises general methodological and metaphysical questions that cannot be canvassed in a book on human nature, specifically. But there is a more fundamental problem with Bayne's claim, which is that it misunderstands the nature of the argument from the unity of consciousness, at least as it was intended by metaphysicians traditionally. Contrary to what Bayne and some contemporary defenders of the argument alike appear to think, it is not an "inference to the best explanation" that posits one possible hypothesis alongside others, where the others can be said at most to be less probable. Rather, it claims that the self qua intellect is simple or non-composite as a matter of *metaphysical necessity*. Suppose someone notes that a series of geometric points, lacking extension, cannot compose an extended thing. To reply that this is one possible explanation of extended things but that there might be others would simply misunderstand the nature of the claim being made. In the same way, it simply misunderstands the nature of the argument from the unity of consciousness, as traditionally intended, to suggest that the simplicity of the self is one possible hypothesis among others and must be weighed according to criteria like explanatory fruitfulness, fit with current empirical evidence, etc. That doesn't mean it can't be criticized, but the *kind* of criticism one might intelligibly level is not the kind one might raise against a scientific hypothesis. And it would beg the question to respond, as the Quinean naturalist would, that the only legitimate metaphysical questions are those susceptible of investigation by the methods of empirical science.

The simplicity of the intellect is thus not a *hypothesis* proposed to account for the data concerning the mind. Rather, it is *itself* among the data with which any sound hypothesizing about the mind must be consistent. Now, precisely because the intellect is simple or not composed of parts, it also cannot be a *system* in Bayne's sense, because that involves functional relationships between parts. Hence, Bayne's purported alternative to thinking of the mind as a substance collapses along with the rest of his response to the argument from the unity of consciousness.[661]

Intellection as dematerialization

In an influential treatment of the contemporary debate over mental representation, Robert Cummins draws a distinction between *representation* in the singular and *representations* in the plural.[662] Representation in the singular is thought's capacity to have *intentionality*, to be *about* something, to have *content* (such as the content that *the cat is on the mat*). Representations in the plural are the particular mental items that have this intentionality, "aboutness," or content. Cummins goes on to note that there have in the history of philosophy been four main views about what, specifically, mental representations are, and four main views about what it is for them to have intentionality or content.[663]

The first view about what representations in the plural are is the Aristotelian-Scholastic view (which I described and defended at the end of chapter 7) that for the intellect to represent a physical thing is for it to consider its *form* or *essence* in abstraction from the matter in which that form is typically embedded. The second is the early modern empiricist view that representations are *images* or copies of sensations. The third is the view that representations are *symbols* of some kind, whether linguistic symbols in a Language of Thought or symbols of some non-linguistic sort. The fourth is the view that representations are *neurophysiological states*.

The first view about what representation in the singular is is the view that it involves a *similarity* between a representation and what is represented. This view in turn is spelled out further either by way of the Aristotelian-Scholastic thesis that a representation and

---

[661] Might the intellect be a system of *immaterial* parts, even if it cannot be a system of material parts? No, because the only way that parts of the relevant kind could be individuated is by virtue of being associated with different bits of matter, or so Thomists argue. Cf. Edward Feser, *Scholastic Metaphysics: A Contemporary Introduction* (Heusenstamm: Editiones Scholasticae, 2014), pp. 198-201. We'll return to this issue in a later chapter.

[662] Robert Cummins, *Meaning and Mental Representation* (Cambridge, MA: The MIT Press, 1989), pp. 1-2.

[663] Ibid., pp. 2-10.

what is represented have the same form, or by way of the early modern empiricist's imagist thesis that images resemble what they represent. The second view about what representation in the singular is is the view that it involves *causal covariance* between a representation and the thing represented, as is claimed by the causal theories of representation considered earlier. The third view is that representation involves *adaptational role,* as is claimed by the biosemantic theories considered earlier. The fourth view is that representation involves *functional or computational role,* as is claimed by the conceptual role semantics approach considered earlier.

To these lists we can add the early modern rationalist view, which is not quite the same as any of those canvassed by Cummins. Unlike early modern empiricism, it would not identify mental representations with images, and unlike materialist theories, it would not identify them either with neurophysiological states or with symbols of a kind that might be encoded in a machine no less than in a human mind. Since it rejects imagism, it also rejects resemblance between a representation and what is represented as the key to intentionality, and since it rejects materialism, it also rejects the idea that content depends on causal covariance between brain states and goings on in the external physical world, or natural selection, or functional relations between symbols encoded in the brain. But it also rejects the Aristotelian-Scholastic view that concept-formation presupposes sensory experience, as well as the hylemorphist metaphysics underlying the idea that the intellect abstracts form from matter. For the rationalist, mental content is at least largely innate and could be just as it is even if the intellect had no contact at all with the material world, indeed even if there were no material world. This dovetails with the Cartesian thesis that the human person is essentially entirely immaterial.

Now, in chapter 7 I argued against this rationalist view, and it is in any event not one to which any materialist could be sympathetic. In chapter 3 I argued against imagism, and in that chapter and the present one I have argued against the view that mental representations are symbols. In the present chapter I have also argued that mental representations could not be neurophysiological states, and that their content cannot be explained in terms of causal covariance, adaptational role, or functional or conceptual role. That leaves the Aristotelian-Scholastic view as the "last man standing," and again, I have in the previous chapter already offered positive argumentation for it in any case.

To this we can add the consideration that several mainstream contemporary philosophers with no Aristotelian-Scholastic ax to grind have found that the difficulties plaguing the alternative accounts leave *something like* the Aristotelian-Scholastic view worthy of reconsideration – even if the radicalness of the very idea leads them to stop short of advocating a full-blown neo-Aristotelian or neo-Scholastic position. We have already seen this in the case of Putnam. The basic insight of causal theories, he argues, cannot be developed into a viable account of representation unless we take on board the Aristotelian-Scholastic notion of form as that which objectively demarcates one physical object from another, and which is transmitted from object to intellect when they are causally related in the right way.

Whereas Putnam starts with considerations about what the physical world must be like in order to bear the relevant causal relations to the intellect, BonJour starts at the other end. As we've seen, he argues that we cannot make sense of thought unless we affirm that "at least some of the elements of thought must be *intrinsically* meaningful or contentful, must have the particular content that they do simply by virtue of their intrinsic, non-relational character."[664] But in that case, he goes on to suggest:

> [I]n order for the intrinsic character of the thought to specify precisely *that* particular property to the exclusion of anything else, the property in question must *itself* somehow be metaphysically involved in that character. The rationale for this suggestion is the realization that no surrogate or stand-in of any sort will do, since any account of the relation between such a surrogate and the property itself would raise anew all

---

[664] BonJour, *In Defense of Pure Reason*, p. 180.

the same difficulties that afflict the symbolic theory (of which any such view would in effect be an instance).[665]

Now the way that a property itself is metaphysically involved in a thought about it cannot, as he immediately goes on to note, be by virtue of the thought's *instantiating* the property. For example, a thought about triangles does not instantiate the property *triangularity* – that is to say, the thought is not *itself* a triangle. So we have to allow that "thinking of something as having a particular form or property involves the literal occurrence of that form or property in the mind, but not in the same way in which it occurs in its ordinary instances."[666] And thus, BonJour acknowledges (not entirely comfortably), do "we find ourselves in the dialectical vicinity of the venerable account of thought offered by Aristotle and his followers, especially Aquinas," on which thinking involves taking on the form of the thing thought about but apart from its matter.[667]

We saw in chapter 7 that John McDowell argues that the contingency of the cognitive connection between mind and external world implicit in Cartesianism makes that world not only *unknowable* but *unthinkable*. The mind could not so much as *represent* a world outside it (let alone be justified in affirming its reality) unless there were some intelligible structure common to both. Hence:

> [W]e cannot suppose that intelligible order has completely emigrated from the world we take to be mirrored by intellectual states... We have to suppose that the world has an intelligible structure, matching the structure in the space of *logos* possessed by accurate representations of it. The disenchantment Hume applauds can seem to point to a conception of nature as an ineffable lump, devoid of structure or order. But we cannot entertain such a conception. If we did, we would lose our right to the idea that the world of nature is a world at

---

[665] Ibid., p. 182. As BonJour notes at p. 184, a similar view is expressed by George Bealer in *Quality and Concept* (Oxford: Clarendon Press, 1982), at pp. 187-90.

[666] Ibid., p. 183.

[667] Ibid.

all (something that breaks up into things that are the case), let alone the world (everything that is the case).[668]

Tim Thornton thus characterizes McDowell's position as "an *identity theory of thoughts and facts*."[669] All the same, McDowell does not intend to collapse the world into the mind, after the fashion of idealism. But the idea of an "intelligible structure" common to thought and external reality is hard to distinguish from the Aristotelian notion of form, and the idea that thought is in some way identical to the facts being thought about, but not in an unqualified sense, is hard to distinguish from the Aristotelian thesis that thought involves a *formal* identity of mind and external reality without *material* identity.

To be sure, McDowell himself does not draw the connection. But he at least comes close in remarking on Wilfrid Sellars' treatment of Aquinas's Aristotelian-Scholastic thesis of a "sameness of form" or "*isomorphism* between the intellect and the extra-intellectual realities it can think about."[670] Sellars doesn't interpret Aquinas quite correctly, in McDowell's view, because of Sellars' commitment to a naturalistic "norm-free" conception of the physical world that Aquinas himself doesn't share:

> Aquinas, writing before the rise of modern science, is immune to the attractions of that norm-free conception of nature. And we should not be too quick to regard this as wholly a deficiency in his thinking. (Of course in all kinds of ways it is a deficiency.) There is a live possibility that, at least in one respect, Thomistic philosophy of mind is superior to Sellarsian

---

[668] John McDowell, "Two Sorts of Naturalism," in Rosalind Hursthouse, Gavin Lawrence, and Warren Quinn, eds., *Virtues and Reasons: Philippa Foot and Moral Theory* (Oxford: Clarendon Press, 1995), p. 160. Cf. John McDowell, *Mind and World* (Cambridge, MA: Harvard University Press, 1994), p. 27: "[T]here is no ontological gap between the sort of thing one can mean, or generally the sort of thing one can think, and the sort of thing that can be the case. When one thinks truly, what one thinks *is* what is the case... [T]here is no gap between thought, as such, and the world."

[669] Tim Thornton, *John McDowell* (Montreal and Kingston: McGill-Queen's University Press, 2004), p. 9.

[670] John McDowell, "Sellars's Thomism," in *Having the World in View: Essays on Kant, Hegel, and Sellars* (Cambridge, MA: Harvard University Press, 2009), p. 243.

philosophy of mind, just because Aquinas lacks the distinctively modern conception of nature that underlies Sellars's thinking.[671]

Raymond Tallis notes that human knowledge entails "connection-across-separation."[672] That is to say, it requires both that the gap between mind and world be bridged but also that there really be a gap in the first place. Some metaphysical positions explicitly or implicitly deny the gap, either by absorbing the world into the mind (as idealism does) or by dissolving the mind into the world (as eliminative materialism does). A sound position, he argues, must affirm the reality of the distinction between mind and world while showing how there can be the sort of correspondence between them that makes it possible for the former to know the latter. Tallis notes that a middle ground position of the kind needed is precisely what Aquinas and other Scholastics offer when arguing that knowledge involves the *formal* identity of thought and its object without *material* identity.[673] Because, for example, the same form that is in a triangle is also in the intellect that knows the triangle, we have *connection* between mind and world. But because the intellect considers that form in abstraction from the matter in which the form is embedded in the triangle itself, we maintain *separation* between mind and world.

Again, though they come close, none of these writers is quite willing at the end of the day to adopt the Aristotelian-Scholastic position. But neither does any of them offer good reasons for this reluctance. Though McDowell acknowledges the possibility that Aquinas's conception of nature gives his philosophy of mind an advantage over its naturalistic rivals, he also hints that it is nevertheless deficient "in all kinds of ways." Yet he doesn't offer even one specific example of these alleged myriad deficiencies. BonJour resists the Aristotelian idea that one and the same universal (*triangularity*, for example) is to

---

[671] Ibid., p. 255.

[672] Raymond Tallis, *Logos: The Mystery of How We Make Sense of the World* (Newcastle upon Tyne: Agenda Publishing, 2018), p. 168.

[673] Ibid., pp. 69-70.

be found both in a thought and in the thing thought about. He suggests instead that what is to be found in each are "distinct, though presumably intimately related universals."[674] But this defeats the whole purpose of BonJour's project of developing an account of thought on which the property the thought represents "must *itself* somehow be metaphysically involved in [its] character," and where "no surrogate or stand-in of any sort will do." For if the universal instantiated in the thing thought about is "distinct" from that which exists in the thought, then the property represented will *not* after all be "metaphysically involved" in the thought's character, but *will* instead be a mere "surrogate or stand-in."

In an exchange with John Haldane, wherein Haldane urges Putnam to follow out the Aristotelian implications of his critique of naturalism, Putnam offers one concession but gives three reasons for not going all the way.[675] The concession is to agree that "talk of properties and talk of concepts represent two sides of the same coin, two ways of talking about the same things" so that "when I think that something is that way, and when the thing *is* that way, the 'way' in question is one and the same."[676] To that extent, Putnam accepts the Aristotelian-Scholastic thesis that thought involves a formal identity between mind and world. But he is unwilling to go further than that – first of all because to say, for example, that thinking about a triangle involves taking on the form *triangularity* "too much suggests" the absurdity that the thinking is *itself* a triangle.[677]

The trouble with this objection is that it simply ignores, without answering, the details of the Aristotelian hylemorphist analysis of physical objects (which I defended in chapter 5). For on that analysis, it is only form and matter together that make up a physical object.

---

[674] BonJour, *In Defense of Pure Reason*, p. 183.
[675] John Haldane, "Realism with a Metaphysical Skull" and Hilary Putnam, "Comment on John Haldane's Paper," in James Conant and Urszula M. Zeglen, eds., *Hilary Putnam: Pragmatism and Realism* (London: Routledge, 2002).

[676] Putnam, "Comment on John Haldane's Paper," p. 106. Again, see Bealer, *Quality and Concept*, pp. 187-90 for a similar view.

[677] Ibid., p. 107.

Hence the form of a triangle – that is to say, the form of *being a closed plane figure with three straight sides* – is not itself a triangle or any other physical object. It is only matter together with this form which constitutes a triangle. But in that case, to say that thinking of a triangle involves the mind's taking on the form of a triangle does not at all "suggest" ("too much" or otherwise) that the thinking *itself* amounts to a triangle. It would suggest that only if it were claimed that the *matter* of a triangle, as well as the form, is taken on by the mind. But that is precisely what the Aristotelian denies. Hence a thought about a triangle no more counts even *prima facie* as a triangle than the form of a triangle all by itself, and without matter, could count as a triangle.

Putnam's second objection is that there is with at least some things no one pattern that could plausibly count as *the* form or essence of the thing.[678] He gives the example of a dog, and says that for a molecular biologist, the DNA of a dog would count as what is essential; for a population biologist, being part of a certain reproductive population would be what is essential; for a pet lover a wild dog might not count as a true dog, while it might count as a dog from the point of view of a scientist; dingos might count as dogs from an Australian aboriginal point of view, but as members of a different species from an American point of view; and so forth.

The problem with this is that Putnam here runs together features of very different types, which Aristotelian-Scholastic philosophers would carefully distinguish before trying to determine the essence of a thing. As we saw in chapter 5, we need to distinguish between a thing's essence and the "proper accidents" or properties that flow from its essence; between these proper accidents and merely contingent accidents; between substantial form and accidental form; and so on. Putnam conflates the very different phenomena captured by these distinctions and lumps them together as equally plausible candidates for *the* form or essence of a thing. But an Aristotelian looking for the essence of dogs would say, first of all, that cultural associations and linguistic practices of the sorts some of Putnam's examples involve are not relevant to determining the essence of any natural substance like a dog. For these mix together aspects of a thing deriving from its substantial form and those involving merely accidental

---

[678] Ibid., pp. 107-8.

forms. Finding the essence is in part a matter of separating these out. The Aristotelian would also note that reproductive capacities follow from deeper physiological facts about an animal, so that an animal's status as a member of a reproductive population is less fundamental to *what it is* (that is to say, to its essence) than its DNA would be. But the Aristotelian would also caution against flatly *identifying* the essence of a thing with some "hidden structure" like DNA. And so on.

Furthermore, it is no good to cite a random example of a kind of thing (whether dogs or anything else), note some complications or controversies in determining its essence, and suppose that one has thereby identified a grave difficulty for Aristotelianism. This presupposes that the Aristotelian takes a thing's essence to be determinable fairly easily, on the basis of a cursory examination. Nothing could be further from the truth. Neither cursory inspection, nor even cursory inspection together with the conceptual distinctions I've referred to, will typically suffice to tell us the essence of a thing. Detailed investigation of a physiological, chemical, or other scientific kind is often required in order to discover its essence, to determine what are really only proper accidents rather than part of the essence, and so forth. No Aristotelian supposes these questions can be settled from the armchair. Nor does the overall Aristotelian account of physical objects and our cognition of them ride on how such an investigation turns out – as if the entire system stands or falls with what the facts about dogs turn out to be! The most that would ride on the results of such an investigation is how we *apply* this system of concepts to a particular case, not the soundness of the system itself.

Putnam's third objection is that the notion of form does no real explanatory work. For the claim that the form of *being a triangle* is what makes some particular triangle a triangle "sounds either tautological or nonsensical."[679] But the answer to this objection should be clear from what has already been said. The form of *being a triangle* (or, as I put it above, *being a closed plane figure with three straight sides*) does not suffice to make something a triangle, because both *triangles* and *thoughts about* triangles have that form, and the latter are not triangles. Being a triangle requires having both the form in question *and*

---

[679] Ibid., p. 108.

matter. Hence the claim that *the form of being a triangle is what makes some particular triangle a triangle* is not tautological or trivially true. It could be tautological or trivially true only if the presence of the form of *being a triangle* sufficed all by itself for the presence of a triangle, and it does not. It might also sound tautological if the phrase "being a triangle" was claimed to capture the entirety of what it is to be a triangle, but of course that is not the case either.

The claim Putnam says "sounds either tautological or nonsensical" is really shorthand for something like "The form of *being a closed plane figure with three straight sides*, when combined with matter, is what results in a triangle (as opposed to a circle, a square, a dog, etc.)." And when put that way, it is clearly not a tautological claim. (Especially not when we go on to explicate form and matter in terms of the theory of actuality and potentiality, etc. For this hylemorphic analysis, far from being trivially true, is one that critics of Aristotelianism claim to be *false*, and a claim can't be both false and trivially true.) Nor is the claim in question nonsensical. It is clear what it *means*, whether or not one goes on to *agree* with it.

Though also not entirely unsympathetic to the Aristotelian-Scholastic position, Tallis criticizes the notion of formal identity of thought and object on the following grounds:

> Unfortunately, while this may help to identify what it is about mental contents that makes them be about the world, it does not address the question of why or how there are such truthful mental contents, such that thought can be "adequate" to things. What is more, precisely what is meant by "a common form" between thought and its objects remains obscure. We do not have a clear idea of what the form of a thought is – other than the thought itself – or what aspect of its object it captures – other than that specified in the thought.[680]

The problem with the first of these objections is that appears to criticize the Aristotelian position for failing to answer a question it is not addressing in the first place. What it is addressing is the question of *what it is to think*, not the question of *how thinking things came to be*

---

[680] Tallis, *Logos*, p. 69.

(which is presumably what Tallis means by "why or how there are" true thoughts). The correctness of an answer to the first question does not ride on whether it can answer the second.

The problem with Tallis's second objection is that it misses the point. He says that "we do not have a clear idea of... what aspect of its object [a thought's form] captures – other than that specified in the thought." But the whole point of the idea of formal identity of thought and object is that it just the form of the object, *considered apart from its matter or any other "aspect,"* that the thought captures. It will seem "obscure" what more the form of the thought captures only if one wrongly supposes that it is *claimed* to capture more. Tallis also says that "we do not have a clear idea of what the form of a thought is – other than the thought itself." This seems to presuppose that there is more to the thought than its content-conferring form. But as I have argued, thoughts are formal signs rather than instrumental signs. With instrumental signs we can distinguish between their content and that which bears the content, but we cannot do that with formal signs. They *just are* their content and nothing more. It will seem "obscure" what more there is to the content-conferring form of a thought other than the thought itself only if we wrongly suppose there *is* more.

Having said that, it cannot be denied that there is nevertheless *some* obscurity to the nature of thought as the Aristotelian-Scholastic account understands it. But it would beg the question against that account simply to assume that this is a reason to reject it. For the Aristotelian-Scholastic tradition denies that all aspects of reality are, or should be expected to be, transparent to us. Indeed, other philosophical traditions deny this too, even if not for exactly the same reasons. Kantianism denies that we can know things as they are in themselves; constructive empiricism holds that what we can reasonably believe about a scientific theory is at most only that it is empirically adequate, but not that it is true; Noam Chomsky distinguishes between the *problems* that minds of our kind are capable of solving and the *mysteries* that they cannot solve; and so on. In the case of the intellect, the Aristotelian-Scholastic tradition holds that given its immateriality, our conception of it must be largely negative. We can say more about what it *is not* than what it *is*. That this result is intellectually unsatisfying simply does nothing to show it is incorrect. We cannot expect reality to conform to our ambitions.

Let's take stock. I have, in the previous chapter, made a positive case for the Aristotelian-Scholastic account of cognition, and as we have seen in this section, even some mainstream contemporary philosophers without an Aristotelian ax to grind think that something at least in the ballpark of that account must be correct. I have just argued that none of their remaining reservations about the account are well-founded. And again, I have also argued that none of the rivals to the Aristotelian-Scholastic account can succeed. Now, it would be naïve to hope that all of this will in practice suffice to melt most resistance to it. Modern philosophers, when they have any awareness of the Aristotelian-Scholastic position at all, are used to thinking of it as a relic of premodern philosophy rather than a live option. But I have, I think, said enough to indicate that this is more a reflection of entrenched prejudice than serious engagement with the view.

In any event, the Aristotelian-Scholastic account of intellectual cognition affords one further argument for the immateriality of the intellect, one the basic thrust of which goes back to Aristotle's *On the Soul* and was reiterated by Aquinas and other later Aristotelians.[681] The argument is this. When the intellect understands a thing, it takes on the same form as the thing itself. For example, when it understands triangles, it takes on the form of *being a closed plane figure with three straight sides*. Now, for a material thing to take on a form is for it to become a thing of the kind that the form defines. For example, when the ink you smear across a marker board takes on the form of a triangle (given the direction in which you are moving the pen), it *becomes* a triangle. But when the intellect takes on a form, it does *not* become a thing of the kind the form defines – it does not, for instance, become a triangle when it takes on the form of a triangle, as it does when it

---

[681] Aristotle, *De Anima*, Book III, Chapters 4 and 8; Thomas Aquinas, *Summa Theologiae*, Part I, Question 75, Article 2. As Aristotle notes, in fact the basic idea goes back even earlier than him, to the Pre-Socratic philosopher Anaxagoras. My own understanding of the argument has been greatly influenced by Herbert McCabe, "The Immortality of the Soul: The Traditional Argument," in Anthony Kenny, ed., *Aquinas: A Collection of Critical Essays* (Garden City, NY: Doubleday, 1969).

understands triangles. It follows that the intellect is not a material thing. It could not carry out its characteristic activity if it were.

A critic might ask how conceiving of the intellect as "immaterial stuff" taking on the form of a triangle is any less problematic than conceiving of it as a material thing taking on that form. For wouldn't this too amount to the intellect's becoming a triangle, albeit not a physical triangle? But it cannot be emphasized too strongly that such an objection would completely miss the point of the argument. The Aristotelian is not positing a kind of ghostly "stuff" in which forms are instantiated. The whole point is that intellection involves taking on a form in a manner that does not involve *instantiation* of any kind, either in a bit of matter or in a bit of non-matter. And the reason is that the Aristotelian agrees with the critic that to conceive of thought in this way would indeed just raise the same problem over again. I have emphasized throughout this chapter that a thought is to be understood as a *formal sign*, a representation that is *nothing more than* a representation, rather than a representation that has some nature over and above its representational content. For if it did have such a further nature, it would be precisely what thoughts are not. It would be a mere *instantiation*, within that further nature (whether we think of that further nature as material or immaterial), of the form of a thing – rather than being a grasp of the form *itself*, of that that which is distinct from and common to all instantiations.

The critic will no doubt reply that this makes thought mysterious, but that is no objection to the argument. Thought *is* mysterious. As we have seen, the Aristotelian-Scholastic tradition argues that we simply cannot make sense of the character of thought unless we regard it as involving a *formal* identity with its objects but without *material* identity. If it turns out to be very difficult to say more of a positive nature about it (as opposed to saying what it is *not* like), that is a reflection of the fact that intellects like ours are, as I have argued, deeply dependent on the body and the senses for their input. The primary objects of the human intellect's knowledge are precisely composites of form and matter. Hence when it turns to contemplate that which is *im*material, it finds itself flatfooted and unable to move much beyond negative characterizations of it. But to criticize the Aristotelian analysis for this result is to blame the messenger, and certainly to beg the question against the message. Only if the materialist can provide an alternative analysis that both does justice to the character of thought while reducing the mystery will noting the mysteriousness of the Aristotelian analysis have any force. It cannot *by itself* cut any ice.

But the materialist will no doubt reply that such an alternative analysis has indeed been made available by modern neuroscience and by Artificial Intelligence and the computer model of the mind more generally. It is to dispelling this illusion – and an illusion is all that it is – that we turn in the next chapter.

9. Neither Computers nor Brains

Thinking versus computing

The arguments of the previous chapter are *logically* sufficient to establish the immateriality of the intellect. But there is a further, *rhetorical* barrier to be overcome before the case against materialism is completed. For there are two sets of considerations which, in the contemporary intellectual culture, are widely assumed to render enormous plausibility to materialism, or even to establish its truth. And this assumption has spread into the larger popular culture. The first set of considerations concerns modern computer science and Artificial Intelligence research, and the second concerns modern neuroscience. The latter is assumed to have established that thinking is just neural activity, and the former that it amounts, specifically, to the running of a kind of software on the hardware of the brain. Hence, no matter how powerful a philosophical argument one gives for the immateriality of the intellect, these purported scientific results will be taken by many readers to indicate that there must be *something* wrong with it.

But the idea that science has established either of these things is an illusion, albeit a pervasive one. Dispelling that illusion will remove the main obstacle many readers might have to seeing the force of the preceding chapter's arguments. Intellects are not computers, and they are not brains either (even if the intellect relies on brain activity for input in the manner discussed in the previous chapter). This chapter is devoted to explaining why.

It is important to emphasize at the outset that I am addressing here only the nature of the *intellect*, specifically. As we've seen in previous chapters, there are other aspects of the mind, which we share with non-human animals – sensory experience, mental imagery, the passions, and so on. I am not going to be arguing that *those* mental phenomena cannot be accounted for in neuroscientific or computational terms (though some of the criticisms I will be raising against the idea that the intellect is a kind of computer will, as it happens, imply similar criticisms of computational models of other mental phenomena). Rather, I will be arguing only that the capacities identified in chapter 3 as distinctive of the intellect – grasping concepts, putting concepts together into propositions, and reasoning logically from one proposition to another – cannot be accounted for in those terms. We'll begin with a critique of computational models of thought, and then turn later in the chapter to the neuroscientific considerations.

Now, it so happens that properly to understand what a computer *is* in the first place ought to enable one to see why it really makes no sense to suppose that the intellect might be a kind of computer. To start with a definition borrowed from Tim Crane, "a computer is a machine that processes representations systematically according to rules."[682] But exactly what this means needs spelling out. The rules in question are algorithmic, and to understand the general idea of an algorithm, it will be useful to begin with an example also borrowed from Crane.[683] Consider the following procedure for finding the answer to any multiplication problem. We take two pieces of paper and mark them X and Y, respectively, for the two numbers being multiplied. We also take a third piece of paper and label it ANSWER, for the product of the two numbers. We write whichever two numbers we want to multiply on the X and Y pages, and then follow these steps:

Step (i): Write 0 on the ANSWER page, then go to step (ii)

Step (ii): Does the number written on X = 0? If YES, then go to step (v); if NO, then go to step (iii)

Step (iii): Subtract 1 from the number written on the X page, then go to step (iv)

---

[682] Tim Crane, *The Mechanical Mind: A Philosophical Introduction to Minds, Machines, and Mental Representation*, Third edition (London: Routledge, 2016), p. 75.

[683] Ibid., pp. 61-63.

Step (iv): Add the number written on the Y page to the ANSWER page, then go to step (ii)

Step (v): STOP

If, for example, you write "3" and "2" on the X and Y pages, respectively, and carry out the procedure, you'll find that "6" is what is left on the ANSWER page when you finish. And of course, 3 multiplied by 2 is indeed 6. The procedure is tedious, and only gets more so the larger the numbers you start with on the X and Y pages. But the algorithm will always give you the correct answer for any numbers you want to multiply.

Now, among the features of algorithms that this example illustrates is that they are *effective procedures* in the technical sense that they guarantee a correct outcome simply by following a finite number of explicitly articulated rules, with no insight or special knowledge required beyond the rules themselves. For this reason it is often said that an algorithm is a procedure that can be followed "mechanically." In our example, one needn't have much in the way of mathematical ability to find the right answer to any multiplication problem, no matter how large the numbers being multiplied. One need only be capable of basic adding and subtracting, and have the patience and stamina to keep applying the procedure through to the end.

But that brings us to a feature of the example that is especially important for our purposes. As what I just said indicates, our sample algorithm allows someone to generate the correct answer to any multiplication problem *even if he does not know how to multiply*, and indeed *even if he does not understand what multiplication is*. Following the algorithm will nevertheless guarantee that he behaves *as if* he understands. And notice that that is *all* it guarantees. That someone follows the algorithm does not suffice to show that he knows how to multiply, and could not in principle do so, precisely because it is written in such a way that no understanding of multiplication is necessary.

Now, algorithms can have sub-algorithms as component parts. For example, to follow our sample algorithm requires adding and subtracting, and these involve following further algorithms (such as the addition and subtraction algorithms learned in grade school). Suppose we write algorithms for finding the answers to addition and subtraction problems that don't require actually knowing how to add or subtract at all (just as our algorithm for finding the answers to multiplication problems doesn't require knowing how to multiply). Then someone who followed these algorithms together with our multiplication algorithm would behave *as if* he knew not only how to multiply but also how to add and subtract even if he lacked the latter arithmetical skills as well, and indeed even if he did not so much as understand what addition and subtraction (let alone multiplication) are.

So far we have been talking about human beings following algorithms, but a computer is, again, a *machine* that does so. The classic model for such a device is the *Turing machine*, named for mathematician Alan Turing (1912-1954), who discovered the idea.[684] The specific physical mechanisms Turing described are not essential. It is the abstract properties they illustrate that matter. Still, those mechanisms greatly facilitate exposition, so I'll follow custom by describing them. Consider a machine which consists, first of all, of a long tape divided into squares. The machine moves the tape either left or right, one square at a time. It is also able to read what is on a given square or to write on a square, where what can be read or written on any square is one of two symbols, either a 0 or a 1. The machine is also able to change its "internal state." At the basic physical level, the machine does nothing more than move the tape back and forth, read and write symbols on the tape, and change its internal state. The specific series of operations a particular Turing machine carries out is described in what is called its "machine table" or program. This specifies everything the machine will do given whatever internal state it is in together with a certain input, i.e. whether it is reading a 0 or 1 on the tape. For example, the machine table might state: *If the machine is in state A and reads a 0, then it will change to state B and move the tape one square to the right; if the machine is in state A and reads a 1, then it will stay in state A and move the tape one square to the left; etc.* The "internal states" of the machine are entirely defined by such a machine table. That is to say, there is nothing more to such a state that what the table says about them. For instance, in the example just given, to say that the machine is in state A just means nothing more than that if it reads a 0, then it will change to state B and move the tape one square to the

---

[684] Crane's *The Mechanical Mind* provides a lucid brief exposition of the idea of a Turing machine, at pp. 64-75.

right; if it reads a 1, then it will stay in state A and move the tape one square to the left; and so on.

Now, we can assign various possible *interpretations* to the symbols on the tape. For example, we can interpret different sequences of 0s and 1s as different numbers. And we can write a machine table that describes a sequence of operations that can be interpreted as *adding* numbers. In particular, it can be interpreted as the following of an algorithm for addition. In that case, the Turing machine will produce outputs (such as moving the tape and writing symbols) that can be interpreted in such a way that it is *as if* it were adding, just as a human being who knew no addition but followed the right algorithm would behave as if he could add. We could also write machine tables that describe sequences of operations that can be interpreted as subtracting, multiplying, etc., and in that case we would have a Turing machine that produced outputs that could be interpreted in such a way that it is *as if* it had general arithmetical competence (just as a human being following the right algorithms would behave *as if* he knew arithmetic even if he knew no arithmetic at all).

It turns out that, just as we can code numbers into sequences of 0s and 1s, even a machine table itself can be coded as a sequence of 0s and 1s. But a given machine table is a complete description of the operations of a certain kind of Turing machine. For example, the machine table for the Turing machine we imagined behaving as if it had general arithmetical competence describes a simple calculator. Another machine table could be written that describes operations that can be interpreted as moves in a game of chess. Indeed, any algorithm can be represented in a machine table for some Turing machine. And these can all be encoded as sequences of 0s and 1s. In that case, though, a sufficiently complex Turing machine could encode any of these sequences, and thus encode any other Turing machine. Such a machine is known as a *universal Turing machine*. For anything that could be done by some Turing machine or other, a universal Turing machine can do it.

The notion of the universal Turing machine is the foundation of the modern digital computer. Of course, the computers we are familiar with in everyday modern life are not made up of tapes divided into squares with 0s and 1s written on them, etc. But as I said earlier, the particular physical mechanisms Turing described are not what matter. What matter are the more abstract properties embodied in the machine he described, which can be embodied instead in machines of very different physical designs. What is essential is that there be *something* in the machine that is interpretable as the sequences of 0s and 1s that encode the representations processed by a Turing machine. That *could* be marks written on tape as in Turing's model, but it could instead be something else. For example, it could be a series of switches or a series of valves, or electrical currents in the circuity of an electronic computer.[685]

Following Crane, we defined a computer as a machine that processes representations systematically according to rules. And now we can see more clearly what that means. For a machine to process representations is for it to do the kind of thing a Turing machine does when it takes sequences of 0s and 1s as input and gives sequences of 0s and 1s as output, where these sequences can be assigned an interpretation as arithmetical questions and answers, moves in a chess game, or whatever. For the machine to do this processing systematically according to rules is for the processing to be interpretable as the following of an algorithm (insofar as the 0s and 1s processed by the machine can be interpreted as encoding not only the inputs and outputs, but also the algorithmic rules that mediate between them).

The difference between a human being who follows an algorithm such as our sample multiplication algorithm, and a computer which follows it, is this. The human being need not understand how to multiply or even what multiplication is, but he does understand the rules of the algorithm. The computer, by contrast, not only need not understand multiplication, but need not understand the algorithm either. How can it follow the algorithm, then? The answer, of course, is that human designers and programmers, who *do* understand the algorithm, have constructed the machine in such a way that its operations parallel in crucial respects those a human being would carry out when following the algorithm. The human being behaves *as if* he understands multiplication, but *really does* understand the algorithm. The

---

[685] For a lucid discussion of the way computers can be built out of a variety of physical mechanisms, see W. Daniel Hillis, *The Pattern on the Stone: The Simple Ideas That Make Computers Work* (New York: Basic Books, 1998), especially chapter 1.

computer behaves only *as if* it understands multiplication and also only *as if* it understands the algorithm.

Human beings and computers do not follow algorithms in the same sense, then. There is an *analogy* between what a human being does and what a computer does, but they are still crucially different. Suppose you are in a restaurant and the waiter says to you: "Restrooms are next to the entrance." And suppose that as you walk through the restaurant you see a sign on the wall reading: "RESTROOMS ARE NEXT TO THE ENTRANCE." There is a sense in which the waiter and the sign each told you the same thing, but of course, they did so in very different ways. The waiter understood what he was telling you, but the sign did *not* understand what it was telling you, and indeed does not understand anything at all. Moreover, it is only because there are human beings around who do understand, and who construct such signs to convey messages of that kind, that the sign exists in the first place. Computers are exactly like that. Like the sign on the wall, they do not understand the algorithms they follow, or indeed anything at all. Like the sign, they exist at all and do the things they do only because there are human beings around who do understand, and who construct computers in such a way that they can mimic what human beings do when they follow algorithms.

We are now in a position to see why it simply makes no sense to suggest that the intellect might be a kind of computer. For the way a computer works is to generate outputs that are similar to those an intellect would produce but *precisely in a way that requires no intellect actually to be present*. As one important critique of the notion of machine intelligence puts it, "in mechanizing, one has not endowed... [a] device with intelligence, *one has substituted for intelligence altogether*."[686] Hence a computer qua computer can in the nature of the case only ever *mimic* or *simulate* an intellect, and never actually amount to one. When a human being follows an algorithm like our sample multiplication algorithm, the role of the intellect is *reduced* insofar as actual understanding of multiplication is rendered unnecessary. Only understanding of the algorithm is required. But when a computer follows

---

[686] Graham Button, Jeff Coulter, John R. E. Lee, and Wes Sharrock, *Computers, Minds, and Conduct* (Cambridge: Polity Press, 1995), p. 138.

such an algorithm, the role of the intellect is *eliminated altogether* insofar as even understanding of the algorithm is no longer necessary. More precisely, the intellect is absent from the operations of the machine itself, though it is of course present in the designers and users of the machine. But precisely for that reason, it is only something *outside* the computer that can be said to possess intellect (again, the designers and users) and not the computer itself. In short, computer algorithms of their nature *subtract* intellect from the picture, so that it is incoherent to suppose that to put such an algorithm into a machine would be to *add* intellect to it, or that the human intellect might itself be a kind of computer algorithm.

Some readers are bound to object at this point that the argument is purely semantic, an appeal to how we use words like "intelligence" and "machines," and one that can be rebutted by simply adopting different definitions. But there are two problems with this objection. First, the argument is *not* semantic. I am not appealing to what the words "intelligence" and "machines" *mean* but rather to what intelligence and machines themselves *are.* When I point out that the waiter in my example possesses intelligence and the sign on the restaurant wall does not, that is, of course, not a semantic claim. The sign conveys an intelligible message not because it is itself intelligent, but because something else that is intelligent (a human being) put the message on it. That is just an obvious fact about the nature of signs (rather than about the word "sign"), with which no one would think to quibble. But exactly the same thing is true of machines. They exhibit behavior that conforms to the rules of an algorithm not because they are themselves intelligent, but because something else that is intelligent (human beings) constructed them so that they would do so.

A second problem with the objection is that even if my argument were semantic, for the defender of the view that machines can think to propose alternative definitions would be self-defeating. Claims that the intellect is a kind of computer, that a sufficiently complex "artificial intelligence" would literally be intelligent, etc. crucially presuppose that words like "intellect" and "intelligence" do indeed have the same meanings when applied to machines as when applied to us. The claims would not be very interesting or controversial otherwise. To try to salvage these claims by proposing an alternative definition of "intelligence" would thus defeat the whole purpose.[687] One might as well say that while the sign on the restaurant wall is not intelligent in the same sense the waiter is, it might be said to be "intelligent" in some different and novel sense the word. Needless to say, that would not be a very interesting claim. But neither would it be interesting to hold that while machines are not intelligent in the same sense human beings are, they might be said to be "intelligent" in some different and novel sense of the word. It would in this case be the *defender* of the claim that computers can think, and not the critic, who would be putting forward a merely semantic rather than substantive thesis.

A second objection that might occur to some readers is that the argument I've been giving doesn't *prove* that a machine can't think. But such an objection would miss the point. One might as well say that my remarks about the waiter and the sign on the restaurant wall don't *prove* that the sign can't think. Suppose we concede for the sake of argument that the sign *might* in theory be thinking, absurd as this would be. That would not undermine the point I was making, which is that the fact that the sign conveys the message "RESTROOMS ARE NEXT TO THE ENTRANCE" does not provide any evidence whatsoever that the sign can think, for the simple reason that we know that that message did not come from the sign itself, but from the human beings who made the sign. Hence, if one wanted to show that the sign was thinking, one would need to appeal to something *other than* the message it conveys. Similarly, even if we conceded for the sake of argument that a machine might think, that would not undermine my argument. For the point is that the fact that the machine's behavior conforms to an algorithm (for arithmetic, chess, or whatever) does not provide any evidence whatsoever that it is thinking, for the simple reason that we know that it does so not because of anything the machine by itself is capable of, but rather because of the way its human makers have designed it. Hence, if one wanted to show that the machine was thinking, one would need to appeal to something *other than* the fact that its behavior conforms to an algorithm.

Another analogy might help. Good illusionists (such as Penn and Teller, Ricky Jay, and David Blaine) can produce effects that *seem*

---

[687] Ibid., pp. 20-21.

to be magic. But of course, they are not magic, and we know this precisely because we know that they are designed merely to *simulate* the effects of magic. It would obviously be silly to try to argue that magic is real on the basis of what Penn and Teller and the others can do. Even if magic were real, what these illusionists accomplish cannot *itself* be evidence for it, because what they do is a mere simulation rather than the real McCoy. Similarly, even if machines could be intelligent, what modern computers do cannot *itself* be evidence for this, because what they do too is mere simulation. The difference, of course, is that intelligence is real and magic is not. But that reinforces the point that the simulation of a thing, no matter how convincing, cannot establish its reality.

A third objection that might be raised against the argument I've been giving is that it understates the similarities between computers and intellects. For example, like human beings, computers are said to possess *language* (which, I allowed in chapter 3, may be a concomitant of intellect in rational animals). However, as with arithmetical performance that results from the following of an algorithm, here too there is less than meets the eye. For one thing, as one critique of the idea that computers can think says of so-called "computer languages":

> Of course, these supposed 'languages' are not themselves languages. The translation of something into machine code is no more a translation between two languages than is the translation of a message into Morse code. One can indeed be said to translate a message into Morse but one has not, therefore, transformed a statement in English into a statement in Morse – the statement translated into Morse remains, of course, a statement in English. This is why it would be pointless to translate an English statement into Morse in the hope of communicating with someone who understood Morse code, but spoke – say – only Russian. The transformation into and out of Morse is not, in that sense, a *linguistic* operation, for Morse itself is no language, though in it can be conveyed all the things which can be said in languages. Just as Morse is a device for relaying messages through telegraph wires, so computer languages are devices for manipulating the inner states

of computers, using them, sometimes, to simulate linguistic and mathematical expressions and operations.[688]

For another thing, as this last quoted sentence indicates, "computer languages" or codes are, strictly speaking, not used by computers *themselves* at all, but by the human programmers and users of computers.[689]

Yet another objection might be that my argument presupposes Turing's model of computation, whereas there are other models. For example, there is *parallel distributed processing* (PDP) or *connectionism*, a model of computation that is much closer than Turing's is to the way the brain operates.[690] A connectionist machine is a network of interconnected units or nodes related to one another in a way that is analogous to the connections between neurons. There is an input layer of units, an output layer, and one or more intermediate or "hidden" layers. Activation of the input units generates a pattern of activation in the intermediate units which in turn generates a pattern of activation in the output units. But whether a given unit or units will excite or inhibit other units depends on the strengths of the connections between the units, and these strengths vary over time depending on the activation history of the network. One difference between the PDP or connectionist model on the one hand and Turing machines on the other is that the operations of the former run in parallel whereas the operations of the latter run serially. Another difference is that the representations processed by a Turing machine are localized, whereas a connectionist machine can feature distributed representations. For example, what might be represented by a particular sequence of 0s and 1s in a Turing machine might be represented by an activation pattern spread across the whole network in a connectionist machine.

---

[688] Ibid., p. 101.

[689] Ibid., pp. 100-101.
[690] For a basic exposition, see Crane, *The Mechanical Mind*, pp. 105-10. For a philosophically illuminating comparison of the Turing machine model of computation and the connectionist model, see Hubert L. Dreyfus and Stuart E. Dreyfus, "Making a Mind Versus Modeling the Brain: Artificial Intelligence Back at a Branch-point," in Margaret A. Boden, ed., *The Philosophy of Artificial Intelligence* (Oxford: Oxford University Press, 1990).

Do such differences make a difference to the argument I've been defending? Not at all. Indeed, it is if anything even less plausible to suggest that a connectionist machine might have an intellect than to suggest that a Turing machine has one. The first and most fundamental point to make here is that with connectionist machines as with Turing machines, it is the programmers and users of the machine who assign an interpretation of its operations. The machine itself merely operates *as if* it is processing representations (distributed or otherwise) according to rules (those of a connectionist kind or otherwise), because of the way these human beings design and interpret it. So the differences between Turing machines and connectionist machines are irrelevant to the point I have been making. The problem with the idea that a computer mind be said to think lies in what the models have in common.

Another problem is that the advantages of connectionist machines over Turing machines lie in areas other than those relevant to modeling the operations of the intellect, specifically. Connectionist machines are good at tasks like pattern recognition, such as the identification of faces. In that way they can to some extent mimic what human beings and non-human animals do when they recognize something as a tree or a dog or what have you.[691] But connectionist machines are not as good as Turing machines at producing outputs that simulate what we referred to in chapter 3 as the compositionality, productivity, and systematicity of thought.[692] For these properties require representations having a combinatorial structure, which localized representations possess but distributed ones do not. Hence connectionist machines are even less promising than Turing machines as models of distinctively intellectual operations. (We'll come back to this issue when considering "machine learning," an approach to artificial intelligence descended from connectionism that has moved to the center of discussions of AI in recent years.)

---

[691] Even here the performance depends crucially on parameters set by the designers of the machine. Cf. Button et al., *Computers, Minds, and Conduct*, pp. 115-17.

[692] Cf. Jerry A. Fodor and Zenon W. Pylyshyn, "Connectionism and Cognitive Architecture," in Alvin I. Goldman, ed., *Readings in Philosophy and Cognitive Science* (Cambridge, MA: The MIT Press, 1993).

A fifth objection might be to suggest that there is nothing more to intelligence than exhibiting the kind of behavior we do when we engage in intelligent conversation, so that if an algorithm allowed a machine to do that, we'd have to judge it to be intelligent. This, of course, is the famous Turing Test criterion of intelligence, also developed by and named for Turing.[693] But the Turing Test is hopeless as a criterion for intelligence. To see what is wrong with it, imagine someone suggested that if a clever illusionist could produce an effect so impressive that no one was able to tell it apart from magic, then it would *be* actual magic. Obviously, it would *not* be magic, not only because there is no such thing, but because the way illusionists work is precisely to find ways to *simulate* magic without actually having to do it. In the same way, writing an algorithm for solving arithmetic problems, playing chess, or engaging in conversation is precisely a way to *simulate* intelligent behavior without actually having to produce it. The trouble with the Turing Test is that, far from giving us a way to tell real intelligence apart from mere simulation, it completely ignores the distinction between them. It arbitrarily rules out precisely the evidence that would show that we are dealing with mimicry rather than real intelligence (namely, evidence that the behavior was produced by an algorithm). It is like a purported test for distinguishing pyrite from real gold that is sensitive only to what the two metals have in common. Or it is like a would-be criterion for detecting a con man that allows us to consider only evidence of the kind a con man could falsify.[694]

Let us reiterate the key points. When a human being follows an algorithm like our sample multiplication algorithm, that is precisely a way of *substituting for* a certain kind of intelligent behavior rather than actually producing it. It is a way of behaving *as if* one knew

---

[693] Alan M. Turing, "Computing Machinery and Intelligence," in Boden, ed., *The Philosophy of Artificial Intelligence*. Turing himself doesn't flatly assert in this paper that machines can think or that human-like conversational performance strictly entails intelligence, though he certainly gives the impression that that is what he believes. His various statements on the subject over the years are not entirely consistent. In some places he explicitly declines to offer any definition of thinking, while at other times he speaks as if studying what machines do can help us to discover what thinking is. Cf. B. Jack Copeland, *Turing: Pioneer of the Information Age* (Oxford: Oxford University Press, 2012), p. 209.

[694] Button, et al., *Computers, Minds, and Conduct*, p. 144.

how to multiply, rather than a way of actually knowing how to do it. All the same, a human does at least understand the algorithm itself. But a machine that follows such an algorithm does not understand even that much. It not only merely behaves *as if* it understood how to multiply, but also merely behaves *as if* it were following an algorithm in the sense in which we follow algorithms. The machine's behavior is thus *doubly* removed from actual intelligence. Hence it is quite absurd to suggest that doing what a computer does might suffice to generate the operations of an intellect. That is one thing we can be quite certain is not happening.

It is important to emphasize that the points I have been making having nothing to do with the *immateriality* of the intellect. That is a separate issue. The point is rather that, whether the intellect is material or immaterial, a machine's running an algorithm cannot suffice to give it an intellect. One could agree with this judgment even if one is nevertheless convinced that the intellect is material (and some philosophers who take the intellect to be material *do* agree with it).

Other arguments against machine intelligence

In contemporary philosophy, several other arguments against the thesis that computers can think have been put forward, and some of them have gotten a great deal of attention. In my view, these arguments are sound and important, though less fundamental than the points we have been considering so far. But they illuminate and reinforce those points, so let us have a look at them.

Searle's arguments

Perhaps the most famous critique of the idea that computers can think is the one developed by John Searle. Searle's position consists of two main lines of argument. The first and better known is his famous Chinese Room argument. The second, less well-known but no less important, is his argument against what he calls "cognitivism." Let's consider each in turn.

The Chinese Room argument begins with the following scenario.[695] Imagine that Searle, who does not know any Chinese, is put in a room with a collection of Chinese symbols and a set of instructions written in English explaining how to combine the symbols into response to questions in Chinese slipped into the room to him. To Searle, the questions and the collection of symbols look like meaningless squiggles. But the instructions tell him that when he sees such-and-such a sequence of squiggles in the question put to him, he should give out a certain other sequence of squiggles in response. We can imagine further that Searle gets good enough at producing answers in accordance with the instructions that those outside the room who are sending him questions suppose that he is a native speaker of Chinese. But in fact he has no idea what he is saying.

In this scenario, Searle, like a computer, is following an algorithm for processing symbols. And in virtue of doing so, he passes the Turing Test for understanding of Chinese. But he does not in fact understand Chinese at all. He merely behaves *as if* he did. What this shows, then, is that running a computer program or algorithm is not sufficient for having genuine understanding. There is more to intelligence than that. Searle has summed up the basic thrust of the argument in the following four steps:

1. Programs are entirely syntactical.

2. Minds have a semantics.

3. Syntax is not the same as, nor by itself sufficient for, semantics.

4. Therefore, programs are not minds.[696]

To say that programs are syntactical is to say that they consist of rules for manipulating symbols according to their formal features rather than their semantic content. A Turing machine will read and write 0s and 1s the same way whatever interpretation the machine's

---

[695] John R. Searle, "Minds, Brains, and Programs," in Boden, ed., *The Philosophy of Artificial Intelligence*.
[696] John R. Searle, *The Mystery of Consciousness* (New York: New York Review of Books, 1997), pp. 11-12.

programmer gives them, or indeed whether any interpretation is assigned at all. Similarly, Searle, by following the instructions provided him in the Chinese Room, will manipulate the Chinese symbols the same way as someone who understood their meaning would, even though he does not himself know it. To say that minds have a semantics is to say that intelligence *does* involve a grasp of the meanings or contents of symbols, and not just their formal properties. Truly to understand a language, for example, is more than just knowing how to parrot the right sequence of words. It requires knowing what the words mean. What the Chinese Room scenario illustrates, says Searle, is the truth of his third premise, that syntax is not the same as and does not suffice for semantics. For in the thought experiment, Searle has mastered the syntax of the Chinese symbols perfectly, but nevertheless remains entirely ignorant of the semantics or meaning of the symbols. Hence, again, following the syntactical rules of a program simply does not amount to having a mind or intelligence.

This argument has been extremely controversial and generated an enormous literature.[697] Many objections have been raised, but variations on two of them in particular are especially influential and important, and were addressed by Searle in his original article on the argument. The first of these is known as the *systems reply*. Searle, it is acknowledged, does not understand Chinese. But he is only part of a larger system, which includes the Chinese symbols, the instructions, and indeed the room as a whole. For all Searle has shown, the reply claims, maybe this whole system understands Chinese by virtue of his following the algorithm, even though he himself does not. In response to this, Searle notes that the room is not actually essential to the argument. We can imagine instead that he memorizes the symbols and the rulebook and carries on answering questions in Chinese put to him by consulting his memory of what the symbols look like and how the instructions tell him to respond. In this revised scenario, Searle himself is the entire system, but still does not understand Chinese. Hence the lesson of the original thought experiment is upheld.

---

[697] For a useful survey of the debate, see Josef Moural, "The Chinese Room Argument," in Barry Smith, ed., *John Searle* (Cambridge: Cambridge University Press, 2003). For an anthology on the argument, see John Preston and Mark Bishop, eds., *Views into the Chinese Room: New Essays on Searle and Artificial Intelligence* (Oxford: Clarendon Press, 2002).

Some attempt to get around Searle's response by suggesting that there is a third scenario distinct from Searle's understanding Chinese and the room as a whole understanding it. The proposal is that Searle's mind is merely one mind in the overall situation, which thinks in English and does not know any Chinese. But for all Searle has shown, when he follows the algorithm for answering questions in Chinese, this yields a *second* mind, which *does* understand Chinese. Even when Searle memorizes the symbols and instructions, he is not aware of the thoughts of this second mind but only of his own. But that does not entail that there is no such second mind, and if there is, then the following of an algorithm would after all generate understanding of Chinese.[698]

But like the Turing Test, this proposal simply ignores the distinction between simulation and reality. To insist that the following of an algorithm *must* generate understanding of Chinese *somewhere* (even if not in Searle's own mind) is like insisting that the sleight of hand of a skilled illusionist simply *must* generate real magic *somewhere* (even if not on the stage on which the illusionist is performing). In reality, that an illusionist is capable of skilled sleight of hand strictly entails only that he can simulate magic, not that he can actually produce it. Hence, if someone wanted to claim that he was capable of real magic, he'd have to appeal to more than just his capacity for sleight of hand. And in the same way, that something runs an algorithm for giving answers in Chinese strictly entails only that it can simulate understanding of Chinese, not that it really has such understanding. Hence, if someone wants to claim that *something* in the scenario (even if not Searle himself) does have genuine understanding, he'll have to appeal to more than just the following of the algorithm. Again, it is only if we collapse the distinction between reality and simulation that it can appear plausible that Searle's following of the algorithm *must* yield genuine understanding *somewhere*.

The second of the main replies to the Chinese Room argument is the *robot reply*. Here we are asked to imagine that the algorithm for giving answers in Chinese is being run by a computer situated in the

---

[698] Variations on this idea can be found in David Chalmers, *The Conscious Mind* (Oxford: Oxford University Press, 1996), p. 326; and Ned Block, "Searle's Arguments against Cognitive Science," in Preston and Bishop, eds., *Views into the Chinese Room*, at pp. 73-74.

head of a robot, which can detect what is going on outside it via cameras, microphones, and the like, and can interact with the world via robotic limbs. It is claimed that this causal engagement with the world, which is very different from Searle's sitting in a room isolated from the world, would yield genuine understanding of Chinese.

Searle responds by asking us to imagine that he is controlling the robot from the Chinese Room. The Chinese symbols he processes now come in through the robot's perceptual apparatus rather than through the door to the room, and the answers he gives now go out through the robot's motor apparatus. But this in no relevant way changes the outcome of the original thought experiment. He still has no idea what the symbols he's processing mean, so that we still have the lesson that following the algorithm is not sufficient to yield genuine understanding. (We might add that the defender of the robot reply owes us some account of exactly *how* the causal relations to the world in question would yield meaning or semantic content in the symbols. The answer would have to be in terms of one of the naturalistic theories of meaning that we addressed in the previous chapter. But as we saw there, all such theories are hopeless.)

More could be said about the Chinese Room argument, but it is Searle's second, later argument that goes deeper to the heart of the problem with the idea that the intellect is a kind of computer. The Chinese Room argument essentially allows, for the sake of argument, that the brain might be said to be running algorithms, and simply holds that this is nevertheless insufficient for genuine intelligence. But Searle's second line of argument challenges the assumption that the brain is a kind of digital computer which can be said to run algorithms – a thesis he labels "cognitivism."[699] The basic criticism is very straightforward. Computation is a matter of manipulating symbols according to syntactical rules. Yet symbols and syntax are not *intrinsic* properties of the physical world, but merely *observer-relative* features of it. Something counts as a symbol or as following syntactical rules only insofar as we assign such an *interpretation* to it. But in that case, neither the brain nor anything else can be said to be *intrinsically* a digital computer. The brain, like anything else, is a computer only in the

---

[699] John R. Searle, *The Rediscovery of the Mind* (Cambridge, MA: The MIT Press, 1992), p. 202.

trivial sense that anything could be interpreted as carrying out computations if we wanted so to interpret it.[700]

The upshot of this argument is that it makes no sense to try to explain the human mind in terms of computation, because something counts as computation in the first place only relative to the human mind. Cognitivism puts the cart before the horse. The Chinese Room argument shows only that running an algorithm is not by itself *sufficient* for explaining intelligence, though it leaves it open whether running an algorithm might be part of the story. The argument against cognitivism goes deeper by pointing out that in fact something's running an algorithm actually *presupposes* intelligence. Hence appeal to algorithms and the like cannot be even part of the explanation of intelligence. The contemporary obsession with computers as a model for the human mind is a wild goose chase.

An objection sometimes raised against this second argument of Searle's is that computation cannot be entirely observer-relative, but presupposes something's having, as a matter of objective fact, the right sort of causal organization.[701] For example, for a physical system plausibly to count as implementing the computation "1 + 2 = 3," it is not sufficient that it has states corresponding to "1" and "+" and "2" and "=" that are followed by a state corresponding to "3." For what it does genuinely to count as addition, it must also be true that, had the input instead been states that correspond to "2" and "+" and "3" and "=," the output would have been a state corresponding to "5," and that yet other inputs would yield outputs of the kind we'd expect from something doing addition. The causal organization of any system which we could plausibly interpret as following an algorithm for addition would have to allow for all of these possible computations, and whether a particular physical system has such an organization is a matter of objective fact rather than being observer-relative.

But while this is true, it does not undermine Searle's point. Consider once again the example of the sign on the restaurant wall. In

---

[700] Ibid., p. 225.
[701] Cf. Block, "Searle's Arguments against Cognitive Science," pp. 76-78; and Chalmers, *The Conscious Mind*, pp. 219-20.

order for something to function as a sign of that sort, it has to have certain physical properties like solidity and durability. You can't make a sign that says "RESTROOMS ARE NEXT TO THE ENTRANCE" using cigarette smoke, or liquid water, or yogurt. You need something like wood or metal or plastic. And that is a matter of objective fact rather than being an observer-relative feature of the world. All the same, that the sign carries that message, specifically, *is* an observer-relative feature. Similarly, in order for a machine to be interpretable as processing representations in accordance with the rules of an algorithm, it too will have to have, as a matter of objective fact, certain physical features. All the same, that it counts, specifically, as processing such representations and following algorithms *is* an observer-relative feature. Searle is not saying, and need not say, that *all* the features of a computer are observer-relative, but only that those particular features of it are.

Elsewhere I have analyzed Searle's argument against cognitivism at greater length and defended it against other critics.[702] The point to emphasize for present purposes is that Searle's arguments illustrate and reinforce the point emphasized in the first section of this chapter, that there is simply nothing in what computers do that can justify attributing to them anything more than a simulation of what intellects do. Searle's critics sometimes allege that the Chinese Room argument amounts to an appeal to intuition, or a failure of imagina-

---

[702] Edward Feser, "From Aristotle to John Searle and Back Again: Formal Causes, Teleology, and Computation in Nature," *Nova et Vetera* 14 (2016): 459-94; and Edward Feser, *Aristotle's Revenge: The Metaphysical Foundations of Physical and Biological Science* (Neunkirchen-Seelscheid: Editiones Scholasticae, 2019), pp. 351-74. In these works, I argue that if we assume a naturalistic rather than Aristotelian conception of the natural world (as Searle and his critics alike do), then Searle's argument is unanswerable. I also argue that if instead we assume an Aristotelian conception of nature that recognizes formal and final causes, then natural objects and processes can be said objectively to have something *like* computational properties. However, this does not affect the arguments of the present chapter. For one thing, I do not claim that they would have properties like the ones posited by computer models of the mind. For example, there would still be nothing objectively in nature that corresponds to the 0s and 1s of a Turing machine. Those would remain observer-relative. My point is rather that there is an analogy between the relationship between software and hardware on the one hand and the relationship between formal and material causes on the other, and an analogy between following an algorithm and being directed toward an end or final cause. For another thing, intellectual powers would remain immaterial and thus irreducible to bodily powers even on an Aristotelian account of the latter.

tion with regard to what an algorithm might be capable of producing.[703] But this is like saying that the claim that what an illusionist does is not real magic rests on intuition, or that it is only a failure of imagination that could lead someone to think that the sign on the restaurant wall would not be intelligent. Of course, neither intuition nor a failure of imagination has anything to do with those claims. We know how illusions are achieved and we know how signs get their meaning, and it is on the basis of this knowledge (rather than some exercise in intuition or imagination) that we judge that there is no real magic in the one case or intelligence in the other. By the same token, we know how things come to be symbols and how there come to be algorithms for manipulating symbols. Human beings create these things for the purpose of simulating intelligent activity. And on the basis of that knowledge we can judge that there's no reason to attribute anything more than a simulation to symbols and algorithms, any more than there is any reason to attribute real magic to what illusionists do.

One is tempted to say that the reason some people fail to see all this is not because it is *difficult* but precisely because it is so *obvious*, like the tip of one's nose that one fails to see precisely because it is so close and familiar. Yet on this failure to grasp the obvious rests the whole project of explaining intelligence in terms of computation.

Kripke's argument

In chapter 8, we had reason to consider Saul Kripke's example of the "quus" function, which he defines as follows:
$$x \text{ quus } y = x + y, \text{ if } x, y < 57;$$
$$= 5 \text{ otherwise.}$$

We saw that there is nothing in the facts about behavior, neurophysiology, or any other physical aspect of human nature that could by

---

[703] Cf. Eric Dietrich, Chris Fields, John P. Sullins, Bram van Heuveln, and Robin Zebrowski, *Great Philosophical Objections to Artificial Intelligence* (London: Bloomsbury Academic, 2021), p. 96; and Paul M. Churchland and Patricia S. Churchland, "Could a Machine Think?" in their collection *On the Contrary: Critical Essays, 1987-1997* (Cambridge, MA: The MIT Press, 1998).

themselves determine that a person is doing *addition* rather than *quaddition*. I appealed to this result in support of the conclusion that the intellect is not corporeal.

As Kripke argued, the example can also be deployed in an argument against the claim that the mind is a kind of computer.[704] For there are no physical features of a computer that can determine whether it is carrying out addition or quaddition, no matter how far we extend its outputs. No matter what the past behavior of a machine has been, we can always suppose that its next output – "5," say, when calculating numbers larger than any it has calculated before – might show that it is carrying out something like quaddition rather than addition. Of course, it might be said in response that if this happens, that would just show that the machine was *malfunctioning* rather than performing quaddition. But Kripke points out that whether some output counts as a malfunction itself depends on what program the machine is running, and whether the machine is running the program for addition rather than quaddition is precisely what is in question.

Another way to put the point is that the question of what program a machine is running always involves *idealization*. In any actual machine, gears get stuck, components melt, and in other ways the machine fails perfectly to instantiate the program we say it is running. But there is nothing in the physical features or operations of the machine *themselves* that tells us that it has failed perfectly to instantiate its idealized program. For relative to an eccentric program, even a machine with a stuck gear or melted component could be doing exactly what it is supposed to be doing, and a gear that *doesn't* stick or a component that *doesn't* melt could count as malfunctioning. Hence there is nothing in the behavior of a computer, considered by itself, that can tell us whether its giving "125" in response to "What is 68 + 57?" counts as an instance of its following an idealized program for addition, or instead as a malfunction in a machine that is supposed to be carrying out an idealized program for quaddition. And there is nothing in the behavior of a computer, considered by itself, that could tell us whether giving "5" in response to "What is 68 + 57?" counts as

---

[704] Saul A. Kripke, *Wittgenstein on Rules and Private Language* (Cambridge, MA: Harvard University Press, 1982), pp. 35-37; Jeff Buechner, "Not Even Computing Machines Can Follow Rules: Kripke's Critique of Functionalism," in Alan Berger, ed., *Saul Kripke* (Cambridge: Cambridge University Press, 2011).

a malfunction in a machine that is supposed to be carrying out an idealized program for addition, or instead as an instance of properly following an idealized program for quaddition.

As Jeff Buechner points out, it is no good to appeal to counterfactuals to try to get around the problem – to claim, for example, that what the machine would have done had it not malfunctioned is answer "125" rather than "5."[705] For such a counterfactual presupposes that the idealized program the machine is instantiating is addition rather than quaddition, which is precisely what is in question.

Naturally, we could always ask the programmer of the machine what *he* had in mind. But that simply reinforces the point that there is nothing in *the physical properties of the machine itself* that can tell us. But if there is nothing intrinsic to computers in general that determines what programs they are running, neither is there anything intrinsic to the human brain specifically, considered as a kind of computer, that determines what program *it* is running (if it is running one in the first place). Hence there can be no question of explaining the human mind in terms of programs running in the brain.

Might we appeal to God as the programmer of the brain who determines which program it is running? No, for that would make of human thought something as extrinsic to human beings as the program a computer is running is extrinsic to a computer, indeed as extrinsic as the meaning of a sentence is to the sentence. Just as the meaning of "Restrooms are next to the entrance" is not really in the ink marks in which the sentence is written, but rather in the mind of the user of the sentence, so too the idea of God as a kind of programmer or user of the brain qua computer would entail that the meanings of our thought processes are not really in us at all but only in him.

Neither, as Buechner points out, will it do to suggest that natural selection has determined that we are following one program rather than another. For any program we conjecture natural selection has put into us, there is going to be an alternative program with equal survival value, and the biological facts will be insufficient to determine which of them is the one we are actually following. For example,

---

[705] Buechner, "Not Even Computing Machines Can Follow Rules," pp. 356-58.

suppose it is suggested that the capacity for addition has survival value, and thus would have been favored by natural selection. In that case, it might be thought, we have good reason to think that the brain is running the program for addition. The problem is that we could also postulate instead that the brain is running a program for something like *quaddition*, because there is always going to be a form of quaddition that will yield exactly the same results as addition in all cases where survival depends upon it. So there is no argument from natural selection for the conclusion that the brain is running a program for addition that wouldn't be an equally good argument for the conclusion that the brain is running a program for quaddition.

Like Searle's argumenta, Kripke's argument illustrates and reinforces the point that there is nothing in what a computer does that can guarantee more than a *simulation* of what the intellect does. For while it is true that a computer can operate *as if* it were adding, any such computer also thereby operates *as if* it were quadding rather than adding, and there is nothing about it that rules out one interpretation rather than the other.

Dreyfus's arguments

Hubert Dreyfus developed an influential and especially detailed critique of the project of artificial intelligence in a series of publications.[706] Most relevant for our purposes is what he says about the two fundamental aspects of the notion of a computer as we have defined it, namely that it processes *representations* and does so by following *rules*. Now, in a Turing machine, both of these are and must be explicit. In particular, both the symbols the machine processes (such as the representations for numbers in a machine that solves arithmetic problems) and the algorithmic rules by which it processes them must be encoded in certain specific series of 0s and 1s. If the human mind is a kind of Turing machine, then, the representations it processes and the rules by which it processes them must be present in it in a similarly explicit way.

---

[706] See especially Hubert L. Dreyfus and Stuart E. Dreyfus, *Mind over Machine* (New York: The Free Press, 1986); and Hubert L. Dreyfus, *What Computers Still Can't Do: A Critique of Artificial Reason* (Cambridge, MA: The MIT Press, 1992).

But in fact neither such representations nor such rules are or can all be in the mind in such a way. Take the purported rules first. One problem here is phenomenological. We simply do not in fact experience the use of language, for example, as a matter of applying rules. Not only do we typically not consciously apply rules when speaking, but we are also often able to make sense of what people say when they make odd utterances or even commit outright linguistic errors, despite their thereby failing to follow whatever rules are supposedly guiding linguistic behavior.[707] And if it is claimed that, despite appearances, such speakers really are following subtle rules that govern our usage, then this would leave it unintelligible why we find the utterances odd or erroneous. The supposition that linguistic competence involves the following of rules implies that all utterances would have to be either rule-governed even in cases where it seems not to be, or utterly arbitrary. But actual human linguistic practice shows that there is a third possibility, in which utterances can be intelligible despite not being governed by rules.

But a deeper, conceptual problem would remain even if we were to grant that we are, appearances notwithstanding, really following rules at some unconscious level. The problem is that any explicitly formulated rules are susceptible of different possible interpretations and applications. So, if linguistic competence and other mental capacities rest on the following of explicitly encoded rules, then we will need a *second* level of rules telling us how to apply the first set to whatever concrete situation we find ourselves in. But now these rules too would be susceptible of alternative interpretations and applications, which would call for a yet *higher* level of rules directing us how to understand and apply *them*. And so on *ad infinitum*. The supposition that all mental activity presupposes explicitly formulated (albeit unconscious) rules thus entails a vicious regress. There is no way all the relevant rules could be explicitly encoded.[708]

Analogous problems face the supposition that all thinking involves the processing of representations. The idea here is that in a computer, and in the human mind if it is a computer, everything that

---

[707] Dreyfus, *What Computers Still Can't Do*, pp. 199-200.

[708] Ibid., pp. 203-204 and 286. Cf. Dreyfus and Dreyfus, *Mind over Machine*, pp. 80-81.

is known is embodied in a set of explicitly formulated facts or items of information.[709] Now, actually making use of facts or items of information in a concrete situation requires knowing which are *significant* or *relevant to* the situation. For example, there are innumerably many things we know about restaurants, but most of them are irrelevant to the activity of going to a restaurant for dinner. For instance, when ordering, we needn't bring to bear our knowledge that the air in the restaurant is made up of molecules, that each member of the restaurant staff has a hippocampus, or that there is groundwater at some point below the restaurant's floor. But we do need to keep in mind facts such as that usually one has to order from the menu and that one needs to have a credit card or enough cash to pay for the meal. On the other hand, there might be circumstances where some facts of the former kind might become relevant. For example, if a restaurant was considering adding a basement, facts about groundwater would obviously be important. And if you were a building contractor who was eating at the restaurant and wanted to offer your services to the management, this might, accordingly, become an item of information as important to you as what's on the menu.

To be usable, then, facts or items of information need to be put into a *context*. Now, suppose that this context was itself embodied in a further set of explicitly formulated facts or items of information, so that it could be added to the computer (and to the mind, if it is a computer) and thereby allow the computer to make use of the first set of facts. The problem now is that what was true of the first set of facts is true also of the second set that provides the context for the first. Applying that set of facts too requires knowledge of relevance, which entails *further* context. And if that further context is itself embodied in an explicitly formulated set of representations, that will just raise the problem yet again at a higher level. Once again, a vicious regress looms.[710] And once again, we find that the information that a computer needs in order to function cannot all be explicitly encoded in it.

But this model of knowledge too is in any event not true to the phenomenology of actual human experience. In reality, observes

---

[709] Dreyfus, *What Computers Still Can't Do*, pp. 206f.
[710] Ibid., pp. 220-21. Cf. Dreyfus and Dreyfus, *Mind over Machine*, p. 80.

Dreyfus, we don't engage with the world as if it were a set of innumerable facts none of which possesses significance or relevance until that is brought in from outside. Rather, we encounter things precisely in such a way that some of them already have special significance or relevance. The significance or relevance is itself already built in to our experience of things, rather than something that has to be tacked on to otherwise uninterpreted bit of data.[711] And that significance reflects factors beyond the purported symbols and algorithms the computer model of the mind claims are implemented in the brain, such as our embodied nature and our cultural circumstances.[712]

Now, in the case of the computers with which we are familiar, what provides the interpretive context for the rules and for the facts encoded in it is, of course, the *programmer* of the computer – what he, a human being, takes to be relevant or significant given the purposes for which the computer is being programmed.[713] It is not anything in the rules and representations encoded in the computer *themselves* that determines interpretive context, and it could not be.

The upshot of all this is that the processing of representations and the following of rules *presuppose* the existence of minds which are capable of interpreting the representations and rules. In that case, though, it simply makes no sense to try to explain the mind itself in terms of representations and rules. That gets things the wrong way around. Dreyfus's arguments too, then, illustrate and reinforce the point that the most we could attribute to a machine is the *simulation* of intelligence rather than the real thing, and that the simulation is possible in the first place only because human beings design the machine with that end in mind, rather than because of anything in the machine itself.

---

[711] Dreyfus, *What Computers Still Can't Do*, pp. 224 and 288.

[712] Ibid., p. 290.

[713] Ibid., p. 289.

Arguments inspired by Gödel

There is one further well-known family of arguments against machine intelligence which is more problematic, but which I will address briefly for completeness' sake. These are arguments inspired by the famous First Incompleteness Theorem of logician Kurt Gödel (1906-1978). Gödel showed that for any consistent formal system capable of expressing arithmetical statements, there will be some statement which is true but not provable within the system.

Here is one way briefly to state the basic idea of the theorem, which I borrow from Dietrich et al.[714] Let's assign the label A to a system of formal logic powerful enough to express arithmetic. And let's assign the label G to the statement "I am not provable," as expressed in the language of A. Suppose that A is a *consistent* system, meaning that it is not possible to prove within it any contradiction – that is to say, one cannot prove, within the system, both some statement S and its negation *Not-S*. Then it would follow that G is true. For if we *could* prove G, then it would follow that G is true (since you can't prove a statement that isn't true). But it would also follow that G is *not* true, since what G says is that it is *not* provable, and we will in fact have just proved it. So we will have a contradiction, insofar as both G and *Not-G* will be true – which is not possible given that A is consistent. If A really is consistent, then, G must *not* be provable (which is, of course, precisely what G itself says). So, for any system like A, there will be statements in it that are true but not provable within the system itself.

The philosopher John Lucas and the physicist Roger Penrose have argued that Gödel's theorem entails that the human mind cannot be a computer.[715] To take Lucas's version of the argument, the basic idea is that if the mind were a machine, then it would embody a formal system of the kind described by Gödel. In that case, there would be statements expressible in the formal system that are true but that the mind could not *know* to be true. For a machine could arrive at such

---

[714] Dietrich et al., *Great Philosophical Objections to Artificial Intelligence*, pp. 11-12.

[715] Cf. J. R. Lucas, "Minds, Machines, and Gödel," *Philosophy* 36 (1961): 112-27; Roger Penrose, *The Emperor's New Mind* (Oxford: Oxford University Press, 1989); and Roger Penrose, *Shadows of the Mind* (Oxford: Oxford University Press, 1994).

truths only by way of algorithms, and Gödel's theorem shows that there will be truths expressible in the system that cannot be proved algorithmically. However, *we* can in fact know these truths, as the example in the previous paragraph makes clear. Hence, our minds cannot be machines.

Such arguments have gotten a great deal of attention, though few think they succeed. One objection would be that a machine *could* in fact prove, and thus know, a statement of the sort in question by adopting the perspective of a higher-order formal system, just as a human mathematician would.[716] The trouble with this response, though, is that it raises the question of exactly *how* a machine could do this. If the answer is that the machine could be programmed by us to do so, then that is true, but hardly a problem for Lucas's argument. For in that case it remains the case that the machine cannot come to know such statements *on its own*, without our assistance. Human minds, by contrast, do not need such outside assistance.

A more serious objection is raised by Searle.[717] The most Lucas has shown, Searle argues, is that if the mind were a machine, there will be truths it cannot know by way of *theorem-proving* algorithms, specifically. But not all algorithms are of that kind. For all Lucas has shown, it may be that the human mind is a machine that arrives at knowledge of such truths by way of algorithms of some other kind.

However, even if this is true enough as far as it goes, it does not suffice to defuse all challenges to machine intelligence inspired by Gödel's theorem. As Storrs McCall has argued, in a *Turing* machine, specifically, there is no difference between truth and provability.[718] What a Turing machine programmed to do arithmetic can recognize as true is only what is in its axiom base or what can be proved as a theorem from that base. But Gödel's theorem shows that truth and provability *diverge*, since there can be true statements that are not

---

[716] Dietrich et al., *Great Philosophical Objections to Artificial Intelligence*, p. 14.

[717] Searle, *The Mystery of Consciousness*, pp. 65-66.

[718] Storrs McCall, "Can a Turing Machine Know that the Gödel Sentence is True?" *Journal of Philosophy* 96 (1999): 525-32.

provable. And we can see the difference, whereas a Turing machine could not. Thus, concludes McCall, the mind cannot be a Turing machine.

This is hardly an insignificant result, even if one grants Searle's point that for all Lucas has shown, the mind might embody algorithms other than the theorem-proving kind. For it would arguably undermine the *paradigmatic* version of machine intelligence, even if it left open the possibility that computers of a kind other than Turing machines might be said to think.

All the same, Gödel-inspired arguments against machine intelligence, though interesting, seem to me to be less decisive and fundamental than the kinds developed by Searle, Kripke, and Dreyfus. They are not as decisive for several reasons. For one thing, while I've loosely sketched the basic idea of such arguments, when spelled out in detail various technical issues arise, and these have proven difficult to settle. For another thing, and as I've just indicated, even if successful, such arguments may succeed in showing only that the mind is not a *Turing* machine, specifically, while leaving it an open question whether it might be a computer of another kind.

Such arguments are less fundamental because they do not touch on the point that there is nothing about *any* machine, whether a Turing machine or some other kind, that could ground the judgment that it is doing anything more than merely *simulating* intelligence, behaving *as if* it were doing arithmetic or some other intellectual operation. The argument I developed in the first section of this chapter emphasizes this basic fact, and the arguments of Searle, Kripke, and Dreyfus at least point to it. Gödel-inspired arguments do not. But once this basic point is made, any considerations related to Gödel's theorem are rendered of secondary importance.

Artless artifice

I have been emphasizing that computers are able to do what they do only because they are made to do so by human intellects. They have no capacity to do anything that even *simulates* intelligence, let alone really exhibiting it, apart from human designers and users. In chapter 3, we noted Searle's distinction between the intrinsic intentionality that concepts and thoughts have, and the merely derived intentionality that words and sentences have. The meaning or semantic content that the representations in a computer possess is of the derived kind, not the intrinsic kind that a mind possesses. In chapter 2, we saw that an intelligent thing is a kind of substance rather than an artifact or an aggregate. And in chapter 5, we noted the Aristotelian distinction between the substantial forms and intrinsic teleology that true substances have, and the accidental forms and extrinsic teleology that artifacts possess. Insofar as computers exhibit capacities to mimic intelligent behavior, that is by virtue of accidental rather than substantial forms and extrinsic rather than extrinsic teleology. They are not true substances, but mere artifacts.

These points together imply a further, distinctively Aristotelian argument against the possibility of machine intelligence. The basic idea can be summarized in three steps. First, an intelligent thing is a kind of substance, not an artifact. But second, a machine is an artifact, and not a true substance. Therefore, no machine can be an intelligent thing.

But the difference between computers and the human intellect is even more radical than what has been said so far indicates. Pyrite or fool's gold is not true gold, and neither are papier-mâché painted to look like gold, or a two-dimensional painting of a piece of gold. But papier-mâché painted to look like gold is a more convincing simulacrum than the two- dimensional painting, and pyrite is an even more convincing simulacrum still. Now, compared to the human intellect, computers, I submit, are typically more like papier-mâché or even the two-dimensional painting than they are like pyrite. They are not only not genuine intellects, they are not even close simulacra. They operate on principles not closely analogous to those on which the human intellect operates.

To see how, recall first Dreyfus's point that in order to know what facts are relevant in a given situation, we need to fit them into a context. In the case of ordering at the restaurant, for example, the context tells us that facts about what is listed on the menu are relevant, whereas facts about the groundwater in the earth beneath the floor of the restaurant are not. Some of the relevant facts are determined by custom (such as that you put in an order by telling a waiter what you want) and some are determined by human biology (such as that a steak is among the things you might enjoy eating, but the plate it is served on is not). Most of this context, and the judgments about which facts are relevant that follow from it, are typically not consciously and explicitly considered when you order at the restaurant, but implicit and taken for granted. They are part of what, in chapter 7 and following Searle, we called the *Background* against which conscious judgements are made. As we saw in that chapter, this Background involves a set of capacities, dispositions, and the like which embody *knowing how* to act rather than *knowing that* such-and-such propositions are true.

Now, figuring out how to put this sort of Background knowledge into a computer is known in research on artificial intelligence as the "commonsense knowledge problem."[719] And as we have seen, it cannot be solved simply by putting further rules or facts into a machine, because determining how those further rules and facts are to be interpreted and applied would *itself* be yet a further task calling for the application of commonsense Background knowledge. An especially famous sub-problem within the larger difficulty of figuring out how to embody commonsense knowledge is known as the "frame problem."[720] The difficulty here is not just that how to apply rules and interpret facts presupposes a context, but that this context *changes* over time, and in innumerable ways. For example, as you sit in the restaurant deciding what to order, the waiter may come and inform you that they are out of chicken, the couple at the table next to you may abruptly get up and leave, the person behind you might complain about the taste of the spaghetti, the temperature in the room may decrease slightly, a red car may drive past the window, and so on. Some

---

[719] Dreyfus and Dreyfus, *Mind over Machine*, pp. 77-78.

[720] The problem was brought to prominence by John McCarthy and Patrick Hayes in their article "Some Philosophical Problems from the Standpoint of Artificial Intelligence," in B. Meltzer and D. Michie, eds., *Machine Intelligence, Vol. 4* (Edinburgh: Edinburgh University Press, 1969). For a brief overview of the nature of the problem, see Dreyfus and Dreyfus, *Mind over Machine*, pp. 82-90. For a somewhat more detailed discussion, see Daniel C. Dennett, "Cognitive Wheels: The Frame Problem of AI," in Dennett's *Brainchildren: Essays on Designing Minds* (Cambridge, MA: The MIT Press, 1998). For an overview of the history of the debate about the problem, see Dietrich et al., *Great Philosophical Objections to Artificial Intelligence*, chapter 6.

of this would be irrelevant to what you decide to do, some of it would be highly relevant, and some of it may or may not be relevant. (Why did the couple leave? Was the service bad?) Let a "frame" be a set of factors that are relevant to a context, so that changes in those factors (such as learning that the restaurant is out of chicken) would need to be taken account of when deciding what to do while other changes (such as a red car's going by) could be safely ignored. How can a machine determine what should be part of the frame?

The frame problem and the commonsense knowledge problem more generally have been notoriously difficult to solve. If it is approached as a matter of storing information and drawing inferences from it, one problem is the staggering size of the database and number of calculations this would entail. A computer would have to know that the absence of chicken will make a Caesar salad less satisfying, but a slight decrease in room temperature will not; that people abruptly leaving may be an indicator of bad service, but a red car passing by the window is not; that if the waiter bothers to tell you that they are out of chicken, it is highly unlikely that they will have it back in stock within five minutes; that if another diner complains about the taste of the spaghetti, that is some evidence that the restaurant serves bad spaghetti, though there is also a possibility that the other diner is just cantankerous, or wants to get the cook fired, or was joking; and so on and so forth indefinitely. The computer would also then have to draw an enormous number of inferences to the effect that the absence of chicken should be considered; that the change in room temperature can be ignored; that the red car passing the window can be ignored; that the people leaving early and the other diner's comment might need to be investigated further; and so on and on. And to approximate human performance, these inferences would all have to be carried out within the short time the normal person would take to order dinner.

One approach would be to bite the bullet and attempt the herculean task of loading common sense into a computer in the form of millions of items of information, as researcher Douglas Lenat's CYC project (for "encyclopedia") does.[721] Naturally, this runs up against the problem that *any* body of information and rules, no matter how

---

[721] Dreyfus discusses and criticizes this project in *What Computers Still Can't Do*, at pp. xvi-xxx.

large, will still itself need to be interpreted and applied. Merely adding to its size does not solve this basic problem, but just disguises it by making the computer's mimicry more convincing. Indeed, it reinforces the point that mere mimicry is all that is achieved, because *this is not how human intellects themselves possess common sense.* It is not a matter of their containing millions of explicitly formulated propositions about matters such as the irrelevance of small air temperature changes to the taste of Caesar salad, or of drawing innumerable inferences about the relevance of such esoteric facts to how to act in the present moment. An artificial intelligence like CYC is no more a genuine mind than a painting of a piece of gold is real gold.

A more realistic approach would be to put into a machine some heuristic principle by which the number of factors that need to be considered in the first place in a context like the restaurant can be cut down considerably. But as Jerry Fodor points out, the problem with this is that it just raises the same difficulty again at a higher level.[722] How could a machine come to know that it should consider the absence of chicken and ignore the slight change in air temperature? By applying a heuristic, says the proposal under consideration. But how could the machine know that the heuristic is the right one? That would require having reason to judge that the heuristic is *correct* to allow considering factors like the absence of chicken and to disallow considering a slight change in air temperature. But how could the machine make *that* judgment without knowing precisely the things the heuristic was supposed to allow it to avoid having to consider?

Nor, as Fodor notes, can it plausibly be said that a connectionist machine might deal with the frame problem better than a Turing machine would.[723] The problem here reflects the fundamental difference between Turing machines and connectionist machines. A computer has to determine whether to include within a frame some particular factor (concerning the restaurant being out of chicken, the red

---

[722] Jerry Fodor, *The Mind Doesn't Work That Way: The Scope and Limits of Computational Psychology* (Cambridge, MA: The MIT Press, 2000), pp. 41-46.

[723] Ibid., pp. 46-53.

car driving by, or whatever). That entails that the computer's representation of that factor has to be either moved into the frame or kept out of it. And that entails in turn that *one and the same* representation persists through this process. For example, the representation of *the restaurant's being out of chicken* might initially not be part of the frame, and then gets moved into it. But with connectionist networks, observes Fodor, it is difficult to see how there could even be such a thing as the same representation persisting over time. If a representation is distributed across the entire network and its content determined by the state of the network, then if the state of the network changes over time, the representation and its content change over time. Hence, whatever representation exists after a change to the network is just a *different representation* from the one that existed before the change. Connectionist networks thus seem to lack the basic structural preconditions for dealing with the frame problem, let alone dealing with it better than a Turing machine can.

The intractability of the frame problem has led work in artificial intelligence to focus on what computer scientist Erik Larson calls "narrow AI" and what Dietrich et al. characterize as "monointelligence."[724] This involves designing machines dedicated to some very limited and well-defined task. Examples would be chess-playing computers, IBM's *Jeopardy!*-playing machine Watson, and the marketing programs used by companies like Amazon and Google to determine customer preferences. Precisely because the domains such programs deal with are so extremely narrow, the frame problem can be ignored. But the cost is that such computers are simply not at all closely analogous to human intellects. Even what they do well, they do not do *the way* that human beings do it. (For example, they may operate with vast databases of explicitly formulated representations or carry out a staggering number of calculations, which is not what human beings do when they play chess or *Jeopardy!*) But they are also incapable of going beyond the narrow range of problems they're designed to solve.

---

[724] Erik J. Larson, *The Myth of Artificial Intelligence: Why Computers Can't Think the Way We Do* (Cambridge, MA: The Belknap Press of Harvard University Press, 2021), p. 28; Dietrich et al., *Great Philosophical Objections to Artificial Intelligence*, p. 154.

They lack what Dietrich et al. call the "open-ended intelligence" that even the simplest human being possesses.[725]

As Larson observes, this narrowness is an unsurprising consequence of the fact that Turing's approach to intelligence essentially reduces it to the single task of "problem-solving."[726] This was necessary if intelligence was to be modeled on what a Turing machine does, because what such a machine can do is what can be reduced to problem-solving. Now, more recent work in artificial intelligence purports to acknowledge and move beyond the limitations of the approach represented by Turing, which is often referred to as GOFAI (an acronym coined by philosopher John Haugeland for "good old fashioned artificial intelligence"). Brian Cantwell Smith characterizes the GOFAI approach as "first-wave" artificial intelligence, and observes that "GOFAI no longer has imaginative grip as 'how intelligence works'; it is widely disparaged in cognitive science and neuroscience; the center of gravity of AI thinking has shifted to machine learning and other second-wave approaches."[727]

Machine learning (ML) includes techniques such as applying the connectionist approach to computation to massive amounts of data, and drawing statistical regularities out of it.[728] Facial recognition programs and the like would be examples. As with every other kind of computer, the way the inputs to the system and the outputs from it are conceptualized reflects the purposes of its designers and users rather than anything about the machine itself.[729] ML architectures also mimic only what is common to higher mammalian brains rather than

---

[725] And of course, it must always be kept in mind that what narrow competence they do possess is only what *human designers* put into them in the first place, not something they somehow acquired on their own. Cf. Larson, *The Myth of Artificial Intelligence*, pp. 29-30.

[726] Ibid., p. 23.

[727] Brian Cantwell Smith, *The Promise of Artificial Intelligence: Reckoning and Judgment* (Cambridge, MA: The MIT Press, 2019), p. 23.

[728] Cf. Margaret A. Boden, *AI: Its Nature and Future* (Oxford: Oxford University Press, 2016), pp. 46-50 and chapter 4.

[729] Ibid., pp. 64-66.

anything distinctive of human beings qua rational animals.[730] Moreover, ML's so-called "facial recognition" competence has nothing to do with a *conceptual* grasp of what is "seen" by the computer, but is merely a matter of detecting correlations between pictures on the one hand and names or the like on the other.[731] So there is no basis for attributing anything analogous to *intellectual* activity to so-called "machine learning."

But might ML at least be doing something analogous to what we do at the *sub*-intellectual, perceptual level? No. As Gary Smith points out, image recognition software does not identify objects the way we do.[732] For example, that something has the paradigmatic appearance of a STOP sign is enough to allow us quickly to recognize it as one. Secondary features like size variations or stickers attached to the sign, defects like dents and rust, and obscuring factors like a branch partially hanging in front of the sign don't prevent us from doing so. But they can prevent an image recognition program from doing so, because it responds to images at the pixel level rather than by considering the object as a whole, and is sensitive to fundamental and secondary features alike until it "learns" from a large number of examples that the latter are less common.

Naturally, that ML is sensitive only to superficial statistical regularities rather than the significance of the information it processes is even more obvious in its mimicry of linguistic behavior. A computer can be programmed to detect instances of the word "betrayal" in scanned texts. But because it lacks the *concept* of betrayal, if it scans a story about betrayal that happens not to use the actual word "betrayal," it will fail to detect the story's theme.[733] And if it scans text that does contain the word, but without deploying the concept of betrayal, the computer will erroneously classify it as a story

---

[730] Ibid., p. 55.

[731] Ibid., p. 50. Cf. Gary Smith, *The AI Delusion* (Oxford: Oxford University Press, 2018), p. 50.

[732] Smith, *The AI Delusion*, pp. 50-53.

[733] Ibid., p. 46. Cf. Larson, *The Myth of Artificial Intelligence*, pp. 148-49.

about betrayal. Due to the rough correlation that exists between contexts in which the word "betrayal" appears, and contexts in which the concept is deployed, the computer will loosely simulate the behavior of someone who understands the word. But the simulation breaks down where the meaning conveyed by an utterance does not correlate with frequency of usage. For example, ML does poorly detecting sarcastic uses of words and phrases, because these are much less common than straightforward usage.[734] Nor is it just the frequency of occurrences within the data set a program is working from that limit ML. It is also, of course, what is in the data set itself in the first place. When the real-world facts begin to diverge from what is in the data set, an ML simulation will fail badly.[735] It lacks the capacity to cope with novelty that goes along with genuine intelligence.

Again, even the best AI programs simulate what the intellect does no more closely than painted papier-mâché simulates real gold. Or to borrow an analogy from Smith, to suppose ML's crude simulation even approximates real intelligence is like supposing that climbing a tree approximates flying.[736]

Arguments from neuroscience

Let's turn now to the neuroscientific considerations that might be claimed to support or even establish materialism. Let me remind the reader once again that what I am addressing here is the idea that *intellectual* operations, specifically, can be explained in materialist terms. I am not challenging the thesis that sensory experiences, the passions, and other mental attributes we share with non-human animals are corporeal.

---

[734] Larson, *The Myth of Artificial Intelligence*, p. 151.

[735] Ibid., p. 140.

[736] Smith, *The AI Delusion*, p. 23.

The basic materialist argument from neuroscience is very simple.[737] For one thing, it has long been known that there is at least a general dependence of mental activity on what goes on in the brain. A blow to the head can leave one unconscious. Alcohol and narcotics can affect one's emotional state and impair the exercise of our rational capacities. Damage to the brain can impair memory, perception, linguistic ability, and so on. For another thing, modern neuroscientific inquiry has established somewhat more fine-grained correlations between specific areas and activity within the brain and specific kinds of mental functioning – visual, auditory, linguistic, and so on. Even if neuroscience has not explained every aspect of the mind, its understanding is continuously increasing. While this does not strictly demonstrate that all mental activity will turn out to be entirely explicable in neuroscientific terms, Ockham's razor (so the argument goes) supports that judgment. Science has not so far *needed* to posit any immaterial factors in order to explain the mental phenomena it has shed light on, and it is at least highly improbable that it will have to do so in the future.

The first thing to be said in response is that, whatever challenge one might suppose this sort of argument to pose to other forms of dualism (such as the Cartesian kind), it has no force whatsoever against the distinctively Aristotelian position I have been defending in this book. As I have emphasized, the Aristotelian position acknowledges that sensory experience, mental imagery, emotion, and other mental attributes we share with non-human animals are entirely corporeal or bodily. It also holds that the intellect depends on the senses, and thus the body and brain, for informational input. Moreover, the Aristotelian allows that even when concepts have been abstracted from mental imagery, the intellect still, in the normal course of things, makes use of imagery when entertaining even the most abstract ideas and lines of reasoning. That too depends on brain activity. And it cannot be emphasized too strongly that these are not concessions the Aristotelian has been forced to make in light of modern neuroscientific findings. On the contrary, these are things that Aristotelians have been saying for centuries. Hence there is nothing in what modern

---

[737] Cf. Paul M. Churchland, *Matter and Consciousness*, Third edition (Cambridge, MA: The MIT Press, 2013), pp. 29-35, 43-45, and chapter 7.

neuroscience has discovered about the mind that need be remotely troubling to the Aristotelian. Indeed, it is precisely the sort of thing Aristotelian philosophy of mind would lead us to expect.

The second thing to say is that the arguments for the incorporeality of the intellect defended in the previous chapter are not *empirical hypotheses*, but purport to be *metaphysical demonstrations*. They claim to establish, not that it is merely *improbable* that the intellect will be explained in purely material terms, but that this is strictly *impossible*. Naturally, as with any philosophical argument, a critic might raise various objections (albeit I have argued that none of those objections succeeds). But to weigh probabilities and appeal to Ockham's razor is simply to miss the point. If you are trying to show that someone's attempt at a proof in geometry is mistaken, it would be quite ridiculous to weigh the probabilities of the conclusion's being true, or to object to the conclusion on grounds of parsimony. That is simply not how that sort of reasoning works. In order to rebut such an attempted demonstration, one will either have to show that the conclusion does not follow from the premises or that one of the premises is doubtful. The same thing is true of metaphysical arguments like those defended in the previous chapter. If the arguments succeed, then they will have flatly shown that the intellect is immaterial, and questions about probabilities and Ockham's razor drop away as irrelevant. They will have established absolute limits to what neuroscience might account for.

Mind reading?

Hence, if the materialist has nothing to appeal to but the general success of neuroscience in illuminating various aspects of the mind, then that is entirely consistent with the arguments of the previous chapter and thus casts no doubt on them. However, it might seem as if there are certain specific findings of neuroscience that should be more troubling to the Aristotelian than the ones mentioned so far. In particular, this might seem to be true of claims to the effect that neuroscience has discovered ways to *read minds*.

Sensationalistic claims to that effect appear in the popular press from time to time, but even more sober and well-informed accounts can seem, at least at first sight, very impressive.[738] The most dramatic results occur with a combination of functional magnetic resonance imaging (fMRI) of brain activity together with statistical pattern recognition techniques.[739] As one scientist sums up the findings:

> It has been possible to read increasingly detailed contents of a person's thoughts... to read out which visual picture a person is looking at, which visual image they are conjuring up in their mind, which memory item they are remembering, which specific intention they are holding in mind and planning to pursue in the future, or which emotion they are communicating to their romantic partner... In the case of thoughts it is now possible to read out... which concepts are figuring in a person's mental states ('cat', say, versus 'dogs').[740]

This makes it sound as if observation of the brain allows researchers to know what is going on in a person's intellect in something like the way that inspection of the throat can reveal oral thrush or a colonoscopy can detect polyps. But that is not at all what is going on. First of all, researchers do not, of course, directly observe mental states, but rather draw *inferences* about what is going on in the mind from what they observe to be going on in the brain. Second, they can draw these inferences with at most a significant degree of probability rather than with certainty. Third, the inferences cannot be drawn just by inspecting the brain straightaway. The researcher has to rely on the introspective reports of the subject in order to establish a set of correlations between certain kinds of observed patterns in the brain and certain kinds of mental state.[741] And this is possible only for a

---

[738] For a collection of academic articles on the subject, see Sarah Richmond, Geraint Rees, and Sarah J. L. Edwards, eds., *I Know What You're Thinking: Brain Imaging and Mental Privacy* (Oxford: Oxford University Press, 2012).

[739] John-Dylan Haynes, "Brain Reading," in Richmond, Rees, and Edwards, eds., *I Know What You're Thinking*, at p. 30.

[740] Ibid., pp. 30-31.

[741] Ibid., p. 33.

finite number of mental states. Only after this set of correlations has been built up can the researcher begin to draw inferences in future cases about what is going on in the subject's mind.

Fourth, it is easier to draw such inferences when a mental state is described in a coarse-grained way rather than a fine-grained way. For example, one might conclude that a subject is lying but be unable to determine exactly which part of what they have said is false.[742] Fifth, the development of any particular subject's brain is to some extent idiosyncratic, so that the correlations established for one subject to not necessarily apply to another subject.[743] Hence, even when researchers can draw significant inferences about what is going in one person's mind, it doesn't follow that the correlations would allow them to do the same with another person. Sixth, even in a single individual, the correlations might change over time, so that what might be inferred with some confidence at an earlier time might not remain inferable later on.

As Tim Bayne has pointed out, yet another consideration involves what philosophers call the "multiple realizability" of mental states.[744] The same mental state can be correlated with diverse kinds of neural activity, and the same kind of neural activity can be associated with different kinds of mental state, so that correlations are not airtight. How mental states and brain events are classified is also crucial. There are several distinctions to be drawn, not only between mental states characterized at a coarse-grained level (such as being conscious) versus a fine-grained level (such as being conscious that there is a cat in the room), but also between particular mental *episodes* (such as a sudden twinge of anxiety) versus general mental *dispositions* (such as being depressed), and between sensory and affective mental states (such as seeing a red object or feeling fear) versus higher sorts

---

[742] Ibid., pp. 34-35.

[743] Ibid., pp. 32-33.

[744] Tim Bayne, "How to Read Minds," in Richmond, Rees, and Edwards, eds., *I Know What You're Thinking*.

of cognition (such as entertaining the abstract concepts of color and of emotion).[745]

Finally, even the most well-established correlations will not by themselves allow the researcher to infer mental states *beyond* those for which correlations have been established in the past. For that, we would need some kind of compositional principle.[746] For example, we would need to be able to know that if one kind of brain activity has in the past been correlated with thoughts about cats, and another kind of brain activity has in the past been correlated with thoughts about dogs, then when, in some novel situation, these kinds of activity occur together, we can infer that the subject is entertaining the thought that *the cat sees the dog*. But no one has established any such compositional principle. Nor would doing so be an easy task. We would need, among other things, some way to justify the conclusion that what the subject is thinking really is that *the cat sees the dog* – as opposed to thinking that *the dog sees the cat*, or that *the cat does not see the dog*, or that *either there is a cat present or a dog present*, or some other possible mental state concerning cats and dogs.

As all of this shows, so-called "mind-reading" is actually a much messier and less certain affair than one would initially suppose from the more dramatic claims made about it. In particular, it is fraught with *indeterminacy* in the sense operative in the previous chapter. What shows up in an fMRI or some other method of imaging what is going on in the brain requires *interpretation*, and there are always alternative possible interpretations. No one even pretends that the neuroscientific evidence all by itself determines that we can exclude all interpretations but one, and the arguments of the previous chapter show that it *could not* do so. Nor is there anything in the neuroscientific evidence that indicates in the first place that what shows up in an fMRI or the like correlates directly with anything but *images* or *phantasms*, as opposed to *concepts*. As I have emphasized, for the Aristotelian, the intellect makes use of imagery even when entertaining the

---

[745] Ibid., pp. 47-48.

[746] Haynes, "Brain Reading," pp. 33-34, and Bayne, "How to Read Minds," p. 44.

most abstract ideas, and imagery is corporeal. Hence we should expect there to be at least a *loose* correlation between what can be detected in brain activity and what is going on in the intellect, but not a *tight* correlation that would eliminate all indeterminacy. And that is exactly what we find.

In short, the neuroscientific evidence concerning so-called "mind-reading" not only does not conflict with the Aristotelian position defended in this book, but in fact confirms it.

The limits of localization

But even this perhaps concedes too much to the materialist. For the significance of even the loose correlations between the mental and the neural posited by modern neuroscience is often overstated. As psychologist William Uttal has argued, it is much more difficult confidently to establish a correlation between some particular kind of mental activity and a certain location in the brain than is often realized, and arguments for such correlations are often fallacious.[747] There are three main problems here, concerning, respectively, the way mental phenomena are conceptualized, the known anatomical and physiological facts about the brain, and the technology by which researchers try to map the mental onto the neural.

First, in order to establish a location in the brain for some particular kind of mental capacity or activity, we need a crisp and clear characterization of the latter. But researchers typically do not have that.[748] In ordinary usage, terms like "consciousness," "intelligence," "thought," and so on are not well-defined, so that they can hardly form the basis for a rigorous search for neural correlates. But even more technical characterizations of the mental are problematic. As Uttal points out, a wide variety of taxonomies have been proposed over the centuries. These include Plato's tripartite division of the psyche; Aristotle's distinction between vegetative, sensory, and rational

---

[747] William R. Uttal, *The New Phrenology: The Limits of Localizing Cognitive Processes in the Brain* (Cambridge, MA: The MIT Press, 2001).

[748] Ibid., chapter 3.

souls; Descartes' divide between *res cogitans* and *res extensa*; early modern empiricist theories of the association of ideas; Wolff's faculty psychology; phrenology; Freud's theory of the id, ego, and superego; Chomsky's Language Acquisition Device theory; Fodor's theory of mental modules; Gardner's theory of multiple intelligences; and so on. There is no general agreement on any one taxonomy, and the empirical evidence does not force us to accept one of them to the exclusion of the others. Moreover, the empirical methods available to us may bias us in favor of an approach. As Uttal writes, "mental taxonomists must appreciate that *how* we measure in large part determines *what* we measure – or, perhaps more precisely, what we *think* we are measuring."[749] We may adopt a taxonomy not because there is objectively good reason to think it accurately captures mental phenomena, but rather because it would make it easier for us to study them if it were correct. We thereby let our methods determine what we will take to be real, rather than letting reality determine the suitability of our methods.

Note that I am *not* saying that mental phenomena cannot be clearly defined or that there are no good grounds for preferring one taxonomy to another. On the contrary, I have, of course, been defending distinctive conceptions of the intellect, the will, and other mental capacities. But I have given *philosophical* arguments in their defense, rather than claiming to read them off from the neuroscientific facts. Uttal's point is that it is an illusion to suppose that *any* taxonomy could be read off from the neuroscientific facts. All proposed taxonomies rest on background theoretical assumptions that they bring to bear on the interpretation of the neuroscientific facts, so that it is hopeless to assume that neuroscience by itself can settle these matters.

The only crisp and clear localizations that can be established, Uttal argues, are those associated with sensory input to the brain and motor output.[750] With other kinds of mental activity, the corresponding neural activity tends to be distributed across the brain rather than clearly localized. (Notice that it is precisely where mental activity of

---

[749] Ibid., p. 91.
[750] Ibid., pp. 143 and 208.

the kind that we share with non-human animals is concerned that localization within the brain is most plausible.)

The second problem, again, has to do with certain facts about the anatomy and physiology of the brain. In order to establish that a certain kind of mental capacity or activity can be located at a specific region of the brain, we need to be able clearly to identify the relevant regions. But Uttal points out several serious difficulties.[751] First, while the brain is not homogeneous, different brain regions are nevertheless not sharply demarcated from one another. Moreover, even clearly distinct regions are interconnected in complex ways. Apart from relatively simple sensory and motor functions, the neural activity relevant to most mental phenomena is distributed across the brain. To be sure, researchers often appeal to specific sorts of impairment that follow upon brain injuries or lesions to argue that the relevant kind of mental activity is localized to the damaged area. But there are several problems with these arguments too. Some of the evidence from these cases reflects factors that may be idiosyncratic to the specific people involved, and not plausibly generalizable to all human beings. Sometimes subjects eventually recover lost functionality despite the damage to the parts of the brain in question. And the loss of function after damage to some specific region of the brain can establish, in any case, only that activity in that region is *necessary* for proper functioning, not that it is *sufficient* for it.

The third problem discussed by Uttal has, as I have said, to do with the technology used to try to establish correlations between the mental and the neural.[752] The significance of what such methods reveal is highly subject to interpretation. For example, consider images of brain activity generated by fMRI.[753] The basic idea is that an increase in blood flow in a certain area of the brain indicates an increase in oxygen use, which in turn indicates an increase in neural activity,

---

[751] Ibid., pp. 152-67.
[752] Ibid, pp. 167-72.

[753] For a brief and lucid summary of how such images are arrived at, see Paolo Legrenzi and Carlo Umiltà, *Neuromania: On the Limits of Brain Science* (Oxford: Oxford University Press, 2011), pp. 14-29.

which in turn reflects a change in mental activity. Now, when a subject is asked to perform some cognitive task, neural activity increases across the brain. So, comparison is made between results arrived at under different conditions with the aim of isolating which bit of neural activity is likely to be the one responsible for the task. False colors are then assigned to the image by the experimenter to represent different levels of neural activity. And then a conclusion is drawn about the relationship between what is in the image and what is going on at the mental level of description.

Naturally, all of this reflects fallible judgments about the significance of the multiple factors considered. In particular, Uttal notes, the method rests on challengeable assumptions about the relationships between metabolic activity, neural activity, and cognitive activity.[754] For example, when assigning the false colors to the image, "a conservative assignment could hide localized activity and a reckless one suggest unique localizations that are entirely artifactual."[755] Raymond Tallis notes several other problems.[756] Neural activity lasts for mere milliseconds whereas detected changes in blood flow last 2-10 seconds. Hence it is possible that blood flow changes are providing oxygen to more than one bit of neural activity. Moreover, many millions of neurons have to be activated for a blood flow change to be detected, so that activity in smaller groups of neurons will not be spotted. Yet such smaller-scale activity may nevertheless have significant effects at the cognitive level. In other ways too, activity that is detected may not be the whole story. It might play whatever role it plays only against the background of neural activity that precedes what is detected. And of course, attributing specific content to any mental activity alleged to be correlated with what shows up in an fMRI image

---

[754] Uttal, *The New Phrenology*, p. 169.

[755] Ibid., p. 168.

[756] Raymond Tallis, *Aping Mankind: Neuromania, Darwinitis, and the Misrepresentation of Humanity* (Durham: Acumen, 2011), pp. 76-77. Cf. Sally Satel and Scott O. Lilienfeld, *Brainwashed: The Seductive Appeal of Mindless Neuroscience* (New York: Basic Books, 2013), pp. 14-22.

faces all the indeterminacy problems described in the previous chapter.

That is by no means to deny that methods like fMRI have value. The point is that their use is very far from a simple reading off of mental activity from what is going on in the brain. Background theoretical assumptions are always in play, and if one changes those assumptions, what we might conclude from the imaging techniques will also change.

Psychological research indicates that non-experts who would otherwise reject an implausible theory will tend to accept it if neuroscientific information is added to the presentation of the theory, even when this addition does not actually change the content of the theory itself.[757] I submit that this is often what happens with arguments for materialism. References to neuroscience appear to many to lend plausibility to such arguments, though, considered more closely, they do no such thing. As with artificial intelligence research, the results of modern neuroscience cast no doubt whatsoever on chapter 8's arguments for the incorporeality of the intellect.

---

[757] Legrenzi and Umiltà, *Neuromania*, pp. 53-61.

Part IV:
What is the Soul?

10. Immortality

Survival of death

In chapter 1, I adopted Boethius's definition of a *person* as *an individual substance of a rational nature*, and chapters 2 through 4 established what it is to be such a thing – that it entails being a persisting self, having an intellect, and possessing free will. Chapters 8 and 9 established that rationality is incorporeal and indeed entirely immaterial. A person or rational substance that is *nothing but* a rational substance would therefore be purely incorporeal. It would be an *angel*, as angels are understood in the Scholastic tradition in philosophy and theology represented by thinkers like Aquinas.

To think of human beings as incorporeal substances only contingently related to their bodies, as the Platonic and Cartesian traditions do, would thus in effect be to conflate them with angels. But that is not what human beings are. In chapters 5 and 6 I established what it is to be corporeal, and what it is to be a corporeal substance of an animal nature, specifically. Chapter 7 established that animality, and thus corporeality, is part of human nature too, alongside rationality. It thereby vindicated Aristotle's conception of human persons as *rational animals*.

All the same, just as Plato and Descartes were correct to take human beings to be at least *partly* incorporeal (even if they are not entirely so), so too were they correct to hold that the human mind, and thus the self, survives the death of the body. And it survives precisely because it is incorporeal.

Philosophical proofs

What I take to be the main philosophical argument for this claim, which derives from Aquinas, is as follows.[758] There are three fundamental ways a thing might cease to exist. The first is as a consequence of the destruction of some other thing on which it depends for its existence. To borrow an example from Robert Pasnau, a fresco might be destroyed because the wall on which it is painted is destroyed.[759] The second is as a result of the decomposition of its own parts. As explained in chapter 5, this is ultimately a matter of prime matter losing one substantial form and taking on another, as when a cow is slaughtered for beef or a tree is reduced to ash. The third is utter annihilation, which entails the thing and its parts going out of existence altogether, rather than the latter taking on some new form. This is not something that occurs in the natural order of things, insofar as, when material substances go out of existence naturally, the matter simply takes on the form of some other sort of thing. For Aquinas, it involves instead God ceasing to conserve a thing in being.

Aquinas calls the first of these three ways of going out of existence corruption of the *accidental* kind, and the second corruption of the *per se* kind. Corruption of the *per se* kind amounts to a substance's going out of existence, whereas corruption of the accidental kind does not, though it might be a byproduct of a substance's going out of existence. That can be what happens in the case of the fresco going out of existence, if this involves, say, the stone wall on which the fresco was painted being blasted into dust. The fresco itself is not a substance, but rather results from something that is a substance (namely the stone that makes up the wall) taking on a certain accidental form. When that substance goes, it takes this accidental form with it, as it

---

[758] The *locus classicus* is Thomas Aquinas, *Summa Theologiae*, I.75.6. See also Aquinas's *Summa Contra Gentiles* II.55. Variations can be found in many Thomistic manuals of philosophy. See, for example, H. D. Gardeil, *Introduction to the Philosophy of St. Thomas Aquinas III: Psychology* (St. Louis: B. Herder, 1956), pp. 226-28; George P. Klubertanz, *Philosophy of Human Nature* (New York: Appleton-Century-Crofts, 1953), pp. 312-13; Michael Maher, *Psychology: Empirical and Rational*, Ninth edition (London: Longmans, Green, and Co., 1933), pp. 533-37; and Henri Renard, *The Philosophy of Man* (Milwaukee: Bruce Publishing Company, 1948), pp. 33-36.

[759] Robert Pasnau, *Thomas Aquinas on Human Nature* (Cambridge: Cambridge University Press, 2002), p. 364.

were. But imagine instead a case where the paint is simply scraped off of the wall. In this case, the fresco is destroyed, but the underlying substance is not. Or imagine a club which disbands. The club is not a substance, but exists only insofar as certain relations hold between substances (namely, the members of the club). When these relations cease, the club ceases, but the substances carry on. A substantial form too can go out of existence in this accidental way. For instance, when the stone of the wall is reduced to dust, the substantial form of stone is no longer present, any more than the accidental form of the fresco is.[760] This counts as corruption of the accidental kind insofar as, though a substantial form is, of course, constitutive of a substance, it is not *itself* a substance.

Now, a person, including a human person, cannot go out of existence by way of the accidental sort of corruption. For as we saw in chapter 2, a person is a kind of substance, rather than an attribute or collection of attributes or an aggregate of substances. But might a person go out of existence by way of corruption of the *per se* kind?

Corruption of the *per se* kind, as I have said, ultimately involves prime matter losing substantial form. Let's now expand on this. I say it *ultimately* involves this, because while other kinds of damage to a thing may be involved in corruption of the *per se* kind, it is only when the loss of substantial form results that such corruption actually occurs. For example, an animal may die as a result of an explosion occurring next to it, which severely damages its body. But it is not the damage to the body itself which *constitutes* the animal's corruption, as is obvious from the fact that an animal might in some cases survive such damage. It is only when the damage is severe enough to result in the loss of the substantial form of the animal that corruption occurs. Or consider a case where the animal dies as a result of the lack of water. It is not the deprivation of the water that constitutes the animal's corruption, but rather the loss of substantial form, which results from the deprivation of water.

---

[760] I am assuming for the sake of argument that stone is a true substance rather than an aggregate. But nothing rides on this particular example, and, if one wishes, another example that does involve a true substance can be substituted in order to make the point.

I say that corruption of the *per se* kind involves *prime matter losing substantial form* because in order for a change of any kind to occur, there must be a *potential* for that change already present. In the case at hand, there must be something in the substance that corrupts that has the potential to lose its substantial form. As we saw in chapter 5, that is precisely what prime matter is. Qua potential to take on substantial form, it never locks on to one particular form and thus is always ready to lose whatever form it has and receive another, should the right causal factors be present. It is, accordingly, the principle by virtue of which physical substances can be generated and corrupted.

A corollary of this is that a substance of which prime matter is not a constituent *cannot* be corrupted. For if there is nothing in it that has the potential to take on some different substantial form, then there is nothing in it that can lose the substantial form that constitutes it as the substance it is. Hence there is nothing in it by virtue of which it can go out of existence.

Now, since rationality is incorporeal, an angel, which is a rational substance that is *nothing but* a rational substance, would be entirely incorporeal and thus lack prime matter. Accordingly, it would not be capable of corruption of the *per se* kind. But what about human beings, who are rational animals? Being animals, they are partly corporeal, but being rational, they are not entirely so. Hence, they are not entirely corruptible *per se*.

In particular, at death, the prime matter that is the substrate of the human body loses the substantial form of a human being. But that substantial form, and the substance of which it is the form, do not themselves thereby go out of existence, because not everything a human being does depends on the body, and thus on prime matter, in the first place. The rational powers of intellect and will, which are incorporeal, carry on, and thus the substance of which they are powers carries on. To be sure, the substance in question is not *complete*. As a rational animal, a fully mature and undamaged human being not only thinks and wills, but also takes in nutrients, grows, reproduces, and has sensory experiences, appetites, and locomotion. Since the latter, animal capacities are lost, death greatly diminishes the substance that is the human being. But it does not destroy it altogether.

The situation is analogous to an amputation. Suppose a human being's arm is cut off and destroyed. The prime matter that was the substrate of that arm loses the substantial form of a human being. But of course, that does not entail that there is nothing left having that substantial form – that is to say, that the substance of which the arm was once a part has gone out of existence – because a human being is more than his arm and can survive its amputation. The substance that is the human being carries on, albeit in a diminished state. Now, death can be thought of as a *full body amputation*.[761] The person loses not only arms and legs, but the entire corporeal side of his nature, since all of the prime matter that had been its substrate loses the substantial form of a human being. But here too, that does not entail that there is nothing left having that substantial form – that the substance of which the body as a whole was a part has gone out of existence. For a human being is never entirely bodily in the first place, but has a non-bodily or incorporeal part, namely the intellect with its powers of thinking and willing. That part carries on – or more precisely, the substance that is the human being carries on, reduced to that part (just as a human being after a quadruple amputation carries on, reduced to just his head and torso).

Commenting on this sort of argument, Pasnau raises the question whether the intellect, even if distinct from the body, may nevertheless depend for its continued existence on the body, especially given that (as we saw in chapter 7) its normal mode of operation involves making use of mental imagery, which is corporeal.[762] He draws an analogy with an unborn baby which, though distinct from its mother, would die without the umbilical cord that attaches it to her. Now, as Pasnau goes on to acknowledge, just as a baby after birth shifts to a different way of taking in nutrients and oxygen, so too, one could hold (as Aquinas does), does the human intellect shift to a different mode of cognition after death. And in that case, one could also hold

---

[761] Cf. Edward Feser, "Aquinas on the Human Soul," in Jonathan J. Loose, Angus J. L. Menuge, and J. P. Moreland, eds., *The Blackwell Companion to Substance Dualism* (Oxford: Wiley Blackwell, 2018).

[762] Pasnau, *Thomas Aquinas on Human Nature*, pp. 366 and 373. Cf. Norman Kretzmann, *The Metaphysics of Creation: Aquinas's Natural Theology in* Summa Contra Gentiles II (Oxford: Clarendon Press, 1999), pp. 413-18.

that, just as the baby can in such circumstances survive apart from the mother, so too can the intellect persist apart from the body. This analogy, Pasnau grants, suffices to keep the objection in question from being decisive. But Pasnau overlooks the more basic point that the *reason* an unborn baby will die without the umbilical cord is because its body is a composite of form and matter, and the matter will lose the form without sufficient oxygen and nutrition. But the intellect is *not* a composite of form and matter, and this (rather than the possibility of shifting to an alternative mode of cognition) is the fundamental reason why no dependence it has on the body could be strong enough to entail that it cannot survive without it.

Even apart from this point, though, Pasnau overestimates the force of the objection. Aquinas holds that while the body is present, the intellect always brings phantasms or mental imagery to mind when entertaining even the most abstract of concepts, and in chapter 7, I expressed agreement with this position. However, the considerations Aquinas raises in defense of this thesis, and the ones I appealed to in that chapter, neither establish nor are claimed to establish that the intellect depends on imagery *of metaphysical necessity*.[763] They establish at most only that the relationship between the intellect and the body is so intimate that, as *a matter of contingent empirical fact*, intellectual activity always makes use of imagery. But it is only if the former, stronger claim were true that the intellect's indirect dependence on imagery (and thus on the body) would tell against its incorruptibility – though again, as I argued in the previous paragraph, in fact it would not tell against it even in that case.[764]

---

[763] Cf. Adam Wood, *Thomas Aquinas on the Immateriality of the Human Intellect* (Washington, D.C.: Catholic University of America Press, 2020), p. 263.

[764] Indeed, the objection Pasnau considers is even weaker than these points indicate. For the intellect's persistence after death need entail only that it then retains the *power* to entertain concepts, propositions, and inferences (since, if a substance persists – even if, in this case, only in an incomplete way – then the distinctive powers that follow from its having the form it does must persist as well). It need not entail that it will then actually *exercise* those powers. (Cf. Wood, *Thomas Aquinas and the Immateriality of the Human Intellect*, p. 264.) Having said that, I would argue that it does in fact exercise them even then, for reasons to be addressed below.

Note that what I am here claiming is contingent is *only* the fact that the human intellect, while associated with the body, brings imagery to mind when entertaining concepts *that it has already acquired*. I am *not* claiming that it is merely a contingent fact that the acquisition *itself* depends on abstraction from imagery, and thus on sensation. One can consistently hold *both* that the intellect can, after death, entertain concepts without resorting to imagery *and* that said concepts would nevertheless not have been acquired in the first place had the intellect not first abstracted them from images, and thus been associated with the body and its sense organs. Note also that what I am saying is consistent with the intellect's not only *happening* to make use of imagery when together with the body, but having a *positive, natural inclination* to do so.

This is in no way an *ad hoc* collection of claims about the intellect, but rather the picture that one is naturally led to when taking account of all the relevant metaphysical and empirical considerations. On the one hand, metaphysical arguments demonstrate that the human intellect is incorporeal and carries on beyond the death of the body as an incomplete substance, and that as a substance it retains the rational and volitional powers that are characteristic of it. *In those respects* it is like the mind as the Platonic-Cartesian tradition conceives of it. On the other hand, empirical considerations reveal that we are intellectual substances *of the kind* whose natural condition is to be associated with a body, and which, in particular, require sensory experience and imagery for the acquisition of concepts, and a have a natural inclination to make use of imagery even after they are acquired. *In those respects*, the human intellect is *unlike* the mind as the Platonic-Cartesian tradition conceives of it.

Now, does the line of argument I have been developing here entail that the human being, though reduced to his intellect after death, could not be utterly annihilated? No, because at least as Thomists understand the relationship between God and things he creates, nothing that is distinct from God can continue in existence or exercise its natural causal powers, even for a moment, without God conserving it in being and concurring with its operations.[765] That is as true of the

---

[765] Cf. Edward Feser, *Five Proofs of the Existence of God* (San Francisco: Ignatius Press, 2017), pp. 232-38.

human intellect after death as it is of anything else, so that if God were to cease conserving it in being, it would be annihilated. However, the argument we've been considering does entail that *only* such a cessation of divine conservation could destroy the intellect. Nothing either in its own nature or in that of any of the other things that God creates can destroy it. In that sense, it is by nature immortal.

So far I've been defending what, as I have said, I take to be the main philosophical argument for the intellect's incorruptibility. A second, related argument appeals to the intellect's *simplicity*. I argued at length in chapter 8 that the intellect is simple or non-composite in the sense that it lacks parts of either a quantitative kind (namely, extended parts) or a constitutive kind (in particular, form and matter). This, it was claimed, establishes the intellect's immateriality. But it also establishes its incorruptibility, insofar as what makes a thing susceptible of corruption or perishing is that it can be broken down into its extended parts or, more fundamentally, its constitutive parts (when its matter loses the form distinctive of it). Since the intellect lacks such parts, it cannot be corrupted.[766]

To be sure, the intellect is not simple or non-composite in an absolute or unqualified sense. Thomists would say that there is, for example, a real distinction between its essence and its existence, and that anything in which there is such a distinction can be annihilated by God if he ceases to conserve it in being. But the point is that the intellect lacks the kind of composition necessary for it to be destroyed by *natural* means (that is to say, short of divine annihilation).[767] The intellect, as an incomplete substance, also possesses attributes which can be distinguished from the substance and which are gained and

---

[766] Cf. D. Q. McInerny, *Philosophical Psychology* (Elmhurst, PA: Alcuin Press, 1999), pp. 265-66; Gary R. Habermas and J. P. Moreland, *Beyond Death: Exploring the Evidence for Immortality* (Eugene, OR: Wipf and Stock, 2004), pp. 23-31.

[767] Shelly Kagan thus misses the point when he suggests that the possibility that God might annihilate a simple substance undermines the argument from simplicity (in Shelly Kagan, *Death* (New Haven: Yale University Press, 2012), at p. 92). Rightly understood, the argument claims to show only that there is nothing *within* the natural order, conserved in being by God from moment to moment, that could destroy the intellect. That is consistent with its being the case that God might cease conserving the particular part of the natural order that is the intellect, thereby annihilating it.

lost. But the point is that the substance *itself* lacks parts the decomposition of which could result in its destruction.[768]

Obviously, this argument is similar to what I characterized as the main proof of the intellect's incorruptibility, which appealed to the intellect's lack of a certain specific part, namely prime matter. The argument from simplicity can nevertheless be thought of as a distinct argument, because versions of it have been defended by thinkers who are not arguing within the framework of Aristotelian-Thomistic hylemorphism that informs the other argument.[769]

Now, against this sort of argument, some have held that there are ways other than decomposition into parts by which a simple substance could go out of existence. Richard Swinburne offers the example of a table which is suddenly liquefied, while its constituent molecules are nevertheless kept in the shape of a table by being contained within a table-shaped mold.[770] Though its parts have not been separated, the table can be said to have gone out of existence. The problem with this objection, though, is that Swinburne's conception of what counts as a "part" and as the separation of parts is too narrow. The Aristotelian will say that the matter of the table has in this example lost the accidental form of a table, and has lost it because the underlying wood has lost the substantial form of wood. Since these are "parts" in the relevant sense, the scenario is not the counterexample Swinburne thinks it is. But even someone who does not endorse the notions of substantial and accidental form and the rest of the hylemorphist analysis could hold that the spatial configuration and bonding of

---

[768] In their discussion of the argument in *Beyond Death*, Habermas and Moreland note that the self has parts in this sense and for that reason say they reject the argument for survival from *simplicity*. But they nevertheless accept what they call an argument for survival from *unity*, according to which the substance that underlies the self's attributes possesses sufficient unity for it to persist beyond the death of the body. But I would argue that what they call the argument from unity *just is* the traditional argument from simplicity, *properly understood*.

[769] For a useful collection of essays on the history of this line of argument, see Thomas M. Lennon and Robert J. Stainton, eds., *The Achilles of Rationalist Psychology* (Springer, 2008).

[770] Richard Swinburne, *The Evolution of the Soul* (Oxford: Clarendon Press, 1986), pp. 305-6.

molecules, and not just the molecules themselves, are parts of the table in the relevant sense.

Kant raised the objection that even if simple or non-composite, the intellect could go out of existence by virtue of a gradual diminution of the intensity of consciousness to zero.[771] Kant was replying to a version of the argument developed by Moses Mendelssohn (1729-1786), yet he overlooked the fact that Mendelssohn had already anticipated such a response.[772] As Mendelssohn pointed out, while diminution in intensity involves a gradual change in degree, a transition from existence to non-existence would involve a sudden leap of a very different kind, one that does not follow from the former. Suppose you used a dimmer switch gradually to decrease the intensity of a light bulb until it went out. Obviously it would not follow that further turning of the switch would cause the light bulb to go out of existence, or even to lose its power to illuminate. The bulb would remain, as would its power to illuminate, should the switch ever be turned in the other direction.

Nor is it correct in the first place to suppose that the intellect's activity after death might decrease in intensity to zero. For a living substance does not merely happen either to carry out its distinctive operations or to fail to do so. Rather, it has a positive inclination to do so (as, for example, a corporeal living substance has a positive inclination to maintain its metabolism). Hence, as Aquinas notes, an entirely incorporeal intellectual substance or angel would always be engaged in intellectual operations, which are the only kind it has.[773] Now, the reason human beings are not always engaged in such operations is that, unlike angels, we are associated with bodies, and the corporeal operations this entails can interfere with the intellectual ones.[774] But

---

[771] Immanuel Kant, *Critique of Pure Reason*, Transcendental Dialectic, "Refutation of Mendelssohn's Proof of the Permanence of the Soul."

[772] Brigitte Sassen, "Kant and Mendelssohn on the Implications of the 'I Think,'" in Lennon and Stainton, eds., *The Achilles of Rationalist Psychology*, pp. 219-21.

[773] Thomas Aquinas, *Summa Contra Gentiles* II.97.

[774] Ibid.

these drop away at death, so that, like an angel, the disembodied human intellect will always engage in the intellectual operations that are the only ones left to it.

A third sort of argument for the intellect's incorruptibility is known as the *conceivability argument*. It was made prominent in early modern philosophy by Descartes and has defenders in contemporary philosophy.[775] The basic idea is that it is *conceivable* that I could continue to exist as a thinking thing even if my body were destroyed. From this, the argument claims, it follows that my essence is that of a substance which *can in fact* exist as a purely thinking thing, with the continued existence of the body being inessential. Otherwise, my continuing to think beyond the death of the body should not be even conceivable.

Naturally, there is more to the argument, and sophisticated expositions and defenses of it in the contemporary literature. All the same, I do not think it works. Arguing from what is conceivable for a thing to the essence of the thing simply gets things the wrong way around. In fact, you need first to know the essence of a thing in order to be able to judge that what seems to be conceivable for it really is conceivable, and not just a cognitive illusion. Hence, only if I could independently show that thinking is incorporeal could I know that it really is conceivable for me to continue to exist as a thinking thing beyond the destruction of my body. But in that case, I would already have established the intellect's immateriality and incorruptibility, and the appeal to conceivability would be doing no work.

That the Thomistic position I've been defending in this chapter is different from that of Descartes is crucial to emphasize for yet another reason. Antony Flew argued that there are three possible ways we might conceive of the survival of the self after the death of

---

[775] Cf. Rene Descartes, *Meditations on First Philosophy*, Meditation Six; W. D. Hart, *The Engines of the Soul* (Cambridge: Cambridge University Press, 1988); and Richard Swinburne, *Are We Bodies or Souls?* (Oxford: Oxford University Press, 2019). I reviewed Swinburne's book critically in "Soul Proprietor," *First Things* (February 2020).

the body, and that none of them holds up to scrutiny.[776] The first he calls *the Platonic-Cartesian way*, which takes the body to be entirely extrinsic to the self. The problem with this view, he says, is that bodies are essential to how we identify and individuate persons. We attribute personal characteristics like speaking, acting, and the like on the basis of bodily criteria, we distinguish persons by associating them with distinct bodies, and we re-identify the same person over time by determining that we are dealing with the same body. Hence the body is *not* extrinsic to the self. The second approach Flew calls *the way of the astral body*. This takes selves to be distinct from bodies as usually understood, but nevertheless not entirely incorporeal. Rather, they are to be identified with some more ethereal sort of matter, along the lines of ghosts as represented in movies. The trouble with this view, Flew says, is that if it emphasizes the ways astral bodies are like ordinary bodies, then it faces the problem that there is no good evidence for the existence of such things. But if, to avoid this problem, the view emphasizes instead the differences between astral bodies and ordinary bodies, then it is hard to distinguish the way of the astral body from the Platonic-Cartesian way. The third approach identified by Flew is what he calls *the reconstitutionist way*. On this view, a person just is his body, so that the only way for him to survive the destruction of his body is for it to be somehow reconstituted. But if there is nothing that persists between the time the original body is destroyed and the time the later body is brought into being, then the latter, however similar to the original, will be only a *replica* of the original person and not genuinely the person *himself*.

The astute reader might have noticed that none of these views corresponds to the position I have been defending in this book. Indeed, the Thomist would, with qualifications, agree with Flew's criticisms of the three views he describes, and simply note that Flew has overlooked a fourth possibility. As I have emphasized, a human being is a substance with both incorporeal and corporeal attributes, which is why this substance is *incomplete* when the latter disappear at death. Hence the Thomist position does not take the body to be extrinsic to

---

[776] Antony Flew, *God, Freedom, and Immortality: A Critical Analysis* (Buffalo, NY: Prometheus Books, 1984), Part III; and *Merely Mortal? Can You Survive Your Own Death?* (Amherst, NY: Prometheus Books, 2000), chapter 1.

the person, as the Platonic-Cartesian way does. Moreover, though the view I am defending does allow (as we'll see in the next chapter) for the possibility of a person's body being restored, it is perfectly compatible with Flew's point that there must be something that persists between the death of the body and its reconstitution, so that what results from the latter is not a mere replica. For the substance that is the human being continues after death reduced to just the intellect, so that the restoration of the body would not be a matter of bringing some new and different substance into being. Rather, I would involve restoring to the incomplete substance that has persisted the corporeal attributes it had lost. Meanwhile, the notion of an astral body is simply no part of the Thomistic view. So, the Thomist can happily accept Flew's battery of objections against the views he criticizes, and note that they do not apply to the Thomist's own position.

To be sure, Flew does briefly note that Aquinas himself was aware of the replica problem, and formulated his position in a way that would avoid it.[777] But he characterizes Aquinas's position as if it essentially amounted to adding a variation of the Platonic-Cartesian way to the reconstitutionist way. What he does not appreciate is that it is a different view altogether. It does not reduce the human person to his incorporeal component, as the Platonic-Cartesian view does, nor does it reduce him to his corporeal component, as the reconstitutionist view does. But neither does it take the human person to be an aggregate of distinct corporeal and incorporeal substances. A human being is one substance, with both corporeal and incorporeal attributes.

Now, in Aristotelian-Thomistic metaphysics, it is *matter* that individuates distinct substances of the same specific kind – stones, trees, dogs, and cats no less than human beings.[778] So, the Thomist already has, independently of the debate about survival of death, reason to agree with Flew that the identity and individuation of human persons is tied to corporeality. The difference, of course, is that Flew assumes that this rules out survival of death, and the Thomist denies

---

[777] Flew, *God, Freedom, and Immortality*, pp. 107-8 and *Merely Mortal?*, pp. 10-11.

[778] Cf. Edward Feser, *Scholastic Metaphysics: A Contemporary Introduction* (Heusenstamm: Editiones Scholasticae, 2014), pp. 198-201.

this. For the Thomist, the fact that all human beings *start out* with distinct bodies is sufficient to individuate them.[779] It is not necessary for individuation that they retain these bodies at every stage of their existence. Nor is this an *ad hoc* modification to the Thomist account of physical substance for the purpose of upholding the possibility of survival of death. It follows naturally from the fact that the intellect makes human beings unique among corporeal substances in having incorporeal operations. If not *everything* a human being does is, in the first place, tied to the body even during life, then the persistence after death of an incorporeal residue should not be surprising. Moreover, even after death, this residue, the incomplete substance that is the human intellect, remains naturally ordered to its body, in a way analogous to how the body which has lost an arm or leg remains naturally ordered to having that missing limb. A man who has lost a leg does not cease being a thing of the type that, in its normal condition, would have that leg. He still *tends toward* having it, even if that tendency is frustrated by the damage his body has suffered. Similarly, you remain, after death, a thing of the type that in its normal condition would have a body, and indeed would have *your body* in particular. You still *tend toward* having it, even if that tendency has been frustrated by the "full-body amputation" that is death.

Empirical considerations

It may seem odd that the immortality of the intellect can be established in just a few pages of argumentation, as this relatively brief discussion might seem to imply. But it follows directly from the claims that corruptibility is tied to corporeality and that the intellect is incorporeal. I devoted an earlier chapter to the nature of corporeality and two long chapters to the intellect's incorporeality, and that is where the heaviest lifting needed to be done. Our discussion here could be relatively short once these presuppositions were established.

Still, our treatment would not be complete without at least briefly addressing one further matter. In the popular imagination, the case for survival of death is associated, not with abstruse metaphysical

---

[779] Cf. David S. Oderberg, "Hylemorphic Dualism," *Social Philosophy and Policy* 22 (2005): 70-99.

arguments, but with near-death experiences, purported encounters with ghosts, alleged memories of past lives, and the like. Needless to say, much testimony of this kind can reasonably be dismissed as reflecting fraud, wishful thinking, or a failure adequately to consider mundane explanations. But not all of it can be, and some academic writers have tried to marshal the best evidence of this sort into an argument for the probability or at least plausibility of survival of death.[780]

Hence, consider near-death experiences (NDEs), and especially the subset of such experiences known as out-of-body experiences (OBEs), reported by patients who were resuscitated after a prolonged period in which their hearts had stopped and brain activity had ceased. At least some such experiences, it is argued, cannot plausibly be explained away as mere hallucinations or vivid dreams. In some cases, patients report having perceived what was going on around them as doctors tried to revive them, but from a position outside their bodies. In some cases, they accurately report on objects or events that would not have been visible *except* from such a position. Or they convey accurate information based on alleged encounters with people who had died.

The most impressive cases of this type have features like the following. First, the objects or events the patients report having perceived were not only not visible from where their bodies were lying, but could not have been known to them before the NDE nor deduced by them from what they may have heard others in the room saying. For example, a patient might report a detail such as the fact that there were two coins lying atop a certain cupboard, where these coins were unknown to, and not visible to, anyone else in the room, but whose presence was verified when a staff member checked the top of the cupboard.[781] Or a patient might accurately report on who was present in

---

[780] Cf. Paul and Linda Badham, *Immortality or Extinction?* (Totowa, NJ: Barnes and Noble Books, 1982); Stephen E. Braude, *Immortal Remains: The Evidence for Life after Death* (New York: Rowman and Littlefield, 2003); Habermas and Moreland, *Beyond Death*; and Gary R. Habermas, "Evidential Near-Death Experiences," in Loose, Menuge, and Moreland, eds., *The Blackwell Companion to Substance Dualism*.

[781] Badham, *Immortality or Extinction?*, pp. 74-75.

another room in the hospital and what they were doing and saying.[782] In some cases OBE patients have allegedly even accurately described what was on the roof of the hospital.[783] Second, in some cases where NDE patients report on meeting persons who had died, the fact that the person was dead was not known to the patient or anyone else beforehand, but only verified later. For example, in one case a patient reported seeing someone who, it turned out, had died in a traffic accident just an hour before.[784] Furthermore, NDE patients do not report experiences of meeting people who are *not* dead, such as still-living relatives and friends. These facts make it difficult to dismiss NDEs as mere hallucinations of people the patient might have expected to see in the afterlife, or whose presence the patient might find comforting. Third, NDE patients report their experiences as having been the opposite of dreamlike, and indeed as more vivid than ordinary waking experiences. They also report them as being very different in character from the dreams and nightmares they may have experienced around the same time. Moreover, such dreams and nightmares quickly fade in the patients' memories just as dreams and nightmares in general tend to do, whereas the NDEs remain as clear in patients' memories as waking experiences do, and are so convincing that they result in the patient's being permanently convinced of the reality of survival of death, even when he had no such belief prior to the NDE.

Where testimony about encounters with ghosts is concerned, the most impressive cases have features like the following. They are attested to by multiple witnesses, especially people independently known not to be credulous or prone to wishful thinking, or whose education would make them sensitive to signs of trickery or other possible mundane explanations.[785] Or they involve witnesses purportedly acquiring information from a ghost that could not have been known

---

[782] John W. Cooper, *Body, Soul, and Life Everlasting* (Grand Rapids, MI: William B. Eerdmans, 1989), pp. 232-33; Habermas, "Evidential Near-Death Experiences," p. 239.

[783] Habermas, "Evidential Near-Death Experiences," p. 235.

[784] Badham, *Immortality or Extinction?*, p. 80.

[785] Cf. the cases recorded in Braude, *Immortal Remains*, chapter 7; Herbert Thurston, *Ghosts and Poltergeists* (Chicago: Henry Regnery Company, 1954); and Alan Gauld and A. D. Cornell, *Poltergeists* (London: Routledge and Kegan Paul, 1979).

to the witness otherwise, but which is later confirmed. In an example that featured in a court case, the location of a lost will was allegedly revealed by an apparition.[786]

Naturally, a determined skeptic will insist that *all* such phenomena are either fraudulent, or misinterpreted by credulous people, or would otherwise be explicable naturalistically if only we had sufficient knowledge of the circumstances. For example, it is sometimes suggested that NDEs and OBEs can be sufficiently explained in neuroscientific terms.[787] One such proposal would be that they are nothing more than hypnopompic dreams, that is to say, those that occur during reawakening and are thus remembered.[788] Comparable experiences sometimes occur in contexts where one is not near death, such as with military pilots centrifuged into unconsciousness.[789] Skeptics note that the details of NDE patients' experiences of a world beyond this one differ in ways that correlate with their different cultural backgrounds and religious assumptions, which tells against there being a common objective reality they are in contact with.[790]

On the other hand, certain other elements of NDEs tend to be common across cultures, such as the experience of leaving one's body. Moreover, the skeptic's focus on causal factors in the brain or otherwise internal to NDE patients does not account for such patients' knowledge of *external* objects and events they have no way of accessing by normal means.[791] Nor, it might be argued, is it plausible to suggest that *all* the many reports if this type can be dismissed as dishonest,

---

[786] Badham, *Immortality or Extinction?*, p. 93.

[787] Cf. Susan Blackmore, *Dying to Live: Near-Death Experiences* (Amherst, NY: Prometheus Books, 1993).

[788] Michael N. Marsh, "The Phenomenology of Near-Death and Out-of-Body Experiences: No Heavenly Excursion for 'Soul'", in Loose, Menuge, and Moreland, eds., *The Blackwell Companion to Substance Dualism*.

[789] Ibid., p. 253. Cf. Braude, *Immortal Remains*, p. 272.

[790] Marsh, "The Phenomenology of Near-Death and Out-of-Body Experiences," p. 249.

[791] Habermas, "Evidential Near-Death Experiences," pp. 241-42.

deluded, or mistaken. Suppose, then, that there are a number of cases that cannot plausibly be explained away by existing skeptical hypotheses. The case for survival will still not yet have been completed, because one first has to rule out explanations that are not likely to be favored by naturalists, yet don't involve survival. For example, it might be claimed that clairvoyance, telepathy, psychokinesis, or some combination of such paranormal abilities is responsible for the unusual phenomena described, perhaps unbeknownst to those involved. For instance, one could argue that when NDE patients acquire knowledge of events in other rooms in the hospital, this involves a kind of extrasensory perception (ESP) rather than their minds leaving their bodies. One could argue that poltergeist phenomena are not caused by the ghosts of the dead, but by psychokinetic activity on the part of witnesses to these phenomena, who do not realize they are the ones producing them. And so on. Such paranormal abilities would, of course, be unusual and in need of explanation themselves, but no more so than survival of death, or so the argument goes.[792]

Impressive cases of apparent mediumship and reincarnation are, on this view, susceptible of explanation in terms of telepathy. When a medium claims to relay information to a person about a dead relative, it might be suggested that what the medium is actually doing is not getting this information from the dead relative, but rather from the mind of the still living person, via telepathic means, and misinterpreting what is going on.[793] Or consider cases in which someone has what appear to be the character traits and memories of some deceased person he otherwise has no information about, and the deceased person's relatives confirm the accuracy of these memories and similarity of the character traits. What is really going on, it might be claimed, is not reincarnation, but a telepathic transfer of information about the

---

[792] Braude's *Immortal Remains* emphasizes the challenge that appeal to ESP, psychokinesis, and the like poses to the survival hypothesis, though he does not think that all of the evidence for survival is in fact best explained that way.

[793] Badham, *Immortality or Extinction?*, pp. 94-95.

dead person from the relatives into the mind of the person who thinks he has been reincarnated.[794]

Naturally, to find explanations of this sort plausible, one would have to find it plausible that there really are such phenomena as ESP, psychokinesis, and telepathy, and needless to say, that is itself a highly controversial matter. Moreover, even if one grants the reality of such phenomena, it doesn't follow that *all* the evidence claimed to support survival of death is better explained in terms of ESP, psychokinesis, and the like. For example, as Paul and Linda Badham point out, if we suppose that NDE patients are really just exhibiting a kind of extrasensory perception, we'd have to suppose that they are somehow capable of *far more powerful* feats of ESP than the stereotypical cases of alleged extrasensory perception, even though, unlike in those cases, there is *little or no* brain activity associated with the exercise of these powers.[795] That does not seem plausible. Moreover, Stephen Braude points out that the survival hypothesis has the advantage that it can account for all the phenomena at issue (NDEs, hauntings, mediumship, etc.) in terms of a single cause, namely survival of death.[796] By contrast, the appeal to alleged powers such as ESP, psychokinesis, and telepathy has to posit several causal factors. In some cases, it has to posit them operating all at once to produce the effect –as, for example, when psychokinesis is claimed to be the cause of the physical manifestations of purportedly ghostly hauntings, and telepathy the source of the information purportedly conveyed by a ghost. The survival hypothesis thus has parsimony in its favor.

At the same time, Braude emphasizes, exactly *what* conclusions about survival these empirical considerations support should not be overstated.[797] Considered just by themselves, he argues, they indicate at most that *some* people survive death, not that everyone

---

[794] Stephen T. Davis, "Philosophy and Life after Death: The Questions and the Options," in Brian Davies, ed., *Philosophy of Religion: A Guide and Anthology* (Oxford: Oxford University Press, 2000), pp. 701-2.

[795] Badham, *Immortality or Extinction?*, p. 77.

[796] Braude, *Immortal Remains*, pp. 301-6.

[797] Ibid., p. 306.

does. And they show only that those who survive do so for a limited time, not necessarily indefinitely.

My own view is that while such considerations are not without interest, they are of only secondary importance, and that it would be a serious mistake to treat them as if they were the main considerations in favor of immortality. They can support at most a probabilistic judgment to the effect that survival is a better explanation of the phenomena than the alternatives. But it is by no means clear what degree of probability they afford, and they certainly do not strictly rule out alternative explanations. Moreover, as Braude points out, even in the best cases, they don't establish the immortality of the human intellect as such, but at most only that *some* intellects survive *for a while*. Indeed, they don't even show that it is *human* intellects we are plausibly dealing with in each case. One might instead argue that demonic influence is behind some of the phenomena, such as mediumship and at least some hauntings. Naturally, this presupposes that there are such things as demons, which would have to be independently established before proposing their influence as an explanation of the phenomena in question. The point, however, is simply to emphasize *how little* can be established by appeal only to empirical considerations like those canvassed in this section. Such considerations can by themselves yield at best a "soul of the gaps," confidence in the existence of which is subject to revision in light of future empirical investigation.

By contrast, the arguments I have been defending establish that *all* human intellects as such survive the death of the body, and that they do so *forever* (barring annihilation by God). And these conclusions follow *of necessity* from a sound metaphysics of corporeality and of mind, not merely as the most likely of alternative possible explanatory hypotheses.

Accordingly, they also provide a framework within which to interpret empirical considerations like those we've been addressing. On the one hand, it might seem obvious that, given that we can establish on independent metaphysical grounds that the intellect can carry on without the body, the prior probability of veridical OBEs, ghostly encounters, and the like is higher than it otherwise would be. On the other hand, these same metaphysical considerations raise potential problems of their own for such phenomena. The intellect, I have argued, carries on as an *incorporeal* incomplete substance. But what is incorporeal has no extension. How, then, could be it identified with a ghostly apparition, which is extended? It also lacks sense organs. How, then, could it have visual and auditory experiences (of what is going on in various parts of a hospital, say) during an OBE?

It might be argued that the temporary capacity to manifest itself as an apparition, or to receive sensory input, might, for some special purpose, be imparted by God to at least some disembodied intellects. While I think that is true, such an argument requires appeal to theological premises that go well beyond anything that could be established by way of philosophical anthropology, let alone from the empirical evidence concerning NDEs, hauntings, and the like. That reinforces the point that it is unwise to approach the question of immortality primarily by way of considerations of the latter sort.

In any event, there is at least one interpretation of the empirical evidence for survival that the metaphysical arguments I have been defending decisively rule out, and that is any interpretation that posits reincarnation. Reincarnation would involve the disembodied mind coming to be related to an entirely new body in just the way it was related to its original body. For example, it might involve Socrates's intellect coming to be associated with my body, or with the body of a woman, or with the body of a non-human animal. This would not be a matter of his mind *possessing* a different body, after the manner of demonic possession of a person or an object. That would be a case of one substance exerting causal influence on an entirely distinct substance, but in a way that did not entail any greater unity between them than exists between, say, you and a pencil or hammer you are using. The idea is rather that Socrates' mind and the new body he comes to be associated with would together make up a single, unified person in just the way that his mind and his original body did.

Something like that might be possible on a Platonic-Cartesian conception of human beings, but it simply makes no sense on the Aristotelian-Thomistic conception I have been defending. Socrates is one substance, albeit one with both corporeal and incorporeal powers and operations. Like other substances, he has a substantial form that determines how the matter of his body is configured, and the specific *way* it is configured is, naturally, the way evident to anyone who has inspected Socrates' body. Hence it makes no sense to suggest that something could be Socrates and yet have my body, or the body of a dog. That would be like saying that something could be the tree outside the window of my study, and yet come to have my body or the body of a dog. If something really is the tree outside the window of my study, then the only sort of corporeal properties it could have are those of a tree, and indeed of that tree in particular. And if something really is Socrates, then the only sort of body it could have is a human body, and indeed Socrates' body in particular.

This naturally brings us to the famous Aristotelian-Thomistic thesis that the soul is the form of the body, which I will address in the next chapter. For the moment, let us note that the notion of reincarnation is in any event highly problematic in other ways as well. As John Hick points out, the idea is susceptible of different interpretations along a spectrum.[798] At one end, there is the scenario in which someone not only claims to be a reincarnation of a deceased person, but from the beginning of his life exhibits the memories and character traits of the deceased person in as unambiguous a manner as can be imagined. (Suppose, for example, that from the time I was born, I had all of Socrates' mannerisms and none that he did not have, recalled with crystal clarity all the things Socrates knew at the time of his death, relayed all of this knowledge in Greek, and so on.) At the other end of the spectrum, we have the scenario where none of those traits or memories are present in the purportedly reincarnated person, and it is only something "lying behind or beneath or above the conscious self" that carries over from one body to another.[799]

The problem, as Hick notes, is this. The closer an interpretation of reincarnation is to the first end of the spectrum, the more clearly it conflicts with the empirical evidence, because there simply are no cases of individuals exhibiting the memories and character traits of an earlier, deceased person to that maximally unambiguous degree. All cases of purported recollection of an earlier incarnation fall far short of that. Meanwhile, interpretations of reincarnation at

---

[798] John H. Hick, *Death and Eternal Life* (San Francisco: Harper and Row, 1976), p. 363.

[799] Ibid.

the other end of the spectrum "threaten to end by emptying it of factual content."[800] If neither any bodily traits nor any psychological traits persist from one incarnation to another, it becomes at least more difficult conceptually to explain just what exactly *does* carry over. But even if that problem is solved, the possibility of any empirical evidence that a reincarnation has in fact occurred is undermined.

What about some intermediate interpretation, in which at least a certain number of memories and personality traits persist from one incarnation to another, even if they fall short of the unambiguous display of the deceased person's psychological attributes posited by interpretations at the first end of the spectrum? The best alleged empirical evidence for reincarnation involves precisely this sort of scenario. But now, Hick notes, another problem arises. For if only certain memories and traits of the deceased person are manifest, why suppose that the deceased person *himself* has carried over from one incarnation to another? Why not say instead that it is only those particular memories and traits that have carried over? In particular, why not say that the person who exhibits these memories and traits has somehow acquired them from the earlier person, but without being identical to that earlier person (just as someone might acquire a bodily organ from a deceased person, as in a kidney transplant, but without being identical to that earlier person)?[801]

Hick notes yet other evidential problems with the reincarnation hypothesis.[802] Accounts of the most impressive cases were written up only a significant amount of time after the people involved first showed signs of having the memories and character traits of some deceased person. Hence it is hard to know the extent to which these accounts may have been tainted by errors and exaggerations that affected the witnesses' memories over time. Cases of individuals who claim to recall past lives are far more common in cultures in which belief in reincarnation is already widespread. That is reason to sus-

---

[800] Ibid.
[801] Ibid., p. 376.

[802] Ibid., pp. 373-75.

pect that background cultural assumptions have biased witnesses' interpretations of the behavior they judge to be evidence of reincarnation. Other authors have noted the further problem that purported memories and character traits of a deceased person could be interpreted, not as evidence that someone is the reincarnation of the deceased person, but rather as evidence that he is being possessed by the deceased person, or by a demon masquerading as the deceased person.[803]

So, there are grave conceptual and evidential problems with the reincarnation hypothesis even apart from the specifically Aristotelian-Thomistic objection to it. In any event, the account of human nature I have been defending rules it out. Whatever is going on in cases where people claim to have memories of previous lives, it is not reincarnation. The account I have been defending also raises problems for OBEs. The notion of an "out-of-body" experience might seem intelligible enough given a Platonic-Cartesian account of human nature. For if the mind and the body are two distinct substances, the latter could presumably carry on its vital functions in the absence of the former. However, I have argued that a human being is *one* substance, with both corporeal and incorporeal powers. When the intellect survives the death of the body, what happens is that the same one substance that had its bodily attributes before death loses them, and carries on in an incomplete way, reduced to just its incorporeal intellect. Because it is still a substance (albeit an incomplete one), it retains the *substantial form* of that substance. That entails that the body *loses* that substantial form, which is precisely why it is a *dead* body. But that in turn implies that there can be no such thing as a *living* body from which the intellect has somehow departed. Yet the bodies of those who have "out-of-body" experiences do not die. That is why OBE patients are said to be *resuscitated*, not *resurrected*. If they do not die, though, then they do not lose the substantial form of the body. And in that case, the intellect does not *separate* from the body as an incomplete substance, taking the substantial form with it.

Hence it is difficult to see how an OBE could involve the mind literally separating from the body. And as already noted, there is the further difficulty that it is hard to see how an incorporeal intellect

---

[803] Habermas and Moreland, *Beyond Death*, pp. 240-44.

could have perceptual experiences, given that it lacks the sense organs and brain activity on which such experiences depend. That does not entail that OBEs are mere hallucinations, and it might be argued that they could not be, given that they sometimes involve the acquisition of information in a way that cannot be explained by natural means. Some such experiences might be the result of special divine action. As I also noted already, ghostly apparitions too might reflect special divine assistance to allow disembodied intellects to make themselves seen or heard (at least in cases where we do indeed have reason to attribute the apparition to a human rather than demonic intellect). Hence, even given the difficulties I've raised, one might still try to make an empirical case for survival, at least from OBEs and hauntings, if not from purported cases of reincarnation. Once more, though, it is clear that such arguments can only be of secondary importance, and cannot by themselves tell us much about the *nature* of survival even where they give us grounds to affirm the *reality* of it.

The fixity of the will after death

As we saw in earlier chapters, an intellectual substance is not only a *thinking* thing, but a *willing* thing. It can entertain concepts, combine them into propositions, and reason logically from one proposition to another. But on top of that, it can choose to pursue what these intellectual operations represent to it as the best end, or the best means to an end. Can we know anything about whether and how this volitional capacity is exercised after death?

According to a line of argument developed by Aquinas, we can. In particular, it can in his view be shown that after death, the will can no longer change its basic orientation. That is to say, the end it takes to be the highest, and by reference to which it judges the worthiness of pursuing other ends, becomes unalterably fixed. Now, this end is going to be either God, or something other than God. And in Aquinas's view, for an intellectual substance to be forever fixed on God is for it to be saved, whereas for it to be forever fixed on something other than God is for it to be damned. Hence Aquinas's argument entails that, at death, a human being is either saved or damned. It is important to emphasize that the argument is purely philosophical in character, making no appeal to special divine revelation. Hence it falls within the purview of philosophical anthropology, and not just theology.

In my view, Aquinas's argument, rightly understood, is compelling. What follows is an exposition and defense. My focus will be on what I take to be the basic thrust of the argument, rather than on sticking closely to Aquinas's own way of formulating it or on exegesis of the key texts from his works (which I have provided elsewhere).[804]

The core idea of the argument is that after death, the human intellect is relevantly like that of an angel, where the basic orientation of an angel's will is fixed immediately after its creation. So, in order to understand why the human will's orientation becomes unchangeable after death, we need to understand why an angel's will becomes unchangeable immediately after its creation. But in order to understand that, we must in turn understand Aquinas's account of action – an account developed by way of an analysis of human action, specifically, but an analogue of which applies to angelic action.

Naturally, the skeptic will object to the reference to angels. But for the specific purposes of the argument, one needn't presuppose that angels actually exist. We need consider only what would be true of them *if* they existed. In particular, we need to consider what would be true of an intellectual substance that was, unlike human beings, *entirely* incorporeal and thus devoid of perceptual experience and bodily appetites.

Let's consider first, then, the relevant themes from Aquinas's account of action. Then we will turn to his account of the fixity of angelic wills, after which we will be in a position to understand why the human will must be fixed after death.

Following Boethius, I have characterized a person as an individual substance of a rational nature. The difference between angelic and human persons is that angels are *incorporeal* substances of a rational nature and human beings are *animal* (and thus corporeal) substances of a rational nature. As we have seen, for a substance to be rational is for it to possess intellect, the power to grasp concepts and

---

[804] Cf. Edward Feser, "Aquinas on the Fixity of the Will After Death," *New Blackfriars* 104 (2023): 651-67.

their logical relationships. Human beings form concepts by abstracting universal natures from the individual things instantiating them that are revealed to us in sensory experience. For example, we form the concept of *being a man* by attending to what is common to the different particular men we perceive around us. We then put concepts together into complete thoughts or judgements (as when we judge that *all men are mortal*), and reason discursively from judgement to judgement (as when we reason from the thoughts that *all men are mortal* and that *Socrates is a man* to the conclusion that *Socrates is mortal*).

Since angels are incorporeal and thus lack sense organs, their concepts are not acquired in this way. Instead, Aquinas holds, they are connatural or innate to them.[805] Nor do angels need to put concepts together into complete thoughts or reason discursively from one thought to another.[806] Rather, all at once, in a single act, they grasp the relationships between concepts and between premises and conclusions.

For Aquinas, all substances are naturally inclined or directed toward distinctive goods. For example, a tree is directed toward the goods distinctive of plants, such as taking in water through its roots. A squirrel is directed toward goods such as gathering nuts and acorns, and unlike a tree, the squirrel has sensory knowledge of these goods. A person or rational substance, unlike a squirrel (let alone a tree), can conceptualize the goods toward which he is inclined, and thereby have intellectual knowledge of them. As we saw in chapter 4, the will, for Aquinas, just is the inclination of a rational substance toward what the intellect judges to be good. Indeed, as we also noted in that chapter, for Aquinas the will inclines of necessity toward what the intellect judges to be good, and in particular at what we judge will bring happiness. That does not entail that we cannot will what we judge to be in some way bad. Aquinas's view is rather that whenever we will some end, it is because of some good we judge it to have, even if the intellect acknowledges it to be bad in other respects. At the moment of choice,

---

[805] *Summa Theologiae* I.55.2

[806] *Summa Theologiae* I.58.3-4

it is the good that the intellect sees in it that it focuses on, and the will opts for it *under that* aspect.

Though I follow here the common practice of speaking about what the intellect sees, what the will opts for, and so on, it is important to emphasize that strictly speaking, it is only the *person* or rational substance who does these things. The intellect and will are powers or capacities of this substance rather than substances in their own right. When it is said that the intellect knows something, this is to be understood as a shorthand way of saying that the person knows it, by virtue of his intellect. Similarly, when it is said that the will chooses some end, this is a shorthand way of saying that the person chooses it, by virtue of his will.

Now, many ends are pursued for the sake of further ends. You labor in order to earn an income, you want to earn an income in order to feed your family, and you want to feed your family in order to ensure that they survive and flourish. But Aquinas holds that there must be one *ultimate* end toward which all our actions are directed, and as we noted in chapter 4, he holds that that end is happiness. Moreover, he argues that what alone can bring happiness is to know and love God.[807] That is not to deny that people disagree about what will bring happiness, and that many seek it in something other than God. The point is that whatever ultimate end they seek, they seek it *as* that which they suppose will bring happiness. And, Aquinas holds, what alone can really bring it *is* in fact God, even if some do not see that.

John Lamont helpfully characterizes Aquinas's conception of action as "life-driven," by contrast with the "goods-driven" conceptions that predominate today.[808] For on Aquinas's account, "the goal that ultimately rules human action is that of living a life of a certain sort" such that one's choices "give life a certain pattern... a complete narrative structure, a structure that is the story of a person as such."[809]

---

[807] *Summa Theologiae* I-II.2

[808] John Lamont, "The Justice and Goodness of Hell," *Faith and Philosophy* 28 (2011): 152-73.

[809] Ibid., pp. 159-60.

A goods-driven account, by contrast, does not conceive of actions and the goods they are directed towards as fitting into any larger narrative structure. In effect, it takes these actions and goods to amount to just one thing after another. "Life goals" of the kind one might aim at on a life-driven account include "those of a revolutionary or a monk, but there are [also] many everyday kinds of human lives," as when "people decide to get married and raise children, or to dedicate themselves to a certain career."[810] Now, there are also people who do not consciously entertain any such life goal, whose pattern of actions approximates the model that the goods-driven conception attributes to human action in general. But this pattern too, Lamont argues, amounts to a tacit choice of a life goal, namely that of "a shallow irresponsible wastrel."[811] Such a life in fact has a narrative structure no less than that of someone who consciously tried to construct a life narrative.

Conceiving of action in such narrative terms elucidates why Aquinas and like-minded thinkers put such emphasis on virtues and vices when analyzing the moral life. Virtues are habits of action that facilitate the realization of the true end of human life, and vices are habits that frustrate the realization of that end. Hence the story of a life well lived will be a narrative of the acquisition of the virtues, and the story of a bad life will be a narrative of enslavement to the vices. This also contributes to making intelligible how a person's will can become fixed on either good or evil. Richard Swinburne's account of the matter emphasizes how repeatedly giving in to the temptation to do evil can gradually dull one's ability even to perceive what is truly good, let alone to want to do it.[812] The basic idea is familiar from Aristotle, who contrasts the incontinent or weak-willed man (the *akratēs*) from

---

[810] Ibid., p. 160.

[811] Ibid.

[812] Richard Swinburne, *Providence and the Problem of Evil* (Oxford: Clarendon Press, 1998), pp. 141-47. A similar account is defended in Jerry L. Walls, *Hell: The Logic of Damnation* (Notre Dame: University of Notre Dame Press, 1992), chapter 5.

the licentious man (the *akolastos*).⁸¹³ The former does wrong with regret and is capable of reform, whereas the latter has become so thoroughly addicted to immoral pleasures that he can no longer repent of pursuing them.

However, to leave it at that might give the impression that it is only gradual habituation into evil, as a result of a series of immoral acts, that can result in orientation toward the wrong life goal. As Lamont notes, that is not the view of Aquinas, for whom "the commission of one mortal sin constitutes the rejection of friendship with God as one's life goal."⁸¹⁴ To be sure, such a sin can be repented of, and for Aquinas this is true even with the *akolastos*, though his sins are more grave and repentance more difficult.⁸¹⁵ The point, though, is that *unless* it is repented of, even a single mortal sin will suffice to take one's life narrative in the wrong direction.

For Aquinas, a necessary condition for repentance is the recognition of a higher good the realization of which is frustrated by the action of which one repents.⁸¹⁶ He compares this to correcting an intellectual error by reasoning back to first principles (an example of which would be the law of non-contradiction). If one is correct about which principles are truly first, then rectifying the error is possible. But if one is incorrect about that, rectifying an error is far more difficult, because one will not have anything more fundamental to appeal to in order to correct one's mistake about which principles are truly first. Similarly, if one correctly understands which ultimate end will conduce to human happiness, repentance of sin will be much easier than if one is wrong about the ultimate end. This is why the *akolastos*

---

⁸¹³ Aristotle, *Nicomachean Ethics*, Book VII, Chapters 7 and 8. For a useful discussion that relates Aristotle's analysis both to Aquinas and to work in contemporary philosophy, see Kevin L. Flannery, SJ, "Anscombe and Aristotle on Corrupt Minds," *Christian Bioethics* 14 (2008): 151-64.

⁸¹⁴ Lamont, "The Justice and Goodness of Hell," p. 161.

⁸¹⁵ *De Malo*, Question III, Article 13.

⁸¹⁶ Ibid.

is in much greater spiritual danger than the *akratēs*, though Aquinas thinks that at least in this life the former can still discover his error about the ultimate end. But if it should somehow become impossible to correct that fundamental error, so too will repentance become impossible. That is exactly what Aquinas thinks occurs at death.

The reason he thinks this occurs at death is, as I have said, because he takes the disembodied human soul to be in relevant respects like an angelic intellect. Let's now turn, then, to Aquinas's reasons for thinking that angelic intellects are fixed in their orientation toward either good or evil immediately after their creation. He addresses this topic in several places.[817] This is not the place for exegesis of the relevant texts, which, again, I have in any event examined elsewhere.[818] Suffice it for present purposes to note that Aquinas's account of the obstinacy of the demonic will is essentially as follows. A fallen angel is analogous to the *akolastos* as Aristotle conceives of him, so thoroughly hardened in evildoing that he is incapable of reconsidering the ultimate end that orders all his actions. In particular, once he has forsaken the supernatural end of the beatific vision, an angel is incapable of repenting of this choice. For whereas the *akolastos* can in fact repent, the prerequisites to repentance, which exist in the *akolastos*, are absent in an angel. For one thing, unlike a human being, an angel does not arrive at judgements about the ultimate end through any sort of reasoning process. Hence there can be no correction of such a process, as there can be in the *akolastos*. For another thing, the factors that lead human beings into culpable errors in the reasoning process in the first place are also absent in an angel. In particular, an angel lacks either passions that might surge or be calmed, or sensory appetites that might be habituated. Hence he lacks the avenue to repentance open to the *akolastos*, namely the reform of disordered passions and sensory appetites. There is in an angel simply the single appetite of will, which after the angel's creation locks either onto the

---

[817] He does so at greatest length in four works: his *Commentary on the Sentences* II.7.1.2; *De Veritate*, Question 24, Article 10; *Summa Theologiae* I.64.2; and *De Malo*, Question XVI, Article 5. Shorter discussions can be found in *Summa Contra Gentiles* IV.95.8, *Compendium Theologiae* I.184, and *On Free Choice*, Article X, but these essentially summarize points developed at greater length in the other works referred to.

[818] Cf. Feser, "Aquinas on the Fixity of the Will After Death."

beatific vision as its ultimate end, or onto something else, depending on the intellect's judgement. Precisely because whatever it locks onto becomes the *ultimate* end, there is no end more fundamental by reference to which the angel might go on to alter this judgment.

That, as I say, is the basic argument. But there are some further issues to be addressed. One of them concerns the precise nature of the error made by the demonic intellect. It might seem that this must involve ignorance of a true proposition or even the affirmation of a false proposition. But while that occurs in the case of human sin, Aquinas holds (at least in the later version of his argument) that angelic error is of a different character. Because of the influence of passion or habit, the human intellect can wrongly judge something evil to be good. But this is not how angels are led into sin, since they have neither passions nor any habit that might incline them to sin prior to their first sin.[819] There is, however, a further way the intellect can go wrong, which involves neither affirming a falsehood nor lacking knowledge of some truth, but instead culpably *failing to attend to* a truth it knows. With the demons, Aquinas holds, it is not that they were ignorant of the beatific vision or wrongly denied its possibility, but rather that in their pride and envy they did not attend to the fact that it can be attained only by grace and not by their own power.[820]

A second issue concerns whether the various differences between human beings and angels noted in Aquinas's argument are equally fundamental to it. Again, Aquinas notes that human beings, unlike angels, arrive at judgments through a reasoning process, and that this process can be affected by fleeting passions and badly habituated sensory appetites. But the angels' lack of passions and sensory appetites is more fundamental to the argument than the fact that they do not go through a reasoning process. For one thing, passions and sensory appetites are corporeal, whereas the human intellect, even given its differences from the angelic intellect, is like the angelic intellect in being incorporeal. And Aquinas emphasizes that it is only

---

[819] *Summa Theologiae* I.63.1

[820] *Summa Theologiae* I.63.2-3

insofar as we retain our corporeality that we are capable of repentance, while he also emphasizes that it is the angels' lack of corporeality that makes them incapable of it.[821]

For another thing, it is precisely because human intellection depends on the body that it involves a *process* in the first place. For Aquinas, though angelic intellects possess concepts innately, the human intellect has no innate concepts but initially has only the potential to acquire them.[822] This potential is actualized by way of sensory experience, and thus sense organs, over time. Moreover, even after concepts are acquired, the intellect makes use of mental imagery when combining them into judgements and drawing inferences, and this imagery too requires corporeal organs.[823] Aquinas indicates that after death, when it is entirely divorced from the body, the intellect's mode of cognition will be more like that of the angels.[824]

So, what is doing the main work in Aquinas's argument for demonic obstinacy is not the thesis that angels know what they know all at once rather than as a result of a reasoning process, but rather the fact that angelic intellection is free of any influence of passions or habituated sensory appetites.

These issues are important not only for the proper understanding of Aquinas's argument about the fixity of angelic wills, but also for the question of the fixity of the human will after death. For if angels can become impenitent even just as a result of a failure to attend to some truth they know, how much more susceptible of impenitence are human beings, who are not only ignorant of truths known by the angels but also positively affirm falsehoods? If even creatures whose mode of intellection is neither discursive nor reliant on the senses can fall into permanent error, how much more likely is such error in the case of human beings, who know what they know through

---

[821] *Compendium Theologiae* I.184.

[822] *Summa Theologiae* I.84.3.

[823] *Summa Theologiae* I.84.7 and I.85.5.

[824] *De Veritate*, Question 19, Article 1. Cf. *De Anima*, Article XVIII.

a fallible reasoning process and limited empirical evidence? Even before we consider the specifics of Aquinas's argument for the fixity of the human will after death, the thesis that even angels can become obstinate in evil makes it *a priori* likely that human beings can do so as well.

Let us turn, then, to Aquinas's argument for the fixity of the will after death. The key passage is in *Summa Contra Gentiles*:

> The desire of this thing or that thing under the aspect of beatitude and ultimate end arises from some special disposition of nature; hence, the Philosopher says that "as a man is, so also the end appears to him." Therefore, if that disposition in which something is desired as ultimate end cannot he removed from the man, neither will his will be able to be changed in respect to desire of that end.
>
> Dispositions like these, of course, can be removed from us so long as the soul is united to the body. For, that we desire a thing as the ultimate end sometimes happens from our being so disposed by a passion which quickly passes; hence, too, this desire of the end is easy to remove, as appears among the continent. Sometimes, however, we are disposed to the desire of a good end or a bad one by a habit, and that disposition is not easily taken away; hence, such a desire for an end persists rather strongly, as is clear among the temperate. For all that, an habitual disposition can be removed in this life.
>
> Thus, therefore, it is manifest that so long as the disposition persists in which a thing is desired as ultimate end, the desire of that end is not changeable, because the desire of the ultimate end is an extreme; hence, one cannot be called from desire of the ultimate end by something more desirable. The soul is, of course, in a mutable state so long as it is united to the body, but it will not be after it has been separated from the body. A disposition of the soul is changed incidentally with some change in the body, for, since it is at the service of the soul for its very own operations, the body was given to the soul by nature with this in view: that the soul existing within

the body be perfected, be, as it were, moved toward its perfection. When it shall, then, be separated from the body it will not be in a state of motion toward the end, but in a state of rest in the end acquired. The soul's will, therefore, will be immovable regarding a desire for the ultimate end.[825]

Note first that we see here, once again, the Aristotelian theme that an agent can become so habituated to the pursuit of some end that it is no longer possible for an alternative end to *appear* to him as more ultimate. We also see again the thesis that such habituation is not absolutely fixed in a bodily agent, because fleeting passions or even deeply habituated desires that aim one toward a certain end can still be changed, resulting in a change in the ultimate end that is aimed at. And we see once more the idea that where there are no such bodily influences on the will, its orientation toward an ultimate end is *not* changeable. With angels (as Aquinas repeats a little further on in this chapter from *Summa Contra Gentiles*), their orientation is not changeable because they never had bodies in the first place. What Aquinas argues here is that the human soul is similarly unchangeable once it loses its body at death.

The key idea, here as in the case of angels, is that in the absence of the body there is only a single appetite, the will, which is directed at what the intellect judges to be good. Now, where the good in question is judged less than ultimate, the will might be changed in its orientation if some other lesser good comes to seem to the intellect to be a better means to the ultimate end. If my ultimate goal is to get to San Francisco, I might change my initial plan to take an airplane there if I find out that the bus would be much cheaper and the extra travel time not onerous. As Aquinas goes on to say after the passage quoted above, the will of the separated soul "is changeable from this object of will to that so long as the order to the same ultimate end is preserved." But where the *ultimate* end is concerned, no change is possible where there is only the single appetite of the will. For there is in

---

[825] *Summa Contra Gentiles*, Book IV, Chapter 95. Quoted from Saint Thomas Aquinas, *Summa Contra Gentiles, Book Four: Salvation*, translated by Charles J. O'Neil (Notre Dame: University of Notre Dame Press, 1975), pp. 343-44.

that case nothing that might pull the intellect away from its judgement that some end is highest.

Hence, suppose that reasoning leads me to conclude that the highest end would be a life of political activism. But suppose also that I have a weakness for alcohol. The pull of the bottle might distract my intellect from the considerations that led me to judge political activism the highest good, and repeated indulgence might even lead me no longer to pay them any attention at all, so that drinking comes to seem a worthier pursuit. All other factors being equal, had I not had that distracting bodily appetite for alcohol, my intellect would have remained focused on the end of political activism.

A critic of Aquinas might object that it is not only fleeting passions and habituated bodily appetites that might pull the intellect away from a judgment like the one in question. For obviously, I might change my mind about political activism for reasons having nothing to do with a weakness for alcohol or the like. For example, I might read a book that convinces me that some other pursuit would be more worthwhile, or I might have a conversation with someone who convinces me of that. But reading a book or holding a conversation involves sensory experience, which requires a body. So, just as the absence of the body would prevent an appetite for alcohol from altering the intellect's judgement, so too would it prevent a book or a conversation from doing so. In general, sensory experience cannot influence the judgements the human intellect makes after death any more than it can influence the judgements made by an angelic intellect.

The application of the basic thrust of Aquinas's argument concerning angelic wills to the case of the human will after death is straightforward enough. But there is a crucial new element to the story added in the passage from *Summa Contra Gentiles* quoted above. Note that Aquinas does not say merely that the body influences the judgements of the intellect. He makes a stronger claim. He says that by nature the body exists for the sake of moving the soul towards its perfection or completion, and that at death this task will be completed. The body's influence on the intellect is therefore *necessary* and *teleological* in character. It's not that the intellect operates in a freestanding way, where bodily influences contingently might (but also might not) influence its operations. Rather, the intellect is initially in an unfinished state with respect to its basic orientation, and requires corporeal influences to direct it to its completion. This completion occurs when these influences drop away at death. The soul with its intellectual powers is like wet clay, which initially can be molded into any number of shapes. Bodily influences are like the hands that mold the clay into some particular configuration, and death is like the kiln fire which hardens the clay permanently into that shape.

Thus, even though the body is the source of the human will's initial changeability with respect to its ultimate end, Aquinas holds that the restoration of the body after death would not make the will once again changeable. He writes:

> For all that, one should not think that the souls, after they take up their bodies again in the resurrection, lose the immutability of will; rather, they persevere therein, because... the bodies in the resurrection will be disposed as the soul requires, but the souls will not be changed by means of the bodies.[826]

Wet clay is malleable, but after it has been hardened by the fire of the kiln, it cannot be made malleable again by wetting it. Before firing, the clay will conform itself to the water you apply to it; after firing, the water will conform itself to the clay, rolling off its surface or, if poured into a pot the clay has been fashioned into, taking on the shape of the pot. Similarly, though the intellect conforms itself to bodily influences before death, after death it becomes like clay which has set or hardened into a certain shape. The body, if restored to it, will then conform itself to the intellect rather than the other way around.

Aquinas's conception of the influence the body has on the intellect thus reflects what Lamont calls a "life-driven" rather than "goods-driven" account of human action. Passions and habituated appetites are not merely one set of factors among others that may or may not influence the intellect's choice of an ultimate end, and at any point in its existence. Rather, they play an essential role within a *narrative* that is the story of a rational animal, a narrative that has a climax at death.

---

[826] Ibid., p. 345.

An interpretive controversy among Thomists concerns whether, given Aquinas's account, we should think of the intellect as making its immutable choice of an ultimate end before death or immediately after death.[827] Cajetan held that it is just after death, when the human will becomes relevantly like that of an angel, that the fatal choice is made. Sylvester of Ferrara held that the choice is made before death but that it is fixed after death. To explain the latter view by way of the analogy of the clay, the fatal choice before death would be like the final motions of the hands which form the clay into the shape of a pot, say, rather than a figurine. Death is like the fire which hardens the shape in place. The choice has a permanent effect even though it was made before death, just as the hands have a permanent effect even though their action stopped before the fire was applied. Or to take another analogy sometimes used to explain Sylvester's position, if a tree falls either toward the north or the south, it will, of course, lie wherever it lands.[828] The falling of the tree in a certain specific direction is like the choice made before death, and the tree's landing in a certain definite spot is like the fixing of this choice after death.

The dispute over these interpretations is in part motivated by theological concerns, but Sylvester's position is more plausible even on purely philosophical grounds. The thrust of Aquinas's argument is that, after death, the choice of ultimate end cannot be altered. Hence, if one has opted for some ultimate end before death, how could that choice be reversed after death, consistently with Aquinas's position? For that would require some bodily influence on the will, and all such influences are absent. So, it must be the final choice made while still alive, and not (contra Cajetan) a first choice made after death, that fixes the will immutably.

Another interpretive question concerns the specific reason why the choice of end cannot be altered without bodily influences. Abbot Anscar Vonier appears to hold that it has to do with the sepa-

---

[827] For a brief overview of the debate, see Reginald Garrigou-Lagrange, *Life Everlasting* (Rockford, IL: TAN Books, 1991, chapter IX.

[828] Ibid., pp. 65 and 67. The analogy is inspired by Ecclesiastes 11:3.

rated soul's taking on an angelic mode of intellection, and in particular, it's knowing what it knows all at once rather than through a process of reasoning.[829] Now, as we have seen, when discussing the obstinacy of the angelic will, Aquinas does indeed note that angelic cognition is not successive or processual as ours is. We have also seen that Aquinas does indicates that the soul's cognition after death will be more like that of the angels. However, in the passage from *Summa Contra Gentiles* quoted above, Aquinas himself does not actually appeal to the distinction between knowing all at once versus knowing by way of a process of reasoning. And as I suggested earlier, even in the case of angelic obstinacy, this distinction is not in fact what is most fundamental to the argument.

What *is* fundamental, I would suggest, is the absence of both any new information and any competing appetites that might effect a change in the will's basic orientation. In the case of an angel, these are absent because an angel knows what it knows all at once and lacks any sensory appetites. In the case of the human soul after death, they are absent because it no longer receives any input from the senses and loses its sensory appetites. And that would remain the case whether its cognition continues to be successive in nature or instead takes on the non-successive character of angelic cognition. Hence the question of whether the soul's cognition after death is successive or non-successive is, it seems to me, not really essential to Aquinas's argument for the fixity of the will after death.

Now, David Bentley Hart alleges that Aquinas's thesis that the will is immutable after the loss of the body is "just a blank assertion," and raises two objections to it.[830] First, if it were true, then the fallen angels, lacking bodies, could not have made even their initial choice of ultimate end, let alone chosen differently later on. Second, even if it were true, the restoration of the body at the resurrection would nevertheless restore the will's mutability.

But all of this misses Aquinas's point. Given Aquinas's account of action, all choices are for the sake of what the agent takes to be the

---

[829] Abbot Vonier, *The Human Soul* (Bethesda: Zaccheus Press, 2010), chapter 29.
[830] David Bentley Hart, *That All Shall Be Saved* (New Haven: Yale University Press, 2019), p. 46.

ultimate end, and thus wills as such. But what is willed as an ultimate end is whatever the agent's intellect attends to in the first moment it is able to operate without distractions from competing appetites. For an angel, this occurs immediately upon its creation. For a human being, it occurs immediately upon death. Let's label the end in question E. The only way an agent could abandon E is if there were some other end it took to be more ultimate, and in light of which it judged that E was not ultimate after all. But the whole point, of course, is that the agent does *not* take any other end to be more ultimate than E. If it did, then E would not in fact be in the first place the end it takes to be ultimate. Hence, supposing that an intellect takes some end E to be ultimate, it can never revise this judgment, because any revision would presuppose that some end *other* than E is taken to be ultimate – which contradicts the initial supposition.

But isn't it Aquinas's view that what the human intellect takes to be the ultimate end can and does in fact change, at least before death? I would say that this is true only in a loose sense but not in a strict sense. Strictly speaking, it is not that the will, before death, first fixes on one end as ultimate, and then fixes on another. Rather, before death, it doesn't fix on any end at all. It's not like a bullet that reaches one target but can be pulled out, reloaded, and fired at another. Rather, it's like a bullet that has not yet reached any target at all, and which is on a *trajectory* toward some particular target but might yet be diverted. And, like a bullet, once it reaches its target – at creation in the case of an angel, at death in the case of a human being – it *cannot* be fired again.

In light of these considerations, we can see that all three of Hart's claims are mistaken. First, Aquinas's position is by no means "just a blank assertion," but is grounded in a theory of action. Second, there is no contradiction in Aquinas's view that the angels can opt for an ultimate end immediately after their creation but cannot opt for some other ultimate end afterward. For the initial act involves precisely the attended to and willing of something as the ultimate end for the sake of which all other choices will be made. To say that this can happen once but only once is no more incoherent than saying that a bullet can be fired once but only once, or that a bit of clay can be molded into a pot once but only once. Third, there is also no contradiction in holding that the will is mutable before death but will not regain its mutability when the body is restored at the resurrection. For mutability is possible only where the will has never settled on an end. The will is mutable before death because it has not yet settled on an end, and is immutable after death because it then does then settle on an end, and this remains the case whether or not the body is ever restored.

The upshot of this chapter is that the soul's immortality and its salvation or damnation after death, though today commonly regarded as purely theological doctrines, can in fact be established by way of philosophical arguments. However, other than in the quotes from Aquinas, the word "soul" has not been used. Indeed, up until now, I have almost entirely avoided using it in this book. But it is time at last to see how the notion of the soul relates to the claims and arguments I have been defending in the book.

11. The Form of the Body

What is the soul?

Throughout this book, I have followed Boethius in taking a person to be a substance of a rational nature. And in the course of the last ten chapters, I have argued that to be a *human* person, specifically, is to be a substance of a rational *and animal* nature. What that entails, as we have seen, is this. First, a human person is neither less than nor more than a substance. He would be less than a substance if he were merely a bundle of mental states, as Hume claims. He would be more than a substance if he were a composite of two substances, as Descartes maintains. In reality, he is a substance, and one substance.

Second, by virtue of having an animal nature, a human person is, in part, of a *corporeal* nature. In particular, the animal powers of nutrition, growth, reproduction, sensation, appetite, and locomotion entail the possession of a body and it organs. Third, by virtue of having a rational nature, a human person is also in part of an *incorporeal* nature. In particular, the rational powers of forming concepts, putting them together into propositions, reasoning logically from one proposition to another, and willing actions on the basis of what these intellectual capacities present as ends worth pursuing, do not directly involve any bodily organs.

Fourth, because the human person is, therefore, not an entirely corporeal substance, the death of the body does not entail the entire destruction of the substance. Rather, the substance carries on after the body's death in an incomplete state, reduced to its rational operations. The end of your *body* is not the end of *you*, because you are only partly, and not entirely, bodily.

Perhaps it goes without saying that this position amounts to an endorsement of the traditional doctrine of the immortality of the soul. Yet I have, so far in this book, almost entirely avoided using the word "soul." That was deliberate. The term has many connotations, and even if I had started with an explicit definition, many readers would inevitably have read into the various claims and arguments I've been defending in this book things I did not intend. Rather than beginning with an account of what the soul is, and then repeatedly qualifying my remarks throughout the course of the book, it was better, in my judgment, first to say whatever could be said without using the word, and only afterward to explain what I mean by "soul" in light of those results. And after ten chapters, it turns out that quite a lot can be said about human beings, and even about survival of death, without using the word "soul."

All the same, the term is indispensable, and not only because it so deeply embedded in the tradition that it cannot be avoided. The different connotations of "soul" capture aspects of human nature that are interconnected in just the way you'd expect from the fact that the same word has been used to refer to all of them.[831] The words most commonly translated "soul" in scripture (the Hebrew *nephesh* and the Greek *psychē*) connote that which makes a body a living thing. In Greek literature too, the soul is that without which the body loses its life, and also connotes the inward part or personality of someone. "In primitive religions," as Paul Badham notes, "talk of the soul expresses a conviction that after bodily death life continues in some shadowy mode of being."[832] Many religions agree in taking the soul to be rewarded or punished for the deeds of this life, even if they differ over the nature and duration of these rewards and punishments. For Plato, the soul is what moves the body, knows the forms or natures of things, exhibits virtues or vices, and survives the body's death. For Aristotle, the soul is the form of the body and what gives it its distinctive powers.

Is the term irredeemably equivocal? Or is there some one component of human beings to which all these things can indeed be attributed? My view is that there is such a component, and that it is precisely the incorporeal incomplete substance that persists beyond the death of the body, but is, before death, integrated with the body

---

[831] For a useful overview of the ways the soul is conceived of in biblical and Greek literature, see the article "Soul," in Colin Brown, ed., *The New International Dictionary of New Testament Theology*, Volume 3 (Grand Rapids: Regency Reference Library, 1978), pp. 676-89.
[832] Paul Badham, "Soul," in Alan Richardson and John Bowden, eds., *The Westminster Dictionary of Christian Theology* (Philadelphia: The Westminster Press, 1983), at p. 548.

so as to make up a single complete substance. That incorporeal *part* of you is *your soul*.

Subsistent form

Now, the position I have been defending in this book is Aristotelian-Thomistic. The Aristotelian-Thomistic tradition famously holds that the soul is the substantial form of the living body. How does that relate to the characterization of the soul I just gave? Is my characterization compatible with the Aristotelian-Thomistic thesis? It is, if that thesis is properly understood. However, it is often *not* properly understood. In particular, it is misunderstood by those who suppose that there is something mysterious or even incoherent about Aquinas's view that though the soul is the form of the body, it can nevertheless survive the death of the body as a "subsistent form" or form existing on its own apart from matter. They hold that you can either agree with Aristotle that the soul is the form of the body, or with Plato that it survives the death of the body, but not both. Aquinas, they think, is vainly trying to reconcile two positions that are inconsistent with one another. In fact there is no inconsistency, and what I've said in this book allows us to see why.

But let's understand why people find the Aristotelian-Thomistic thesis puzzling, before making it explicit why they shouldn't.[833] Then we can return to the question of how that thesis is compatible with the characterization of the soul that I gave. What often happens when people consider the claim that *the soul is the substantial form of the body* is, I think, this. They know that, on the Aristotelian analysis, when a material substance like a stone loses its substantial form, nothing of that individual stone survives. The form of the stone carries on only in the sense that some other thing could always come to have the form of a stone. But that *particular* stone is gone for good, and there is no sense in which its form persists *as a particular thing*. So far so good. Then the listener recalls that for the Aristotelian, a plant or a non-human animal can be said to have a soul, since a plant or animal

---

[833] I have addressed this issue before, in "Aquinas on the Human Soul," in Jonathan J. Loose, Angus J. L. Menuge, and J. P. Moreland, eds., *The Blackwell Companion to Substance Dualism* (Oxford: Wiley Blackwell, 2018).

is a living substance and thus must have the substantial form of a living thing. But, the listener recalls, Aristotelians also hold that the soul or substantial form of a plant or non-human animal too does not carry on beyond death, any more than the substantial form of a stone carries on after its destruction. Again, so far so good.

But now the listener makes a mistake. He supposes that when Aquinas, following Aristotle, says that:

(1) The human soul is the substantial form of the body.

then he is saying something that entails:

(2) The human soul is the substantial form of a substance which is entirely bodily or corporeal.

As a result, the listener is puzzled when Aquinas goes on to say that the human soul persists beyond the death of the body. After all, stones, trees, and non-human animals are all entirely bodily or corporeal, and their substantial forms don't carry on when the substances in question perish. And the human body is by definition bodily or corporeal. So, why should *its* substantial form carry on after it perishes any more than these other substantial forms do? Hence the listener concludes that if Aquinas were consistent, then he ought to think *either* that the soul survives the death of the body but therefore is not really the form of the body but rather a substance in its own right; or that the soul is the form of the body but therefore does not persist beyond the death of the body. But to think both that it is the form of the body and that it survives the death of the body is (the listener judges) not consistent.[834]

---

[834] Cf. Denys Turner's worry in *Thomas Aquinas: A Portrait* (New Haven: Yale University Press, 2013) that to hold that the form of the body can survive the body's death seems comparable to supposing that a patch of yellow could survive the destruction of the surface of which it was the color, or that the Cheshire cat's smile could survive the demise of the cat (p. 73). I take William Hasker to be making a similar point in *The Emergent Self* (Ithaca: Cornell University Press, 1999) when he objects that Aquinas's use of "form" is ambiguous between form conceived of as an abstract universal and form conceived of as the concrete "configurational state" of some one particular thing (pp. 161-70). A form considered as an abstract universal does not depend on the continued existence of any particular material thing that instantiates it. But, supposes Hasker, for the form of the body to survive death would be for the concrete "configuration" of its parts to survive its death, and this is impossible (p. 164).

But in fact there is no inconsistency, because *proposition (1) simply does not entail proposition (2)*, and Aquinas would reject (2). For in Aquinas's view, the human soul is the form of a *substance*, that substance is *a human being*, and a human being has both corporeal *and incorporeal* operations. Hence the soul is not the form of a substance which is *entirely* bodily or corporeal. Rather, it is the form of a substance which is corporeal *in some respects* and *incorporeal in others*. Now, those corporeal respects are the ones summed up in the phrase "the body." Hence the soul is, naturally, the form of the body. But it simply doesn't follow that the soul is the form of a substance which is *exhausted* by its body and bodily operations.

This is why there is nothing terribly mysterious about why the soul, as Aquinas understands it, can persist beyond the death of the body. For the *substance* of which the soul is the form does not go out of existence with the death of the body. Rather, the *corporeal or bodily* properties and powers of that substance are no longer manifest, while *the incorporeal properties and powers continue*. To be sure, the substance in question has been severely reduced or damaged. That is why Aquinas thinks of the disembodied soul as a substance that is not *complete*.[835] But an incomplete substance is not a non-substance. Thus, to say that the soul persists beyond the death of the body is *not* to say that the form of a substance persists after the substance has gone out of existence (which certainly *would* be a very mysterious thing for an Aristotelian like Aquinas to say).

I would suggest that these considerations shed light on a dispute that has arisen among Thomists in recent years over how to understand the relationship between the postmortem soul and the human being whose soul it is. There are two main views. One of them has come to be called *corruptionism*, and it holds that at death the human being ceases to exist (unless and until God resurrects him), even though the soul carries on. The other view is called *survivalism*, and it holds that the human being persists in existence after death and even before any resurrection, though only as constituted by his soul. Among the many philosophers who have contributed to this debate are Patrick Toner on the corruptionist side, and David Oderberg on the

---

[835] Cf. *Summa Theologiae* I.75.4.

survivalist side.[836] There are two main questions where these views are concerned. First, which of them is the most plausible view to take in light of Thomistic metaphysical principles? Second, which of them did Aquinas himself actually hold? I will focus on the first question rather than say much by way of exegesis of Aquinas's texts. It is worth noting, however, that the two questions are not unrelated. If one of the two views is in fact more plausible in light of Aquinas's own principles, then that is at least some evidence favoring the attribution of that view to him, and reconsidering our interpretation of those passages that seem at odds with it.

It will no doubt be obvious from what I've said so far that the position I favor is the survivalist one. For I have said that after death the human being persists, albeit in a severely reduced or incomplete state. Now, the survivalist view is characterized as the view that after death but before resurrection, the *soul* constitutes the human being. The way I would suggest interpreting this claim is as follows. Consider first that the soul, considered just as a kind of form, cannot *by itself and without qualification* either subsist or constitute anything, because a form *qua form* exists only together with the substance of which it is the form. However, since the substance of which the human soul is the form is not entirely corporeal, that substance subsists and continues beyond the death of the body because the death of the body involves the cessation of only the corporeal aspect of said substance, not the incorporeal aspect. Hence, because the substance that the human soul is the form of persists beyond the death of the body, the *soul* persists beyond the death of the body.

Consider next that the substance in question (i.e. the human being) persists only in a greatly diminished and incomplete state, indeed diminished to the bare minimum possible consistent with the substance's existing at all. So, you might say that the substance has gotten as close as anything possibly could get to being a substantial form existing all by itself. Moreover, the corporeal side of this substance is completely gone, so that we do have a form without *matter*,

---

[836] See e.g. Patrick Toner, "Personhood and Death in St. Thomas Aquinas," *History of Philosophy Quarterly* 26 (2009): 121-38, and David S. Oderberg, "Survivalism, Corruptionism, and Mereology," *European Journal for Philosophy of Religion* 4 (2012): 1-26. See Oderberg's footnote 2 for a list of philosophers on each side of the debate.

even if it is not exactly a form existing apart from any *substance*. So, there is a loose sense in which we can say that we have a substantial form by itself; and there is a strict sense in which we can speak of a substantial form without a *body*, specifically. So, since the soul just is that substantial form, it is quite natural to speak of the soul existing all by itself – even if, were we speaking more strictly, we'd speak instead of the soul continuing to exist together with the substance of which it is the form, but without the *corporeal* features of that substance being present any longer.

So, since there is a sense in which we might think of this thing that persists beyond the death of the body as the soul, and this thing that exists beyond the death of the body is also a substance – albeit an incomplete one – and, since this incomplete substance just is the human being in a radically impaired state, it is quite natural to say that the soul that survives death just is the human being surviving death (again, in a radically incomplete state). Now, that is just what the survivalist position says. So, the position I have been defending in this book is essentially the survivalist position.

Now, I think that one of several good reasons for a Thomist to take the survivalist position rather than the corruptionist position is that the corruptionist position would make Aquinas's view as mysterious as people sometimes suppose it to be (mistakenly, as I have argued). For the corruptionist position holds, again, that at death the human being ceases to exist, even though the soul carries on. Yet the human being is the substance of which the soul is a form. So, if the human being ceases to exist at death, then that means that the substance of which the soul is the form ceases to exist at death. And in that case, how could the soul carry on? How could a form exist apart from the substance of which it is the form? Corruptionism seems to make Aquinas's position as incoherent as its critics accuse it of being. But survivalism does not have this problem, precisely because it does *not* say that the human being ceases to exist at death.

There are two further important arguments for survivalism, one philosophical and one theological. The first is this. On Aquinas's philosophical anthropology, just as it is the *human being* who sees, and not the eye, it is the *human being* who thinks, and not the intellect. The eye sees only in a loose sense, and the intellect thinks only in a loose sense. Now, on both the survivalist view and the corruptionist view, the intellect survives the death of the body and thought occurs as well. But if thought occurs and if on Aquinas's own principles it is strictly speaking only the human being, and not the intellect, which thinks, then it follows that there must be a sense in which the human being survives as well.[837]

The second, theological argument is this. Being a Christian theologian, Aquinas holds that, after death, the soul is rewarded, punished, or purged in light of the deeds of this present life. But it makes sense to reward, punish, or purge only persons, not mere parts of persons. It makes no sense, for example, to speak of rewarding or punishing Bob's foot or his pancreas for Bob's good or bad deeds. But then the soul as it exists after death must in some sense be the human person existing after death, rather than a mere part of the person.[838]

Naturally, corruptionists present arguments of their own. One of them appeals to the *Weak Supplementation Principle*, a widely accepted thesis of mereology (the study of parts and wholes). The principle holds that a thing cannot have only a single proper part, where a proper part is a part that is less than the whole. Now, the disembodied soul is merely part of a human being. If the human being persisted after death as the disembodied soul, then the human being would exist as a single proper part of a human being, thus violating the Weak Supplementation Principle. So, concludes the corruptionist, the human being does not persist.

There are several things that could be said in response to this. Oderberg suggests that the Weak Supplementation Principle seems like a universal truth of mereology because the examples we tend to focus on when thinking about mereology are material objects, whose parts are spatially smaller than the whole. But what is true of material things will not necessarily be true of immaterial things, and the soul is immaterial.

---

[837] Oderberg, "Survivalism, Corruptionism, and Mereology," p. 8.

[838] Cf. David Hershenov and Rose Koch-Hershenov, "Personal Identity and Purgatory," *Religious Studies* 42 (2006): 439-51.

It seems to me, though, that a more important point is that here as elsewhere when thinking about the metaphysics of substance, we need always to keep in mind the distinction between the properties which flow from a thing's substantial form and the actual manifestation of those properties, and the corresponding distinction between the normal or paradigm case and the aberrant case. All dogs by virtue of their substantial form are four-legged, and this is not falsified by the existence of three-legged dogs, because such dogs are defective instances. The manifestation of one of the properties they would naturally tend to exhibit (four-leggedness) is in this case being blocked. And if we consider a more radically damaged dog – say, one which has lost all its limbs and sense organs and has thereby been reduced to its merely vegetative functions – we can see how a thing might be reduced to something close to a single one of its proper parts.[839] Now, I would suggest that this is exactly what happens in the case of the disembodied soul. The human being has been reduced to a single one of its proper parts. This doesn't violate the Weak Supplementation Principle if we interpret that principle as applying to a thing *in its mature and normal state*. For the human being qua disembodied soul is *not* in his normal state.

Another corruptionist argument appeals to Aquinas's remark in his Commentary on St. Paul's First Letter to the Corinthians that "my soul is not I."[840] Doesn't this entail that Aquinas himself denied that the human being survives death as a disembodied soul, and was therefore a corruptionist rather than a survivalist?

It does not entail that. It would entail that only if, when making such remarks, Aquinas was addressing the *specific* issues in dispute between corruptionism and survivalism. And he was not. I would suggest that the target of such remarks was not what we would today call

---

[839] Oderberg makes a similar point and illustrates it with the vivid example of a human being reduced to just his head, kept alive through futuristic technology as in a science fiction story. I prefer my example of the radically damaged dog, since even the human being preserved as a severed head is not *just* a head, but the head plus the incorporeal aspect of the human being.

[840] *Commentary on the First Epistle to the Corinthians*, Chapter 15, Lecture 2, in Thomas Aquinas, *Commentary on the Letters of Saint Paul to the Corinthians*, translated by Fabian Larcher, Beth Mortensen, and Daniel Keating (Lander, WY: The Aquinas Institute, 2012).

survivalism, but rather Platonism.⁸⁴¹ The Platonist takes the view that a person is an *entirely* incorporeal thing, which is only *contingently* related to the body. The survivalist certainly rejects that view, but it was one which would have been very familiar in Aquinas's day, and one to which many thought (and many still think) belief in the immortality of the soul tends to lead. What Aquinas intends in making remarks like "My soul is not I" is to indicate that he rejects this Platonist view. He means "I am not *merely* my soul," or "I am not *reducible to* my soul," because the body is essential to me and thus something I would have when in my mature and normal state.⁸⁴² It doesn't follow that there is no sense at all in which I am my soul. Nor does this follow from Aquinas's view that it is St. Peter's soul, rather than St. Peter, to whom we pray.⁸⁴³ For just as it is a person who thinks, rather than part of a person, it is only a person to whom we can intelligibly pray, not part of a person. It would make no sense to say "Left foot of St. Peter, pray for us," or "Pancreas of St. Peter, pray for us." But it does make sense to say "Soul of St. Peter, pray for us." The only way that can be true is if there is a *sense* in which St. Peter's soul just is St. Peter.

In any event, Aquinas *can* be read this way, and I would argue that it is certainly what he *should* say given the general metaphysics of substance in the context of which he develops his philosophical anthropology. But I am less interested here in questions about Aquinas exegesis than in what is actually the truth of the matter. And the truth of the matter, as I have argued, is that the human person carries on after death as an incorporeal incomplete substance.

---

[841] Adam Wood, who is a corruptionist himself and who takes the most natural reading of the relevant texts from Aquinas to be a corruptionist one, concedes that that is not the only possible reading and that Aquinas's actual target may be Platonism rather than survivalism. See Wood's *Thomas Aquinas on the Immateriality of the Human Intellect* (Washington, D.C.: Catholic University of America Press, 2020), p. 269.

[842] In the same passage where he says "my soul is not I," Aquinas says that "the soul... is not an *entire* man," which leaves it open that it is an *incomplete* man.

[843] *Commentary on the Sentences* 3.22.1.1, ad 6; and *Summa Theologiae* II-II.83.11, ad 5, and III.50.4, ad 2.

A unified conception

The soul, I suggested earlier, is best thought of as the incorporeal incomplete substance that persists beyond the death of the body, but is, before death, integrated with the body so as to make up a single complete substance. Since I have, in this book, established the existence of such an incorporeal incomplete substance, I have also thereby established he reality of the soul.

I also suggested that this conception allows us to unify the various ways the soul has been conceived of historically. The soul, as I have noted, has been characterized as *that which makes a body alive*; as *what persists beyond the death of the body*; as *what nevertheless has only a shadowy or imperfect mode of being after death*; as *what moves the body*; as *the inward self or personality* that is manifested through the body; as *that which thinks, and in particular what understands the forms or natures of things*; as *that to which virtue and vice is attributable*; as *what is saved or damned after death*; and as *the form of the body and ground of its powers*. How does my characterization unify these different notes of the idea of the soul?

If we start with the thesis that the soul is an incorporeal incomplete substance, then the next step is to note that like any substance (whether incomplete or complete), it must have a *form* that grounds its distinctive properties and powers. And its form is, of course, that of a rational animal. To be more precise, it is the form of a substance of the kind which in its *complete* state would exhibit both the incorporeal powers of intellect and will, and the corporeal powers of nutrition, growth, reproduction, sensation, appetite, and locomotion. This is so even though, in its incomplete state, only the incorporeal powers are manifest (just as someone who has lost his sense organs or limbs is still a substance of the kind that would, in its *complete* state, exhibit the powers of sensation and locomotion).

Now, that this incomplete substance has this form is the key to the other characteristics traditionally attributed to the soul. Because the form in question is that of a rational animal, when the soul is conjoined to the body, that body exhibits the powers characteristic of animal life, namely nutrition, growth, reproduction, sensation, appetite, and locomotion. In that sense the soul is indeed *that which makes the body alive.* Because this incomplete substance nevertheless does not lose its incorporeal powers when it loses those corporeal animal powers, the soul is also *that which persists beyond the death of the body.*

The incorporeal powers that remain operative when the soul persists beyond the death of the body are intellect and will. Now, to be a person or self just is to have these powers. Because these distinctively personal powers are operative whether or not the body is present, they are in that way more fundamental to the soul than the corporeal powers. Intellectual and volitional activity, being incorporeal, is also imperceptible in a way that bodily activity is not. In these ways, the soul can indeed be said to be *the inward self or personality* that is manifested through the body.

It is by virtue of having the intellectual powers that we can understand the forms or natures of things. And it is by virtue of having wills that we can possess the moral virtues and vices. Since these powers are, again, the ones that are operative whether or not the body is present, there is a sense in which the soul is *that which thinks* and *that to which virtue and vice are attributable.* Since it is by virtue of its volitional powers that we perform the actions we do, the soul can also be said to be *what moves the body.*

As I argued in the previous chapter, at death the soul becomes locked onto its ultimate end, either that which is as a matter of objective fact the highest good, or on something less than that. Since that is, at least on one historically influential view, the core of what it is to be either saved or damned, the soul can be said to be *what is saved or damned after death.*[844] Since what persists after death is nevertheless only an incomplete substance, and one whose normal operation requires bodily organs, the soul has in that sense *only a shadowy or imperfect mode of being after death.*

---

[844] Naturally, there is much more to the topics of salvation and damnation, but addressing them requires attention to theological matters that go well beyond the purely philosophical claims and arguments I am defending in this book. The point for present purposes is simply to show how much of the traditional understanding of the soul can be defended on purely philosophical grounds, even if not *everything* we would like to know about the soul's destiny after death can be known via philosophy alone.

Thus can the various traditional notes of the idea of the soul be seen naturally to fall out of the theses that *the soul is a kind of incorporeal incomplete substance* and that as such *it has the substantial form distinctive of such a substance*. These theses, which I am proposing capture what is fundamental to the soul, reflect what is true in the Platonic and Aristotelian approaches to the soul while avoiding what is erroneous in them. The Platonic approach correctly notes that the soul is a kind of substance that can persist beyond the death of the body, but wrongly judges it to be a complete substance, to which the body is entirely extrinsic. The Aristotelian approach correctly notes that the soul is related to the body as form to matter, but, if not qualified, so overemphasizes the notion of form that it becomes mysterious how the soul could persist beyond the death of the body. The correct, middle ground position is that of Aquinas, as interpreted by "survivalism."

Hylemorphic dualism

The position I have been defending in this book is sometimes known as *hylemorphic dualism* or *Thomistic dualism*.[845] It is a kind of dualism insofar as it holds that there are two irreducibly different aspects of human nature, corporeal and incorporeal. It thereby rejects the *materialist* position that all reality is ultimately material or physical, and the *idealist* view that all reality is ultimately mental. However, it also rejects the *substance dualist* view, associated with Plato and Descartes, that the body and the incorporeal mind are two distinct substances, each complete in its own right, and that a human being is a composite of these substances. Rather, it holds that a human being is a single substance, albeit one with both corporeal and incorporeal properties and powers.

---

[845] The label "hylemorphic dualism" goes back at least to David S. Oderberg, "Hylemorphic Dualism," *Social Philosophy and Policy* 22 (2005): 70-99. The label "Thomistic dualism" goes back at least to Hasker, *The Emergent Self*, pp. 161-70.

Yet it is also at the same time different from what contemporary philosophers refer to as *property dualism*.[846] Property dualism takes a human being to be a material substance, with matter conceived of in the manner inherited from what I referred to in chapter 5 as the mechanical philosophy. It holds that human beings have, in addition to the physical properties they share with other material substances, at least some mental properties that are of a non-physical kind. The view I have been defending conceives of material substances in Aristotelian hylomorphic terms rather than in mechanistic terms. And it takes the intellect to be an incomplete substance rather than merely a collection of properties, which is why it can persist beyond the death of the body. That hylomorphism informs its conception of matter is what makes "hylomorphic dualism" an apt label. That it is inspired by Thomas Aquinas is, naturally, the reason for the "Thomistic dualism" label.[847]

But fully to understand how different hylomorphic dualism is from other forms of dualism requires noting that most of the puzzles and objections commonly raised in connection with substance dualism and property dualism do not arise with hylomorphic dualism. For instance, if the intellect were, as substance dualism holds, a complete incorporeal substance in its own right, it would be odd that intellectual activity would be affected in the ways we know it to be by changes to the body and brain (as with drunkenness, neurological disorders, and the like). But this is not surprising given that the incorporeal intellect and the body only together make up a single complete substance, and given the complicated relationships, discussed in earlier chapters, between intellection and volition on the one hand and sensation, imagination, and the sensory appetites on the other.

---

[846] For more detailed discussion of property dualism, substance dualism, idealism, materialism in its various forms, and other approaches to the mind-body problem, see Edward Feser, *Philosophy of Mind* (Oxford: Oneworld, 2006).

[847] Some Thomists eschew the "dualism" label, because they associate it with Platonism and Cartesianism, from which they rightly want to dissociate Aquinas's position. But in contemporary philosophy of mind, "dualism" has a broader connotation, covering any position that recognizes irreducibly different corporeal and incorporeal aspects to human nature. Hence the Thomist position is clearly "dualist" in the modern sense of the term, so that to resist the label seems to me more likely to generate confusion than to dispel it.

Then there is the "interaction problem" famously raised by Princess Elisabeth of Bohemia against Descartes and reiterated by others many times over the centuries.[848] If, like Descartes, we think of the body as a purely extended substance and the mind as a separate, purely thinking substance, then it is difficult to understand how there can be causal relations between them. The causal relations holding between two extended objects (such as one billiard ball knocking into another) cannot provide a model, because the mind is not extended. Nor can the causal relations holding between thoughts (as when the thought that it will rain triggers the thought that you will need an umbrella) provide a model, since the body is unthinking.

Now, angels are said to have effects on the physical world, as when Gabriel announced to Mary that she would bear the Messiah, and when demons possessed the Gadarene swine or caused furniture to move about the room in the movie *The Exorcist*. But there are two reasons why this cannot provide a model for causal interaction between Cartesian extended and thinking substances. First, even if it indicated how the mind could affect the body, it could not explain how the body affects the mind. After all, though a demon can possess a swine, a swine cannot possess a demon. Second, it does *not* in fact provide a model even for the mind's effects on the body. For there is no special connection between an angelic intellect and any physical thing it might affect. The swine or the bed moved about by a demon is no more a part of it than the pencil you move across a piece of paper or the horse you ride across the desert is part of you. A demon would no more experience the swine's sensations and bodily appetites than you would experience the horse's, and the bed it causes to float above the floor no more possesses sensations, passions, and appetites than the pencil you write with.

By contrast, you do have a special connection to your body that you do not have to any other physical object. It *is* experienced as part of you, and you *do* feel the sensations, passions, and appetites that characterize its everyday operation. You and your body make up a unity that is not exhibited by an angelic intellect and any part of the

---

[848] Princess Elisabeth of Bohemia, "Selections from Her Correspondence with Descartes," in Margaret Atherton, ed., *Women Philosophers of the Early Modern Period* (Indianapolis: Hackett, 1994).

physical world it might affect. It is this that makes especially apt Gilbert Ryle's famous characterization of Descartes' conception of human nature as "the dogma of the Ghost in the Machine."[849] If the human mind and body really were two distinct substances, each complete in its own right, then the relation of the former to the latter *would* be like that between a demon and the swine it possesses, or between a ghost and the dead mechanism it might haunt.

But it is not like that, and hylemorphic dualism, unlike Cartesian substance dualism, can make sense of why it is not. For, again, it takes a human being to be, not a composite of two distinct substances, but *one* substance with both incorporeal and corporeal operations. And the incorporeal incomplete substance that is the soul is related to the body not as an *efficient* cause but as its *formal* cause. Their relationship is as intimate as that between the form and matter of a stone, a tree, or a dog, which is why we experience the body as *part of* us rather than as some instrument extrinsic to us. Soul and body do not "interact" any more than the substantial form of a stone and the matter that makes up the stone interact. Hence there is no "problem" of explaining *how* they interact. An "interaction problem" can arise only if, like Descartes, one misconceives them as two distinct substances related by efficient causation.

Two other puzzles generated by substance dualism, but also by property dualism, are the "problem of other minds" and the closely related notion of a "philosophical zombie." A "zombie" in the sense familiar in contemporary philosophy is a creature whose behavior and bodily attributes are utterly indistinguishable from those of a normal human being, but which is nevertheless devoid of any conscious awareness whatsoever.[850] Your zombie duplicate would look and act exactly like you, and insist, if asked, that it had the conscious thoughts and experiences that you have, but in fact there would be no consciousness at all. Substance dualists and property dualists argue that if zombies are possible at least in principle, then this refutes materialism, since it would show that facts about conscious awareness are fur-

---

[849] Gilbert Ryle, *The Concept of Mind* (New York: Barnes and Noble, 1949), pp. 15-16.
[850] An especially influential treatment of this idea is David Chalmers, *The Conscious Mind* (Oxford: Oxford University Press, 1996).

ther facts over and above the facts about bodily attributes and behavior. But the possibility of zombies would also generate a puzzle about how one could ever know that anyone else really has a mind. For if you would look and behave exactly as you do whether you are genuinely conscious or whether you're merely a zombie, then how can I know that you are *not* a zombie? Indeed, how can I know that there are *any* minds at all other than my own?

But all of this essentially presupposes a mechanistic conception of matter of the kind discussed and rejected in chapter 5. Recall that on this conception of matter, there is nothing in the physical world itself that corresponds to our experiences of so-called secondary qualities like color, sound, odor, taste, smell, heat and cold. These exist only as the qualia of conscious experience rather than in the material world. If the body, conceived of in light of this notion of matter, is a complete substance in its own right, then considered all by itself it would be a mere zombie, regardless of how closely its behavior corresponded to that of someone who was truly conscious. The qualia of conscious awareness would be something utterly extrinsic to the body, either located in a distinct immaterial substance (as substance dualism holds) or comprising a set of non-physical properties somehow tacked on to the physical substance (as property dualists hold).

However, if one rejects this extrusion of so-called secondary qualities from the material world, as Aristotelian hylemorphists do, then one has *ipso facto* rejected the metaphysical preconditions of the possibility of zombies. For we are in that case no longer working with a conception of matter on which there can be nothing in the material world that corresponds to color, sound, etc. as we experience them. Moreover, there is, for hylemorphism, no such thing as a living human body without the substantial form of the human body, and thus no such thing as a zombie. For if something has the substantial form of the human body, then it is a rational animal, and thus has a mind with all that that entails (such as conscious awareness). But a zombie would be a living human body *without* all that is entailed by having a mind, and thus *without* the substantial form of a human body. Hence, if we are dealing with a living human body that exhibits all the behavior normal to human bodies, then we know we are dealing with a rational animal, and thus with something that is not a zombie and has a mind.

The notion of a zombie, and with it the so-called problem of other minds, disappear with the rejection of the Cartesian mechanistic conception of matter that generated them.

Similarly, thought experiments of the kind modern philosophers like Locke appeal to in order to motivate revisionist accounts of personal identity go by the board with the recovery of Aristotelian hylemorphism. For example, recall Locke's scenario, discussed in chapter 2, in which a prince awakens in the body of a lowly cobbler and the cobbler awakens in the body of the prince. If it is truly the *prince* in the cobbler's body, then we would have a case where the *substantial form* of the prince informs the cobbler's body. And that simply makes no sense. Any body that had the substantial form of the prince would *ipso facto* be the prince's body, with all of its characteristics rather than those of the cobbler's body. The thought experiment may seem to make sense given a mechanistic conception of matter, but not on a hylemorphic conception.

Of course, these remarks do not answer every question that one might reasonably ask about the neural correlates of distinctively intellectual activity, the causal relations between the mental and the physical, our knowledge of other minds, the status of secondary qualities, or personal identity. I have said more about these issues in earlier chapters. The point is just that they became especially problematic only with the rise of the mechanical philosophy, and take on a very different complexion when looked at in light of an Aristotelian hylemorphic account of the natural world.

The past and future of the soul

When does a person's soul come into existence? Since its natural state is to be integrated with the body so intimately that it functions as the form of the body, the natural answer is that the soul comes into existence when the body does. But here a few questions arise. First, it might be objected that since the intellect and will are the most distinctive and fundamental powers of the soul, the soul must not be present in the body until intellectual and volitional activity is manifest. Yet that happens long after the human body comes into existence. So, doesn't it follow that the soul comes into existence long after the body does?

But this does *not* follow, and the objection confuses the *exercise* of a power with the power *itself*.[851] Some of an organism's powers are exercised from the time it comes into existence, and some are exercised only after it has reached the appropriate developmental stage (such as the reproductive powers, which are exercised only after puberty). But both powers can be present in the organism prior to the exercise. What if the organs associated with these powers are also not yet present in the organism? Even here, the organism is from the beginning by nature *directed toward* developing such organs, and through them toward the exercise of the associated powers once the right developmental stage has been reached. For example, even before an embryo actually develops eyes, it is by nature *directed toward* developing them, and toward having the visual experiences that will begin when the eyes are fully developed and the right circumstances are in place. In the same way, even before the embryo's brain is developed, it is *directed toward* developing it, and toward the rational activity that the brain is normally necessary for (even if, since intellectual activity is incorporeal, the brain is not *sufficient* for it).

Nor is it correct to say that, until all this happens, we are dealing only with a *potential* rational animal. Rather, we are dealing with an *actual* rational animal that has not yet realized all its potentials. A human embryo is, after all, a *human* embryo, and not a dog or bird embryo or a thing of some indeterminate nature. It is a substance whose *teleology* or *final cause* is to manifest all the properties and powers distinctive of rational animals, even if this end is realized only gradually. Thus it must have from the beginning a *substantial form* appropriate to a substance with such a teleology, which entails that it has a soul. Here we see yet another significant difference between hylemorphic dualism and Cartesian substance dualism. If soul and body really were, as Descartes supposes, distinct substances each complete in its own right, then there arguably would be no reason to take the soul to be present until the rational powers are actually exercised. By contrast, if the soul is what gives form to the body, then it must be present as soon as the body is present, whether or not all the organs

---

[851] David S. Oderberg, *Real Essentialism* (London: Routledge, 2007), p. 250.

characteristic of such a body are yet formed or all the powers it gives the body are yet exercised.

Here some might object that Aquinas himself, though a hylemorphist, took the human soul to be present only long after conception.[852] But that is not because he thought a human body was present even before the human soul was present. Rather, he thought that conception yields something that is not yet a human body but which gives way to a human body precisely when it loses its substantial form and takes on the substantial form of a human body – that is to say, a human soul.[853] So, Aquinas by no means disagreed with the claim that a human body is present only when a human soul is present. Rather, he supposed that the human body existed only some time after conception. Moreover, this supposition was grounded in an erroneous understanding of the relevant biological facts. When we combine Aquinas's principles with what we know from modern embryology, the natural conclusion to draw is that the human body is present from conception.[854]

Because of its relationship to the heated controversy over the ethics of abortion, the question of whether human beings come into existence at conception or only some time afterward has itself become highly controversial. I cannot address here every issue that arises in connection with that controversy.[855] Nor can I address every issue

---

[852] *Summa Contra Gentiles* II.89

[853] Oderberg, *Real Essentialism*, p. 250.

[854] The relevance of modern biological knowledge to interpreting Aquinas's view about ensoulment has been debated by Robert Pasnau and John Haldane and Patrick Lee. Haldane and Lee argue that, when interpreted in light of modern biology, Aquinas's position entails that the soul is present from conception, whereas Pasnau denies this. See Robert Pasnau, *Thomas Aquinas on Human Nature* (Cambridge: Cambridge University Press, 2002), pp. 105-20; John Haldane and Patrick Lee, "Aquinas on Human Ensoulment, Abortion, and the Value of Life," *Philosophy* 78: 255-78; Robert Pasnau, "Souls and the Beginning of Life (A Reply to Haldane and Lee)," *Philosophy* 78: 521-31; and John Haldane and Patrick Lee, "Rational Souls and the Beginning of Life (A Reply to Robert Pasnau)," *Philosophy* 78: 532-40.

[855] For a detailed defense from an Aristotelian hylemorphist point of view of the thesis that a human being is present from conception, see David S. Oderberg, *Applied Ethics: A Non-Consequentialist Approach* (Oxford: Blackwell, 2000), chapter 1, and Oderberg's articles "Modal Properties, Moral Status and Identity," *Philosophy and Public Affairs* 26 (1997): 259-98; and

that arises in connection with the question of when the life of a human being ends, which has become no less heated because of its relationship to the ethics of euthanasia.[856] But as with the embryo, so too with human beings whose rational faculties no longer function due to brain damage, the fact that the *exercise* of a power is absent does not entail that the power *itself* is absent, or that the substantial form that grounds the power is absent. Recall what was said in chapter 5 about the relationship between a substance's properties and the essence from which they flow or follow. The manifestation of the properties that flow from a substance's essence can be blocked because of either damage or incomplete development, but the essence itself is nevertheless still there.

The bottom line is that given hylemorphism, if a living human body is present, then its substantial form is present, which entails that the soul is present. Hence we are dealing with a rational animal or human being, whether or not the human being happens to be capable of exercising all his distinctively human powers.

Aristotelian hylemorphism also provides a framework within which to evaluate so-called "transhumanism." According to the most extreme versions of this view, the bodily and cognitive enhancements that modern technology makes possible might so radically alter human beings that the result would essentially be a new species.

For example, consider inventor Steve Mann, who has popularized the use of "wearable computers" to augment a person's perceptual experience of the surrounding world.[857] He sports computerized eyeglasses that filter out aspects of his environment that he would rather not see (such as advertising), reveals information not available to normal vision (such as temperatures of distant objects), enhances text, and so on. So routine has such use become that removing the glasses

---

"The Metaphysical Status of the Embryo: Some Arguments Revisited," *Journal of Applied Philosophy* 25 (2008): 263-76.

[856] For treatment of the subject from an Aristotelian hylemorphist point of view, see Oderberg, *Applied Ethics*, chapter 2, and David S. Oderberg, "Death, Unity, and the Brain," *Theoretical Medicine and Bioethics* 40 (2019): 359-79.
[857] Steve Mann with Hal Niedzviecki, *Cyborg: Digital Destiny and Human Possibility in the Age of the Wearable Computer* (Doubleday Canada, 2001).

can be disorienting. Mann thinks of himself as a "cyborg" and claims that "we are entering the post-human age" in which "we can rebuild ourselves, transcend the supposed limitations of the human form – both physical and mental."[858]

But a human being wearing such technology is no more "post-human" than stones that have been arranged to form a wall are "post-stones" or horses which have been attached to a buggy they are pulling are "post-horses." In all three cases, all that is going on is that a certain substance has taken on new accidental forms, to use the jargon introduced in earlier chapters. But for a substance to take on a new *accidental* form is not for it to lose its *substantial* form and thereby give way to a different substance – which is what would have to happen for a substance of the human type to become a substance of a different, post-human type. Nor does the fact that technology might even give a human being Iron Man-like physical strength or afford him some analogous level of cognitive power change anything. Differences in degree do not entail any difference in kind.[859]

It is also sometimes claimed that advances in artificial intelligence (AI) are leading to a "singularity" event which will yield "superintelligence" that dwarfs not only what computers can currently do, but what human intelligence is capable of.[860] Such a "superintelligence," it is feared, might be beyond the control of human beings, and perhaps threaten civilization itself. In reality, as we saw in chapter 9, no AI that operates on the principles that computers do will ever be *super*intelligent, because it won't really be *intelligent* in the first place. Hence, if fears about future "superintelligent" computers reflect the assumption that they will do what we do, but do it better, they are

---

[858] Ibid., p. 2.

[859] Cf. David S. Oderberg, "Could There Be a Superhuman Species?" *The Southern Journal of Philosophy* 52 (2014): 206-26, at p. 222.

[860] Ray Kurzweil, *The Singularity is Near: When Humans Transcend Biology* (New York: Viking, 2005); Nick Bostrom, *Superintelligence: Paths, Dangers, Strategies* (Oxford: Oxford University Press, 2014).

entirely groundless. Computers don't *at all* do what we do in the first place, and thus they can hardly do what we do *better* than we do it.

This is by no means to deny that we might develop computer technology so sophisticated that it spirals out of our control. That could certainly happen, though serious thinking about the specific *ways* it might happen is hampered by the muddleheaded supposition that computers are literally intelligent. If computers ever pose a threat to our civilization, it will be for the same reason nuclear weapons, bioweapons, and other technology might pose a threat to it – not because *they* are intelligent, but because *we* too often fail to use our intelligence wisely. Nor are my remarks meant to deny that technological enhancements of human beings might have a dramatic effect on the character of everyday human life, just as other technological developments have. The point is simply that while the *ethical* implications of these technologies may be great, their *metaphysical* implications have been massively oversold. Adding technological enhancements to human beings will never get you anything more than a technologically enhanced human being, rather than something of a radically new kind. Further riffs on the methods and technologies characteristic of artificial intelligence research will never get you genuine intelligence.

How *did* genuine intelligence enter the natural world, then? Against dualism in general and hylemorphic dualism in particular, it is sometimes objected that it is difficult to see how the origin of an incorporeal soul could be explained in evolutionary terms.[861] The first thing to say in response to this is that it gets things backwards. We first have to determine the *nature* of a thing before we can determine whether a certain proposed explanation of it is adequate. If a certain explanation cannot account for every aspect of its nature, then the conclusion to draw is not that the thing in question must not really have the nature we thought it did, but rather that the explanation in question is not adequate and we need to look for a better one. In the

---

[861] This objection is raised against dualism in general in Paul Churchland, *Matter and Consciousness*, Revised edition (Cambridge, MA: The MIT Press, 1988), pp. 20-2; and against hylemorphic dualism in particular in William Hasker, "A Critique of Thomistic Dualism," in Loose, Menuge, and Moreland, eds., *The Blackwell Companion to Substance Dualism*, at p. 127.

case at hand, it has already been established, in chapters 8 and 9, that the intellect is not corporeal. Therefore, if some proposed explanation of the intellect, such as an evolutionary explanation, cannot account for the origin of something incorporeal, the problem is with the proposed explanation, not with the judgement that the intellect is incorporeal.

Second, whether an evolutionary explanation for some biological phenomenon is adequate depends on what *kind* of evolutionary explanation we are talking about, for not all such explanations are of a piece. For example, if interpreted in light of a materialistic metaphysics, evolutionary processes will not have any irreducibly teleological properties. But some such processes could have irreducibly teleological features if evolution is interpreted in light of some different metaphysics, such as an Aristotelian metaphysics.[862] Often, when critics allege that some view is incompatible with evolution, what they really mean is that it is incompatible with the essentially materialist metaphysics in light of which evolution is commonly interpreted. It is hard to see why any dualist should be impressed by this, since to be a dualist is precisely to reject materialism.

Having said that, it is not implausible to doubt that even evolutionary processes more broadly construed can suffice to explain the origin of an incorporeal soul. Traditionally, there have been two main theories of the origin of the soul: *traducianism* and *creationism*.[863] Traducianism holds that a human being's soul derives from his parents, just as his bodily traits do. There are two ways this view could be spelled out further. On one version, the soul derives from the bodies of the parents. But it is at best difficult to see how something *incorporeal* could arise from something *corporeal*. Indeed, that is precisely the point of the objection from evolution raised by the materialist against

---

[862] For discussion of the relationship between Aristotelianism and evolutionary explanations in biology, see Edward Feser, *Aristotle's Revenge: The Metaphysical Foundations of Physical and Biological Science* (Neunkirchen-Seelscheid: Editiones Scholasticae, 2019), chapter 6.
[863] For overviews of the traditional debate over these theories, see Cardinal Mercier et al, *A Manual of Modern Scholastic Philosophy*, Vol. I (St. Louis: B. Herder, 1932), pp. 316-30; Michael Maher, *Psychology: Empirical and Rational* (London: Longmans, Green and Co., 1933), pp. 572-75; and Celestine N. Bittle, *The Whole Man: Psychology* (Milwaukee: The Bruce Publishing Company, 1945), pp. 585-88. Aquinas criticizes traducianism and defends creationism in *Summa Contra Gentiles* II.86-89.

dualism, and hylemorphic dualists can agree with the materialist about that much, even if they draw a different conclusion.[864]

To be sure, William Hasker has proposed a view he calls "emergent dualism," according to which an immaterial mind can emerge or arise out of material constituents when they are "arranged in a suitable way."[865] He compares this to the way a magnet generates a magnetic field. But exactly *how* is this supposed to work? Hasker himself acknowledges the limitations of the analogy.[866] We know the necessary and sufficient conditions for the generation of a magnetic field, but we know of no such conditions for the generation of incorporeal minds out of matter. Moreover, notes Hasker, a magnetic field lacks the unity or simplicity which the self has (as we saw in chapter 8), or the free will it possesses (as we saw in chapter 4). Hasker considers a dilemma he attributes to Brian Leftow, according to which either it is intelligible how mind can arise from matter, but only at the cost of making mind material after all; or matter somehow generates mind *ex nihilo*, which would, absurdly, entail that matter has divine power.[867] Hasker claims there is a third alternative, namely that matter has some *natural* rather than divine power to generate an immaterial mind. But he gives us no account of *how* it could have such a power. Indeed, whether such a power is even possible is precisely what is at issue! Nor is it any help to assert that such a power exists in matter "arranged in a suitable way," for Hasker has little to say about exactly what *makes* such a way suitable other than that it allows for the emergence of an immaterial mind – which, as one critic points

---

[864] For the incorporeal to arise out of the corporeal would violate the Scholastic *principle of proportionate causality*, which holds that whatever is in an effect must in some way first be in its total cause. I expound and defend this principle in *Scholastic Metaphysics: A Contemporary Introduction* (Heusenstamm: Editiones Scholasticae, 2014), pp. 154-59.

[865] William Hasker, *The Emergent Self*, p. 190. Cf. William Hasker, "The Case for Emergent Dualism," in Loose, Menuge, and Moreland, eds., *The Blackwell Companion to Substance Dualism*. As Hasker notes, an earlier emergentist form of dualism was proposed by Karl Popper in Karl R. Popper and John C. Eccles, *The Self and its Brain* (New York: Springer-Verlag, 1977).

[866] Hasker, *The Emergent Self*, pp. 191-92.

[867] Ibid., p. 196.

out, "borders on being tautological."⁸⁶⁸ Hence, "emergent dualism" seems to amount, not to a *theory* of how an incorporeal mind can arise out of matter, but to little more than a novel *label* for the claim that it does so arise.

The other way to interpret traducianism is to hold that the soul derives from the *souls* of the parents, rather than their bodies. This avoids the problem of having to explain how the incorporeal can come from the corporeal. But it faces another problem. Again, for the reasons considered in chapter 8, the soul is simple or without parts. So how can one's soul come from the souls of one's parents? That would seem to require that a *part* of one's father's soul and a part of one's mother's soul be passed down to their offspring. But, again, souls do not have parts. It would also seem to require that those parts be combined in order to make up the soul of the child. But souls cannot be *made up of* parts, because, once again, they lack parts.

So it seems that traducianism, on either interpretation, fails. *Creationism* is the alternative view that, whenever a new human soul comes into being, that is only because it is specially created by God *ex nihilo*. That is not to say that the human being as a whole is so created, or that his parents have nothing to do with his origin. The idea is rather that, though the parents are causally responsible for the body of the person, that this body is conjoined with the incomplete substance that is the soul is the work of God. God and the parents together produce the new human being.

This might seem *ad hoc*, or at best a "God of the gaps" explanation, but it need not be so, provided certain premises are in place. Hence, suppose that the existence of God can be independently established, as I would argue it can be.⁸⁶⁹ Suppose it can also be established that only God can create something *ex nihilo*. And suppose that, by further developing arguments like the ones just surveyed, it can be established that there is no way in principle for a soul to come into

---

⁸⁶⁸ Cf. Brandon L. Rickabaugh, "Against Emergent Dualism," in Loose, Menuge, and Moreland, eds., *The Blackwell Companion to Substance Dualism*, at p. 78.
⁸⁶⁹ Cf. Edward Feser, *Five Proofs of the Existence of God* (San Francisco: Ignatius Press, 2017).

being except by being created *ex nihilo*. Then the appeal to divine action will by no means be either *ad hoc* or a "God of the gaps" explanation. It will be the only possible explanation. My own view is that it is indeed the only possible explanation. But for present purposes, I will put the issue to one side, because further elaboration would require getting into broader theological issues that are beyond the scope of this book. Suffice it to say that, whatever one ends up saying about the *origins* of the soul, that controverted issue casts no doubt on its *nature* as an incorporeal incomplete substance.

What, then, of the soul's future? I have already said something about this in previous chapters. In particular, I have argued that the soul is of its nature immortal, so that, short of God annihilating it, it will and must continue in existence forever. I have argued that its basic moral orientation is unalterably locked at death, either on good or on evil. I have argued that it cannot be reincarnated in the body of another person, much less the body of a non-human animal. What has been said in the present chapter reinforces that conclusion. Socrates' soul is the *substantial form* of Socrates' body, so that any body it might come to inform after death would of necessity be *Socrates' body*, not your body, or a dog's body, or an insect's body.

But *will* the soul of a deceased person ever in fact be reunited to its body? This is the idea of *resurrection*. It has sometimes been suggested that the thesis of the immortality of the soul and the idea of the resurrection of the dead are at odds.[870] But this can seem to be the case only if we conceive of the soul as Plato does, and if we neglect to consider carefully the preconditions of resurrection. If the soul is a complete substance in its own right, what need would it have for reunion with the body? If a person could return to life via resurrection, what need is there for an immortal soul?

But the soul is *not* a complete substance in its own right. Though it can to some extent operate independently of the body, that is not its natural state, and only if the body is restored to it will the complete human *person* be restored. Nor can resurrection be an alternative to the soul's immortality. For suppose a body that is physically

---

[870] Cf. Oscar Cullmann, *Immortality of the Soul or Resurrection of the Dead? The Witness of the New Testament* (London: The Epworth Press, 1958).

indistinguishable from Socrates' body were suddenly to appear. Should we say that Socrates has been resurrected? Or should we say instead that a perfect *replica* of Socrates has come into being? Recall from chapter 10 that Antony Flew raises this problem for the view that reconstituting a person's body suffices to ensure that the person survives death. And recall that Aquinas's conception of the resurrection is not open to this objection, because it holds that the soul of a person persists between death and resurrection, so that there is continuity between the person who died and the later person whose body is indistinguishable from that of the person who died. If Socrates is resurrected, he will be Socrates and not a mere replica because *the same one soul*, which had informed the matter of Socrates' body before he died, comes to inform that matter again.

So, the immortality of the soul is a necessary precondition for resurrection. But, again, will resurrection actually occur? In particular, can philosophical arguments alone tell us? One thing it seems philosophy can tell us is that resurrection is *fitting* given our nature.[871] For, again, it is only when the soul is conjoined with the body that we have a complete substance. The disembodied soul is in an unnatural state, and *aims* or *points toward* the having of its body as its natural condition. It would be most odd if the soul were forever frustrated in this natural tendency – if union with the body lasted only for the fleeting, earliest portion of its unending existence.

Another thing philosophy can tell us is that *if* a resurrection were to occur, only God could bring it about. That, in any event, was Aquinas's view.[872] Natural material causes can no more reunite soul and body than they could generate a soul in the first place. Nor could even an angelic intellect reunite a soul and its body, since angels can only manipulate natural causes, even if they can do so more powerfully than we can.[873] Now, if we consider the fittingness of resurrection together with divine power, goodness, and wisdom, we have the ingredients for an argument to the effect that God can be expected to

---

[871] Cf. Thomas Aquinas, *Summa Contra Gentiles* IV.79; Mercier et al., *A Manual of Modern Scholastic Philosophy*, Vol I, pp. 326-27; and Robert Edward Brennan, *Thomistic Psychology* (New York: Macmillan, 1941), pp. 328-29.

[872] Cf. *Summa Theologiae*, Supplement, 75.3.

[873] Cf. *Summa Theologiae* I.65.3-4 and I.105.1.

restore bodies to souls. Here too, though, elaborating on and defending this line of argument would require a treatment of matters of philosophical theology that are beyond the scope of a book on human nature.

Suffice it to say that philosophy can take us as far as showing not only that the soul is immortal but that its reunion with the body is to be expected. That's pretty far – further even than Plato dared go in the *Phaedo*. But here we reach the limits of what philosophy can by itself establish. If we are to go further, we will have to look for evidence of some special divine revelation about the details of the soul's life after death and the resurrection of its body. It seems relevant to point out in closing that there is one religion, and only one, that grounds its claim to divine provenance precisely on evidence that one such Resurrection has already occurred.

INDEX

abortion, 512
abstraction, 70, 75, 85, 197-98, 206, 240, 292-93, 299-301, 356, 357-59
action, 130-35, 137 *See also* will
actuality and potentiality, 176-79, 196, 200-1, 204-5 *See also* hylemorphism
Adams, Robert Merrihew, 292, 301
Adler, Mortimer, 103, 357
Ahmed, Arif, 323-24
Akins, Kathleen, 244
Allen, Keith, 239
Ameriks, Karl, 376, 383
Anaxagoras, 399
angels, 14, 178, 305, 452, 455, 461, 477, 478, 482-85, 490-91, 507, 520
animals, 14, 65, 68, 117, 141, 210
    Aristotelian conception of, 241-42
    behavior of, 118-20
    intelligence in, 245-56
    language and, 96-102, 245-53
    propositional attitudes and, 251-55
    sentience and, 227-29, 241-45
    souls of, 495-96
Anjum, Rani Lill, 117, 136, 151-52, 155, 156
Anscombe, Elizabeth, 139
anti-realism, 17-18
Aristotle, 2, 13, 306, 328, 391, 445, 452
    on actuality and potentiality, 176-77
    empiricism and, 75-76
    on intellection, 399
    on matter, 172-73, 197, 205
    on nature versus artifice, 181-83
    on the soul, 494, 495, 496

        on weakness of will, 480-81
artificial intelligence, 402-39 *passim* *See also* computers
        connectionism or parallel distributed processing, 412-14, 435-36, 437
        frame problem, 433-39
        Gödel's theorem and, 429-31
        machine learning, 414, 437-39
        singularity, 514-15
atomism, 173, 189, 190, 194, 196   *See also* mechanical philosophy
Augustine, 8-13, 15, 20-21, 23
Avicenna, 376
Ayers, Michael, 69, 234

Bacon, Francis, 193
Badham, Linda, 466, 467, 468, 469, 470
Badham, Paul, 466, 467, 468, 469, 470, 494
Bailey, Andrew, 381
Baker, Gordon, 258
Baker, Lynne Rudder, 350
Balaguer, Mark, 150, 153, 155-56, 157
Barnett, David, 376, 380-81
Bayne, Tim, 56-57, 58, 376, 385-88, 443-44
Bealer, George, 391
Bedau, Mark, 213-14, 215
behaviorism, 91-95, 290, 294-95, 312, 386
Bennett, M. R., 109, 160-61
Berkeley, George, 69, 302
Bermudez, José Luis, 88, 97-101
Bernecker, Sven, 36, 37
Bittle, Celestine, 66, 69, 357, 375, 376, 516
Blackmore, Susan, 468
Blaine, David, 411
Block, Ned, 74, 367, 418, 420
Bluhm, Robyn, 384-85
Bobik, Joseph, 200
Boden, Margaret, 213-14, 437

Boethius, 12-14, 111, 452, 477, 493
BonJour, Laurence, 365-70, 373, 374 390-91, 394
Boscovich, Roger, 190
Bostrom, Nick, 514
Boyle, Robert, 190, 193
Braddon-Mitchell, David, 87, 98
Braine, David, 97
Braude, Stephen, 57-58, 62, 466, 467, 468, 469, 470-71
Brennan, Robert Edward, 58, 228, 292, 520
Brown, Colin, 494
Budd, Malcolm, 288
Buddhism, 41-45
Buechner, Jeff, 312, 423, 424-25
Bühler, Karl, 101
Butler, Joseph, 33-34
Button, Graham, 408, 410, 411-12, 413, 414

Cain, M. J., 298, 350
Cajetan, Thomas De Vio Cardinal, 489
Carroll, Lewis, 271
Cartesianism, 3-4, 5, 258-62, 287, 288-89, 391-92 *See also* Descartes, substance dualism, representationalism
Cartwright, Nancy, 117, 152, 166, 240
causation *See* efficient cause, four causes, powers
Chalmers, David, 231, 235, 376, 418, 420, 508
Chemero, Anthony, 265, 275
Chinese Room argument, 415-19, 420
Chisholm, Roderick, 20-21, 23, 150, 166
Chomsky, Noam, 92-94, 246, 248-50, 294-95, 398, 446
Churchland, Patricia, 313, 422
Churchland, Paul, 103, 110, 242, 263, 313, 329-32, 422, 440, 515
Clark, Andy, 272-73, 274-75
Clark, Austen, 237
Clarke, Randolph, 150, 170
classification, 79
Coffey, P., 69

commissurotomy, 59-62
compatibilism, 149, 151
compositionality, 79-80, 90
computers, computation, 199
 as artifacts rather than substances, 431-32
 connectionism or parallel distributed processing, 412-14, 435-36, 437
 frame problem, 433-39
 Gödel's theorem and, 429-31
 indeterminacy of meaning and, 312-13, 318-19, 422-25
 language and, 411-12, 414, 416-19, 426, 438-39
 machine learning, 414, 437-39
 observer-relativity of, 419-22
 phenomenology and, 426, 427-28
 rule-following and, 425-28
 singularity and, 514-15
 and thought, 402-39 *passim*
 Turing machines, 405-7, 425, 430-31, 435, 437
 Turing test, 414, 416-19
conceivability argument, 462
concepts, 64, 65, 76-91, 139-40, 252-53, 267 *See also* intellect
 abstraction and, 292-93, 299-301, 356, 357-59, 388-401 *passim*
 conceptions versus, 81
 eliminativist approach to, 105-6
 essences or forms and, 292-93, 299-301, 356, 388-401 *passim*
 as formal signs, 88-90, 324-26, 339, 363-64, 373-74, 398, 400
 imagist theories of, 69-76, 77-78, 82, 85
 neo-empiricist versus neo-rationalist theories, 82-91
 neuroscience and, 329-32, 444-45
 origin of, 291-304, 356, 388-401 *passim*
 storage problem and, 357-64
Confucianism, 173, 178
connectionism, 412-14, 435-36, 437
consciousness, 229 *See also* sensation, sentience
 hard problem of, 231
 higher-order theories of, 47, 50

knowledge argument and, 231, 234
panpsychism and, 235-41
qualia and, 230, 231-41, 282-83
unity of, 376-88
zombies and, 231, 234, 508-10
content *See* intentionality
Cooper, John, 467
Copeland, B. Jack, 414
Corbí, Josep, 353
Cornell, A. D., 467
corpuscularianism, 190 *See also* mechanical philosophy
Cory, Therese Scarpelli, 23
Coulter, Jeff, 408, 410, 411-12, 413, 414
Cowie, Fiona, 299, 301, 302-3
Coyne, Jerry, 158-59
Crane, Tim, 65, 233, 237, 341, 403-4, 405, 407, 412
Craver, Carl, 157, 221
Cudworth, Ralph, 234
Cullman, Oscar, 519
Cummins, Robert, 388-89
Cuypers, Stefaan, 150, 168, 169

Dainton, Barry, 41
Davidson, Donald, 129, 131, 142, 154, 252, 285-87, 290, 313
Davis, Stephen, 470
death, 455-56, 464-65, 475 *See also* immortality, near-death experiences
De Haan, Daniel, 221, 225
Democritus, 189
Dennett, Daniel, 54, 74, 95, 229, 284, 313, 314-15, 348, 385, 433
Descartes, Rene, 11, 15, 70, 193, 258, 302, 452, 493, 505, 507, 508 *See also* Cartesianism, dualism, representationalism
        Cogito argument, 11-12, 20-21, 23
        on matter, 190, 191, 205-6, 219, 232, 233, 358
        on *res cogitans*, 219, 259, 261, 263, 446, 462
Des Chene, Dennis, 210, 219

determinism, 117, 141, 149, 151-56, 157, 226
Dietrich, Eric, 422, 429, 430, 433, 436-37
Dijksterhuis, E. J., 191-92
Dillard, Peter, 309, 318-23, 326, 329, 332-39
dissociative identity disorder, 54-58
Donceel, J. F., 210
Dretske, Fred, 341-46
Dreyfus, Hubert, 265-66, 272, 275-76, 277, 278, 412, 425-28, 431, 432, 433, 434
Dreyfus, Stuart, 412, 425, 426, 427, 433
dualism, 232, 233-34
    conceivability argument for, 462
    emergent, 517-18
    hylemorphic, 505-10, 511-12
    interaction problem for, 279, 507-8
    property, 281, 506, 508, 509
    substance, 15, 151, 219, 256, 258, 260, 279, 281, 305, 440, 452, 463-64, 472, 475, 502, 505, 506, 508, 509, 511
Dupré, John, 220, 222-25

Eddington, Arthur, 198, 235
efficient cause, 113, 115, 151-52, 198   *See also* powers
    agent causation versus event causation, 122, 150, 169-70
    downward causation, 221-22
    immanent versus transeunt, 118, 210-12, 214-15, 216-18
    proportionate causality, 301, 517
Elder, Crawford, 195, 278
eliminative materialism, 15, 103-10, 218-20, 282, 330, 393
Elisabeth of Bohemia, 507
embodiment, 263-66, 507-8
    intellection and, 267-73
    perception and, 242-45, 273-85
    social animality and, 285-91
emergence, 383-84, 386, 517-18
emotions, 124, 229
empiricism, 69, 75-76, 78, 291, 301-2, 388-89, 446

Aristotelian-Thomistic version of, 291-304
        neo-empiricism, 82-91
essences, 215, 292, 298, 299-301, 388-401 *passim*, 513
euthanasia, 513
evolution, 213
        computation and, 424-25
        intentional content and, 320-21, 346-49
        origin of the soul and, 515-17

Fellows, Roger, 252-53, 254-55
Feynman, Richard, 174-75, 190
Fields, Chris, 422, 429, 430, 433, 436-37
final cause, 113, 198, 421   See also *teleology*
Fitch, G. W., 323-24
Flannery, Kevin, 481
Flew, Antony, 40, 462-65, 520
Fodor, Jerry, 76, 80, 86, 91, 413, 435-36
        on innate ideas, 296-99
        on intentionality, 340-41, 347-48, 349-50, 353, 366, 369
        language of thought hypothesis of, 90, 97, 370, 373
        on modularity of mind, 377-78, 446
form, formal cause, 113-14, 178-81, 421   See also hylemorphism
        accidental form, 113-14, 181-83, 190, 193, 194, 211-12, 432, 514
        concepts and, 292-93, 299-301, 356, 388-401 *passim*
        corruption as loss of, 178, 208, 453-55, 460
        of living things, 223-26
        soul as, 473, 495-503, 505, 508, 511-13
        subsistent, 495
        substantial form, 113-14, 181-83, 184-86, 187-88, 194-96, 199, 204, 432, 475, 514
four causes, 113, 142-43, 328-29
four-dimensionalism, 31
Frankfurt, Harry, 98, 130, 136
free will, 117, 136-70   See also will
        compatibilist view of, 149, 151

        and determinism, 117, 149, 151-56, 157
        libertarian view of, 149-50, 165-67
        neuroscience and, 157-64
Frege, Gottlob, 72, 327
Freud, Sigmund, 446
functionalism, 385-86
Furlong, Peter, 136

Galileo, 191, 232, 235, 237, 238
Gardeil, H. D., 144-45, 210, 453
Gardner, Howard, 446
Garrigou-Lagrange, Reginald, 489
Gascoigne, Neil, 267
Gassendi, Pierre, 189
Gauld, Alan, 467
Gazzaniga, Michael, 157
Geach, Peter, 300
Gerson, Lloyd, 258
ghosts, 463, 467-68, 469, 470, 471-72, 476
Gibson, James J., 244, 275
Ginsburg, Simona, 229
God, 6, 169, 178, 193, 196, 214, 218, 375, 424, 458-59, 472, 479, 497, 518-19, 520-21
Gödel, Kurt, 429-31
Godfrey-Smith, Peter, 228, 241, 243
Goetz, Stewart, 144
Goff, Philip, 235-41
Goyette, John, 184
Graham, George, 251
Gregg, Justin, 254
Grove, Stanley, 201-2, 203-4

Habermas, Gary, 459, 460, 466, 467, 468, 475
Hacker, P. M. S., 89, 96, 97, 109, 160-61, 288
Haldane, John, 139-40, 300-301, 362, 364, 376, 394, 512
Hanson, N. R., 205

Harris, Sam, 157
Hart, David Bentley, 490-92
Hart, W. D., 462
Harvey, William, 193
Hasker, William, 370, 376, 379, 496, 505, 515, 517-18
Haugeland, John, 266-67, 313, 437
Hayek, F. A., 94
Hayes, Patrick, 433
Haynes, J. D., 163-64, 442-43, 444
Heidegger, Martin, 264, 266, 275, 276
Heisenberg, Werner, 200-1, 204
Hendrie, Phil, 56
Heraclitus, 42, 173, 174-75, 177, 190
Hershenov, David, 500
Hick, John, 473-75
Hillis, W. Daniel, 407
Hobbes, Thomas, 189
Hochschild, Joshua, 91
Hoffman, Tobias, 136
Holden, Thomas, 189, 197
Honderich, Ted, 153
Hood, Bruce, 52-54
Hull, David, 193
Hume, David, 2-3, 69, 391
      on causality, 115-16
      on the self, 26-29, 43, 45-47, 50-52, 493
Humphreys, Paul, 190, 192
Husserl, Edmund, 275-76
hylemorphism, 172-73, 176, 178-89, 194, 241, 318, 333 *See also* form, matter
      concept formation and, 301, 388-401
      dualism and, 505-10
      generation and corruption according to, 178, 208, 453-55, 460
      living things and, 223-26
      quantum mechanics and, 199-205

idealism, 392, 393, 505
imagery, imagination, 66, 67, 291-92, 303-4, 444-45, 456-58
    concepts abstracted from, 292-93
    concepts distinct from, 69-76, 77-78, 82, 85
    corporeal nature of, 293, 309, 331-32, 440
    descriptionalist versus pictorialist theories, 74
immortality, 453-76 *passim*
    Aquinas's argument for, 453-59
    conceivability argument for, 462
    empirical arguments for, 465-76
    reincarnation and, 469-70, 472-75, 519
    and salvation or damnation, 476-92 *passim*
    replica objection against, 462-65, 520
    resurrection and, 519-21
    simplicity of self and, 459-62
indeterminacy of meaning, 72-74, 84, 140, 299, 306-56 *passim*, 369, 422-25, 444-45, 449
indirect realism   *See* perception
innate ideas, innatism, 75-76, 259, 260, 291-304
instinct, 66-67
intellect, 11, 14   *See also* concepts, reasoning
    abstracts form from matter, 291-304 *passim*, 388-401
    active versus passive, 64, 292-93, 298, 299-300, 302-3
    computers and, 402-39 *passim*
    after death, 484, 490
    embodiment and, 267-73, 326-29, 487-88
    imagery utilized by, 303-4, 327-28, 440, 456-58, 484
    imagism and, 69-76, 388-89
    immateriality of, 305-74 *passim*, 399-401
    immortality of, 455-62
    language and, 91-103, 251-53, 285-91
    neuroscience and, 329-32
    and non-human animals, 245-56
    propositional attitudes and, 64-65
    sentience versus, 64-68
    simplicity of the self and, 377-81, 459-62

social animality and, 285-91
  will and, 117-18, 120-23, 137-40, 478-79, 491
intelligence, 245 *See also* intellect, reasoning
intelligent design, 218
intentionality, 76-77, 88, 126, 261-62, 281, 287, 388-89 *See also* indeterminacy of meaning
  Aristotelian-Thomistic approach to, 388-401
  biosemantic theories, 346-49, 389
  causal theories, 84, 331, 340-46, 349-56, 366, 389, 390
  conceptual role theories of, 367-70, 389
  derived, intrinsic, and as-if, 77, 88-90, 431-32
  eliminativist view of, 106-10
  externalist theories of, 317-18, 366
  narrow content versus wide content, 367
interaction problem, 279, 507-8
introspection, 21-23, 235, 284-85, 312

Jablonka, Eva, 229
Jabr, Ferris, 219
Jackson, Frank, 87, 98, 231
James, William, 262
Jay, Ricky, 411
Jensen, Steven, 228
John of St. Thomas *See* John Poinsot
Joyce, G. H., 69

Kagan, Shelly, 459
Kane, Robert, 136, 137, 148
Kant, Immanuel, 30, 376, 381, 383, 461
Kenny, Anthony, 149
Klubertanz, George, 66, 210, 228, 453
Koch-Hershenov, Rose, 500
Koons, Robert, 202-3
Koren, Henry, 186, 206, 210, 216, 228, 230
Kretzmann, Norman, 456

Kripke, Saul, 307, 309-11, 312-13, 315, 318-19, 321-24, 326, 335, 338-39, 422-25, 431
Kurzweil, Ray, 514

Lamont, John, 479-80, 481, 488
language, 101
    animals and, 96-102, 245-53
    computers and, 411-12, 414, 416-19, 425, 438-39
    private, 288-90
    social nature of, 285-91
    and thought, 90-103, 251-53
language of thought hypothesis, 90, 97, 359, 365-70, 373
Larson, Erik, 436-37, 438, 439
Laurence, Stephen, 107
laws of nature, 116-17, 141-42, 152, 157, 165-67
Lee, John R. E., 408, 410, 411-12, 413, 414
Lee, Patrick, 512
Leftow, Brian, 317-18, 517
Legrenzi, Paolo, 447, 449
Leibniz, G. W., 376, 381, 383
Lenat, Douglas, 434-35
Lennon, Thomas, 376, 377, 460
Levine, Joseph, 232
Lewis, C. S., 370
Lewis, David, 31
libertarianism, 149-50, 165-67
Libet, Benjamin, 158-62
Lichtenberg, Georg Christoph, 23-25, 26, 30
life, living things, 118, 210-26   *See also* animals
    immanent versus transeunt causation and, 118, 210-12, 214-15, 216-18
    mechanisms and, 220-26
    sentient, 227-31
    as substances, 223-26
    vegetative, 227, 229-31
Lilienfeld, Scott, 448

List, Christian, 162
Locke, John, 32-41, 43, 69, 75, 190, 233, 510
Lotze, Hermann, 376
Lowe, E. J., 40, 75, 128, 129, 130, 131, 303-4
Lucas, John, 429-31

Machery, Edouard, 86, 103, 105-6
machine learning, 414, 437-39
Maher, Michael, 69, 357, 375, 376, 453, 516
Malebranche, Nicolas, 234
Mann, Steve, 513-14
Marsh, Michael, 468
materialism, 4, 15, 104, 110, 142, 234, 256, 266, 305, 505   *See also* eliminative materialism, physicalism
    artificial intelligence and, 402-39 *passim*
    indeterminacy problem for, 306-56 *passim*, 444-45, 449
    intellection entails falsity of, 399-401
    neuroscience and, 439-49
    reason can't be explained by, 365-74
    simplicity of the self and, 374-88
    storage problem for, 357-64
mathematics, 191-92, 197-98
matter, 172
    extension and, 205-8
    hylemorphic theory of, 172-73, 178-89, 241
    material cause, 113, 178-81
    mathematicized conception of, 191-92, 197-98, 205-8, 235
    mechanical philosophy and, 103, 104, 172, 189-99, 232-33
    primary and secondary qualities of, 232-41, 509
    prime matter, 181, 183, 188-89, 190, 195-96, 199-200, 201-2, 207, 453, 455
    principle of individuation, 208, 388, 463, 464-65
    quantum mechanics and, 199-205, 358
Matthen, Mohan, 243, 274
McCabe, Herbert, 399
McCall, Raymond, 69

McCall, Storrs, 430-31
McCarthy, John, 433
McCulloch, Gregory, 260
McDowell, John, 37, 140, 260, 261-62, 391-93
McGinn, Colin, 190, 302
McInerny, D. Q., 459
McKenna, Michael, 136
McWilliams, James, 206, 207
mechanical philosophy, 103, 104, 172, 189-99, 221, 232-33, 506
    modern epistemologies and, 259, 265, 281, 301-2, 355-56
    zombies and, 508-10
Mele, Alfred, 131, 132, 164
memory, 33-37, 289-90
    sensory, 66, 67
Mendelssohn, Moses, 461
mental maps, 87-88, 98, 331
Mercier, Désiré-Joseph, 358, 375, 376, 516, 520
mereology, 381, 500
Merleau-Ponty, Maurice, 264, 275
Milgram, Stanley, 164
Millikan, Ruth, 313, 346-47, 348
mind, 8, 10, 14-15 *See also* intellect
mind-body problem, 266
Molière, 114
Molnar, George, 198
Moore, Thomas Verner, 66
Moreland, J. P., 376, 386, 459, 460, 466, 475
Morris, Katherine, 258
Mosurinjohn, Sharday, 384-85
Moural, Josef, 417
Mumford, Stephen, 117, 136, 151-52, 155, 156
multiple personality disorder *See* dissociative personality disorder

Nagel, Thomas, 231-32, 234, 244, 282, 306, 322, 323
naïve realism *See* perception
nativism *See* innate ideas

nature, natural, 181-83
naturalism, 62
Neander, Karen, 346, 348
near-death experiences, 466-69, 475-76
neuroscience, 263, 328, 402
    concepts and, 329-32
    eliminative materialism and, 103, 107, 109
    free will and, 157-64
    and localizing mental function, 445-49
    and materialism, 439-49
    "mind reading" and, 441-45
    and near-death experiences, 468
    of perception, 274, 283-85
    self and, 54, 59-62
    of sensation, 242, 446-47
    unity of consciousness and, 384-85
Niedzviecki, Hal, 513
Noë, Alva, 283-84
Noonan, Harold, 35-36
Nozick, Robert, 38
Nyāya-Vaiśesika, 43, 173, 194

O'Callaghan, John, 78
O'Connor, Timothy, 150
Oderberg, David, 185, 199, 202, 210, 214, 216, 225, 230, 357-64 *passim*, 465, 498, 500-1, 505, 511, 512-13, 514
Olafson, Frederick, 263-64, 279, 282
other minds, 338, 508-10

Paley, William, 218
panpsychism, 235-41, 281
Papineau, David, 346
parallel distributed processing *See* connectionism
parapsychology, 469-71
Parfit, Derek, 35, 37, 38
Parker, Francis, 88, 324-26

Parmenides, 173, 175, 177, 190
Pasnau, Robert, 22, 23, 41, 149, 211, 316-17, 364, 453, 456-57, 512
Peacocke, Christopher, 79
Penn and Teller, 411
Penrose, Roger, 429
perception, 5
    embodiment and, 242-45, 273-85
    indirect realism about, 259-60
    naïve realism about, 238-39, 279-81
    unity of consciousness and, 376-78
Pereboom, Derk, 136, 165-67
persons, 12-13, 14, 31, 44, 58, 111, 452, 454, 493 *See also* self
phantasms *See* imagery, imagination
phenomenology, 47-51, 272, 275-78, 284, 426, 427-28
phrenology, 446
physicalism, 194 *See also* materialism, reductionism
Pink, Thomas, 121, 130, 134, 136, 150, 168
Pinker, Steven, 92, 247
Place, U. T., 198
Plantinga, Alvin, 370
Plato, 2, 172, 258, 261, 306, 445, 452, 494, 495, 505, 519, 521
Plotinus, 376
Poinsot, John (John of St. Thomas), 88, 89, 324-25, 339, 363-64
Polanyi, Michael, 264, 275, 278
Popper, Karl, 101, 245, 251, 351-53, 370, 517
Povinelli, Daniel, 254
powers, 114-17, 123-24, 183, 194, 226, 254, 293-94, 302-3
    teleology and, 198-99, 319-20
Prades, Josep, 353
Prinz, Jesse, 76, 83, 84, 85, 86, 89, 295-96, 297, 298-99
properties, 183-84, 206-7, 215, 513
propositional attitudes, 64-65, 92, 98, 251-55, 286
propositions, 64, 72-74, 79-80, 98, 325, 326-27, 368-69, 374, 378-79
proxytypes, 83, 84, 86, 88, 89
Putnam, Hilary, 110, 239, 320, 348-49, 350, 353-56, 366, 390, 394-97
Pylyshyn, Zenon, 80, 86, 413

quantum mechanics, 153, 173, 199-205, 358
qualia, 230, 231-41, 281, 509 *See also* consciousness, sense data
Quine, W. V., 286, 307, 311-12, 313, 314-15, 318, 322, 324, 326, 335

Ramos-Diaz, Antonio, 306, 357, 360-61
Rasmussen, Joshua, 362
rationalism, 75-76, 78, 259, 291, 301, 389 *See also* innate ideas
    neo-rationalism, 82-91
rationality, 64 *See also* intellect, reasoning
Rawls, John, 81
realism, 17-18
reasoning, 64, 85-86, 87-88, 101, 219-20, 482
    and embodiment, 270-72, 483-85, 487, 489-90
    formal, 307-8
    materialism cannot account for, 365-74
reductionism, 17-18, 194-95, 217
    about consciousness, 232-34, 240, 244-45
    in biology, 220-22, 229
Reid, Thomas, 33, 37
reincarnation, 469-70, 472-75, 519
Renard, Henri, 453
Reppert, Victor, 370
representation, mental, 76-78, 82, 261, 265, 388-89 *See also* concepts, intentionality
representationalism, 259-62, 265-66, 278-81, 285
resurrection, 463, 464, 488, 497, 519-21
retorsion arguments, 372-73
Rey, Georges, 79, 81, 92, 106
Rickabaugh, Brandon, 518
Rickles, Dean, 203
Robinson, Howard, 63
Rooney, James Dominic, 173, 178
Rorty, Richard, 313
Rosenberg, Alex, 158, 221, 225
Ross, James, 306-39 *passim*, 363, 364

Royce, James, 358, 375, 376
Rozemond, Marleen, 258
Russell, Bertrand, 21, 69, 198, 235
Ryder, Dan, 84
Ryle, Gilbert, 126, 128, 264, 270-72, 508

Sarkar, Sahotra, 173
Sartre, Jean-Paul, 50, 144
Sassen, Brigitte, 461
Satel, Sally, 448
Scharle, Margaret, 186
Schmaltz, Tad, 234
Schrödinger, Erwin, 282
Schueler, G. F., 133
scientism, 103-4
Searle, John, 77, 88, 312, 322, 425, 430, 431
 on the Background, 267-70, 272, 285, 433
 Chinese Room argument of, 415-19
 on cognitivism, 419-22
 on the will, 121, 130, 146-48
Sehon, Scott, 132-33, 134-35, 144
self, 10, 14, 18-63
 awareness of, 20-23, 47
 in Buddhism, 41-45
 bundle theory, 18, 26-29, 46, 52, 122
 commissurotomy and, 59-62
 dissociative identity disorder and, 54-58
 Lockean theory, 32-41
 phenomenology of, 45-52
 scientific challenges to, 52-63
 simplicity of, 374-88, 459-62, 517, 518
 substantiality of, 23-32
 will and, 122
Sellars, Wilfrid, 103, 140, 277, 282-83, 313, 373, 392-93
sense data, 233, 277, 279-81
sensation, sentience, 65-68, 119, 227-31

      animals and, 227-29
      and appetite, 228-29
      bodily nature of, 242-45
      internal versus external senses, 65-66, 67, 228, 245
      neuroscience of, 242, 446-47
      plants lack, 229-31
      synthetic or common sense, 66, 292
Sharrock, Wes, 408, 410, 411-12, 413, 414
Shields, Christopher, 211
Shoemaker, Sydney, 34-36
simplicity of the self or soul, 374-88, 459-62, 517, 518
singularity, 514-15
skepticism, 261, 278-79, 284-85
Skinner, B. F., 91-92, 94
Smith, Brian Cantwell, 437
Smith, Gary, 438, 439
Smith, Vincent Edward, 206, 207
soul, 3, 492, 493-95, 503-5 *See also* immortality, intellect, reincarnation, self
      after death, 485-86, 487, 488, 493, 495-505 *passim*
      corruptionist versus survivalist views of, 497-503, 505
      creation by God of, 518-19
      and ensoulment, 510-13
      evolution and, 515-17
      as form of the body, 473, 495-503, 505, 508, 511-13
      origin of, 516-19
      resurrection and, 519-21
Spinoza, Benedict, 193
Stainton, Robert, 376, 377, 460
Stalnaker, Robert, 313
Stanley, Jason, 272
Stich, Stephen, 103, 107
Strawson, Galen, 51-52, 167, 168, 170, 228, 235, 237
Strawson, P. F., 277
Stroud, Barry, 239, 290-91
Stump, Eleonore, 148, 149-50, 183

substance, 13-14, 18, 19, 25, 29, 38-40, 112-14, 180-81
    artifacts versus, 181-83, 211-12, 431-32
    in Buddhism, 41-42
    generation and corruption of, 178, 208, 453-55
    immaterial, 208-9, 452, 477
    living, 223-26
    physical, 113, 115, 166, 178, 180-81, 194, 206-8
    soul as incomplete, 495-503 *passim*
    substantial form and, 183-86, 187-89, 514
substantial form   *See* form
Sullins, John, 422, 429, 430, 433, 436-37
Suppes, Patrick, 189, 204-5
Swinburne, Richard, 460, 462, 480
Sylvester of Ferrara, 489

Tallis, Raymond, 161-62, 263, 393, 397-98, 448
Taylor, Charles, 265-66, 277, 278
Taylor, Richard, 136, 150
teleology, 103, 104, 115, 267, 431-32
    and action, 130-35, 143-44, 155, 478-88 *passim*
    in embryo, 511
    evolution and, 516
    life and, 211-12, 226
    mechanical philosophy and, 193, 198-99
temporal parts, 31
Terrace, Herbert, 247, 250-51
Thales, 172
theory of mind, 98, 99
Thomas Aquinas, 2, 14, 16, 303
    dualism and, 506
    empiricism and, 75-76, 291
    on ensoulment, 512
    on freedom, 136-39, 143, 144-46, 149-50, 167-68
    on imagery or phantasms, 327-28, 484
    on the immateriality of intellect, 306, 316-17, 357, 376
    on immortality, 453-59, 461, 464

on intellection, 391, 392-93, 399
　　　on matter, 172, 178
　　　on necessity, 138-39, 146
　　　on resurrection, 520
　　　on self-knowledge, 21-23
　　　on the soul, 495-503 *passim*, 512, 516
　　　on substance, 184-85
　　　on teleology, 115
　　　on the will, 112, 117-18, 119, 120, 121, 122-23, 476-92 *passim*
Thomism, 2, 5, 64, 75, 113, 150, 196, 198, 291-94, 328, 458, 459, 464-65, 489, 495, 497-503, 506
Thornton, Tim, 267, 392
thought　*See* concepts, intellect, intentionality, reasoning
Thurston, Herbert, 467
Toner, Patrick, 498
Torretti, Roberto, 192
Toulmin, Stephen, 172
traducianism, 516-18
transhumanism, 513-15
Turing, Alan, 405, 412, 437
　　　Turing machines, 405-7, 412-13, 425, 430-31, 435, 437
　　　Turing test, 414, 416-19
Turner, Denys, 496
Tye, Michael, 69, 230

Umiltà, Carlo, 447, 449
unity of consciousness, 376-88
universals, 69-70, 179, 186, 292-93, 294, 316-17, 329-32, 357-59
Uttal, William, 445-48

Van Heuveln, Bram, 422, 429, 430, 433, 436-37
Van Inwagen, Peter, 145
Van Laer, P. Henry, 206
Veatch, Henry, 88, 324-26
Viger, Christopher, 384-85
volitions, 124-30

voluntarism, 122, 124
Vonier, Abbot Anscar, 489-90

Walls, Jerry, 480
Wegner, Daniel, 164-65
Weinberg, Jonathan, 86
Whitehead, Alfred North, 135
Wilkes, Kathleen, 54-55, 60-61
will, 11, 111-12, 116
    causality of, 169-70
    emotions and, 124
    fixity after death, 476-92 *passim*
    freedom of, 17-18, 117, 136-70
    intellect and, 117-18, 120-23, 137-40, 478-79, 491
    teleology and, 130-35, 143-44, 155
    volitions of, 124-30
    voluntarist versus intellectualist theories of, 122-23, 124
Williams, Bernard, 24, 37, 313
Williams, Rowan, 15
Williamson, Timothy, 272
Wilson, Margaret Dauler, 381-83
Wittgenstein, Ludwig, 97, 264, 266, 272, 321
    on private language, 288-90
Wolff, Christian, 446
Wood, Adam, 306, 340, 457, 502

Zahavi, Dan, 48
Zebrowski, Robin, 422, 429, 430, 433, 436-37
Zeno, 173, 175-76, 177, 190, 196-97
Zhu Xi, 178
zombies, 231, 234, 288, 508-10

www.ingramcontent.com/pod-product-compliance
Lightning Source LLC
Chambersburg PA
CBHW031539300426
44111CB00006BA/109